A REPUBLIC OF STATUTES

A REPUBLIC OF STATUTES

The New American Constitution

William N. Eskridge Jr. and John Ferejohn

Yale

UNIVERSITY PRESS

New Haven & London

Yale University Press books may be purchased in quantity for educational,
business, or promotional use. For information, please e-mail sales.press@yale.edu
(U.S. office) or sales@yaleup.co.uk (U.K. office).

Set in Electra and Trajan types by Westchester Book Group.
Printed in the United States of America.

Library of Congress Cataloging-in-Publication Data

Eskridge, William N.
  A republic of statutes : The new American Constitution / William N. Eskridge Jr. and
John Ferejohn.
          p. cm.
  Includes bibliographical references and index.
  ISBN 978-0-300-12088-2 (cloth : alk. paper)   1. Constitutional law—United
States.   I. Ferejohn, John A.   II. Title.
  KF4550.E837 2010
  342.73—dc22

                                                          2009043709

A catalogue record for this book is available from the British Library.

This paper meets the requirements of ANSI/NISO Z39.48-1992 (Permanence of Paper).

10   9   8   7   6   5   4   3   2   1

CONTENTS

ACKNOWLEDGMENTS

There are many debts to be acknowledged, too many for us to remember, much less list. We start with gratitude to our bosses who provided research support and leave time, enabling us to complete this massive project. Bill Eskridge thanks Dean Harold Koh of the Yale Law School, and John Ferejohn is just as thankful for generous support from the Hoover Institution, Stanford University, and the New York University School of Law. He also is grateful for thoughtful criticisms of the project and its various pieces to Morris Fiorina, David Brady, Larry Sager, Barry Friedman, Rick Hills, and Michael Levine. Research assistants who have contributed to this project include Amanda Andrade (Yale Law School, class of 2010), Stephen Gilstrap (YLS, '11), Jayme Hershkopf (YLS, '11), Xuan Gui (YLS, '11), Elizabeth Phelps (YLS, '10), and Brian Richardson (YLS, '11).

One or both of us presented chapters from this project to workshops at the Emory University School of Law, the Harvard Law School, the New York University Law School, the University of Pennsylvania School of Law, the University of Texas School of Law, the Vanderbilt Law School, and the Yale Law School, as well as a conference on statutes and constitutionalism held at Banff, Canada. We received helpful comments from participants at those workshops, too numerous to list accurately.

The theoretical points of this book—the centrality of statutes to modern constitutionalism, the notion of "superstatutes," and administrative constitutionalism—have been ones that we have been developing since the millennium began. We have enjoyed excellent feedback as well as inspiration from Bruce Ackerman, Akhil Amar, Lisa Bressman, Steven Calabresi, Philip Frickey, Barry Friedman, Sophia Lee, Sandy Levinson, Roger Noll, Victoria Nourse, Peter Ordeshook, George Priest, Joseph Raz, Larry Sager, and John Yoo.

Each chapter fills out our general theory, within the context of particular superstatutory regimes. In each case, we have benefited from critical comments made by scholars who are more learned in these fields than we are. Thus, chapter 1, on pregnancy discrimination and workplace accommodation of family responsibilities, could not have been written without the benefit of conversations with or feedback from Susan Deller Ross and Sonia Pressman Fuentes, the parents of the Pregnancy Discrimination Act, as well as Justice Ruth Bader Ginsburg and legal scholars Christine Jolls, Kevin Schwartz, and Joan Williams. Chapter 2, on voting rights, builds upon the original work of our friends Brian Landsberg and Bruce Ackerman, with whom we had several conversations, and of the great legal historian David Garrow.

Our colleague George Priest gave us a detailed critique of chapter 3, dealing with the Sherman Act; his comments required us to recast some of our analyses and greatly improved the chapter (errors remain our own, of course). We also received useful comments from Richard Posner, who once helped persuade the Warren Court to apply the law expansively but is now a major critic of such interpretations.

Chapter 4, dealing with social security, draws heavily from the work of political scientist Martha Derthick and conversations with Steven Teles. Although new to legal scholarship, our research associate Amanda Andrade provided unusually keen guidance for chapter 5, on family law. Chapter 6's analysis of the evolving wetlands regulations could not have been written without the expert guidance of Fred Bosselman and Dan Tarlock, whose scholarship, notes to us, and conversations gave us a deeper grasp of the science as well as the law in this area. Our treatment of issues of public finance and money in chapter 7 brought us into an area where we had much to learn, and we learned a lot from conversations with Claire Priest.

In addition to the published scholarship referenced in the endnotes, chapter 8's treatment of our polity's treatment of sexual and gender minorities drew from Eskridge's participation in the California same-sex marriage litigations. Conversations with David Codell, Shannon Minter, and Stephen Reinhardt were particularly helpful. Chapter 9, on the national security constitution, profited from conversations with and feedback from Oona Hathaway, Harold Koh, and John Yoo.

We appreciate the support of our respective families. Sally Ferejohn, in particular, offered constant tolerance and personal reassurance for both of us.

Bill Eskridge dedicates this book to Ben and Mei van Eskridge.

John Ferejohn dedicates this book to the memory of his mother, Olga Collazo, who has now returned to her birthplace in Coamo.

Introduction: America's Working Constitution

This book presents a nontraditional framework for thinking about American constitutionalism. The traditional framework emphasizes the words and structure of the Constitution of 1789, and especially the Bill of Rights and a few other amendments, as interpreted by judges and trumping the political process. Its focus is on limited government and the associated urgency of protecting citizens and especially minorities from government oppression. While this focus is vital to maintaining and protecting our liberal democracy, it neglects the reason why we have a government at all, which is to protect us from each other and from outside enemies. A government strong and decisive enough to protect us is dangerous to liberty, but a government too weak or indecisive to accomplish this primary mission is not worth having at all.

Our framework therefore focuses on the primary instruments of the political process itself—statutes, executive orders, congressional-executive agreements, agency rules—and reveals how those political contrivances have become entrenched, indeed to the point of molding the Constitution itself. These devices have evolved from the early days of the republic to permit the protection of an extensive and flexible system of rights and liberties and other forms of security that exist outside the traditional Constitutional frame. Under our account, the primary governmental actors are legislators, executive officials, and administrators, but the ultimate form of political agency is found in We the People, acting through regular elections and the associated devices of political parties but also by means of political associations and interest groups and through popular social movements. The result, which we call small "c" constitutionalism, does not usually operate as a trump card in the way that the Large "C" Constitution is thought to act. Instead, it is a modality of public life and discourse, facilitating the building and editing of structures within which we as citizens can live flourishing lives. As a legal matter, small "c" constitutional norms and structures are realities that need to be considered when people and businesses make their plans, administrators implement laws, and judges interpret ordinary statutes and even the Constitution.

From the time the colonies were settled, Americans have demanded rights of various kinds. Which rights those are, and whether they are held by individuals or communities, have always been matters of struggle and contention. Many colonists demanded religious liberties of various kinds, including the right of a community to establish its own church as well as an individual right of worship or conscience. The colonists also wanted the right to move to wherever they wanted and to own their own land and have their contracts respected, to marry and beget heirs without too much state interference, and to claim new lands in the frontier. And they wanted the right to govern themselves—to elect their own legislatures and enact their own laws. This claim eventually brought them into conflict with the British government and its principle of parliamentary sovereignty. From the beginning, American citizens have wanted government to do the things the colonists came for, but also a limited government that would generally respect their rights, both as British subjects and as strong-willed American colonists. In this respect, our democracy was liberal from its beginning.

A government is constitutional when its ordinary laws and regulations are regulated by higher order norms and not merely by the will of governmental officials. These higher norms may be enforced as laws, as has been true in this country since the founding period, or they may be religious commands characteristic of some natural law theories, or norms of political morality that guide what policymakers do, as has been the tradition in the United Kingdom. But more is expected of a liberal constitution than the mere establishment of a regulatory structure to limit what the majority and its representatives may do. A constitutional democracy also demands that our leaders will be chosen by majorities and will be subject to specific normative guidance as to which norms and rights are constitutionally sacred and what precisely can be done to those in the minority on various issues. In short, democratic constitutionalism requires the following: popular choice of political leaders, a normative hierarchy embodying substantive rights, and institutions and procedures for enforcing the hierarchy and at least some of the rights. At least since 1689 Britain was understood to have a constitutional government in this sense, and the colonists understood their own governments to be regulated in the same fashion.

The Constitution of 1789, as immediately augmented by the Bill of Rights (1791), formalized many of these understandings: it asserted a hierarchy of legal norms, recognized certain rights, and created institutions of national government that the framers expected to enforce the hierarchy and at least some of the rights. All this was done in a written document. But the written Constitution left many things essentially unresolved, including the extent of the franchise for federal and state elections, the precise authority of the president, the extent and reach of the federal judiciary, and the role of judges in enforcing rights. Although it was not the framers' design, the Constitution's high hurdle for formal amendment limited the extent to which the continuing struggle over the content of our democratic constitutionalism—what rights there are; who holds them; how they can be vindicated—could be resolved as a matter of Large "C" Constitutional law. Rather, if we were to fight about these things— and no vital people could refuse to argue and struggle about them—the field of battle could usually not be confined to the text of the Constitution itself. This is our view, but it is not the conventional wisdom in the legal academy.

At least two generations of law professors and media pundits came of age under the inspiring glow of *Brown v. Board of Education* (1954). In *Brown*, the Supreme Court interpreted the Constitution to render unenforceable state and local statutes requiring that public schools be segregated on the basis of race. Since 1954, Linda Carol Brown, the Topeka schoolchild whose parents brought suit, has been the poster child for the United States Constitution. *Brown* and the Browns have been a powerful symbol for a particular vision of the Constitution as a guardian of individual rights, enforced by fearless federal judges like Chief Justice Earl Warren and trumping squalid statutory regimes such as American apartheid. Indeed, some of our country's most sophisticated Constitutional analysts vigorously argue for a "fusion of [C]onstitutional law and moral theory," on the ground that the Constitution invokes public morality by its terms. Implicitly, such theorists are also relying on the popular notion that in the United States all important political and moral questions ultimately end up as Constitutional questions resolved by the U.S. Supreme Court.[1]

It is not crazy for legal academics to think this way. Especially as it has been amended, the Constitution contains a variety of open-textured guarantees that can be read to support a wide range of social movement objectives, from gay marriage to handguns for self-defense to integration to resegregation. And the dramatic choreography of Constitutionalism is hard to beat, as *Brown* and the Equal Protection Clause illustrate. Purchased with the blood of hundreds of thousands, the Reconstruction Amendments were adopted after a great series of confrontations involving the Radical Republican Congress, President Andrew Johnson, state legislatures (including those of southern states seeking readmission), newspapers, male voters, and others not franchised (such as female abolitionists). The content of these intense and sometimes violent deliberations was basically about who must be recognized as a person within the republic, fully entitled to equal concern and respect. And the resolution of these disputes represents as well as anything our understanding of the basic structure of American civil society.

Because Constitutional change through Article V Amendment requires deliberation, usually over several years, by many different officials and must have the support of large and geographically disparate majorities, such change is usually both legitimate and lasting. Commitments made in this way deserve to be taken seriously and respected. Because the commitments are expected to last a long time, they tend to be broad and elliptical; an example is the Equal Protection Clause, the basis for the NAACP's victory in *Brown* and since then an enduring argument for people of color, language minorities, women, gays, people with disabilities, welfare recipients, the working poor, and nonmarital children. Arbitrating these claims are the justices of the Supreme Court, whose life tenure assures them some insulation from normal politics. For many liberals, the Court is our exemplary deliberative institution.[2]

The foregoing reflects a romantic understanding of the judge-enforced Constitution. It is time to take a more realistic view.

To begin with, the Constitution of 1789 is too old to answer most of the looming social, political, and moral questions that Americans want answered, and there is no process for updating it that is both workable and legitimate. Although the Article V structure has generated some important amendments, it has done virtually no work for an enduring Constitutionalism since 1920, when the Nineteenth Amendment (assuring women the right to vote) took effect. Article V's process, requiring two-thirds support in each chamber of Congress and (much more dauntingly) ratification by three-quarters of the states, is simply too arduous for any but the most process-oriented changes to the Constitution. As a result, Constitutional updating, if any, has fallen to the Court, which most liberals have celebrated. The justices' performance has been erratic—everyone has a long list of the Court's blunders—but the overriding problem is systemic: the Court does not have the legitimacy, the wisdom and expertise, or the enforcement resources to generate important changes in the Constitution.[3]

Moreover, the Constitution, especially as applied by the Court, sets rules applicable to governmental actors, but does not by its own force govern private actors. Heinous as state discrimination was for people of color in earning good educations, exercising the franchise, and riding on municipal buses, even more harmful was the weight of private discrimination against people of color by employers, landlords, banks, real estate agents, hotels, restaurants, lunch counters, professional sports leagues, and country clubs. While norms applicable only to the state may have an educational force, their ability to saturate the public culture is much greater when the norms are applicable to all of us—and

Large "C" Constitutional norms are for the most part not directly applicable to citizens outside government.

Finally, and most fundamentally, neither the Constitution, as amended, nor the Supreme Court, even in the glorious *Brown* era, deeply addresses the duties of government to create and guarantee affirmative and positive legal regimes that provide security and structure for American public finance, families, employment and commercial activities, old-age and disability insurance, and national defense. The Constitution contains a few affirmative platitudes, such as the Preamble's admonition that government "promote the general Welfare," but the Supreme Court shrinks from enforcing even those few platitudes, much less announcing positive state obligations on its own. Yet for Linda Carol Brown Smith, Kansas family law structures her married life and probably has more of an impact on her day-to-day life than the Constitution does. Her ability to flourish in America depends much more on the Equal Employment Opportunity Commission, the Social Security Administration, and the Federal Reserve Board than on our nation's Constitutional Court.

These three huge limitations of large "C" Constitutionalism, explored at greater length in chapter 1, have hardly posed a crisis for the American people. As a general matter, the inflexible Constitution has not stopped Americans from undertaking fundamental commitments, creating new rights, abolishing outrageous injustices. The very obduracy of the Constitution has channeled Americans toward the republic of statutes that is the subject of this book. Americans have created statutory and administrative rights and liberties that are both less dramatic and much broader than Large "C" Constitutional rights. Do we have a right not to be subject to arbitrary employment discrimination against us in the labor market? If we do have such a right, why should it not apply against private as well as public employers? We have fundamental Constitutional rights not to be imprisoned or tortured by the state, but do we have a right to state protection against private violence?[4]

The republic of statutes we describe transcends the libertarian bias in Large "C" Constitutional rights. On the libertarian view, the Constitution works by preventing governmental officials from harming people in various ways. We think this is a partial perspective on the Constitution. But it is not even partial when it comes to the statutory or small "c" constitution. As we shall show, statutes commonly provide positive rights to people, providing them with legal means to combat oppression and discrimination. We are open to the possibility that some of the positive rights we explore have a Large "C" Constitutional basis, even though they are not recognized by the Supreme Court. We agree with Larry Sager, who has argued that many Constitutional rights are (and should be) "underenforced" by the judiciary, for institutional reasons. In some instances, the state action doctrine might be an example of Constitutional underenforcement, but most of the positive rights we describe—from the right to family medical leave (chapter 1), a free market (chapter 3), and old-age pensions (chapter 4)—do not clearly rest on the text or structure of the Constitution. Not only do statutory rights and structures go beyond those required by the Constitution, they interact with Constitutional rights in three interesting ways.[5]

First: Statutes transform Constitutional baselines. The Constitution pervasively depends upon statutes to fill in the huge holes in our governance structure and norms. This is more than mere gap filling. Often, the statutes that fill in Constitutional gaps are themselves transformative, and this was certainly the case with school desegregation. Indeed, what *Brown* means to Americans today is the principle created by statute, not the principle the Supreme Court actually announced in *Brown*. After *Brown*, school districts could no longer categorize and exclude students according to race—but the large majority of districts segregated by law in 1953 remained segregated by practice in 1963. The Constitutional status quo was shattered and the *Brown* norm was transformed by legislation. The Civil Rights Act of 1964 withheld federal funds from public programs discriminating on the basis of race, and the Elementary and Secondary Education Amendments of 1965 greatly expanded the amount of federal money available to local schools. Because those statutes came to be aggressively enforced to require school districts to justify de facto segregation, public school integration occurred all over the country, especially in the South. It was not until 1968, right *after* the 1964–65 statutes, that the Supreme Court even ruled that segregated school districts had an obligation to transition to a *unitary* school system, where there were no discernible black schools and white schools. Although this expanded policy has struggled to produce actual school integration, *Brown's* public meaning was altered by what we call "administrative constitutionalism" (chapters 1–3).[6]

The Topeka School District at issue in *Brown* itself illustrates the critical role played by administrative constitutionalism even in Constitutional lawsuits. In 1955, on remand after *Brown II*, the trial judge ruled that Topeka met the Supreme Court's mandate that there not be formal segregation in the public schools—but of course the schools remained segregated as a matter of practice. It was not until 1974 that this state of affairs was successfully challenged—by the Nixon administration's Department of Health, Education and Welfare (HEW), which ruled that Topeka was in violation of Title VI of the 1964 Civil Rights Act and therefore was barred from receiving millions of dollars in educational funds. Although the district court ultimately ruled that HEW's order could not disturb its own 1955 judgment, in the interim HEW's pressure did bestir Topeka to develop a remedial plan that would actually, rather than formally, desegregate its public schools. It was this process, jump-started by administrators enforcing statutory requirements, that Linda Brown Smith reentered in 1979.[7]

Second: Legislative and administrative deliberation over time can create entrenched governance structures and norms. Some of the nation's entrenched governance structures and normative commitments are derived directly from the Constitution, but most are found in *superstatutes* enacted by Congress, executive-legislative partnerships, and consensus of state legislatures. This body of law is important in its own right and worthy of dedicated study. The Civil Rights Act of 1964 is a classic example of a statute that has broad constitutional reverberations. Like *Brown*, the 1964 act sought to entrench the principle that discrimination on the basis of race is not acceptable. But the statute went considerably further than *Brown*, for it applied to private as well as public institutions and created an affirmative obligation for state officials to eliminate illegal discrimination. As to the former point, Title VII not only extended *Brown* ideas to private employment but also deepened the bite of *Brown* by pursuing discrimination that was not open or obvious. As to the latter point, Title VI of the 1964 act instantiated the principle that federal funds should not even indirectly contribute to possible race-discriminatory programs. Most broadly, the Civil Rights Act, as applied, reflected a more ambitious norm than *Brown* did—actual *integration*, not just *nonsegregation*. What this ambitious superstatutory norm actually means is a matter of debate, but it cannot be denied that the norm has had a powerful effect on American culture.[8]

The process of deep entrenchment we describe in this book has three features, all illustrated by the 1964 act. First, entrenchment involves public deliberation, explained below. Second, the deliberation involves several institutions cooperating together as well as protecting their own authority. While the impetus for most small "c" constitutional innovations comes from social movements and the private sector, public deliberation is driven by executive officials as well as legislators and, to a lesser extent, judges. Thus, the antidiscrimination norm originating in the civil rights movement gained the force of law when Congress adopted the 1964 act, but it acquired greater specificity when agency officials such as Sonia Pressman and her colleagues in the Equal Employment Opportunity Commission figured out how to apply the statute to get at hidden or unconscious racist employment practices. Third, entrenching deliberation occurs over a long period of time, and the norm does not stick in our public culture until former opponents agree that the norm is a good one (or at least an acceptable idea). The consensus that has formed around the antidiscrimination norm has come rather quickly, but that consensus ought not to obscure the fact that new disputes and polarities have formed around precisely what that norm requires.[9]

Consider a distinction drawn from Max Weber's theory of power (or "domination"). One kind of power is based upon the *authority to command*, such as the power delegated by the social contract. The Large "C" Constitution announces a hierarchy of commands. State law rules trump private ordering; valid federal statutory rules trump state law; and the Constitution trumps federal as well as state law. Within that hierarchy, superstatutes fit with other federal laws: they trump state law but must give way to the Constitution. Weber also understood that power can flow from what he termed a "constellation of interests," or a social consensus establishing various norms that people will follow because it is in their interest. Power based on the *force of social norms* operates differently from Weberian authority, and we now suggest that law typically operates within both of Weber's spheres. Indeed, this is the space where we situate superstatutes: like ordinary legislation, their authority yields to the Constitution, but like the Constitution itself superstatutes have generated strong social entrenchment that not only makes them resistant to change but also gives them a power beyond their formal legal ambit. For example, small employers are not covered by Title VII of the 1964 act, and under traditional common law rules (the employment at will doctrine) they are legally free not to hire people of color unless they are covered by state antidiscrimination laws. That Title VII is a superstatute means that its norm will be a weighty reason for the noncovered employer to consider in its own hiring decisions, and for a state supreme court to consider if an employee is sued under contract law. We expect that few noncovered employers would openly discriminate, and if they did most state courts would find a way to overrule such discrimination, perhaps modifying the employment at will doctrine to account for the norm. To repeat: the Weberian power of superstatutes rests upon *both* their authority to command *and* their social gravity that induces people to apply or consider the norm beyond its formal command. Notice the similarity to traditional British constitutionalism, where judges interpreted the common law and ordinary statutes in light of landmark statutes; one finds similar discourse in French and German law as well.[10]

Third: The evolution of Large "C" Constitutional law ought to be guided by legislative and administrative deliberations. The Constitution's rules and purposes are announced at a high level of generality, which has contributed to their social entrenchment but has made authoritative application to specific circumstances more tricky. This dilemma has been ameliorated by the fact that federal superstatutes, agency elaborations, and state statutory convergences do address many of those specific issues, and the extent of their social entrenchment does and should influence Constitutional elaboration. Although the Constitution as a formal matter trumps statutes inconsistent with its terms, as a practical matter Constitutional law's evolution is generally—and ought to be—influenced by the norms entrenched in other ways, such as by the development of a state statutory consensus, or through the creation of a federal superstatute.

Accordingly, the Supreme Court's proper Constitutional triumphs have been in cases where the Court enforced Constitutional norms consistent with clear statutory consensus, reached after repeated public deliberations and reflecting an overlapping consensus within the polity. *Brown's* core norm, that public schools should not be racially segregated by law, reflected a state statutory consensus in 1954, whereby virtually all states outside the South had repudiated the school segregation policy, *and* reflected substantial agreement at the national level, consistent with the United States' *amicus* briefs in *Brown* and previous cases. The Warren Court's expansions of *Brown* came in cases that similarly followed statutory principles: *Green v. New Kent County School Board* (1968), whose norm of a school system that is actually *integrated* followed the Civil Rights Act and the Education Amendments as administered; and *Loving v. Virginia* (1967), which followed the convergence of all state legislatures outside the South in holding antimiscegenation laws unConstitutional.[11]

For many Americans, *Brown* was an illustration of a larger point, that the Constitution is our nation's Grand Blueprint and the Guarantor of Its Democracy as well as the Embodiment of Our Highest Aspirations. It is this larger point—this grander myth—that our book questions in a sustained manner. At the same time, we want to present a new and more modest vision. What we are calling small "c" constitutionalism is more mobile in responding to important social movements and social needs, addresses its vision and commands to all Americans and not just government officials, and creates positive structures and affirmative rights in an effort to assure opportunities for personal flourishing by Americans. Modest as this view may appear to be, it is also more demanding of ordinary citizens, for it suggests that there is no "Great Guarantor" of our liberties and insists that, ultimately, the creation and preservation of our freedoms is a never-ending project and a burden that falls on us all.

AMERICA'S REPUBLIC OF STATUTES, TREATIES, AND AGENCY RULES

America's Large "C" Constitution is one of the shortest such documents in the world, and reading the document and its illuminating history would not tell you everything you'd want to know about the fundamental institutions, practices, and norms of our polity, what we shall be calling our small "c" constitution, our working constitution. You would not know where most legal rules come from, how democratic our polity is, and what principles represent our highest aspirations; nor would you have any idea about the details of institutional arrangements and public values. You can only begin to know those things by studying statutes, their implementing regulations, treaties, and executive orders—as well as the political discourse in the myriad associations, social movements, and interest groups by which Americans express themselves and seek to shape our civil society as well as government. The reason we have government is to ensure positive protections for the citizenry. Thus, the state has an affirmative responsibility to ensure everyone's security, to protect us all against personal harm and collective attack, and to guarantee institutions such as the national market and a stable financial system. These are the essence of the modern consumerist state, and it is the republic of statutes, implemented by agencies, and not the Constitution, implemented by judges, that carries out this deepest role of government.[12]

Consider another intriguing point. Statutes, treaties, and rules are of course adopted within the framework authorized by the Constitution—but American practice under the Constitution has transformed our polity into a governance structure that transcends the original Constitution. Here are a few examples.[13]

The U.S. Constitution sets forth the basic structure of government (three-branch national government; bicameralism and presentment for statutes; federalism) and some qualifications for officials. These are the most entrenched features of our government, even as participants quibble over precisely what those commitments mean in practice. Statutes and institutional rules not only fill in important details of the Constitutional structure, they also have altered that structure and have ultimately created a somewhat different structure. The biggest change in the Constitutional structure has been the creation of the modern administrative state, through congressional delegations of *lawmaking* authority to independent agencies such as the Equal Employment Opportunity Commission, executive branch agencies such as the Department of Justice, and even the Supreme Court and various advisory committees. Scholars debate whether such agencies and such lawmaking authority are Constitutional, but almost no one seriously denies that both phenomena are here to stay and have the effect of altering the structure of power in our national government, against as well as beyond the expectations of the Constitution's framers. The framers expected national lawmaking to be the product of the carefully deliberative structure established by Article I, Section 7: statutes have to gain the approval of both chambers of the legislature and, in most cases, the president as well. Yet in the modern administrative state, commissions and bureaus promulgate most legally binding rules. The framework for understanding most national lawmaking and much national adjudication in this country is no longer Article I,

Section 7, of the Constitution, but is instead the Administrative Procedure Act of 1946, which codified the new public order.[14]

Moreover, the Constitution has little to say about the institutions that matter the most to people's lives, such as state and local governments, the family, and the market. Article IV's injunction that the "United States shall guarantee to every State in this Union a Republican form of Government" is one of the most open-ended provisions in the Constitution, and judges have declined to enforce that provision. The fundamental rules structuring families and markets have traditionally been set by state common law of marriage, property, contract, and tort. Indeed, at the time of our nation's founding, the people's fundamental rights and duties were mainly defined by state common law; America's original small "c" constitution was outlined, for the most part, in Sir William Blackstone's *Commentaries on the Law of England* (1765), which went through many American editions. Although the American Revolution in constitutionalism after 1789 has been the creation of national superstatutory regimes administered by agencies, a big part of our small "c" constitution to this day is defined by state common law or codifications of it like the Uniform Commercial Code.[15]

Consider also our nation's democratic structure. Although the Constitution of 1789 was more electorally inclusive than other contemporary frameworks, from today's perspective it had many gaps. We the People, in 1789, did not mean All of Us. Political citizenship did *not* extend to people, like Linda Brown Smith, who were female or African American. Our current status as a democracy with wide participation is a product of wrenching, sometimes violent, social movements that built on, molded, and pushed popular expectations about who ought to participate as political actors. In the first two generations of American history, the Jeffersonian and Jacksonian periods, expansion of the franchise came entirely through state statutory and constitutional change. The Fifteenth (1871) and Nineteenth (1920) Amendments barred discriminations because of race and sex, but the former was nullified by state statutory and constitutional impediments— impediments that were ultimately overthrown through the Voting Rights Act of 1965, discussed in chapter 2. Indeed, since 1920, most of the important changes in America's democratic constitution have come through federal statutes, state and local law, and sometimes state constitutional amendments.[16]

The Constitution is most famous for its protection of individual rights, enumerated in the Bill of Rights and the Fourteenth Amendment. When people think that issues of public morality invariably end up in court, they are thinking of the open-textured assurances of these rights-protecting provisions. As the legislative implementation of *Brown* suggests, however, statutes typically play an important role here as well—and sometimes (unlike in *Brown*) they are the exclusive mechanism by which public norms have formed around the protection of individual or minority rights. Like protections against race discrimination, protections against sex discrimination enjoy both Constitutional and statutory recognition. The difference is that in the arena of sex discrimination, the statutory protections came first and remain much more extensive. Thus, more than a decade before the Supreme Court formally recognized sex as a Constitutionally suspect classification (1976), Congress barred private (and after 1972 public) employers from discriminating because of sex. Title IX of the Education Amendments of 1972 barred private as well as public schools receiving federal funds from practicing sex discrimination, which the Department of Education and the Supreme Court have interpreted to include sexual harassment by other students as well as teachers and staff. Most dramatically, the Supreme Court ruled that discrimination based upon pregnancy, a form of exclusion potentially faced by Linda Brown Smith and most other women, was not *actually* discrimination "because of sex"—a ruling promptly overridden, for public and private employers, by the Pregnancy Discrimination Act of 1978, discussed in chapter 1.[17] Following the PDA model, equality guarantees for most minority groups are substantially or entirely creations of federal or state statutes—including laws against discrimination on the basis of age, disability, and sexual or gender orientation. The purpose of these statutes is to extend *Brown's* antidiscrimination principle to groups the Supreme Court has not protected under the aegis of the Equal Protection Clause.[18]

When the Browns of Topeka participated in the Constitutional litigation that bore their family name, they were seeking more than just formal equality; they were seeking security and opportunities for their daughter and her future progeny. The Constitution of 1789 says little or nothing about the right to a solid education that was their core goal, nor had it much to say about rights to compete in a free and fair market, to decent housing and adequate medical care, or to security against old age, sickness, accident, and unemployment. To the extent these securities are guaranteed by law, it is through federal statutes and state law. Although most Americans like the Browns did not appreciate the Sherman Anti-Trust Act of 1890, it provided structural protections for consumers like them when it gave teeth to the ideal of a free market (chapter 3), and the Federal Reserve Act of 1914 delivered a similar assurance of a sound financial system (chapter 7). The Social Security Act of 1935 was the starting point for a national program of social insurance against old age, disability, and unemployment (chapter 4).[19]

ENTRENCHMENT OF STATUTORY NORMS THROUGH REPUBLICAN DELIBERATION

The first theme in this book is that America enjoys a constitution of statutes supplementing and often supplanting its written Constitution as to the most

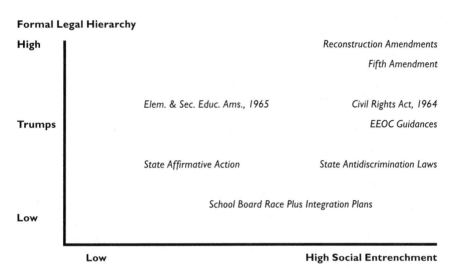

Formal Legal Hierarchy

High
                              Reconstruction Amendments

                                 Fifth Amendment

Elem. & Sec. Educ. Ams., 1965   *Civil Rights Act, 1964*

Trumps   *EEOC Guidances*

State Affirmative Action   *State Antidiscrimination Laws*

School Board Race Plus Integration Plans

Low

Low   **High Social Entrenchment**

Figure 1. Weber's hierarchy of commands and continuum of social entrenchment

fundamental features of governance: Which institutions make which rules? To whom are these institutions accountable? What rights do we citizens have, and what institutional structures and protections does the state provide us? A second theme is the ongoing deliberative process by which small "c" constitutional norms and institutions become *entrenched* in our polity. We use the term "entrenched" to refer to norms and practices that are accepted not just because of their Weberian authority to command but also because of the force of a Weberian constellation of interests, namely, a popular consensus that the norm or practice is a good thing to believe or do. Figure 1 maps this contrast.

As figure 1 suggests, most (though not all) Constitutional rules are socially entrenched as well as hierarchically supreme. Indeed, the standard account of American Constitutionalism posits that our foundational national institutions and commitments are incorporated in a timeless document whose interpretation and elaboration are largely entrusted to judges but which can only be fundamentally changed through a supermajoritarian politics of an energized populace. Paralleling the process by which the Constitution of 1789 came into effect, Article V of the Constitution lays out that process, as in figure 2, on the next page.

As figure 1 suggests, this institutionally interactive, deliberative process usually contributes to normative entrenchment, such that a Constitutional rule added through Article V is powerful *both* because it is legally authoritative *and* because its strong deliberation requirement usually generates a constellation of

---

Constitution of 1789 + Existing Amendments

⇓

Supreme Court implementation of Constitution in concrete cases, but an
important problem is addressed badly or not at all

⇓

Supermajority (two-thirds) in Congress proposes Constitutional Amendment

⇓

Supermajority (three-fourths) of states ratify Amendment, and
it becomes part of the Constitution

⇓

Supreme Court interprets the Amendment (dynamically) and adjusts Constitution in light of its
precepts

Figure 2. New Large "C" Constitutional norm

interests that reinforce its normative power. But a central dilemma confronting the standard account of American Constitutionalism is that the Article V
process has not worked for big issues since 1920 (when it yielded women the
right to vote), while judicial expansions in post-*Brown* decisions have been
controversial and, sometimes, disastrous. Chapter 1 shows how leading Constitutional theorists have grappled with this dilemma by amending the standard
account to recognize functional equivalents to the big showdown for Constitutional change contemplated by Article V.

By the standard account, entrenchment of fundamental institutions and
norms comes through a process of a supermajoritarian higher politics, followed
by judicial elaboration. Chapter 2 suggests the outlines of a different understanding of what entrenchment is and how it comes about. America is now, and
long has been, a *republic of statutes*. In such a republic, normative commitments are announced and entrenched *not* through a process of Constitutional
amendments or Supreme Court pronouncements but instead through the
more gradual process of legislation, administrative implementation, public
feedback, and legislative reaffirmation and elaboration. Although such statutes
are legally subject to the superior authority of the Constitution, in practice they

rival and sometimes supplant the Constitution because of the way in which their norms have stuck in American society as the result of this process of *republican deliberation.*

What is republican deliberation? Deliberation, as we are using the term, is the interactive process by which a group of people decides what to do. Republican deliberation is that process engaged in by or through popularly accountable organs of governance. Three features characterize republican deliberation. First, all kinds of deliberation are *purposive.* Deliberation is not only seriously problem solving, it also considers solutions in light of larger public purposes as well as their capacity to solve the problem. Deliberation considers trade-offs. Problems cannot usually be completely solved at an acceptable cost, and certainly not immediately solved under those circumstances. Deliberation takes into account not only the costs and benefits (broadly understood) of different solutions or norms but also their consistency with the polity's larger commitments.[20]

Second, all kinds of deliberation are *dialogic.* Deliberation requires individual participants to be at least somewhat open to facts, hypotheses, and other viewpoints about the nature of the problem, possible solutions, and the scope and content of proposed norms. The dialogic feature of republican deliberation requires differently situated participants and institutions to provide inputs that reflect their comparative advantages: agencies provide information about the problem, including social and economic structures framing the problem and affecting solutions; legislators balance incommensurable values and create compromises as well as new governmental structures and programs to deal with the matter; judges fit and sometimes evaluate legislative directives and agency rules in light of the nation's larger body of law. The dialogic features of deliberation assure that both its process and its substance will be dynamic. Indeed, deliberation about important applications of larger public norms changes those norms and those commitments.

Third, republican deliberation is *accountable* to stakeholders: the decision makers have to answer for the choices they make and the trade-offs incurred. Thus, private participants are accountable to their sponsors and social movements, while governmental participants are ultimately accountable to the voters as well as public critics in the media and academe. Voter accountability is strongest for House members, who run for reelection every two years, and weakest for federal judges, who effectively have life tenure. Accountability is linked to reason giving. The House members who face the voters most often are most closely attuned to the electorate's raw (that is, needing little justification) preferences and are most prone to defending their choices and trade-offs in terms of political *will.* Agency officials and, even more, judges do not face the voters at all and have a much higher burden of justifying their decisions as *judgments* rationally consistent with the policy choices already made by a past Congress or likely to be acceptable to the current or a future one.[21]

Article V draws much of its power from the republican deliberation that its process induces. The requirement that both Congress and three-quarters of the state legislatures must agree to a Constitutional amendment assures that only proposals with wide public support will even be seriously advanced and that a diverse array of constituencies will have to go along for ratification to occur. The strenuous procedural hurdles, however, have also made Article V a process that cannot accomplish big changes—a point many critics have made—but our additional problem with Article V is that it front-loads deliberation: our representatives must sign onto a normative commitment without knowing exactly how it will work, either substantively or institutionally. As we learned from Prohibition, a Constitutional mistake is very costly and hard to revoke. For these reasons, significant Constitutional amendments dried up after 1920, and a more lengthy and polycentric statutory process has essentially superseded it.

In America's republic of statutes, republican deliberation over fundamental national commitments has migrated, relatively speaking, away from Constitutionalism and toward legislative and administrative constitutionalism. Specifically, there are three different kinds of sub-Constitutional law that have been the situs for this kind of entrenched national commitment to institutional structure or norms:

- *State statutory convergences*, such as state expansions of the franchise in the Jeffersonian and Jacksonian eras (chapter 2), state criminalization of abortion and birth control in the second half of the nineteenth century and the decriminalization and then espousal of birth control in the middle part of the twentieth (chapter 5), and the denigration followed by tolerance of gay people in the latter half of the twentieth century (chapter 8).[22]
- *Federal superstatutes*, such as the Civil Rights Act of 1964 (chapter 1), the Voting Rights Act of 1965 (chapter 2), the Sherman Anti-Trust Act of 1890 (chapter 3), the Social Security Act of 1935 (chapter 4), the Family Planning Services and Population Research Act of 1970 (chapter 5), the Clean Water Act of 1972 and 1977 (chapter 6), the United States Bank Acts of 1791 and 1816 and the Federal Reserve Act of 1914 (chapter 7), the Defense of Marriage Act of 1996 (chapter 8), and the Uniform Code of Military Justice of 1950 (chapter 9).[23]
- *Transnational agreements and conventions*, such as the Geneva Conventions of 1949, which served as a focal point of opposition to the constitutional innovations of the Bush-Cheney administration (chapter 9).[24]

In a series of (nonexhaustive) case studies, this book explores the process by which a superstatutory principle or policy becomes entrenched. Every superstatutory policy begins with an important public need and, usually, strong political demand, as through a social movement such as the civil rights, populist, women's rights, and old-age assistance movements, but also the very different new capitalist (chapter 7) and the national security (chapter 9) movements of the early twentieth and early twenty-first centuries, respectively. Enactment of ambitious statutes demanded by We the People is just the beginning, for many highly popular statutes do not have social legs. The process of implementation by administrators and judges and feedback from the citizenry is essential if a popular statute is to develop the supportive constellation of interests that Weber identified as a deeper source of power. Entrenchment usually entails the following three features. First, the statute's strong supporters and administrators (an overlapping group if the statute is to succeed) have to figure out practical and cost-effective ways to implement the putative superstatute, with evidence that it is making progress toward its stated goal(s). Second, the statutory application has to avoid the disasters predicted by opponents and, even better, ought to find ways to appeal to the values and concerns held by opponents. Third, the emerging superstatute must be sufficiently valuable to an important and expanding group in American society that it generates an enthusiastic and dynamic and growing base of popular support. If all three of these conditions are met, it is likely that a subsequent legislature will reaffirm the putative superstatute and expand upon its principle or policy. As illustrated by case studies of the pregnancy (chapter 1), voting rights (chapter 2), antitrust (chapter 3), and social security laws (chapter 4), federal superstatutes are consolidated after a new and differently constituted Congress reaffirms the original, ambitious statutory initiative.

Popular and ambitious laws mature into superstatutes through a process of entrenchment that is *institutional*, but without the rigid supermajoritarian process required by Article V; that is *deliberative*, but with the focus on agencies and legislatures rather than courts; and that is *popular*, but with feedback occurring over time in a series of episodes rather than in one big Constitutional poll. In short, rather than changing fundamental institutional structures and normative commitments through a big showdown requiring immediate supermajorities at both the national and the state level, as the Article V model recommends, the superstatutory model produces change through a series of statutes, together with implementational feedback, that stick in our public culture over a period of time. Chapters 1 and 2 of this book develop the theoretical and practical bases for our different understanding, using antidiscrimination and voting statutes as our templates. The remaining chapters illustrate and fill in the details of this theory.

The central procedural feature of constitutional entrenchment is repeated legislative refinement and reaffirmation of the new norm or institution over a period of time—in contrast with the more linear supermajoritarian process of an Article V Constitutional Amendment (figure 3). This central feature works somewhat differently when constitutional entrenchment occurs through state statutory convergences. (Federal superstatutes, by the way, are often themselves copies or adaptations of successful state experiments, as illustrated by the Civil Rights Act of 1964 and the Social Security Act.) In that event, the repeated legislative affirmation of the new norm or institution is a process that occurs across most of the states. For example, New York was a pioneer in adopting married women's property laws; the entrenchment of the *national* norm came through constant pressure by feminist groups not only on the New York legislature to reassert and expand the norm (often to override foot-dragging judicial decisions) but also on legislatures in other states, a story we tell in chapter 5. The evolution of the gay-tolerant constitution is a story of state statutory convergences, recounted in chapter 8.

This is how constitutional change works in a republic of statutes. We shall also maintain that this process of constitutional change is typically superior to the models laid out in Article V or suggested by *Brown v. Board of Education.* Without denigrating the importance of the Large "C" Constitution, which establishes the basic structure of our government and remains a potential path toward entrenched commitments, we maintain that the small "c" constitution of statutes is a better way to develop and express our foundational institutions and norms. It is better in that it is more adaptable to changed circumstances (now including developments around the world), is more legitimate than the Constitutional updating that unelected judges routinely accomplish in the default of a workable Constitutional amendment process, and produces more robust results than the Article V or *Brown* approach standing alone.

The chapters in this book develop this hypothesis through case studies in arenas as different as the responsibility of the workplace to accommodate women (chapter 1), voting rules (chapter 2), state responsibility for free markets (chapter 3), social security (chapter 4), regulation of the family (chapter 5), environmental nondegradation (chapter 6), monetary policy (chapter 7), treatment of sexual and gender minorities (chapter 8), and national security (chapter 9). Each of these traces the process by which federal superstatutes or state statutory convergences took shape (often after experimentation) and became entrenched. As noted above, our accounts begin with an important social or economic problem that becomes a political problem because of social movement demands, then move toward the enactment and implementation of superstatutes, and finally trace the perceived success of those new statutory regimes.

Social movement or economic problem creates demand for state action.
Norm entrepreneur (such as the president) secures spot on public agenda

⇓

Legislative deliberation, supported by public, generates statute embodying new norm or
addressing critical economic problem

⇓

Administrative implementation/expansion of new statute, with feedback and pushback from
media, experts, public, judges

⇓

Legislature revisits statutory norm and reaffirms it in the face of opposition

⇓

Administrative elaboration of the norm, with further public and official (judicial, etc.) feedback
and legislative revision

Figure 3. New small "c" constitutional norm (federal superstatutes)

Another way of thinking about the case studies in this book would be to focus on the way in which our country's republic of statutes addresses the core values that the state offers to its citizens. One value is equality, where all citizens are given reasons to consider themselves stakeholders because the state treats them all the same, with no social group outside the equal protection of the law and the state poised to be responsive to new groups and new demands. Another value is the state's guarantee of market and financial structures facilitating economic opportunities for all Americans. A third value of the state, and one that has been front and center since 9/11/2001, is to provide security for all Americans—not just against foreign attacks but also against the violence we commit against one another and the longer-term threats our activities pose to the environment. Arrayed according to the process and institutional themes of our book in its table of contents, our case studies can also be arrayed according to these fundamental subjects, as follows:

Equal Citizenship

- The constitution of equality and administrative constitutionalism (chapter 1)
- The democratic constitution and our episodic republic (chapter 2)
- The antihomosexual constitution and its dis-entrenchment (chapter 8)

MARKETS

- The constitution of the market and state legitimacy (chapter 3)
- The monetary constitution and administrative experimentation (chapter 7)
- The green constitution and the politics of judicial deference (chapter 6)

SECURITY

- The safety net constitution and the politics of entrenchment (chapter 4)
- The constitution of the family and state statutory convergences (chapter 5)
- The national security constitution and the balance of powers (chapter 9)

The book's themes can also be arrayed as in table 1.

As you read the accounts we have provided for the working through of institutional structures and public values by legislators, administrators, and judges, consider larger normative lessons that statutory constitutionalism suggests. For starters, our theory raises the stakes of administrative law and statutory interpretation. The sharp differences between Constitutional and statutory interpretation ought to be questioned in the light of the account we provide for civil rights, voting, social security, finance, antitrust, environmental, and national security statutes in the first seven chapters. Not only do Large "C" Constitutional issues formally connect to statutory issues, statutory interpretation involving legislative or administrative efforts to entrench new norms that have big consequences for society ought to consider the broader matters typically consigned to theories of Constitutional interpretation. What role should broad and ambitious statutory purposes play in understanding technical statutory language and structure? Is the original meaning binding, or does it give way as the statute evolves? How should subsequent legislative action, or inaction, figure in statutory interpretation? Should

Table 1. Themes of this book: process (vertical) and substance (horizontal)

	Equality	*Market*	*Security*
Process of small "c" constitutionalism	Job discrimination (ch. 1) Voting rights (ch. 2)	Antitrust (ch. 3)	
Process of entrenchment		Green regulation (ch. 6)	Old age (ch. 4) Family (ch. 5)
Cycles of entrenchment & dis-entrenchment	Gay rights (ch. 8)	Money/Finance (ch. 7)	National security (ch. 9)

courts defer to agency visions in these matters, or does the judiciary have an independent contribution to make? Chapter 6 sets forth our preliminary views as to these issues, but we invite readers to form their own conclusions.

In addition, our theory makes *deliberation* central to fundamental law but suggests an understanding of deliberation different from that reflected in much legal scholarship. For example, we do not understand the Supreme Court as our exemplary deliberative body. A Court-centered understanding of deliberation values detachment from politics, principled reasoning from uncontested premises, and case-by-case incrementalism. This understanding leaves out half of what "deliberation" is and ought to be. In a modern complicated democracy, deliberation should be politically engaged as well as rational, should be forward-looking and openly normative as well as principled, and should engage in wholesale and not just retail rule making. Perhaps like some theories of judging, legislative and administrative deliberation should deploy practical reasoning to manage or accommodate what appear to be incommensurable values and options. Deliberation should be complicated, polycentric, experimental, forward-looking, problem-solving.[25]

Our book is about America's *republic* of statutes. Such a title mobilizes not only the interactive, forward-looking understanding of deliberation suggested here but also the classic republican notion of citizens and public leaders acting for the common good. This notion is often marginalized or ridiculed on liberal grounds: everyone acts in his or her own self-interest, and appeals to the common good are cynical ploys to trick people into voting against their economic interests. But even the most beady-eyed liberal concedes that "self-interest" often entails altruism or public happiness. This book contains many post-1789 examples of republican engagement—often in the context of social movements but also in the context of the social safety net, market regulation, and public finance. Modern republican heroes include not only the Reverend Martin Luther King Jr. but also Wendy Webster Williams, Susan Deller Ross, Ruth Weyand, Eleanor Holmes Norton, Marsha Berzon, Ruth Bader Ginsburg, and others who spearheaded a revolution in the relationship of the workplace to pregnancy and family (chapter 1); Burke Marshall, Nicholas Katzenbach, and Lyndon Johnson, who drafted and implemented the Voting Rights Act of 1965 (chapter 2); Senators John Sherman, George Edmunds, and George Hoar, the legislators who created our first nationwide antitrust statute (chapter 3); Margaret Sanger, Mary Dennett, and other birth control and family planning advocates (chapter 4); Abraham Epstein, Frances Perkins, and Franklin Roosevelt, the parents of the Social Security Act (chapter 5); Rachel Carson and Aldo Leopold, theorists who advanced green thinking decades before Earth Day, 1970, as well as Senator Edmund Muskie and Representative Morris Udall, prime movers in environmental legislation (chapter 6); Nelson Aldrich, Paul Warburg, and Carter Glass, important architects of the Federal Reserve System (chapter 7); Frank Kameny, Del Martin and Phyllis Lyon, José Sarria, and other early leaders of the lesbian and gay rights movement (chapter 8); and President Dwight Eisenhower and other military heroes who championed the Geneva Convention and norms against abuse and torture in international conflicts, as well as Senators John McCain and John Kerry, Vietnam-era veterans who defended our country's Geneva Convention values under fire during the war on terror (chapter 9).

Finally, our project has implications for the broader transformation of what We the People expect from the state. Large "C" Constitutional scholars have devoted millions of pages to the Constitutional "switch in time" during the New Deal, *Brown* and ensuing equal protection jurisprudence, and the present relationship among presidential power, civil liberties, and congressional authorizations—and only a few thousand pages to the more fundamental transformation of the republic and the conditions of its legitimacy. When read in its entirety, this book documents Philip Bobbitt's suggestion that state legitimacy has evolved toward a *consumerist constitution*, though we trace the origins of that constitution back to the New Deal (much earlier than Bobbitt does). That is, the state's legitimacy is no longer tied to rules of recognition or the belief that the state is promoting the public welfare, it is more closely tied to the state's affirmative assurance to every citizen of the security and institutions giving those citizens ample room to make the *choices* that fulfill their needs and desires. The consumerist constitution is the product of a statutory mosaic that includes the expansion of democracy and voting, to assure that every social group is represented in our multicultural republic (chapter 2); the consumer welfare turn in federal antitrust law (chapter 3) and public finance (chapter 7); the government's assurance of fair employment opportunities (chapter 1) and a prosperous retirement (chapter 4) for all Americans; the progression of family law away from marriage with two children toward families we choose (chapter 5), including lesbian and gay families (chapter 8); and the American government's promise to win the war on terror, where the goal of the adversary is to undermine states of consent such as ours (chapter 9).[26]

JUDGES IN THE REPUBLIC OF STATUTES

Is there a productive role for unelected judges in a republic of statutes? On the one hand, we argue for a much more modest role for judges in Constitutional cases. Large "C" Constitutional judicial review is and should be *deliberation-*

respecting. The normative power of the small "c" constitution arises from the fact that it emerges from a robust type of deliberation—elected representatives responsive to popular needs and demands craft a bold statute, administrators work with affected groups to devise a workable implementation, popular response feeds into the agency and legislators and may figure in a presidential election, and legislators reaffirm and expand upon the statutory scheme. This kind of deliberation enjoys three kinds of legitimacy: it operates within the *formal* Constitutional structure (like ordinary statutes); is distinctively *democratic* in operation and thus enjoys some participatory legitimacy; and meets functional needs of citizens in ways that impose reasonable burdens on other citizens and thus enjoys a *pragmatic* legitimacy. Most of the chapters in this book contain examples where the Constitution accommodates superstatutory initiatives through deliberation-respecting judicial review. For example, the Constitution's arguable original meaning did not stand in the way of Congress's imposing a duty of accommodating families on state employers (chapter 1), placing the South into electoral receivership for a generation (chapter 2), regulating local anticompetitive agreements and conspiracies (chapter 3), funding and managing state old-age assistance programs (chapter 4), regulating localized and episodic estuaries (chapter 6), chartering the Bank of the United States or imposing legal tender status on mere paper money (chapter 7), and forbidding the commander in chief to authorize torture and other inhuman treatment of persons detained for allegedly violating the laws of war (chapter 9).

Deliberation-respecting review is available to aggressively enforce some Constitutional rights. For example, judicial review might be the only mechanism available for jump-starting institutions of public deliberation that are broken. Thus, the apartheid regime in the deep South was not deliberative in the republican sense: its laws were adopted after whites disenfranchised and terrorized voters of color and hence reflected a pale democracy and were implemented through secretive and violent processes, including lynching, rape, and economic terror. Judicial review is also a mechanism for enforcing rights that are particularly relevant to republican deliberation, including rights to vote, publish and criticize, form normative associations, and engage in political activities. Deliberation-respecting review is also a mechanism for bringing outlier jurisdictions into conformity with national norms under exceptional circumstances. The best example involves antimiscegenation laws. Right after *Brown*, the Supreme Court dismissed an appeal from the Virginia Supreme Court's affirmation of its law criminalizing marriage between persons of a different race, in part because most states still barred different-race marriage. Surely in part because of *Brown*, legislatures in one state after another repealed their antimiscegenation laws. By the time the issue returned to the Court, in *Loving v. Virginia* (1967), only sixteen (southern) states had such laws. Chapter 8 and the Conclusion offer other examples of this phenomenon.[27]

If our understanding of the judicial role in enforcing the Large "C" Constitution is modest, we believe the more significant judicial role lies in the incremental elaboration of superstatutes and treaties through statutory interpretation, a topic that is the focus of chapters 6 and 9. Indeed, as Professor Philip Frickey has classically argued, the Supreme Court's Large "C" Constitutional vision is frequently expressed through canons of statutory interpretation that enforce those values indirectly. By interpreting statutes, including superstatutes, to avoid Constitutional problems or to reflect Constitutional structures and values, the Court can reverse the burden of inertia when those values are in play: if Congress does not consider those values and its statute is ambiguous, the Court will essentially remand the issue for further consideration. The political interests seeking Constitutional innovation bear the burden of pointing this out to legislators and securing their explicit agreement that such innovation is merited. Such an approach is *deliberation-inducing* as to such fundamental matters.[28]

In chapter 6, we apply these ideas to judicial review of agency interpretations. By far, most of the interpretive work in the modern state is carried out by agencies, and what we are calling "administrative constitutionalism" is aggressive agency application of superstatutes to carry out their purposes in a manner that is workable, coherent, and consistent with the nation's other normative commitments. Modern judges say they are deferential to agency interpretations; although judges are not as deferential as they claim to be, our theory provides one justification for deference. Sometimes, however, administrative constitutionalism goes wrong, and we provide examples of that in chapters 7–9. Judicial review is not always the most effective institutional response to administrative constitutionalism gone wrong, but judges do provide a backstop for aggressive interpretations that go beyond legislative authorizations, betray superstatutory purposes, or fall athwart larger normative commitments. Most important, we argue that judges should engage in *deliberation-rewarding* review of agency interpretations. Where the agency has engaged in republican deliberation (serious attention to statutory purposes, input from the public and other relevant institutions, and consistency with larger norms), its rules should generally be accepted. Where there is scant evidence of such deliberation, judges should be undeferential; they might agree with the agency's interpretation on the merits, but they cut the agency no slack under those circumstances.

Part I

STATUTES AND CONSTITUTIONALISM

Aristotle understood a polity's "constitution" to be its most fundamental practices, institutions, and norms. Modern Americans have lost this understanding of constitutionalism. Although some believe the Constitution of 1789 to be America's version of Aristotle's constitution, most believe it is a higher law—a definitive statement of the terms of our social contract or of our best aspirations. In the first part of this book, we re-present Aristotle for a modern audience and outline a theory of small "c" constitutionalism that is richer and exercises a greater influence in our lives and on our identities than the Large "C" Constitution does. In the process, we suggest a theory of deliberation and a more complicated understanding of the role of statutes in American public law.

The Constitution of 1789 is a great document but suffers from three weaknesses that prevent it from serving as anything but a partial statement of our country's institutions, norms, and rights. First, the Constitution is old and too hard to amend. Its generalized and often vague terms allow the Constitution to accommodate most governmental innovations needed to meet evolving social and economic needs, but those same terms deprive the Constitution of sharp relevance to modern issues. In lieu of Article V amendments, the official Constitutional updating is up to judges through dynamic interpretations, but judges have neither the legitimacy nor the expertise to do a proper job of Constitutional updating. Second, the Constitution is largely structural and process oriented, which is a great virtue for judge-enforced documents that need to last a long time, but which limits the Constitution's relevance for the substantive values and commitments important to the polity. Combined with the fact that judges are the primary interpreters, this feature ensures that the Constitution will mainly be a source of negative limits on government and will not provide positive aspirations for government or the details for carrying out those aspirations. Third, the Constitution is primarily addressed to state actors and says little to nonpublic sources of authority and power. For example, the Constitution of 1789 did not perfectly reflect the extent to which the United States, even then, was a polity saturated with democratic, egalitarian thinking. Even as amended to expand the franchise and to add equal protection guarantees, the Constitution understates We the People's commitment to democracy and egalitarian baselines in private as well as public workplaces, schools, and social institutions.

As we argue in chapter 1, these and other features of the Constitution have generated enormous academic interest in new theories of Constitutionalism outside the courts—theories that focus on Constitutional deliberation by the legislature, the president, and the citizenry. We applaud those projects, but ours is more radical. The most exciting features of citizenship, governance, and public values today are those for which pitifully little, if anything, can be pried out of the Constitution. Nowadays, these issues are typically addressed through *superstatutes* rather than through Constitutional litigation. Each chapter in this first part explores the dynamic history and normative power of a particular superstatute: the Pregnancy Discrimination Act of 1978 (chapter 1), which amended the Civil Rights Act of 1964 (Introduction); the Voting Rights Act (VRA) of 1965 (chapter 2); and the Sherman Act of 1890 (chapter 3). What these superstatutes have in common is that each (1) embodied a new principle or policy displacing common law baselines, responsive to important social or economic challenges facing the country; (2) was drafted and enacted after a process of publicized institutional deliberation responsive to the voices and needs of We the People; and (3) stuck in the public culture, after a period of implementation and formal confirmation by Congress after further public discussion.

The norm entrepreneurs for each of the statutes in this part are legislators and executive officials. A central focus of each chapter is the process of "administrative constitutionalism." Administrative constitutionalism is the normative, problem-solving vision held by political (as opposed to judicial) officers as they work to enact, implement, and administer landmark statutes. As we are using the term, administrative constitutionalism includes norm entrepreneurship by legislators and their staffs, chief executives and their advisers, and agency officials. We could label this congressional-presidential-administrative constitutionalism, a move we resist because of its terminological clunkiness. And unlike prior authors who focus effective governance within the White House or Congress, we want to emphasize the primary role played by agencies and administrative officials.

Going beyond earlier work claiming that legislators and presidents have an independent authority to interpret the Large "C" Constitution, our argument is that deliberation serving the public good by administrators as well as legislators is central to the fundamental structure and values of American public policy. Administrative constitutionalists will consider and interpret the Large "C" Constitution, but that process is not independent of the process by which legislative and executive officials deliberate about how best to address a pressing public problem proactively, practically, and prophylactically. The process by which statutory principles and policies are entrenched in our polity usually depends on the ability of administrators to flesh out those principles and policies into a coherent and attractive statutory scheme.

As a matter of law's hierarchy of formal authority, superstatutes are subordinate to the Constitution—but in the functional terms of public values and social norms, superstatutes resemble Constitutional rules in the following ways. They reflect foundational principles that influence law and policy beyond their formal authority. They are durable, adaptable, and dynamic as applied across decades. They spawn both legal chains (rules building on them) and legal webs (rules and practices related to their precepts). They exercise normative gravitational force, bending other legal rules to their principles and policies. Indeed, superstatutes sometimes rival Constitutional rules, bending an ambiguous or even hostile Constitutional tradition to acquiesce in superstatutory innovations. For example, the Voting Rights Act has not only changed the character of our democracy, it has altered our Constitutional federalism as well. The Sherman Act was an inspiration for a whole line of nontextual Constitutional doctrine. The phenomenon we describe is not unfamiliar in modern public law. Before Great Britain's membership in the European Union, British constitutionalism was articulated through statutes, conventions, and the common law. Civil law countries such as Germany, France, and Israel recognize additional normative principles (which the French call "fundamental principles of the republic") that exercise normative rather than directory force in their public law.

By our account, a central feature of America's republic of statutes is that they are products of deliberation, the process by which our polity evaluates and chooses among policy options, implements those choices, and then reconsiders them in light of experience. (As explained in the Introduction, we have a dynamic, problem-solving, and republican understanding of deliberation.) Under our theory, deliberation plays several different roles. On the one hand, deliberation explores the intrinsic merits of different proposals, their likely ability to contribute positively to the common good or the purposes for which a state response is needed. Call this the *merits value* of deliberation. On the other hand, deliberation contributes to the content-independent reasons for accepting a statutory rule. Call this deliberation's *legitimating value*. The traditional content-independent reason for following a legal rule is based on acceptance of appropriate exercises of state authority. The deliberative process helps citizens understand the principle or policy behind the rule as well as some of the accepted elaborations. Another reason for following a legal rule is the web of norms that accumulate around the rule helping to coordinate social behavior; under norm-based legitimation, I follow or support the rule because others are attached to the rule, and it connects me to a desirable network. The deliberative process helps create network effects by creating or signaling a consensus around the rule, suggesting reasons why various groups will benefit from it, and associating even perceived rule violation with bad consequences. Thus, repeated congressional and agency deliberations over voting rights between 1965 and 1982 went beyond the obvious goal of justifying as well as explaining the VRA's regulatory regime; they also strongly contributed to the norm that no adult should be denied the right to vote. The deliberative process built a coalition of different interests that aligned to support that norm, and once it was put in operation almost all elected officials covered by the VRA had strong incentives to support it—for otherwise they would be viewed as disrespecting some of the citizens whose votes they needed.

This is a key feature of superstatutes: they are supported not just by the normal obligation to obey the law but also by a broader social network, including but not limited to the group directly helped by the statute and its administrators. Superstatutes instantiate both social norms and legal rules—and the two processes interact. Accordingly, the superstatute's rules are ones that most people *want* to follow, for their own reasons and not just because they fear state penalties. In turn, the legal rules provide a focal point for social norms arising in connection with the superstatute. And the norm associated with the superstatute has bite beyond the four corners of the statute itself. We explore and elaborate these ideas in the first three chapters.

The Constitution of Equality and Administrative Constitutionalism

Carolyn Aiello supported herself as a hairdresser at Salvatore's Hair Cutting Company in San Francisco. But her livelihood was (temporarily) cut off when complications associated with her pregnancy required her to take a medical leave on June 21, 1972. The doctors discovered that Aiello had an ectopic pregnancy and performed surgery to terminate her pregnancy. Although she would ultimately return to work on July 28, she could not afford the loss of even a month's income. Like millions of other Americans, she applied for unemployment benefits on the basis of her physical disability. But, unlike almost all other applicants having serious even if temporary disabilities, her claim was denied. California's unemployment compensation program excluded from its coverage disability claims based upon pregnancy.[1]

Living in Portsmouth, Virginia, Sherrie O'Steen worked on the assembly line of a local General Electric factory. When she became pregnant in 1970, GE forced her to take unpaid sick leave for the remainder of her pregnancy. "One day my boss came and told me, 'You're too big now, you're going to have to go.'" Being thrown out of work cost O'Steen not only her needed wages but also her husband, who accused Sherrie of losing her job on purpose, because she was lazy. Like a flame, he flickered out of Sherrie's life. Without income for herself and the child she was carrying, O'Steen lived without heat and sufficient food until she could return to work after the pregnancy.[2]

Most Americans today would consider the treatment of Aiello and O'Steen to be unConstitutional sex discrimination. Not necessarily. Under the standard account of American Constitutionalism, We the People, in an act of supermajoritarian commitment, created a foundational document that protects us against oppression through jurisdictional limits on government authority and through enumerated rights that individuals have against the state. Judges are the primary or ultimate enforcers of those limits and those rights. The standard account is libertarian and negative rather than affirmative and demanding as to state responsibility for injustices. Accordingly, Sherrie O'Steen, the wronged General Electric employee, had no *Constitutional* claim, because her grievances were against a private company and not against the state. What if O'Steen's lawyer had filed a complaint against the state, for tolerating and therefore enabling private centers of economic and political power to subject women to discriminatory and degraded conditions? This would have satisfied the state action requirement for Constitutional claims but would still have been laughed out of court. Federal courts will generally not recognize Constitutional claims based upon the state's failure to help its citizens, as opposed to its commission of harm against them. O'Steen's lawyer knew not to make such a claim.[3]

Because she was excluded from a state-sponsored unemployment insurance program, Carolyn Aiello's Constitutional claim satisfied the state action requirement, and the state had harmed her by denying her benefits almost everybody else received. Aiello's lawyers, Wendy Webster Williams and Peter Weiner, argued that California's exclusion of pregnancy-based unemployment from its compensation scheme constituted discrimination against women in violation of the Constitution's equal protection guarantee. Their claim was perfectly intelligible under the standard account—but the Supreme Court rejected the claim because the justices did not consider discrimination because of pregnancy to be *sex* discrimination and, if sex discrimination, considered it justified by the company's showing that female employees (on average) derived as much benefit from its insurance program as male employees.[4]

In this chapter, we identify systematic problems with the standard account of American Constitutionalism as the primary way of thinking about our nation's fundamental public commitments and close with an examination of new waves in Constitutional thought. Academics across the intellectual and ideological spectrum have abandoned the standard account in large part and are moving toward an account of fundamental commitments that emphasizes the role of legislatures and statutes, as opposed to courts and precedents.

Well before Wendy Williams and Peter Weiner filed their Constitutional sex discrimination claims, staff attorney Sonia Pressman (now Sonia Pressman Fuentes) was making a similar argument in the General Counsel's Office of the Equal Employment Opportunity Commission (EEOC). Title VII of the Civil Rights Act of 1964 prohibited workplace discrimination "because of sex" as well as because of race, and dozens of complaints and inquiries asked whether this prohibition barred employer policies discriminating because of pregnancy. Because pregnancy fell only upon women and because antipregnancy rules were severe barriers to careers for many working women, Pressman argued that it was a sex discrimination under the statute. Susan Deller Ross, who joined the EEOC's staff in 1970, supported Pressman's general position and refined it in light of new liberal feminist thinking and, specifically, proposals developed by Catherine East and the Citizens' Advisory Council on the Status of Women. When the EEOC issued its initial Sex Discrimination Guidelines in 1972, it followed Ross's suggestion that discrimination against pregnant workers was, presumptively, sex discrimination in violation of Title VII. Williams and Weiner relied on those guidelines in their Constitutional litigation, and they were the basis for the Pregnancy Discrimination Act adopted by Congress in 1978.[5]

Sonia Pressman, Susan Deller Ross, and other officials in the EEOC were engaged in what we are calling administrative constitutionalism. They were responding to an important public problem, namely, the perseverance of employer policies discharging or otherwise penalizing pregnant workers—policies that were inconsistent with the legitimate needs of female workers and with the norms advanced by the women's rights movement. As a general matter, administrative constitutionalism is both the primary means by which social movements interact with the state and the primary means by which governmental actors *deliberate* about how to respond to social movement demands or needs. Lawyers often assume that administrative deliberation is simply a process of applying expertise and responding to political pressures in deciding rules for regulation. But agencies also engage in higher-level deliberation, and that is the only way to understand the EEOC's decision making regarding pregnancy discrimination. The deliberation was neither a mechanical application of expertise nor a simple response to political pressure; instead, it was deliberative in the deeper sense we discuss in the Introduction. The administrators considered new evidence and experiences, not fully documented, from which they had to extrapolate conclusions and proposals. They considered counterarguments, easily generated by more old-fashioned officials within the agency. The administrative constitutionalists considered not only (speculative) monetary costs and benefits of different rules but also incommensurable costs and benefits, including long-term efficiency of the workplace and women's satisfaction in their careers. And they came up with an experiment—the 1972 pregnancy guidelines, which did not have the force of law but which did put employers on notice that old pregnancy rules would probably be challenged, as they immediately were.

Normatively, the EEOC's internal deliberations were also informed by higher-level normative considerations. Specifically, Sonia Pressman and Susan Deller Ross considered the following normative vectors as they argued (with one another and with their EEOC colleagues) and deliberated about the best way to interpret "discriminate . . . because of sex" in the statute:

- *Title VII's Purpose.* Reflecting her background in labor law as well as a sensitivity to women's careers, Pressman believed Title VII's purpose was to protect women's place in the job force and to provide individual women job security when they were having children. Reflecting ERA-style liberal feminism, Ross believed that Title VII's purpose was to remove business rules and practices that impeded women's ability to participate in the workplace on an equal basis with men and to eliminate an arbitrary and irrational trait (sex) from workplace decisions. Although they had overlapping but different conceptions of the statutory purpose, Pressman and Ross worked together on the pregnancy issue and persuaded the agency that pregnancy discrimination fell within the statute for all these reasons.
- *Constitutional Equal Protection.* Ross, in particular, believed that the EEOC's interpretation of the statute ought to be informed by the proper construction of the Equal Protection Clause, which Ross read the same way Williams and Weiner would in 1972. Even though the agency did not have to interpret the Constitution to announce its statutory interpretation, Large "C" Constitutional ideas informed the staff discussions. More important, agency interpretation of the Constitution preceded the Court's interpretation later in *Aiello.* Ross was unpersuaded by the Court's reasoning; if she had been at the EEOC in 1973, she would have been influenced still by the liberal feminist constitutional vision.
- *America's Public Norms.* At the most general level, both Pressman and Ross were influenced by their understanding of America's public needs. From their own experiences and friendship networks, they understood that many women wanted careers and that pregnancy discrimination was a structural mechanism by which employers thwarted those careers. That was both intolerable and inefficient. Because neither Ross nor Pressman was the official decision maker, it is notable that they had to persuade older male decision makers that they were right about this. Some of the EEOC's legal staff were skeptical that many women wanted "careers" outside the home, but the EEOC's general counsel, Charles Duncan, supported Pressman's views in the early years of the agency; General Counsel John Pemberton subsequently supported Ross's specific proposals for drafting the 1972 pregnancy discrimination guidelines; and male commissioners acquiesced in the judgments about pregnancy and other forms of sex discrimination pioneered in the Office of the General Counsel.

In short, administrative constitutionalism considers superstatutory purposes, Large "C" Constitutional commitments, and small "c" constitutional public norms and needs when officials deliberate about what the legal rules should be. The argument of this chapter is that administrative constitutionalism, including but not limited to Constitutional analysis by executive and legislative officials, is the dominant governmental mechanism for the evolution of America's fundamental normative commitments.[6]

An important feature of administrative constitutionalism is that it is not the final word; the trial balloons hoisted by agencies are subject to public critique as well as veto by courts, legislatures, and other executive branch officials. The EEOC's pregnancy guidelines, in fact, were rejected by the Supreme Court—but the Court was itself overridden when a mobilized coalition of traditionalists and feminists persuaded Congress to codify the EEOC's rule in the Pregnancy Discrimination Act of 1978 (PDA). The PDA created a statutory entitlement binding on private employers and trumping state law to the contrary. But the campaign to secure the statute did not stop after 1978; rather, it intensified, and the PDA became part of a larger reform movement focusing on the workplace's accommodation of families. The leaders of the broader reform movement included prominent feminists and labor leaders, but also both state and federal administrators. The PDA's principle evolved, and early on revealed a normative force beyond the four corners of the statutory text. Today, there is an emerging statute-based norm that employers should affirmatively accommodate the needs of workers who are new parents and caregivers, rights partially recognized by the Family and Medical Leave Act of 1993 (FMLA), which expanded upon the PDA. The national conversation that generated the PDA has continued after the FMLA. In short, Congress and state legislatures have not so much reversed as transcended the Supreme Court's stingy Constitutionalism. Legislators and administrators have inaugurated a small "c" constitutional process that has delivered what even a more generous American Constitutionalism could not: affirmative rights applicable to private as well as public workplaces.[7]

What we are calling administrative constitutionalism is the process by which legislative and executive officials, America's primary governmental norm entrepreneurs, advance new fundamental principles and policies. The contrast with judicial Constitutionalism is not just an institutional contrast—agencies rather than judges are the primary interpreters—but also operational and normative. Administrative constitutionalism is explicitly policy oriented, experimental, and practical; judicial Constitutionalism often operates that way, too, as we argued in the Introduction, but its underlying architecture is rule oriented, definitive, and principled. Administrative constitutional norms achieve their entrenchment primarily through their appeal to practical reason, while Constitutional norms announced by judges achieve entrenchment primarily through their appeal to higher authority. The goal of this chapter is to situate administrative constitutionalism within a larger story of the collapse of the highly romantic "standard account" of American Constitutionalism and the proliferation of theories of the Constitution outside the courts. In the latter discourse, the role of agencies is virtually ignored, a gap we aim to fill. But by leaving out agencies, popular theories of the Constitution also leave out the deep and pervasive ways that Large "C" Constitutionalism interacts—and ought to interact—with the small "c" constitutionalism of superstatutes and their implementation.

THE STANDARD ACCOUNT OF AMERICAN CONSTITUTIONALISM

When Wendy Williams and Peter Weiner crafted the 1972 complaint for equal protection violations in *Aiello v. Hansen* (the original caption of their lawsuit), they accepted and assumed three central premises of conventional American Constitutional law. *First*, the Constitution is a written legal text whose meaning is authoritatively elaborated primarily through Supreme Court precedents applying that text to trump ordinary state and federal laws. *Second*, the legitimacy of Constitutional law—the validity of its trump as against laws adopted by current legislative majorities—is derived and justified by the supermajoritarian and popular process through which the document was ratified and amended. *Third*, the primary role of the Constitution is to be a bulwark protecting We the People against government oppression or discrimination; when the state traverses those limits, the Constitution overrides. Although partial readings of the Constitution, these premises seized the imagination and monopolized the attention of lawyers and academics in the latter half of the twentieth century and are often treated as inevitable features of constitutionalism generally. Of course they are not.

THE DOCUMENTARY PREMISE: JUDICIAL REVIEW AS A TRUMP

Unlike British constitutionalism, American Constitutionalism is closely connected to a single unified document whose canonical text is not in serious dispute. One implication of such a "documentary premise" is that Constitutional claims must be linked to the written Constitution, as amended. When drafting Aiello's complaint, for example, Williams and Weiner knew they had to connect their grievance with a Constitutional provision. They maintained that California's treatment of Aiello violated the Equal Protection Clause of the Fourteenth Amendment: "[N]or shall any State . . . deny to any person within its jurisdiction the equal protection of the laws." What does this language prohibit, exactly? Surely it cannot be applied to invalidate all statutory distinctions (discriminations)?[8]

To answer questions such as these, another implication of the documentary premise has been critically important. Judges are trained and competent to analyze written legal texts—from wills and contracts to statutes and *constitutions*. Historian William Michael Treanor has shown that the notion of judicial review was widely accepted as a corollary of a written and legally enforceable Constitution during the colonial and Revolutionary periods, well before 1787. This idea stuck in our public culture and expanded in the early decades of the republic. At the hands of a brilliant judge like John Marshall, chief justice of the United States from 1801 to 1835, the written Constitution came alive as a document that could not only provide guidance for governance but could also be a font of enduring principles. As an expositor of the document, presenting "neutral" legal arguments with a political deftness, Marshall had no peer in the early republic. His landmark opinions in cases like *Marbury v. Madison* (1803) and *McCulloch v. Maryland* (1819) enabled the Supreme Court to assume primacy as the authoritative interpreter of the Constitution. In the process, Marshall exploited another implication of the documentary premise: the Constitution, as interpreted by judges, *trumps* ordinary laws, nullifying them. Even if legislatures fail to repeal laws inconsistent with the Constitution, they are dead letters after a judicial invalidation.[9]

The Supremacy Clause says: "This Constitution, and the Laws of the United States which shall be made in Pursuance thereof; and all Treaties made, or which shall be made, under the Authority of the United States, shall be the supreme Law of the Land; and the judges in every State shall be bound thereby, any Thing in the Constitution or Laws of any State to the Contrary notwithstanding." Implementing Article III, the Judiciary Act of 1789 gave the Supreme Court jurisdiction to review state as well as federal judicial decisions applying federal statutes, treaties, and the Constitution to an issue. Hence, those state and federal judges had strong incentives to follow Marshall's interpretations, and to anticipate his construction when new issues arose, especially when state laws were inconsistent with federal statutes, treaties, or the Constitution itself. Because judges followed the Supreme Court's interpretations, state government officials and private parties had incentives to do so as well. Rights and duties created by statutes inconsistent with the Constitution were not enforceable in state or federal court, and so neither state officials nor private citizens could rely on unConstitutional state statutes or policies—a status that could only be determined, finally and authoritatively, by the U.S. Supreme Court. Although the Court did not aggressively exercise its judicial review power until after the Civil War, it was from the beginning an important rule of American governance.[10]

Another reason judges have become central to Constitutional interpretation is that their body of *written* opinions has filled in the details of open-textured

Constitutional provisions in an authoritative lawlike way. In our common law system, not only are lower court judges absolutely bound by Supreme Court decisions, the Supreme Court itself is obliged to follow its own earlier interpretations under the doctrine of *stare decisis* ("the decisions will stand"). That judges at all levels could be expected to follow Supreme Court precedents has meant that other officials would likewise find it in their interest to do so; otherwise, their own directives would be in danger of disobedience. Because of the *settlement function* served by precedent, the justices have become masters of Constitutional interpretation. So long as their interpretations demonstrated general neutrality and adherence to the terms of the document, predictability has been a great boon for Constitutional law.[11]

The common law method by which the Supreme Court has filled in Constitutional details is inevitably evolutive, because every precedent creates possibilities for new Constitutional arguments called forth by fresh social injustices and political grievances. Thus, even though in 1972 the Court had never ruled that pregnancy discrimination posed serious equal protection problems, Weiner and Williams were hopeful because of inviting rhetoric in the Court's precedents. The Court had interpreted the Equal Protection Clause to render race-based classifications "suspect" and therefore highly vulnerable to judicial review, and feminist litigators like Williams were pressing the Court to apply strict scrutiny to sex-based classifications as well. In good common law fashion, they argued by analogy to the race precedents. Sex was, they maintained, a suspect classification for the same reasons race was: one's sex is immutable, beyond the individual's control, and is generally unrelated to rational public goals; sex discriminations are grounded upon irrational stereotypes that reflect and contribute to the subordination of women. It required little argumentation, plaintiffs' lawyers hoped, to show that pregnancy-based discriminations are sex discriminations, as their burden falls entirely on women.[12]

Representing California, Deputy Attorney General Joanne Condas distinguished the race discrimination cases. Protecting African Americans just freed from slavery, the Fourteenth Amendment's core purpose was to sweep away racist state policies. California's unemployment compensation scheme was a far cry from the black codes, and women (as a majority of voters) were better positioned to remedy any sex discrimination through the political process. Moreover, the "real differences" between women and men—such as the fact of pregnancy—justified some sex-based policy choices. Data showed that, even with the pregnancy exclusion, female workers derived greater per capita benefits from California's unemployment compensation fund than male workers did. Adding benefits for pregnancy would not only exacerbate this existing imbalance but might bankrupt the program, according to California's lawyers.

Finally, as many as half the women who took work leaves because of pregnancy never returned to their jobs. Given the limited resources available for unemployment compensation, California felt it was best to distribute them to temporarily unemployed workers who planned to return to work as soon as the disability eased or could be managed.[13]

Although it did not do so, the state could also have relied on the specific expectations of the framers, an approach associated with the documentary premise. While the *Aiello* case was litigated, the solicitor general of the United States was Robert Bork, who is now the prime advocate of an original meaning approach to the Constitution. (When the Supreme Court took the case, Bork recused himself from participating in *Aiello*; the acting solicitor general authorized the EEOC to file a brief supporting Williams and Weiner's clients.) Adopted in 1868, the Fourteenth Amendment itself assumed that sex discriminations were permissible. Its framers rejected early feminist demands that sex discrimination be outlawed specifically; they and their contemporaries considered sex-based exclusions natural and not discriminatory. In short, the authors and ratifiers of the Constitutional text would *not* have found a pregnancy-based exclusion a violation of the Fourteenth Amendment. In this way, the documentary premise gives the Constitution a conservative character: because it is an *old* document, its text and certainly its original meaning are bound to reflect the problems of yesterday and not those of today. This is a potentially huge problem, unless the Constitution can be reliably updated, either through formal amendment or dynamic judicial constructions. The former is politically impossible, and the latter is often unsuitable for reasons of institutional competence and legitimacy.[14]

THE BIG SHOWDOWN PREMISE: CONSTITUTIONAL CHANGE THROUGH SUPERMAJORITY RATIFICATION

An important feature of our Constitution is its recognition that sovereignty rests in We the People. (Eighteenth-century England, in contrast, viewed sovereignty as resting in Parliament.) Practically speaking, however, the way in which We the People create Constitutional text is more significant for our analytical purposes. In Article VII, the Constitution stipulated that it would not come into effect unless nine of the thirteen states approved it. Article V provided that the Constitution could be changed if Congress proposed amendments by two-thirds majorities in both chambers and three-quarters of the states ratified those amendments.[15]

A key reason for such high procedural hurdles is the notion that We the People must be engaged and decisively inclined when new Constitutional text is being created. Most Article V amendments have been significant additions requiring the same quality of momentous normative struggle and debate that marked the ratification of the original Constitution. The Bill of Rights (Amendments I–X) represented a concession by the Federalists, delivered (as promised) after they won adoption of the Constitution following an arduous national debate. The Reconstruction Amendments (XIII–XV) were purchased at the cost of civil war and tremendous effort by the governing Republican Party afterward. Amendment XVI, authorizing the federal income tax without apportionment among the states, was a swift rebuff to a Constitutional ruling by the Supreme Court. Two other progressive era Amendments (XVII, XIX) broadened democracy, the latter giving women the right to vote after two generations of political mobilization. The exception that proves the rule, the Prohibition Amendment (XVIII, repealed by XXI), sneaked through the Article V process at the tail end of World War I. It was a national experiment in values, but undertaken without the vigorous debate generating broad consensus contemplated by Article V. We the People have not always chosen wisely, but our most significant Constitutional failures (slavery and Prohibition) were corrected through formal amendment to the foundational document.[16]

The grand textual changes—from the adoption of the original Constitution (plus the Bill of Rights), to the Reconstruction Amendments, and concluding with the Progressive Era Amendments—were the result of *big popular showdowns*. The progression usually looks something like this: Popular movement demanding change in the structure or norms of our polity → Public debate and resistance → Popular endorsement of change, yielding Article V amendment by consensus or decisive margins. In each showdown, competing normative visions faced off: the Federalists versus the Anti-Federalists in the 1780s, the Radical Republicans versus President Andrew Johnson and the defeated South in the 1860s, and the Progressives versus the Old Guard in the early 1900s. In each showdown, one normative vision prevailed: its adherents won elections waged over these issues of governance and values, and they persuaded moderates to support their important Constitutional changes. The winners swept the political field to such an extent that their Constitutional proposals procured the needed supermajorities required by Article V. The texts produced by these episodes had a superlegitimacy—and thus a justification (in addition to the rule of law idea discussed above) for the Constitution's trumping authority—that owed much to the decisive triumph of the amendment after intense popular engagement and focused public deliberation.[17]

Wendy Williams participated in a similarly dramatic political episode, but with a different conclusion. After decades of division on the issue, feminists came together in the late 1960s to support the Equal Rights Amendment (ERA), which followed the classic model of Constitutional change, outlined above. In

1972, just before Williams and Weiner filed their complaint in *Aiello*, Congress passed the ERA by huge margins. Half the states ratified it within a year. Section 1 of the ERA provided: "Equality of rights under the law shall not be denied or abridged by the United States or by any State on account of sex." The ERA, if ratified by the requisite thirty-eight states, might have assured Carolyn Aiello victory in her lawsuit. Under the ERA, she could make the following textual argument:

(1) California's exclusion "denie[s] or abridge[s]" her "equality of rights," on account of her pregnancy.
(2) Pregnancy-based exclusions are "on account of sex," because they fall exclusively on women such as Carolyn Aiello.
(3) California's denial of Aiello's "equality of rights" "on account of sex" violates the plain meaning of the ERA.

Even if the ERA were not read literally, to ban all sex discriminations, California's pregnancy exclusion did not rest upon a compelling state justification. The substantial cost of adding pregnancy might constitute a "rational" basis for the state exclusion, but it did not constitute a compelling interest as the Court had defined it.[18]

A powerful argument for Aiello's ERA claim was that state pregnancy-based exclusions were not only a formal discrimination against women but also a symbolic reaffirmation of the notion that women's place was at home, bearing and raising children. Recall that one reason California gave for excluding pregnancy from its disability and unemployment programs was that female employees usually did not return to work after having children, and so unemployment compensation would be nothing more than a severance package for these women. But this phenomenon was changing, as more women were necessary or sole wage earners for their families. Moreover, one reason women did not return to work—did not have "careers"—was pervasive sex discrimination in the workplace and by the state. If employers denigrated women as "temporary" workers and the state refused to help them when they became pregnant, many female workers rationally concluded that they needed to marry a man and to subordinate their careers to those of their husbands. This, Williams and other ERA supporters maintained, was morally intolerable and economically inefficient.

There are some rough parallels between feminist critics of sexist state policies in the 1970s and Republican critics of censorship laws of the 1790s. In his *Report on the Virginia Resolution* (1800) condemning the Alien and Sedition Acts of 1798, James Madison called on We the People (through the states) to stand against federal statutes that represented an affront to genuine Constitutional precepts. For Madison, We the People were acting in their "highest sovereign capacity" when they engaged in such civic activism. Wendy Williams was acting as Madison would have advocated, seeking to engage the people in their highest sovereign capacity—and not just through Constitutional amendments but also through political activism and, in Williams's case, through litigation as well. As we shall see later in this chapter, Williams and her feminist allies were tracking Madison in another way. Madison's activism against the Alien and Sedition Acts was channeled not through the judiciary exercising judicial review but through the Virginia and Kentucky legislatures. (Jeffersonian Republicans considered the judiciary filled with Hamiltonian Federalists to be an unfriendly forum.) Likewise, feminists later channeled their energies through Congress rather than an all-male Supreme Court that refused to see pregnancy-based discrimination as sex discrimination.[19]

THE LIBERTARIAN PREMISE: NO AFFIRMATIVE CONSTITUTIONAL GUARANTEES?

Joanne Condas's brief defending California's pregnancy exclusion in *Aiello* said this: "There is no [C]onstitutional requirement that governments establish comprehensive public welfare assistance programs, subsidized housing programs, social security and workmen's compensation plans, or unemployment compensation programs." Wendy Williams and Peter Weiner did not challenge this assertion. As construed by judges, the U.S. Constitution was designed to protect, against state interference, people's liberty to design their own life plans, pursue their economic and social goals, and enjoy pleasures and happiness, so long as these activities do not harm their neighbors; this meta-norm is the vision of the judge-developed common law. Reflecting both input from lawyers and the narrow philosophy of judges, the Constitution of 1789 protects liberty through jurisdictional rules, process-based checks and balances, and rights whose phraseology is so broad that they could only have been implemented in common law fashion.[20]

Although the Constitution can be read more broadly, the Supreme Court has interpreted the document to valorize the individual's right to be left alone by the state. Of course, the state is always present in our lives, because it stands ready to discipline us if we violate someone else's property, contract, or tort rights. This way of thinking about liberty conceives of it as a right to be left to the regime of state property, contract, and tort law. The First Amendment, for example, tells the federal government that it cannot arrest the protester burning his flag or the newspaper printing irresponsible antigovernment screeds. But judges have not interpreted the First Amendment to require the government to provide the protester with the flag or to subsidize the newspaper (though state-supported newspapers must be open forums to an extent).

The Constitutional abortion claims raised by feminists in the 1960s and 1970s transcended this traditional emphasis: women not only argued for a right to be left alone by the state in making abortion decisions, they also argued that the state had a duty to pay for abortions under circumstances (poverty) where it was willing to pay for other needed medical procedures. Even this limited appeal for affirmative Constitutional responsibilities was not successful. Resting upon the Due Process Clause, *Roe v. Wade* (1973) vindicated feminist libertarian claims, but the Court in subsequent cases declined to read *Roe* to require the states to pay for abortions when pregnant women could not afford them and even allowed municipal hospitals to refuse to perform abortions.[21]

Feminist and other academics have criticized strong versions of the libertarian premise. For some scholars, *Brown v. Board of Education* (1954) stands for the proposition that public education is a fundamental Constitutional right, one that the state is affirmatively obliged to provide its citizens to ensure equal citizenship and their personal flourishing. From that kind of premise, prominent scholars have maintained that the Constitution requires the state to provide citizens with a minimum standard of living, to protect them against private violence, and to eradicate private expressions of prejudice and harassment. Unsurprisingly, the Supreme Court has not agreed with these academics. The year before it decided *Geduldig v. Aiello,* the Supreme Court handed down *Rodriguez v. San Antonio Independent School District* (1973). Rejecting claims that Texas's school financing system violated the Equal Protection Clause, the Court narrowly but decisively ruled that there is no Constitutional right to a good public school education and that the state has wide leeway in tolerating and even encouraging local variation in school funding levels. Although the Burger (1969–87) and Rehnquist (1987–2005) Courts sometimes imposed additional process requirements upon the state, they were unreceptive to Constitutional claims that would have required the state to reallocate tight budgetary resources to satisfy affirmative rights for disadvantaged or excluded citizens.[22]

Even before *Rodriguez*, Wendy Williams and Peter Weiner fully understood this. Their complaint for Carolyn Aiello did not demand that workers were *entitled* to state support during periods of unemployment. Instead, their claims were that the state discrimination "places said women employees at a serious disadvantage in the pursuit of their chosen occupations." Their brief before the Supreme Court emphasized the ways in which the state had *oppressed* and *discriminated* against women. Much of Williams and Weiner's brief consisted of a demonstration of the ways in which pregnancy-based discrimination in workplace entitlements hindered women's ability to engage in gainful employment and even to support their families. All they asked of the Supreme Court was to stop California from harming Carolyn Aiello through a segregation of benefits. One reason they lost the case was that the justices felt that the proposed Constitutional right was too much of an affirmative obligation for them to impose on the state unemployment compensation program, and other programs that could be affected.[23]

NORMATIVE PROBLEMS WITH THE STANDARD ACCOUNT

The standard account of American Constitutionalism—the judicial review, big showdown, and libertarian premises—is a romantic understanding of that glorious document, and one constructed primarily by and around judges. But it is also narrow, obsolete, unresponsive to the needs of our polity, and certainly not desirable as the sole or primary basis for our nation's fundamental law, broadly understood. The continuing allure of the standard account owes much to our admiration for the Warren Court (1953–69), whose aggressive judicial review recognized libertarian rights of criminal defendants, political dissidents, racial and religious minorities, and married couples, as well as the equality rights associated with *Brown*. But the Warren Court was neither as progressive nor as successful as its fans have assumed, and the time has come to jettison our romantic vision of a Constitution sanctioned by big popular showdowns, implemented by far-sighted federal judges, and protecting people's liberties against government interference.

Our primary criticism of the standard account is that it is too narrow an understanding of constitutionalism. A deeper constitutionalism, even a libertarian one, *starts with* why we have the state in the first place, namely, to provide *security* for people to form families and relationships, engage in economic activities and pursue careers, and participate in larger communities. These are affirmative, positive rights. Therefore, not only does constitutionalism have to include affirmative as well as negative rights, but effectual negative rights oblige the government to give *all* citizens equal access to state forums for recognizing and enforcing limits against government. If negative rights were only enforceable by some citizens and not by others, and if the state could victimize those same citizens without access, the social contract begins to unravel, as excluded groups opt out of it through migration, rebellion, or terrorism. Once some groups respond to public violence with private violence, there is a genuine danger that the polity will dissolve.[24]

Additionally, we focus on the oddest feature of our Constitution of 1789, its absurdly difficult amendment process, which has assured that its terms are superentrenched but frequently obsolete, delphic, or irrelevant. Article V guarantees

that the Constitution will never specify anything close to the full range of constitutional assurances required by classic theory. Into the breach has stepped the
Supreme Court, with its academic commentators, and to this we address our
third criticism. The Court is institutionally incapable of developing much of the
affirmative protective features the constitutional state, extending constitutional
protections to private centers of power, or enforcing the Constitution's open-ended
equal treatment and libertarian guarantees.

AFFIRMATIVE OBLIGATION OF GOVERNMENT TO PROVIDE SECURITY FOR ALL CITIZENS

The biggest shortcoming of America's judge-centric Constitution is its seem-
ing emphasis on negative rights or, in common parlance, its libertarianism. The
Supreme Court has focused Constitutionalism upon negative rights and governmental limits—much more than is justified even by the classic "liberal" political
philosophers such as Thomas Hobbes. In *Leviathan* (1651), Hobbes argued that
government is justified, and earns our consent, by allowing us to escape the
"state of nature," a "war of all against all." The civil state exists so that citizens
can pursue their lives without fear that other citizens, or outside invaders, will
interfere with those natural rights. To protect citizens thus, the civil state needs
legislatures to enact laws serving the public interest, police to enforce those
laws, and courts to adjudicate controversies without resort to private feuds and
duels. These protections, moreover, need to be made available to more or less
everyone. The state's failure to preserve and protect, and to make these protections broadly available, so that people can live their lives secure from fear, is for
Hobbes a justification for revolution. While other features of Hobbes's philosophy are controversial, his "mutuall Relation between Protection and Obedience" is not, and it expresses an essentially positive right: the right of all citizens
to the state's protection of their lives. If the state protects only some, or provides
protection ineptly, this is a justification—and according to Hobbes the *only*
justification—for civil disobedience and self-defense.[25]

An even more affirmative role for government was sounded by John Locke, the
political philosopher who was probably most influential among America's founding generation. Like Hobbes in *Leviathan*, Locke in *A Second Treatise of Government* (1689) put security as the first duty of government, even creating two special
departments: the executive, charged with maintaining internal security, and the
federative, for external security.[26] While Hobbes was mostly concerned that citizens be able to preserve their lives and perhaps also their existing property, Locke
argued that the civil state not only saved people from the "inconveniences" of the
state of nature but also provided citizens with the ability to add to their liberties
and possessions, and enrich their lives beyond what they could possibly enjoy in

the state of nature. To do this the state invented such institutions as money (permitting accumulation), instituted civil rights in the place of natural ones, and established a (responsive) legislative process and so forth. The *Second Treatise* also offered a more permissive theory for justified disobedience or even revolution. If the legislature were to "take away or destroy the property of the people, or reduce them to slavery under an arbitrary power," the government has breached the trust invested in the state by popular consent, and the people "have the right to resume their original liberty, and, by the establishment of a new legislat[ure], (such as they think fit) provide for their own safety and security, which is the end for which they are in society."[27]

Lockean arguments were important justifications for the American Revolution against the arbitrary rule of King George III—and for the peaceful repudiation of the Articles of Confederation by the Constitution itself. The first sentence of *Federalist* No. 1 echoes Locke: "After an unequivocal experience of the *inefficacy of the subsisting federal government*, you are called upon to deliberate on a new Constitution for the United States of America." Creating a much more puissant central government, the new Constitution stirred anxieties for a liberty-loving people. Publius responded that "the vigor of government is essential to the security of liberty," and that the energetic governance structure contained in the proposed Constitution was faithful to the "*true principles of republican government*" and would provide "*additional security . . . to the preservation of that species of government, to liberty, and to property.*" Overall, the federalist case for the Constitution emphasized the affirmative obligations it placed on the state, and the means by which the state could accomplish ambitious goals. Given some emphasis, too, was the federalist promise that a national judiciary would provide neutral forums for private as well as public disputes. Indeed, the charge that most troubled the supporters of the Constitution of 1789 was that it did not provide affirmative guarantees to citizens, a defect that was ameliorated by the due process and jury trial assurances of the Bill of Rights in 1791.[28]

Faithful to the Lockean vision, nineteenth-century American governments understood their mission as creating a society that served the Lockean *salus populi*, the welfare of the people. Accordingly, municipal and county governments structured business through licensing laws, engendered neighborhoods through prophylactic land use restrictions and early versions of zoning regulations, provided a comprehensive code of criminal prohibitions (including such crimes as cross-dressing and spitting), created elaborate fire codes and public health regulations, prohibited disorderly houses, and regulated liquor sales and consumption, among other activities. Increasingly, local governments provided free and compulsory public schools for children in the community; proponents such as Horace Mann argued that education was a public right and an obligation. State governments did more than enforce common law rights of property, contract, and tort; legislatures created elaborate codes of morals, engaged in great projects such as building canals and roads, regulated shipping and commerce, limited immigration, and so on. Even the national government, hamstrung by a modest bureaucracy and dependent on the tariff for revenues, carried out large projects of its own: the operation of a national mail service, land purchases and wars that doubled and redoubled the size of the country, the creation of a national bank and a workable if flawed currency system, an elaborate jerry-rigged bureaucracy for regulating steamboats and preventing accidents, the construction of the transcontinental railroad, and the dispersal of federal lands to homesteaders.[29]

These great projects went well beyond the night watchman role that some libertarians entertain as the ideal for government. (Even a "night watchman" state requires a fair amount of energy to do its job well, namely, providing forums for citizens to maintain and enforce contracts and other forms of private law, to seek redress for crimes and nuisances, and by the mid-nineteenth century to provide police and other officials to deter, seek out, and eradicate crimes and nuisances.) For many Americans, government was purposive and problem solving. Oftentimes it was ambitious. The Civil War, of course, was ambitious liberty-restricting government at its most dramatic: the Lincoln administration and the period immediately following not only flexed the national government's military muscle to preserve the union but also embargoed southern ports, created the foundations for a paper currency, abrogated the institution of slavery, initiated the transcontinental railway project (through land grants), handed over millions of acres in property to homesteaders and freed slaves, and expanded Americans' understanding of equal treatment and national citizenship. After the Civil War, the government of a fast-industrializing country engaged in significant and much-deliberated interventions to manage labor disputes, maintain and closely regulate interstate transport systems, protect the public health through regulatory agencies, regulate unfair trade practices, create a federal reserve system, and suppress pornography, contraception, abortion, cross-dressing, and oral sex. Many of these efforts were unsuccessful, and some appear ridiculous to us today, such as Prohibition (1920–33), which created an unprecedented bureaucracy to enforce a republic of temperance and sobriety.[30]

The Great Depression of 1929 shattered the notion that unregulated markets and property entitlements provided a sufficient context for the average American to construct a good life. The dramatic collapse of the economy changed attitudes and cast old players in new roles. As secretary of commerce, Herbert Hoover had headed a massive government relief effort that prevented a socioeconomic meltdown after the Great Mississippi Flood of 1927; this relief effort catapulted Hoover to the presidency in 1928. But President Hoover was perceived as too passive in responding to the economic crisis of 1929, and he lost the presidency in 1932 to Governor Franklin Delano Roosevelt (FDR), who promised a more activist governmental response. In his landmark speech to the Commonwealth Club in San Francisco on September 23, 1932, on the eve of his election, Roosevelt called for a "redefinition of rights in terms of a changing and growing social order." He proposed "an economic constitutional order" that would assure ordinary Americans rights to work, to a decent standard of living for honest work, and to security in the event of disability and old age. FDR's New Deal represented a fundamental (though rarely radical) reconsideration of basic public entitlements in this country.[31]

The most mature expression of this new philosophy came in FDR's State of the Union Address, on January 11, 1944. The president announced a Second Bill of Rights, available to all Americans, "regardless of station, race, or creed." He identified rights [1] "to a useful and remunerative job"; [2] "to earn enough to provide adequate food and clothing and recreation"; [3] of a farmer "to raise and sell his products at a return which will give him and his family a decent living"; [4] of a businessman "to trade in an atmosphere of freedom from unfair competition and domination by monopolies"; [5] "to a decent home"; [6] "to adequate medical care" and "good health"; [7] "to adequate protection from the economic fears of old age, sickness, accident, and unemployment"; and [8] "to a good education."[32]

FDR did *not* believe these rights were already in the Constitution, nor did he seek an Article V amendment. His project was to recognize these affirmative rights as fundamental commitments that a democratic government should be making to its citizens; FDR's deeper project was to perfect the Lockean state and recast government legitimacy as resting on its capacity to create structures allowing every American to create a flourishing life—the concrete starting point for the *consumerist constitution* that has governed our country for the past two generations. The primary mechanism for Roosevelt's grand project was superstatutes. Various economic stimulus laws such as the Agriculture Adjustment Act of 1935 and the 1935 amendment to the Federal Reserve Act sought to create conditions for economic revival that could see family farms regain profitability and businesses bring workers back to their jobs. The Sherman Act of 1890 already embodied Right Number 4, and the Roosevelt administration was committed to a vigorous enforcement of that law. The Social Security Act of 1935 substantially implemented Right Number 7. Various New Deal programs sought to assure Rights Numbered 1–3. Roosevelt and his successor, President Harry S. Truman (1945–53), wanted federal legislation guaranteeing Right Number 7, but political opposition postponed this initiative until it was partially fulfilled in the Medicare amendment to the Social Security Act in 1965. Interestingly, Right Number 8 became the situs for Constitutional litigation—the desegregation cases and their progeny. Echoing President Roosevelt, Chief Justice Warren's opinion in *Brown* recognized "the importance of education to our democratic society," the "very foundation of good citizenship," and for these reasons "perhaps the most important function of state and local governments."[33]

The school desegregation cases highlight another feature of a Lockean Constitution that has been very important in American history: the government's affirmative obligation to protect life, liberty, and property applies to *everyone's* life, liberty, and property. In particular, if officials exclude significant social groups from the affirmative benefits of governance, members of those groups will be alienated from the state and will leave (if they can) or revolt against its tyranny. This notion has a substantive component, a procedural component, and a political component, all of which can be illustrated by reference to the most divisive social category of the founding era, religion. The substantive element is that *all* men are created equal and *all* possess inalienable rights. One religion might in fact be right about everything, but as to that the state is agnostic, and the Catholic or the Buddhist must be treated by the state with the same respect it gives adherents of the majority religion. The procedural component is that every American, however despised (for one's religion, for example) or marginal, must have access to state processes for challenging the government when it violates its promise to secure our lives, liberties, and property. The heretic who is beaten must receive the same protection of police, prosecutors, judges, and juries that the acclaimed saint receives. Finally, the political component insists that all proper citizens have a political voice, at least in having an opportunity to vote. (More on this in the following chapter.)[34]

Now apply these fundamental precepts to the pregnancy discrimination claimants. The government was not "interfering" with Carolyn Aiello's freedom to work, but the government's safety net unemployment program was not available to her the way it was to male employees. She was, literally, denied equal "protection" of the unemployment compensation law because of her pregnancy, and indirectly because of her sex. Notwithstanding this logic, the Supreme Court denied Aiello's claim and extended her case to cover Sherrie O'Steen's statutory claim as well. An angry and engaged Congress responded with the Pregnancy Discrimination Act of 1978, which treated employer discrimination because of pregnancy as a sex discrimination actionable under Title VII of the Civil Rights Act of 1964. The PDA carried out Locke's constitutional philosophy: the government must ensure everyone's economic security, in the sense that everyone ought to have fair economic opportunities; female workers were subject to pervasive disadvantages in the workplace because of pregnancy rules that were usually irrelevant to their ability to do their jobs; the state played a productive role in sweeping these discriminatory policies off the books. That this Lockean equality was delivered by Congress in a landmark statute, rather than by the Supreme Court in a landmark precedent, is normal rather than unusual in modern America.

OUR OLD, SHORT, AND HARD TO AMEND CONSTITUTION

At a minimum, a country's rules of governance ought to include the following: (1) affirmative commitments the state makes to its citizenry, to secure their lives, liberties, and property; (2) negative protections against government arbitrariness; and (3) equal treatment guarantees, including access to a trustworthy forum for enforcement of affirmative guarantees and protection against private as well as state oppression. Many nations enshrine all these commitments in their written Constitutions, but the United States does not. The reasons relate to three central and interconnected features of that document—its age, its brevity, and the difficulty of formally updating it—as well as to deeper problems with hard-wiring affirmative security-protecting commitments in a hard-to-change legal document.

Most framers of the Constitution of 1789 expected it to last a long time, an expectation that has been borne out beyond their hopes. Our Constitution is the oldest continuously operating document of its kind in the world; at 221 years, it beats most others by decades or centuries. This is a source of national pride, but it also helps explain why the Constitution leaves out so many guarantees that seem obvious to us today, especially affirmative commitments. More recently adopted state constitutions guarantee their citizens an "efficient" education, for example. If our national document were the Constitution of 1989 rather than 1789, it might also include assurance of a fair competitive marketplace, protection against poverty because of old age or illness, a mandatory network of federal trial and appellate courts, and so forth. We do not assert that such a Constitution would be *better* than the one we now have, but it would be a more complete statement of national commitments that we currently view as important. Conversely, the Constitution of 1789 is loaded with anachronisms that would probably not be included if We the People had started from scratch in 1989, including the equal representation of the states in the Senate, the Electoral College method for choosing presidents, diversity jurisdiction for federal courts, and perhaps the Second (a right to bear arms) and Third (no quartering of troops) Amendments.[35]

Partly because they expected the U.S. Constitution to last a long time, the framers did not specify most of its guarantees in any detail. The Constitution has four thousand three hundred words, shorter than the initial constitution for every one of the states, most of which were more than twenty-five thousand words. When the Constitution does touch on some fundamental guarantees, it speaks only in general terms. Thus, protections against government arbitrariness include abridgments of "freedom of speech or the press" (First Amendment); "unreasonable searches or seizures" (Fourth Amendment); "cruel or unusual punishments" (Eighth Amendment); or denial of the "equal protection of the law" (Fourteenth Amendment). Nondiscriminatory access to the franchise is set forth in a more straightforward way in the Fifteenth (no denial because of race), Nineteenth (sex), Twenty-fourth (no poll taxes), and Twenty-sixth (eighteen year olds can vote) Amendments, with the notable caveat that the Fifteenth Amendment was the most ineffectual part of the Constitution for almost a century. Access rights are expressed with similar brevity but even greater uncertainty: Congress can suspend the writ of habeas corpus only in cases of invasion or rebellion (Article I, Section 9); no law can limit the people's petition for redress of grievances (First Amendment); and the government cannot deprive any person of "life, liberty, or property without due process of law" (Fifth and Fourteenth Amendments).[36]

Associated with and contributing to both our Constitution's longevity and its brevity is its intractable process for updating, which has generated an amendment rate for the U.S. Constitution that is much lower than for any state constitution. As the normal process for amendment, Article V requires two-thirds majorities in each chamber of Congress *plus* ratification by three-quarters of the states. In contrast, almost all the states allow simple majorities in the legislature, followed by a majority vote of the people, to amend their state constitutions. (Some states require votes in two successive sessions of the legislature; many states allow constitutional initiatives that do not require legislative votes.) This is significantly easier than the Article V juggernaut. It can hardly be surprising that the average state constitution has been amended more than a hundred times, and all states have had more than one constitution; the U.S. Constitution, in contrast, has been amended only twenty-seven times. Political scientist Donald Lutz estimates that the U.S. Constitution's amendment rate would triple if the state ratification requirement were reduced to two-thirds (still a formidable supermajority). The inference that Article V is a modern outlier is supported by expanding the comparative eye. Our Constitution is also the most difficult to amend among all Western constitutions, and we have the third-lowest amendment rate in the industrialized world.[37]

The wisdom and experience of the framers, as well as the resiliency of We the People, are surely the main reasons the Constitution of 1789 has proven so durable, but Article V may have contributed to that durability by keeping all but the most popular innovations out of the Constitution (with one short-lived exception: Prohibition). As John Hart Ely famously argued, once you start putting substantive commitments into a Constitution, you open up a hornets' nest of complexities. The difficulty of amendment has very probably contributed also to the Constitution's brevity: by expressing fundamental commitments at a high level of generality, the Constitution can avoid superstrong entrenched rules that prove disastrous. The flip side of this equation is problematic, however: the Constitution purchases durability through brevity and difficulty of amendment that remove thorny questions of detail from the popular ratification process that is the source of the Constitution's superlegitimacy.[38]

The frustrations of this conundrum were deeply felt by Wendy Williams and other legal feminists in the early 1970s. When it comes to modern women—more than half of We the People—the Constitution of 1789, written and debated by men and only men, effectively gave them too few of Hobbes's or Locke's promises of security, equal treatment, and access to process. The Constitution of 1789 and the Bill of Rights say next to nothing about women and the rights particular to them. A product of its era, the original document assumes that women were not legally equal to men. The text of Article II, for example, assumes that the president would be a man; by our count, there are thirteen references to the president using the gendered pronoun "he" in Article II. Section 1 of the Fourteenth Amendment is ungendered, and its equality, due process, and privileges and immunities protections apply to women as well as men, but Section 2 says that southern states might lose representation based upon the number of *males* disenfranchised. This Reconstruction-era provision assumes that women can be denied the right to vote; this is an assumption reinforced by women's exclusion from the Fifteenth Amendment guaranteeing people of color voting rights. The Nineteenth Amendment overrode that assumption but went no further.[39]

As it read in 1972, the U.S. Constitution did not speak to the conditions of modern society, where women *were* workers and social and political leaders, and where women *should be* assured equal treatment. Yet state and federal laws pervasively denied women employment opportunities and paid them a small fraction of what a man would earn for the same work; pregnant women were treated as disposable by the state as well as by private employers; women were pervasively subjected to sexual harassment in schools and the workplace and rape within marriage and families—all without any state remedy or even recognition that there was a problem. The only thing *approaching* sufficiency that women had was the right to vote, and that right suggested a Constitutional remedy: amend the Constitution to add the ERA, which also threatened to break the logjam blocking major amendments—until Phyllis Schlafly, a conservative activist, organized STOP ERA in 1973. Once articulate women objected to the ERA in great numbers, supporters were ultimately unable to achieve the thirty-eight states needed for ratification. Even a congressionally authorized extension of the period for ratification (until 1982) failed to save the ERA. The failed ERA illustrates how the Article V process is far *too* arduous and is an insuperable barrier for anything but housekeeping and process-based reforms.[40]

Even if the ERA had been ratified, the Constitution would not necessarily meet the political needs of women as citizens. A major theme of feminist theory has been critique of the public-private distinction and, therefore, of the state action doctrine that is a central feature of the judge-enforced Constitution. Constitutional precedents have overwhelmingly focused on protecting male-valued liberties (physical freedom, ownership of property, enforcement of contracts) against state deprivation. Women value their physical freedom and economic liberties, too, but face different threats to those freedoms and liberties. Private violence and fraud, by husbands and fathers as well as strangers, have been a pervasive problem for women, a much bigger problem than it has been for (white) men. Yet the state has traditionally been laggard in protecting women against private violence. The state action doctrine, developed by judges, has ensured that women's grievances against the lackadaisical state have not been understood as Constitutional violations. Indeed, if private violence and discrimination are a central problem for women, then the liberty-loving Constitution constructed by (male) judges may be an impediment to women's security, freedom, and equal treatment. According to some feminists, libertarian Constitutional rights protect rapists from paying for their crimes and even from being arrested or prosecuted; provide public expressive spaces to sexists who humiliate, harass, and denigrate women; and afford immunity to misogynistic pornographers to profit from the sexual degradation of women, children, and others. In short, American women, especially, have urgent complaints that the United States is not fulfilling even the most basic job of government outlined by Thomas Hobbes.[41]

UNDERENFORCEMENT OF CONSTITUTIONAL NORMS BY THE JUDICIARY

Notwithstanding our first two critiques, we believe that the Constitution of 1789 *could* and *should* be read and understood to address at least some affirmative guarantees instinct in the modern state. Because positive assurances of security are preconstitutional conditions for the state's legitimacy, even under social contract theory, the Constitution ought to be read to provide for at least some affirmative protections. Our own Constitution does not lack provisions that could be read this way. For example, the Preamble that announces the sovereignty of

We the People also provides an impressive array of affirmative goals for our Constitutional governance: "to form a more perfect Union, establish Justice, insure domestic Tranquility, provide for the common defence, promote the general Welfare, and secure the Blessings of Liberty to ourselves and our Posterity." Read in a Hobbesian or Lockean way, the Constitution is a purposive document—and every institution and every right ought to be read in light of these purposes. Some of the rights enumerated in the document, as amended, are written in a manner that reflects affirmative rather than negative freedom; the Equal *Protection* Clause is the best-known example, but an even more dramatic one is the Protection Clause of Article IV, which commits the federal government to "protecting" citizens of the various states against domestic violence and invasion.[42]

Consider an example of this kind of Constitutional thinking. When Congress was considering old-age and unemployment insurance legislation in 1930, opponents argued that "Congress may only levy taxes . . . in execution of express grants of authority made to it, or directly implied therefrom." Because there was no allowance for Congress to provide for insurance, the bills were unConstitutional. Supporters invoked the Taxing Clause, which authorizes Congress "[t]o lay and collect Taxes [etc.] to . . . provide for the common Defence and general Welfare." Opponents responded that "general Welfare" was a limitation on Congress's authority, to be narrowly construed in light of the document's federalist structure. Supporters replied: "What is the whole purpose of our Government? Is it not in order to guarantee equal rights and mak[e] possible 'the pursuit of happiness'?" Indeed, Congress had a "duty . . . to see that poverty, at least, is abolished in this country, and that we make the poor somewhat happier."[43]

What is noteworthy about the foregoing exchange is that the argument for positive obligations was made by social reformers but not by lawyers. The latter have internalized a culture that has been created by narrow Supreme Court opinions. As read by the New Deal and Warren Courts, even the Equal Protection Clause has been retrofitted into a limited government, negative rights framework. Contrary to its apparent text and dramatic history, judges insist that this provision does not require that the state actually protect anyone from risk or danger and certainly does not require that the state enrich the lives of its citizens—it only requires that state programs not adopt arbitrary exclusions. As Joanne Condas argued in the *Aiello* litigation, the Constitution does not require that California establish an unemployment compensation program for workers—but, as Wendy Williams and Peter Weiner maintained, once it had done so, the state could not exclude racial minorities or women from the program's benefits. Narrowly understood in this way, the Equal Protection Clause reinforces, rather than undermines, the judge-entrenched libertarian premise of Constitutional law. It has been deployed as a structural disincentive for government to get too involved in people's lives, either by telling them how they must live them *or* providing them with positive support for their chosen life projects. If the state considers legislation that meddles with people's choices, it cannot exempt the rich and the privileged; this requires lawmakers to think twice before enacting liberty-depriving laws. If the state considers legislation giving people support and benefits, it cannot carve out women or unpopular minorities; this requires lawmakers to include more recipients and fund programs at higher levels than they would otherwise desire.[44]

Because judges and lawyers dominate public discourse about the authoritative commands of our American Constitution, it is understood primarily as a *legal* rather than as a larger normative document; as a charter of *liberties*, negatively defined, rather than as a charter of affirmative obligations; as a statement of *limited* government rather than as an authorization for energetic governance. That negative rights and restrictive limits are now the main things that Americans associate with the Constitution is less a product of what the document says and what its goals were, and more a product of the legalized reading of the document by the Supreme Court. As legal philosopher Robin West and other scholars have demonstrated, the Court's narrow reading is not the only legal reading of the Constitution. While some believe that the Court's libertarian interpretation of the Constitution has been driven by ideology, our view is that the Court's approach is best understood as adaptive and pragmatic. It is primarily for *institutional* reasons that the Supreme Court has declined to announce or enforce affirmative obligations and has focused on enforcing limits and negative rights.[45]

This institutionally driven focus on Constitutional limits would have come as no surprise to the framers who were sophisticated lawyers. In *Federalist* No. 78, Alexander Hamilton posed this question: What comparative advantage do courts bring to Constitutional governance? Hamilton and his collaborators appreciated the ability of the president to give energy to the federal government and of the legislature to set policy; these institutions were well designed to provide the affirmative advantages of government. Because the judiciary is the "weakest of the three departments of power," however, it is unable to carry out the affirmative powers of government; hence, our liberties "can never be endangered from that quarter." Indeed, "the courts of justice are to be considered as the bulwarks of a limited Constitution against legislative encroachments" as well as against "dangerous innovations in the government, and serious oppressions of the minor party in the community." Left in the hands of judges—as *legally enforceable* rights have been—Constitutionalism in operation is "naturally" going to focus more on limits and negative liberties, and less on affirmative obligations of government.[46]

An important institutional difference between adjudication (courts) and statutes (legislatures) is that the former normally cannot resolve problems that are polycentric, future oriented, and reallocational. Classic adjudication involves plaintiffs and defendants whose controversy is focused on resolving questions about past violations of right and present remediation, through a "neutral" decision reasoning from widely accepted sources of binding law. Classic adjudication is activity judges are well trained to handle, is suited to the resource limitations of the judiciary, and carries out an important Lockean function of government that judges are uniquely capable of accomplishing, namely, the peaceful and orderly settlement of disputes among citizens or between citizens and government. In our view, federal judges usually do an excellent service to the country in the expert way they handle classic adjudications involving breaches of contract, violations of property rights, accusations of criminal conduct, and governmental activities claimed to violate a provision of the Constitution. When the Court errs in Constitutional cases, it is usually by *underenforcing* Constitutional norms or principles, as the justices may have been doing in *Geduldig v. Aiello*. The caution evidenced by an underenforcing Court might, however, be preferable to excessive judicial review from a Court that overenforces the Constitution and thereby cuts off democratic debate, as we argue in our Conclusion to this book.[47]

Assume, moreover, that the Court had decided *Geduldig* in favor of the claimants. Standing alone, *Geduldig* would have provided few benefits for working women, most of whom labored for private employers whose practices were not covered by the Equal Protection Clause. That is, merely declaring a right to be free of state pregnancy-based discrimination would not have fully implemented the abstract principle of equal protection. To fully enforce the principle required more affirmative state action and a more complete statute than even Title VII and the PDA proved to be. From a progressive feminist perspective, an antidiscrimination rule does not fulfill the entire promise of equal protection, because employers have no obligation toward pregnant workers if they simply drop their disability and leave programs for all workers. The deep problem is that what pregnant workers *most* need is workplace policies that provide *reasonable accommodations* for their pregnancies—and this was not the policy advocated for by Williams and Weiner in *Geduldig*, nor was it even the policy explicitly adopted in Title VII or the PDA. So even if Williams and Weiner had prevailed in *Geduldig*, they and their feminist allies would not necessarily have won enough for their clients and would have turned to the legislature for more complete Constitutional relief in any event.

These points were hardly lost on contemporary feminists. Susan Deller Ross and Ruth Weyand, feminists who headed the campaign that persuaded Congress to enact the PDA, believed that women's workplace inequality was a polycentric problem that would not have been solved by *Geduldig* or even by the PDA. Female workers were held back by employer discharges of pregnant workers—the problem targeted by the PDA—but they were also held back by gender-neutral employer benefit packages that were insufficient, by stingy employer leave policies for all employees (and therefore not a "discrimination" just against women), and by employer refusals to work with pregnant workers who needed workplace accommodations for pregnancy-based limitations. None of these problems was solved by the PDA, and another big problem may have been exacerbated by the statute. Many feminists maintain, persuasively in our view, that the biggest impediment to women's careers and to workplace equality is *stereotyping*. On the one hand, women are often marginalized in the workplace because employers consider them more family oriented than work oriented, a stereotype that might be reinforced by pregnancy protections alone, and even more by maternity-only leave statutes such as the statute California enacted in 1978. On the other hand, so long as employers and society view the *ideal worker* as one embodying male sex and gender features, women will always lag behind. For feminists such as the ACLU's Ruth Bader Ginsburg in the 1970s and Professor Joan Williams of WorkLifeLaw today, the goal of workplace equality cannot be achieved until everyone's understanding of masculinity and their gender role evolves toward a pro-family stance.[48]

Addressing the broader feminist agenda requires more affirmative government interventions, in the form of positive mandates for employers to provide greater benefits and to accommodate family needs, government daycare programs, and ultimately even paid leaves for family responsibilities. Accompanying such programs would have to be massive educational efforts aimed at corporate officials and attorneys. In our system, the judiciary is debarred by precedent and (even more) by practical institutional limitations from teasing any of these affirmative requirements from the Constitution. By the way, a great deal of Supreme Court jurisprudence reflects the Court's deep institutional practice of ceding to the political branches the duty of fleshing out and implementing positive Constitutional norms and principles. Thus, the Court requires plaintiffs to show an actual and particularized injury in order to have *standing* to sue; a plaintiff harmed by government action easily has standing to sue for a negative injunction, but a plaintiff seeking to prod the government to carry out its affirmative obligations will often not have standing. The Court's *political question* doctrine of nonjusticiability gives wide berth to executive branch discretion, which is much more prominent when you are talking about the state's affirmative obligations than its negative limitations. Accordingly, a judge is highly unlikely to adjudicate claims that the EEOC has failed to develop a comprehensive approach to workplace equality, as opposed to claims by individual companies that the EEOC has misconstrued the law when it seeks to impose accommodation-for-family-responsibility requirements on them.[49]

The most that judges can usually do—and this is the glory of *Brown*—is to jump-start the political process by forcing a fundamental normative discussion when the political system has not been responsive. But this role must not be overstated, for the Court often drops the ball, as it did in *Geduldig* and *Gilbert*. As these cases illustrate, courts are sometimes *less* responsive to the public good, and more influenced by the interests of well-financed repeat-player litigants than legislatures and agencies are. The Supreme Court didn't get the deep and pervasive sex discrimination reflected by pregnancy-excluding rules—but Congress did, at least in part. The Campaign to End Discrimination against Pregnant Workers found legislators more open to their arguments and more accountable to women's normative voices. Congress was a forum for feminist arguments, in part, because women constitute a majority of voters, and a legislator has no room to dismiss their perspectives the way the Supreme Court did. Also, the deliberative norms structuring congressional deliberations are not straitjacketed by legal doctrines of the kind discussed above. Thus, Congress can hear vaguely expressed claims that resonate in the shared experience of many Americans. The legislative process allowed Sue Ross, Ruth Weyand, Wendy Williams, and their allies a full opportunity to articulate reasons and evidence supporting a norm that pregnancy-based discriminations unfairly undermined working women's careers and their ability to support themselves and their families. After Congress enacted the PDA, the EEOC issued implementing regulations and commentary that gave sharp teeth to the statutory norm. The agency's commentary said that employers were prohibited from denying pregnancy benefits to the wives of male employees and subsequently took the position that employers could not discriminate on the basis of sex in rules against worker exposure to hazardous substances in the workplace. Although many employers objected to these requirements, the agency was broadly and intelligently responsible to the congressional mandate and to the legitimate interests of working women like Carolyn Aiello.[50]

The foregoing discussion does not suggest that legislators and administrators are *always* accessible and accountable to We the People, and judges never are. All we are arguing here is that as regards the great foundational principles of our polity—including the equal protection principle associated with *Brown*—legislators and administrators are sometimes accountable to new popular needs and interests in ways that judges are not. Indeed, this phenomenon relates back to Lockean constitutionalism and two kinds of equal treatment rights that citizens have. One kind is equal access to courts as forums to hear everyone's grievance; another is equal access to the political process, through the franchise, political expression, and other activities. These process rights provide two complementary channels of government accountability, one involving courts and adjudications, the other involving elections and political actors. Moreover, these two channels interact: when the political channel is weak or absent (as in the South in the 1950s), judges have been under greater pressure to protect minorities; when judges are behind the times, the political process—often at the state or local level—is sometimes available for rights enforcement. It has been local, state, and national legislatures, not judges, that have established norms against discrimination because of pregnancy, age, disability, and (at the state and local levels alone) sexual and gender orientation. Indeed, the lawyerly Supreme Court has construed the Americans with Disabilities Act of 1990 so narrowly that many analysts have accused the Court of deliberately undermining the statute.[51]

The case of pregnancy discrimination also reveals the link among Constitutional (1) limits on government, (2) affirmative duties for government, and (3) presumption of equal treatment. The PDA, which applies to governmental as well as private employers, reflects both a negative and an affirmative program: not only must state as well as private workplaces avoid discrimination *against* pregnant workers, they must sometimes *accommodate* those workers as well as workers with pregnant wives. To be sure, the PDA did not go very far toward a pregnancy-accommodating norm and said little about postpregnancy family responsibilities, but many PDA supporters had a larger vision of restructuring workplaces to make them more family friendly for all workers. Such a vision required legislation imposing positive duties on employers to provide time off for all workers to accommodate family needs (caregiving as well as childbirth needs). This was a constitutional vision in the sense that these supporters believed that women would never achieve workplace parity so long as employers treated them, and only them, as needing family-based accommodation. This disparity not only reinforced traditional gender stereotypes (female but not male workers need "special" accommodation for family demands), it also as a practical matter rendered female employees more expensive to the employer. This small "c" constitutional vision had a connection to the Large "C" vision, for the disparity literally denied female workers equal *protection* of the law.[52]

In light of *Geduldig*, it is hard to imagine the Supreme Court reading this proposition into the Constitution—but Congress did when it enacted the Family and Medical Leave Act (FMLA). Because Congress rested its authority to apply the FMLA to state employers upon its Fourteenth Amendment power to "enforce" the Equal Protection Clause, legislators gathered evidence and concluded that the PDA had not adequately solved the Constitutional problems identified by feminists and that a more affirmative and gender-neutral remedy was needed, in the form of mandatory leaves for male as well as female workers. Faced with these congressional findings, Chief Justice Rehnquist understood the Constitution much more affirmatively than he and his brethren had in *Geduldig* (and understood sex discrimination more capaciously than his own opinion for the Court in *Gilbert* had done). Upholding the FMLA's application to state employers, Rehnquist's opinion for the Court in *Nevada Department of Human Resources v. Hibbs* (2002) reasoned thus: "By creating an across-the-board, routine employment benefit for all eligible employees [in the FMLA], Congress sought to ensure that family-care leave would no longer be stigmatized as an inordinate drain on the workplace caused by female employees [protected by the PDA], and that employers could not evade leave obligations simply by hiring men." To hold that the FMLA was an exercise of Congress's Section 5 power to "enforce" the Equal Protection Clause, the Court had to be saying that all these concerns were of a Constitutional magnitude. Put more gently, the Court was saying that there was space in Section 5 of the Fourteenth Amendment for Congress to push more affirmatively and creatively for positive protections for women in the workplace.[53]

Notice how Congress and the Court, working together, were able to transcend the limitations of a purely judge-enforced Constitutionalism. But make no mistake: the primary actors were social movement leaders, executive and agency actors, and legislators, with judges merely confirming and acquiescing. Ironically, nowhere in his *Hibbs* opinion did the chief justice overrule *Geduldig*, and indeed all nine justices treated *Geduldig* as good law. Hence, the Constitutional floor that judges will enforce on their own remains low—but it is a floor that Congress has elevated by statute, with the Court going along.

A further point needs to be made. The FMLA reflects the fact that small "c" constitutionalism (like its Large "C" cousin) is an ongoing conversation. This superstatute is itself only a partial fulfillment of the Lockean promise of equal protection for female workers. Based on data compiled in 2000 by the Department of Labor, as many as thirty-seven million employees are not covered by the FMLA; 3.5 million covered workers wanted to take family or medical leaves but did not do so because they could not afford to lose their salary or feared losing seniority or opportunities for job advancement. Fifty-eight percent of the leave-takers are female employees, still a significant gender gap. If the ultimate feminist goal of the FMLA and other statutes is to discredit workplace gender stereotyping (women are more interested in their families, men in their careers), much more work needs to be done. What our book maintains is that almost all the legal work will be accomplished by state and federal administrators, state legislatures (some of which are adopting paid-leave policies for state employees and, in California, for private ones as well), the national legislature, and chief executives.[54]

As we shall see to be the case with other superstatutes, the constitutional conversation reflected in the FMLA is seeping over into other statutory schemes as well. The point that must not be missed is that the ongoing constitutional conversation among social movement leaders, administrators, legislators, and judges has changed the way we as a people think about "discrimination" itself. Americans have long considered discrimination to be a bad idea, but our understanding of that term has traditionally been a crude one: employers ought not to say they'll never hire a black man or a woman for a job. But what if there is a pregnant woman perfect for the job, but the employer fears it will have to accommodate her pregnancy? Many Americans do not consider this "discrimination" and feel it would be unfair to "impose" an accommodation duty upon the employer. But the PDA imposed an accommodation duty on employers, to include pregnancy in the disabilities for which the employer will allow leave-taking. The FMLA imposes an across-the-board accommodation duty on employers, to give all workers time off for family or medical reasons. The Americans with Disabilities Act of 1990 imposes reasonable accommodation requirements for persons with disabilities. As legal scholar Noah Zatz has demonstrated, the EEOC has imposed accommodation requirements on employers in its sexual harassment guidelines (and lower court judges have generally gone along with that). Zatz's bigger point is even more important: refusal to provide reasonable "accommodation" for many employees amounts to "discrimination." When? Under what circumstances? For what kinds of traits? These are normative decisions that America's republic of statutes will be deliberating about for the next several decades. And the key deliberators will be social movement leaders, economists and sociologists, administrators, and state and federal legislators, with judges playing a peripheral (and we hope not an unproductive) role.[55]

CONSTITUTIONAL THEORY IS BACKING AWAY FROM THE STANDARD ACCOUNT

The standard account, without our emendations, of American Constitutionalism remains the assumed model for most scholarship and law teaching. It dominates all but one of the leading Constitutional law casebooks, including the book one of us has coedited. The overwhelming number of law review articles on the subject, including theoretical articles, operate within its premises. Moreover, popular culture and both political parties subscribe to the standard account as an article of faith. Anyone nominated to the state or federal bench has to pay lip service, at least, to the standard account, as illustrated in the 2009 confirmation hearings for Justice Sonia Sotomayor.[56]

Conceptually, however, the standard account is in intellectual freefall. Most of the interesting theoretical work in the past generation has refocused Constitutional law on what can broadly be termed "popular constitutionalism." This body of work takes the notion of popular sovereignty and democracy seriously and uses it to reject some or all features of the standard account. In *Taking the Constitution Away from the Courts* (1999), for example, legal scholar Mark Tushnet calls upon We the People to take the Constitution back from the Court. Jettisoning the standard account altogether, Professor Tushnet would deprivilege the written Constitution and its amendments in favor of what he calls the "thin constitution," namely, the aspirational principles found in the Declaration of Independence, the Bill of Rights, and so forth. Tushnet maintains that constitutional discourse should involve ordinary Americans and should focus on current values and the needs of the modern republic. There should be open debate on these issues, where lawyers have no privileged position, and judges no role at all.[57]

Our main quarrel with Professor Tushnet is that he provides no compelling reason to remove the judiciary entirely from this great debate. Courts are often the institution *best* situated to enforce limits on the other branches. For example, America's response to terrorists is its iterated public devotion to the rule of law, an ideal the executive is always tempted to sacrifice and Congress only occasionally inclined to insist upon. Tushnet's specific thesis has much less bite in post-9/11 America, when even conservative jurists have enforced rules of law against overreaching executive and military officials, as we document in chapter 9. We are also less impressed than Tushnet is with the tendency of activist conservative judges to impede progressive constitutionalism when it is successful in the political process. The typical move of a cautious judge is to deny some worthy Constitutional claims, such as in *Geduldig v. Aiello*, but the Court's stingy opinion in Aiello's case only galvanized feminists politically. When Congress responded with the PDA, the Court has applied the new public norm, albeit sometimes stingily. Nonetheless, Tushnet is onto something. A great deal of recent public law scholarship has advanced mechanisms for Constitutional evolution outside the Article V process. The evolution is driven institutionally by the president and legislators, with judges playing a peripheral role; is ongoing and dialectical rather than the result of a big popular showdown; and seeks to empower government to solve new problems and to redistribute rights and power more equally. The new scholarship increasingly integrates Constitutional doctrine, statutory interpretation, and administrative law in ways that call into question the central role the Constitution of 1789 and judicial review are thought to play in American public law. The Pregnancy Discrimination Act of 1978 and the Family and Medical Leave Act of 1993 exemplify this new public law.[58]

THE NEW DEAL AND THE CIVIL RIGHTS ERA AS CONSTITUTIONAL MOMENTS

A generation of legal academics grew up in a period of our history when the New Deal and its jurisprudence were the conventional wisdom and the civil rights revolution was the most exciting thing happening in law. The culmination of New Deal jurisprudence was the Warren Court and *Brown*. These scholars were critics when the Burger and Rehnquist Courts cut back on or declined to expand Warren Court precedents. Most would like to revive the Warren Court, an unrealistic aspiration. For starters, Supreme Court appointments after 1968 revealed a steady progression to the right. New Deal liberalism died off with the departures of Justices William Brennan (1990), the mastermind of the Warren Court, and Thurgood Marshall (1991), the mastermind of the *Brown* triumph. This practical dilemma was not occurring by accident. We the People did not approve of an unelected judiciary that imposed expensive duties on the state, unless those duties comported with strict legal requirements or public opinion. The Supreme Court had a legitimacy problem, which legal academics have dubbed the "countermajoritarian difficulty." The Burger and Rehnquist Courts invoked notions of democracy and accountability in retracting aggressive remedies and pressuring lower courts to wind down *Brown II* cases. Within the Court liberal and conservative justices fell into debates within the frame of a very conservative and legalistic understanding of the Constitution, a far cry from *Brown*.[59]

Bruce Ackerman challenges this conservative citadel on what he considers rule of law grounds. Yes, the Constitution of 1789, 1791, and 1868 has long been obsolete. One reason it is obsolete is that the modern regulatory state, replete with affirmative and group rights, has replaced the night watchman state that the framers assumed for the federal government. Don't hold your breath for Constitutional amendments to reflect this new reality. Yet Ackerman argues that the Constitution as a legal document, and the popular sovereignty that it embodies, not only authorize *Brown* but also require the Court to monitor the political process for various structural and prejudicial dysfunctions. In a series of books, collectively entitled *We The People*, Ackerman has brilliantly expanded the standard account to support this conclusion. His key move is to represent the New Deal (and, recently, the Civil Rights Era) as a revolution in the

Constitution itself, and not just in the way it was applied by sympathetic judges. In the process, he reconceptualizes and strengthens the big showdown premise, which he assumes to be central to the legitimacy of activist judicial review.

Ackerman has famously argued that there have been at least three authoritative Constitutional "Moments": the Founding, Reconstruction, and the New Deal. Although the third did not produce new Constitutional text, Ackerman argues that this detail is not critical to the normative story. For one thing, the texts produced by the first two Constitutional Moments were of questionable pedigree. The original Constitution provided that it would take effect when nine states ratified it, contrary to the Articles of Confederation, which required unanimity to amend or supersede. The Fourteenth Amendment's ratification owed everything to Congress' refusal to readmit rebel southern states unless they ratified the amendment and its refusal to recognize the effort by two states to rescind their ratifications. Notwithstanding the questionable claim these moments have to be considered authoritative "texts," they have undoubtedly been considered part of the Constitution—and properly so, because they reflected foundational realignments of our national normative commitments.[60]

Ackerman argues that the Constitutional legitimacy of all three moments is a consequence of the higher lawmaking engagement of We the People, repudiating prior governance regimes and adopting new models. Accordingly, the New Deal's regulatory statism was ratified by a similar popular process that characterizes the other two moments: popular demand for change that produces a political crisis and an interbranch impasse → generates an intense period of high-politics debate and a popular electoral ratification of a new order of governance → after which, the old guard stands down and acquiesces in the new Constitutional norm. In effect, therefore, Ackerman relaxes the documentary premise, based upon the same kind of big deliberative showdown that gave us the Constitution and the Reconstruction amendments, and uses that triumph of one normative regime after public deliberation to open up Constitutionalism to affirmative rights and other progressive readings.[61]

If it is a Constitutional Moment, the New Deal transforms the Constitution itself. Once Constitutional law is viewed as having three rather than two defining Constitutional Moments, *Brown* becomes an exercise not just in translating the precepts of Reconstruction to current circumstances but rather in applying the core precepts of Reconstruction in light of the New Deal. In this manner, Ackerman's Constitutional synthesis updates the obsolescent, unamendable Constitution and renders it freshly relevant for today's normative debates. And it does so by reference to objectively determinable legal materials. Thus, *Brown* and other liberal precedents can appear consistent with both the rule of law and our supermajoritarian democracy. Indeed, Ackerman's defense of *Brown* is more lawlike than defenses by more conventional theorists. For example, Mark Tushnet has defended *Brown* as an exercise in "translation" of Reconstruction equality values onto modern circumstances, namely, the regulatory state that provides universal, compulsory public education. Even conservative theorists, ranging from mavericky Richard Posner to archoriginalist Robert Bork, have accepted *Brown* based upon the Constitutional learning curve that we have had since citizens expected state and local governments to provide public education. All of these theorists interpret the Constitution dynamically by pitching the inquiry at a high level of generality—a move that allows the interpreter to import current values (or her own values) into old texts, without much legal analysis. In contrast to these "conservatives," Ackerman grapples with the reasoning in *Plessy v. Ferguson* (1896) and provides a reasoned *legal* basis for overruling that line of precedent as inconsistent with the document itself.[62]

Our central problem with Constitutional Moments theory is that a simpler and more defensible story can be told about the evolving Constitution. After 1933, the open texture of the Constitution was and should have been reinterpreted in light of the public deliberation accompanying the New Deal's superstatutes, as we demonstrate occurred in connection with the Social Security Act of 1935, which the Supreme Court upheld before what Ackerman considers the New Deal Moment (chapter 4). That it is more legalistic than even Robert Bork could imagine reveals how Ackerman's account of *Brown* neglects the central role played by the civil rights movement, state legislatures, and the national executive branch in discrediting the *Plessy* understanding of the Equal Protection Clause.

Partly in response to our criticism that fundamental rights have often been delivered by superstatutes rather than Constitutional Moments, Ackerman has recently expanded his theory to identify eight "cycles" of Constitutional history. The seventh cycle is the post-*Brown* civil rights era, starting around the March on Washington (1963) and focusing on national legislation; the eighth cycle begins with 9/11 and reflects a broad rethinking of the relationship between national security and individual rights. Under Ackerman's new theory, it seems as though America is always in the throes of a Constitutional Moment—but notably missing from Ackerman's Moment-Studded Constitution is women's citizenship. Ackerman now recognizes that landmark statutes are part of the nation's canon, but he seems to marginalize superstatutes such as the PDA, the FMLA, and other sex discrimination laws, as well as landmark precedents such as *Roe v. Wade.* We are second to none in recognizing the constitutional importance of the civil rights movement, but any theory that elevates that movement while substantially ignoring the women's rights movement is missing the most important changes in America's constitution in the past generation.[63]

Examine the FMLA in greater detail. Legislation guaranteeing work leave for all employees for family and medical reasons originated in intramural debates within feminist communities. A majority of states adopted such legislation between 1978 and 1993, and the administrative experience with these statutes provided a solid basis for nationalizing the idea. Congress considered national legislation every year starting in 1985. Energized feminists and labor activists assembled a persuasive case for such legislation, and some employers as well as traditionalist religious groups (notably the Roman Catholic Church) joined their coalition. In 1990 and 1992, Congress passed the FMLA—but President George H. W. Bush both times vetoed it on employer-cost grounds. The FMLA was a major issue, perhaps the most discussed issue, of the 1992 presidential campaign. Governor William Clinton seized upon this issue as a way to position the Democratic Party as pro-family and to attract the lion's share of women's votes. It was featured in his acceptance speech at the July convention as well as in the party's platform, in both presidential and vice-presidential debates, in the Clinton-Gore campaign book, and in numerous speeches. Clinton beat the incumbent by a modest but decisive margin, all of which could be traced to the largest gender voting gap at that point in American history. The FMLA was the first statute that President Clinton signed into law, and by 1996 Republicans supported the statute; the Rehnquist Court in 2002 ruled that the FMLA Constitutionally applied to the states.[64]

Why was this not a Constitutional Moment? It not only fits Ackerman's higher politics model, but we can document just as much if not more focused public engagement on this issue than Ackerman documents for public engagement on the Court-packing and other New Deal controversies. This inquiry not only illustrates the myopia of Constitutional Moments theory as regards women's citizenship but also motivates this question: Would it be a good thing that the FMLA should be Constitutionalized? We do not see the legal cogency or the political wisdom of routinely converting landmark legislation into Constitutional obligation. In the Weberian terminology of our Introduction, Ackerman would seem to insist that at least some superstatutes have the same authority to command that Constitutional text has, while we argue that superstatutes lack that formal authority but do have normative weight derived from social consensus and reliance. Our disinclination to Constitutionalize superstatutes as a formal matter (though we happily constitutionalize them) is related to our understanding of one big virtue of such laws: they are experiments that evolve through agency application and subsequent updating by Congress.[65]

The main payoff to considering the PDA or the FMLA a Constitutional Mini-Moment would seem to be symbolic, making those landmark statutes an even bigger deal. Is bigger better? Not necessarily. Insisting upon the Constitutionalized PDA or FMLA raises its stakes, an experience that has proven highly corrosive in the abortion, gay marriage, and other national debates. Constitutionalizing the PDA or the FMLA also shifts discursive power away from legislators, administrators, and state officials and toward judges and academics. As a realistic as well as aspirational matter, it is better to view the PDA and the FMLA for what they were—normative experiments carried out by administrators, companies, states, and private groups. This reflects our notion of what *should* be the public law agenda: more focus on statutory and administrative policy, and not so great a focus on Constitutional Law. Ta-da: administrative constitutionalism.[66]

THE EXECUTIVE BRANCH AS AN ENGINE OF CONSTITUTIONAL DYNAMISM

John Choon Yoo is the anti-Ackerman. Where Ackerman concedes the revolutionary nature of his theory, taking it as a virtue that Constitutional law need not be moored to Constitutional text, Professor Yoo presents his theory as utterly conventional. He devoutly supports the documentary premise for Constitutional law, but he and his allies are innovative in separating the judicial review corollary from that premise for selected issues. Yoo's recent book *The Powers of War and Peace* (2005) is an exegesis of Constitutional text, read in light of background history, the Philadelphia deliberations, and the ratification debates. Yoo argues for virtually unlimited presidential authority in foreign affairs, including the power to involve the country in foreign wars, to make and terminate treaties, and to provide authoritative interpretations of international agreements. This book has stirred intense discussion, and other scholars are following Yoo's lead, with pragmatic and legal arguments taking the "National Security Constitution" away from the courts, a move that must give Mark Tushnet nightmares.[67]

Notwithstanding his conventional presentation, Professor Yoo is an intellectual revolutionary who destabilizes the standard account of American Constitutionalism as much as Ackerman does—and in this regard he is the ultimate-Ackerman. Yoo's critics claim that he exploits the documentary premise, allegedly by a slanted presentation of textual and original meaning evidence. For example, the Constitution is relatively specific in its apportionment of war-making authority: it belongs with Congress, which has the sole authority to "declare war" and to regulate the armed forces; as commander in chief, the president conducts but does not initiate war. Deliberations at Philadelphia suggest an exception in cases of "sudden invasions," which the president is empowered to "repel." The leading Constitutional scholars have endorsed this reading of the document—a reading that Yoo rejects, based upon a fascinating account of the eighteenth-century difference between "declare war" (announce a state of war, and national emergency) and "make war" (send troops against foreign enemies). This debate between Yoo and his critics reveals yet again the difficulty of teasing determinate Constitutional directives for modern problems using traditional legal analyses. That the indeterminacy exists in an arena with specific Constitutional text and plenty of framers' discussion is significant.[68]

Professor Yoo's larger point is his most persuasive: the Constitution does not settle the specific questions of war power and foreign affairs but instead sets up a structure through which these issues are decided over time. As Yoo points out, Congress has the power of the purse, as well as the power to declare war, and so theoretically Congress has the final say even as to temporary foreign engagements. If the commander in chief has no troops, or the troops are not being paid, he cannot lead the nation into battle. (Contrary to Yoo, we read the Take Care Clause of Article II to bind the president to legislative directions as well as funding limitations.) In an interesting analytical move, Professor Yoo then maintains that the Constitution's apportionment of responsibilities must also be informed by post-framing *practice*. Congress has only declared war five times in our nation's history, but as a nation we have entered into foreign hostilities more than a hundred times. (Sometimes Congress has authorized the hostilities, sometimes it has not.) When the president has taken the initiative, there has rarely been large-scale congressional or popular objection. Indeed, some of the initiatives, such as President Lincoln's famous response to the confederacy, are celebrated today. One might call this form of argument "Constitutional Adverse Possession." Note here a similarity between this approach and Professor Ackerman's Constitutional Moments: both seek to elevate essentially political controversies into hard Constitutional text or determinate meaning.[69]

Professor Yoo makes another big point that reveals a way in which he is the transnational ultimate-Ackerman: just as the Constitution evolved to accommodate *nationalization* of regulation and security during the New Deal, so it is now evolving to accommodate *globalization* of regulation and security. This occurs through a "dynamic" (Yoo's word) understanding of the Constitution that, again, avoids the cumbersome Article V process. For example, Yoo argues that subConstitutional texts (executive-legislative agreements) are the legal instruments by which new constitutional norms should be implemented. For example, congressional-executive agreements implementing the North American Free Trade Agreement (NAFTA) and joining us to the World Trade Organization (WTO) have revolutionized American commercial and trade law, but without treaty ratification that might have been impossible to achieve. Like Article V, Article II's supermajority requirement for treaties is too hard to obtain for anything controversial, which probably was the framers' purpose when they adopted Article II, as Professor Oona Hathaway has demonstrated.[70]

To bring this argument to fruition, however, Yoo needs to go beyond Acker-man, for there was no dramatic confrontation during the Bush-Clinton-Bush period—a big popular showdown—analogous to the Roosevelt-era Constitu-tional Moment. The lack of a big showdown does not trouble Yoo, nor should it in our view. Thus, Yoo rejects Ackerman's claim that the New Deal's Constitu-tional Moment essentially rewrote the Treaty Clause as well as the Commerce Clause and therefore renders congressional-executive agreements interchange-able with treaties. Yoo argues that there has been no popular engagement on this particular issue and insists that there is no functional reason to reject Arti-cle II's vesting foreign affairs matters, including human rights and arms control treaties, with the president. By endorsing the WTO and NAFTA, however, Yoo is accepting a fundamental transformation of American federalism. By endors-ing *Dames and Moore v. Regan* (1981), where the Court ruled that an executive agreement overrode a federal jurisdictional statute, Yoo is accepting the propo-sition that an executive agreement (like a treaty) can actually alter congressio-nal legislation. These Constitutional moves are just as dramatic as those endorsed by Ackerman, and Yoo needs a legitimacy-conferring theory to sustain these changes.[71]

Professor Yoo's aggressive reading of Article II relies, ultimately, upon small "c" constitutional national security values that not only affirmatively protect our country against external enemies but also have been ratified by We the People (according to Yoo's account). Substantively, 9/11 reminds us that the most im-portant role, a pre-Constitutional one, of the federal government has always been national security; as Hobbes and Locke agreed, the government's failure to provide security for its citizens is the primary justification for disobedience or creation of a new government. Consistent with the affirmative liberalism of Hobbes and Locke, Article II vests the president with the primary role in pro-tecting our national security, a role that Yoo claims must be exclusive to be ef-fective. Presidents from Jefferson and Lincoln to Reagan and the Bushes have repeatedly exercised those powers broadly, and with popular approval. In mak-ing this claim, Professor Yoo is aligning himself with Professor Steven Cala-bresi's famous theory that Article II vests *all* executive power (including foreign affairs power) with the president, and that Congress cannot Constitutionally deny the president plenary authority over all federal agencies and administra-tors. Calabresi supports his theory, in part, by the same kind of adverse posses-sion justification as Yoo's theory. Presidents of all parties and persuasions have consistently insisted upon the "unitary executive" with plenary authority over federal agencies and administrators, and We the People have acquiesced in this position because We have reelected these specific leaders and because our primary criterion for choosing a president is the ability to lead the country in a coherent direction. Moreover, Congress has acquiesced in these assertions by not objecting or not doing so strenuously enough.[72]

The unitary executive idea strikes us as a plausible theory for dynamic and practical reasons, not because it is hard-wired into the U.S. Constitution, which carves out an elastic exception to the theory in its Appointments Clause (Article II, Section 2, Clause 2). The presidency is the branch of government that is capable of providing quick responses to crises, greater coherence to over-all government policies, and focal-point leadership in both foreign and domestic affairs. Presidents of both parties have concentrated power within the White House, and this approach has proven workable. Congress and We the People have quietly acquiesced in most of the presidential expansions, and we agree with Calabresi that this has normative force. Debates about presidential power usually occur at the margins, and nowadays they almost always occur in the shadow of a federal statute. In our view, there has been a stable Constitutional understanding that the president must "take Care" to follow and enforce federal statutes (Article II, Section 3), even as there has been vigorous constitutional debate about the meaning of those statutes and the validity of the president's dynamic interpretations of them. Perhaps contrary to Professor Calabresi, we insist that debates about those statutes *cannot* be resolved by wooden invocation of plenary executive power and *must* address the small "c" constitutional issues involving the proper circumstances for presidential innovation. Those circumstances must follow a deliberative model: the president must be addressing an issue or a new wrinkle unanticipated by the enacting Congress, must do so openly and not in secret, and ought to bow to persuasive feedback from citizens and their representatives.

Note some surprising similarities between Professor Yoo's and Professor Calabresi's constitutional method and that of the feminists who pioneered the notion that pregnancy-based exclusions are unacceptable discriminations on the basis of sex. To begin with, both feminist progressives of the 1970s and national security experts of the new millennium emphasize the affirmative duties of the state, to protect citizens against external threats (Yoo and Calabresi) and against job discrimination (Williams and Ross). More than Ackerman, these theorists are shifting public discourse away from judges enforcing the Constitutional limits on government, and toward legislators and administrators implementing projects that provide the national and internal security needed for individual citizens to pursue their life projects. Finally, all four of these scholars believe that the executive branch should be a primary normative entrepreneur in the modern security-assuring state. Yoo and Calabresi believe that the president ought to take the lead in developing frameworks and practices for fighting the war on terrorism, while Williams and Ross believe that the EEOC was, rightfully, the key institutional player in developing a norm against pregnancy discrimination.[73]

POLYCENTRIC CONSTITUTIONALISM (AND ADMINISTRATIVE CONSTITUTIONALISM)

Another important challenge to the standard account of American Constitutionalism was revived by Attorney General Edwin Meese in 1986: "Each of the three coordinate branches of government created and empowered by the Constitution—the executive and the legislative no less than the judicial—has a duty to interpret the Constitution in the performance of its official functions." Thus, "constitutional interpretation is not the business of the Court only, but also properly the business of all branches of government." Meese was questioning the legitimacy of a system where judges, alone, contributed to Constitutional law. Without taking the Constitution *away* from the courts, the attorney general said that it ought to be shared by the other branches, namely, Congress and, especially, the president. As a positive matter, political scientists have provided important support for the Meese thesis: the meaning of the Large "C" Constitution is primarily molded by the political rather than the judicial process.[74]

As a matter of normative aspiration, legal academics have been surprisingly receptive to this notion, which might be called *polycentric Constitutionalism* (a term suggested by Dean Robert Post and Professor Reva Siegel). The thesis is that Constitutionalism, like public policy generally, should be institutionally interactive rather than linear. Constitutional discussions within state governments and other organs of the national government usefully set the stage for Supreme Court review, which in turn may stimulate Constitutional responses from other branches that ought to affect the ultimate or ongoing resolution of a Constitutional issue. It is good governance for each institution to anticipate the perspectives of other institutions and adjust their moves accordingly. A deep reason why a unilateralist position on torture (the president decides) is unacceptable in our polity is that we are committed to consensus-based decision making as to matters of morality and long-term strategy, where Congress, the Supreme Court, and the president are required to cooperate in the setting of national policy; outside the Bush-Cheney administration (2001–09), the lawfulness of official torture has been overwhelmingly rejected.[75]

This institutionally interactive process can be viewed mechanically as a rational choice game, but we agree with scholars who understand it organically as an institutional *dialogue.* "Our Constitution is interpreted on a daily basis through an elaborate dialogue as to its meaning. All segments of society participate in this constitutional interpretive dialogue," says legal scholar Barry Friedman. Unlike Professor Tushnet, Professor Friedman and other dialogic scholars are fans of judicial review and defend it in part on the ground that judicial pronouncements are not the final word on issues of great public importance yet do contribute to thoughtful constructions of public values as well as reconsiderations of hasty decisions. Thus, courts participate with citizens and other branches of government to create what Friedman calls "shared [C]onstitutional meaning."[76]

Such a dialogic understanding of judicial review is well illustrated by the Supreme Court's sex and pregnancy jurisprudence. For most of the twentieth century, the Court sustained one sex discriminatory state policy after another, usually without significant push back from the political process or even from the women's rights movements. Responsive to a new consciousness among younger women and men, the President's Commission on the Status of Women concluded in 1963 that women's equality "is so basic to democracy and its commitment to the ultimate value of the individual that it must be reflected in the fundamental law of the land." Founded in 1966, the National Organization of Women (NOW) galvanized millions of women into political activism around the core notion that equality of citizenship *requires* the state to provide affirmative job security for female workers and to create conditions under which gender stereotyping (e.g., women work only until they have children) is delegitimized in the workplace and in society. Responding to this civic activism, the Supreme Court sent up a trial balloon in *Reed v. Reed* (1971), the first time the Court had invalidated a state sex discrimination on Constitutional grounds. As if to confirm the Court's suggestion that women's equality was an idea whose time had come, the Ninety-second Congress (1971–72) passed legislation extending the federal sex discrimination protections to public employees in 1972, expanding the mandate of the U.S. Commission on Civil Rights to include sex discrimination, and prohibiting sex discrimination by educational institutions receiving federal funds, and of course sent the ERA to the states for ratification, after the Senate voted 84–8 on March 22, 1972.[77]

The next year, the Supreme Court struck down a federal sex discrimination in *Frontiero v. Richardson* (1973), and four justices would have applied strict scrutiny to all governmental sex discriminations; four others wanted the ERA process to play out before making a further determination. The year after that, the Court decided *Geduldig*, Aiello's pregnancy discrimination case. Friedman's theory provides us with a deeper understanding of *Geduldig* that supplements the old-male-judges-cannot-understand-pregnancy theory. The feedback after *Reed* revealed the emerging consensus, after popular inputs and congressional deliberation, that discrimination against women based on stereotypes or prejudice was no longer acceptable—but that feedback did not address the deeper issue of family and gender role that were raised by pregnancy-based exclusions. The EEOC's Sex Discrimination Guidelines (also issued in 1972) addressed this issue in the context of the workplace, but there remained room for dispute as to whether the antidiscrimination norm required accommodation for women's pregnancies. Dialogic theory does not *require* the result in *Geduldig*, for the Court could easily have followed the EEOC's lead and gauged Congress's reaction, but such theory does provide a more reasonable explanation for the normative work that was going on.[78]

After the Supreme Court applied the *Geduldig* reasoning to Title VII, in Sherrie O'Steen's case, Susan Ross, Ruth Weyand, Marsha Berzon, Wendy Williams, Marcia Greenberger, Mary Dunlap, and their allies created the Campaign to End Discrimination against Pregnant Workers. The campaign included religious traditionalists as well as feminists, labor activists as well as academics, and Republicans as well as Democrats. In detailed testimony before both House and Senate committees, the campaign and its allies made three important points. First, employer discrimination against pregnant women was catastrophic for many female workers. Almost 44 percent of American adult women were in the workforce, most of them because their income was necessary to support themselves or their families—women like Sherrie O'Steen, who testified in person before Congress.[79]

The campaign's second point was systemic: the workplace would *never* be one where women would stand on an equal plane with men, so long as companies could discriminate against them on the basis of pregnancy. Pregnancy-based leaves or dismissals interrupted the careers of female employees. Even the possibility of pregnancy was a common excuse for not hiring or promoting women. Because there was no evidence that pregnant women were unable to do their jobs as well as men or nonpregnant women, this kind of pervasive discrimination suggested the perseverance of gender-based stereotypes or even prejudices against women in the workplace. Those old-fashioned attitudes were not only unfair to women as a group—a group which Congress realized constituted a majority of voters—but also economically unproductive. Women were in the workplace to stay, and practices that made their careers unnecessarily rough ought not to be tolerated. Some employers argued that workplace efficiency required some discretion as to treatment of pregnant employees, but the campaign enlisted government experts and some employers to refute excessive cost claims.[80]

Finally, and perhaps most powerfully, the campaign argued that pregnancy discrimination was antifamily. Both the pro-life Roman Catholic Church and pro-choice feminists like Williams and Ross pressed the norm that pregnant women should be supported rather than discharged or discriminated against. For Sherrie O'Steen, pregnancy-based discrimination literally destroyed her marriage and almost cost this mother the life of her child. The campaign and its allies argued that the state has an obligation to protect not only these women but also their children and their families against arbitrary treatment. Buried within the campaign's case for the PDA was an overarching policy that the state should make the workplace more "family-friendly" for mothers and fathers.[81]

After extensive hearings, debate, and some popular feedback, Congress enacted the PDA as an amendment to Title VII. Its sponsors and supporters understood the PDA to be a renunciation of a normative stance that could not understand pregnancy-based discrimination as sex discrimination. With an engaged Congress across the street, the Supreme Court beat an immediate retreat from *Gilbert* and has largely construed the PDA in accord with the new public norm supported by congressional and administrative deliberations. That process, in turn, contributed to a feminist campaign to persuade state legislatures and, in 1993, Congress to require employers to afford all employees leave time for family and medical needs. Ironically, the same justice who authored *Gilbert* also authored the Court's opinion upholding the Family and Medical Leave Act of 1993: William Hubbs Rehnquist.[82]

Like Susan Ross and Wendy Williams, legal historian Reva Siegel believes that the PDA is a Constitutional repudiation of *Geduldig*, but she does not rest that repudiation upon an Ackermanian claim that We the People were mobilized into an exercise of higher lawmaking and so forth. Instead, she rests her case on Congress's Constitutional obligation to "enforce" the Fourteenth Amendment, which carries with it a Meesean obligation on the part of Congress to make its own determination as to whether antifamily policies in private as well as public workplaces deny women and men the equal "protection" of the law. No one disputes that Congress and President Clinton adopted the FMLA only after a serious, fact-based inquiry, and the statute represented a public-regarding response to a significant problem that was flagged by an important social movement. The process by which the FMLA was developed and enacted is one not well characterized as a big showdown pitting an obdurate institution against a mobilized We the People; instead, it was marked by institutional problem solving, disagreement and compromise, and ultimately a fair amount of consensus, achieved within the forum of our elected and accountable representatives.[83]

Previous accounts of polycentric Constitutionalism have emphasized the initiating role of social movements and the legitimizing role of Congress, and we build on that work in this book. One of the conceptual themes that we add to the existing literature is the central (rather than peripheral or mechanical) role played by agencies; another theme is that the important normative role of agencies goes way beyond that of giving life to judicially "underenforced" Constitutional norms. Consider, as an illustration, three different and interlocking ways of understanding the EEOC's pathfinding normative move in its 1972 pregnancy guidelines:

- Title VII's sex discrimination bar is best understood in light of the statutory purpose to integrate women into the national workforce and provide them with the same kind of security in their jobs and careers that men enjoy.
- The Constitution requires the agency to monitor and regulate workplace practices, such as pregnancy discriminations, in a fair manner that assures female as well as male employees the "equal protection of the law."
- Even if neither Title VII nor the Constitution requires the agency to regulate workplace discrimination, these legal sources permit the agency to issue such regulations, based upon the agency's judgment about how the workplace should be reformed.

(A similar account can be rendered for the EEOC's pregnancy guidelines issued after the PDA was enacted and for the Labor Department's guidelines following enactment of the FMLA.) Administrative constitutionalism embraces all three of these understandings of the agency's normative role in superstatutes—not just giving life to underenforced Constitutional norms but also implementing statutory purposes and improving our society within its realm of broadly delegated authority. Polycentric Constitutionalism, in contrast, embraces only the second understanding.

While far from comprehensive, our survey of important post-*Brown* theories suggests that thoughtful scholars, officials, and citizens are retreating from a Constitutionalism that relies on Article V and the Supreme Court to update our nation's fundamental commitments and to keep them relevant for a millennial era where political citizenship has expanded dramatically, where the main threats to national security come from nonstate networks of antimodern vigilantes, and where inaction spells decline or disaster. Article V is a virtual dead letter, or maybe a Constitutional Scarlet Letter given the fate of the ERA: even amendments with wide support cannot gain the support of thirty-eight states; it is much easier to secure Constitutional rights through dynamic judicial constructions or landmark statutes than through the Article V process.

The feminist experience also suggests a third way between Tushnet's notion that the Constitution should be taken away from the Court and the older notion that all things good and liberal should be Constitutionalized. That third way, the project of this book, is that important frameworks and values, especially those carrying out the state's affirmative duties, are entrenched through federal super-statutes, state statutory convergences, and legally enforceable treaties and conventions. The chapter that follows will explain in greater detail the political theories from which small "c" constitutionalism draws.

THE DEMOCRATIC CONSTITUTION AND OUR EPISODIC REPUBLIC

On June 22, 1957, Louise Lassiter, a forty-one-year-old black woman in Sea-bord, North Carolina, presented herself to register to vote, for the first time in her life. Helen H. Taylor, the registrar, offered her a copy of the North Carolina Constitution and asked her to read designated portions of it. State law required Taylor to follow this procedure, and then to ask for the applicant to copy a portion of the document, in order to be certain that Lassiter was literate. Eighteen states then had literacy requirements for voting, but only five (Alabama, Georgia, Mississippi, and North and South Carolina) imposed on potential voters a formal examination such as this one. Just Mississippi and North Carolina required the potential voter to do more than write her name.[1]

Lassiter believed that North Carolina's literacy requirements were inconsistent with the Equal Protection Clause of the U.S. Constitution and, for that reason, refused to cooperate in Taylor's exercise. That is, literacy requirements in the South were motivated by, and had the effect of, excluding people of color from the franchise. In 1956, only 24.9 percent of African American adults in the South were registered to vote; in North Carolina, the figure was 24.0 percent, a little lower than the regional average, probably because of the literacy test. On June 28, the Board of Elections for Northampton County, in which Seabord Precinct was located, rejected Lassiter's arguments that application of the state literacy requirements was unConstitutional, and her NAACP lawyer appealed. Lassiter's case is a classic example of the standard account of American Constitutionalism in action—and of the problems identified in the previous chapter. The central problem is the tension between the greatness and urgency of Lassiter's claim, a central tenet of the civil rights movement whose moral rightness was sweeping world opinion, and the inhospitality of the traditional legal materials. Justice William O. Douglas, perhaps the most liberal justice in the Court's history, wrote the opinion denying Lassiter's claim, and no one dissented.[2]

Louise Lassiter's case marked the end of one epoch of democratic change in the United States, and the beginning of a new one. Recall that the Constitution of 1789 did not assure electoral participation by many Americans. The participatory democracy we enjoy today was the result of three waves of republican activism that expanded the franchise, each followed by a period of withdrawal and limitation. This phenomenon inspires our notion that the United States is an *episodic republic.* Even as to the most fundamental rights associated with the democracy we have long considered definitional of our nation, advancement of participatory values has involved focused struggle and republican deliberation, followed by lethargy and, often, reaction. Consider our history in a nutshell.

The first republican surge occurred at the local level and resulted in *state constitutional convergences.* During the Jeffersonian period, the states amended their own constitutions to eliminate most property- and income-based requirements for voting. Although the Jacksonians continued some of this surge, they fell into deep division over the issue of slavery and even citizenship for free blacks. The abolitionist movement and, ultimately, the Civil War represented the second wave of democratic activism, which was encoded in *Constitutional amendments* barring state franchise discrimination based on race (1871), sex (1920), inability to pay a poll tax (1964), and age (1971). As Lassiter's case reflects, the Fifteenth Amendment barring race discrimination was largely a dead letter in the South, whose jurisdictions created a forest of nonrace barriers that affected poor whites as well as citizens of color. The civil rights movement had some success persuading federal judges to invalidate some of the subterfuges, but like the hydra two new forms of exclusion immediately replaced every old one that judges attacked. The only effective solution was a third wave of electoral transformation—through *federal superstatutes.*[3]

The Civil Rights Acts of 1957 and 1960 authorized the Department of Justice to bring lawsuits opening up the franchise in the face of discriminatory state practices. Under the leadership of Assistant Attorney General Burke Marshall (1961–65), the department successfully sued a number of districts, but its attorneys also concluded that case-by-case adjudication was an ineffective process: many southern federal judges tended to be foot-dragging, it was hard and very expensive to "prove" discrimination, and southern registrars were often one step ahead of the federal lawsuits. The structure of case-by-case adjudication—the classic enforcement for Constitutional rights under the standard account—was disappointing at best. Its failure to solve a national problem that reached crisis proportions in 1964–65 motivated Congress and President Lyndon Johnson to enact the Voting Rights Act of 1965 ("VRA"). The VRA addressed Louise

Lassiter's complaint by suspending literacy tests in specified southern jurisdictions (including Northampton County) and addressed the larger problem of discriminatory evasions by requiring "preclearance" of voting changes by covered southern jurisdictions.[4]

The Supreme Court's decision in *Lassiter* illustrates the previous chapter's argument that Constitutionalism is an insufficient way of understanding and pursuing our nation's fundamental values, and provides a springboard for this chapter's argument that statute-based constitutionalism is richer and more realistic. Our small "c" constitutionalism is a more embracing understanding of our nation's fundamental commitments, an understanding that includes common law baselines, state statutory convergences, federal superstatutes, and the primary provisions of the Constitution itself, as amended. Most of the VRA's reforms could not have been adopted as an Article V amendment simply as a matter of politics; three-quarters of the states would not have ratified such an amendment. But neither would an Article V amendment have been the best way to develop and entrench a new approach to regulating the electoral process. The VRA was experimental, administrative, and time limited—and those very features setting it off from a Constitutional amendment proved valuable in developing and then entrenching new franchise norms. In our episodic republic, there is more than one path toward constitutional entrenchment.[5]

Another important feature of the episodic republic is that our nation's constitutional commitments entail an affirmative role for government. A republican answer to Lassiter's complaint is that an educated, literate electorate is a good aspiration for a democracy, and some southerners sincerely believed that literacy tests fulfilled such a public-regarding purpose. Another republican answer, suggested by Lassiter's attorneys, was that such tests were administered in a discriminatory manner, and so had to go. A deeper answer was developed by the Justice Department administering the VRA: if the state demands literacy as a franchise requirement, it has an obligation to provide a good education for all its citizens, an obligation that southern school segregation flunked cold and that job discrimination also impeded. Under conditions of inequality, and state defaults on its duties to educate, literacy requirements were a poor mechanism to motivate citizens. The broader point is that the conditions of democracy are interconnected with the duty of the state to secure everyone's "liberties"—a term we use to include not just a right to be left alone by the government but *also* each citizen's right to state institutions protecting his and his family's security against private abuse or oppression *and* each citizen's right to opportunities for active civic and political engagement.[6]

Thus, we see the episodic republic as one whose commitments are embodied in federal statutes and state constitutions, not just the U.S. Constitution, *and* where statutory protections impose obligations upon government and not just safe harbors against state intrusions. A third feature of our episodic republic is deliberative. Recall, from the Introduction, that republican deliberation is problem solving, interactive, and accountable. We now enrich that discussion of deliberation with the further observation that republican deliberation in our complex government structure involves *institutional interaction*, where different institutions perform different roles. Executive institutions are usually initiators and motivators, as well as implementers. Legislative actors recast and calibrate such problem-solving initiatives to earn a broader acceptability among the public and various groups that mold opinion. Courts soften the edges of the legislative product, integrate it into the nation's other normative commitments, and monitor agencies. Important to such institutionalized deliberation is *feedback*— not just direct feedback from We the People (Is the statutory program popular?) but also responses from more particular groups, including experts (Is the statutory program working?), the regulated group (Are they internalizing the statutory norm?), and critics (Are some of them persuaded that it was a good idea?).

The Voting Rights Act epitomizes successful deliberation along these lines. The statute was responsive both to grievances by citizens of color and to the public interest in a democracy integrating all groups; its content was a product of executive department experts and drafters, congressional compromises, and judicial construction; and feedback was formalized in the sunset features of the 1965 statute and its 1970, 1975, 1982, and 2006 reenactments. These deliberative features contributed to the law's success on the merits—citizens of color now vote in numbers approaching or exceeding those of white voters—and to its legitimacy. Can you imagine that Senator Barack Hussein Obama, a candidate of color, would in the 2008 presidential election have carried North Carolina, Louise Lassiter's long-segregated state, had it not been for the VRA?[7]

SMALL "c" CONSTITUTIONALISM

Louise Lassiter's attorneys and the justices of the Warren Court faced a dilemma when they contemplated the Constitutionality of North Carolina's literacy requirement for voter registration. Their dilemma originates in an irony. Theories of republican governance demand participation and deliberation by engaged citizens, and literacy tests could be connected to such an admirable theory. But they could also be connected to American apartheid, a system of practices and rules designed to exclude citizens of color from full participation. Even if not malignantly inspired and arbitrarily applied, the literacy requirement bore disproportionately upon racial minorities, working-class persons, and the poor—assuring their marginalization in the democratic process. In short, literacy tests in the South set republican aspirations for an engaged citizenry against the demands of an inclusive democracy. By 1961, those demands had become pressing, and the nation was in crisis. Yet it was not clear how such tests violated the Constitution, which explicitly delegates the voter-qualification rules to the states. The Fifteenth Amendment bars franchise exclusions "on the basis of race," but literacy tests are not explicitly race based, and the Supreme Court had by 1961 repeatedly upheld more restrictive literacy tests than North Carolina's against Fourteenth and Fifteenth Amendment attack. Although Lassiter's claims were expressed within the standard account, they were less grounded in Large "C" Constitutional law than in an older tradition of what we call small "c" constitutionalism. Our purpose here is to retrieve that tradition, which looks not to a single authoritative document and is a political discourse dominated by social movements and administrators, rather than a legal one dominated by judges.[8]

ARISTOTLE'S NOTION OF SMALL "C" CONSTITUTIONALISM

We begin with the writings of some illustrious visiting observers of popular governments: Aristotle, who lived much of his life in Athens as a resident foreigner or "metic" rather than as a citizen, was a constitutional comparativist; he and his students did studies of hundreds of constitutions all over the Greek-influenced world. Polybius, a Greek hostage of the Romans, who became a close friend of Scipio Africanus (victor over Hannibal in the Second Punic War), wrote his brilliant analysis of Rome's constitution for a Greek audience. The baron de Montesquieu's most important writings on republican government resulted from the French noble's visit to Great Britain almost exactly one hundred years prior to Alexis de Tocqueville's celebrated American travels. Tocqueville himself is the paradigmatic example of the outsider whose observations are still teaching us about America's special political genius. Each of these visitors took a comparative view of constitutions, a view external to the political practices of the places they studied. Although they wrote in different eras and about different polities, these political theorists had some fundamentally similar things to say about constitutionalism.[9]

Each of these observers treated constitutions as descriptions of the institutions and practices by which a people is governed; a polity's constitution can only partly be described by official documents. Constitutions, in their eyes, were robust and foundational in the sense that they could *not* easily be changed or abandoned. When the Athenian democracy was overthrown, for example, in 411 B.C. or, again, in 404 B.C., Aristotle would not have thought that its constitutional identity changed at those moments (as these changes didn't last long). Regime change is different from constitutional change. For an unwritten constitutional change to occur takes a long time, perhaps generations. Notwithstanding the endless disputes among historians as to when the Roman Republic ended, virtually all of them believe the republic did not end in a day. Probably all could agree that by the time Octavian became princeps in 27 B.C., the republic was finished—but some believe that Octavian's accession as Augustus Caesar was only the end of the end. And the consensus that the republican constitution was over by 27 B.C. depends on the fact that the republic did not make a comeback after Octavian's death in A.D.14.[10]

Consider a related historical point. The Athenians distinguished fundamental laws (the *nomoi*) from the particular decrees or commands (*psephisma*) that emerged from the popular assembly (the *ekklesia*). Indeed, they criminalized proposed decrees inconsistent with the nomoi. (They also rejected proposed nomoi that were inconsistent with the body of the laws overall.) In effect, the Athenians instituted an early form of judicial review whereby courts could invalidate actions of the assembly. Moreover, by the beginning of the fourth century they no longer permitted the assembly to enact nomoi; instead, they erected a special and separate process for that purpose, a judicial process in which the popular assembly could play no direct part. In this way, Athenians distinguished general laws from particular commands and insisted that the former were legally superior to the latter. We can think of the set of laws as forming (part of) the real constitution of Athens—the institutions and enduring principles and values that constituted the Athenian public space. These included, of course, the narrowly political laws that defined and regulated citizenship, specified offices, established institutions, established and regulated voting rights in various bodies, and outlined legal duties of public service. But there were also other laws that regulated the interaction among citizens as well as between citizens and the city.[11]

Like contemporary Americans, Athenians identified deeply with their constitution and the way of life it protected. The brilliant reputation of orators such as Pericles and Demosthenes rested partly on their ability to tie particular arguments and occasions to practices of citizenship that Athenians considered to be at the core of their polity. Perhaps the most striking example of this commitment can be seen in the *Crito*, where Plato described Socrates's last meeting with his friends and his explanation for declining their offer to rescue him from the state-imposed death penalty. Although an "internal" critic of Athenian democracy, Socrates identified himself deeply with Athens nevertheless. For him to accept his friends' offer of escape would be to undermine the laws (nomoi) that made possible his birth, his education, and his lifelong practice of public philosophy. It would be to break what Socrates considered the underlying bargain between the citizen and the state by undermining the basis of political order. His only moral options were either to convince the jury or, failing that, to accept its verdict. If the *Crito* is any guide, a constitution commands loyalty and respect insofar as it makes it possible for persons living under it to live morally attractive lives. Such constitutions do this by establishing effective governmental institutions and protecting certain basic values.[12]

Plato and Socrates thought about "constitution" in a wider sense than Americans do. The Athenians had no official document called "the Constitution," but they believed that they had a unique form of government that differed significantly from those of their neighbors. Consistent with *Crito*, Aristotle thought that a constitution was something like the soul of a city: more than territory or the inhabitants, he thought that a city's constitution accounted for its civic identity across time. "This community *is* the constitution," Aristotle says in the *Politics*. "[T]he constitution is so to speak the life of the city." It is a description of the institutions and practices by which a people were governed. "A constitution is the organization of offices in a state, and determines what is to be the governing body, and what is the end of each community." He described Athens's constitution as democratic, because citizenship was widespread and all of its citizens were entitled to vote in the ekklesia, to serve on juries, and to act as magistrates. In contrast, Sparta's constitution mixed aristocratic with democratic elements, but tilted strongly toward aristocracy because its base of citizenship was narrow and the exercise of political authority was more tightly controlled.[13]

Aristotle did not confine himself to certain documents when thinking of constitutions. Instead, he posed a practical question: How are a people actually governed? Asking the question this way has a number of implications. In contrast to the traditions of American Constitutionalism, Aristotle did not necessarily consider the constitution legally superior to ordinary decrees (unless part of the nomoi). Indeed, the constitution may have no special legal status at all. For a modern example, the eighteenth-century British constitution consisted of conventions and symbolic declarations having no legal force, as well as statutes having legal force but not the formal trumping authority Americans associate with our Constitution. But an Aristotelian constitution is nevertheless superior, as a matter of political morality, to everyday decrees and legal rules, in the sense that a constitution helps make the city what it is. Thus, "the laws are, and ought to be, framed with a view to the constitution, and not the constitution to the laws." This is more or less the same way that the British have traditionally thought about their constitution, and this distinction finds an echo in Max Weber's distinction between rules we follow because of their authority to command

and those we follow because of a constellation of our own and other people's interests (our Introduction).[14]

In addition to the internal analysis he applied to rules as a matter of description, Aristotle was an external critic as well, applying a normative analysis to appraise the Athenian constitution and recommend changes. For example, Aristotle thought that the Athenian government of his time was too radical because its institutions were too much dominated by one class (the poor people who happened to constitute the majority) who pursued their own class interests rather than common interests. He preferred a moderate democracy (*politaia*), which included middle and upper classes, as better attuned to pursuing the common good, rather than class interests. Accordingly, Aristotle favored property qualifications for citizenship, which he thought would produce rule by the middle class, whose class interests best resembled the interest of the city. The framers of the Constitution of 1789 followed Aristotle in this respect, and latter-day literacy tests such as the one in *Lassiter* could be defended on similar grounds.[15]

Aristotle's constitutionalism, both its descriptive and normative elements, has been pervasively important in Western history, influencing Polybius, Machiavelli, Montesquieu, and Rousseau. Like Aristotle, each of these writers thought that a good constitution would mix popular and elite elements and that such a balanced constitution would be the best guarantee of liberty. In various ways, each of these later writers elaborated his theory in consideration of the development and decline of the Roman Republic, where the major elements of Rome's constitution—the Senate and the tribunes—represented classes in Roman society. Like Aristotle, Polybius, Machiavelli, and Rousseau all accepted a binary political ontology that included the wealthy class and the masses of people. Unlike Aristotle, the later writers (except for Machiavelli) did not envision a middle class that might play a distinctive role in politics; therefore, each saw constitutionalism as in some way balancing sharply opposed class interests of the rich and the poor. Polybius was the clearest in seeing the genius of the Roman constitution in its institutionalization of class conflicts; he was pervasively influential in thinking that the preservation of Roman liberties was anchored in the hard-won balance between the fundamental social elements reflected in its constitution. Montesquieu agreed that it was important to involve various classes in government, as much for their peculiar virtues as for their social weight, but he adopted (possibly from Locke or possibly from contemporary governmental practices) a functional notion of mixture that permitted him to distinguish executive, legislative, and judicial powers. Montesquieu provided a powerful analysis for why any combination of authorities—the legislative with the executive, the executive with the judicial, and the judicial with the legislative, as well as all three in the same hands—was dangerous to liberty.[16]

AMERICAN CONSTITUTIONALISM AT THE FOUNDING

Modern thinking ought not to be limited by the precise descriptions found in Aristotle, Polybius, and Montesquieu, who embraced now-outmoded beliefs that society consisted of clearly defined classes and that a good constitution would reflect the different classes of society. Modernists follow Hobbes and Locke in understanding society as a collection of individuals, not classes. What we draw from these foundational theorists are the ideas that a small "c" constitution is integrated with a polity's identity (Aristotle), that it emerges and evolves as a result of political struggle (Polybius), and that it ought to reflect the interests of all those in the polity (Montesquieu). Consider their approach as a contrast with the standard account of American Constitutionalism. Rather than expressing a set of positive rules negotiated by long-deceased framers, the central metaphor of a Large "C" Constitution as social contract, an Aristotelian small "c" constitution consists of the basic rules of political participation and citizenship, fundamental institutions and frameworks for governance, and foundational normative precepts for state practice as well as private behaviors. Small "c" constitutionalism is reasoning from those values to address new problems confronted by the nation. As Aristotle documented in his famous history of the Athenian experience, constitutionalism is relentlessly dynamic.[17]

Notwithstanding the standard account, an Aristotelian constitutionalism has flourished in America, alongside the post-Independence Constitution. (The pre-Independence colonies, of course, were familiar and comfortable with the evolving constitution of England and the republican Commonwealth tradition.) The Constitution's framers themselves viewed their product in small "c" constitutional terms, as illustrated by Madison and Hamilton's view that the governmental structure rendered a Bill of Rights unnecessary. Were Aristotle revived in 1797 to describe America's early constitution, he would not have confined himself to the Constitution of 1789, as modified by the Bill of Rights (1791). He would have inquired into our foundational laws and civic practices. Early statutes establishing four cabinet offices, an independent federal judiciary, a postal system, and the Bank of the United States would be just as important for an Aristotelian constitution as the Constitution's Articles I to III, which set forth the framework for the three national branches of government. The internal rules and practices of the House and the Senate would be included. The Washington administration's practices in executive branch appointments and removals, foreign relations, and deployment of armed and naval forces were part of the constitution. Even more fundamental to America's constitution circa 1797 would have been the common law rules followed in the states that assured rights of exclusion for holders of private property, enforced contracts, held people accountable for injuries they caused to other persons or property, defined the rights of husbands over wives and children, and so forth. Normatively, the common law rules of marital rights were more important than the Bill of Rights to the lives of Americans in 1797.[18]

From Aristotle's point of view, a key feature of American constitutionalism in 1797 would have been rules or practices involving political citizenship and participation, especially franchise rules: Who can hold office? Who can vote? And for what? The Constitution of 1789 answered few of these questions, largely deferring to state voting rules and setting forth only a few qualifications for holding office (mainly generous minimum age requirements). Ever the social scientist, Aristotle would have been happy to conduct surveys of state practice. In the 1790s, he would have found the United States in some ways less democratic than ancient Athens had been: more people could vote in America, but they had less voice on particular issues. In 2010, he would be bewildered by the level of political participation in this country—a product of three waves of popular surges, which have been encoded in state constitutional, federal Constitutional, and federal statutory mechanisms and entrenched in our political culture.

AMERICA'S DEMOCRATIC CONSTITUTION: CONSTITUTIONAL RULES PLUS STATE STATUTORY CONVERGENCES PLUS SUPERSTATUTORY STRUCTURE AND RULES

Our founders were fearful of democracy, especially in its populistic or direct form. They distrusted institutions that were directly democratic; even for the representative democracy they favored, elections would not be too frequent and districts would be large enough to create deliberative distance between the representatives and popular whims. Some of this fear was abstract and theoretical, grounded partly in eighteenth-century views of the excesses of radically democratic Athens and of the populist Roman demagogues, and partly in the tumultuous experiences of the American states during and following the Revolution. These fears were embodied both in the Constitution and in the important writings surrounding it, such as *The Federalist*, where the authors ("Publius") celebrated the anticipated role of elites in refining and enlarging (or sanitizing) public opinion as it made its way into the policy process. Like many other eighteenth-century writers, Publius found it a virtue that the American Constitution eschewed direct democracy in favor of a representative form of government, where We the People could be kept at arm's length. Article I, Section 1,

Clause 2 says that House members will be elected every two years, by vote of the "electors for the most numerous Branch" of the state legislature, the same organ that elected U.S. Senators under the Constitution of 1789. For presidential elections, Article II, Section 1, Clause 2, recognizes an Electoral College, whose members are chosen in each state "in such manner as the Legislature thereof may direct." These Constitutional defaults were moderately democratic for the time but appear seriously underinclusive today, as most states limited the franchise to white men who owned property.[19]

One of the great ironies of American history is the rapidity with which these beliefs and expectations were immediately upended by the first republican surge. In his magnificent *Radicalism of the American Revolution* (1991), historian Gordon Wood shows just how quickly democratic and egalitarian expectations came to dominate the American political landscape, and how quickly the founding generation was swept from office. As most of the founding elite sorted themselves into unpopular sides of issues, contested elections produced a new class of politicians, who appealed directly and successfully to public sentiments. By the time Tocqueville arrived in the United States (1831), he found and described a governance that had become democratic well beyond the imaginings of the founding era. During the Republican presidencies of Jefferson (1801–09), Madison (1809–17), and Monroe (1817–25), the political system not only rejected the Federalist notion of rule by elites but also partially democratized the voting process. By 1824, most states had dropped the property-holding requirement for voting in state and congressional elections, and all but a handful of states were choosing presidential electors by popular vote. When Tocqueville published *Democracy in America* (1835), he could say, with only some exaggeration, that "all the states of the Union ha[ve] adopted universal suffrage," as regards white men.[20]

For Tocqueville, what was most striking about the United States under President Andrew Jackson (1829–37) was the widely held democratic beliefs and practices. Although Tocqueville devoted a long chapter to the Constitution of 1789, he saw that the document represented no more than a partial view of American public values. For example, the Constitution seemed to envision what Aristotle would have called a mixed government, where the populist House of Representatives worked with the oligarchic Senate and the potentially monarchical president to create public policy. By the 1830s, however, the government that white male Americans actually enjoyed was substantially democratic, in both form and substance. Tocqueville's take-home point in *Democracy in America* was that American culture was saturated with democratic practices, including expanded rules for political participation and a greater voice of We the People in public policy. Thus, white males of all social classes and incomes voted for House members, state legislators who chose senators, and the electors who chose the president. Moreover, President Jackson had triumphed over the elites supporting the United States Bank, and his successor brought public finance under democratic control in the Treasury Department. Even the Whig Party, which had acidly ridiculed Jackson's appeal to the common man, swiftly shed the antidemocratic, elitist airs they had inherited from the Federalists. They won the presidential election of 1840 by depicting their candidate, General William Henry Harrison ("Old Tippecanoe"), as the heir to Jackson's populist mantle and deriding President Martin Van Buren (Jackson's hand-picked successor) as a dandy out of touch with ordinary Americans. Consistent with Tocqueville's report, historians depict Jacksonian democratic practices and the spirit of equality as dominating our culture, affecting public policy, the popular press, emerging public education, and everyday life. Virtually the only thing untouched by democracy was Constitutional text and precedent.[21]

Unremarked in Tocqueville's book, there were great gaps in America's democratic constitutionalism. Thus, in 1835, neither women nor, in most states, people of color could vote, and these formal franchise rules belied Tocqueville's sunny assessment that women and servants had indirect voices in public policy. These gaps were challenged, directly by the women's rights movement launched at Seneca Falls in 1848, and indirectly by the movement to abolish slavery. Although it required decades of fierce activism, and a tragic civil war, to accomplish the goals of these social movements, they were successful in amending the Constitution to bar race (Fifteenth Amendment, 1871) and sex (Nineteenth Amendment, 1920) as grounds for denying citizens the franchise. Although half the states already allowed women to vote in at least some elections, the Nineteenth Amendment was the greatest expansion of the franchise in American history. Tocqueville also failed to discuss the interesting fact that the United States was one of the few democracies in either ancient or modern times *not* to put some issues to a direct vote of the people. The progressive movement of the early twentieth century changed that at the state level. In 1904, Oregon created the first statewide initiative, allowing popular petitions to place measures on the ballot that, if ratified by a majority of voters, would become law. Since 1904, almost all the states have adopted initiatives or referenda for some issues, though the United States remains unusual in its not having a national referendum for any issue. Popular lawmaking has significantly affected public policy at the state level and has introduced many important issues that have shown resonance with voters, from property tax stabilization to affirmative action to restrictions on state benefits given to illegal aliens.[22]

In other ways, however, the period between Reconstruction and the New Deal saw the franchise narrow; local retrenchment almost immediately followed adoption of the Fifteenth Amendment. New franchise restrictions, adopted at the state level, included residency requirements, poll taxes, literacy tests, felony disqualification rules, the all-white primary, and other measures designed to keep African Americans (especially in the South), European American immigrants (North), Asian Americans (West), and poor whites (everywhere) from voting. Contrary to Tocqueville, the expansion of the right to vote was not self-propelling; it was two steps forward and one step backward, or vice versa, for most of American history between 1828 and 1938. In the South, it was a temporary step forward and then back to square zero for people of color such as Louise Lassiter's ancestors. As before, the franchise rules reflected as well as molded social attitudes: people of color were not considered equal citizens, and the illiterate and poor of all races were second-class at best. Also important was the introduction of the secret ballot, which had large but hard-to-pinpoint consequences for the incidence as well as nature of voting in this country.[23]

By the 1930s, however, America's self-understanding as an inclusive democracy took a third turn, primarily in response to the republican surge of the civil rights movement. Complaints by people of color that they were systematically excluded from participation in the South and other areas received increasing attention (outside the South), partly because of the populism of the New Deal and partly as a self-defining reaction to the totalitarian governments of Nazi Germany and the Communist Soviet Union. Americans insisted on contrasting our polity from these unchristian societies—a contrast that brought our own exclusionary practices into sharper relief. World War II and the Cold War created new pressures to democratize. Some of the previous race-based restrictions fell. Constitutional lawsuits spelled the end of the all-white primary, and the Twenty-fourth Amendment (1964) abrogated the poll tax in federal elections. The Supreme Court's one-person, one-vote cases relieved the states of gross malapportionment that favored rural over urban interests, but the Court's decision in *Lassiter* left literacy tests in place. After 1930, America's redefinition as a truly inclusive democracy came largely through statute—state-level repeals or narrowing of franchise-restricting laws, the Civil Rights Acts of 1957, 1960, and 1964, and most important the Voting Rights Act of 1965, including its reenactment and expansion in 1970, 1975, 1982, and 2006.[24]

So it was that America's first constitutional shift toward greater democracy was the political as well as social triumph of Jeffersonian thinking in our episodic republic. As a legal matter, this period saw a state statutory convergence around the norm of universal (white) manhood suffrage (1789–1861). Our second great shift was Lincolnian or (Susan B.) Anthonian, reflecting the new industrial, entrepreneurial society that the United States was becoming. Its legal expression was largely Constitutional—adoption of the Fifteenth (1870),

Nineteenth (1920), and Twenty-fourth (1964) Amendments, as well as the Supreme Court's one-person, one-vote decision interpreting the Equal Protection Clause in *Reynolds v. Sims* (1964). Starting in 1965, the third era is (Dr. Martin Luther) Kingian, as disenfranchised social groups—Latino or Hispanic Americans and Asian Americans as well as African Americans—have demanded equal citizenship and full access to the franchise. This current era has witnessed much Constitutional litigation and two amendments, but the most dramatic changes have occurred under the aegis of the VRA—through administrative implementation by state governments and the Department of Justice, dynamic Supreme Court constructions (typically driven by the department's suggestions), and congressional amendments expanding this law in light of experience and practice. Like the Civil Rights Act of 1964, the VRA is a super-statute because it (1) was responsive to the new shape of America's pluralism and adopted new principles and new institutional frameworks to assure the franchise for newly significant social groups, (2) was drafted and enacted after a process of publicized institutional deliberation responsive to the voices and needs of We the People, and (3) was accepted by We the People and formally reaffirmed by Congress after a period of implementation and public discussion of the controversial new ideas advanced in the law or its implementation.

Consider some important changes introduced by the VRA that have become entrenched in America's democratic constitution. First, this statute responded to Louise Lassiter's critique of literacy tests as a prerequisite to voting registration. Section 4 of the 1965 Act suspended the use of literacy tests and other education or moral requirements in those states where the attorney general found that fewer than 50 percent of minority adults were registered or voted in the 1964 election; jurisdictions could reinstate their tests if they could show that they did not abridge minority rights. The 1970 VRA reauthorization extended the suspension nationwide, and the 1975 reauthorization made the preemption of literacy tests permanent. Second, section 10 of the act announced Congress's finding that poll taxes unConstitutionally taint state elections (unregulated by the Twenty-fourth Amendment) and directed the attorney general to seek a judicial invalidation, which came swiftly on the heels of the VRA declaration. Third, section 5 of the 1965 Act sought to head off evasion by barring covered (southern) jurisdictions from adopting any changes in their voting rules or districting without an explicit "preclearance" from the Department of Justice or a three-judge court in the D.C. Circuit; to preclear, the decision maker must find that the change would not diminish minority voting efficacy. These three new franchise policies, and increasingly vigorous implementation by the Department of Justice, contributed to higher registration rates for black adults in North Carolina, Lassiter's state, and in the South more generally, as illustrated

Table 2. Percentage of African American adults registered to vote, 1940–70

Year	North Carolina	South Carolina	Alabama	Eleven southern states
1940	7.1%	0.8%	0.4%	3.0%
1952	18.0%	20.0%	1.2%	20.0%
1964	46.8%	38.7%	23.0%	43.1%
1968	55.3%	50.8%	56.7%	62.0%
1970	54.8%	57.3%	64.0%	66.3%

Source: David Garrow, *Protest at Selma: Martin Luther King, Jr., and the Voting Rights Act of 1965* (New Haven: Yale University Press, 1978), 7, 11, 19, 189, 200.

by table 2. Note, however, that registration rates were climbing all over the South, especially North Carolina, before the 1965 Act. The VRA, alone, did *not* cause the revolution in southern voting. The revolution came as a complicated interaction of civil rights consciousness among blacks, a softening of resistance from whites uneasy about the moral and economic problems with apartheid, and resistance to the old practices from civil rights leaders, judges, and federal administrators. (In addition, huge victories for liberal Democrats in the 1958 and 1964 elections rendered the old southern Democrats, defenders of apartheid, a minority within their own party.) Thus, the superstatute fueled a revolution that had already started and removed the formal barriers that had suppressed the political voices of the Louise Lassiters for a century.[25]

The interaction between the VRA and the Constitution has been complex and interesting. Section 4, of course, had the effect of overriding the rule of *Lassiter v. Northampton County Board of Elections.* Did Congress have that authority? Ruling in an original jurisdiction lawsuit brought by South Carolina, the Supreme Court immediately sustained the new statutory rule. Without overruling *Lassiter,* the Court in *South Carolina v. Katzenbach* (1966) unanimously held that Congress was within its Fifteenth Amendment authority to find that a regional suspension of literacy tests and imposition of the preclearance requirement were needed to head off state evasion that Congress had documented in detail in legislative hearings and committee reports. In *Rome v. United States* (1980), the Court ruled that Congress also had the power to disallow voting changes (under section 5) that had a disparate impact on racial minorities, even though only rules adopted with discriminatory intent or motivation are violations of the Fifteenth Amendment that the Court would enforce. In the 1982 reauthorization of the VRA, Congress amended section 2 to follow a discriminatory impact approach as well. (Section 2 is national in scope and prohibits the use of any voting qualification or procedure to "deny or abridge the right to vote on account of race or color.") In each instance, the Supreme Court effectively announced that Congress has authority to "enforce" the Fifteenth Amendment even though the Court was not willing to go that far.[26]

There are three kinds of rules that now govern districting and voting requirements in the South, the only region covered by the section 5 preclearance requirement:

- *Constitutional* rules barring practices that are racially motivated, which the Supreme Court says can even include some race-based gerrymanders that seek to increase minority participation in legislatures;
- *Superstatutory* rules preempting state literacy tests, requiring affirmative assistance for language minorities, and barring districting and voting practices that have a "retrogressive" effect on minority voting rights; and
- *State statutory and constitutional rules* that are not currently inconsistent with the Constitutional and superstatutory rules, such as practices in most states of not allowing prisoners and persons on probation to vote, of discouraging third parties and write-ins, and so forth.

If Tocqueville returned to the United States in 2010, he would consider all of these in describing America's democratic constitution—as well as the informal norms and practices that have grown out of American social and political history. To take an important example, Toqueville would appreciate how our two-party system structures democratic politics and pervasively affects the operation of state statutory convergences and federal statutes such as the VRA. Thus, a key reason the VRA has dramatically increased African American representation in the House of Representatives is that both the Democratic and (especially) Republican Parties have found it in their self-interests to create majority-minority House districts.[27]

LIBERTY AS SECURITY AND ENGAGED CITIZENSHIP

In 1960, when the Supreme Court dismissed Louise Lassiter's claim, most of the justices tended to think about "rights" as individual assurances that the state would not actively interfere with private choices. Understanding that, Lassiter's attorneys phrased their Constitutional claims in terms of registrar Helen Walker's interference with Lassiter's ability to register. But the board had an easy answer: there was no evidence that the registrar had coerced or bullied Lassiter. Moreover, this narrow statement of her Constitutional claim did not reflect Lassiter's underlying grievance: in historical context, the North Carolina law empowered white registrars, disempowered black citizens, and reinforced social beliefs that citizens of color were not capable of fulfilling the responsibilities of the franchise.[28]

In this way, Louise Lassiter confronted the same kind of problem that Sherrie O'Steen faced in the previous chapter: they felt they were subject to demeaning as well as arbitrary treatment by officials wielding private or public power. The dearth of judicial remedies for this kind of arbitrariness inspired our criticism that the traditional model of Constitutionalism is impoverished. We now deepen that criticism by exploring classical theories of liberty, security, and responsibility that have been episodically important in our nation's history but have been suppressed in judge-dominated Constitutional law.

One interpretation of classical theories, championed by political philosopher Philip Pettit, understands liberty itself as *nondomination* rather than *noninterference*. Domination without interference is exemplified by the relationship of the benevolent master and the happy slave, or the good parent and the well-raised child; interference without domination is exemplified by the relationship between the citizen and the just law. We consider Professor Pettit's interpretation a useful but incomplete reading of classical authors. We read these authors to insist that liberty, equal treatment, and the rule of law are interconnected. The primary connecting principle is *security*: the state provides each citizen with security, namely, conditions for her flourishing; these include protection against arbitrary exercises of private as well as public power. This idea allows us to reinterpret Louise Lassiter's grievance. In the context of southern apartheid, North Carolina's literacy test not only *interfered* with Louise Lassiter's exercise of a fundamental right but also subjected her to *domination* by racist or paternalist registrars and unresponsive legislators, and sought to *discourage* blacks like her from even trying to vote and participate politically.[29]

Unlike Professor Pettit, we view liberty as security against unreasonable interference and arbitrary domination as essentially grounded in liberal (or perhaps liberal republican) theory, for this conception of liberty creates conditions in which citizens can pursue their private domestic and economic projects. But, like Pettit, we believe there is a distinctly civic republican conception of liberty that is different from either liberal conception. It is a more positive conception, the notion that liberty entails civic responsibility to participate in self-government. The joy of freedom is the civic happiness of participating with others in sharp dialogue about what is best for the community and how best to achieve it. It is even making short-term sacrifices to cooperate in common projects. As we shall see, Louise Lassiter's case was, implicitly, asserting all three kinds of liberties: liberal noninterference, the thinnest understanding of her claim; liberal republican nondomination; and republican civic engagement.

RENAISSANCE REPUBLICANISM: LIBERTY AS SECURITY
AND AS CIVIC ENGAGEMENT

One popular conception of "liberty" is that espoused consistently by the Cato Institute and episodically by the ACLU and the Republican Party: get government off our backs! This is what Pettit considers a "noninterference" or noncoercion understanding of liberty. Interestingly, this modern popular conception is not prominent in the works of classical philosophers. Aristotle's history of the Athenian constitution does praise the tyrant Pisistratus because he "burdened the people as little as possible with his government," but praises him more lavishly because "he was accustomed to observe the laws, without giving himself any exceptional privileges." In the *Republic*, Plato criticizes a society where "each lives along, day by day, gratifying the desire that occurs to him," without interference or reprimand from the state. Such a formless society inevitably degenerates, because citizens end up "paying no attention to the laws, written or unwritten, so that they may avoid having any master at all." True freedom and the flourishing of the polity are only possible when there are strict laws that everyone feels obliged to follow. Reflecting the axiom that Rome was an "empire of laws, and not of men," Roman authors were even more explicit. Livy, for example, celebrated the expulsion of the kings as a triumph of the neutral rule of law. Cicero summed up the Roman philosophy: "[A]ll of us—in short—obey the law in order to be free."[30]

These classical expressions suggest two further understandings of liberty that are analytically separate from noninterference. Both were ideas revived at the beginning of the Italian Renaissance, and found early expression in Leonardo Bruni's "Funeral Oration for Nanni degli Strozzi" (1428), a Ferranese general. Following the lead of Pericles' famous funeral oration, Bruni delivered an ode in praise of Florence, Strozzi's birth city. Bruni announced that Florence was the home for the new humanistic studies that were revolutionizing Western thought, but emphasized that intellectual flourishing depended upon the city's republican politics and the liberty engendered from that politics. "True liberty" is "not to have to fear violence or wrong-doing from anybody, and to enjoy equality among citizens before the law and in the participation in public office." The notion of "equal liberty" meant that any citizen was entitled to honors based upon his contribution to the common good, "for our commonwealth requires *virtus* and *probitas* in its citizens." Later authors, notably the sixteenth-century philosopher Niccolò Machiavelli, clarified these two features of liberty, one we call "liberty as security" and the other "liberty as civic engagement."[31]

A core theme in Machiavelli's *Discourses on Livy* (1531) is the notion of liberty as security within the rule of law. Discourse 16 explores the difficult task whereby a freed people retains its newfound liberty. Machiavelli announces the "common advantage" of the self-governing state to be "the possibility of enjoying what one has, freely and without incurring suspicion, for instance, the assurance that one's wife and children will be respected, the absence of fear for oneself." The discourse then digresses into a recommendation for a prince who wants to reassure the people of their freedom, namely, "to live in security." Their needs can be satisfied "by introducing such institutions and laws as shall . . . make for the security of the public as a whole. When the prince does this, and the people see that on no occasion does he break such laws, in a short time they will live in security and contentment." In Discourse 58, Machiavelli savages the adage that the "masses" are more fickle than oligarchs or princes. Whatever the identity of the governors, "it has been essential for them to be regulated by laws. For a prince who does what he likes is a lunatic, and a populace which does what it likes is unwise."[32]

An assumption of the *Discourses* is Bruni's idea that political liberty entails civic obligation. The free man not only limits his own choices to conform with the laws adopted through the regular process but also sacrifices his time, money, and even life to serve the commonwealth. In *The Art of War* (1521), Machiavelli argued that a state relying on mercenaries for its defense is in trouble, because only citizen militias will capably defend the commonwealth. In both works, Machiavelli is mesmerized by the image of the citizen who drops his plow in response to a call from the city to lead its defenses—and then returns to the plow once his mission is completed. This is the essence of *virtù* for Machiavelli, the robust, machismo-soaked eagerness to sacrifice for the common good.[33]

As historian J. P. G. Pocock has demonstrated, Machiavelli's work inspired the "republican" tradition in Anglo-American political theory. Written in the wake of the English Civil War, James Harrington's *Commonwealth of Oceana* (1656) maintained that the English constitution was founded upon the king's dependence on parliamentary checks. Harrington followed Machiavelli in distinguishing between "liberty or immunity *from* the laws" and "liberty or immunity *by* the laws." Both the Turk in despotic Constantinople and the Lucchese in republican Lucca, says Harrington, enjoy liberty *from* the laws whenever the laws of their respective states are silent. But only the Lucchese enjoys liberty *by* the laws, for only he lives in an "empire of laws, and not of men." Whereas the "greatest Bashaw" in Constantinople lives "at the will of his lord," even the "meanest Lucchese" is "not to be controlled but by the law." Harrington's widely influential distinction between liberty as noninterference and liberty as nondomination was foundational to the "Commonwealth tradition," whose adherents rejected the English Crown's claims to unchecked power.[34]

Montesquieu's *Spirit of the Laws* (1748) defines liberty as "that tranquility of spirit which comes from the opinion each one has of his security." Because the mere possibility of arbitrary interference would disturb such tranquility, the rule of law which reduces the chance of arbitrary disruption enhances rather than diminishes true liberty. In a just regime, liberty consists in "the right to do everything the laws permit." Echoing Harrington, Montesquieu declares that "a man against whom proceedings had been brought and who was to be hung the next day would be freer than the pasha in Turkey." Liberty as security is important for all kinds of governments, but according to Montesquieu liberty as civic engagement is only essential for republics, as they depend on popular devotion to the common good. "When virtue is banished, ambition invades the minds of those who are disposed to receive it," and "they were free while under the restraint of laws, but they would fain now be free to act against the law."[35]

American eighteenth-century intellectuals (such as Benjamin Franklin and Thomas Jefferson) and some lawyers (such as James Wilson and James Madison) were familiar with these thinkers, especially Montesquieu and the Commonwealth writers. A primary inspiration of the American Revolution was outrage against being subject to what they thought of as arbitrary domination, and many Americans saw it as their civic duty to oppose this kind of domination. Their attitude can be seen most clearly in the opposition to the Stamp Act, which imposed a small and quite bearable tax. What the colonists opposed was the idea that the King-in-Parliament could impose a tax of its own choosing, without even giving the colonists any voice in the proceedings. The Americans had been relatively free from British interference with their economic and social affairs until the end of the Seven Years' War, and enjoyed high standards of living for that era—but they felt deeply aggrieved when King George III imposed duties and taxes upon them without their consent, and hence arbitrarily. Their shibboleth, "taxation without representation," reflected that objection. In Harrington's metaphor, Americans felt they were treated more like Turkish subjects than Lucchese citizens, and they revolted.[36]

In this way, the American understanding of liberty as security and equal treatment under the rule of law sounds like Machiavelli's understanding, but there was at least one major change in focus. Unlike Machiavelli, Harrington, and Montesquieu, the Americans understood freedom from a more individualistic rather than classist point of view. The earlier thinkers tended to view freedom through the prism of classes. The Commonwealth thinkers, for example, defended the English constitution as one where the Crown could do nothing without the cooperation of the nobility (the House of Lords) and the people (House of Commons). This need for cooperation assured the freedom of these social classes. Reflecting the philosophy of Hobbes and Locke, our founding generation generally viewed all the branches as accountable to the entire citizenry and viewed liberty in both republican (Harringtonian) and liberal (Hobbesian) terms, as both security within the rule of law *and* noninterference by the state. After the founding era, moreover, the Hobbesian conception of liberty as noninterference has gained in popularity, at times overshadowing the older conception of liberty. But, as we shall now show, the republican conception of liberty as security has not only persevered, it has gained new traction in an interdependent world.[37]

THE EPISODIC REPUBLIC: LIBERTY AS SECURITY AND CIVIC ENGAGEMENT IN AMERICAN HISTORY

Although American constitutional history is often presented as relentlessly libertarian, that is far from the case, as illustrated by our discourse about liberty itself. In our episodic republic, the noninterference understanding of liberty ebbs and flows in tension and sometimes in harmony with liberty as security and liberty as civic engagement. We cannot present a comprehensive history here, but a few examples from our history may suffice. Thus, in the founding era, the Federalist case for the Constitution rested in large part upon the argument that a puissant national government best provided for national as well as social security. As Hamilton put it in the first of the *Federalist Papers*, "the vigor of government is essential to the security of liberty," and "their interests can never be separated." In *Federalist* No. 51, Madison put the matter classically: "It is of great importance in a republic not only to guard the society against the oppression of its rulers, but to guard one part of the society against the injustice of the other part." Responding to Anti-Federalist fears of domination of minorities by factions, Madison famously argued that even in a world of factions the republican aspiration of "the necessity of sacrificing private opinions and partial interests to the public good" could be preserved through representative governance over a larger territory and (more cogently) through a separation of powers structure whereby "[a]mbition must be made to counter ambition." Because any law would have to pass through both chambers of Congress and, usually, secure the approval of the president as well, it was unlikely that factional legislation would be enacted. If it were, the states would surely resist it. Hamilton added that an independent judiciary was a protection against "unjust and partial laws" through its powers of judicial review and narrow statutory interpretations.[38]

The republican understanding of liberty as security within the rule of law and as civic engagement continued to have bite in the nineteenth century, as illustrated by Francis Lieber's *Manual of Political Ethics* (1838–39). Lieber went so far as to assert that the "very condition of right is obligation; the only reasonableness of obligation consists in rights." Echoing Plato as well as the

Commonwealth tradition, he rejected the liberal conception: "Let us, then, call that freedom of action which is determined and limited by the acknowledgment of obligation, Liberty; freedom of action without limitation by obligation, Licentiousness. The greater the liberty, the more the duty." Interestingly, Lieber's understanding of liberty as entailing obligation was invoked by Chief Justice Taney in *Dred Scott v. Sandford* (1857). To support his ruling that a person of color could *never* be considered a citizen under the Constitution, Taney relied on the fact that Congress since the early days of the republic had excluded black persons, "in marked language," from military duties. Because the obligations of citizenship were reserved for whites only, so were the benefits, Taney reasoned.[39]

Chief Justice Taney's slavery-protective construction enraged the abolitionists, who maintained that it was their civic obligation to oppose an institution that denied both republican and liberal liberty to human beings. The abolitionist agenda was pervasively republican: decent citizens had an obligation to oppose an institution that flaunted the liberty rooted in the Declaration of Independence and the small "c" constitution of this country. As elected leaders moved slowly toward their position, it was vindicated by the Civil War experience. Overriding *Dred Scott*, the Thirteenth Amendment (1866) abolished the institution of slavery; the Fourteenth Amendment (1868) assured the freed slaves *and* everyone else fundamental privileges and immunities, equal protection of the law, and due process guarantees; the Fifteenth Amendment (1871) promised that voting would not be closed off on account of race. Republican liberty as security is the glue that holds together this cluster of Constitutional amendments: no one can assert mastery over another person; everyone will be treated the same under the neutral rule of law, with no "class legislation" oppressing a minority by treating its members arbitrarily; everyone will have an opportunity to participate in the creation or repeal of the laws neutrally enforced. The reconstruction amendments illustrate how the modern United States is an episodic republic, from time to time witnessing great public triumphs for a citizenry engaged in and making sacrifices for the common good, but triumphs followed by let-down and normal interest-group politics. After 1877, the civic republican moment of reconstruction was overwhelmed by a self-interested compromise between southern Democrats and northern Republicans and by a new liberal understanding of liberty as state noninterference with economic rights held by vested interests.[40]

Even as it was subordinated in the national political culture, liberty as security and as civic engagement continued to have a robust appeal among ordinary Americans. "Of all dangers to a nation," wrote the poet Walt Whitman in *Democratic Vistas* (1870), "there can be no greater one than having certain portions of the people set off from the rest by a line drawn—they not privileged as others, but degraded, humiliated, made of no account." Even people considered socially spoiled have a role to play in the body politic. As "Nature's stomach is fully strong enough not only to digest the morbific matter always presented, not to be turn'd aside, and perhaps, indeed, intuitively gravitating thither—but even to change such contributions into nutriment for highest use and life—so American democracy's." Whitman famously espoused republican sentiments for women as citizens as well as men. Spearheaded by Elizabeth Cady Stanton and Susan B. Anthony, the ongoing social movement seeking rights for women epitomized the republican understandings of liberty. Feminists argued that the state was in default of its obligation to provide female citizens the same security it provided male citizens. As Anthony told a congressional committee in 1881, men-only suffrage "makes all men sovereigns and all women subjects;" it makes "all men, politically, superiors and all women inferiors." The exclusion inflicts "not just political degradation, but . . . also social, moral, and industrial degradation" on women, an old republican trope.[41]

One of the arguments for female suffrage was that women had special insights about social legislation. An insight suffragists may have had in mind was the notion pioneered by Jane Addams (the founder of Hull House), that a democracy has an obligation to provide education and other opportunities for the poor to better themselves. Democracy cannot flourish in neighborhoods where residents want for the necessities of life. Just as women were revealing their aptitude for civic engagement through their energetic campaign for suffrage, so the immigrant and the ethnic laborer should be invited to similar activism. This progressive message, of course, was espoused by male progressives as well— labor leader and socialist politician Eugene V. Debs, economist Gardner Means, and corporate law professor Adolf Berle. They argued that large concentrations of corporate power were the primary threats to individual security and that the national government was the best hope for individual freedom, through protective legislation. During the era of normalcy, the 1920s, the popular audience for these messages was modest.[42]

The dominance of liberty as noninterference in our public culture came crashing down with the stock market in 1929. In his 1932 Commonwealth Club speech (described in the previous chapter), presidential candidate Franklin D. Roosevelt (FDR) reimagined business as a public trust and proposed "an economic constitutional order" that would assure ordinary Americans rights to work, to a decent standard of living for honest work, and to security in the event of disability and old age. This speech reflected a neorepublican philosophy but went beyond the classical republican understanding of liberty as security in three ways. First, the promise of security was to a broad constituency of individuals, including those considered politically marginal or irrelevant by the Renaissance writers—the working class, the elderly, the unemployed, and people of color. "Democracy in order to live must become a positive force in the lives of its people. It must make men and women whose devotion it seeks, feel that it really cares for the security of every individual." Second, FDR's philosophy entailed a much broader understanding of *security*. Security of life meant not just protection for one's person and one's family but also "the right to make a comfortable living" and the right to a financially secure retirement. Security of property meant not just protection against thieves and brigands but also "a right to be assured, to the fullest extent attainable, in the safety of his savings."[43]

Third, FDR's philosophy understood security in structural, future-oriented terms. Like founding father Thomas Jefferson, Roosevelt sought to protect the security of farmers, small businesspeople, and workers—but like Hamilton (Jefferson's rival), Roosevelt believed that security depended on regulatory institutions that would create productive incentives and structures. In the regulation of financial markets, labor-management relations, agricultural production, old-age and unemployment insurance, and other problem areas, FDR proposed long-term solutions. He called on Americans "to cooperate through the use of government." This came in the form of "carefully-drafted statutes" such as the securities laws (1933–34), the Social Security and National Labor Relations Acts (1935), and so forth. Running for reelection in 1936, President Roosevelt's platform emphasized the "inescapable obligations" the government has to protect people's families and homes, as well as establish a "democracy of opportunity" for all Americans. In one speech, Roosevelt analogized the American Revolution to the New Deal: the first had secured Americans freedom from British despotism, the second was securing Americans from the despotism of big business. Rather than noninterference from the government, liberty requires affirmative government action to protect people's rights to work and live productively. "Better the occasional faults of a Government that lives in a spirit of charity than the consistent omissions of a Government frozen in the ice of its own indifference," he said.[44]

In the Second Bill of Rights, discussed in the previous chapter, President Roosevelt laid out an ambitious statement of the liberal-republican notion of liberty as security: the state has an affirmative obligation to create conditions for individual flourishing, which is a precondition for the operation of a robust democracy that meets the needs of all relevant groups in our society. At the same time FDR announced the Second Bill, he had also called up the republican notion of liberty as civic engagement when he had mobilized the country for participation in World War II. Our episodic republic revives republican notions of citizenship obligations and self-sacrifice in times of war or crisis—but not just war and crisis. An even more direct example of that republican notion was already afoot. The civil rights movement stirred people of color, religious folk, and progressives to seek liberty for African Americans—freedom against police brutality and private lynchings; freedom to earn a living and raise families under decent circumstances; and freedom to participate in the civic life of the community without denigration. Philip Randolph's March on Washington Movement on the eve of the war impelled President Roosevelt to issue an executive order banning racial discrimination in federal employment, and similar pressure after the war resulted in President Truman's executive order desegregating the armed forces (almost a century after *Dred Scott's* invocation of military service as a reason to treat blacks as noncitizens).[45]

The NAACP's Legal Education and Defense Fund, Inc., carried out a litigation campaign to provide some protection for racial minorities against oppression by southern police, juries, and registrars. Having renounced its liberty of contract activism, the New Deal Court tentatively initiated a jurisprudence protecting civil rights, including a relentless campaign against "white primaries" and other voting rights decisions that encouraged people of color to register and vote in numbers unheard of since Reconstruction (see table 2). In this way, the civil rights movement was more deeply republican than the social activism network created by Jane Addams or the political movement spearheaded by Franklin Roosevelt, for this was a social movement not just seeking liberty as security so that people of color could pursue their private projects and happiness but also mobilizing growing numbers of Americans to demand dignified treatment of racial minorities. The civic republican ideal thrives in America through waves of social movements: in addition to the civil rights movement, important waves have included the women's rights movements (chapters 1 and 3), the old-age assistance movement (chapter 4), the Earth Day environmental movement (chapter 6), the lesbian, gay, bisexual, and transgendered persons as well as the traditional family values movements (chapter 8), and the gun rights movement (Conclusion). Fittingly, these twentieth-century social movements were populated by Americans who were exhibiting the same kind of republican *virtù* Machiavelli had praised, but shorn of its masculinist associations.[46]

DR. KING, CIVIL RIGHTS REPUBLICANISM, AND THE VOTING RIGHTS ACT

Because racial segregation and prejudiced attitudes were deeply entrenched in American society, the civil rights campaign made slow progress until the 1960s. *Lassiter* illustrates these limitations. Some justices in the *Lassiter* majority understood that literacy tests masked deeper injustices but felt that the record in the case was too weak to support a Constitutional ruling. Indeed, the South's massive resistance to *Brown* had yielded an openly racist politics that secured governorships for George Wallace in Alabama, Ross Barnett in Mississippi, and Orval Faubus in Arkansas. It is far from clear that the Eisenhower administration would have lent any support to the Court, and its order would probably have been a dead letter in the South. Nor would support have been forthcoming from the American Bar Association or the prestigious Harvard Law School, which were already assailing the Court as a bunch of lawless politicians masquerading as judges. The justices probably felt they had no plausible alternatives in *Lassiter*. But the civil rights movement was not so limited, as activists registered new voters without the Court's help, engaged in sit-ins at segregated lunch counters, and brought its petition to the nation's capital for federal civil rights legislation in the massive August 1963 March on Washington.[47]

In his "I Have a Dream" speech capping off the event, Dr. Martin Luther King Jr. eloquently deployed the old republican understanding of liberty as security and civic engagement to announce an ambitious small "c" constitutional agenda. He started with the Emancipation Proclamation (1863), which freed some of his ancestors from slavery, but lamented that "one hundred years later, the Negro is still not *free*. One hundred years later, the life of the Negro is still sadly crippled by the manacles of segregation and the chains of discrimination." Dr. King defined freedom in terms of nonarbitrary and equal treatment, not in terms of noninterference, even though apartheid could easily have been indicted on that ground as well. The consequences of not being free are alienation, for the black man "languish[es] in the corners of American society and finds himself an exile in his own land." The opposite of such an exile is the engaged citizen, the classic republican theme, and Dr. King's entire speech was a call to civic engagement for black and white Americans alike.[48]

The government *owes* people of color the same dignified treatment it accords white people. Invoking the Declaration of Independence, Dr. King focused on the "inalienable Rights" of "Life, Liberty and the Pursuit of Happiness"—positive rights denied African Americans. Delivery on those rights was urgent: "Now is the time to make real the promises of *democracy*." Denying one group of worthy Americans rights of civic engagement places the legitimacy of the state on the line. "This sweltering summer of the Negro's legitimate discontent will not pass until there is an invigorating autumn of freedom and equality." For "there will be neither rest nor tranquility in America until the Negro is granted his citizenship rights." Dr. King closed his petition with the words, "We cannot be satisfied as long as a Negro in Mississippi cannot vote and a Negro in New York believes he has nothing for which to vote. No, no, we are not satisfied, and we will not be satisfied 'until justice rolls down like waters, and righteousness like a mighty stream.'"[49]

The March on Washington inspired a generation of Americans and contributed to the enactment of the 1964 Civil Rights Act. But Dr. King and his allies, including President Johnson, understood that the antidiscrimination statute was only a first step and that the next step was a statute assuring people of color the right to vote. Literacy tests epitomized the African American's lack of freedom, understood from a republican perspective. Well before the 1964 Act, the U.S. Commission on Civil Rights had documented the depressive effect literacy tests had on minority voting. Such tests vested a terrible discretion, deployed by vicious bigots to deny as many people of color the franchise as possible, and deployed by nicer bigots to deny "uppity" blacks the vote while delivering it to more compliant blacks. And because literacy tests had the effect of discouraging as well as excluding black adults from registering and voting, those tests undermined the security of all African Americans. So long as people of color did not vote, openly racist officials were elected in the South—men like James G. Clark Jr., a county sheriff who ruled the roost in Selma, Alabama. And that was the place that Dr. King chose as the situs for his campaign to shame the nation into supporting voting rights legislation with regional bite.[50]

Selma was a brilliant choice, because it perfectly illustrated the insecurity of a people denied the right to vote. A bully expected to overreact to peaceful protests, Sheriff Clark lived down to his reputation and supplied a steady stream of stories and headlines for the newspapers across the nation in January and February 1965. Every story brought forth bipartisan demands that the Johnson administration deliver a strong voting rights bill. The Department of Justice originally wanted to press a Constitutional amendment, as it had done for the poll tax, but such a strategy was too slow to meet the needs of an engaged electorate. On March 7, at 4:15 P.M., fifty helmeted Alabama state troopers violently assaulted peaceful marchers at Pettus Bridge, outside Selma. As photographs of thuglike officers beating defenseless youths with their clubs saturated the country, "Bloody Sunday" forced the administration to deliver a statutory proposal immediately, and it drew bipartisan support. Congressional hearings detailed the need for remedial national legislation. Given the overwhelming record, the deep and wide support for strong legislation, and continuing pressure from civil rights protests, congressional leaders papered over disagreements as to details. In record time for such major legislation, the Voting Rights Act was signed into law on August 6, five months after Bloody Sunday.[51]

Before proceeding, we suggest a pause to reflect on the different kinds of constitutional entitlements (liberal, liberal republican, and republican) and the visions of liberty each entails (noninterference, security, participation). Table 3

Table 3. Various ways to understand "rights" and "liberty"

	Liberal: Liberty as noninterference	*Liberal republican: Liberty as security*	*Republican: Liberty as civic engagement*
Negative rights	Woman's right to choose an abortion, without state interference (*Roe v. Wade*); competing parental right to notification for a minor's abortion (state laws)	Employee's right not to be penalized on the job for his or her race, sex, or pregnancy (CRA 1964; PDA); antiharassment rules (EEOC)	State cannot deny voting rights on the basis of race (XV Amendment), sex (XIX Amendment), literacy (VRA 1964)
Affirmative duties	State obligation to pay for abortion and/or provide counseling for women seeking abortions (state laws)	Employer duty to accommodate family and medical needs of employees (FMLA 1993); employer duty to monitor coworker harassment (EEOC rule)	State has an obligation to produce an educated citizenry (DOJ on VRA); state must accommodate needs of non-English-speaking voters (VRA 1964 and 1975)

combines that triad with the negative-versus-affirmative-rights analysis in the previous chapter. The table is largely self-explanatory, but note how large a role state statutory convergences and federal superstatutes play in understanding one's rights even in arenas (privacy, antidiscrimination, and voting) that the Court has Constitutionalized. Although the Supreme Court as a formal matter plays a critical role in okaying ambitious congressional enactments, evaluating state rules, and interpreting federal statutes, as a functional matter the Court is marginal to the process by which constitutional values are advanced and structures are created. Social movements dominate the former, and legislators and agencies dominate the latter.

ENTRENCHMENT BY DELIBERATION

The republican understanding of liberty depends on the distinction between laws serving the public interest and those arbitrary measures serving private or factional agendas. But one person's "public interest" is often another person's "arbitrary" result. In *Lassiter*, the Board of Elections and North Carolina made the classic republican argument that literacy tests were public-spirited means to assure an informed electorate and to encourage citizens to pursue state-supported education. Lassiter responded that, in the context of school and other forms of segregation, the literacy requirement was a subterfuge to discourage citizens of color from engaging politically. It is often hard to tell the difference between the public interest and factional positions. Such a dilemma can be arbitrated through procedural mechanisms. The epitome of a fair procedure to allocate a piece of cake is for me to cut the cake in half and you to choose a piece. This logic inspired Montesquieu's admonition that the power to legislate (cut the cake) be separate from the power to execute and adjudicate (who gets precisely which piece). From Lassiter's perspective, apartheid maintained by significant franchise exclusions is a corrupt system where I cut the cake and devour both pieces.[52]

Postclassical republican theory also emphasized the late Roman and medieval notion that "what affects all must be decided by all." This feature of republicanism has an analogue in modern pluralist theory, which insists that all relevant interest groups be represented in the political process that divides the pie. Thus, both republican and liberal theories demand a model of *deliberation*. A substantial academic literature discusses the matter, often in high platitudes along the lines of the previous sentences. Continuing the discussion initiated in the Introduction, we offer an account of deliberation going both to its goals and to its method. The goals of deliberation include the usual republican purposes of securing the common good and advancing participatory values of citizen engagement, corresponding to the republican understandings of liberty. Viewed in a longer time horizon, the goal of deliberation is to confirm or create conditions for establishing the *legitimacy* of state action affirmatively pursuing the more immediate republican goals.[53]

For aggressive government action to be considered legitimate, the process of deliberation matters, as does the quality of thinking brought to the issue from social movements, experts, and statesmen. The remainder of this chapter outlines in greater detail key features of legitimating deliberation in the modern regulatory state. First, the deliberation must be responsive to the deep as well as urgent needs of We the People. The biggest problem with Large "C" Constitutionalism is the unresponsiveness of the Article V structure for deliberation that formally changes the Constitution. Small "c" constitutionalism, usually through superstatutes such as the VRA, is more immediately responsive—but is it capable of deep responsiveness? The second feature of modern deliberation helps us to say, "Often, yes": the initial response is not the end of the matter, for deliberation continues among different institutions. Executive officials and agencies staffed by proponents of the new norm typically take the lead, with important inputs from Congress through appropriations, oversight hearings, and discussions of follow-up legislation often demanded by judges. The third feature of modern deliberation, typically overlapping with the second, is feedback from outside the government. Popular opinion, evaluation by experts, and criticisms all play a role in the nation's ongoing deliberation. Small "c" constitutionalism is usually experimental. If the statutory response to a deep public need is administered by its core supporters in a way that meets the need at an acceptable cost, and without the disadvantages predicted by critics, then such a response stands an excellent chance of entrenchment in the nation's public culture.

MECHANISMS FOR GOVERNMENT RESPONSIVENESS TO DEEP AND URGENT CHALLENGES

According to classical republican theory, public debate ought to address the great controversies and class conflicts of the day. The framers of the Constitution were familiar with how "differences of opinion . . . often promote deliberation and circumspection," but they also contemplated deliberation as the mechanism by which the Constitution would be updated to address new national challenges. Their model was the process by which We the People jettisoned the Articles of Confederation and adopted the Constitution of 1789: recognition of a great public need requiring constitutional change; drafting a proposal to address the need in a national body; and ratification by a supermajority of the states. Article V replicates this process as a mechanism for changing the Constitution through amendment. Article V has the big advantage of producing recognizable Constitutional law, legitimated by a popular consensus dramatically achieved. It has the big disadvantage of setting the ratification goalpost much too high, as illustrated by the fate of the Equal Rights Amendment (chapter 1).[54]

Thus, Article V was the means by which We the People purged federal elections of the poll tax that had long been used to disenfranchise potential black voters in the South and immigrants or working-class voters elsewhere. The success and obvious legitimacy of the Twenty-fourth Amendment (1964), nullifying the poll tax in federal elections, inspired the Department of Justice to draft an even broader amendment in response to Dr. King's Selma campaign. Section 1 of the department's January 8, 1965, draft would have added this to the Constitution: "The right of citizens of the United States to vote shall not be denied or abridged by the United States or any State for any cause except (1) inability to meet residence requirements not exceeding sixty days or minimum age requirements, imposed by State law; (2) conviction of a felony for which no pardon or amnesty has been granted; (3) mental incompetency adjudicated by a court of record; or (4) confinement pursuant to the judgment or warrant of a court of record at the time of registration or election." This draft Twenty-fifth Amendment would have solved the gap of the Twenty-fourth, would have overridden *Lassiter* and swept away all literacy tests, and would have empowered Congress to clean up residual or new problems—and all of this needed reform would have been accomplished through the superlegitimate Article V process.[55]

But everyone realized that the odds of thirty-eight states ratifying such an amendment were slender, and even if ratified it would take years to address a problem that demanded *immediate* attention, especially after Bloody Sunday. (That drawback has spawned theories allowing Constitutional updating outside of Article V's mechanism for legitimacy, theories discussed in chapter 1.) Although Article V contains an excessively high threshold for ratification of Constitutional amendments, it has other features that guide us in thinking about fundamental normative change, namely, (1) strong political demand for a reform, initiated by an engaged popular movement, (2) translation of the demand into a proposal by one branch of government (Congress), and (3) institutional confirmation (by the states) after a period of popular as well as legislative debate. Small "c" constitutional change through superstatutes involves a similar framework, but without supermajority requirements and with deliberation and feedback over a longer time period, in response to administrative implementation. Thus, small "c" constitutional changes come about in this way: (1) strong political demand for a reform, initiated by an engaged popular movement, (2) translation of the demand into a proposal by the legislative or executive branch of government, which is implemented administratively, and then (3) institutional confirmation by subsequent legislation, after considering popular feedback and evaluating the success of the administrative implementation. This is a different process, admittedly, from Large "C" Constitutional change, which requires supermajorities and state involvement. Neither of those differences ought to deter us from considering superstatutes such as the VRA and the PDA to be fundamental constitutional developments, however.[56]

COMMONSENSE INSTITUTIONAL REASONING

When deciding what to do or how to act, we exercise what philosophers call practical reason. We deliberate about or weigh alternative considerations and decide, in light of the best reasons we can find, which is the best course of action. Collective deliberation is how we make such practical judgments as a group. Deliberation, or practical reasoning, concerns not only what to do but also, in a certain way, what to want. Philosopher Henry Richardson argues that ends and means interact in practical reasoning; part of deciding whether to pursue some goal must take account of available means and their costs. Ends and means need to fit together in a kind of reflective equilibrium, to borrow John Rawls's language. So a deliberative theory aims to explain not only policy choice but also the evolution of public values and commitments. It is this aspect of deliberation that we are principally concerned with here—the process by which our values, our ends, evolve deliberatively over time. Sometimes, this process involves a kind of interpretation: that when deciding what to do, we are considering which choice best "fits" with our historical identity and values and the range of values we currently hold. For our purposes, it is not necessary to go into the technicalities involved in these debates. We only insist that the evolution or development of fundamental values is a vital part of our constitutional culture and that this evolution is partly guided by democratic expectations.[57]

Democratic deliberation in this country occurs within a complex institutional context, and this is invariably so at the national level. Although We the People are the ostensible authors and ratifiers of the Constitution, we acted through representative bodies and not a popular plebiscite, such as those followed to amend most state constitutions. So our nation's public values evolve through a process that occurs within institutions, with popular initiation and feedback. Inspired by *Brown v. Board of Education* (1954), important liberal thinkers such as John Rawls and Owen Fiss consider the Supreme Court the exemplary deliberative institution, suggesting that it is in the setting of Supreme Court cases that our public commitments are shaped and reshaped. We believe their focus is too narrow. In *Rhetoric*, Aristotle distinguished forensic speech (backward-looking speech proper to adjudication) from the (forward-looking) deliberative speech of a legislator. Aristotle's distinction between forensic and deliberative speech does not map onto our institutions perfectly well but still has bite: deliberative speech is aimed at lawmaking, not law application. It is still legislative speech whether or not it takes place inside the chamber of a legislature, inside a court (acting not as a place for correcting errors but as a source of norms), or outdoors, among the people themselves. The relevant considerations are principally forward looking, anticipating consequences of various policies in the future. It remains important to recognize that most deliberation takes place in the context of policy formulation, whether in legislative or administrative settings. Courts play a role too of course, especially concerning the content of the Constitution, but that role neither monopolizes nor dominates actual deliberative processes, particularly with respect to the small "c" constitution.[58]

Picking up themes sounded by political philosopher John Dewey's *The Public and Its Problems* (1927) and the language of Governor Roosevelt's speech accepting the Democratic nomination for president (1932), we suggest that deliberation about fundamental structures and values reflects a kind of "commonsense" reasoning whose legitimacy is established when it is both institutionally based and democratically responsive. It is a kind of ideal or aspiration according to which each person is supposed to have an equal voice in deciding what to do. We may try to persuade him to prefer one policy over another, but at the end of the day, there will be a vote to decide what to do, and each vote will count equally no matter how unreasonable the beliefs of the voter. No one is required to defer to others on the basis of wealth, status, fear, or any other extrinsic factor, and everyone is free to stand up to any of the others in stating her views and casting her ballot. Obviously, there are many ways in which this commonsense ideal can be, and has been, corrupted in our history, but to expose a *corruption* in our public culture is to recognize the preexistence of the norm that is corrupted, to announce an embarrassment or hypocrisy, and to suggest a need for reform. We may lack the strength or focus to bring about effective reform, but that does not alter our appraisal of the corruption. Thus, even though commonsense democracy may be honored in the breach at times, what is important for us is that it *is* honored. It stands not so much for our actual practices as for our normative expectations.[59]

Now consider a modern polity that has relatively well-functioning political institutions, thus, a relatively fair and open electoral process for selecting a legislature/government, a more or less free flow of information, and a system of effective public agencies and courts. In commonsense democratic theory, the people or electorate stand as political principals in relation to the other institutions and their occupants. This is true for formal reasons: the U.S. Constitution announces that We the People are sovereign. This formal reason is strongly reinforced by a battery of functional reasons: popular acceptance and not just passive acquiescence is needed to preserve the legitimacy and effectiveness of our government *and* to encourage citizen engagement. A government that is unresponsive to mobilized citizen viewpoints is democratically illegitimate and, more important, risks alienating and the citizenry and making them passive or even rebellious. Our choices and decisions are to be treated, for this reason, as needing no justification, at least if those decisions are made within a certain institutional context (an election or perhaps a referendum) and have not been obviously corrupted so that they are "our" decisions. Indeed, seeking or demanding reasons from voters might be discouraged as a sign of respect for the sovereign nature of the voters' decisions. No small "c" constitutional change can occur unless We the People accept it; if there is popular resistance to a change propounded by the institutions of government, not only does that change fail to be of constitutional significance, it stands as a threat to the rule of law and, in extreme cases, to government itself.

One step removed from the citizenry are members of Congress, who are both chosen by democratic elections and accountable to the people, because they can be turned out in a future election. These representatives for the actual voters can also act for political or other reasons more or less as they choose. They are expected to give reasons of a certain kind in the form of political justifications or party platforms. Directed toward the electorate, legislators' reasons tend to be forward looking and purposive: here is a problem We the People have recognized, and our statute is the best way to deal with this problem as a matter of the public interest, while fitting into a larger understanding of our country's characteristic features and its ideals. In the commonsense theory we are articulating, manifestos or campaign promises are important politically. If the legislative program fails to solve the problem or creates new ones, the legislator can expect electoral retribution. Thus, the standard account of the VRA gives due credit to norm entrepreneurs such as Dr. King and his congressional allies from both parties, but emphasizes that this sweeping legislation was only possible because legislators everywhere outside the South felt it was not only justified on policy grounds but also acceptable to their constituents. This phenomenon made it much easier for risk-averse legislators to support the VRA's strong regulatory response.[60]

Take another step away from the electorate and we get to agencies that often translate popular movements and public problems into legislative proposals and then administer the enacted statutes by filling in substantive details through rule making, policy guidances, opinion letters, pamphlets, manuals, and speeches. Although they are appointed by and typically are removable by the elected chief executive, agency officials are themselves not elected, and their decisions tend to be well below the radar of the media and most voters. Because there are many statutory gaps to fill, these below-the-radar decisions are important ones, often of constitutional significance. For example, the Department of Justice in the 1960s devoted few resources to monitoring southern compliance with section 5 of the VRA, and as a result southern jurisdictions simply failed to report electoral changes for preclearance. After the bipartisan 1970 reauthorization, Department of Justice practice grew more aggressive, and preclearance became an effective mechanism to prevent southern backsliding in the next generation, under both liberal and conservative administrations. Most statutes are not subject to the VRA's sunsetting, and agencies implementing those laws often proceed through notice-and-public-comment rule making when they engage in substantive elaboration of statutory imperatives.[61]

Yet another step removed from We the People are federal judges. Courts are the branch most insulated from politics and thereby are usually the least accountable. The nature of classic adjudication and the political insulation of judges require them to give reasons; indeed, reasoned justification in light of public-regarding purposes and the legal landscape is the great comparative advantage that judges bring to our nation's constitution. Judge-given reasons tend to be more backward looking and less openly consequentialist than reasons given by legislators and agencies—but part of the backward-looking legal landscape that judges weigh heavily is the authoritative statements of legislators in committee reports and agencies in rules, guidances, and the like. Accordingly, the Supreme Court's interpretation of the VRA not only paid close attention to and rarely departed from political consensuses reflected in committee reports but also followed executive department interpretations in about two-thirds of the cases. Appropriate in light of commonsense democratic theory, the Court has been more faithful to the congressional preferences than the administrative ones and has often overridden agency interpretations. In turn, Congress was not bashful in announcing its agreement or disagreement with Supreme Court interpretations when it reauthorized the VRA in 1970, 1975, 1982, and 2006.[62]

Commonsense democratic theory lays out the normal structure for institution-based practical reasoning in our democracy. It doesn't say where it is that decisions are reached, but it does say if they are made in one kind of setting, certain kinds of justifications are expected. This set of expectations is supposed to embody, in principle, basic democratic norms of equal concern and respect for all citizens and of majority-based decision making at the end. The core expectation is that even remote decision-making centers ought to be open to influence from ordinary people and willing to change their views as a result of that input. Commonsense theory also helps us understand why the legal process was, basically, at an impasse over the literacy test issue in 1960. Southern white voters and legislatures were committed to such tests for ideological or emotional reasons; they not only wanted to preserve their monopoly on authority, they devoutly believed that their continued dominance served the public interest. Congress had the authority to trump state law on this issue but was stalemated because southern representatives intensely favored the status quo, while most nonsoutherners did not consider voting rights an urgent issue; both sets of legislators well reflected the views of their constituents. Not wanting to raise the stakes of this issue, local administrators such as Helen Taylor behaved reasonably when the spotlight was on them, and open race-based discrimination was the rare exception by 1960. Many administrators discriminated unconsciously, based upon paternalistic attitudes or stereotype-based thinking. Theoretically, the Supreme Court could have reversed the burden of inertia for the literacy test issue, perhaps by vacating and remanding *Lassiter* for state judges to determine whether there was a compelling public interest in literacy tests that outweighed Louise Lassiter's fundamental right to vote. But even the liberal Warren Court hesitated, for standard judicial reasons: the Constitutional text did not create a general fundamental right to vote, and the Court had repeatedly upheld literacy tests with much greater race-based effects than North Carolina's. In light of the Court's institutional weakness and the certainty of a big backlash (on top of the ongoing backlash against *Brown*), even the most liberal justices went along.

Commonsense democratic theory also tells us that the foregoing impasse might be broken by a combination of pressure from *both* the bottom up (the people pressing their representatives) *and* the top down (representatives taking initiatives and awaiting popular response). The response to *Lassiter* and continued exclusion of blacks from the franchise in the South predictably combined grass-roots civic republican engagement with institutional interaction that responded to the urgent problem. Inspired by his successes in 1963–64, Dr. King and his allies entered the Selma campaign with a thoroughly national focus. The state troopers and media played their roles more perfectly than anyone could have imagined, and Bloody Sunday on Pettus Bridge moved minority voting rights to the top of the national agenda. By the time voting rights arrived at that desirable political location, its success was assured, because all the relevant institutions had themselves been deliberating about the issue, softening up political preferences throughout the national government. After almost a decade of study, the U.S. Commission on Civil Rights had already endorsed federal preemption of state literacy tests and other measures as the only way to break antidemocratic logjams in the South. Since 1960, the Department of Justice had been seriously litigating voting rights cases in the South, and federal judges like Frank Johnson had been issuing opinions not only finding outright discrimination but also fashioning aggressive structural remedies for such violations. Bursting with pride over the 1964 act, Congress felt vindicated by the election of 1964, which gave President Johnson a Rooseveltian landslide and returned a Congress thoroughly dominated by liberal Democrats and pro–civil rights Republicans.[63]

Based upon its remarkable experiences in voting rights cases, the Department of Justice came up with proposed legislation that was both practical (merely suspending literacy tests on an experimental basis) and bold (the preclearance requirement). Both features of the administration's bill found deep support and factual justification from the Civil Rights Commission, Constitutional law experts, departmental line attorneys as well as officials, and other knowledgeable experts. Even farm state conservatives like Senator Everett Dirksen (Illinois) and Representative William McCulloch (Ohio) were personally committed to strong legislation and thus inclined only to quibble over details. Particularly notable was that even southern opponents agreed that no one ought to be denied the right to vote because of her race. During the VRA's extensive and expertly managed hearings, southern opposition was grounded in largely accurate claims that people of color were already voting in increasing numbers in their region.[64]

The VRA nicely reflects the aspirations of commonsense constitutionalism. The statute reflected a practical reasoning process by which the simple end (nondiscrimination in voting) became universally accepted but was immediately complicated by the fact that it was not possible, as a practical matter, to effectuate such a goal without intruding on the independence of southern states. With important input from the Department of Justice, the Civil Rights Commission, and civil rights groups and with full opportunity for southern representatives to explain the damning studies, Congress moved ahead and enacted the Voting Rights Act of 1965 by large bipartisan margins. The election of 1966 provided an opportunity to hear directly from voters, who substantially ratified this move. Although the election was viewed as a setback for President Johnson and the Democrats, it was a strong reaffirmation of voting rights. Not one of the winning statewide Republican candidates ran against the VRA, and virtually all supported voting rights for minorities. In the South, the big losers were diehard segregationists.[65]

IMPLEMENTATION, FEEDBACK, AND ENTRENCHMENT

The large congressional majorities and popular support for the initial Voting Rights Act did not ensure that it would effectuate a small "c" constitutional change. Commonsense democracy has to keep on working for a statute with the greatest popular and partisan support in order for it to become what we call a superstatute. Specifically, the statutory principle and operational framework have to "stick" in our polity. To accomplish *that*, the statute has to be implemented in a way that builds upon and reinforces the social change that has already occurred, successfully advances the great principle it represents, and does these feats without the crippling costs and disadvantages identified by critics and opponents. If the statute accomplishes the former, it creates a loyal constituency among beneficiaries, media pundits, and experts. If it also does the latter, it wins over skeptics, sweeps moderates and the next generation of voters to its agenda, and very likely will induce a subsequent Congress to eagerly and publicly reaffirm and even expand its core principle. If all of this comes together, the statutory norm and framework have become *entrenched* in America's constitution, and we'd say the law has become a superstatute.

The events leading up to the 1965 act itself took the country a long way toward entrenching the norm that people of color ought to be encouraged to register and vote, and certainly not excluded, even through indirect mechanisms. The application of that meta-norm to literacy tests was not so entrenched, however. Section 4 of the VRA itself just suspended southern literacy tests for five years, and also provided a process by which jurisdictions could argue they were entitled to reinstatement, because they had not manipulated their tests or applied them in a discriminatory manner—precisely the argument the Supreme Court accepted as a sufficient defense in *Lassiter*. Under the common-sense theory we have expounded, it is important that the force and meaning of section 4 were contingent upon the administration of its requirements and its opt-out process by the Department of Justice. Although the department was initially lethargic in enforcing the new statute, it insisted that the law be interpreted to carry out its great purposes. In response to a claim by Gaston County, North Carolina, to be relieved of the section 4 literacy test ban, Department of Justice lawyers reasoned that Congress wanted to break down barriers that *actually*, not just *intentionally*, prevented African Americans from registering and voting, and that broader purpose justified an interpretation of section 4 that looked to results (Does the test keep a lot of black adults from voting?) and not just intent (Did the legislature intend to disenfranchise blacks?). Moreover, the state itself bore responsibility for the disproportionate effect of literacy tests on blacks, because pre-*Brown* segregated education shortchanged black children. This was a dynamic interpretation of the VRA, which altered the statutory goal, but in a republican manner. The department was pushing the statute beyond a tougher nondiscrimination goal toward a goal of proportional registration, where about the same percentage of adult blacks and whites would be registered. In 1968, when a three-judge federal court rejected Gaston County's petition to reinstate its literacy test, North Carolina's registration figures included 78 percent of all white adults, but only 55 percent of black adults—a significant increase from 1964 but nowhere close to parity. With only one dissenting justice, the Supreme Court in *Gaston County v. United States* (1969) affirmed the lower court and accepted the Department of Justice's dynamic construction of the law.[66]

From the perspective of commonsense theory, *Gaston County*, involving statutory law, strikes us as a resolution that better advanced the project of democratic constitutionalism than *Lassiter*, involving Constitutional law. *Gaston County* not only contributed to an expansion of the franchise but also represented a superior process of norm elaboration. The department's interpretation, adopted by the courts, reflected a better-informed understanding of North Carolina society and politics, and for that reason alone it was less likely to be an arbitrary decision. Another legitimating feature of the aggressive administrative application of the VRA was the congressional review necessitated by the sunsetting feature of the 1965 act. During 1969 congressional hearings, the Civil Rights Commission and the attorney general reported the significant progress people of color had made in registering to vote in the South but urged renewal of the VRA to make the registration numbers closer to parity. Ongoing school segregation meant that people of color remained more vulnerable to literacy tests than white people, the *Gaston County* point being accepted by conservatives as well as liberals in Congress. Even southern representatives retreated on section 4; the Mississippi attorney general conceded: "Illiterate voters we can abide if forced to." Indeed, Nixon administration attorney general John Mitchell (a northern conservative) not only endorsed *Gaston County* but also recommended that the renewed VRA include a nationwide ban against literacy tests. Mitchell placed on the table an expansion of the original VRA norm: not only were literacy requirements discriminatory against blacks in the South, they burdened Latinos in the North and West, as well as the poor everywhere in the country. Indeed, in an age where most Americans learned the news from radio and television, was literacy really *essential* for the intelligent exercise of franchise? Moreover, representatives from both parties recognized that illiterate citizens paid taxes and served their country in many ways, and thus it was unfair to exclude them from voting. Congress not only renewed the VRA in 1970, it added a nationwide suspension of all literacy tests until the act expired again in 1975. When Congress returned to the VRA in 1975, it permanently preempted literacy tests all over the country. By then, there was a virtually unanimous consensus not only that literacy tests had been an unfair impediment to minority voting in the past but also that their abrogation had no malign effects on the quality of our democratic deliberations and practices. Southerners had cried wolf, and the country observed a lamb.[67]

The VRA's settlement of the literacy test issue reveals genuine advantages of provisional statutory resolution of constitutional issues. A Constitutional amendment to ban literacy tests (like the one abrogating poll taxes in federal elections) would not only have been politically difficult to carry off in 1965, it would have been a bad idea. Literacy tests had a plausible republican justification: one of the duties of citizenship is to be educated and literate, and an informed citizenry ought to be more deliberative and perhaps make better political choices. The Department of Justice believed this ideal had no connection to the way such tests were administered, whereby perfectly witless whites were routinely registered, while the most literate blacks were often turned away or discouraged from trying to register. The department was probably right about that, but from a legitimacy perspective it was important for its lawyers not only to persuade legislators from both parties but also to hear from articulate spokespersons from the jurisdictions that would be affected by a suspension (1965 and 1970) or preemption (1975) of such tests. It was a useful strategy for the country to adopt a provisional ban on literacy tests, in the South where they were most abused, and then see how that worked. Once southern tests were suspended, not only did a majority of black adults finally register to vote and participate more actively in politics, southern politics improved in overall quality, a huge republican boon (and, coincidentally, a boon to the Republican Party as well). A process by which preemption came step by step rather than in a big national referendum under the auspices of Article V was, in this sense, a legitimate as well as common-sense approach. The key was that the VRA *created conditions for falsification* of oppositional claims, an experimental process that is easier to accomplish by agency implementation of a statute than by judicial implementation of the Constitution. Once they were forced to live without literacy tests, southern whites as well as blacks came to accept the norm that no one should be denied the right to vote on account of race, or even literacy. Once blacks could vote, some congressional segregationists started paying close attention to their minority constituents, while others retired and were succeeded by moderates such as South Carolina senator Ernest Hollings (1966–2005), Alabama senator Howell Heflin (1979–97), and Mississippi senator Thad Cochran (1978–present). Embracing constituents of all races, Senators Hollings, Heflin, and Cochran represented an improved southern politics.[68]

When the VRA was reauthorized in 2006, the entire political spectrum accepted the demise of literacy tests as a good thing, and a majority also reaffirmed an important extension of that norm. Section 4(e) of the 1965 VRA had required states to assist non-English-speaking voters who had received a sixth grade education or better in Puerto Rican schools. Expanding upon that idea, section 203 of the 1975 VRA reauthorization barred voting discrimination on the basis of language and required jurisdictions to accommodate language minorities by making ballots and other voting materials available in different languages. Section 203 requires affirmative accommodation and not just non-discrimination. Those cost concerns have been overwhelmed by bigger anxieties about cultural and linguistic diversity raised by large-scale immigration from Latin America, and this was one of the issues that divided Congress during the 2006 VRA reenactment. An amendment to drop section 203 lost by 238–185, a decisive albeit not overwhelming margin.[69]

The norm that literacy is *not* a prerequisite for exercising the franchise is *entrenched* in America's democratic constitution at this point. By "entrenched" we mean that it is beyond partisan debate. Had anyone questioned that conventional wisdom during the 2006 VRA reauthorization debates, for classical republican reasoning based upon the idea of an informed and invested electorate, she would have been met with stunned silence or even laughter. Opponents of section 203 went out of their way to stress that they were *not* calling this norm into question; they merely objected to "special treatment" for language minorities and said they accepted the nondiscrimination idea. As the foregoing account suggests, entrenchment of the norm has occurred without an overruling of *Lassiter*, which remains a citable Constitutional authority. Indeed, entrenchment of the norm through a superstatute rather than through a Constitutional amendment allows us to contemplate the different paths toward entrenchment in our polity. These are mapped out in table 4.

Consider some interesting points relating to table 4. First, all three entrenchment mechanisms have precedent in Large "C" Constitutionalism, viewed from a comparative perspective. In fact, the VRA model is more popular than the Article V model and competes with or complements the *Brown* model when written constitutions are drafted. Donald Lutz's study of constitutions found no constitution in the world that is as hard to amend as ours, while a number of countries follow something like the VRA model; such democracies allow amendments through extended legislative deliberation across more than one session of Parliament. This is also true for American state constitutions. There is no state constitution that is as hard to amend as is the U.S. Constitution. Most states amend their constitutions by legislative proposals ratified by popular majorities. Interestingly, several states allow constitutional amendment only after majority (or in four states supermajority) votes in two successive sessions of the legislature, followed by popular votes.[70]

Second, there are different paths toward entrenchment of norms and institutions into the small "c" constitution. The hardest path is the Article V model, but when successfully deployed it has an excellent record of entrenchment. The *Brown* model has the greatest romantic appeal (for lawyers especially), but we think it does the least entrenchment work of all three models, for it depends on the Court's remaining steadfast in its purpose and usually depends on supporting legislation to achieve its goals. The VRA model has the most impressive record of actually achieving entrenched public values and is virtually the only mechanism for creating new institutions that serve affirmative purposes.

Third, the three models can interact in ways that assure a superentrenchment. Adopted in March 1964, the Twenty-fourth Amendment abrogated poll taxes for federal elections. In April 1965, the House Judiciary Committee added a provision to the proposed VRA banning poll taxes in all elections, state as well as federal. The Department of Justice opposed this move on Constitutional grounds, and conservative Republicans also expressed reluctance. As a compromise, Congress in section 10 of the VRA "found" that poll taxes were Constitutional violations because the right to vote is fundamental and directed the department to seek judicial invalidation of poll taxes in state elections (i.e., those not covered by the Twenty-fourth Amendment). Closely following the department's argument but ignoring section 10, the Supreme Court in *Harper v. Virginia Board of Elections* (1966) ruled that the right to vote is "fundamental"

Table 4. Different models of entrenchment for new fundamental norms

	Article V model	Brown model	Voting Rights Act model
Initiation of new fundamental norm	Social movement political activism or a pressing national need	Social movement litigation (often class action) seeking to overturn an unjust status quo	Social movement political activism or a pressing national need
Institutional deliberation	Congressional deliberation: evidence gathering and consensus sought by committees; debate and voting in both chambers; two-thirds supermajority	Judicial deliberation: evidence gathering in trial court hearing; debate and voting among justices; simple 5–4 majority	Congressional/executive deliberation: evidence gathering and consensus sought by committees; debate and voting in both chambers; legislative majority + president
Popular and other feedback	Proposed amendment goes to the state legislatures for debate; big media attention	Precedent implemented by lower courts; media and academic attention to ongoing litigation	Election following statutory enactment; critical scrutiny of statute's administration, including congressional oversight hearings
Ratification of fundamental norm	Three-quarters of the states ratify	Supreme Court treats the resolution as a superprecedent	After new deliberation, subsequent Congress reaffirms and expands new norm/institution
Virtue of the model	Usually successful in entrenchment: new norm sticks in public culture, because must attract cross-regional support and broad coalition to meet the state ratification requirement	Institution outside of politics is able to reverse the burden of inertia impeding legislative or Article V Constitutional change	Incremental approach to entrenchment, taking advantage of administrative expertise and fresh legislative deliberation; only model likely to create new institutions and provide significant state resources
Limitation of the model	Much too difficult to accomplish, especially the state ratification requirement (DOJ draft XXV Amendment)	Popular frustration with norm creation by nonelected judges (Southern Manifesto); reliant on legislation implementing the new norm (Brown II)	Much of the norm elaboration comes from agency implementation, below the popular radar

and therefore any abridgment of it was Constitutionally suspect; because Virginia had only weak arguments in favor of its poll tax for state elections, it was invalid. Astonishingly, within two years, a Constitutional amendment, a superstatute, and a landmark Supreme Court ruling worked together to eliminate a longstanding state practice—albeit one that had already been abandoned everywhere except in a few southern states by 1964. This may be an example of constitutional overkill.[71]

The VRA is a classic example of a superstatute. Like the PDA, analyzed in chapter 1, the VRA propounded a bold new principle of law that was enthusiastically received in Congress, was aggressively implemented by the Department of Justice and the Supreme Court, has been accepted by Americans of all political persuasions, and has been repeatedly reaffirmed by Congress. The process of VRA (or PDA) entrenchment reflects its administrative workability, its strong support from the group benefiting from the principle, and the falling away of opposition as costs proved unimpressive and a new generation was persuaded the VRA was a good idea. We the People, including most southern Americans, have embraced the VRA's core principle, and any effort to upend it would be met with popular unease or outrage. Unlike the PDA, the VRA has also created a new institutional structure: section 5's preclearance requirement, which establishes the Department of Justice and the Supreme Court as monitors of southern voting changes. (Admittedly, this structure is not as entrenched as the VRA's core principle.)

Over time, the VRA has had the liberty-protecting effects that Dr. King prophesied: in the past forty-five years, people of all colors have been more engaged in the political process, open racists have rarely been elected to office (Selma's villain, Sheriff Clark, was turned out in the next election), conservatives have been more responsive to their black constituents, and people of color have been elected to local, state, and federal offices in numbers unheard of since Reconstruction. Indeed, the superstatute has been so successful that its 2006 reauthorization has been challenged on the ground that there is no longer need for section 5's preclearance requirement, which grates on federalist values. In *Northwest Austin Municipal Utility District No. 1 v. Holder* (2009), the challengers relied on the facts that minority voter turnout in the South is often higher than it is in other parts of the country, and that there is no voting mechanism anywhere in the country nearly as discriminatory as the old literacy tests that were core targets of the 1965, 1970, and 1975 statutes.[72]

What is the Court's obligation if a majority of justices believe that the VRA has become inconsistent with Supreme Court precedents requiring that statutes regulating the states be grounded in state Constitutional violations? In our view, the Court's first obligation is to read its precedents in light of the VRA's deliberations, reasoning, and experience and to give Congress a wide berth. In the 2006 VRA reauthorization, Congress found that "40 years has not been a sufficient amount of time to eliminate the vestiges of discrimination following nearly 100 years of disregard for the" Fifteenth Amendment, as evidenced by "second generation barriers constructed to prevent minority voters from fully participating in the electoral process." These were not casual findings. Congress held twenty-one separate hearings, heard from eighty-six witnesses, and gathered more than fifteen thousand pages of evidence to figure out whether discrimination against minority voters continues in jurisdictions covered by section 5. Congress concluded that discrimination continues and, more important, that latent discrimination would return if the section 5 prophylactic were removed. It would be an act of judicial daring for the Court to override these findings.[73]

If most of the justices believe there remains a Constitutional problem with the VRA or its application, their next duty is to figure out if there is a narrowing interpretation of the superstatute. In earlier cases, the Supreme Court rejected Department of Justice applications of the statute that pushed jurisdictions toward districts created only to assure racial balancing, in tension with the Fifth Amendment's implied equal protection guarantee. In June 2009, a near-unanimous Court handed down a narrowing construction of the VRA in *Northwest Austin*, thereby avoiding a Constitutional ruling that would have divided the Court down the middle. What about the next case challenging the validity of section 5? If there is no narrowing interpretation the justices can swallow, then . . . we come to a corollary of our presentation of America's statutory constitution: it can still be trumped by the Large "C" one. More precisely, if the justices believe that a politically entrenched practice such as section 5 is inconsistent with important and foundational Constitutional principle such as federalism, they have the power to reverse the burden of political inertia and force the political process to reconsider the practice.[74]

3

The Constitution of the Market and State Legitimacy

Martin Manion and Mathilda Fitzpatrick were officers in the firm Manion & Company, a pipe-laying firm located in New Orleans, Louisiana. In February 1895, Manion, the managing director, submitted a bid for a contract to lay pipes and extend the mains of the New Orleans Water Works Company. At first, he did not think he could bid on the project, because all the leading southern foundries were demanding the same high prices (about $21.75 per ton) for pipe. At the last minute, he discovered he could get pipe for $14–15 per ton from Radford Pipe and Foundry in Virginia and successfully bid on the New Orleans contract under that assumption. Nothing went right after that, though. The Radford company repeatedly changed the terms of the bargain, apparently at the behest of a cartel of pipe companies seeking to keep prices high. Delivery of the pipe was mysteriously delayed, and when delivered the price was much higher than that originally bargained. Manion & Company sustained heavy losses on the project. Ultimately, the firm went bankrupt.[1]

Like most of the other aggrieved citizens we examine in this book, Manion and Fitzpatrick had no conventional claim under the judge-enforced Constitution, because their harm was at the hands of a private cartel that refused to deal with their company except at elevated prices and that pressured other pipe companies not to deal either. Some other source of law would have to protect Manion & Company against this unfair conduct. The common law of contracts, for example, might have provided a claim for relief against the cartel, perhaps for "restraint of trade" or (more likely) "unlawful interference with contractual relationships." In 1895 a number of states had "antitrust" laws protecting against local cartels. It does not appear that Louisiana offered Manion and Fitzpatrick these specific protections, however. A larger problem with state antitrust statutes or common law remedies was that they might be unConstitutional as applied to the interstate pipe cartel that discriminated against Manion & Company. For example, the cartel members could in 1895 have argued that state regulation of an interstate cartel violated the Commerce Clause. Article I of the Constitution grants Congress plenary authority to regulate "commerce between the states," which the Court construed as a limit on state regulation of the same. (In 1886, the Supreme Court had relied on this idea to limit the authority of state railroad regulatory commissions, a decision that generated popular demand for the Interstate Commerce Act of 1887.) It is striking that the Constitution not only offered no solution to unfair treatment but also posed potential barriers to state remedies.[2]

Yet today we take it for granted that cartels cannot set prices or coerce companies into anticompetitive arrangements. Not only is this considered a fundamental economic right, businesses expect the government to enforce this right against violators such as the pipe cartel. And businesses can ask courts to enforce it themselves, in private antitrust actions, if the government drags its heels, or the businesses want the treble damages bounty that antitrust law awards successful lawsuits. The right to an unrestrained market guaranteed by the government, like the right to be free of pregnancy-based discrimination, is based upon a federal statute—the Sherman Anti-Trust Act of 1890, as expanded by subsequent laws. By its brief terms, the Sherman Act makes it unlawful for anyone to enter into a "contract, combination . . . , or conspiracy, in restraint of trade or commerce among the several States" (section 1) or to "monopolize" or "combine or conspire" to monopolize any part of trade or commerce among the states (section 2). Indeed, the Department of Justice invoked section 1 of the Sherman Act as the basis for a lawsuit which successfully prosecuted the pipe cartel that victimized Manion & Company.[3]

As amended and expanded, the Sherman Act is an important foundation of America's constitution of the market. (Far from the *most* important foundation, as that honor would go to the Uniform Commercial Code, an example of state statutory convergence and a classic codification and reform of the Anglo-American common law of sales contracts, bank notes, and, especially, secured transactions.) That is not to deny there are important exemptions to the Sherman Act, including exemptions for labor activities, professional baseball, agricultural cooperatives, and railroads. More important, there are other federal superstatutes that, with the Sherman Act, help structure America's constitution of the market—the Federal Reserve Act of 1913, the Securities Act of 1933 and the Securities Exchange Act of 1934, the Bankruptcy Act of 1978, and the World Trade Agreement entered into by the United States in 1994, to name some important examples. As the Supreme Court has recognized, other superstatutes do sometimes overlap and potentially collide with the Sherman Act's regulatory regime, and the Court has recognized implied exemptions to the antitrust laws when Congress has delegated regulatory authority to another agency (like the Securities and Exchange Commission) and there is a risk of inconsistent regulation within the core area of the other agency's jurisdiction.[4]

The Sherman Act's enduring principle is that the government is responsible for the operation of a "competitive market." Under our view of constitutionalism, this is a great principle, assuring businesses and consumers a security against certain predatory practices and inflated prices. Although we take it for granted today, the Sherman Act's great principle became entrenched in America's constitution through a process that was even more jagged than the entrenchment of the no-pregnancy-discrimination and no-literacy-test norms examined in the earlier chapters. That process illustrates the themes developed in the earlier chapters: statutory constitutionalism often grows out of social movement demands that government create affirmative programs to regulate private as well as public institutions and behaviors; successful entrenchment of statutory principles and structures depends upon astute administrative strategizing as well as having a good idea; and the implementation process is highly dynamic, as administrators apply the statutory principle to ever-changing social and economic circumstances.

The Sherman Act's history illustrates all these points and reveals that the exciting dynamism of our theory is hardly limited to civil rights statutes, with which we started the book. Thus, the Sherman Act norm that the government should guarantee a competitive marketplace is a broad idea whose current implementation reflects values and practical analyses very different from those assumed by its supporters in 1890. What is a "competitive market"? Senator Sherman and the early Department of Justice officials considered it a market with a lot of small as well as large competitors, a market in which the size of a competitor does not restrict its capacity to bargain over price and quantity (though size may matter in production costs if there are scale economies). The department today believes that a competitive market may be one dominated by a few large firms—the kind of firms that would swallow Manion & Company for breakfast. Congress and the Department of Justice in 1890 probably understood that some industries were "natural monopolies," where regulation should be more substantive than antitrust (procedural) in nature, but they felt that this justification was highly exceptional and that industrial concentration and coordination were causes for great concern. The primary *purpose* of antitrust law has changed in the past century—from protection of diffused industry structures and of small competitors such as Manion & Company to maximization of consumer welfare, with tolerance for a great deal of market concentration, to the extent that concentration is consistent with welfare maximization.

The evolutive potential of superstatutes represents the greatest advantage that our republic of statutes has over a Constitutional republic. Although they represent great principles, an important virtue of superstatutes is that they are responsive to public needs and values under changed circumstances. These can be expressed in Congress, or by agencies like the Justice Department, or in more public settings. A theme of this book is that *few* of the fundamental institutions, principles, and policies of our republic should be hard-wired into the impossible-to-change Constitution. Our republic of statutes provides a mechanism whereby a great principle can be recognized and entrenched, but the details worked out by experts and institutions. A related theme is that as superstatutes like the Sherman Act are applied, their purpose and principle will change. This chapter's big story about the Sherman Act is the evolution of its public-regarding purpose, from the notion that democracy best thrives in an economy of small farmers, shopkeepers, and businesses, to the notion that democracy requires maximizing consumer satisfaction. Another way of putting it would focus on shifting emphasis as to what constitutes economic justice in our country: within this framework, the Sherman Act has evolved from a statute emphasizing justice to competitors, who invest their money and sweat to build their businesses, toward a greater focus on justice to consumers, who deserve a fair price and participation in the bounty of America's market economy. However put, this evolution parallels an evolution in our polity's understanding of what gives government its political legitimacy, from the notion of government protecting traditional forms of economic organization, toward the notion of government providing citizens security to ensure their flourishing through free choices. (By the way, the dramatic evolution of the Sherman Act, far from its original purpose, has been ratified by so-called strict constructionists like Robert Bork and Antonin Scalia as well as liberal constructionists like John Paul Stevens and Stephen Breyer. We return to the inevitability of dynamic statutory interpretation in chapter 6.)[5]

We leave to others the task of providing a bottom-line evaluation of this evolution, but our account can helpfully structure the normative debate. For example, critics might object to the current state of antitrust law on the ground that it has departed from the original civic republican or justice-to-competitors purposes of the Sherman Act. By our account, it is no response to say that the Sherman Act, from the beginning, was primarily concerned with economic efficiency or consumer welfare; as a matter of history, that is erroneous. Indeed, the Department of Justice's interpretation of the Sherman Act is more dynamic than its construction of the Voting Rights Act or the EEOC's construction of Title VII and the Pregnancy Discrimination Act. It is more accurate to recognize the Sherman Act's evolution, through an aggressive administrative constitutionalism, and then to consider justifications stronger than the now-traditional ones. That the current Sherman Act incorporates sophisticated principles of economics is a partial defense; defenders would better serve their position if they added an account of democratic legitimacy. We outline such a response at the end of the chapter, one that focuses on the kind of republic we have become—a republic of consumers. Although this new form of state legitimacy helps justify as well as explain the current Sherman Act purpose, it is subject to a meta-critique: Has the focus on consumer welfare been applied in ways that actually benefit consumers? Are there long-term disadvantages to the current lenient approach to antitrust policy? Is there a better strategy?

ENTRENCHMENT OF THE SHERMAN ACT'S NORM, 1890–1921: A REPUBLIC OF SMALL PRODUCERS

The process by which the Sherman Act's norm that the federal government is the guarantor of an unrestrained free national market became entrenched in America's statutory constitution is similar to the stories we told in the preceding chapters for the Civil Rights Act of 1964 and the Voting Rights Act of 1965. (Virtues of the Sherman Act story are that it involves an economic regulatory statute and covers a much longer stretch of our nation's history, a pattern we replicate in the next two chapters, on the safety-net constitution and the constitution of the family.) As with the previously discussed superstatutes, the Sherman Act's story involves three stages: (1) The antitrust principle started as a deliberated congressional response to a social movement insisting on federal governmental action against a threat to the security that should be enjoyed by small businesses as well as consumers. Entrenchment began with the political energy that generated the original law, but received important boosts from (2) vigorous and strategic executive deployment of the law and political feedback that reinforced the norm and urged more aggressive agency action. (3) Congress responded to the episodically aggressive executive application and positive political feedback by enacting subsequent statutes that reaffirmed the Sherman Act norm, provided greater specifications, and expanded the regulatory apparatus for enforcing it.

STAGE ONE: CONGRESS RESPONDS TO A POPULAR DEMAND AND NEED, 1890

The U.S. economy boomed in the generation after the Civil War, with nine billion dollars in production by 1890. Industrial capacity expanded exponentially and fueled a dramatic restructuring of American business between 1880 and 1920. Firms in a variety of sectors sought to concentrate the expanded capacity in a few corporate hands. As business historian Alfred Chandler explains it, the movement toward formal concentration, through monopolies and trusts (where several companies joined together under a central directorate), was most successful in what he calls "center" industries, with large economies of scale due to technological advances or mass production possibilities. Center companies dominated the oil, food processing, rubber, chemical and pharmaceutical, machinery, and transportation sectors. In the other sectors without such economies of scale, such as textiles and construction materials, "peripheral" companies sought to achieve the same concentrated power through cartels and trade associations (such as the pipe and foundry cartel that bedeviled Manion & Company in *Addyston Pipe*), but they were usually not successful for long periods of time.[6]

With center companies visibly ballooning into mega-firms, trusts, and monopolies, and peripheral companies forming cartels and coercive associations, most Americans were alarmed. Complaints were heard from farmers bitter over railroad price gouging and forced rebates, from small businesses (such as Manion & Company) facing cartel-fixed prices or ruinous competition, and from workers and labor unions claiming that big business forced them to work for slave wages and in deplorable conditions. As a judge would later put it, "processes of manufacturing have resulted not only in putting practically the entire manufacturing industry of the country into the hands of the corporations, but have enabled the latter to put an end to competition among themselves by the creation of trusts, to monopolize the production of a particular thing." The fact that "the public hated trusts *fervently*," however, rested on something more than economic self-interest and reflected a larger set of civic republican fears. People from all walks of life were concerned that big business was gobbling up everything, and destroying the farmer and the small business in the process. Thomas Jefferson's, Andrew Jackson's, and Abraham Lincoln's vision of a United States populated with thriving small businessmen, craftsmen, and farmers was becoming obsolete as a matter of economic fact—but Americans were not prepared to relinquish that arcadian ideal, updated by the Horatio Alger myth of the young man who could rise to the top by his own wit and entrepreneurial initiative. Most important, many Americans believed that the rush to corporate bigness threatened the foundations of democracy itself. Concentration of economic power in a few hands would support greater concentration of political power, fatal to a thriving democracy.[7]

With farmers, unions, small businesses, consumers, and lawyers openly alarmed at the threat that great collectives posed to individual economic initiative, there was tremendous bipartisan pressure for legislatures to respond. "The kind of remedy that the public desired was also clear enough: it wanted a law to destroy the power of the trusts." Policymakers realized that state laws could not do this in a timely manner, and the new Interstate Commerce Act of 1887 only addressed some abuses by railroads. In an 1887 message to Congress, President Grover Cleveland, a Democrat, objected to the way that trusts "strangled" competition and destroyed free enterprise; he called for national legislation. Both political parties assailed oppressive business combinations in their 1888 presidential platforms, and during the election campaign Senator John Sherman of Ohio introduced legislation to declare all contracts and combinations preventing full and fair competition and increasing prices to be contrary to public policy, unlawful, and void.[8]

Senator Sherman's original bill was criticized for its broad coverage, embracing acceptable as well as harmful restrictive agreements and business combinations, and for its failure to justify the Constitutional basis for Congress's regulation in this area. In 1889, President Benjamin Harrison (who had unseated President Cleveland) urged the Fifty-first Congress to give "earnest attention" to antitrust legislation. "When organized, as they often are, to crush out all healthy competition and to monopolize the production or sale of an article of commerce and general necessity, they are dangerous conspiracies against the public good, and should be made the subject of prohibitory and even penal legislation." Senator Sherman introduced an expanded version of his bill, designated as "S.1," the first Senate bill introduced in the new Congress. After hearings, committees in both the House and the Senate issued reports detailing the growing power of trusts, and the economic oppressions accompanying this accumulation of private power.[9]

The antitrust bill was the focus of Senate debate in March 1890. Responding to objections, Senator Sherman conceded that the line between legality and illegality was not entirely clear, but the details could be left to case-by-case adjudication. What was important was to preserve "the rights of individuals as against associated and corporate wealth and power." Reflecting the views of small businesses, farmers, and unions, Senator Sherman presented his proposal in terms that these core constituencies of the post–Civil War Republican Party found valuable. "I am not opposed to combinations in and of themselves . . . but when they combine with a purpose to prevent competition, so that if a humble man, solitary and alone, in Ohio [Sherman's state] or anywhere else, they will crowd him down and they will sell their product at a loss or give it away in order to prevent competition . . . then it is the duty of the courts to intervene and prevent it."[10]

Only one senator disagreed with the Sherman critique of trusts and combinations, but many senators continued to object to his inattention to Congress's Constitutional authority, and the bill was referred to the Senate Judiciary Committee. Six days later, Senator George Edmunds, the learned chair, reported a revised form of the Sherman bill, similar to the version that was later enacted: section 1 prohibited (as a felony) contracts and so forth in restraint of trade; section 2 prohibited monopolization (also a felony); the law rested on Congress's authority to regulate interstate and foreign commerce, with sections 1 and 2 drafted to reflect that jurisdictional basis. Both Senator Sherman and the House Committee on the Judiciary (in its April 25 report on revised S.1) expressed dissatisfaction with the structure and wording of the bill but endorsed it upon a sense of "general acquiescence in the recommendation of its passage as perhaps the only legislation possible under existing conditions by this Congress." After two conference committees to resolve minor differences between the bills voted by the two chambers, the revised Sherman bill was passed unanimously by the Senate and almost so by the House.[11]

What principles and values did the Sherman Act embody? Former judge Robert Bork maintains that the original intent of the Sherman Act Congress was to enhance overall social welfare (e.g., lower consumer prices) through rules supporting efficient markets. This is an incomplete understanding of the statute, unfortunately. To begin with, the bill's supporters generally did not use the language of economic efficiency to describe the rules laid down by the proposed legislation, and some of their analysis was contrary to the teachings of modern neoclassical economics. For example, members of Congress focused on injuries to *both* competitors *and* consumers, usually without any effort to differentiate those injuries. When legislators analyzed consumer welfare, they did so unsystematically. The original (1888) Sherman bill targeted combinations seeking "to prevent full and free competition" that had the effect of "advanc[ing] the cost to the consumer," but Senator Sherman's stated concern was also for the "humble man, solitary and alone, in Ohio or anywhere else," who was "crowd[ed] down" by big business combines and trusts. The primary examples of abusive combinations were the oil and sugar trusts, which had engaged in "ruinous competition" eliminating small businesses but which had also significantly lowered prices during the 1880s. Even the iron and steel industry had experienced price declines during this period of consolidation—yet the supporters of the Sherman Act were adamant that they were core examples of illegal bigness.[12]

What most of the senators did not appreciate—or refused to admit in public—was that trusts and monopolies often yield lower prices *and* that overall economic efficiency is often served rather than undermined by trusts and other business combinations. One of the few legislators who conceded that the sugar and oil trusts had actually lowered prices, Senator Edmunds defended the bill in terms that mixed political and economic justifications: "[I]n the long run, however seductive [trusts] may appear in lowering prices to the consumer for the time being, all human experience and all human philosophy have proved that they are destructive of public welfare and come to be tyrannies," which had provoked "riots" elsewhere in the world. In light of these representative statements by the Sherman Act's sponsors, it is clear that the enacting coalition sought to protect competitors as well as consumers. Although the sponsors ignored or minimized the tension between their two purposes for the legislation—protection of competitors versus protection of consumers in the form of lower prices—the original balance probably favored the protection of competitors.[13]

We believe Judge Bork is anachronistically assuming that Sherman Act sponsors sought to maximize welfare as modern neoclassical economists would recommend, an understandable error, but an error nonetheless. In 1890, the large majority of Americans still lived on farms and in small towns; industry and trade, as well as agriculture, were dominated by many small or medium-sized companies. The mega-firm was a frightening anomaly to such a culture. As historian Richard Hofstadter put it, the trusts and monopolies inspired "a fear founded in political realities—the fear that the great business combinations, being the only centers of wealth and power, would be able to lord it over all other interests and thus to put an end to traditional American democracy." The political theory undergirding the Sherman Act was one drawing from Presidents Jackson (for the Democrats) and Lincoln (for the Republicans) the notion that concentration of economic and social power would undermine democracy itself.[14]

STAGE TWO: INCREASINGLY STRONG ADMINISTRATIVE IMPLEMENTATION, 1890–1914

During the congressional debates over the wisdom of adopting the Sherman Act, no one mentioned how hard it would be to implement the law. The Department of Justice, the primary enforcement agent, had in 1890 only eighteen lawyers. Every minute of their time was needed to handle the thirteen thousand claims then pending against the federal government. Until 1902, therefore, the attorney general had much less to do with initiating Sherman Act prosecutions than did local U.S. attorneys (with the approval of the attorney general). In early 1892, these prosecutors filed two landmark lawsuits, one against the sugar trust for its proposal to buy out its four largest competitors and another to dissolve the Trans-Missouri Freight Association, a cartel of railroad companies cooperating to fix prices. Notwithstanding this desultory record of prosecutions, the Republican Party trumpeted its support of the antitrust law in the 1892 campaign. In their winning effort to return Cleveland to the White House, the Democrats were even more enthusiastic: "[W]e believe [the trusts'] worst evils can be abated by law, and we demand the rigid enforcement of the laws made to prevent and control them, together with such further legislation in restraint of their abuses as experience may show to be necessary."[15]

While there can be little doubt that the antitrust principle was popular, there is much doubt as to precisely what that principle *was*, and how it fit into the Constitution. Responding to the early prosecutions, the Supreme Court sent mixed signals. In *United States v. E.C. Knight* (1895), a divided Court ruled that the Sherman Act's regulation of monopolization of "any part of trade or commerce among the states" did not cover an intrastate manufacturing enterprise, even one like the sugar trust that shipped its goods in interstate and international commerce. *E.C. Knight* was a notable issue in the 1896 presidential campaign, with Democratic candidate William Jennings Bryan lambasting the Court for its narrow construction, even as he was lambasting the Court for its broad understanding of federal regulatory power in *In re Debs* (1895), where the Cleveland administration had wielded the Sherman Act to procure injunctions crushing the Pullman Strike of 1894. After the election (and Bryan's defeat), the Court held in *United States v. Trans-Missouri Freight Association* (1897) that a railroad association formed for the purpose of fixing prices and other terms of competition met the interstate commerce (jurisdictional) requirement of the Sherman Act and violated section 1.[16]

The case involving Manion & Company was a turning point that both clarified and expanded the statute. Attorney General Judson Harmon only reluctantly authorized suit against the iron pipe manufacturers' conspiracy late in 1896. He cautioned U.S. Attorney James Bible: "I leave the whole matter to your own judgment, with full authority and discretion, only I would be careful not to shoot until I was sure of my aim." Much was at stake in this lawsuit. After *E.C. Knight* had narrowed section 2 (monopolization), losing the pipe case would have crippled section 1 (agreements in restraint of trade). The defendant companies argued that their prices were reasonable and their market share was not so large as to preclude competition from plenty of other pipe makers. Every judge who considered those arguments rejected them in *United States v. Addyston Pipe & Steel* (1898). Delivering the opinion of a Sixth Circuit panel including Justice Harlan and Judge Lurton, Judge (and former Solicitor General) William Howard Taft read section 1 liberally and pragmatically. Section 1 allowed restraints that were "ancillary" to legitimate business purposes, but price fixing was not such a purpose. "[W]here the sole object of the parties in making the contract as expressed therein is merely to restrain competition, and enhance or maintain prices, it would seem that there was nothing to justify or excuse the restraint, that it would necessarily have a tendency to monopoly, and therefore would be void." Nor was the alleged reasonableness of the price a defense to the Sherman Act. A unanimous Supreme Court affirmed Judge Taft, with a minor modification in the judgment.[17]

The iron pipe cartel also made some important Constitutional arguments. Defendants invoked *E.C. Knight* for the proposition that Congress had no authority to regulate their essentially intrastate business of manufacturing cast iron pipes. Because *Trans-Missouri* had read section 1 more broadly than *E.C. Knight* had read section 2, to cover agreements affecting interstate shipments, this argument had substantially been rejected by the Supreme Court. The pipe makers further maintained that a broad interpretation of section 1 would violate their due process "liberty of contract" rights, which the Court had recognized (and would enshrine in the Constitutional canon with *Lochner v. New York* [1905]). Here, *Trans-Missouri* was less authoritative, as the railroads fixing prices in that case were quasi-public entities the Court considered especially susceptible to public regulation. But in *Addyston Pipe* the government responded that "the liberty contended for by [the cartel] is the liberty to destroy liberty," such as the contractual freedom of Manion and Fitzpatrick to conduct their business affairs in New Orleans. For this reason, the Sixth Circuit and the Supreme Court, both unanimously, rejected the cartel's argument. In an opinion by Justice Rufus Peckham, a liberty of contract champion who would later write the Court's *Lochner* opinion, the Supreme Court ruled that the cartel was "restricting the right of each of the members to do business in the *ordinary way*," as well as affecting the market. Under the common law, no one enjoyed a "liberty" to harm others or destroy public goods. Although Justice Peckham did not deny the civic republican features of the Sherman Act, he read its policy through a libertarian lens.[18]

Addyston Pipe is a landmark in the constitution of the market. Reflecting the balance of expert as well as popular opinion, Judge Taft believed that there was a "fair market" structure that preserved productive opportunities for all American businesses, that the Sherman Act rendered the federal government a guarantor of that structure (which was beyond the ability of the states to protect), and that business combinations and monopolies directly threatened that structure and, with it, American democracy itself. Some of the most conservative liberty of contract judges were moved by this last point. Justice David Brewer, a devout ally of Peckham's liberty of contract jurisprudence, was converted to the Sherman Act by 1893, when he observed that "the drift today is toward the subjection of the individual to the domination of the organization. The business men are becoming slaves of the combine, the laborers of the trades union and organization. Through the land the idea is growing that the individual is nothing, and that the organization, and then the State, is everything." Notice that Justice

Brewer saw the civic republican features of antitrust policy more clearly than his friend Peckham.[19]

Although there were only sixteen federal prosecutions in the first twelve years of the antitrust law, the Sherman Act was a provisional legal landmark when Theodore Roosevelt became president upon the assassination of President William McKinley in 1901. Its unrestrained competition principle (rife with ambiguities, to be sure) was accepted by bipartisan consensus and was reaching beyond the common law and transforming American markets, and even core Constitutional commitments were being reshaped to accommodate the constitutional one. Whatever doubts there legitimately were about this statute's potential for changing business practices were further diminished by the prosecution of the Northern Securities holding company in 1902. Under orders from President Roosevelt, Attorney General Philander Knox prosecuted a holding company formed by railroad titan James Hill and banking tycoon J. Pierpont Morgan. The purpose of the company was not to fix prices but instead to call a truce in their financially exhausting battle for control of two western railroads. Although the Northern Securities prosecution went well beyond the core principles of the Sherman Act and antagonized prominent Republican moguls, it was a public relations success—dramatizing the point that even the most wealthy barons of industry were accountable to the legal norm of unrestrained competition. A closely divided Supreme Court went along with this regulatory adventure, affirming the convictions in *Northern Securities v. United States* (1904). The Republicans touted the successful prosecution in President Roosevelt's 1904 campaign for election to a full term of the office. The Democratic candidate took a more passive attitude toward the antitrust law—and garnered only 37.6 percent of the vote, against Roosevelt's 56.4 percent, the poorest showing for a Democrat in the history of presidential elections.[20]

Buoyed by this popular wave, Roosevelt's attorneys general Knox (1901–04), William Moody (1904–06), and Charles Bonaparte (1906–09) continued to file aggressive Sherman Act prosecutions. In 1903, at the behest of the administration, Congress specifically funded antitrust enforcement ($500,000 worth), including money for an assistant to the attorney general for antitrust matters; the first such assistant was William Day (1903–05), and he was followed by a regular stream of similar officials. Brisk enforcement continued during the administration of Roosevelt's handpicked successor, former judge Taft. Indeed, President Taft's attorney general George Wickersham (1909–13) initiated many more antitrust prosecutions in four years than the Roosevelt administration had in seven and successfully pursued the Roosevelt administration's prosecution of the Standard Oil and American Tobacco monopolies. Although the Court upheld these prosecutions, Chief Justice Edward White's opinion for the Court in

Standard Oil of New Jersey v. United States (1911) rejected the government's theory that *all* contractual restraints of trade were illegal, as had been suggested by the Court in *Trans-Missouri*. Consistent with Judge Taft's opinion in *Addyston Pipe*, the chief justice ruled that challenged business practices should be evaluated by a "rule of reason." Because the lower court had found that Standard Oil engaged in predatory practices designed to eliminate "potential competition" and raise prices, the Court had no difficulty finding a Sherman Act violation: its conduct violated the rule of reason. But it was unclear how this standard would apply in future cases.[21]

The debate between the Supreme Court and the Department of Justice had echoes in the election of 1912, which confirmed the entrenchment of the Sherman Act. Recall our rule of recognition for entrenchment: a statutory principle gains such traction in public culture that no one is able to attack it successfully, and so it becomes a consensus principle that is reaffirmed and expanded by statute. In the election of 1912, the political Right (GOP), the Left (Progressives and Socialists), and the Center (Democrats) all explicitly endorsed an aggressive government role in maintaining a competitive market. A new Progressive Party nominated former president Roosevelt, the original trustbuster; the Republicans renominated President Taft, a booster of the Sherman Act since his opinion in *Addyston Pipe*; and the Democrats nominated Governor Woodrow Wilson on the strongest antitrust platform of all. The Democrats regretted that "the Sherman anti-trust law has received a judicial construction depriving it of much of its efficacy," referring to *Standard Oil*'s rule of reason, and advocated "the enactment of legislation which will restore to the statute the strength of which it has been deprived by such interpretation." Wilson ran away with the election, partly because of the Roosevelt-Taft split in the Republican vote.[22]

In 1912, the Sherman Act was at a crossroads. It was unquestionably popular, and the reasons for its popularity were complex. Reflecting the views of Senator Sherman, conservatives as well as progressives supported the antitrust norm because they saw the rise of business trusts and monopolies, labor unions, and redistributive state policies as profound threats to American individualism and, hence, democracy. This is the same philosophy that was reflected in the labor injunction cases such as *Debs* and the liberty of contract cases such as *Lochner*. This normative parallelism helps us see how Justice Peckham, the author of *Lochner*, could also write for the Court in *Trans-Missouri* and *Addyston Pipe*. Peckham did not see himself protecting overall market efficiency and was more concerned with assuring a political economy of "small dealers and worthy men," to use his precise language. Eager to advance popular prosecutions, the Department of Justice seemed to take this view in cases like *Northern Securities* and *Standard Oil*. But theirs was not the vision of the future. Others rejected the assumption that industrial bigness was necessarily bad and took a more modern view of the Sherman Act, asking what rules would promote an efficient market or maximize consumer welfare. Examples of the more modern view were Judge Taft's *Addyston Pipe* opinion, Justice Holmes's *Northern Securities* dissent, and Chief Justice White's *Standard Oil* opinion.[23]

STAGE THREE: CONGRESSIONAL CONFIRMATION AND
EXPANSION OF THE SHERMAN ACT (1914–21)

During the 1912 presidential campaign, Governor Wilson issued an open letter outlining the economic policy of his New Freedom platform. As a general matter, the letter committed Wilson to the consensus policy that the federal government has a responsibility that "competition can and should be maintained in every branch of private industry." Responding to the open-ended rule of reason approach of *Standard Oil*, Wilson promised to buttress the Sherman Act with a new statute specifying particular practices that violated the rule of reason, including prohibitions targeting "methods" by which the great trusts "commonly crush their rivals," providing stronger remedies for antitrust violations, and creating "a board or commission to aid in administering the Sherman law." Because Wilson's views of antitrust policy were still evolving, this important letter was written by his adviser, Louis Brandeis. It is noteworthy that Brandeis approached antitrust policy from an antibigness perspective inflected by his Jacksonian/Lincolnian vision of an America of small businesses. To the extent Brandeis was a student of economics, it was study profoundly biased by his political views. For example, he opined that large business units are, inherently, not as efficient as smaller ones; "if it were possible today to make the corporations act in accordance with what doubtless all of us would agree should be the rules of trade no huge corporation would be created, or if created, would be successful." This was not a sound understanding of business economics.[24]

In 1914, President Wilson secured enactment of two new laws that not only reaffirmed the Sherman Act's principle but also strengthened the law in precisely the ways Wilson had promised during the campaign. With significant presidential arm-twisting and no small amount of compromising, Congress passed the Clayton Act of 1914. The new statute included a specific list of prohibited practices that supplemented the Sherman Act's established bar to price fixing and market division (*Trans-Missouri* and *Addyston Pipe*) and monopolization (*Northern Securities*). Thus, the Clayton Act barred price discrimination (section 2), tying and exclusive dealing agreements (section 3), and stock acquisitions (section 7) when the effect of such practices would be "to substantially lessen competition or create a monopoly." The Clayton Act also prohibited interlocking directorates (section 8), a prophylactic structural measure to head off opportunities for collusion, price fixing, and the like. (The concern was that if the same people served as directors of competing companies, there would inevitably be collusion as to prices, and so on.) Although this grab bag of prohibited practices have proven highly controversial as a policy matter, they were a significant policy response by Congress reaffirming a serious commitment to antitrust policy and providing substantive details in response to *Standard Oil*.[25]

The remedial provisions of the Clayton Act reaffirmed and expanded those of the Sherman Act. Section 4 of the Clayton Act expanded the Sherman Act's private treble damages cause of action to include claims by any person "injured in his business or property by reason of anything forbidden in the antitrust laws." Going beyond the Sherman Act's treble damages cause of action, section 16 of the Clayton Act gave injured private parties a claim for injunctive relief (as well as the damages under section 4) for violations or threatened violations of the antitrust laws. These Clayton Act provisions transformed enforcement of the Sherman Act, as they effectively deputized businesses and their attorneys to be private attorneys general to enforce the antitrust laws, with injunctions as well as treble damages. An immediate consequence of section 16 was that it also unleashed the notorious "labor injunction," whereby employers would use the antitrust laws as a legal way to break union boycotts and strikes through injunctions and then through contempt proceedings when union leaders violated the injunctions.[26]

This last point was ironic, because the Clayton Act was billed as protecting organized labor against antitrust prosecutions. Section 20 prohibited federal courts from issuing injunctions in cases "involving or growing out of, a dispute concerning terms or conditions of employment, unless necessary to prevent irreparable injury to property, or to a property right." Section 6, moreover, said that "nothing contained in the antitrust laws shall be construed to forbid the existence and operation of . . . labor . . . organizations . . . or to forbid or restrain individual members of such organizations . . . from lawfully carrying out the legitimate objects thereof; nor shall such organizations . . . or members thereof, be held or construed to be illegal combinations or conspiracies in restraint of trade, under the antitrust laws." In *Duplex Printing Press Co. v. Deering* (1921), the Court ruled that sections 6 and 20 did *not* exempt secondary boycotts (third-party refusals to buy goods of an antiunion employer) from antitrust liability and legitimated a decade of labor injunctions against union activities. Although the labor injunction could be defended on civic republican grounds, as a way to prevent big unions from tyrannizing small businesses, in practice they tended to be weapons wielded by big businesses to discourage labor organizing, a setback to civic republican ideals.[27]

The Federal Trade Commission Act of 1914 outlawed "unfair methods of competition" as well as "unfair or deceitful practices in commerce" and created a new agency (the Federal Trade Commission, the FTC) to enforce this Sherman-inflected norm through cease-and-desist orders. Although we shall not explore the FTC's interesting history here, its creation was significant, for after 1914 there were three sources for enforcing rules against price fixing and other anti-competitive practices: Department of Justice prosecutions, FTC administrative proceedings or enforcement actions in court, and private actions for injunctions and/or treble damages. As an organ of potential administrative constitutionalism, however, the FTC was less than successful. Its failure, certainly in the short term, was a classic illustration of what can go wrong with administrative constitutionalism (a theme we explore more systematically in part 3 of this book). Although the FTC was charged with enforcing a procompetition mandate as to which there was substantial agreement, the vagueness as to details and the greater public focus on the Clayton Act made it important that the agency have energetic leadership early on, which it decidedly did not have. Like the Justice Department in the 1890s, the FTC had no overall strategy for implementing its statutory duties, but unlike the department, the FTC had no room for experimentation, for its window of regulatory opportunity closed unexpectedly. Indeed, the commission got started just weeks before a German U-boat sank the *Lusitania* in 1915. After the *Lusitania*, the Wilson administration and the country were preoccupied with the Great War in Europe. By the time the war ended, the United States entered an era quite unfriendly to vigorous antitrust enforcement by an agency like the FTC. After a slow start, the FTC never became the dynamite agency the Securities and Exchange Commission would later be.[28]

Although the FTC failed to get off the ground, the Department of Justice continued to enforce the Sherman Act, as amended by the Clayton Act, especially under Attorney General Thomas Watt Gregory (1914–19) and his antitrust assistant, George Todd (1913–19). What the department was calling the "Antitrust Division" by the end of the Wilson administration had eighteen attorneys. Although the department did not file as many splashy indictments against mega-firms as the Roosevelt and Taft Justice Departments had done, it did file on average eleven prosecutions each year.[29]

CHALLENGES AND EVOLUTION OF THE SHERMAN ACT, 1921–69: A REPUBLIC FREE OF MARKET BOTTLENECKS

Although we consider the Sherman Act's core principle to have been entrenched by 1921, there remained ambiguity in 1921 as to precisely what that principle was. Much of the public support for antitrust regulation rested upon the Horatio Alger myth that anyone, however humble his origins, can rise to the top through good old American ingenuity, hard work, and pluck. There was also a general alarm against bigness, a preconception that strongly motivated even sophisticated thinkers such as Louis Brandeis. The institutional interaction among President Wilson, the Department of Justice, the Supreme Court, and Congress valued the Horatio Alger aspiration but also understood the policy to help assure "competitive" markets, another concept as to which there were several different understandings. The next two generations saw the Sherman Act principle swoon in the face of economic crisis, and then rebound stronger and more conceptually developed than before. The new understanding of the Sherman Act was that it was structural, a promise by the federal government that it would assure the operation of a free and efficient national market. The operation of a free national market was for the common good, and the governing paradigm was that the role of the federal government was to unblock practices and institutions that were *bottlenecks* in the emerging national market that New Deal administrators wanted to ensure. ("Bottleneck" is neither a statutory nor an economic term; we use it here to capture the still-ambiguous conceptualization of antitrust policy by the leading figure during the New Deal.) Institutionally, the removing-bottlenecks understanding of the Sherman Act was the dominant one, but the republican concerns with concentrated economic power retained strong bite throughout this period, though a bite expressed in the reigning economic language of the New Deal. That is, New Deal regulators expressed and transformed the old protect-small-competitors justification for the Sherman Act in the language of economics: market concentration was objectionable because it provided a structure where administered prices and other anticompetitive practices were easier to accomplish.

EXOGENOUS SHOCKS: WORLD WAR I AND THE GREAT DEPRESSION

Even superstatutes may have a roller-coaster history when political or other circumstances change. World War I not only derailed the feeble FTC but also raised questions about whether the Department of Justice should be aggressively pursuing the Sherman Act. The wartime administration sometimes encouraged corporate cooperation, and that nonconfrontational approach dominated the next decade, the return to normalcy. Secretary of Commerce (1921–29) and then President (1929–33) Herbert Hoover's philosophy of corporate cooperation drove the Sherman Act into mild desuetude—except for the stream of labor injunction suits by private businesses against unions, labor organizers, and striking or boycotting workers. Although the Antitrust Division boasted several capable assistants during this era, notably William ("Wild Bill")

Donovan (1925–29) and John Lord O'Brian (1929–32), there were very few major prosecutions. Notably, however, the post-1900 merger and trust boom dissipated, and political concerns with business concentration were not prominent in the 1920s. Moreover, neither the Department of Justice nor the Supreme Court retreated from the Sherman Act's core commitments to the rule against business practices designed to suppress competition, a rule applied by Justice Brandeis in *Board of Trade of the City of Chicago v. United States* (1925), a leading restatement of the rule of reason.[30]

A bigger challenge faced the superstatute during the Great Depression that commenced in 1929: Sherman Act enforcement fell off dramatically, and policymakers wondered whether its principle of fair competition ought to be replaced or modified by a principle of mutual cooperation by competing businesses as well as labor enterprises. (It is no coincidence that the Norris–La Guardia Act terminating federal court involvement in labor disputes was enacted in 1932.) During the first term of President Franklin Roosevelt (1933–37), a dominant theme was to stimulate higher wages through cooperative business practices, or government-sponsored cartelization. In 1933, Congress enacted the National Industrial Recovery Act (NRA), which authorized distressed industries to create their own "codes of fair competition," including the power to fix prices. Under the NRA regime, the Antitrust Division of the Department of Justice (formally recognized by Congress in 1933) spent most of its time *enforcing* rather than *challenging* industry-wide price-fixing regimes. Although the Supreme Court would later strike down the NRA as a violation of the Constitution's vesting all legislative authority in Congress, the statute reflected the dominant thinking during Roosevelt's first term.[31]

An attitude friendly toward corporate cooperation was reflected in Chief Justice Hughes's opinion for the Court in *Appalachian Coals, Inc. v. United States* (1933). Quotably hailing the Sherman Act as a "charter of freedom," the chief justice compared the "generality and adaptability" of its language to "that found to be desirable in [C]onstitutional provisions." Like the Constitution, however, the constitution of the market bent to the uncertainties created by the Depression. The Court unanimously upheld, under the rule of reason, an agency scheme entered into by 167 Appalachian coal-mining firms to set prices and negotiate deals with suppliers. (Ironically, the actual mechanism was a joint sales agency, functionally the same as the mechanism struck down in *Addyston Pipe*.)[32]

Nonetheless, there was ongoing support for antitrust law within the Roosevelt administration. In "Industrial Prices and Their Relative Inflexibility" (1935), a document prepared for Congress, economist Gardiner Means argued that concentrated industries had caused the Depression, because they fostered anticompetitive tendencies, including the practice whereby a few companies would "administer" fixed prices above what ordinary supply and demand would generate. Implicit in Means's analysis was that the federal government was needed as a countervailing power, to monitor predatory practices and prevent concentrated market structures that were inherently anticompetitive. Although many New Dealers were reflexively opposed to market concentration for social and political reasons (such as the purported inconsistency between democracy and concentrated industry), Means's point of view gained the upper hand during President Roosevelt's second term (1937–41). The president handed over antitrust policy to brilliant administrators influenced by the modernized critique of business concentration provided by Means and other economists.[33]

Implementing this philosophy were the heads of the Antitrust Division for a critical decade in the statute's history: Assistant Attorneys General Robert Jackson (1937–38), Thurman Arnold (1938–43), and Wendell Berge (1943–47). The key figure was Arnold, a brilliant, mercurial Yale law professor who turned out to be the quintessential twentieth-century administrative constitutionalist. He not only sought to articulate and implement a more coherent approach to the Sherman Act, he also tied that vigorous philosophy to big public themes of democracy and consumerism. Arnold was determined to enforce procompetitive market structures upon unwilling barons of business policies that were in the public interest and contributed to greater economic and job security for ordinary Americans. Arnold and his allies argued that the New Deal's commitment to an expanded federal role in America's constitutional governance required an aggressive regulatory philosophy like that which James Landis and William O. Douglas had brought to the Securities and Exchange Commission. Not only did Arnold serve notice on big business that antitrust law was back in vogue, during the interminable deliberations of the Temporary National Economic Committee (1937–42) he and his allies stood against the New Dealers who thought that all business bigness is bad.[34]

Arnold was a classic example of the kind of official whose practical skills as well as conceptual vision made administrative constitutionalism the driving force of American public policy. He cajoled President Roosevelt and Congress to increase the budget and size of his division (to five hundred employees by 1943, from the fifteen it started with in 1933) and brought great publicity to his antitrust message and his many prosecutions. Arnold's approach to prosecution was innovative. Once the division was able to identify an industry or sector where anticompetitive practices were prevalent, Arnold brought a cluster of prosecutions, accompanied by much publicity as well as detailed public explanations of what the division was redressing. The large majority of cases were settled by consent decrees outlawing the objectionable practices and sometimes restructuring the industry along lines that Arnold thought would reduce opportunities for future predatory behavior.[35]

After half a generation of reduced enforcement, Arnold found plenty of cartels and oligopolies worth suing, including the big three automobile manufacturers, the motion picture industry, the dairy industry, the American Medical Association, the insurance industry, a cartel of oil firms, and the Alcoa company, which had achieved a virtual monopoly in aluminum sales. Arnold won all of these cases, and many more. His most notable victory was the Supreme Court's decision in the oil case *United States v. Socony-Vacuum Oil Co.* (1940), which all but overruled *Appalachian Coals* and announced a *per se* rule that price-fixing conspiracies can never meet the rule of reason. A weaker but well-publicized victory was the Second Circuit's judgment in *Alcoa* (a case Arnold inherited from Jackson), where Judge Learned Hand essentially found a violation of section 2 based upon the company's market share and without the strong evidence of monopolistic practices that had characterized most of the monopolization prosecutions (such as *Standard Oil*). According to his biographer, with the appropriate level of overstatement for this genre, "Arnold destroyed the moral and economic basis for the culture of cartels in America and abroad" and "delegitimated [price fixing] by making it both anticonsumer and unAmerican, created a stable mandate for antitrust as part of an expanded role of the federal government in policing a healthy national economy, and made it impossible for antitrust to be repealed in the future or completely undermined by changes in the prevailing political winds." What we would add to this encomium is that Thurman Arnold imported from Gardiner Means an economic theory that modernized the civic republican rhetoric of the first generation of antitrust law. We now turn to that vision.[36]

THE SHERMAN ACT'S NEW DEAL VISION: REMOVING "BOTTLENECKS" AND ENSURING A PROCOMPETITIVE MARKET STRUCTURE

Although Thurman Arnold insisted that Sherman Act policy was simple and straightforward, his own public justifications were more complex and sometimes inconsistent with his grand vision. Thus, he stated that antitrust law was a weapon against the "evils of concentrated economic power in a democracy," namely: (1) the ability to fix prices, with the result that "resources are not efficiently allocated," and (2) "the tendency of such empires to swallow up local businesses and (3) drain away local capital." The first evil (inefficient allocation of resources) was economic and drew from administered-price and other economic theories; the second sounded economic but did not reflect sound economic analysis and probably reflected the earlier civic republican concerns held by the parents of antitrust law (Senator Sherman's concern that localized businesses like Manion & Company would cease to exist); and the third (draining away local capital) was probably a political bow to continuing localist sentiments, because there is no economic efficiency concern with draining away "local capital" so long as funds are available from somewhere. To modern ears, there is greater tension between the statute's economic efficiency purpose and the save-little-companies and localism purposes than Arnold would have admitted. It is often inefficient to save little companies. From an economic perspective, it is also inefficient to preserve localism for its own sake; localities not only lose economies of scale but also tend to be magnets for subsidies and inefficient services.[37]

These tensions are illustrated by the Alcoa case. Initiated by Robert Jackson but vigorously pressed by Arnold, the Alcoa prosecution was reminiscent of the Northern Securities prosecution in its lack of justification under what today would be considered sound economic analysis. Alcoa was a big center industry with a near monopoly, but as with typical center industry giants, Alcoa's market share owed more to economies of scale than to unfair business practices. Upholding a judgment that Alcoa violated section 2 of the Sherman Act, Judge Learned Hand invoked the original goal of the statute, namely, "[Congress's] desire to put an end to great aggregations of capital because of the helplessness of the individual before them." Officials like Arnold and Hand understood and appreciated economic efficiency as an important purpose of government generally and the antitrust laws in particular, but they believed that a concentrated market structure was inherently inconsistent with efficiency. Like modern theorists, we are skeptical and believe that the Alcoa prosecution was an example of the tendency of the old civic republican goals to persevere even when economic efficiency was becoming the primary justification for antitrust law.[38]

When Thurman Arnold and other New Dealers in Roosevelt's second and third terms invoked economic concepts, they placed great importance on structure-based economic theory of the sort Gardiner Means advanced in 1935. Thus, the procompetition New Dealers believed that the federal government was obliged to guarantee structures and institutions that would allow all Americans to pursue their individual projects. A central institution of this sort is the market. It is hard for markets to exist without the state and the legal rules of contract, currency, and fair trade practices. From Arnold's perspective, an important role of the market-guaranteeing state was to clear away market bottlenecks impeding the efficient allocation of human and other resources in the economy. Two such bottlenecks were cartels such as the iron pipe cartel that ran Manion & Company out of business decades earlier, and monopolies such as Alcoa. Hence, cartels and monopolies also impeded economic recovery and had to be attacked as vigorously as possible. The Department of Justice and the Supreme Court were the "cop[s] on the beat" or the "referee[s]" protecting the fair and unrestrained operation of the market. To be a little more speculative, we also believe that Arnold's thinking reflected the pervasive New Deal philosophy that big business was too politically powerful and arrogant, rigging both the economic and political systems in ways that created bottlenecks to individual creativity and productivity.[39]

Guaranteeing the free competitive market by refereeing it and removing bottlenecks is a procedural more than substantive understanding of antitrust law—a viewpoint also reflected in the New Deal Department of Justice's Constitutional jurisprudence. Thus, at precisely the same time that Arnold was pressing his remove-the-bottlenecks interpretation of the Sherman Act, the solicitor general was pressing a very similar concern as a guide for the Court's Dormant Commerce Clause jurisprudence. In the 1937 term, the solicitor general argued for Constitutional invalidation of South Carolina's exceedingly restrictive limits of the weight and width of trucks passing through the state. The argument was that the restrictive regulations posed an unreasonable burden on interstate commerce, specifically interfering with the "development of a national interconnected and interstate highway system," which had been created and reinforced by the Federal Highway Act of 1921 and the Motor Carrier Act of 1935. The Department of Justice did not argue that those statutes preempted the state law but argued instead that the Commerce Clause barred "unreasonable burdens" on interstate commerce, and that the state's large departure from the uniform safety standards developed by the federal Bureau of Public Roads was decisive evidence of such a burden. Although the Supreme Court was unpersuaded by these arguments in the 1937 term, the Court adopted virtually the same arguments to strike down state train length regulations in *Southern Pacific Co. v. Arizona* (1945). The balancing approach followed by the Court in *Southern Pacific*, taken almost verbatim from the department's brief, was the governing standard in Dormant Commerce Clause cases for the next forty years.[40]

We should note some larger points that emerge from the evolution of antitrust thinking between 1890 (when the Sherman Act was enacted) and 1945 (when *Southern Pacific* was decided). One point is that the post-1936 Justice Department—not just Thurman Arnold but also Solicitors General Stanley Reed and Robert Jackson (head of the Antitrust Division before Arnold)—had a small "c" constitutional vision of the federal government as a police officer blowing the whistle on all manner of commercial bottlenecks, not just monopolies and conspiracies but also captured state laws that impeded the operation of an efficient national market. This constitutional vision unified the administration's broad understanding of Congress's Commerce Clause power (the topic most discussed among law professors) with its broad understanding of the "negative" Commerce Clause's dynamic limit on state authority and of the antitrust statutes. The Old Court did not follow this vision (1938), but the New Deal Court in place by 1945 did, as reflected in *Southern Pacific* as well as the antitrust precedents. The foregoing also suggests that Arnold's stated concern with preserving local capital formation was a throwaway point in his litany of anticompetitive "evils." The reason for our surmise is that Arnold, like the solicitors general, was committed to the New Deal's nationalist vision, guaranteeing a national market unimpeded by pesky state legal restrictions and local cartels.

Another point returns us to our discussion of the different conceptions of *liberty* in the previous chapter. In neither 1890, the beginning of the so-called *Lochner* era, nor 1945, the height of the New Deal, was the federal government committed to a libertarian, noninterference understanding of liberty. Public officials and voters alike apprehended that small businesses like Manion & Company were effectively deprived of their liberty by monopolies or by firms or cartels engaged in "predatory" practices. The biggest liberty difference between the two eras is that the earlier era, which witnessed the birth of the Sherman Act, gave greater attention to what we are calling liberty as civic engagement. By allowing firms to conspire and monopolize, the government would be undermining the conditions for democracy, namely, the flourishing of small shops, businesses, and farms that populate the Jeffersonian arcadia. Conversely, there is greater emphasis in the latter period (the New Deal) on liberty as security, whereby each citizen feels he has an opportunity to participate in an economic system that is not bottled up with inefficient obstacles (whether private or public) to private enterprise. The latter period was skeptical of monopolies (even ones like Alcoa that were probably the result of economies of scale) and bigness in business, but expressed the skepticism more often in the language of economics than in the language of politics. In prosecutions like *Alcoa*, Thurman Arnold and Learned Hand may have been doing little more than modernizing the Sherman Act's original civic republican philosophy: big capital concentrations will be tempted to corrupt political processes; this temptation would be nearly impossible to control through regulation; hence, as a political prophylactic measure, bigness should be headed off through antitrust and other policies. The difference in the eras is that Arnold felt compelled to express antibigness in economic terms, and he did not press that approach too far very often.

In short, many liberty of contract devotees were enthusiastic about antitrust as an area of aggressive government regulation and, potentially, restructuring of entire industries. This was an expanded role for government, and many conservatives went along with it through gritted teeth. Note how our account of the Sherman Act cuts against some conventional wisdom, whereby the *Lochner* era was one of triumphant (negative rights) libertarian constitutionalism. This is false: the period from 1890 to 1940 was one of rapidly escalating state regulation responding to the new economic forces unleashed by large-scale industrialization—and the Supreme Court upheld almost all of it, *Lochner* notwithstanding. Even the most adamant judicial libertarians such as Justices Peckham (who wrote *Lochner* as well as *Addyston Pipe*) and Brewer (who wrote *Debs*) favored aggressive federal interventions to protect each citizen's right to pursue a livelihood and even a career without undue interference from the new leviathans, namely, trusts, monopolies, and (for some) unions. Effectively, the Court upheld the creation of a new regime of positive rights, which was enforced through administrative and legislative action. The New Deal continued this line of thought but adapted it in fundamental ways too. The first New Deal (1933–37) firmly entrenched the Norris–La Guardia policy of removing unions from antitrust law and replaced that regulation with the corporatist model of the National Labor Relations Act of 1935, where economic peace was secured by facilitating worker organization into countervailing institutions (unions). The second New Deal (1937–41) was more procompetitive and was ultimately antilocalist. In both Sherman Act prosecutions and Dormant Commerce Clause *amicus* briefs, the post-1936 Department of Justice sought to protect a national market, not just the series of local markets that was a premise of *Addyston Pipe* and other early cases. Especially after 1935, the New Dealers engaged in a more structural analysis and connected their antitrust policy with a larger philosophy, whereby the government promised We the People that its own programs, and not just the "free" market, would assure citizens opportunities to pursue their own economic projects. Carrying forth the philosophy of Machiavelli and Locke, the legitimacy of government was grounded more ambitiously than ever before on the promise of *economic security*, guaranteed directly by the state. We pursue this theme in the next chapter, on social security.[41]

THE PERSEVERANCE OF ANTICONCENTRATION
AS A SHERMAN ACT GOAL

Throughout the 1940s, the Department of Justice and (especially) the FTC pressed Congress to amend the Clayton Act to give them broader authority to regulate market concentrations even where there was no evidence of predatory practices. The agencies presented evidence to Congress that business concentration was again on the upswing and that the agencies did not have sufficient regulatory tools to head off further ruinous concentration. (The agencies' fears were greatly overstated, but no one in Congress confronted them on this point.) In addition to the economic problems with concentration, Assistant Attorney General (Antitrust) Wendell Berge (1943–47) argued that cartels and monopolies were "threats to American democracy" itself, because economic power translates into political power. To prevent a recurrence of out-of-control corporate power, it was necessary to have big countervailing institutions—unions (the NLRA), the federal government (the antitrust laws), and perhaps consumer groups too.[42]

The agencies pointed out that the Supreme Court had construed the Clayton Act too narrowly, in one case declining to expand section 7's regulation of stock acquisitions to include acquisitions of assets. In *United States v. Columbia Steel Co.* (1948), Justice Douglas dissented from this interpretation, explicitly recalling Justice Brandeis's "bigness is bad" philosophy. Two years later, the Democratic Congress elected in the Truman landslide responded to *Columbia Steel* by amending section 7 of the Clayton Act to bar a company's acquisition of the assets of another company when its effect "may be substantially to lessen competition, or to tend to create a monopoly." The Celler-Kefauver Act of 1950 was a legislative attempt "to cope with monopolistic tendencies in their incipiency and well before they have attained such effects as would justify a Sherman Act proceeding." Congress justified the law, in part, by reference to economic theories insisting that concentrated industries were most prone to anticompetitive conduct. Price leadership and even direct price fixing were easier under these circumstances—and revised section 7 was a prophylactic measure to head off these dangers. As with the original Sherman Act, Congress's economic analysis sometimes involved unverified concerns that reflected underlying civic republican or localist motivations. (Indeed, the electoral structure of Congress, where short-termed House members represent small constituencies, encourages a localist bias in legislation.)[43]

The Eisenhower administration brought several prophylactic prosecutions under revised section 7, and the Warren Court followed the FTC and the Department of Justice in deploying procompetition justifications to regulate market concentration. In *Brown Shoe Co. v. United States* (1962), the first Celler-Kefauver Act case to reach the Supreme Court, the Court unanimously upheld the Department of Justice's challenge to the merger of the nation's third- and eighth-largest sellers of shoes. Chief Justice Earl Warren's opinion was a classic statement of an anticoncentration theory of antitrust: "Their [the shoe companies'] expansion is not rendered unlawful by the mere fact that small independent stores may be adversely affected. It is competition, not competitors, which the Act protects. But we cannot fail to recognize Congress's desire to promote competition through the protection of viable, small, locally owned businesses. Congress appreciated that higher costs and prices might result from maintenance

of fragmented industries and markets. It resolved those competing considerations in favor of decentralization. We must give effect to that decision." Just as
gung-ho were the Kennedy administration's solicitor general Archibald Cox and
assistant attorney general Lee Loevinger (1961–63), whose brief laid much of the
groundwork for Warren's *Brown Shoe* opinion. Indeed, Loevinger went even
further when he was appointed to head the Antitrust Division: "[T]he problems
with which the antitrust laws are concerned—the problems of distribution of
power within society—are second only to the questions of survival in the face of
threat of nuclear weapons in importance for our generation."[44]

Whatever the motivation, the revival (or survival) of an anticoncentration philosophy was, we repeat, rationalized in economics-based terms more than it had
been earlier in the century. Even an efficient big company will be tempted to
behave noncompetitively and in ways that will be hard to regulate—so the argument was that such tendencies should be thwarted by a preemptive antitrust rule.
Indeed, the Great Society's assistant attorney general for antitrust Donald Turner
(1965–68) justified aggressive enforcement of strong antitrust norms largely in
economic terms. Turner argued that concentrated industries were inherently anticompetitive and that the best policy for the Sherman Act was "protection of
competitive processes by limiting market power." In another prosecution initiated during the Eisenhower administration, *United States v. Von's Grocery Co.*
(1966), Turner and his assistant Richard Posner defended the department's effort
to prevent a grocery store merger that would occupy 7.5 percent of a local market
that had shown increasing concentration. That there was no persuasive economic justification for the Von's Grocery prosecution bothered Turner and Posner a bit but did not seem to bother the Warren Court, which summed up the
purpose of antitrust laws as "prevent[ing] economic concentration in the American economy by keeping a large number of small competitors in business." Implementing Turner's philosophy and the recommendations of the White House
Task Force on Antitrust Policy, the Department of Justice in 1968 issued Merger
Guidelines that codified rules seeking to prevent market concentration even
when particular mergers demonstrated overall economies of scale. Underlining
this anticoncentration philosophy, Attorney General Ramsey Clark filed a
section 2 Sherman Act prosecution against IBM (whose dominant market position was probably the result of technological superiority and economies of scale)
on the last day of the Johnson administration.[45]

While the Department of Justice was enforcing the Celler-Kefauver Act to
head off market concentrations, it and private litigants were also enforcing section 1 of the Sherman Act with renewed vigor. One important target was vertical
restraints, whereby a manufacturer would impose restrictions on downstream
distributors, franchisees, or retailers. In *Dr. Miles Medical Co. v. John D. Park &*

Sons Co. (1911), the Supreme Court had held that seller imposition of minimum resale prices was *per se* illegal under section 1, for the same reason horizontal price fixing among competitors was illegal (*Trans-Missouri*). In the 1960s, the department took the position that many vertical restrictions were presumptively illegal, as unfair impositions on competitive choices available for retailers. As it had in *Von's Grocery*, the Warren Court pressed the point further, holding in *United States v. Arnold, Schwinn & Co.* (1967), that vertical restrictions on goods sold to retailers or franchisees were *per se* illegal under section 1. (Also as in *Von's Grocery*, Richard Posner argued the government's successful appeal but took a more moderate approach to vertical restraints than the Court ultimately took.)[46]

THE MODERN TRANSFORMATION OF THE SHERMAN ACT: A REPUBLIC OF CONSUMERS

Let us return to the government's prosecution of the cast iron pipe cartel in *Addyston Pipe*. Exactly what was wrong with the cartel's price fixing? One focus of criticism is that the cartel drove Manion & Company, a worthy enterprise, out of business by its interference with its contractual relations with the Radford firm. The cartel was using its collective power to coerce and bully other firms, and that was not fair, especially to small businesses. By this understanding, the Sherman Act should protect competitors and prevent big companies from using their market power to ruin small businesses. Another focus of criticism is that the cartel was creating economic inefficiencies. Because its prices were higher than those determined by ordinary supply and demand, the cartel was accruing monopoly profits for its own members and was misallocating resources. By this understanding, the Sherman Act should protect the efficient operation of the market and thereby increase overall social welfare. A variation of this understanding is that the Sherman Act should protect only *consumer* welfare (Manion & Company was actually harmed as a consumer of cast iron pipe). Thus, even if overall social wealth were enhanced by a business practice, it could be vulnerable if none of the wealth increase went to consumers.

Although these are competing understandings of the Sherman Act's purpose, the congressional deliberations over the antitrust bill in 1890 did not recognize such a tension, nor did deliberations preceding the Clayton or Celler-Kefauver Act. Nor was the tension recognized in antitrust prosecutions even as late as the 1960s. In most of the early prosecutions, such as *Addyston Pipe*, these three purposes were probably not opposed. The pipe cartel was harmful to small business competitors, to consumers, and to overall social welfare. An early exception was *Northern Securities*, where the Justice Department and the Court found a Sherman Act monopoly without any evidence that the defendants were engaged in inefficient predatory activities; the Alcoa and Brown Shoe prosecutions were subsequent examples. Concentration of power and the danger of abuse were sufficient in those cases. As was the case with the labor injunction, the Supreme Court pressed this idea harder than the other branches did—and in ways that generated withering academic critique. The primary critique was economic in nature, which was responsive to the primarily economics-based justifications for antitrust prosecutions during the New Deal and in the Celler-Kefauver Act deliberations.[47]

Economics-minded theorists associated with the University of Chicago argued that the purpose of the Sherman Act was overall (society-wide) wealth maximization and that practices contributing positively to society's wealth should be *per se* legal under the rule of reason, even if they hurt small business competitors and produced more concentrated markets. This economic understanding of social welfare as wealth maximization is different from the Progressive Era's and the New Deal's understanding of social welfare. The progressives who demanded the Sherman Act saw social welfare in dynamic terms, with a strong emphasis on preserving room for individual initiative and minimizing concentrated power, which they saw as oppositional. The New Deal reformers largely abandoned the civic republican rhetoric of the earlier antitrust movement but preserved its skepticism of concentrated corporate power, which they often expressed in economics-based analysis along the lines suggested by economists Adolf Berle and Gardiner Means. Most of the new Chicago School economists viewed social welfare in materialist terms and simply excluded the dynamic features of social welfare that the New Dealers valued. Their price-theory approach to economics influenced the Department of Justice and the Supreme Court after 1969.

The Department of Justice and the Court generally have not followed those Chicago School theorists who believe that most concerted business practices should be *per se* legal and have, instead, followed more moderate economic theorists associated with Harvard, Georgetown, and Yale. With this important caveat, we maintain that the Chicago School's focus on material wealth maximization as the only goal of the Sherman Act has been influential—although administrative constitutionalism has short-handed (or, as we think, beneficently altered) that articulation as maximizing consumer welfare. Through the lens of our theory, a statute that began as a reflection of our republic of small competitors has been transformed into a statute reflecting a republic of consumers. This newer economics-based understanding has revolutionized the field of antitrust in the past generation, through an aggressive administrative constitutionalism and judicial embrace of it. We close this chapter with the normative quandary: Has the administrative-judicial transformation of the Sherman Act been legitimate?[48]

THE ECONOMISTS' PRINCIPLE: MARKET EFFICIENCY AND CONSUMER WELFARE

At the same time the Warren Court was expansively interpreting the Sherman, Clayton, and Celler-Kefauver Acts, Professor Aaron Director was developing a critique of the Sherman Act's original goal and its implementation. An economist who was the brother-in-law of future Nobel laureate Milton Friedman, Director was appointed to the faculty of the University of Chicago School of Law in 1946, where he participated in the antitrust course taught by Professor and later Dean Edward Levi. Director's contribution to the course was to criticize Supreme Court opinions that misunderstood how markets work. In *Brown Shoe*, for example, he would have criticized the Court for voiding a merger that revealed no dampening effect on the market and that probably yielded economies of scale and lower prices for consumers. (Director was skeptical of the view adopted by Congress in the Celler-Kefavuer Act, that increasing market concentration tended to create noncompetitive markets.) Even if one accepted, as Director would not, that the antitrust laws sought to protect small businesses, one might ask whether a vigorous antimerger policy would actually help small businesses. A consequence of such a policy would be to undermine the ability of small businesses to sell their assets to larger competitors—an ability that helps many a small business get started. So even under the (economically questionable) normative assumptions of the Celler-Kefauver Act, the Department of Justice's and the FTC's antimerger policy in the 1950s and 1960s was probably too strong.[49]

Director also deployed price theory, Chicago School–style, to argue that many practices disapproved by agencies and judges as *anti*competitive were sometimes or even typically *pro*competitive. The antitrust laws forbade monopolization and price fixing, because these practices enabled firms to earn monopoly profits, which generated deadweight losses to society. But Director denied that vertical restraints, also disapproved by the antitrust precedents, were in any material way similar. While vertical restraints tended to suppress intrabrand competition among retailers or franchisees selling the same product, they also tended to enhance interbrand competition among producers. Typically, Director argued, the procompetitive effects of vertical restraints, including price controls (*Dr. Miles*) as well as territorial limitations (*Schwinn*), outweighed the anticompetitive effects. Certainly, the *per se* rules developed by the Supreme Court were flat wrong. Director and his followers tended to believe that vertical restraints should be *per se* legal, rather than illegal, a stance at odds with the views of other economic theorists.[50]

Professor Director's approach to antitrust policy did not rest upon a deeply considered normative foundation. Like a good market economist, he assumed that the policy goal should be wealth maximization through the enforcement of efficiency-based rules. Although he considered noneconomic theories, such as the civic republican and some anticoncentration theories, a poor basis for public policy, he had no thoroughly considered theory beyond simple welfare economics. Moreover, his descriptive theory rested upon strong assumptions of relative ease of market entry, rationality in corporate pricing, and the like, that are subject to dispute. For example, Director's price theory tended to find efficiency justifications for a broad range of collaborative practices that other theorists believed had anticompetitive potential. Professor Bork has argued from Director's premises that predatory pricing ought to be per se legal under the Sherman Act, while Professors Philip Areeda and Donald Turner maintained that such pricing ought typically be illegal. The latter view still prevails among sophisticated antitrust scholars and officials.[51]

Notwithstanding these criticisms, Director's overall points were powerful: the Sherman Act should advance the material wealth of society; efficient markets maximize material wealth; therefore, antitrust enforcement should target only business practices that cut against market efficiency, and those practices should be determined and tested by empirical examination rather than sociopolitical theorizing. Director persuaded Professor Edward Levi, a staunch legalist, that bushels of antitrust decisions (*statutory* precedents, which Levi had said in print can almost *never* be overruled) were wrong and should be discarded. Perhaps his first important convert was Robert Bork, a 1951 graduate of the University of Chicago Law School who taught antitrust at the Yale Law School (1962–72 and 1977–81) and published a series of articles and books applying and defending Director's theory. A later convert was former regulatory front man Richard Posner, who joined the Chicago faculty in 1969 and translated Director's ideas into antitrust articles, a casebook, and a monograph on the application of Chicago School economics to antitrust cases and doctrines. Between 1966 and 1976, Professors Bork and Posner published up a storm, applying Director's largely unpublished ideas to criticize what they all considered flabby antitrust theory and excessive enforcement against efficient or neutral mergers and business practices. Other economists not associated with the Chicago School, such as William Baumol and Robert Willig, developed their own theories of virtual competition that supported the same deregulatory agenda as the Chicago School price theories.[52]

Notwithstanding these academic critiques, it was not clear that decades of longstanding agency enforcement and Supreme Court statutory precedents would fall under their assault. Indeed, the constitutional history of antitrust suggested an uphill battle for the critics. The amalgam of sociopolitical and economic purposes was apparently what Congress had in mind when it adopted the Sherman Act in 1890 and is consistent with the Clayton and Celler-Kefauver Acts. By 1969, this norm had been the consensus view of candidates in presidential elections since 1912, had been touted by the FTC and the Department of Justice in dozens of successful prosecutions and hundreds of consent decrees, and enjoyed *stare decisis* support from *Dr. Miles, Brown Shoe,* and other Supreme Court precedents. (In 1972, the Supreme Court ruled that erroneous Sherman Act precedents enjoy *superstrong stare decisis* effect, and the proper forum for correcting such errors is Congress, not the Court. As the Celler-Kefauver Act's history suggests, Congress's openness to civic republican arguments, or populist antagonism toward big businesses, rendered it unlikely to override expansive antitrust precedents.) Yet within fifteen years the old anti-concentration approach had been shattered and a new economics-based paradigm had emerged within the corridors of government; within thirty years, the new approach had swept the executive and judicial branches, and silenced the legislative branch on matters of antitrust policy.[53]

THE SIMPLIFIED STATUTORY PURPOSE: MAXIMIZING CONSUMER WELFARE

For two generations after World War II, the United States enjoyed economic prosperity unparalleled in human history. As we have seen in previous chapters, that prosperity was shared by women as well as men, blacks as well as whites, and middle-class as well as rich Americans. This flourishing yielded a culture of individual choice in matters of employment, voting, sexual behaviors, abortion, divorce, retirement, and investment. In the *consumerist constitution* that we now enjoy, the legitimacy of the state is ultimately based upon its ability to create conditions for individual choice and flourishing. In such a culture, the constitution of the market is naturally concerned, primarily (or perhaps exclusively), with maximizing consumer welfare. Among the prophets of this constitution are the economists who are the heirs to Milton Friedman, perhaps the key thinker in the twentieth century's constitution of public finance. In a world of scarcity as well as opportunity, the economist tells us, sometimes accurately, what policies will work and what will produce disasters. In the 1940s through 1960s, economists warned policymakers of the dangers of industry concentration; in the late 1960s and 1970s, newer economic thought criticized the market concentration literature as resting upon poor logic and insufficient evidence. Economists, many of them associated with the University of Chicago, deployed price theory to question the antitrust rules laid down by the Supreme Court, usually at the behest of the FTC and the Department of Justice. At some point, these critiques were bound to influence the evolution of the Sherman Act.

That point came rather quickly after the election of Richard Nixon as president in 1968. The shift from the Great Society to the Nixon era was more than a partisan change. More deeply, the shift was from a vision of public policy as concerned with ex post fairness and political balance, to a more consumerist politics focusing on ex ante efficiency. American politics after World War II had assumed an expanding pie, a luxury that policymakers exploited to engage in all sorts of governmental experiments, some of them successes (civil and voting rights laws, Medicare), some of them failures (wars against poverty and the Viet Cong). The American pie's expansion was more uneven in the late 1960s and even shrank at various points in the 1970s—rendering We the People increasingly receptive to the complaint that government regulatory policies usually created distortions and monopolies impeding economic growth. (In the same period, public choice theorists argued to a receptive academic audience that government programs were typically the distribution of rents to special interests and were not public regarding.) The freshly vocal "Silent Majority" rewarded public officials who promised deregulation that would allow the economy to work without as much deadweight loss and to yield lower prices and more jobs. Thus, starting with the 1968 election (scarcity-conscious Richard Nixon over über-liberal Hubert Humphrey), the American people consistently elected as presidents men who assumed that the pie was not expanding and had to be apportioned in an efficient rather than interest-group accommodating way.

In antitrust law, the Nixon-Ford Department of Justice embraced an efficient markets approach to antitrust enforcement under Assistant Attorneys General Richard McLaren (1969–72), Thomas Kauper (1972–76), and Donald Baker (1976–77), as well as President Ford's attorney general Edward Levi (Director's coteacher). Antitrust experts intimately familiar with economists' criticisms of pre-1969 antitrust policy, Kauper and Baker publicly endorsed the view that the antitrust laws should only have an economic purpose, that the economic purpose should be maximization of consumer welfare, that antitrust enforcement could contribute to consumer welfare by challenging only business practices (like price fixing) or structures (monopoly) that were inefficient, and that most mergers and many vertical restraints were procompetitive and did not meet efficiency standards for appropriate challenge. Agreeing with these principles, Kauper and Levi further entrenched the role of economists in antitrust decision making. Although Aaron Director's specific analyses were not always advanced, his general philosophy was ascendant. During this period, economists of all sorts were invigorating the FTC with new consumer-protection energy and were involved on both sides of the antitrust cases against AT&T.[54]

Economic efficiency and consumer welfare were important antitrust goals before 1969, and the Department of Justice did not entirely abandon the anti-concentration norm after 1969. But there was a shift in departmental thinking during the Nixon-Ford administration, and it continued during the tenure of President Jimmy Carter (1977–81). Although he was a moderately liberal Democrat, Carter was (like Nixon) elected on a platform of shrinking the role of government to reduce waste and inefficiencies. Indeed, the Carter administration did accomplish some serious deregulation, with bipartisan support, in the Airline Deregulation Act of 1978. Assistant Attorney General John Shenefield (1977–80) continued the Antitrust Division's focus on consumer welfare and its skepticism toward many of the Warren Court's precedents.[55]

In short, regardless of the political party in power, the philosophy undergirding the federal guarantee of a competitive market shifted during the 1970s. Administrative constitutionalism in the early twentieth century had credited the Sherman Act's original populist focus on protecting small businesses against big competitors. Abandoning the localism of the original statute, the New Deal (after 1937) had focused on removing bottlenecks from America's national market and sought to check large-scale corporate power with countervailing centers in government and unions; their application of antitrust law was informed and supported by a wide array of economists who maintained that predatory practices were more likely in concentrated industries, to the detriment of the operation of an efficient competitive market. In the new consumerist era, where price theory economists displaced political thinkers and economic structuralists as key to antitrust policy, the prevailing administrative constitutionalism viewed government policy as often part of the bottleneck, and approached business concentration less skeptically. This was the new philosophy. It came from academic economists, public intellectuals, and voters' intuitions—and it took root in the Department of Justice, from which its ideas spread to the other branches.

Notwithstanding precedent supporting the earlier regimes, the Supreme Court was ready to follow the department's lead. Another effect of Nixon's election was an immediate transformation of the Court, as it became populated with justices who were receptive to the economic perspective. By 1975, five or six of the nine justices were business-friendly appointees of Republican presidents. Although none had formal training in economics, you did not need that to understand the economic arguments, which had been digested and clearly spelled out for legal audiences by Department of Justice officials, as well as by Professors Bork and Posner. All you needed was sympathy with the assumption of scarcity, an ability to understand business practices and some basic price theory, and a willingness to revise the law. The reconstituted Court was well qualified along all these dimensions, and there was yet another reason for its members to follow the department's lead. The economic approach maximizing consumer welfare was more lawlike than the hybrid approach combining an anticoncentration political norm with an economic efficiency norm. How can a judge balance those sometimes competing norms? The New Deal and Warren Courts could do so by following the Department of Justice's leads, but once the department deemphasized the anticoncentration norm, how could a judge continue that essentially political balancing act? Reasoning from precedent was not always easy to do, especially if the Department of Justice was telling the judge that precedent was grounded upon erroneous premises and was itself undermining the most defensible goal of the statute, namely, consumer welfare. In this manner, administrative constitutionalism exercised a powerful influence on the branch of government that before 1969 had been the least critical booster of the anticoncentration norm. And presidential elections made a difference: if liberal Democrat Hubert Humphrey had won the presidency in 1968, the justices appointed after 1969 would not have been so receptive to the deregulatory arguments. The fact that Nixon's four justices were business-friendly Republicans made a world of difference as to what kind of "economic" theory would receive serious consideration within the Court. We should be clear: after 1969, there was going to have to be some rethinking of the Court's precedents, some of which were indefensible from most economic perspectives. Precisely what branch of economic theory would drive the rethinking was up for grabs. Some of the most conservative justices have been receptive to Chicago School orthodoxy, probably for political reasons, but the median justice (like the Department of Justice itself) has been more pluralist.

Judicial confirmation of the new administrative constitutionalism arrived in *Continental T.V., Inc. v. GTE Sylvania, Inc.* (1977). In a private treble damages action (and therefore not a federal prosecution), Justice Lewis Powell, one of the nation's preeminent corporate lawyers before his appointment, wrote for six Republican appointees to overrule the *Schwinn per se* rule against territorial restrictions on franchise operators where the distribution was by sale rather than consignment. Quoting and relying on an article by just-retired Assistant Attorney General Baker, Powell described the *Schwinn* sale-consignment distinction as "'an exercise in barren formalism' that is 'artificial and unresponsive to the competitive needs of the real world.'" Drawing from the consensus of economists, the Court majority concluded that manufacturer restrictions on dealer or franchisee territories, however carried out, can be efficient mechanisms for interbrand competition and therefore cannot rationally be subjected to a rule of *per se* illegality, as *Schwinn* held. Whatever the ultimate purpose of the Sherman Act—either ensuring an efficient market or protecting small businesses against predatory practices—a *per se* rule against vertical restraints on territory was not consistent with either economic theory or the available evidence about how businesses actually worked. On the other hand, Justice Powell did not follow the position taken by some Chicago School thinkers (such as Bork and Posner) that vertical restraints should be *per se* legal; instead, he left the legality of such practices to the rule of reason, precisely as the Department of Justice officials had opined.[56]

The *GTE Sylvania* Court did not directly address the question of the Sherman Act's purpose, but that issue came to the Court two years later in a case involving antitrust standing. The issue in *Reiter v. Sonotone* (1979) was whether consumers who had paid higher prices because of anticompetitive practices had standing to sue on the ground that they had been deprived of "business or property" under section 4 of the Clayton Act. In this case, an economic approach to the statute was plaintiff friendly, and the Carter administration's assistant attorney general Shenefield filed an *amicus* brief arguing that consumers ought to have standing to sue. (The brief was substantially written by Deputy Solicitor General Frank Easterbrook, a Chicago Law School graduate and protégé of Professor Posner. Within the administration, the brief also found support in the FTC, whose chair Michael Pertschuk [1977–81] was strongly proconsumer.) The government's reasoning was that section 4 should not be read to undermine the "primary purpose" of the Sherman Act (reaffirmed in the Clayton Act), which was "consumer protection." The Supreme Court agreed, with no dissent. Chief Justice Warren Burger's opinion followed Shenefield and Easterbrook's reasoning in every respect, including its closing quotation from Professor Bork's treatise, which said that "consumer welfare" was the purpose of the Sherman Act. The standing issue did not require the Court to address the premise of the Warren Court merger precedents, that the Sherman Act had at least two purposes, namely, consumer welfare and protection of small businesses. But the *Reiter* precept has, thus far, stood the test of time, as the Court repeatedly invokes consumer welfare—not wealth maximization or protection of competitors—as the sole purpose of the Sherman Act.[57]

Former governor Ronald Reagan ran for president on an unequivocal get-government-out-of-the-way platform and decisively won the 1980 election. Consistent with his platform, President Reagan's Justice Department took a deregulatory economic approach to antitrust issues. Reagan's first assistant attorney general for the Antitrust Division was William F. Baxter Jr. (1981–83), a Stanford Law School antitrust professor who had in the 1970s been converted to an eclectic (i.e., not rigidly Chicago School) economic analysis. Although

Baxter was assistant attorney general for less than three years, he transformed the Antitrust Division into an activist champion of a moderately deregulatory economic understanding of antitrust policy. Like Thurman Arnold, William Baxter is exemplary of the administrative constitutionalism we have been exploring in this book. His innovative tenure illustrates that constitutionalism can be deregulatory as well as regulatory, often (and, we think, typically) speaks to fundamental public commitments on which the Constitution is silent, and exercises normative power through administrators' ability to mobilize a political constituency *and* to persuade skeptics inside and outside of government that their approach is superior to alternatives, including those enshrined in previous administrative and even judicial interpretations. The Baxterian revolution also illustrates how administrative constitutionalism works differently in different areas of law, depending on the normative politics, the institutional structures, and other factors that vary from area to area. In the distinctive realm of antitrust law, policy was enforced through a triadic structure of government prosecutions and guidances, private lawsuits, and judicial decisions. William Baxter understood all this and was administratively innovative in advancing his constitutional vision.

First, Baxter rethought the department's own prosecutions. He insisted that economists be consulted, from the beginning, as to every move the Antitrust Division made. He garnered a great deal of publicity and controversy for withdrawing the department's longstanding prosecution of IBM for predatory practices and for pressing AT&T to divest itself of the Bell operating companies. Baxter's view was that the Johnson administration's IBM prosecution reflected the outmoded philosophy that concentration was *per se* bad and penalized a firm whose outstanding growth had by his lights been the result of efficient practices and technological innovations, not predatory practices. While Baxter took heat from some liberals for letting IBM off the antitrust hook, some conservatives were critical of his insistence on breaking up AT&T, which Baxter thought extended its regulatory monopoly to enterprises that ought to be kept open to competition (what he dubbed the "Bell doctrine"). If his goal was to establish antitrust policy on a sound and relatively nonideological footing, it was a good thing that Baxter took heat from both sides for his most aggressive stances.[58]

Albeit accompanied by less publicity than the IBM and AT&T actions, Baxter's more important move was to revise the Department of Justice's 1968 Merger Guidelines. Both reflecting and revising the department's post-1968 enforcement approach, the 1982 Merger Guidelines explicitly recognized that most mergers do not threaten competition and, instead, benefit consumers by yielding economies of scale that lower prices. Although the revised Merger Guidelines did not abandon the notion that, at some point, market concentration generated an unacceptable risk of anticompetitive practices, the 1982 revision (further refined in 1984 and expanded thereafter) greatly cut back on the mergers that would be subject to challenge through various mechanisms, including (a) an expanded understanding of the relevant "market," to include potentially competing products; (b) explicit consideration of the possibility of market entry from foreign as well as domestic firms; and (c) explicit emphasis on efficiencies flowing from a merger that could trump potential anticompetitive effects. "While challenging competitively harmful mergers, the Department of Justice seeks to avoid unnecessary interference with that larger universe of mergers that are either competitively beneficial or neutral." If they fell within the guidelines' allowance, businesses would have some confidence that their mergers would not violate the antitrust laws, because the Department of Justice would not go after them, and courts would probably defer to the department in private lawsuits.[59]

Finally, Assistant Attorney General Baxter greatly expanded the department's willingness to file *amicus* briefs to persuade courts to throw over other precedents reflecting a regulatory regime considered obsolete by economists. Baxter was persuaded that many of the Supreme Court's remaining *per se* rules were vulnerable for the same reasons *GTE* had invoked to overrule *Schwinn*. In 1982, for example, the Department filed an *amicus* brief in *Monsanto Co. v. Spray-Rite Service Corp.* (1984), a private Sherman Act suit, asking the Supreme Court to overrule *Dr. Miles*, until then a virtually sacrosanct precedent barring producers or franchisers from setting minimum prices by their retailers or franchisees. The Supreme Court dodged the issue of overruling *Dr. Miles* by narrowly construing its *per se* rule—and Congress responded by barring the department from using appropriated funds to challenge *Dr. Miles*'s rule against resale price maintenance in appropriations measures enacted in 1983, 1985, 1986, and 1987. As regards the politics of antitrust law, it cannot be surprising that Congress, especially the localist House of Representatives, would be more protective of small businesses than the Reagan era Department of Justice or the Burger and Rehnquist Courts, which operated from a more national and economics-oriented baseline.[60]

Baxter's successors in the Antitrust Division hewed to his agenda, though the George H. W. Bush administration publicly backed away from the campaign to overrule or narrow *Dr. Miles*. Interestingly, the Clinton administration's assistant attorneys general Anne Bingaman (1993–96) and Joel Klein (1997–2000) revived that campaign and were joined by the FTC and its general counsel Stephen Calkins (1996–97). They had their opportunity in a case involving a producer contract imposing maximum price limitations on dealers. Writing for the Seventh Circuit, Chief Judge Posner (Director's apostle who had been named to the federal bench by President Reagan) upheld liability because it was required by a post-*Schwinn* Warren Court precedent but strongly urged the Supreme Court to reconsider that precedent for standard economic reasons. The FTC and the Department of Justice supported Posner's suggestion, and the Supreme Court unanimously agreed in *State Oil Co. v. Khan* (1997). Closely following the consensus of economists and the path charted by the Bork and Posner publications (as well as Posner's lower court opinion), the Court overruled the earlier precedent for essentially the same reasons it had overruled *Schwinn*. The main innovation, borrowed from the government's brief, was the Court's announcement that economically misguided Sherman Act decisions were *not* entitled to the ordinary superstrong presumption of correctness accorded statutory precedents, as the Court had repeatedly held, because the Act was a "common law statute." Hence, the Court should feel free to reconsider decisions that rested on premises now considered erroneous. This notion freed the Court from the original expectations of the Congresses that adopted the Sherman Act and its amendments, as well as generations of pre-1969 Supreme Court decisions.[61]

The George W. Bush Department of Justice pursued the campaign against *Dr. Miles*. Notwithstanding *GTE* and *Khan*, it was not clear that the Court would go along, nor was overruling *Dr. Miles* necessary to entrench an economic approach to the competition principle. The minimum resale price maintenance covered by *Dr. Miles's per se* rule looks much more like horizontal price fixing that is concededly illegal; as a matter of antitrust economics, it is more likely to be inefficient. As a matter of law, *Dr. Miles* was an older and more foundational precedent than *Schwinn* and the others and had, arguably, been ratified by Congress in the appropriations measures of the 1980s and in the Consumer Goods Pricing Act of 1975. On the other hand, the leading Chicago School thinkers—Robert Bork, Richard Posner, and Frank Easterbrook (who joined Posner on the Seventh Circuit in 1983)—believed that minimum resale price maintenance was often efficient and therefore that *Dr. Miles* had to go. Following their lead, the FTC and Department of Justice persuaded five justices to overrule *Dr. Miles* in *Leegin Creative Leather Products v. PSKS, Inc.* (2007). The most learned justice on theories of antitrust economics, Justice Breyer, wrote a dissenting opinion, accepting the arguments of Clinton-era FTC chair Robert Pitofsky (1995–2001) that there was strong empirical as well as theoretical evidence that resale price maintenance was bad for consumers. It is significant that Breyer's dissent and Pitofsky's analysis accepted the consumer welfare purpose for the Sherman Act, defended *Dr. Miles* within the premises of economics, and ignored the longstanding anticoncentration purpose of the antitrust laws. Breyer was mildly critical of the Court's common law statute evasion of *stare decisis* and, more strenuously, argued that

Table 5. Supreme Court antitrust decisions, 1967–2007

Time period	Sup. Ct. antitrust decisions	% decisions favoring defendants	% decisions citing econ. analysis	% DOJ briefs supporting defendants	% DOJ def. briefs followed by Sup. Ct.
1967–1976	42	34.2% (14/41)	26.2% (11/42)	11.6% (3/26)	00.0% (0/3)
1977–1991	54	44.4% (24/54)	64.8% (35/54)	34.2% (13/38)	84.6% (11/13)
1992–2007	20	90.0% (18/20)	80.0% (16/20)	72.2% (13/18)	92.3% (12/13)

Source: Leah Brannan and (former assistant attorney general for antitrust) Douglas H. Ginsburg, "Antitrust Decisions of the U.S. Supreme Court, 1967–2007," *Competition Policy International* 3(2007): 3, 14–15 (figure 1).

the Court ought not overrule a precedent that found so much continuing support in Congress.[62]

Table 5 demonstrates that the Court's decision in *Leegin* is representative of a broader trend in antitrust law during the past forty years: both the Department of Justice and the Supreme Court have increasingly applied economic reasoning to shift burdens away from defendants in antitrust cases, mainly by abandoning *per se* rules that made plaintiffs' proof burdens easy and by raising the bar for application of the rule of reason in some instances. Because of selection biases in the cases heard by the Court, this evidence neither establishes nor refutes a causal link between the department's increasingly economics-based and prodefendant *amicus* practice and the Court's similar trend. Nonetheless, the historical process we have traced here indicates that the department's economics-saturated *amicus* practice has at least facilitated the Court's dramatic curtailment of antitrust doctrine. Another trend is the decline in judicial partisanship in antitrust cases, a point that advocates of an economic approach take as a marker of great rule-of-law success for their theory. Unlike *Leegin*, few of the decisions are contentious 5–4 splits; since 1992, a majority of the prodefendant, economics-based decisions have been *unanimous*. The Baxterian revolution in antitrust law extends beyond enforcement to a redefinition of antitrust baselines as well as doctrine.[63]

THE LEGITIMACY OF THE BAXTERIAN REVOLUTION IN ANTITRUST LAW?

The revolution in Sherman Act jurisprudence between 1969 and the present is an example of the learning curve inherent in administrative constitutionalism.

That is, agency officials have adapted an old statute's policy in light of modern theory and empirical knowledge about the subject matter (the operation of the market) covered by the statute. We have called this the "Baxterian revolution" in antitrust law, after the assistant attorney general who was the most influential figure, but the revolution neither began with Baxter nor ended with his tenure. Unlike the administrative constitutionalism underlying the Voting Rights Act, there was no Large "C" Constitutional feature to the agency's reasoning, except at the most general level (Baxter would surely have agreed with the banal notion that his policy vision was consistent with the Preamble's directive that Constitutional government support the "general Welfare"). The Department of Justice's administrative constitutionalism was, moreover, connected with a larger economics-driven vision of government generally. That is, market regulation could often hurt the (consumer) interests the statute was designed to advance. The agency advanced this administrative vision to judges through *amicus* briefs, to lawyers through law review articles, to economists through empirical studies and policy papers, and to the general public through presidential jawboning that the American consumer paid lower prices because government policy was protecting, but not overprotecting, the free market.

From our point of view, the big normative question has been whether an important constitutional policy has been dramatically transformed with adequate *public deliberation*. Recall that public deliberation has dual virtues: grounding public policy in an accurate factual and theoretical basis and for sound reasons, as well as providing legitimacy for important decisions. Many experts believe the Baxterian revolution meets the substantive test for public deliberation: its precepts have been well informed, grounded in factually based and theoretically robust approaches to the problem of market abuses, and workable for both businesses and lower level judges and other officials. Many experts agree with Baxter's pure focus on consumer welfare determined by economic analysis but dissent from Baxterian economics as excessively deregulatory; most experts lament the collapse of antitrust enforcement during the Bush-Cheney administration (2001–09) in particular. We place these questions to one side and, instead, address the broader issue: Has the Baxterian revolution in antitrust norms been legitimate?

There are three different kinds of defenses of the legal dynamism entailed in the Baxterian revolution. The first defense is Judge Bork's argument that the original purpose of the Sherman Act was efficiency and wealth maximization, and that this purpose requires administrators and judges to use the best and most rigorous economic analysis. This is a bad defense. For starters, it is unrealistic to think that administrative constitutionalism can possibly remain true to an original statutory vision; in our view, such fidelity neither makes sense nor is achievable. In any event, Bork's argument is wrong on the facts. The original purpose of the Sherman Act cannot fairly be considered pure wealth maximi-zation or even consumer welfare, simpliciter. Senator Sherman's public purpose was to protect competitors as well as consumers, and his ultimate goal was more civic republican than economic (much less economic as understood by Bill Baxter). "The point for us to consider is whether, on the whole, it is safe in this country to leave the production of property, the transportation of our whole country, to depend upon the will of a few men sitting at their council board in the city of New York." (No! said Senator Sherman.) Concentration of economic power would inevitably lead to concentration of political power, Sherman feared. "If the concentrated powers of this combination are entrusted to a single man, it is a kingly prerogative, inconsistent with our form of government, and should be subject to the strong resistance of the State and national authorities." Robert Lande's detailed examination of the statute's legislative background and deliberations demonstrates that Senator Sherman's civic republican under-standing was widely held in Congress.[64]

Subsequent antitrust statutes, specifying the broad commands instinct in the Sherman Act, were likewise grounded on this justification, that a vice of trusts and monopolies is their tendency to undermine democracy by concentrating political power. Thus, the Clayton Act prohibited particular practices, such as interlocking directorates, that Congress believed contributed to the concentra-tion of political as well as economic power; the FTC Act created an administra-tive mechanism to monitor precisely these kinds of power accumulations. Although the rhetoric was less strident, each of these statutes was adopted not only to head off redistribution of economic power but also to prevent concen-trations of political power. These fears remained just as prominent after World War II, when Congress adopted the Celler-Kefauver Act. Reflecting the New Deal, the 1950 act's public justification was the common good, expressed in economic terms. But intermixed with an economic justification was a political one, as expressed by Senator Kefauver himself: "I am not an alarmist, but the history of what has taken place in other nations where mergers and concentra-tions have placed economic control in the hands of very few people is too clear to pass over easily. A point is eventually reached, and we are rapidly reaching that point in this country, where the public steps in to take over when concentration and monopoly gain too much power. The taking over by the public through its government always follows one or two methods and has one or two political results. It either results in a Fascist state or the nationalization of industries and thereafter a Socialist or Communist state." Although the Warren Court has been savagely criticized for its skeptical attitude toward mergers, decisions like *Brown Shoe* are more faithful to legislative expectations than a Baxterian dispo-sition allowing the merger would have been.[65]

An original intent theory of antitrust makes no progress toward justifying the last generation of antitrust law and the administrative revolution epitomized by William Baxter. Defenders of the new regime ought to abandon Bork's original intent defense and concede that statutory interpretation is going to be, and ought to be, dynamic. One dynamic interpretation defense of the Baxterian revolution would run along the following lines: The Sherman Act was or has become a common law statute, where Congress essentially delegated updating authority to judges, who have exercised that authority to trim back the statute in cases where the economics literature does not support *per se* rules of illegality, for such rules would then create rather than eliminate economic inefficiencies. An Achilles' heel of this purposive defense is that it cannot cogently be tied to a real purpose with deep democratic legitimacy. Certainly, the original purpose of the Sherman Act was not simply to maximize consumer welfare, Baxter's aspiration. At best, it was a mix of economic and political goals—and subsequent statutes (the Clayton Act and the Celler-Kefauver Act) synthesized those goals, based on the presumption that concentration undermined the possibility of a fairly competitive market. To be sure, many economists now consider this presumption irrational and inconsistent with the empirical evidence. Other economists at Georgetown, Berkeley, and other schools have argued and shown that predatory conduct is more widespread and profitable than Chicago-style models have admitted.[66]

There is a larger point to be made, relevant to our overall theory of administrative constitutionalism. When Congress adopts an ambitious statute and delegates enforcement authority (as it must) to executive and judicial officers, Congress ought to expect a dynamic application of the statute—not only well beyond original congressional expectations but also in ways that subtly alter the original congressional purposes or balance of purposes. The Sherman Act illustrates this point dramatically: the original purposes were both civic republican (no concentrated power) *and* economic (consumer welfare); during the New Deal, the civic republican purpose was no longer tied to localism and more of the rhetoric was economic, though the economic rhetoric echoed an antimony toward concentrated power; in the past generation, the announced purpose has become exclusively economic, and understood in a way that is not nearly as concerned with concentrated business power.

More broadly, not only does the Baxterian interpretation reflect a different balance of purposes than the original authors of the Sherman Act had in mind, the Baxterian *constitutional* vision is also very different from Senator Sherman's or even Thurman Arnold's. Sherman's constitutional vision saw an economics of many localized markets, accommodated lots of small businesses (such as our friends who ran Manion & Company), and cast a bleary eye on market concentrations even in industries with large economies of scale. Baxter's constitutional vision saw an America where the market is not just national (the New Deal notion) but international, where the relentless logic of the marketplace means that small fry will be and ought to be run out of business or gobbled up by their bigger and more efficient competitors, and where business concentration is often a sign that things are working properly, especially in center industries with economies of scale. IBM and Microsoft would have dismayed Senator Sherman, might have been prosecuted by Thurman Arnold (who, recall, successfully pursued Alcoa), and were celebrated by Bill Baxter. This is a dramatic constitutional shift—as important to American law and society as the much-discussed "switch in time" when the Supreme Court allowed more room for Congress to define as well as regulate the national economy. Unlike the earlier Constitutional shift, which accommodated presidential and congressional demands, the recent constitutional shift has come in the teeth of congressional expectations. As political philosopher Henry Richardson has argued, the dynamics of agency implementation does raise legitimacy problems, and the Baxterian revolution poses the legitimacy question in a dramatic way. (That two of the most aggressive judicial exponents of the Baxterian revolution, Robert Bork and Antonin Scalia, are also the most aggressive critics of "judicial activism" contrary to original meaning renders this dynamism ironic as well.)[67]

We now insist upon the public deliberation requirement outlined in the previous chapter as the most plausible mechanism for legitimating dynamic agency interpretations. That requirement was met in the EEOC's dynamic application of Title VII and the Department of Justice's dynamic application of the Voting Rights Act. In both instances, (1) the agency's dynamism was a thoughtful and well-publicized response to unanticipated statutory problems, (2) was subject to judicial review under circumstances where the substantive grounds for the agency's dynamism were thoroughly examined, which then (3) triggered public lobbying and congressional statutory responses that supported and expanded upon the agency's initiative. The Baxterian revolution in antitrust law substantially meets the first two features of this deliberative model but not the third. Especially in light of the civic republican and some kind of preemptive economic support for an anticoncentration norm, and the fact that Congress has supported that norm in the major antitrust statutes, the deliberation that supports the Baxterian revolution strikes us as insufficient for such a policy shift in a democracy. Is there any way to escape this dilemma?

Antitrust scholar George Priest suggests a third response. The simplified purpose for the antitrust laws is now consumer welfare, which, he suggests, is a democratizing move consistent with the democratization of politics and economics that America celebrated in the twentieth century. If the experts are correct, that efficiency-based antitrust criteria will lower prices and enhance overall consumer welfare, then the Baxterian revolution might be legitimate under the premises of this book. Professor Priest's argument takes on greater cogency in the context of American history. Before William Baxter took the reins of authority in the Antitrust Division, another administrator had blazed the normative trail by making a cogent case for deregulation—Alfred E. Kahn, the Carter administration's head of the Civil Aeronautics Board (CAB). Formerly a professor of economics at Cornell University, Kahn argued not only for deregulation of airplane transportation prices and routes but even for the abolition of his own agency! This is administrative constitutionalism at its most radical, and Kahn's fact-based economics and his brilliant presentation persuaded liberal Democrats, such as Senator Edward Kennedy (whose counsel, Stephen Breyer, was key to Kahn's success), as well as conservative Republicans, such as Senator Orrin Hatch, to substantially deregulate air transportation prices and routes. Out-of-the-way localities raised hell, but on the whole consumers reacted warmly to the significantly lower prices that followed Kahn's coup. In the presidential election of 1980, Governor Reagan promised to get government off the backs of businesses, and the voters went with Reagan, who delivered on his promises with further deregulation of rail transportation and truck hauling, as well as the Baxterian revolution in antitrust.[68]

Smaller-government Republicans won three successive presidential elections, from 1980 to 1988, and when the Democrats finally prevailed in 1992 it was with a centrist candidate, Governor William Clinton, who favored efficient markets. Consistent with that stance, the Clinton administration was not only sympathetic to Baxter's consumerist approach to antitrust, it also proceeded with its own market-enhancing initiatives. The most notable was the president's sponsorship of the North American Free Trade Agreement (NAFTA), creating a much freer transnational market within North America and immediately inducing many industries to relocate outside the United States (as labor union opponents of NAFTA had predicted). In the presidential elections of 1992, 1996, 2000, 2004, and 2008 primary voters in both major parties rejected candidates such as Pat Buchanan and Mike Huckabee (Republican) and Bill Bradley and to some extent Hillary Clinton (Democratic) who retreated from the consumerist, promarket policies of the Reagan and Clinton administrations. Conversely, both major parties nominated candidates who supported the previous deregulation and favored even more, including deregulatory commitments that have come with America's membership in the World Trade Organization. In short, the American electorate has repeatedly opted for national leaders whose platforms support policies that sacrifice localism and antibigness for market efficiency and generally lower consumer prices.

On the other hand, neither Congress nor the electorate has specifically considered and accepted the premises of the Baxterian revolution: there has been neither a legislative validation such as the Clayton Act nor a validating election where antitrust policy itself was a major campaign issue. Also, no presidential or congressional candidate openly advocated abandoning antitrust enforcement of predatory practices or "excessive" market concentration, and so the Bush-Cheney administration's apparent abandonment of such enforcement remains illegitimate under Priest's defense of the Baxterian revolution. The election of 2008 reflected a skepticism of a laissez-faire approach to antitrust policy that characterized the Bush-Cheney administration. Assistant Attorney General Christine Varney, the Obama administration's antitrust chief, has initiated new enforcement priorities, including a more skeptical examination of mergers that significantly increase market concentration

Yet even if the Obama administration opens a new chapter in the history of the antitrust superstatutes, much of the Baxterian revolution has been internalized in the Department of Justice's approach to antitrust policy and in people's attitudes toward big market players. Thus, Americans have voted with their feet on the issue of localism versus lower prices, and the latter have swept the field. Lowe's and Home Depot have supplanted the local hardware store, and thousands of neighborhood five and dimes have given way to Walmart. Indeed, one might argue that legitimacy of this century's *market state* is now grounded in the ability of government to create conditions allowing optimal consumer choice. National security scholar Philip Bobbitt makes precisely this argument for the legitimacy of the modern market state such as ours.[69]

The foregoing arguments are surely the best reason to accept the legitimacy of a shift in antitrust policy toward a consumer welfare model and away from an abstract focus on market concentration. From the civic republican perspective of our project, what seems most significant is that an older positive right—enjoyed by inefficient competitors—has been extinguished and replaced by a new one that is enjoyed by We the Consumers. In effect, we have not replaced republican commitments, we have reshaped them by replacing one kind of positive right with another.[70]

If it sticks, as we think likely, does the Baxterian revolution mean that the Sherman Act is no longer a superstatute, an important foundation for America's constitution of the market? We think that the answer is no and that the Sherman Act remains important, especially in its broad constitutional role as a premise of the free national market. Martin Manion and Mathilda Fitzpatrick, the business partners victimized by the cast iron pipe cartel, would still have a claim for relief under federal antitrust law, even as narrowed in the last generation. To be sure, Manion & Company today would face different economic challenges, and might well be gobbled up by a larger company (for a lucrative price to Manion and Fitzpatrick, by the way), but what Chief Justice Hughes called the nation's "charter of freedom" for business associations has become an axiom underlying not only federal rules of the market but also those adopted in state contract statutes such as the UCC and through transnational agreements like NAFTA and the WTO.[71]

Part II

The Dynamics of Superstatutory Implementation and Entrenchment

A key feature of the statutory constitution is that non-Constitutional institutions and norms become *entrenched* in American political culture—not as strongly as the primary features of the U.S. Constitution, such as the bicameralism requirement for enactment of legislation, but more strongly than ordinary statutes and even some Constitutional rights. Thus, America's social safety net (chapter 4), its constitution of the family (chapter 5), and the green constitution (chapter 6) are not only fundamental to our society but also entail norms and commitments that are as entrenched in our society as most Constitutional rights—and more entrenched than such judge-announced Constitutional rights as the trimester framework for abortion rights in *Roe v. Wade* (1973), the precept of welfare payments as property in *Goldberg v. Kelly* (1970), and the liberty of contract right enforced in *Lochner v. New York* (1906).

The Constitution's model of entrenchment is the Article V process of deliberation and supermajority approval in Congress and among state legislatures. This is a big showdown understanding of entrenchment, and it has influenced Constitutionalism-outside-the-Court theories such as Bruce Ackerman's. Entrenchment can occur in this way, but we maintain that entrenchment more often occurs over a longer period of time, involves compromise and cooperation more than dramatic showdowns and conflict, and is more typically driven by legislative and agency deliberations rather than court decrees. Although the process of entrenchment typically involves showdowns, as when judges or interest groups challenge administrative constitutional initiatives, the showdowns tend to be a series of little ones rather than one big one. In short, political entrenchment usually comes through experimentation and feedback rather than big show-downs.

We use the Social Security Act of 1935 to develop some generalizations about the dynamics of entrenchment (chapter 4). Like the Civil Rights and Sherman Acts, the Social Security Act has become a successfully entrenched superstatute; its norm of federally guaranteed old-age insurance has stuck in our political culture more firmly than many Constitutional norms, such as those of the Contracts Clause or the Prohibition Amendment (both of which were officially buried a few years before the social security law was passed). Like those earlier superstatutes, however, the Social Security Act was not immediately internalized in the political culture; its entrenchment came through an arduous process of successful administration, statutory amendment, and bipartisan commissions. Consider a few generalizations about the process of entrenchment that are illustrated by the social security story.

First, successful entrenchment usually requires committed and strategically savvy administrators to succeed and always involves cooperation of various institutional actors. Responding to the demands of a social movement or to widespread popular perception of a problem, administrative sponsorship and presidential leadership typically elevate the innovative idea on the national public agenda. Congressional deliberation brings together a coalition supporting the statutory norm, and further legislative or administrative deliberation figures out a workable way to implement that norm—that is, delivering benefits expected by supporters, but without the severe disadvantages predicted by opponents. By contrast, federal judges play a much bigger role in Constitutional entrenchment than they do in this process. (Recall from chapter 3 that even the Sherman Act, where judicial proceedings were expected to be the primary forum for enforcement, has seen agencies like the Department of Justice and the Federal Trade Commission supplant the Supreme Court as the dominant mechanism for filling in the details of the statutory scheme and changing its policy course.)

As the agency implements the norm, there will be further feedback from the public. Popular support is essential for a statutory idea to become an entrenched norm or practice. Although agencies are not directly responsible to voters, the House of Representatives, the Senate, and the President are. Each of those institutions reflects a different kind of constituency, and one or more of them are likely to create problems for an agency that is pushing a regulatory idea upon an unwilling public. The trick for the supporters of the statutory idea is to deliver the promised benefits of the superstatute to a significant portion of society, but without the huge disadvantages predicted by opponents of the idea. This is our second generalization about the process of successful entrenchment: for a new public value or institution to take root in American soil, it needs the support of citizens who perceive that the innovation is a good idea and who can persuade others that the innovation is not excessively costly and is in the larger public interest. Social security became entrenched in large part because older Americans soon received old-age benefits greatly exceeding their contributions to the fund, while the next generation came to believe that they were earning the right to a postretirement income and started to plan their retirements around its expected payments. Only the most dedicated critics of big government remained skeptical, and even they bit their tongues for several decades.

Third, entrenchment is a dynamic process, involving compromise, adjustment to meet changed circumstances, and recalibration of the statutory goal itself. Thus, Title VII's goal changed dramatically in response to feminists' campaign against pregnancy discrimination: a law originally focused on fighting race discrimination in the workplace also became a forum for employers to accommodate employees' family needs (chapter 1). Indeed, statutory-constitutional entrenchment is similar to Constitutional entrenchment in this way. As the Introduction's discussion of *Brown* indicates, the Equal Protection Clause has been similarly dynamic, and the meaning of the *Brown* decision itself changed dramatically from the Warren Court to the Burger Court to the Rehnquist-Roberts Court. Unlike Constitutional dynamism, which is mainly ratified or carried out by judges, statutory-constitutional dynamism is mainly carried out by agencies and ratified or modified by Congress itself, and hence with more opportunities for meaningful public input. Thus, the evolution of Title VII to accommodate family responsibilities (chapter 1), of the Voting Rights Act to attack voting practices that have race-based effects (chapter 2), of the Sherman Act to focus exclusively on consumer welfare (chapter 3), and of the Social Security Act to include the medical expenses of the elderly (chapter 4) has been more legitimate and, in our view, more productive than the Rehnquist-Roberts Court's transformation of the Equal Protection Clause into a mechanism to monitor remedial race preferences aimed at integrating schools and workplaces.

Chapter 5 applies our model of entrenchment to a very different, but important, phenomenon. As Professor Robert Ellickson pressed upon us, state and local governments remain the primary face of governmental authority for most of us and create many of the foundational rules that constitute our republic of statutes. Although the Constitution itself assures that different states can adopt different regulatory regimes, many state-supported practices and norms have become part of the nation's statutory constitution. For example, the notion of a social safety net for workers originated in workmen's compensation, old-age assistance, and unemployment insurance laws adopted by the states between 1911 and 1935. Indeed, the original architects of the Social Security Act of

1935—President Franklin D. Roosevelt, Secretary of Labor Frances Perkins, and social security administrators Arthur Altmeyer and Edwin Witte—all got their start on social safety net issues by working on legislation in New York and Wisconsin.

Chapter 5 focuses on America's constitution of the family. The core ideas about family are enshrined in state law, with federal law playing an important but secondary role. The examples explored in chapter 5 involve the transformation of *marriage* (the core state regulatory structure for family law) away from the old common law constitutional model of lifetime commitment of two adults for the purpose of procreation, with the wife having few legal rights outside marital union. Under pressure from feminists and their allies, New York's legislature transformed the institution of marriage through a series of statutes entitling married women to own property, enter into contracts, and bring lawsuits without their husbands' consent; New York administrators and judges interpreted the state anticontraception law to allow married women to secure medical advice and contraceptives for mental as well as physical health reasons. Each of these initiatives was popular in New York—and each was copied by other states, such that there was a *convergence* of state statutes that eventually established a new American family law norm of companionate (rather than just procreative) marriage between two consenting adults, each of whom retains her or his legal independence and individuality. Carrying this norm one step further was California, which in 1969 legislated a new norm of no-fault divorce; like the earlier New York statutory innovations, the California one was borrowed by other states and even more swiftly became part of the national constitution of statutes. In a less-noticed but more fundamental shift, California also pioneered legal innovations that have recognized nonmarital unions as alternatives to marriage and the traditional nuclear family (husband, wife, children). Throughout the United States today, lifetime marriage has been supplanted by families we choose as the institutional basis for state-sanctioned relationships.

Our discussion of the constitution of the family revives the old idea of *stare de statute*, that statutes can be considered precedents, embodying principles that can be the basis for legal reasoning and policies that can be followed or copied by other jurisdictions. Stare de statute is the primary mechanism by which state law becomes the basis for national constitutional precepts today. New York's 1848 married women's property law and California's 1969 no-fault divorce law were both copied and adapted by other states to trump old common law understandings of marriage and revolutionize America's constitution of the family. Conversely, statutory developments can and ought to influence common law reasoning. Thus, California's legislative decriminalization of fornication, adultery, and consensual sodomy was an important legal justification for that state's willingness to enforce contractual obligations in nonmarital unions, an inclination followed in most other states for similar reasons.

Our case studies of social security and marriage illustrate the important role of statutory interpretation in the dynamics of statutory entrenchment. Chapter 6 takes up this theme more systematically, in the context of wetlands regulation and protection of endangered species in America's green constitution. The green constitution reflects the model of entrenchment developed in this part: the environmental movement provided political energy propelling Congress to enact a series of putative superstatutes and energizing agencies to apply those statutes expansively; a series of political push backs and public debates saw judges and legislators confirm that aggressive administrative constitutionalism, in part because public opinion supported the activism; even strong critics of the environmental superstatutes were impelled to acquiesce in the general norm and confine their opposition to local applications. What chapter 6 adds is an account of the inevitably dynamic nature of agency implementation of super-statutes and the incentives that judges have to go along with most agency initiatives, but without giving up their authority to enforce their own understanding of the superstatutory project and its constitutional limits. We argue in chapter 6 for a unified approach to legal interpretation based on administrative experience that ought to inform judicial practice.

Pause at this point for a cautionary note. That America is a republic of statutes does not assure that the republic will successfully solve our many public problems. The case studies in this part all represent political success stories, where social movement ideas have migrated into regimes that have stuck in America's statutory constitution. But entrenchment through the process we describe comes with a price, usually compromises that prevent the constitutional innovation from achieving a more radical adjustment in our national priorities and distribution of resources and rights. Thus, entrenchment of the social security norm came at the expense of a broader social safety net for the elderly poor; for social security to achieve its broad base of support, Americans had to be persuaded that the program was not radically redistributive, and it was not. In family law, marriage remains the primary regulatory mechanism. It has been opened up on both ends, easier to enter and much easier to exit than it was before 1900, but this deeply conservative institution remains the legal linchpin, even as declining numbers of Americans choose its safe haven for their relationships. More troubling, the primary liberalization of marriage, unilateral no-fault divorce, has redistributed resources away from dependent spouses and children. Finally, the green constitution has encountered the continuing force of property rights and their protection, by legislators as well as judges. The tug of war between green regulation and property rights has engendered thousands of compromises that have undermined the green goals and rendered some of the superstatutes powerless to halt continuing environmental losses on the ground. In short, entrenchment of superstatutory norms and institutions does not mean that the superstatute achieves its ultimate goals or achieves partial success without tragic trade-offs.

4

THE SAFETY NET CONSTITUTION AND THE POLITICS OF ENTRENCHMENT

Ida May Fuller was born on a farm outside Ludlow, Vermont, on September 6, 1874. She attended school in Rutland, where she was a classmate of Calvin Coolidge, who would become the nation's thirtieth president. Her own ambitions were more modest; Fuller was a schoolteacher until 1905, when she became a legal secretary, a job she performed diligently for several decades. Like many other Americans in the early twentieth century, she worried about how she would support herself when she grew old. Fuller never married and had no children, and she could not depend on family to care for her; a niece was her closest relative. Perhaps the law firm (one of whose partners was attorney general in the Coolidge administration) would provide for her old age, but she knew better than to rely on the generosity of lawyers. The nation fell into the Great Depression in Fuller's fifty-fifth year. Although she was fortunate to retain her job in hard times, millions of other Americans were not. The Depression hit older workers harder than any other class.[1]

Ida May Fuller was not reassured when the New Deal Congress enacted the Social Security Act of 1935. She certainly did not see this as the announcement of a constitutional right that would mean more to her own personal security than anything else the government did in the twentieth century. The act's preamble contained no ringing proclamation of a new basic liberty, aimed at assuring everyone of the right to a dignified old age. Modestly aiming "to make more adequate provision for aged persons, blind persons, dependent and crippled children, maternal and child welfare, public health, and the administration of their unemployment compensation laws," the 1935 act was intended to provide means-tested benefits to vulnerable and needy people, a class claiming many Americans in 1935, but not Fuller. Social security was a measure focused on alleviating dire but temporary conditions like unemployment, or chronic conditions that had been dealt with by families or localities in the past. Moreover, the various programs were to be administered by the states rather than the federal government, which meant that payments would vary widely, as would administrative standards. The limited ambitions of the original social security law, therefore, barely hint that what was being established was a new right that would ultimately be underwritten by the federal government—a small "c" constitutional right.[2]

This is not to say that the creators of the social security system were modest in their ultimate ambitions for the program. President Franklin Delano Roosevelt (FDR) saw from the earliest days of his administration the need to reconstitute America's system of fundamental rights; central to this reconfiguration would be rights to economic security. He was unapologetic in stating this vision and repeated it many times and in many different forums. FDR was also, above almost all else, a practical politician. He could see that a new right is not created out of thin (or hot) air, but has to be demanded by ordinary citizens and provided with an institutional structure that will permit it to be realized. FDR knew that this was a constitutional undertaking and that he had to persuade more than a mere and temporary majority that it was a good idea. When he and others set out to enact the original legislation, therefore, they said again and again how important it was to start conservatively by keeping the program modest in its scope and commitments, and to keep it well within what was economically manageable. Starting this way, FDR and his advisers thought, gave the fledgling program its best chance to grow into an institutional guarantee of economic rights. This start also committed social security to a conservative vision of the role of government and, ultimately, a confirmation of economic inequalities.[3]

It took a long time for the new program to fulfill this promise. More important for the purposes of this chapter, it took a great deal of political vision and resolve by political leaders and program officials. The prior history of welfare in the United States had produced a patchwork of state and local programs for relief of various categories of indigent and vulnerable groups, combined with federal pensions for soldiers. Each element of this patchwork was a provisional and pragmatic response to an immediate political problem. Compared to citizens in other advanced industrial states, Americans had long resisted the idea that the national government had any general responsibility to provide income security for its citizens. So even though many were prepared to support narrowly targeted poverty relief aimed at those who could not be expected to support themselves, most Americans thought this could be done better at the local level and required no federal role. In view of these considerations, the tentative steps taken in 1935 are hardly surprising.[4]

Moreover, the fragmented nature of twentieth-century politics was usually an obstacle to the introduction of any large new federal program and probably even more inhospitable to the creation of a new entitlement. Historically committed to small government and states' rights, the Democratic Party of the 1930s had only recently acquired a labor-oriented progressive wing, and the party was deeply divided between southerners, devoted to the traditional small-government orientation of nineteenth-century Democrats, and progressive northern Democrats, whose constituency of organized labor, ethnic groups, and city residents favored a larger federal role. With the decline of its own progressive wing, the Republican Party was dominated by fiscal conservatives who were suspicious of governmental intrusions into the economy.

The Depression changed the political situation and produced a chance for the resurgent and reconfigured Democrats to take new initiatives and, particularly, to launch the kind of social insurance program that many European nations had already adopted. The Democrats enjoyed immense majorities in Congress—majorities that increased in an unprecedented four successive elections (1930, 1932, 1934, and 1936)—and a bold president. Still, any big new program launched, even in such circumstances, would be vulnerable when the political winds shifted, as they inevitably would. This might not be so bad if the program was merely aimed to address an immediate crisis. But FDR and his advisers wanted a program that would provide social security for the old age of all Americans; such a program had to endure for decades in order for it to enter into the fabric of people's lives and form the basis for their retirement plans, as FDR wanted. For any program to have that kind of sustainability, it would have to be acceptable across the ideological spectrum, including at least some crusty Republicans.

Roosevelt and his advisers thought that modeling social security as an insurance program—rather than as a means-tested relief program—was the most politically feasible way to work toward the goal of providing a safety net for Americans that would be politically robust. The philosophy was conservative: individuals would purchase an annuity that would pay off in their retirement years. In that respect, it was not supposed to be a program that redistributed wealth between people; instead, its stated purpose was to insure people against the risk of living long after retirement. Unlike private insurance, social insurance can create a larger pool for spreading risks and can expand or contract that pool by fiat rather than market forces, an authority that generated some degree of interpersonal redistribution in the program. Nevertheless, a great selling point for the program, according to President Roosevelt, was that it was not welfare or the dole; each person would be paying (something) for the benefits she was entitled to receive.[5]

The underlying principle of old age pensions as a kind of insurance had originated in Chancellor Otto von Bismarck's Germany half a century before and was widely emulated elsewhere in Europe. Social insurance systems resembled the pension programs that some American firms had recently introduced, and that several of the states were developing. A key attraction of a social insurance program was that it was supposed to be self-financing in the sense of paying out no more than it took in, in the long run. These ideas, taken together, suggested that even though benefits would be related to contributions, such relationship would be imperfect: those whose higher wages led to larger contributions would receive only somewhat higher benefits, and some people would receive benefits that exceeded their contributions. In any case, over the short and medium terms, the revenues raised through payroll taxes would be far higher than the benefits paid out, and so the budget balance condition did not really impose much of a constraint on the program or an impediment to its expansion.[6]

Despite the conservative nature of the insurance principle, it is important to emphasize that American social security also contained, from the beginning, a commitment to equality of status built into the program. Eventually, the program was supposed to guarantee *all workers* a minimal degree of financial security in old age, in exchange for their contributions over their working lifetime. All workers would be eligible to join the program and would be entitled to receive benefits proportional to the wage/contribution history that they experienced and to the actuarial results of their life and health histories. Indeed, the property rights embedded in the Constitution exhibit the same kind of status equality; everyone is entitled to buy and sell property, and anyone who holds property is protected. Of course, that protection is more valuable to those who have more property to protect. Equality of status in this sense could be seen as consistent with the political value of the kind of individualism that Americans generally accept; it also seemed achievable by a social insurance program, at least if the program could be designed in a way that permitted the economics to work.

For the program to work as planned, however, everyone had to be required to participate, and in this respect the program conflicted with American ideals of independence. And the risks that were to be insured, even assuming that the program actually worked as a self-financing insurance program, were those faced by members of the population generally. So there was a collectivization of risk implicit in the program, even if it worked ideally, and this idea may be in some tension with the ideal of individual responsibility. Participation was not an optional feature of the program: enrollment had to be compulsory (with exceptions determined by political considerations) in order to manage the moral hazard implicit in any insurance program. Without it, people who expected not to live long after retirement, or whose financial contributions were relatively great, would opt out of the program, undermining its economic foundation.

Even though American social security never aimed at equalizing outcomes, the status equalization at its base, combined with compulsory financing, had implications that conservatives have always found objectionable. Libertarians objected to the nonvoluntary aspect of social security and to shifting the job of retirement planning away from the individual. Conservatives generally doubted that the government could do as well as individuals and families in investing for the future or in supporting the elderly. They also worried that the program, once begun, would continue to expand and would further undermine what they saw as traditional American values of self-reliance. Fiscal conservatives were skeptical of building a large trust fund, which might distort financial markets and compete with private investors. Yet others opposed the idea of a large system of social insurance, preferring a more targeted means-tested welfare program. These conservative complaints, coming from a weakened Republican Party, could not prevent the passage of some kind of social security legislation. But if the Democrats wanted to build a program that would grow and sustain itself even if the Republicans came back to power, they had to take account of these objections and to rein in the ambitions of the most enthusiastic proponents. This is exactly what executive officials who designed and implemented social security did. The account that follows is a classic example of the *entrenchment* of a statutory right in American history. It is triumphalist in demonstrating how administrative constitutionalists could entrench a robust idea in our republic of statutes—but it is cautionary in demonstrating how the statutory triumph came at the expense of a broader, but more politically difficult, reform that could have helped more people.

Both the triumph and the tragedy can be traced to the compromises that New Dealers built into the 1935 act and to the important 1939 amendments. But credit or blame is also owed to the strategic vision of the administrators who guided the program through its early years. Program supporters in the White House and Congress had a hand in picking these people, but they had no way of knowing that they would remain in place for long or that they would have the patience and sagacity to successfully give birth to an enduring constitutional right. Arthur Altmeyer, who was a member of the original Social Security Board and was then the first social security commissioner until 1953, said that "[a]dministration consists of more than organization, procedures and personnel. . . . Administration also consists of interpreting social legislation in such a manner that it achieves its fundamental purpose most fully." Altmeyer had no doubt as to what that purpose was and said so clearly in an early dispute with the beady-eyed accountants from the Government Accounting Office: "We had quite a time convincing them that this was a different kind of animal—that because of contributions there were certain rights, statutory rights, that had to be recognized and achieved, and that we had an obligation."[7]

In the remainder of this chapter, we trace social security's origins, its political entrenchment, and its resiliency against determined challenges under new circumstances. Within this legislative, administrative, and political story, we shall try to deepen the main conceptual themes of this book. For example, the social security superstatute transformed the federal-state balance for America's socioeconomic safety net, not just for old people, but also for the unemployed, people with disabilities, and widows/widowers. Before 1935, the symbol of the safety net was the local almshouse; after 1935, the government face of the safety net slowly morphed into the Social Security Administration. This expansion of federal government regulatory authority was fiercely contested in the Constitutional as well as constitutional arenas, and its ascendancy in the latter assured its triumph in the former. Within two years, the Supreme Court had not only ratified all aspects of the Social Security Act, it had radically opened up a Constitutional carte blanche for congressional regulation of arenas traditionally left to the states. Even before FDR had appointed a single justice, the Old Court had bowed to the Social Security Act and reduced the Tenth Amendment to a truism.

More important, the social security story is a story of normative entrenchment. Like the antidiscrimination principle, the universal franchise norm, and the state-guaranteed national competitive market explored in the first part of this book, the social security precept is one that did not stick in American political culture immediately. Even though adopted with huge margins in Congress and ratified in the 1936 presidential election, the old-age contribution idea only gradually gained traction, and even after its popular acceptance social security did not radically transform the country, as its academic and labor critics have lamented. Social security became normatively entrenched for the same kinds of reasons we have seen in earlier chapters but want to identify more systematically here. On the one hand is an account grounded in problem-solving deliberation. The social security norm was an intelligent response to a persistent social problem of industrial democracies. Creative administrators made the response a workable and appealing one; the appeal was to established groups as well as to the dispossessed in American society. On the other hand is an account grounded in constituency politics. Once older Americans started to receive benefits, the social security policy created its own constituency, a thoroughly middle-class constituency, people like Ida May Fuller. Its administrators constantly pressed to expand that constituency—pressure that Congress could not resist in times of prosperity. After 1950, small government conservatives as well as big government liberals supported universal social security coverage. Its social safety net was entrenched in America's statutory constitution and survived the antiwelfare revolution during the Clinton and Bush administrations (1993–2009). Whether the perseverance of social security represents the best that America can do is not an issue we address. Like other features of our republic of statutes, this is a matter for ongoing deliberation.

ORIGINS OF THE SOCIAL SECURITY PRINCIPLE

The Social Security Act of 1935 was a far-sighted response by the Roosevelt administration to a social need characteristic of industrial democracies, a need that became urgent with the Great Depression of 1929. To understand how successful the idea was, we shall explore the pre-FDR state law response to the problem of old-age assistance, New Deal administrators' transformation of the preexisting proposals into something that was both more conservative and more radical, and the immediate and complete capitulation of the Old (pre-Roosevelt-packed) Court to the Constitutional vision underlying the Social Security Act. Social security is an example of aggressive administrative constitutionalism. Administrators articulated their own vision of an affirmative problem-solving government that is not only permitted by the Constitution's jurisdictional and rights-protecting provisions, but in their view it is required by the Constitution's general goals and by the purposes of the social contract itself.

THE OLD-AGE ASSISTANCE MOVEMENT, 1907–34

In the early twentieth century, industrial nations of Europe and North America faced a burgeoning social problem of destitute elderly persons. Ida May Fuller, the legal secretary whose story opened this chapter, illustrates this important socioeconomic problem. As the work force changed from an agrarian or small business model, in which old people were cared for by their children on the family farm, to a mass production model, older workers found it hard to keep up and had fewer family and social resources as fallbacks. Additionally, improvements in public health and medicine meant that there were more older persons in the population; someone like Fuller could expect to live into her seventies, at least. The 1920 Census, for example, found that 4.7 percent of the American population was aged sixty-five or older; data collected by state investigating commissions (the first of which was established by Massachusetts in 1907) suggested that as many as a third of the elderly were without either property or significant income. Families supported many of those older Americans, but increasing numbers literally ended up in the poorhouse. This would have concerned Fuller, who was unmarried and without children.[8]

European countries addressed this problem in three different ways: (1) voluntary insurance programs, usually annuities offered by the government to provide income during old age; (2) compulsory insurance programs, where the government required wage earners and their employers to contribute to a fund that would make guaranteed payments upon retirement; and (3) need-based public pensions, paid out of government funds. The second option was the most successful, originating in Germany and adopted also in Great Britain, France, Italy, and most of Scandinavia. In 1911, Representative Victor Berger of Wisconsin, Congress's lone Socialist Party member, introduced a bill proposing option (2) for the United States. Although the bill never came to a vote, it reflected the growing interest in government programs to save the elderly from the almshouse. Labor groups followed Representative Berger to make old-age assistance a legislative priority; the Roman Catholic Church joined their efforts. Founded by Abraham Epstein in 1915, the American Association for Old-Age Security pressed for option (3) at the state level and option (2) or (3) at the national level.[9]

The Great Depression made this problem one of crisis proportions, as the elderly were the most likely to lose their jobs in the wake of the country's economic meltdown. Destitution faced millions, no longer thousands, of older Americans. By January 1934, twenty-seven states had enacted legislation providing public assistance to approximately 114,000 elderly Americans, along option (3) lines. One such state was New York (1930), where Governor Franklin Roosevelt criticized such laws as grossly inadequate. The benefit levels were almost always too low to provide a decent life for the beneficiaries. Also, "those who have given the deepest study to this whole subject and thoroughly understand legislation of this kind as set up in other countries believe that a mere dole or pension for the aged is wrong in principle and bad in practice." The "most successful systems" are those combining options (2) and (3), where a minimum standard of living is assured by the state, but with employee/employer contributions into a fund providing more than a minimum standard of living for most workers in their retirement years. Notwithstanding these objections, Governor Roosevelt signed the "stop-gap" legislation, with the hope that "this will be the forerunner of a proper system of security against old-age want in years to come."[10]

Because the cash-strapped states could not afford to provide sufficient benefits, they and advocates for the elderly turned to Congress for a national solution. Starting in 1927, dozens of bills were introduced in Congress, most of them augmenting the states' ability to provide public benefits or even federalizing the idea (option (3)). As the Depression dragged on, Dr. Francis Townsend demanded legislation paying every American over the age of sixty the sum of two hundred dollars per month, with the stipulation that the recipient spend all of the money within the month. This was a very popular proposal, one that might have appealed to Ida May Fuller, who turned sixty in 1934. The Townsendite movement had echoes in the spread-the-wealth rhetoric of demagogues like Father Charles Coughlin and Senator Huey Long. Seemingly lost in the din of immediate relief demands was Governor Roosevelt's longer-term solution based upon compulsory contributions into a national fund (option (2)). Of course, when Governor Roosevelt was elected president in 1932, he brought to the federal government the same idea he had endorsed as governor in 1930. That proved to be an idea whose time had come.[11]

THE NEW DEAL CONGRESS ENACTS THE SOCIAL SECURITY ACT OF 1935

In contrast to his predecessor, Herbert Hoover, FDR immediately mobilized federal responses to the massive dislocations confronting the economy. In early 1933, he declared a bank holiday to try to put a stop to the recurring waves of banking panics that had decimated the financial structure and dried up credit. To curb deflationary spirals, the Roosevelt administration pushed the National Industrial Recovery Act (NIRA) and the Agricultural Adjustment Act (AAA) through Congress in 1933–34. These early efforts had only mixed success. The bank holiday may have helped stabilize the banking structure, but thousands of the weakest banks had already been purged, so it is not clear how much of an effect to attribute to the administration's actions. The neocorporatist NIRA and the AAA's efforts to limit agricultural production through conditional farm subsidies probably had little positive effect, in part because the Supreme Court promptly invalidated both plans. The Court's decision against the AAA in *United States v. Butler* (1936) ruled that Congress's Tax and Spending Clause authority "may not be used as an instrument to enforce a regulation of matters of state concern with respect to which Congress has no authority to interfere," such as the regulation of local agricultural production. More lasting were the efforts at short-term policies, by which the federal government assumed more of the burden of dealing with big economic shocks.[12]

As during his New York governorship, FDR's goal was to understand socioeconomic problems more deeply and to propound solutions that went beyond short-run responses to the present emergency. President Roosevelt told Congress that the traditional institutions had failed to provide the minimal *security* (by 1933, this was the buzzword) that the American people needed to live their lives. "[S]ecurity was attained in the earlier days through the interdependence of members of families upon each other and of the families within a small community up each other. The complexities of great communities and of organized industry make less real these simple means of security. . . . We are compelled to employ . . . government in order to encourage a greater security for each individual who composes it." Roosevelt went on to outline three kinds of security which had been provided through traditional institutions but which now needed governmental action as well. "[T]he security of the home, the security of livelihood, and the security of social insurance—are, it seems to me, a minimum of the promise that we can offer to the American people. They constitute a right which belongs to every individual and every family willing to work." Articulating and providing for such a right "does not require the creation of new and strange values. It is rather the finding of the way once more to known, but to some degree forgotten, ideals and values. If the means and details are in some instances new, the objectives are as permanent as human nature."[13]

A few months later, Roosevelt established a cabinet-level Committee on Economic Security, with an interdepartmental technical staff, charged with studying "problems relating to the economic security of individuals" and asked to report recommendations and proposals to him by the end of the year. The president instructed the committee to consider a federally financed but state-run unemployment insurance program, a relief program aimed at those on the dole or with no future means of generating income, and an old-age pension program. FDR knew that a government creation of a new right of social security would not be easy to enact in a form that would be sustainable over time, and that such a program could easily be undermined by the temptation of panaceas that were then being bruited around the nation. "I do not know whether this is the time for any federal legislation on old-age security. Organizations promoting fantastic schemes have aroused hopes which cannot possibly be fulfilled" and have "increased the difficulties of getting sound legislation; but I hope that in time we may be able to provide security for the aged—a sound and uniform system." The president conceded that "we cannot work miracles or solve all our problems at once. What we can do is lay a sound foundation on which we can build a structure to give a greater measure of safety and happiness . . . than any we have ever known."[14]

Chaired by Secretary of Labor Frances Perkins, the committee proved eager to take up FDR's challenge in full measure. In its report to the president, the committee recommended a program for old-age pensions that would combine all three of the approaches followed in Europe: benefits for those currently retired or soon to retire (who could not be expected to work and contribute), "compulsory contributory annuities" for those who could contribute during their working lifetimes, and a voluntary annuity program for those who wanted to add to their retirement pensions. The committee's report reached FDR's desk in January 1935; with technical materials, the report ran to ten volumes. On January 17,

President Roosevelt forwarded most of the report and his recommended legislation to Congress.[15]

Although the proposed legislation was ambitious, it rejected the quick fix of the Townsendites and pursued a longer-term goal. "It is overwhelmingly important to avoid any danger of permanently discrediting the sound and necessary policy of Federal legislation for economic security by attempting to apply it on too ambitious a scale. . . . The place of such a fundamental right in our future civilization is too precious to be jeopardized now by extravagant action." President Roosevelt urged Congress to create a structure permanently insuring "the security of men, women and children of the Nation against certain hazards and vicissitudes of life." The details of the new pension program reflected this caution. The initial coverage would exclude large parts of the work force and would not even begin paying benefits for several years. Payroll taxes, at a low level, were to start much sooner; the plan was to build up a reserve fund before benefit payouts were to begin.[16]

The executive department's proposal insisted that the program be self-financed out of payroll taxes, rather than be reliant on general revenues. This was inspired less by fiscal prudence than by the notion that benefit payments, when they began, would be given as a matter of right, since people would have earned them through their contributions. If contributions were put into a designated trust fund, as long as that fund maintained sufficient moneys, payouts could naturally be understood as entitlements—giving back to people what was theirs as a matter of right. Of course this was a *political* tactic, as the president later admitted. "We put those payroll contributions there so as to give the contributors a legal, moral, and political right to collect their pensions. . . . With those taxes in there, no damn politician can ever scrap my social security program." In order to ensure that the program remained solvent, it was to be put on an actuarially sound basis by basing judgments on coverage, taxes, and benefit levels on regularly produced seventy-five-year projections of the program's finances. This insistence too was part of the political strategy. Program leaders, most of whom were civil servants rather than political appointees, were convinced of the importance of fiscal soundness and worked hard to establish the system's reputation for caution. But they also had an almost religious belief that social security was an insurance program and that all had a basic right, a kind of property right, to receive their benefit checks.[17]

FDR's proposals were considered in extensive hearings conducted by the House Ways and Means and Senate Finance Committees. In the congressional hearings, Republicans and their business allies sharply questioned the proposed programs. Former president Hoover depicted the legislation as creating "a system of regimentation and bureaucratic domination in which men and women are not masters of government but are pawns and dependents of a centralized and potentially self-perpetuating government." Some Democrats privately harbored similar objections, and the Ways and Means Committee was originally not in favor of the old-age insurance program, because social security represented big government without any immediate political payoff. President Roosevelt personally intervened to save the old-age insurance program on the ground that it was essential to the New Deal and the long-term fate of the Democratic Party that controlled Congress. The congressional committees revised the social security bill to rely on state implementation of its old-age assistance and unemployment programs and to severely restrict the categories of workers covered by the old-age insurance program (agricultural and domestic workers, the self-employed, and railroad workers were excluded, with different economic and political justifications for each exclusion). But only one major program was dropped, a voluntary pension system that would have operated alongside the compulsory one for those who wanted to enhance their retirement benefits. Congress as a whole approved the committee bills by overwhelming margins. Support was so strong, from Republicans as well as Democrats, that even supporters of the legislation must have wondered if their ambitions had been too modest. Lyndon Johnson once told an interviewer that if she ever saw a bill of his get more than 70 percent of the votes (in Congress) it meant that he had failed to ask for enough. Maybe. But much of the Great Society legislation failed to withstand the Reagan revolution while social security remains a key part of American life. So maybe LBJ had more to learn from his hero than he thought.[18]

The structure of the Social Security Act itself exemplifies both its expansive vision and its modest beginnings. Most of the act was aimed at providing immediate relief for those who could not protect themselves from the economic maelstrom: the blind (Title X), the elderly (Title I), dependent children (Titles IV and V), and the unemployed (Title III). These groups of people could not easily pick themselves up and move or find other ways to earn something to keep body and soul together. They needed some kind of public support, and many would need it until they died. From the vantage of the present, the most significant parts of the act were contained in Titles II and VIII, which set up the compulsory insurance scheme that we know now as "Social Security." It was this part of the legislation that broke new ground by creating a new program of entitlement. The other sections picked up responsibilities that the states were already shouldering to some degree, albeit with much unevenness. Each of the other titles constituted state-run programs; the role of the federal government was restricted to financing these narrowly targeted relief programs and, to a limited extent, maintaining minimum standards. The new pension program, however, was aimed at creating a secure basis for retirement for everyone, at least eventually. Its aspirations were universal, as befits a fundamental right, and the old-age insurance program imposed costs directly upon companies, not out of general tax revenues. Thus, Titles II and VIII drew the sharpest objections from conservatives and the Chamber of Commerce. And these provisions have come under fire in the past few decades as well.

The rhetoric supporting the social security bill invoked the immediate crisis, and the Depression certainly allowed progressives to advance retirement and old-age insurance on the national public agenda. But Title II (the centerpiece of the legislation) had aspirations well beyond the Depression: while it would begin levying taxes almost immediately, no one would receive benefits until 1942. Unlike the old-age assistance and unemployment programs in Titles I and III (respectively), Title II was intended to provide a permanent and reliable safety net for all Americans, rather than solving any short-term problems. The New Deal administrators understood that the development of this new right would take time, and that it could not be established unless people generally came to understand and to rely on it. They accepted, moreover, that not everyone could be offered protection immediately. They wanted to protect the program from foreseeable political pressures, either to expand it unreasonably or to under-mine and destroy it. Thus, supporters would have to balance the pressures emanating from the political left—from the Townsendites and the Huey Longs—with the practical necessity of building a political foundation that could support the new federal promises against attacks from the Right—from the Chamber of Commerce and its GOP allies. This meant not only that social security sup-porters had to deal with congressional conservatives; they also needed to ad-dress their concerns with individual liberties, states' rights, and fiscal caution.[19]

SOCIAL SECURITY'S LARGE "C" CONSTITUTIONAL REVOLUTION

America's Constitutional traditions posed serious challenges to Title II of the Social Security Act. In 1854, based upon the advice of Attorney General Caleb Cushing, President Franklin Pierce had vetoed a federal charitable relief mea-sure on the ground that it went beyond the specific authorities granted Congress by Article I of the Constitution. Pierce's assumption remained the conventional Constitutional wisdom for three generations. The Civil War created an excep-tion for military pensions, which could be justified on the basis of Article I's explicit grant of authority for Congress to set rules for the governance of the armed forces. When Congressman William Wilson introduced the first congres-sional bill providing for old-age pensions a generation later, he feared that a gen-eral measure would be unConstitutional and so engaged in this subterfuge:

his proposed law would have created an Old Home Guard, enlisting all elderly Americans for service to their country while simultaneously pensioning them. This hare-brained scheme died in committee.[20]

Consistent with this history, congressional, business, and media critics of the social security bill maintained that it was at war with "the fundamental principles of our form of Government embodied in our Constitution." The National Association of Manufacturers (NAM) maintained that Congress had no authority to create either welfare or social insurance programs. The Constitutional design was to grant Congress only limited powers, so that the states would retain the primary police powers. According to NAM, "Congress may only levy taxes for the common defense and the general welfare in execution of express grants of authority made to it, or directly implied therefrom." Because there was no allowance for Congress to provide for old-age and other kinds of insurance, the social security bills were unConstitutional.[21]

Supporters vigorously defended the validity of these proposals. The Taxing Clause in Article I of the Constitution authorizes Congress "[t]o lay and collect Taxes [etc.] to . . . provide for the common Defence and general Welfare." Republicans opposed to big government read "general Welfare" as a limitation on Congress's authority, to be narrowly construed in light of the Constitution's federalist structure and, especially, the Tenth Amendment (which preserves to the states powers not delegated to Congress or retained by the people). Supporters read "general Welfare" more broadly, to allow Congress discretion to finance programs that "protect life and make it easier and happier" for the disadvantaged in society. The Department of Justice and other lawyers advising Congress opined that its taxing power was not limited to funding programs specifically enumerated in Article I. These arguments are rich examples of administrative constitutionalism, where agencies develop their own interpretation of their powers and duties under the Constitution.[22]

But administrative constitutionalism also entailed pre-Constitutional arguments about governmental responsibilities flowing from the social contract itself. Abraham Epstein, who had worked on the social security issue most of his professional career, went further than the Department of Justice: "What is the whole purpose of our Government? Is it not in order to guarantee equal rights and making possible 'the pursuit of happiness'?" (Yes.) He urged Congress to declare that "destitution due to forces over which the individual has no control must be remedied at least to some extent. And *it is your duty*, gentlemen, to see that poverty, at least, is abolished in this country, and that we make the poor somewhat happier." Epstein argued that Congress was *obliged* to consider the plight of poor people when it deliberates. Because he was not a lawyer, Epstein did not announce this obligation as a large "C" Constitutional one; indeed, his best authority for an affirmative, obligatory view of "general Welfare" was the Declaration of Independence, not the Constitution. But even as a small "c" constitutional point, it had enormous normative force, grounded upon the purposes of government, the nature of a democracy, and the features of a good and just polity.[23]

Unsurprisingly, businesses challenged the old-age insurance, as well as the public welfare, provisions of the Social Security Act before the ink was dry on the president's signing statement of August 14, 1935. They made precisely the same kinds of arguments Congress had considered and rejected. Relying on the Supreme Court's 1936 *Butler* decision, the Court of Appeals for the First Circuit ruled that Titles II and VIII (the old-age insurance provisions) were un-Constitutional as beyond the power delegated Congress under Article I and the Tenth Amendment. On appeal to the Supreme Court, the attorney general provided a detailed history of the old-age insurance idea and the social and economic needs that it addressed. Surely, the "general Welfare" was capacious enough to accommodate such a program. To the surprise of most outside observers, *seven* of the nine justices agreed with the administration. Justice Benjamin Cardozo's opinion in *Helvering v. Davis* (1937) deferred to the judgment of the CES, Congress, and the administrative experts as to the overwhelming social need ("general Welfare") served by the legislation and the incapacity of the states to serve that need. A closely divided Court ruled, in the companion case of *Charles C. Steward Machine Co. v. Davis* (1937), that Congress's tax-and-spend power could also be exercised to fund state-administered programs conditioned upon the states' following stringent and uniform national guidelines.[24]

The two dissenters in *Helvering v. Davis* did not explain their precise grounds, beyond the assertion that the insurance program was inconsistent with the Tenth Amendment. (Three dissenting opinions put up more of a protest in *Charles C. Steward*, based mainly on the detailed prescriptions Congress imposed upon the states and the strong incentives virtually requiring state participation.) With barely a whimper, the Constitutional conservatives declined to pursue the suggestion they had made in *Butler*, that Congress could not use its tax-and-spend power to impose regulatory authority in an area traditionally handled by the states. Importantly, this concession came a year before President Roosevelt's Court-packing plan and the notorious "switch in time" that sustained other New Deal statutes against Constitutional attack. But *Helvering* and *Charles C. Steward* also came a year *after* the 1936 election, where Republican candidate Governor Alfred Landon had made the Social Security Act a prominent theme of his campaign, and President Roosevelt had, in return, emphasized the 1935 act as one of the central achievements of the New Deal. Handing FDR the biggest electoral landslide since the founding era, the voters sent a strong message of support for the New Deal program, and that reaffirmation probably influ-enced the justices' willingness to accede to all parts of the Social Security Act.[25]

CREATING AN ENTRENCHED RIGHT
TO SOCIAL SECURITY: 1939–74

Notwithstanding the lopsided vote in Congress (1935), the landslide reelec-tion of FDR (1936), and the Supreme Court's dismissal of Constitutional ob-jections (1937), the social security idea was far from entrenched. Ida May Fuller, for one, was unimpressed. A lifelong Republican, she probably voted for Landon; her state of Vermont was one of only two to vote Republican in the 1936 election. Although she started to pay the social security tax in 1937, she never expected to see a return on her investment, probably because she believed the Coolidge- and Hoover-era Republican voices critical of the pro-gram. When she retired at the age of sixty-five, Fuller changed her mind after she received her first social security check, on January 31, 1940. The experts turned out to be right: social security changed the lives of millions of Americans like Ida May Fuller, and they rewarded the program with their loyalty and their votes.

From the contested and modest beginnings described above, the old-age in-surance program grew, and as it did it gained wider political acceptance. The engine for entrenchment of the program was administrative constitutionalism. Recall, from part 1 of this book, that administrative constitutionalism is not just the practical, adaptive construction of the Constitution by executive and legis-lative officials; indeed, that is its least important feature. Administrative consti-tutionalism is also, more important, the recognition of public commitments to positive governmental projects and the construction of a scheme to imple-ment those commitments. Finally, there is the feature of administrative consti-tutionalism we shall explore here—strategizing by program supporters who want their project to become an enduring part of the small "c" constitution. Unlike the Federal Trade Commission, the less-than-successful agency ex-plored in the previous chapter, the Social Security Administration was from the beginning staffed by zealous social reformers and veteran administrators who worked intelligently to design a program that not only worked but also dispelled doubts about its desirability.

At a superficial level, the social security idea followed the classic path of con-stitutional norm creation explained earlier. The original idea borrowed from experience in Europe and some of the states, and it represented a thoughtful long-term response to a deep socioeconomic problem (destitution in old age). The Depression-era Congress was a window of opportunity for such a program, and the New Deal's policy entrepreneurs, empowered by a magnificent spokesman (FDR), persuaded both the legislators and the voters that social security was an idea whose time had come. Especially before benefits started flowing to retirees, social security remained vulnerable, but the program survived the 1939 amendments. When the Republican Party, home to the program's critics, took over Congress in 1947–49, legislators trimmed back the program slightly and were met by vehement opposition from President Harry Truman, who claimed vindication in the 1948 election, when social security was an important issue. The 1950 amendments greatly expanded the program, as well as its constituency, and entrenched the idea so firmly that prominent Republicans became supporters for the next generation.[26]

Note the similarities to the now-entrenched antidiscrimination, voting rights, and national competitive market norms explored in part 1 of this book. In all these cases, aggressive administrative elaboration and politicking found ways to make the putative superstatutes workable and to attract a growing political constituency that protected the statutory principles against dilution or repeal. Figure 4

Social Security Act of 1935 responds to both the immediate and the long-term problem of old-age destitution; survives Supreme Court review and 1939 amendments

⇓

Administrative implementation of new norm, with positive feedback from media, experts, public

⇓

Republican Congress tries to trim back social security coverage; President Truman defies Republicans and triumphs in 1948 election

⇓

Congress reaffirms social security norm and expands coverage, 1950 amendments

⇓

Social security survives GOP control of presidency and Congress, 1953–55, program flourishes and expands, 1950s

⇓

Social security norm is entrenched

Figure 4. Entrenchment of the social security norm

traces the social security norm along the lines we have suggested for entrenchment of policies or principles in America's constitution of federal superstatutes.

In this part of the chapter, we want to deepen this superficial account in several ways. First, every success story conceals the many possibilities for failure, and the social security norm could have been derailed at various points. Indeed, there is a rich theoretical literature demonstrating that administrative entrenchment is usually very difficult; this literature renders the achievements of superstatutes such as the Social Security Act quite remarkable. Second, some of the features of the antientrenchment literature in political science help us develop our own account of how statutory principles triumph. For example, statutory programs are often designed so that regulatory zealots are required to work with skeptics and the regulated community. Although political scientists correctly believe that such arrangements often have an effect of compromising regulatory programs, they may at the same time strengthen them. Because conservatives had input into the design of the social security program, it was in some ways a better program, even if much less radical than its strongest supporters favored. Moreover, the regulatory zealots for various reasons were actually able to convert many skeptics into supporters of the program, which was essential for it to stick on our public culture. A statute like social security becomes truly transformative only when it satisfies two potentially warring conditions: its benefits attract a constituency *and* come to be accepted by skeptics as being in the overall public interest as well. Third, the process of entrenchment requires a dynamic evolution of the statute itself, involving both *conflict* and *consensus*. To gain entrenchment in the nation's public culture, a statutory principle or policy must survive public opposition. That process of conflict is usually followed by a process of consensus building. Both processes change the idea or the program. For social security, program benefits shifted from more or less discretionary payments, at levels set by momentary congressional majorities, aimed at improving social conditions, to a right, backed not merely by a particular promise of the government but by something more enduring and profound. The way in which this right was assured, the way it was insulated from the day-to-day tensions of budgetary politics and the profound shifts of partisan and ideological forces, provides an insight into the promissary structure of the small "c" constitution.

CONFLICT AND CONSENSUS: OVERCOMING OBSTACLES AS A MECHANISM FOR ENTRENCHMENT

Once it is accepted that the significant fact about social security is how it evolved from its modest start as a collection of relief programs into a small "c" constitutional right, the task is to explain how this happened and why. One possibility is that the enacted program contained seeds that were "genetically" programmed to evolve into the program we now see. We can draw insights from recent work on bureaucratic politics, especially that produced by such scholars as Terry Moe and the academic collective known as McNollGast, to see how this might be. The key to establishing a permanent new federal program is building political bases of support to ensure that the interests of those who got the program started (the enacting coalition) are hard-wired in some way into the program. Doing this entails protecting the program, as initially enacted, from political risks arising from new or newly powerful political opponents. For McNollGast, successful programs are likely to maintain the goal orientation of their founders—its enacting coalition—and to be able to persist even when political circumstances are hostile to it.[27]

In contrast, Terry Moe emphasizes that one must focus not only on program advocates but also on program opponents and skeptics who, he argues, are usually able to hard-wire some of their own interests into the program as well. Indeed, because the conflicting desires of opponents are usually embedded in the compromises made in the originating legislation, programs tend to be designed to fail to live up to the aspirations of its strongest supporters. Professor Moe emphasizes that the president is the greatest source of risk for any established program. Presidents have their own priorities, arising partly from their own ideological commitments and electoral incentives, partly from external events and partly from the unique national perspective that the chief executive alone enjoys. Moreover, presidents, being unitary actors, can act decisively. For Moe, therefore, a key to ensuring program stability or bureaucratic autonomy is insulation from the president and his political appointees. But program insulation and autonomy are no guarantee that the program will achieve the objectives of its founders, especially since a new president might be able to strip that insulation away later, if he is willing to pay the political price or shift the program around in the bureaucracy.[28]

So McNollGast and Moe differ on whether a successful program will faithfully reflect the desires of its enacting coalition or whether it will exhibit countervailing structures that undermine the ability of program proponents to achieve its goals. We have no view as to which of these positions is more accurate as a general depiction of the American bureaucracy. But in the case of social security—speaking mainly of its core pension program and, to a lesser extent, the disability and Medicare programs—it appears that things are considerably more complex than either of these two views. To begin with, Moe and McNollGast treat preferences as exogenously formed, and so supporters and opponents of a program are stable categories, at least in the short and medium terms. Consistent with the civic republican literature, one theme of our book is that preferences as to fundamental (constitutional) norms are endogenous: they are a *product* of deliberation and feedback, not anterior to it. Hence, constitutional preferences are often malleable, especially in the early stages of debate about an idea or a program.[29]

Even within the rational choice tradition, we believe deliberation and feedback can trump design. Both Moe and McNollGast emphasize the critical nature of the design stage rather than how the program operates later on and, specifically, how program leaders continue to make strategic choices that can affect the fate of the program. While design issues are surely important, they can be overridden later on by choices coming from inside or outside the program. As Moe has argued, new leaders can be put in place by a skeptical president, agencies can be shifted among departments, and review procedures can be changed. Thus, Republican President Dwight Eisenhower (1953–61) expressed initial skepticism about social security by placing its administration under the new Department of Health, Education, and Welfare and relieving New Dealer Arthur Altmeyer of his duties as social security commissioner. But Eisenhower's skepticism and the administrative reorganization not only failed to kill social security, it actually strengthened it by co-opting Republican leaders in HEW and thereby broadening its political base. Social security easily survived the Eisenhower reorganization, partly because the Social Security Administration itself was led by expert civil servants who passionately believed in the idea, and Eisenhower's political appointees could not really run the program without their cooperation. Within the agency, Robert Ball, Altmeyer's assistant who had extensive experience testifying before congressional committees, simply stepped into the vacuum created by Altmeyer's ouster. He did an even better job selling the program politically (until he was cashiered, in 1973, by President Richard Nixon, who had been Eisenhower's vice president). Moreover, the 1950 amendments had expanded social security coverage and benefits and had taught members of Congress that they could earn easy bonus points with voters by periodic increases in social security benefits. This political payoff attracted the attention of Republican conservatives as well as Democratic liberals, and only the most principled and electorally safe conservatives (like Senator Barry Goldwater) were immune to its siren song.[30]

McNollGast correctly emphasize the importance of long-range institutional strategic choices of program proponents, and in the case of social security, especially those made by FDR and early program leaders. Program opponents and skeptics were able to win some victories from time to time, particularly during the early history of the program—but at least some of the conservative wins were good for the program's long-term prospects. For example, critics were able to force Roosevelt to reconsider the idea of a reserve fund on the ground that such a fund would create too much of a temptation for Congress to spend. The conservatives were probably right about that, and it seems doubtful in retro-spect whether the program needed a reserve fund. As it turned out, the wide political support for the program was sufficient to guarantee its credibility po-litically by making it extremely costly for opponents to try to tinker with it. Moreover, program advocates found it prudent to pace themselves carefully in pushing expansions in coverage to new and hard-to-insure populations and moved slowly to institute increases in benefits. By forcing caution on the expan-sionary plans of zealous administrators, conservative pressure had the effect of making the program more, rather than less, acceptable across the political spec-trum. In short, the fact that the program embodied compromises with skeptics and opponents did not condemn it to bureaucratic futility.[31]

There is a larger point as well. Deciding what kind of old-age insurance pro-gram this country should have is a question that transcends pure normative theories and must involve theories of political legitimacy. On the one hand, the social security contributory insurance program was neither as redistributive as progressives would want nor as small and efficient as conservatives would pre-fer. A program targeted at the old in need, with a voluntary program or a pro-gram with investment choices for middle-class families, might be cheaper to operate, more socially just, and (from a conservative point of view) less of a threat to fundamental American values. On the other hand, efficiency or social justice is not the only standard by which a state policy or program should be evaluated. A fan of both efficiency and social justice, President Roosevelt none-theless opted for the social insurance model of the kind that had been devel-oped in northern Europe, rather than for a social welfare model. The New Dealers believed, astutely, that only a social insurance model offered the pros-pect of political stability over time—both stable support for the program *and* a program that would head off political support for a socialist system. They thought that giving Americans a social insurance *right* would help preserve overall satisfaction with the democratic-capitalist system, and that a rights ap-proach required everyone (namely, the middle class) to be offered protection, not just the indigent. If everyone stood to benefit, the chances were best that the people would support the program even in difficult times. If this account is correct, then the McNollGast theory seems to get things right: the enacting coalition wanted a broad social insurance program (which is by definition an inefficient redistributive program); that is what they created, and that is what persisted through time.[32]

One could argue that these choices undermined social security as a genuine welfare program by redistributing most of its money within the middle class. While the genuinely impoverished might be helped somewhat, it is at the price of extensive, bureaucratically managed, transfers of funds among people who do not really need the money. If this critique is right, one might conclude, with Moe, that the program was flawed from its earliest days. But such a conclusion attributes to FDR and other leaders preferences and goals that they did not have. FDR saw the program as filling a void that was left by the transformation of the American economy, and not as a narrowly targeted poverty program. He announced this aim even before his election in 1932; it was not a compromise he was forced to accept.

DEEP COMPROMISE AND THE ROLE OF BIPARTISAN COMMISSIONS

One of the original compromises made to appease conservatives proved to be a political boon, rather than the kind of landmine that Terry Moe's theory insists upon. The 1935 act required the Social Security Administration (SSA) to consult regularly with advisory councils that would have representatives from business and the insurance industry, as well as from organized labor and the general public. At the behest of Senator Arthur Vandenberg, a thoughtful Republican critic of social security, Congress appointed the 1937–38 Advisory Council on Social Security to review the program and make recommendations. The SSA viewed this process with suspicion: workers such as Ida May Fuller started paying into the program in 1937, but no one would start drawing benefits until 1942, so this was a point of extreme political vulnerability for the program, and the advisory council was viewed as a last chance for conservatives to undo FDR's great vision. Instead, the opposite occurred. After research and investigation, carefully managed by Altmeyer, the agency's staff, and council member Edwin Witte (one of the key New Dealers behind the act), the advisory council's 1938 report reaffirmed the social insurance idea and recommended a significant expansion. The council's biggest recommendation was that social insurance ought to be aimed at supporting *families*, not just individual *workers*. Hence, it recommended expanding social security to include benefits for surviving spouses and dependents (children) of workers who would contribute to the program but not live long enough to receive retirement benefits. It also recommended that retirees start receiving social security payouts in 1940, rather than 1942 as scheduled. Although rejecting its further proposals to expand social security's coverage to include farm and domestic workers, Congress followed the advisory council on these other important matters when it adopted the Social Security Act Amendments of 1939.[33]

The 1937–38 Advisory Council on Social Security and the 1939 amendments were a major event, rivaling the enactment of the original statute. One feature of the process was that it ultimately provided a mechanism whereby the experts in the SSA had an opportunity to educate and win over doubters. As political scientist Martha Derthick has argued, administrators such as Arthur Altmeyer,

Robert Ball, and Wilbur Cohen were effective strategizers and advocates for the social insurance idea. They and their technocrat colleagues (such as the chief actuaries, Rulon Williamson and Robert Myers) had an effective monopoly of information relevant to evaluating how the program operated and how it might prudently be changed. They insisted that this gave them a special responsibility to provide technical advice to congressional staff, their bureaucratic superiors, and other executive branch appointees, as well as to interest groups and the media. Program opponents and skeptics as well as proponents relied on these experts because they, alone, understood the economics and demography of old-age insurance. Nearly everyone believed that social security was so technical that the administrators' advice was indispensable if any programmatic changes were contemplated.[34]

So the advisory council process offered persuasive opportunities for social security experts—even more notable was how a bipartisan representative group of relevant interests worked together and ultimately propounded a *deep compromise* that combined legitimacy and some good ideas. The 1937–38 Advisory Council on Social Security was a body reflecting the range of interests concerned with the program. Its members were leaders from the business and labor communities as well as scholars with interests and expertise in social insurance. (It was too soon of course to recognize what we would now see as a major stakeholder group: retirees such as Ida May Fuller who would receive benefits). Because of the representation of the diverse set of politically salient interests, councils of this kind have come to play an important small "c" constitutional role: they develop recommendations that express a consensus acceptable to business and labor interests as well as to the public. Through their service on the 1937–38 Advisory Council, Marion Folsom (Eastman Kodak's treasurer) and Edward Stettinius Jr. (U.S. Steel's chairman of the board) not only brought financial savvy to the oversight process but also became effective ambassadors for social security in the business community and the Republican Party.[35]

The council's recommendation that the SSA start paying benefits in January 1940, rather than 1942 as originally legislated, was politically significant. This was an important event in the lives of many Americans, as reflected by the experience of Ida May Fuller, who retired from her secretarial job in November 1939, shortly after the social security amendments had been enacted. While running an errand in Rutland, Vermont, she dropped by the Social Security Office. "It wasn't that I was expecting anything, mind you," ventured the cautious New Englander, "but I knew I'd been paying for something called Social Security, and I wanted to ask the people in Rutland about it." To her surprise, the "people in Rutland" told her she was now eligible for benefits and helped her file the necessary paperwork. On January 31, 1940, the agency issued Fuller its first old-age benefits check (number oo–ooo–oo1), which she received the same day. The amount was $22.54, and the recipient was delighted.[36]

This kind of experience was the beginning of the program's political ascendancy. People liked getting their checks, and everyone getting checks in the early days was getting back much more than he had contributed. Ida May Fuller, for example, had contributed less than twenty dollars in the two years before her retirement, an amount smaller than the first monthly check she received; she ultimately drew $22,888.92 in benefits, a spectacular return on the most modest of investments. Knowing that microevents like this built political capital, program administrators such as Altmeyer and Ball suggested to Congress that it could safely increase the benefits paid out and enlarge the pool of eligible recipients while postponing tax increases. The result was a period of slow program growth from the time of the 1939 amendments to the much more expansionary amendments of 1950. Given the budgetary stringency of the war years, slow programmatic growth was perhaps to be expected, and the postwar boom and inflation probably inhibited any thirst for expansion. Social security remained smaller than the means-tested welfare programs and still excluded large fractions of the work force (especially agricultural workers). By the end of the 1940s, program leaders had cemented fairly strong support in Congress, especially in the finance committees, but social security had not yet fulfilled Witte's, Altmeyer's, and Ball's broader vision. For that to happen, its coverage would need to become universal, and Congress would have to exhibit some willingness to accept its financial burdens.[37]

The midpoint of the twentieth century marked another turning point for social security. The GOP-controlled Congress created another advisory council in 1948. As before, conservative critics assumed that a fair and balanced assessment would require some curtailment of the program. As before, the advisory council was composed of representatives from the business, labor, and academic communities. As before, the council's deliberations were strongly influenced by information provided through SSA staff member Robert Ball (playing the role in 1948 that Arthur Altmeyer played in 1938). As before, the council roundly endorsed the social security old-age insurance idea, recommended that eligibility for the program be expanded (and expanded much more than the 1938 council had recommended), and urged that benefits be increased. Although appointed during the Republicans' control of Congress, the council delivered its report to a Congress controlled by the Democrats, basking in the wake of their triumph in the 1948 presidential and congressional elections.[38]

Not surprisingly, Congress enthusiastically followed the council's recommendations. The Social Security Act Amendments of 1950 expanded coverage by about ten million more workers (out of the twenty-five million not previously covered). Through the efforts of the administrators and a friendly Congress, social security was coming closer to the universal "right" prophesied in FDR's Second Bill of Rights (chapter 2). In addition, the 1950 amendments increased benefits an average of 80 percent, to reflect the cost of living increases since 1940. Like thousands of other beneficiaries, Ida May Fuller received her first social security increase on October 3, 1950—right before the off-year elections. Rather than the monthly check of $22.54 that she had been receiving since 1940, Fuller received a check for $40.53; by the expression on her face, preserved for posterity on the SSA's Web site, she was even more delighted than she had been in 1940.[39]

Egged on by administrators, members of Congress realized that this kind of legislation was electoral gold. In every even-numbered year for the next two decades, Congress enacted cost of living increases in social security benefits. By the time the Republicans regained Congress (and the presidency, with Dwight Eisenhower) in 1953, there was a solid bipartisan majority that not only supported the social security idea but also supported its expansion. Hard-line anti–New Dealers such as Senator Carl Curtis of Nebraska suffered one humiliating rebuff after another, culminating in President Eisenhower's 1954 State of the Union address reaffirming the social security idea and urging its expansion to include farm workers and state and local employees, which the GOP Congress promptly enacted as the Social Security Amendments of 1954.[40]

We agree with Martha Derthick that, at least in its early decades, the social security program was successful in doing most of what its proponents wanted, although at a measured pace that built political foundations prior to taking action. Ultimately, the political foundation that was established in those years permitted the program to weather the political threats that arose during and after the 1970s. One might complain (as we are inclined to do) that the program achieved little redistribution to the elderly poor. A more efficient redistributive program would have required means-tested benefits, so that the well-off would not receive them. But the mantra of program executives was that "a program for the poor is a poor program"—if a program's constituency was small and poor (and likely to be politically weak and uninvolved), it was likely to be vulnerable to political shifts. The sad fate of the means-tested Great Society programs after 1980 is testimony to the political wisdom of this saying. Moreover, a means-tested program tends to stigmatize recipients and to marginalize a program from the everyday lives of most people. Program advocates wanted social security to be a central theme in the lives of all Americans—a part of their planned retirement which they could enhance if they wished—and therefore resisted stigmatizing it by means-testing benefits or by detaching payouts from contributions. This vision shares much with the social insurance ideology prevalent in northern Europe where, it is believed, virtually anyone could fall into a state of need for reasons not fully under her own control. Although a private insurance model is very different from social security—requiring larger premiums to insure against catastrophic risks—ordinary people liked the feeling that they were participating in their own retirement. Social security acquired the aura of a public-private partnership: the government was providing a mechanism whereby working Americans could plan responsibly for their retirements (itself a new concept).[41]

Achieving this vision required more than gradually expanding benefits while keeping tax rates relatively low and not very visible, at least at the beginning. It also entailed constructing a financial chassis for the program that would make its promise credible as a right that every American could count on. The program administrators envisioned a robust right to social security, but (like FDR) they were also tactically cautious and strategically clever. They had signed up to the idea that the program should be based on the insurance model, which implied that people would have an entitlement to retirement benefits based on their contributions. The insurance model implied that the tax rates should be raised as quickly as possible to a level sufficient to finance benefits over the long run. Program administrators also wanted to build up an interest-generating trust fund that could be counted on to contribute substantially to revenues over the long run. These proposals would prove to be politically controversial in Congress, and administrators were forced to compromise some of their ideas as to how the program should be financed. Specifically, they gave up on the idea of a rapid rise in payroll tax rates and therefore in the creation of a large trust fund. Even the modest tax increases envisioned in 1939 were effectively postponed for a decade. These decisions compromised the idea that the program was really an insurance program at all, a point not lost on congressional critics. Still, by compromising on financing, the program became so popular that antigovernment Republicans could not mount much resistance to its steady expansion. (On the other hand, this compromise meant that when the ratio of retired to working people increased in the 1970s and afterward, the program became more expensive.) In contrast to some of the earlier compromises that strengthened the program, these compromises had short-term political advantages but longer-term costs, namely, significant financial weaknesses in the underlying structure, that would lead to financing crises down the road.

EXPANSION OF SOCIAL SECURITY: THE MEDICARE ACT OF 1965

Right number 7 of President Roosevelt's Second Bill of Rights was "the right to adequate protection from the economic fears of old age, sickness, accident, and unemployment." By the end of the Eisenhower administration, the federal government had delivered programs addressing this economic right. Old-age insurance was available to almost all workers by 1961, every state in the union had an unemployment compensation program funded in large part under Title III of the 1935 act, and the Social Security Act Amendments of 1956 funded a program providing income support to Americans who were disabled from working because of sickness or accident.[42]

Presidents Roosevelt and Truman were also committed to item number 6 of the Second Bill of Rights: "The right to adequate medical care and the opportunity to achieve and enjoy good health." They and the administrators advising them were aware that federally sponsored health care would be a major governmental initiative that would be politically difficult. FDR's 1934–35 Committee on Economic Stabilization considered federally funded health insurance, a proposal that was met by determined opposition from the American Medical Association (AMA). The committee's report on public health was not even submitted to Congress, because President Roosevelt decided that including health insurance would imperil the already controversial social security bill. After the adoption of the 1935 act, however, the new Social Security Board and other agencies gathered information and episodically published reports on public health and possible federal responses to systemic problems. In 1937, Dr. Thomas Parran Jr. of the Public Health Service suggested, in an administrative memo, that health insurance could be limited to social security recipients.[43]

World War II cut off serious debate about national health insurance proposals. President Truman proposed a national health insurance program in 1945, but the postwar politics of the Truman and Eisenhower administrations were unfriendly to any such program, especially given the AMA's fervent opposition. But administrators kept Dr. Parran's idea alive, and Congress in 1956 adopted a "military medicare" program, assuring medical care for the dependents of service personnel. The same year, Congress handed the AMA a rare defeat when it amended the Social Security Act to fund income-maintenance payments to disabled workers, over the medical profession's opposition and quiet lobbying. After that defeat, congressional reformers in 1957 introduced a Medicare bill for the benefit of retirees such as Ida May Fuller, who was then eighty-three years old and still receiving her monthly social security check, augmented every two years by congressional increases. The Eisenhower administration conceded that America's aged (by then almost 9 percent of the population, and growing) faced genuine problems of health care affordability. Fuller's senators, Republicans Ralph Flanders and George Aiken of Vermont, were strongly in favor of such federal legislation, and Flanders had introduced a weaker bill during the Truman administration. With bipartisan support, Congress in 1960 enacted the Kerr-Mills Act, which funded assistance to elderly "medical indigents," people who were ill and could not afford standard medical treatment.[44]

The 1960 presidential election saw both candidates criticize Kerr-Mills as only the first step, and the prevailing candidate, Senator John F. Kennedy, openly favored health insurance for the elderly. Medicare bills remained bottled up in Congress throughout the Kennedy administration. In the wake of President Kennedy's assassination in November 1963, Congress came within one vote of enacting a Medicare bill—Ways and Means Chair Wilbur Mills killed the measure in conference committee. The 1964 election, however, provided a strong mandate for such legislation. President Lyndon Johnson was running for a full term; his opponent was Senator Barry Goldwater, the most articulate congressional critic of social security. Although Johnson's best-known achievement after a year in office was the Civil Rights Act of 1964, which Goldwater had opposed, the issue that probably hurt the GOP challenger even more was social security. During the primary season, Senator Goldwater voted against Medicare and said this: "I would like to suggest . . . that Social Security be made voluntary, that if a person can provide better for himself, let him do it." The Democrats lampooned Goldwater as an enemy of social security, and conservative older voters abandoned the Republican Party in droves. We suspect that even Ida May Fuller voted against him; her rock-ribbed Republican state (one of only two to buck the Roosevelt landslide of 1936) voted for the Democrat. Goldwater lost the election by one of the largest margins in American history, and congressional Democrats outnumbered Republicans two to one. His case buttressed by the report of a 1965 Advisory Council on Social Security, President Johnson won the enactment of Medicare in 1965.[45]

When President Johnson delivered Medicare to the still-increasing aged population, Ida May Fuller was ninety years old and in failing health, so this measure came just in time for her. In a few years, she would move to live with her niece, Hazel Perkins, in Brattleboro, Vermont, but most of her doctor and hospital bills would be paid by the federal government. Her doctors, who had fought tooth and nail against "socialized medicine," soon found Medicare to be a pot of gold. Although we shall not provide a detailed account, the entrenchment of Medicare came more easily than the original social security idea, because Medicare swiftly won the loyalty of the medical community as well as America's aging population.

DEFENDING THE RIGHT TO SOCIAL SECURITY

The golden age of social security, capped by the addition of Medicare, ended rather suddenly in the early 1970s. When Ways and Means Chair Wilbur Mills and President Richard Nixon (both tight-fisted fiscal conservatives) agreed to automatic cost of living adjustments in 1972, it seemed a recognition that social security had become the center of the American version of the modern state of consent, where the government assures every citizen of an economic and institutional structure allowing all of us the discretion to make life choices that satisfy us. But the Mills-Nixon compromise meant that there would no longer be congressional-executive agreements every two years to increase benefits and expand coverage. Program leaders had been divided on the wisdom of indexing, with Social Security Commissioner Robert Ball and analyst Richard Myers supporting the idea, and former HEW Secretary Wilbur Cohen opposing it. Cohen believed that, by requiring regular congressional action, the program would more effectively maintain political support. This debate illustrates how administrative constitutionalism is far from monolithic; program administrators sometimes disagreed among themselves as to the best course of action. Cohen was probably right. Even though beneficiaries such as Ida May Fuller (at the age of ninety-eight, still receiving her monthly check) appreciated indexing, it deprived the expanded social security program of political oomph in a decade when it faced a demographic dilemma.

Shortly after the 1972 Mills-Nixon deal, the economy entered into a long period of low growth and double-digit inflation ("stagflation").[46] This was a double whammy for social security: with an automatic cost of living adjustment, benefits expanded rapidly with inflation, while tax revenue growth slowed with the economy. Even worse, the postwar baby boom had been followed by much smaller birth cohorts, so long-run financial projections became even less optimistic. The actuaries almost immediately began projecting deficits that extended far into the future. The 1976 projection, for example, was that the Social Security Trust Fund would be exhausted as early as 1979. In this time of increasing challenge, the program lost its most brilliant strategist, as Commissioner Robert Ball was discharged by President Nixon; the old generation of dedicated experts came to an end precisely as the program faced huge new challenges. Would social security suffer the same fate that soon befell Nixon and Mills, both of whom resigned from high office in disgrace two years after their historic agreement?[47]

In 1975, the nation's first social security beneficiary, Ida May Fuller, died. She had been an invalid living with her niece before she passed away at the age of one hundred. Would social security follow her into the grave?

Presidents Gerald Ford and Jimmy Carter each proposed adjustments to benefit formulas, increases in the retirement age and payroll taxes, and expansion of the tax base. Congress went along with these initiatives. But neither presidents nor legislators had the courage to pursue any of these fixes far enough to do more than to put off the problem for a few years. So the chronic deficit problem remained on the agenda, triggering another emergency fix in 1983 and arising again early in the twenty-first century. The program adjustments seemed to undermine, at least a little, the idea that social security was a basic right; the promises of the social security program began to look shaky. Indeed, public confidence that benefits would actually be paid fell sharply. Whereas 63 percent of survey respondents said they were confident in the future of Social Security in 1975, when Ida May Fuller died, that number fell to 37 percent three years later. Specifically, the idea that there was a firm right of the kind that Edward Witte, Frances Perkins, Arthur Altmeyer, and Franklin Roosevelt had envisioned became vulnerable in the minds of many Americans. When combined with substantial political changes that were sweeping through the political system more generally, these shifts emboldened critics of social security.[48]

As a result of these developments, the program became vulnerable to a new kind of objection. Traditionally, conservatives attacked social security either because it was compulsory or because it was a seductive road to big government. (The two criticisms were linked, but they were not the same.) Both criticisms gained force insofar as the program was actually beneficial to most Americans in a material sense. After all, what would have been seductive about a program that offered little in the way of benefits? And why would people accept compulsion for such a program? But once the program started to look like a bad deal for many Americans, conservatives came up with more appealing arguments: Americans could do better investing in their own retirement, or the government could make better use of the money in other programs. That social security survived these arguments is a testament to its enduring place (for better or for worse) in America's statutory constitution.

THE REAGAN ADMINISTRATION'S ASSAULT ON SOCIAL SECURITY

In 1976, Ronald Reagan lost the Florida primary, and with it the GOP nomination, to President Gerald Ford, in part because of Reagan's perceived opposition to still-sacrosanct social security. Many older Republican voters otherwise opposed to big government still supported the social security safety net for themselves and their parents. To avoid being "Goldwatered" on the issue again, Reagan took the social security oath in 1980 and was elected president. But he and his advisers still hated the ever-growing program. And when Reagan assumed office, he found on his desk an administrative report saying that the trust fund would be exhausted within a year or so.[49]

Seizing the initiative within the administration was its director of the Office of Management and Budget (OMB), David Stockman. Like his boss, Stockman thought the program was objectionable because it was compulsory and undermined individualist values. Social security was a kind of creeping socialism; from Stockman's point of view, it was inevitably inefficient, like any other governmental program. Moreover, as the nation's premier budgetary politician, Stockman thought that he could make better use of social security revenues than to dedicate them to paying benefits in the distant future. He had better things to do with money—cutting income taxes and building Reagan's six-hundred-ship navy, for example—and no interest in solving "some other guy's problem in 2010." Money is fungible, and Stockman believed that the trust fund was simply a paper fiction without any economic meaning. The program looked like a loser taken altogether, but it did drag in lots of revenue through its payroll taxes. To Stockman, it made fiscal sense to exploit social security for his own purposes; such tactics were hardly unprecedented. Years before, in order to hide Vietnam era deficits, LBJ had pioneered the idea of a unified federal budget that ignored the distinction between general revenues and dedicated payroll taxes that were at the basis of Social Security. A unified budget made Keynesian sense as an instrument for guiding fiscal policy, for assessing the total effects of public taxing and spending in the economy.[50]

Rejecting conventional responses to the social security deficit proposed by Republican senators and social security administrators, Stockman proposed several cuts in the program: (1) reducing early (age sixty-two) retirement benefits from the long-promised 80 percent to only 55 percent of the standard benefit; (2) cutting disability benefits; and (3) drastically curtailing benefits to dependent children. House Speaker Tip O'Neill, the highest-ranking Democrat in the country, lustily denounced Stockman's package of proposals as the most "rotten thing to do" to ordinary Americans who had been promised these benefits, "a despicable thing." Democrats feasted on Stockman's proposals like famished dieters and forced the administration to beat a hasty retreat on all but the third proposal. Unfortunately, the most vulnerable group, the ones who could not vote (dependent children), were the only interests sacrificed for budgetary reasons. In the wake of the Stockman disaster, the Reagan administration suffered losses in the 1982 House elections and agreed to the conventional mechanism for solving social security problems—a bipartisan commission.[51]

The 1983 commission was different from the earlier councils, in that the House, Senate, and President Reagan were each entitled to appoint five members. Business and labor interests were amply represented, and the panel was chaired by conservative economist (and former Ayn Rand protégé) Alan Greenspan, taking his first star turn. While the commission recommended controversial benefit cuts and tax increases, the political effect was similar to the effects of the earlier constitutional moments. As it did with the recommendations of the ad hoc councils of 1937–38 and 1947–48, Congress accepted the commission's recommendations virtually without amendment.[52]

It is hard to miss the constitutional aspects of such practices, however ad hoc and exceptional they may have seemed at the time. This should alert us that cynical interpretations of the "bipartisan model" of safe political reform is only part of the story. President Reagan created the commission to give him the cover needed to cut back on benefits and increase taxes, but in operation the 1983 bipartisan commission represented a successful institution of ongoing administrative constitutionalism. To meet the government's commitment to older Americans, the program needed to be overhauled, but the ordinary organs of government were insufficient to the task: the SSA and the Supreme Court did not have the authority or legitimacy to do so, and Congress and the president were paralyzed by partisan bickering. Like the earlier councils and advisory committees, the 1983 Greenspan Commission treated social security as a system for protecting fundamental rights and worked out a bipartisan plan for continuing to implement that program. Legislators were important for the legitimacy of this process, and administrators played their accustomed key role in providing statistical information, enthusiasm for the program, and ideas about what would work and what would not.

THE NEW CRITIQUE OF SOCIAL SECURITY, 1980–97

Even though conservatives had suffered a tactical setback in the early Reagan administration, they continued to see the social security deficit issue as a long-term strategic advantage. At the very least, it would force social security onto the national agenda and, more important, would make people unsure that they would ever receive the benefits they had paid for. Indeed, at the very point when the deficit was gaining public attention, conservative think tanks, particularly the Heritage Foundation (established in 1973) and the Cato Institute (1977), were developing sophisticated policy critiques of social security. This was an important development, for the imbalance between the information and data possessed by defenders of the modern administrative state and their conservative opponents undergirded the durability of liberal programs.[53]

Starting with Peter Ferrara's *Social Security: The Inherent Contradictions*, published by Cato in 1980, conservative intellectuals mounted a powerful assault on social security. The neoconservatives avoided the mistakes of the past. Rather than railing against "socialism security" and threatening to cut back on benefits, the new critics raised empirical doubts about the likelihood of future benefits, demonstrated that retirees could obtain superior returns on their investments through private rather than public mechanisms, and developed concrete proposals for attractive alternatives. As Martha Derthick and Steven Teles put it, they "recognized the need to move from 'normal' politics to a long-term strategy of disentrenchment. Disentrenchment required that conservatives weaken the public's certainty that they would receive benefits (thereby reducing their belief that future benefits were a right to which they were entitled) while simultaneously increasing their certainty in and experience with an alternative."[54]

The neoconservative critique was especially timely because of unrelated changes in pension law. Many large employers had traditionally offered defined-benefit pension plans, in which retired employees would receive a certain percentage of the salaries earned near the end of their period of employment. The formulas differ, but the defining feature of such plans is that they do not depend on contributions to fix benefit payments. As the baby boom aged, the weaknesses of these plans became apparent. Employers often underfunded the plans and used plan revenues to make risky investments; if a firm failed, its pension plan could disappear completely. Newspapers filled with stories of workers retiring without promised pension benefits and of opportunistic or shortsighted employers. In 1974, Congress passed landmark pension legislation aimed at shoring up defined-benefit plans, but the new regulations had the predictable effect of making such plans much less attractive to employers. In 1978, Congress added a new section 401(k) to the Internal Revenue Code to give employers another option; the law permitted employers to contribute to a tax-deferred individual retirement account (IRA) that would be owned by the employee. Numerous restrictions were placed on these 401(k) defined-contribution plans, limiting their size and the investments that could be made by them, but employers and many employees found them attractive. Over time, such pension systems have become the standard way most people plan for retirement. The switch to defined-contribution plans would seem to produce a large shift in who bears the risks of retirement income (though how much risk shifting there is, is a very hard question given the regulatory restrictions on how these plans can invest). And active retirement planning probably also produced a new mindset for many people.[55]

It is not obvious how the changed private pension environments affected support for the social security system. The shift to defined-contribution plans might have shored up support for a relatively secure governmental pension guarantee as a component of retirement portfolios. Conversely, the new mentality might have worked the other way, making people comfortable with the idea of controlling their own investments and less willing to support a tightly managed and very conservative pension scheme. When combined with enlarged public uncertainty that benefits would actually be paid, the public might have become less supportive of social security and more accepting of shifting away from reliance on government promises. This was the belief of the neoconservative critics: "IRAs can ease the transition toward structural reform of the Social Security system."[56]

Because we do not have relevant public opinion polling data before 1984, the neoconservative faith in the erosive effect of IRAs cannot be refuted, but the data we do have are inconsistent with their hypothesis. From 1984 to 2000, the percentage of respondents saying that either too little or about the right amount was spent on social security never fell below 90 percent in the National Opinion Research Center's General Social Survey. This was true even as many people lost confidence that the program would continue to exist or pay benefits. This is a remarkable pattern in public opinion and one that program opponents seemed not to understand. What could it mean, for example, for someone to think we are spending too little on a program that will soon fail to pay benefits? In our view, such a pattern probably implies that the loss of confidence is not a simple prediction about the program but is partly an implied criticism of those who would try to abolish it. As Lawrence Jacobs and Robert Shapiro wrote, "Super-majorities support Social Security but fear that politicians or an economic downturn will ruin it."[57]

Jacobs and Shapiro show that the general level of support for social security is not only stable over time, and their finding also applies to key features of the program. The general public opposes reductions in benefits to any recipients (including those with high incomes), reductions in the cost of living adjustments, and increases in the retirement age. While the public disfavors increasing payroll taxes, that opposition disappears when there would be benefit cuts unless taxes are increased. It seems evident from this pattern that the American people have accepted the ideas that there is a basic right to retirement security earned by paying payroll taxes, that this right should be available to everyone, and that this is a right worth paying for. Moreover, Jacobs and Shapiro demonstrate that the pattern of public support is visible in the young as well as the old, and in the well-off as well as the not-so-well-off.[58]

As the stock market took off in the 1990s, people flocked to IRAs by the millions and became optimistic about the returns they could expect to earn. While there was a sharp drop in the market after 2000, the stock market soon resumed a long upward trend (an ascent that ended in October 2008). At the time, conservatives seemed justified in thinking that they could induce younger cohorts away from social security by offering a transition to private accounts. Indeed, the Democrats made their own contribution. President Clinton and other "New Democrats" seemed to encourage the belief that there was some kind of funding crisis for the program that might be solved by devoting some of the large bubble-driven budget surpluses into shoring up the trust fund. Clinton's "Save Social Security First" was a potentially attractive wedge issue for Democrats looking forward to 2000.

Remembering the Reagan-era debacle, the Republican-controlled Congress moved cautiously on social security issues. Thus, the only mention of social security in House Speaker Newt Gingrich's Contract for America was a promise to expand the benefits that could be received by reducing taxes and earned income penalties on middle-income recipients. Ironically, the Republicans' most important critique came from the 1994–96 Advisory Council on Social Security. Unlike earlier councils, the 1994–96 body included well-informed critics of the whole social security idea, most prominently Carolyn Weaver, a member of Senator Robert Dole's staff and an outspoken supporter of privatization. Also unlike earlier councils, the 1994–96 body declined to endorse the social security idea and, instead, openly advocated alternatives. In its 1997 report, a plurality of the council (the Weaver group) recommended privatization. Although not joining Weaver's critique, council chairman Ed Gramlich advocated an integration of personal investment accounts, indexed and managed by the government, into the social security monthly payments. In the wake of the council's report, prominent New Democrats, such as Senator Daniel Patrick Moynihan of New York, proposed diversions away from the traditional social security payroll tax and toward IRAs. None of these serious reform proposals was considered by Congress, which was consumed with impeachment fever during the latter part of the Clinton administration.[59]

THE GEORGE W. BUSH ADMINISTRATION'S TURN

Seizing the initiative on the social security issue was Governor George W. Bush, in his acceptance speech to the GOP's national convention on August 3, 2000: "Social security has been called the third rail of American politics, the one you're not supposed to touch because it might shock you. But if you don't touch it, you cannot fix it. And I intend to fix it. To the seniors in this country, you earned your benefits, you made your plans, and President George W. Bush will keep the promise of Social Security, no changes, no reductions, no way. . . . For younger workers, we will give you the option, your choice, to put part of your payroll taxes into sound, responsible investments. This will mean a higher return on your money in over 30 or 40 years, a nest egg to help your retirement or to pass on to your children." This was, politically, a brilliant move—reassuring middle-class aging Americans that the Republicans had learned their lesson (don't mess with people's entitlements) but the Democrats had not learned theirs (social security needs to be modernized to reflect better consumer choices). With this smarter conservative message, Governor Bush defanged the social security reform issue and won the presidency.[60]

What had changed in the twenty years since the 1983 bipartisan commission to convince conservatives that the country would be more receptive to fundamental changes in social security? Was there reason to think that the program had become less popular or that the public had grown less suspicious of politicians seeking to undermine or change it? Was there some reason to believe that Republicans were more trusted to deal with social security now than in the past? One elephant in the room was the fact that the baby boomers were getting close to retirement age, which would have an impact on short-term fund flows in the program. But this was really foreseeable long before then and had indeed been a part of SSA projections for decades. In 1934, Robert Myers had estimated that 12.7 percent of the population would be over the age of sixty-five in the year 2000—very close to the actual fraction of 12.4 percent. So while the short-term payouts were changing, these changes were already anticipated in past projections. Maybe there was a concern that people were now living longer than had been anticipated at the inception of the program. But while there has been an increase in longevity, this is mostly due to changes in infant and child mortality; expected life span conditional on reaching sixty-five has increased only modestly. As far as we can see, there was really nothing about the program or public attitudes that had changed since the time of the bipartisan commission. We need to look elsewhere for an explanation.[61]

Conservatives gained confidence from their congressional victory in 1994 and subsequent presidential wins in 2000 and 2004. Plenty of new findings of public support for privatization were being churned out by polling organizations for conservative think tanks. Of course, as any public opinion researcher will tell you, you can fiddle with question wordings and orderings enough to produce a pretty wide range of results for a paying client. As far as we can see, none of the new findings contradicted the earlier results reported in Jacobs and Shapiro. The program remained almost as popular as ever, and the public was just as suspicious of political attempts to undermine it. And the much-touted generational or income class divisions were not very great. For these reasons, the situation was perfectly set up for the farce that sometimes succeeds a tragedy.[62]

President Bush assumed office with a carefully articulated and rational social security reform proposal. But it had one huge problem: it would cost hundreds of billions of dollars to double fund the existing program *plus* the new accounts. Following Clinton's lead, Bush might have used the inherited budget surpluses for that purpose—but for political reasons the surpluses were spent on large tax cuts instead. (After 9/11/2001 the surpluses turned into large deficits to fund a series of foreign wars.) That political decision removed privatization from Bush's first-term agenda, and the president in May 2001 followed the time-tested approach of appointing a bipartisan social security reform commission, this time headed by former senator Moynihan and Time/Warner CEO Richard Parsons. Packed to the gills with Cato alumni and other avid privatizers, the commission advocated privatization, which the president officially proposed for congressional enactment in 2005.[63]

Notwithstanding his decisive 2004 reelection victory, President Bush's 2005 proposal was a train wreck. Social security prevailed and helped bring down the Bush administration's domestic agenda. Political scientists Steven Teles and Martha Derthick have identified reasons for the debacle: moderate Democrats supportive of privatizing reform died or left Congress, leaving the Bush proposal completely partisan and therefore ripe for attack rather than deliberation and compromise; labor unions and the American Association of Retired People (AARP) unleashed ferocious public relations and lobbying campaigns against the proposal, while business groups remained quietly supportive at best; and burgeoning deficits from the tax cuts and the foreign wars dimmed the enthusiasm of fiscal conservatives, the group the president expected to beat the drums for his initiative. We agree with their analysis but suggest it underemphasizes the most important reason for Bush's failure: the American middle class considered social security an entrenched element in America's statutory constitution; although people recognized pressing problems, they were never persuaded by the Cato-Bush case that social security was obsolete.[64]

There may well be ways to operate private retirement accounts to produce reliably safe income streams for people during their retirement years, while at the same time permitting them some choice about how their funds are invested and how much risk they want to bear. Fighting for private accounts is not where President Bush went wrong. Rather, he fouled up in failing to see that the only way to make massive structural changes to social security would involve a kind of constitutional politics—and in this case, it probably required something like a bipartisan supercommission that would ensure that the changes were acceptable across the political spectrum. Such a supercommission would have to be composed more or less in the image of the earlier commissions, so that it would be genuinely representative of the various "stakeholders" in social security. Certainly this would have to include large and small businesses and labor, but also would have to include interest groups like the AARP and academics (both left and right).

Securing agreement in such a body requires supermajoritarian approval. In 1983 Robert Dole (as a commission member) was able to reach agreement with Edward Kennedy (as well as with fellow commissioner Daniel Patrick Moynihan) on the reform package—and this was key to its acceptability. Supermajoritarian politics of this kind requires compromise among divergent viewpoints, and it is possible that private accounts would not emerge from such a process. We cannot know that in advance. Neither can the president. But changing fundamental rights necessarily requires reaching a broad consensus and cannot be accomplished by ordinary legislative politics. Consensus politics does not mean that hard choices are off the table: the 1983 Greenspan Commission succeeded in producing painful recommendations that secured the program's financial condition for a generation. Creating private accounts would require no less. In retrospect, of course, President Bush's failure to replace social security with private retirement accounts probably saved thousands of aging Americans from financial destitution following the stock market collapse in 2008. Between September 2008 and March 2009, institutional and individual investors lost 30–40 percent of the value of their stock portfolios. After March 2009, there was a rebound, but the 2008 collapse is a cautionary tale for privatizers. For risk-averse retirees or near-retirees, the whole idea of social "security" is undermined if income flows are unpredictable and if there is a danger of flows drying up altogether. Notwithstanding criticisms by economists and some policymakers, there may be wisdom in the social security idea, and practical utility in its entrenched status in America's statutory constitution.

THE CONSTITUTION OF THE FAMILY
AND STATUTES AS PRECEDENTS

At the founding, America's small "c" constitution consisted, in large part, of state common law. If Aristotle had surveyed the American constitution in 1789 or even 1829, he would have focused on neither the Constitution nor federal statutes. Instead, he would have homed in on the body of interconnected rules and exceptions founded upon judicial precedents the states inherited from England and continued to rely on as the basis for private law after Independence. If Machiavelli had visited the United States during the founding generation, the security-assuring rules of law that would have most impressed him would have been the largely common law regime governing family law. As roughly articulated in Sir William Blackstone's *Commentaries on the Law of England* (1765), the common law regime had three fundamental features: coverture, lifetime commitment, and sexual monopoly. The legal rules associated with this regime were interwoven with our customs; together, they were pervasively constitutive of Americans' life choices and identities, a classic example of the wedding of Max Weber's two different duties of obedience (following the commands of law and conforming to social norms). As an Indiana judge put it in 1857, American marriage law was itself "a great public institution, giving character to our whole civil polity."[1]

"By marriage, the husband and wife are one person in law," said Blackstone. This idea is often expressed as marital "unity," but the more accurate term is "coverture," whereby the wife's legal identity was "covered" by that of her husband; it was (again to quote Blackstone) "consolidated" into her spouse's identity. Thus, a wife enjoyed legal rights of support from her husband, but her dealings with the outside world fell under the husband's presumably benevolent control. Hence, wives ordinarily did not own property in their own names, could not enter into contracts except as agents of their husbands, had no right to control earnings their labor generated for their families, and were subject to reasonable discipline by their husbands. Founding father James Wilson elaborated: Although "peculiar" to the common law, marital unity was "not uncongenial to the spirit of a declaration from a source higher than human—'They twain shall be one flesh.'" While Wilson appreciated the common law's consistency with American religious beliefs, we should add that the common law rules were also functional for a society that was largely agrarian, with large households and many children; similar rules existed in early Louisiana, a civil law jurisdiction.[2]

Coverture created and helped define marriage as a cooperative enterprise, with the husband as the presumptive legal decision maker as regards relations between the family and the outside world. The common law further defined marriage by proclaiming the illegality of procreative (penile-vaginal) conduct outside marriage and of nonprocreative conduct within or without marriage. Thus, the American colonies and the early states criminalized (increasingly by statute) fornication, or procreative sex between unmarried persons; open and notorious sexual cohabitation by unmarried men and women; adultery, or procreative sex with a person married to someone else; incest, or procreative sex with a related person one was not allowed to marry; and seduction, or procreative sex with a minor female. This criminal law regime established marriage as the compulsory situs for procreative activities. Marriage's monopoly on procreative sex was complemented by common law and statutes imposing the death penalty for engaging in the "crime against nature," namely, nonprocreative anal sex with an animal or a human, including one's spouse. This sexual monopoly not only reinforced the notion that marriage was the situs for bearing and rearing children but also provided a strong incentive for sexually thirsty Americans to wed.[3]

Finally, the common law understood marriages as lifetime commitments. Given the spiritual and legal merger of the wife and the husband into the marital household, the common law was loath to recognize divorce. Indeed, English and most American judges in the eighteenth century refused to recognize divorces sought because the marriage had been a disaster, or even because the husband had abused, assaulted, or cheated the wife. New York chancellor Reuben Wallworth said this in 1828: "It would be aiming a deadly blow at public morals to decree a dissolution of the marriage contract merely because the parties requested it." In a liberalization of the common law, however, most American legislatures provided for divorce when a public crime had been committed. In 1813, for example, New York adopted a statute permitting divorce for adultery or extreme cruelty. But even these liberalizations were justified within the agrarian ideology of lifetime marriages producing boatloads of children. When the husband was guilty of adultery, divorce might be considered as a "protection of the innocent party, and the punishment of the guilty."[4]

For most Americans, and virtually all married women, the foregoing common law regime was of greater constitutional significance than anything written in the U.S. Constitution. Marriage was transformational: when a man and woman wed, each of them assumed new rights and obligations—toward one another, toward the children they were expected to bear, *and* toward the community—and took on new identities. The security Machiavelli praised in states operating under the rule of law was most centrally the security of the family: as a public citizen, the husband was concerned that his family would be protected against the arbitrary exercise of the law, which would also create conditions for the family to flourish. Conversely, the common law family had a civic republican feature, for the husband's protective governance of the household was considered a model for the public-regarding citizen. Responsible for the welfare of the household, the husband was expected to make decisions that were in the interests of all members, especially the children, and was subject to severe criticism if he placed his own needs and desires ahead of the household's welfare. Literally, early Americans considered the good husband/father to be the model for the good citizen.[5]

Elizabeth Cady Stanton (1815–1902) and other nineteenth-century feminists found the foregoing regime deeply objectionable. From their perspective, coverture reduced wives to the legal status of servants or virtual slaves, anticontraception rules condemned sexually active wives to everlasting motherhood, and divorce often trapped good wives in relationships with barbarous husbands. The daughter of Judge Henry Cady and the wife of New York legislator Henry Stanton, Elizabeth was attuned to the ways marriage was constructed by law—and could therefore be undone by law. As a girl, she had ripped from her father's law books the portions that explained coverture; Judge Cady had explained to her that removing the pages was not as effective as persuading the legislature to override the objectionable rules. In an unpublished paper, "Why Legislatures Should Make Precedents," Elizabeth argued that elected legislatures existed as forums for critique of outmoded legal rules and for deliberation about what should replace them. As a young woman, she lobbied the New York legislature for such reform; and as a leader of an organized feminist social movement, she pressed for repeated liberalizations. By the middle of the nineteenth century, there was a significant and growing audience for her view that marriage and divorce needed to be reconceived. With the growth of a robust urban middle class and sharply declining fertility rates, more women (like Elizabeth Cady) were receiving higher educations and demanding greater rights, *and* more men (like Judge Cady) viewed the issue of married women's rights through their altruistic roles as fathers than their selfish roles as husbands.[6]

In the twentieth century, fertility rates further declined, women's economic opportunities outside the home greatly expanded, and the technology of contraception and abortion underwent a revolution. As a result of these broad trends, social patterns changed; the law accommodated those new patterns and molded them to some extent. Accordingly, the constitution of the family today is dramatically different from the common law regime prevailing in the founding period: wives enjoy separate legal personalities, divorce is available without fault, nonprocreative and nonmarital sex is no longer a crime. The norm entrepreneurs for these changes have been birth control pioneer Margaret Sanger (1879–1966) and law professor Herma Hill Kay (born 1934). Few legal transformations have been as constitutionally important for the lives, identities, and experiences of ordinary Americans as the transformation of family law. That transformation has been primarily through state statutes, which displaced the common law and have since the nineteenth century been the primary mechanism for the transformation of our constitution of the family. In this chapter, we provide an abbreviated account of several of the most important moments in this transformation, from statutory overrides of coverture to no-fault divorce. As you read this account, keep in mind several larger themes significant to this book.[7]

To begin with, America's republic of statutes involves *state* statutes as well as federal ones. Although norms and legal rules often varied from state to state in the nineteenth century, many of the fundamental norms and rules were quite similar, as reflected in the idea of the common law itself. Even today, the common law rules are often very similar from state to state, contributing to a national constitutional culture—but the more common pattern nowadays is statutory convergence. As Willard Hurst magisterially demonstrated, the early nineteenth century saw states displace the common law with statutory regimes. The states were becoming "laboratories of experimentation," a metaphor suggesting that legislatures can learn to avoid failed experiments—and that successful experiments can be copied or improved upon. Recall Elizabeth Cady's paper on legislatures as creators of precedent. Like a judicial decision that represents a thoughtful, rational solution to a legal quandary, a law that represents a deliberative, rational solution to a public problem can be treated as a precedent, to be followed or modified. The notion of *stare de statute* (follow a statute like a precedent) is most attractive when a prominent state adopts a statute in response to a common social problem, and the people of that state find the new law workable and congenial. As other states address similar social and economic problems, they will encounter the first state's solution as a policy precedent: If this idea worked in New York, won't it work here, too? Or, even better: Why not take the New York solution and improve on it in the following way? When the process is working this way, state statutory convergences can be a "best practices" statutory common law that both reflect and entrench a policy framework and a cluster of values for a particular area of law.[8]

An early example, explored in this chapter, of the statutorification of common law subjects is the married women's property laws adopted in New York (home to the Cadys and the Stantons) and picked up in other jurisdictions in this *stare de statute* manner. This has remained the typical pattern, and this chapter closes with the California no-fault divorce law, which has also been widely copied, such that no-fault divorce now reflects a national constitutional commitment. But many states have not entirely copied California's law, which also allowed unilateral divorce and arguably provided too few protections for dependent spouses and children upon the consensual dissolution of marriages. This is a little-explored defense of the states as laboratories of experimentation: subsequent states may do more than just copy the early state statute; they may improve upon it, based upon the experience of earlier-adopting states or their own independent study. Thus, statutory precedents evolve as they are applied, and later-adopting jurisdictions may make them better. That such a process occurs in legislatures directly accountable to citizens and with access to expert recommendations from study commissions makes the process especially useful in our republic of statutes. While we remain concerned with the documented faults of no-fault divorce (especially when unilateral), its state-by-state statutory process has proven to be a useful ongoing laboratory of serial experimentation.[9]

The middle of this chapter tells a statutory story which reflects a different process, one that most directly tracks the administrative constitutionalism theme of this book. By the mid-twentieth century, state criminal law was decidedly obsolescent, especially with regard to issues of sexual behavior (not just fornication and sodomy laws but also statutes criminalizing abortions and the use of contraceptives). This obsolescence did not produce an immediate crisis, because local and state police, prosecutors, and other administrators took the edge off harsh criminal statutes by applying them only in situations where a third party was harmed or the public peace was breached (usually both). Although racial and sexual minorities were not treated with such lenity, these ameliorative policies spread throughout the country between 1920 and 1945, through cross-jurisdictional administrative deliberation about what were "best practices." Inspired by this development and by professorial embrace of it, the prestigious American Law Institute between 1955 and 1962 deliberated and adopted a "Model Penal Code," an idealized and systematic European-style code that modernized both the jurisprudence and the details of criminal law. It was explicitly utilitarian, humane, and pro-choice—so long as your choice to use contraceptives, engage in sodomy, or have sex outside marriage is voluntary and does not harm someone else, the academic code drafters provided no criminal penalties. Like other model codes of the era (especially the Uniform Commercial Code), the Model Penal Code provided the basis for a state-by-state administrative constitutional deliberation with regard to the issues it treated; that process began in 1955 and continued for the next generation.

A second theme illuminated in this chapter is that legislative and administrative constitutionalism is the primary mechanism by which the state adapts to and accommodates important technological and socioeconomic changes. The increasing recognition of women's legal independence from their husbands, the legal tolerance and then deregulation of sexual cohabitation and adultery, and the allowance and later facilitation of divorce—all of these legal developments reflected larger social and economic realities in this country. We do not contribute new insights into the sociology of changing American family values, for we draw many of our assumptions from historian Carole Shammas's theory that shrinking household size and fertility rates after 1783 undergirded most of the social changes, such as new opportunities outside the home for women and replacement of sex for companionship and pleasure for the traditional notion that sex was valuable only insofar as procreative within a marriage. What we argue is that the social changes occasioned by these demographic ones required a shift of some sort in America's small "c" constitution and that legislators and administrators were the primary means by which states adapted to these new developments. When implementation has been left to judges alone, adaptation has been rockier and sometimes perverse.[10]

The constitution of the family strikingly reflects the theme that Large "C" Constitutional law is parasitic on statutory and administrative developments that, in turn, reflect underlying social, economic, and political shifts. The history of the Constitutional right of privacy has included both uncontroversial applications when the Court simply removes outlying laws (as in the contraception cases) and the controversial ones when the Court is ahead of small "c" constitutionalism (as in the early abortion cases). The larger and more important point, however, is the relationship between constitutional law and social attitudes. Family law surely illustrates the many ways the latter influence the former, but is the converse also true? We offer no answers. Empirical evidence remains ambiguous, but cultural analysis argues for pervasive influence. For example, it is hard to demonstrate, conclusively, that unilateral no-fault divorce has causally affected actual divorce rates over the long term, but thoughtful scholars in the field believe (without either definitive proof or refutation) that unilateral no-fault divorce has contributed to a transformation of Americans' attitudes about the duration of marital commitments, their choices to cohabit rather than marry, women's decisions about education and career, and even parents' attitudes toward child rearing.[11]

Third, while federal statutory and Constitutional law is not the primary legal expression of these fundamental shifts in constitutional norms, it is far from insignificant. Indeed, it plays important, albeit quite different, roles in the three scenarios we are exploring. Federal law played no significant role in the enactment of state laws substantially curtailing coverture. There was no equal protection guarantee before 1868, and the Fourteenth Amendment's Equal Protection Clause was understood to apply to race but not sex discriminations. On the other hand, the married women's property rights social movement overlapped significantly with the sociopolitical movement seeking the right to vote for women, and such laws did help prepare the way for one of the most important expansions of the Large "C" Constitution, namely, the Nineteenth Amendment, assuring women equal access to the franchise. The Nineteenth Amendment, in turn, gave greater political gravity to women's interests, for female voters have since 1920 been one-half or more of the population eligible to vote. This has not assured women of truly "equal protection" by state criminal codes, but it has motivated legislatures to revise their criminal codes to be more responsive to women's interests *when* there has been a consensus among women as to what those interests are. Rape law, for example, evolved swiftly, and almost entirely through legislative reform, after the second wave of feminists insisted on it in the 1960s onward. Abortion law, for another example, has followed women's (and men's) consensus views that there should be room for choice, but that states ought to be able to regulate the right to choose through waiting periods and educational requirements, parental notification or consent (for minors), as well as banning "partial-birth" abortions altogether.[12]

In contrast, federal law played a surprisingly large role in the regulation of contraceptives. The federal Comstock Act was a putative superstatute; under *stare de statute*, the Comstock law was a precedent that twenty-six states followed in their own criminal codes. But Comstock's project of quashing contraceptive knowledge and devices was thwarted by a skeptical administrative constitutionalism—the failure of police, prosecutors, and juries to cooperate. In turn, the birth control movement had greater success keeping criminal prosecutions at bay than persuading state officials to fund and support family planning programs. Support for such local programs came in part from federal financial encouragement, another New Deal legacy. Statutes adopted during the Johnson and Nixon administrations confirmed family planning as a national policy, delinked from marriage and funded much more lavishly than prior state programs had been. Federally funded family planning was a more important development for the constitution of the family than the Supreme Court's 1965 decision Constitutionalizing contraceptive choice (within marriage) as a privacy right had been.

The issue of liberalized divorce saw the Large "C" Constitution strongly influence the small "c" constitution. Specifically, the Full Faith and Credit Clause in Article IV of the Constitution had a greater effect on the constitution of the family than the Constitutional privacy right has had. As interpreted by the Supreme Court, Article IV requires states, virtually without exception, to enforce valid judgments entered by state courts in sibling states. Because divorce is a state court judgment, the Full Faith and Credit Clause required states with restrictive divorce laws to recognize divorce judgments from states with more liberal laws. Once a single state had adopted no-fault or unilateral divorce, not only did unhappily married couples often turn to its courts for relief from their marriages, those quickie divorces exercised a hydraulic effect on state legislation everywhere, speeding the adoption of no-fault divorce across the nation.

The universal adoption of unilateral no-fault divorce can be criticized on a number of grounds, but as a positive matter it is one of the hallmarks of America's constitution of choice, or our *consumerist constitution*. At the outset, note an irony in today's constitution of the family. Unlike in previous eras, most American adults today are not married; many cohabiting couples are not married, and a lot of children are raised in nonmarital households. Changes in the law, relaxing strict rules for sexual intercourse and interpersonal contract rights, have probably contributed to the relative decline of marriage as a social matter—but what is more striking is the fact that marriage remains the keystone to America's constitution of the family, long after the social basis for this central role has faded. Even the consumerist constitution of the family holds out old-fashioned committed relationships as the romantic ideal in our modern republic of statutes.[13]

MARRIED WOMEN'S PROPERTY LAWS
AND STATUTES AS PRECEDENTS

In colonial America, the typical free white household was large and patriarchal: the husband governed his wife, their children, indentured servants, and slaves. After Independence, these forms of authority came under increasing challenge, as inconsistent with the equality norm that many observers considered instinct in the American constitution. A leading critic in the 1840s and onward was Elizabeth Cady Stanton, who as an abolitionist and feminist objected to slavery, indenture, and coverture on moral and social grounds. As a woman, Stanton could neither vote nor hold office, but she and like-minded thinkers persuaded male legislators that this level of patriarchal control was wrong. By 1880, all three forms of legal patriarchy had been revoked or ameliorated—one by a Constitutional amendment (abolishing slavery), one by a federal statute (the Debt Peonage Act of 1867), and one by statute in most states (married women's property laws). These reforms were responsive to larger changes in American society, including an expansive understanding of the liberal ideals of the American Revolution by an urbanizing society, a trend toward fewer children and smaller households, and desires by middle-class fathers to protect their married daughters against destitution. The legal reforms, moreover, interacted with the social movement and the demographic trends. Once married women gained property and contract rights, they were more willing to work outside the home, a socioeconomic development that has for the past 150 years had ripple effects on constitutional practices and norms regarding sex for money, homosexual intimacy, demand for contraception and abortion, divorce without a showing of fault, and surely other important developments.[14]

THE NEW YORK MARRIED WOMEN'S PROPERTY LAW OF 1848

Early married women's property laws were the consequence of changes in state inheritance law, rather than feminist political pressure. Historians Mary Beth Norton and Richard Chused have demonstrated that women in the first two generations after Independence assumed significantly larger roles in household governance, in part because state statutes abolished primogeniture (inheritance by the eldest son) and provided for inheritance by widows and progeny of both sexes. As Professor Chused has shown through an examination of bequests, the period 1800–1850 saw wives inheriting and bequeathing property at rates unprecedented in the colonial period or in England, which did not abolish primogeniture until 1826. In the jurisdictions Chused examined, wills by both men and women favored women as beneficiaries. The common law, of course, would have considered bequests to married women the property of their husbands, but equity intervened: following English practice, chancery courts recognized equitable estates whereby married women could exercise control (and therefore make their own bequests) of property, without their husbands' permission.[15]

From this legal evidence, Chused and other historians suggest that women were assuming more responsibility within middle-class and wealthier households and that fathers in particular were acting on concerns for the welfare of their married daughters. The state itself also recognized an interest in protecting the family unit against destitution occasioned by economically irresponsible husbands, an interest dramatically underscored by the thousands of bankruptcies of the Jacksonian era. In 1835, Arkansas adopted a statute protecting a wife's property from debts incurred by her husband prior to marriage, and after the Panic of 1837 most states expanded upon that approach to provide substantial protection for wives and families against the husband's debts acquired at any point. These laws aimed to ameliorate the effects of coverture in times of distress, and so were usually quite narrow. Some states, however, went considerably further.[16]

In 1837, New York assemblyman Thomas Herttell introduced a bill providing that all property, both real and personal, owned by a woman at the time of marriage, or acquired in her own name after marriage, would remain under her control as an estate separate from that of her husband. In a pamphlet entitled *The Right of Property of Married Women* (1839), Herttell argued that his bill was needed to rationalize the state's law on equitable trusts. The common law was plainly inadequate to meet the needs for wives to have access to resources bequeathed to them by their fathers, and an 1828 statute had only created confusion. Herttell was also writing against the backdrop of the codification movement of the 1820s and 1830s. Eminent lawyers such as David Dudley Field maintained that the common law should be replaced by statutory codes as the primary body of legal rules: codes were simpler, more accessible, and more legitimate, as they would be adopted by democratically accountable legislators. In the spirit of Field, Herttell denounced the fictions and complexities of the common law as post-Independence vestiges of "the dark ages" of "human vassalage."[17]

Herttell also argued that property coverture was inconsistent with "the just and moral principle of equal rights; and equal protection, which constitutes the objects of free government." Indeed, coverture was uncomfortably close to "negro slavery," which most New Yorkers condemned on humanistic and religious grounds. This argument revealed the explicit influence of contemporary feminist thinking, for Sarah Grimké's *Letters on the Equality of the Sexes* (1838) made the same point. Herttell ridiculed the legal fiction of unity: If a husband and wife were really "one person," then why was the wife not hanged when the husband committed a capital crime? Anticipating opponents' primary argument, that abolition of coverture would create discord within the family, Herttell followed Gimké in asserting the opposite: recognizing the wife's right to hold property would *protect* the family against the husband's debtors and would vest at least some of the household's resources in the hands of the parent who was usually more likely to use those resources for the good of the family, and not for private goods.[18]

Although Herttell's 1837 bill was defeated in the assembly, it triggered an unprecedented *public* debate over the rules of marital property and the status of wives. Responding to the concern that widows and their children needed safety nets, the New York legislature in 1840 passed a law enabling a wife to benefit from insurance against the life of her husband, exempt from the claims of the husband's creditors; five years later, married women were vested with rights to own patents in their own names. Every year, dozens of petitions were submitted to the legislature seeking reform and protection of married women's rights; eight major bills were introduced. Newspapers and popular magazines were filled with articles discussing the issue. Although there was no organized feminist lobby, individual women advocated reform. Elizabeth Cady Stanton spent the winters of 1844, 1845, and 1846 lobbying legislators and the governor. Politicians were reluctant, however. As the assembly's Judiciary Committee put it in 1844, "laws and customs which have stood the test of time . . . should not be changed without due consideration or for slight causes," perhaps especially when any change would take away power and authority from the state's key stakeholders, married white males.[19]

In 1846, New York held a Constitutional Convention which laid out ground rules for legal modernization and codification. One of the delegates, Ira Harris of Albany, proposed a married women's property allowance in the new Constitution. The Harris proposal prompted a fierce debate; it was adopted on October 2, by a 58–44 vote and then revoked three days later, 50–59. The primary opponent was a pro-slavery Democrat, Charles O'Connor, but the new Republican Party swept into control of the next session of the legislature; its antislavery ideology was open to the emancipation of wives as well. Former Judge John Fine sponsored such a bill, because he and his propertied wife had been frustrated by the difficulty of assuring her property in the event of the judge's death. Senator George Geddes cosponsored the bill in large part to allow his own married daughter to inherit from him without fear of spousal appropriation or dissipation. The Married Women's Property Act of 1848 sailed through the legislature by overwhelming margins and was signed into law by Governor William Seward (who had been personally lobbied by Stanton) on April 8, 1848.[20]

Following Herttell's bills in the previous decade, the act provided that the "real and personal property" of a woman who marries "shall not be subject to the disposal of her husband, nor be liable for his debts, and shall continue her sole and separate property, as if she were a single female." The statute did not allow husbands to transfer assets to their wives in order to escape creditors, nor did it allow wives to sue their husbands, enter into contracts, or retain earnings for work outside the home. The statute's intended effect was to create assets dedicated to family use and exempt from the husband's debts.[21]

New York was not the first state to legislate space for wives to own and manage their own property. Arkansas and at least nine other states had provided more limited protection before 1848. Statutes going beyond the Arkansas approach and broadly assuring ownership of personal as well as real property had been adopted in Michigan (1844), Maine (1844), Massachusetts (1845), Alabama (1845), Florida (1845), Ohio (1846), and New Hampshire (1846). But New York's law was the most influential *precedent*, because a great deal of publicity accompanied its enactment, New York was the largest and most important state, and the reported decisions of its judiciary could be expected to fill in the details of the statute with judicial precedents that could be followed in other states. Applying Elizabeth Cady Stanton's precocious notion of stare de statute, other state legislatures did follow New York's lead with broad statutes: Pennsylvania (1848), Missouri (1849), Connecticut (1849), Wisconsin (1850), and New Jersey (1852). Because of the association of feminist demands and the abolitionist movement (illustrated in Elizabeth Cady Stanton's life), married women's property laws were much more popular in northern Republican states than in southern Democratic ones. Northern states were also more urbanized and had smaller families, which correlated with fatherly and even husbandly concern for the welfare of their daughters and wives.[22]

FEMINISM AND PROPERTY LAW REFORM AFTER 1848

The 1848 act (and an 1849 act that followed) were not immediately revolutionary, but they did spark a revolution that was carried forth most aggressively in Massachusetts, Ohio, and New York, our focus. The politics that pressed for follow-up legislation was one where women participated as citizens claiming their place at the table. Recall our theme that the United States is an episodic republic, where the old notion of liberty as obligation, self-sacrifice, and participation episodically calls forth energized political pressure for important constitutional reforms. An important occasion for civic republican engagement came three months after enactment of the first New York married women's property act.

On July 16, 1848, Elizabeth Cady Stanton and other feminists assembled at Seneca Falls, New York. In Stanton's words, the new statute "encouraged action on the part of women, as the reflection naturally arose that if the men who make the laws were ready for some onward step, surely the women themselves should express some interest in the legislation." On July 19, the convention issued a "Declaration of Rights and Sentiments" denouncing the legal doctrines of coverture and marriage for life. In 1853, women's rights activists held a new convention in Rochester and resolved to support equality for women in education, workplace, and politics. Specifically, the convention requested that the New York legislature consider "suitable measures for the full establishment of women's equality with men." Inequalities not addressed by the 1848 and 1849 acts included women's inability to control their own earnings, to enter into contracts, and to become guardians of their own children in the event of divorce or the husband's death. At the same time the abolitionist movement was demanding an end to slavery, the women's rights movement was demanding an end to domestic servitude. Not surprisingly, the two social movements overlapped considerably, with feminists like Stanton strongly engaged in the abolitionist movement and abolitionists and leaders of the new Republican Party providing critical support for women's rights.[23]

The 1853 demands raised the stakes of the debate. Unlike the practical demands for married women's property ownership, pressed by fathers and husbands, these new demands were broader and were pressed by wives themselves. That lent them an air of radicalism that was sure to provoke hostility in the New York legislature. Opponents derided feminist demands as anti-Christian, because they revoked the "one flesh" understanding of civil marriage, and socially destabilizing, because they would allow women to step out of the domestic sphere where they "naturally" belonged. Notwithstanding such objections, each chamber of the legislature appointed a special committee to consider Stanton's petition. Stanton, Anthony, and Evangeline Rose deposited with the committees two petitions, each with ten thousand signatures: one for wives' equal property and contract rights and one for female suffrage.[24]

On February 15, 1854, Stanton formally addressed the committees, in a statement that was promulgated throughout the state as her "Address to the Legislature." She started the address with a bang: "The Tyrant Custom," namely, the common law of coverture, largely untouched by the 1848 act, "has been summoned before the bar of Common Sense." Stanton objected that women were "classed with idiots, lunatics, and negroes [*sic*]. . . . [I]n republican America, we, the daughters of the revolutionary war heroes of '76, demand . . . a new code of laws." Coverture was "in open violation of our enlightened ideas of justice," Stanton announced. She identified victims of injustice with particularity: the wife whose husband squandered his wages on alcohol; the widow who might be left in poverty; the mother who lost her children because her husband improvidently apprenticed or indentured them. Stanton's presentation tied women's demands to the natural rights of liberty and equality for which the Revolution was fought, while at the same time exposing the inconsistencies within the cult of domesticity that protected coverture from repeal. The men who believed marriage to be a uniting of man and wife, with special protection for the wife, were confronted with the fact that many husbands abused their authority, to the detriment of children as well as wives. And the wives were no longer willing to suffer in silence.[25]

This was a new kind of politics. Few legislators were genuinely sympathetic, but many felt the petitions could not be ignored. As Rose put it, "These are not the demands of the moment or of the few; they are the demands of the age." In light of this pressure, the committees recommended legislation requiring the mother's assent before a child could be apprenticed or subjected to guardianship and giving wives the right to collect earnings or those of her children if needed to support the household if the husband were unable or unwilling to support or educate the family. Bills embodying these proposals failed in that session, but this only fueled feminists' determination to extract reform out of the legislature.[26]

Stanton's protégée and lifelong friend, Susan B. Anthony assumed the role of general agent for the women's rights movement. She traveled to fifty-four of the state's sixty counties between December 1854 and May 1855. In each county, she helped create a leadership structure, organize conventions to discuss and advocate women's equal rights, and raise enough money to finance her trip to the next county. At every session of the legislature, Anthony and Stanton presented fresh petitions signed by thousands of supporters for women's equal rights. Although few of the signatories could actually vote, an increasing number of legislators took their petitions to heart. While the 1856 New York legislature ignored the petitions after a judiciary committee report belittled their demands, the 1858 legislature updated the married women's insurance law, and the 1859 legislature saw the assembly pass a married women's earnings law.[27]

Anthony barnstormed the state in 1859–60, when she and her colleagues sponsored conventions in forty counties and delivered lectures in 150 municipalities. The newspapers were filled with debates about wives' property rights *and* suffrage for all women, and finally the legislature was receptive. Populated by Republicans inspired by the Declaration of Independence to fight a Civil War to end slavery, the February 1860 session of the legislature was a totally different audience. Stanton addressed the legislators in a joint session. Her words were, again, eloquent, but her audience was already set for action. Engineered by natural rights advocates in the legislature, the Act Concerning the Rights and Liabilities of Husband and Wife sailed through the state senate by a vote of 18–3 and the assembly by 95–5. It was signed into law on March 20, 1860.[28]

The 1860 Married Women's Property Act went well beyond the 1848 and 1849 acts and was a "radical change in the common law," according to the New York Court of Appeals. The new law allowed a married woman to engage in economic activity outside the home and to retain the earnings in her own separate account, free from her husband's control. Married women could freely convey their personal property and could convey real property with the assent of their spouses. They could henceforth bring lawsuits in their own names to enforce their economic rights. Not least important, married women were joint guardians of their children, with "equal powers, rights and duties in regard to them, with the husband." Inheritance law was also changed, to give wives life estates in their intestate husbands' real estate during the minority of the youngest child.[29]

The ripple effects of Stanton and Anthony's campaign for the 1860 act were as important as its substantive provisions. Just as coverture had been an impetus for the Seneca Falls Convention, so ending it was an organizing issue for feminist groups in New York and all over the country. Women in other states followed the Stanton-Anthony model of lobbying for married women's equal rights *and* suffrage for all women, which simultaneously created an organizational structure for a feminist social movement. Leaders following this model and creating their own emendations included Mary Upton Ferrin in Massachusetts, Jane Swisshelm in Pennsylvania, Clarina Howard Nichols in Vermont and Kansas, and Frances Gage, Hannah Tracy Cutler, and Elizabeth Jones in Ohio. Their efforts bore fruit, as state after state adopted statutes assuring married women the right to retain the money they earned for economic activities outside the home. Although some states like Massachusetts (1855) did so earlier than New York, most followed New York through a combination of local activism and practical "they did it in New York and the world did not end" arguments.[30]

An important lesson of the New York feminists' struggle was that it did not end with the 1848 and 1860 acts, which together seemed to overthrow the common law regime of coverture. As feminists learned immediately, winning legal rights is an incremental process—for not only is it important to persuade legislatures to adopt needed measures, further effort is required to implement those measures and, then, to persuade a reluctant citizenry that they are good or at least benign measures. Historian Peggy Rabkin has demonstrated that, in New York, implementation of the married women's property laws fell to a judiciary that was inclined to read statutes to disturb the common law as little as possible. In *Birkbeck v. Ackroyd* (1878), for example, the New York Court of Appeals allowed a husband to sue to recover for his wife's outside earnings; the Court construed the statute to segregate the wife's earnings from the unified control of the husband only when there was a clear indication that the wife intended to maintain a separate account. This requirement was quite difficult for working-class households to establish. Feminists returned to the legislature, which in 1884 adopted another married women's property act authorizing married women to "contract to the same extent, and with like effect and in the same form as if unmarried, and she and her separate estate shall be liable thereon, whether the contract relates to her separate business or estate or otherwise." Even this important statute was construed narrowly, and the legislature finally overrode the common law with success in 1902. As Rabkin argues, the various court decisions were probably responsive to equities in the individual cases, such as allowing the family to obtain a fair recovery in *Birkbeck*, but the case-by-case adjudication characteristic of the common law was not suited to a modern regulatory regime.[31]

Contrast Rabkin's account of the laggard judicial implementation of married women's property laws with our earlier accounts of administrative implementation of the Civil Rights Act of 1964, the Voting Rights Act of 1965, the Sherman Act of 1890, and the Social Security Act of 1935. Where putative superstatutes are initially interpreted by sympathetic administrators who have direct access to the social movement securing the law's enactment, implementation will be more aggressive, and perhaps better informed, than it will be if left entirely to older judges who have no connection to the social movement. This remains true even for superstatutes where the agency has no formal lawmaking authority but announces public statutory interpretations backed up by cogent reasoning. The agency retains a large first-mover advantage when its informed and mobilized officials interpret the statute early on, for judges will tend to follow reasoned agency constructions even where they have the primary authority to interpret superstatutes such as the Civil Rights Act of 1964 (chapter 1), the Voting Rights Act (chapter 2), and the Sherman Act (chapter 3).

STATE STATUTORY CONVERGENCE AND FUNDAMENTAL NATIONAL NORMS

By the 1870s, there was a state statutory convergence around a new fundamental norm: married women could possess and inherit property on their own account, could enter into contracts and bring lawsuits in their own names, and could control their outside earnings, all without a formal veto by their husbands. As before, this convergence tracked the fortunes of the Republican Party and its willingness to espouse rights for the freed slaves; during Reconstruction, most of the South followed New York and Massachusetts in adopting these reforms. Observe the limits of this norm: it did not challenge the unity of the family in most instances, especially for families with few property resources. Husbands remained in control of property and earnings in most families, retained substantial freedom to discipline both wives and children, and of course were the only family members who could vote, serve in the military and on juries, and participate in public life as citizen-deliberators. As legal historian Reva Siegel has shown, wives after the partial end of coverture still remained under their husbands' authority with regard to household and parenting tasks and suffered from economic destitution and physical abuse without any effective legal remedy. On the other hand, such women had more of an opportunity to leave abusive marriages and to take property with them.[32]

The married women's property laws constituted an important shift in America's constitution of the family. And the shift occurred along something of the same lines we suggested in part 1. Thus, the starting point was new social and economic circumstances creating a problem for the republic and the conditions for a social movement. The social movement then petitioned for a norm-shifting statute, which generated public deliberation and feedback. There is an important difference from the national superstatute model of part 1 in that the feedback for the innovative state statute is at two different levels: local and interstate. Within the originating state, there is implementation of the "junior superstatute," further mobilization of the beneficiary group and its allies and new proposals, and ultimately legislative reaffirmation of the new norm and perhaps some elaborations. Outside the originating state, the proposed "precedent-statute" inspires similar beneficiary groups and provides them with good arguments for their states to adopt something similar, generates discussion about variations as well as elaborations of the precedent-statute, and (ultimately) leads to some degree of copying by other state legislatures *(stare de statute)*, without the barn-burning political struggle accompanying adoption in the focal states, New York and Massachusetts. One can think of this process as the gradual creation of a model code (the series of laws adopted in New York after 1848) that represents the best practices available to address an important social or economic problem. Figure 5 illustrates that process.

Figure 5 of course reflects a successful process of state law change and convergence. At any point, this process can be disrupted: the new statutory norm suggested by State 1's proposed precedent-statute might be adopted by only a few other states; the norm might be trimmed back or even nullified through stingy implementation by judges (typical nineteenth-century implementers) or agencies (twentieth-century); or legislatures might have second thoughts and, rather than reaffirm the norm, might trim it back, revoke it, or simply ignore it. The figure reflects a successful state chain reaction supporting and amplifying a new norm, and the idea that married women ought to have independent economic rights is one of the greatest revolutions in American legal history. The ripple effects of New York's 1848 act extended beyond property ownership and included wives' rights to retain earnings, enter into contracts, prevent exploitation of children, and inherit property.

An important ripple effect of the married women's property law movement was in the Large "C" Constitution itself. At Seneca Falls, Elizabeth Cady Stanton and her allies claimed the franchise as one of the equality rights women ought to have. Because the right to vote could not plausibly be sold to male legislators as necessary to protect the family (wives and children) against destitution occasioned by irresponsible or unlucky husbands, it was not likely to be

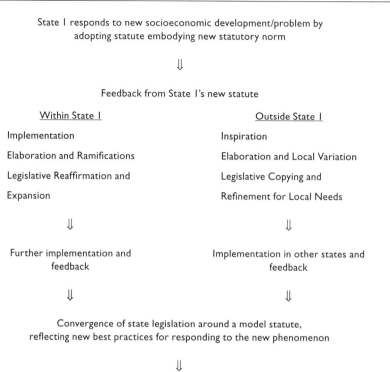

Figure 5. Small "c" constitutional norm from convergence of state laws

adopted in the 1840s and 1850s. But a right that was unthinkable in 1847 became a hot topic of discussion starting in 1848. Stanton understood the intimate connection between married women's property rights and their enfranchisement. On the one hand, demanding the right to vote gave moderate legislators cover to vote for married women's property rights, as the less radical demand. On the other hand, as women came to be property owners, that became an argument for the franchise: "What is property without the right to protect that property by law? It is a mockery to say a certain estate is mine, if, without my consent, you have the right to tax me when and how you please, while I have no voice in making the tax-gatherer, the legislator or the law. The right to property will, of necessity, compel us in due time to the exercise of our right to the elective franchise, and then naturally follows the right to hold office." It took longer than Stanton thought. She and many other feminists were bitterly disappointed when their abolitionist allies did not support women's right to vote during Reconstruction. Under the leadership of Susan B. Anthony, Stanton's best friend and lieutenant in the property rights campaigns, it took more than a generation for feminists to win the right to vote, which finally occurred through the Nineteenth Amendment (1920). While the struggle for women's property rights was an important precondition for women's suffrage, the Nineteenth Amendment provided a political basis for other items on the feminist agenda, starting with the birth control movement and continuing with rape reform. Once women had the right to vote, any issue about which there was substantial agreement among women was an issue to which the statutory constitution would be responsive.[33]

ENDING THE MONOPOLY OF PROCREATIVE MARITAL SEX

At the same time wives were claiming individual economic rights within the marital relationship, Elizabeth Cady Stanton and other feminists were advocating for broader "human rights," including "the sacred rights of a woman to her own person." Stanton wondered: "Did [man] ever take in the idea that to the mother of the race, and to her alone, belonged the right to say when a new being should be brought into the world? Has he, in the gratification of his blind passions, ever paused to think whether it was with joy and gladness that she gave up ten or twenty years of the heyday of her existence to all the cares and sufferings of excessive maternity?"[34]

Although Stanton, Anthony, and their contemporaries were ultimately successful in securing some economic rights and, ultimately, the franchise, they had much less success securing rights of the body. To the contrary, doctors and moralists persuaded legislators to adopt *new* laws reaffirming and modernizing the traditional understanding of a woman's ultimate goal: conceiving and bearing children within marriage to a man. Between 1845 and 1870, when most states were passing statutes allowing wives to own property on their own account, those same states adopted laws making abortion a serious crime. (The common law had left unregulated abortion of a fetus before "quickening," about the two-thirds point of most pregnancies.) Between 1855 and 1885, when most states were passing statutes allowing wives to retain and manage earnings from work outside the home, those same states were passing statutes barring the sale or use of contraceptives, which had also been unregulated by the common law. Indeed, the leading statute was the federal Comstock Act of 1873, which made it a crime to disseminate any book, pamphlet, other printed material, or article "of an immoral nature, or any drug or medicine, or any article whatever for the prevention of conception." Like the married women's property laws described above, these new contraception and abortion laws were not just a codification, they were a major expansion of America's small "c" constitution. These statutes not only reaffirmed Anglo-American law's longstanding condemnation of sex outside of marriage (fornication, adultery) and of nonprocreative sex (sodomy) under any circumstances, but by criminalizing advertisements or trade in contraceptives, the new laws were modernizing the traditional condemnation and were attempting to create a new administrative apparatus for enforcing the constitution of traditional sexual mores. They were also a rebuke to feminist demands for women's sovereignty over their own bodies.[35]

So the constitutional regime of family law changed in the latter half of the nineteenth century, weakening the notion of marriage as a legal unity under the economic control of the husband, but reaffirming and strengthening the notion that sexual activity was wrong unless conducted in a procreative way between a man and a woman married to one another (for life). This updated constitutional regime came under sustained assault from the beginning and, even more, in the generations after women secured the right to vote, when families in a rapidly urbanizing America accepted and then hailed the idea that sexual pleasure could serve sociable as well as procreative functions. After World War II, it became clear that Americans had abandoned the notion that sex was only legitimate if it were procreative intercourse between husband and wife. Contraception laws were nullified for middle-class women by mother's health allowances, while fornication laws were little-enforced dead letters. Most Americans, and many lawyers, believe that the elimination of contraception and fornication laws has been solely a product of the Supreme Court's Constitutional privacy precedents—a belief that this part of the book will refute. Instead, state deregulation of consensual conduct was a product of administrative constitutionalism, with judicial Constitutionalism coming much later and playing a clean-up role. From the perspective of family planning, more important than the Supreme Court's much-discussed privacy right were state and federal programs affirmatively educating American couples about contraceptive techniques and ever-expanding medicines and devices.

ADMINISTRATIVE NULLIFICATION OF CONTRACEPTION LAWS

The author and chief lobbyist for the federal law (and many state laws) criminalizing the distribution of contraceptives or advertisements was Anthony Comstock, one of the most ambitious administrative constitutionalists in American history. President of the New York Society for the Suppression of Vice (1872–1915) and a special agent of both New York and the U.S. Post Office, Comstock personally arrested and prosecuted thousands of Americans for violating his and other antiobscenity statutes. His neopuritan philosophy rested on the belief that sexuality outside marriage or without procreative expectations was not only immoral but also socially corrupting; sexual activities for pleasure or even sociability were abominations that the polity ought to stand against and aggressively prosecute. The Comstock Society and Boston's Watch and Ward Society were the primary prosecutors for obscenity in late nineteenth- and early twentieth-century America. Notwithstanding all the headlines and drama arising out of Comstock's activities, historian Andrea Tone has demonstrated that the "Roundsman of the Lord" was a great constitutional flop. Altogether, between 1873 and 1898, the heyday of Comstock's activities, only 105 persons were arrested for selling or advertising contraceptives in New York; virtually no one went to jail for this offense. Instead of a neopuritan renaissance, Comstock presided over, and fulminated against, the most flourishing contraception market in American history.[36]

Professor Tone identifies several reasons why Comstock failed as an implementer of his normative vision. One reason was insufficient resources. Although Comstock himself had boundless energy, neither the federal government nor New York was willing to provide him with assistants or the budget needed to track down and prosecute the hundreds of contraceptive products and their typically clandestine purveyors. Apparently, state prosecutors devoted virtually no resources to enforcement. Given the large and expanding demand for contraceptives by the nation's ballooning urban population, scanty enforcement resources meant that a tiny fraction of those violating the law were ever apprehended or prosecuted. And those who were apprehended, usually by Comstock himself, almost never went to jail and usually got off scot-free. Tone reports no documented example where a contraceptive distributor went to jail unless she or he injured a victim and many examples where grand juries refused to indict, petit juries refused to convict, and presidents issued pardons to purveyors of contraceptives. Although a putative superstatute, the Comstock Act was, for the most part, a constitutional black hole.[37]

That very few violators went to jail for violating the Comstock Act's bar to contraception materials does not mean the law was utterly without effect, however. An important effect of the federal and similar state laws was to keep birth control inside a social closet and to discourage the formation of public birth control clinics, where poor as well as middle-class women could be educated about methods of birth control, not just condoms (contraception controlled by men) but also pessaries and diaphragms (contraception controlled by women). The leading activist was Margaret Sanger, who opened the country's first public birth control clinic, in Brooklyn, New York, in 1916. The New York police arrested Sanger and her sister, Ethel Byrne, for violating a state law prohibiting circulation of "articles of indecent or immoral use," including articles "for the prevention of conception." The sisters were both convicted in well-publicized trials and went to jail as martyrs for the new cause. The New York courts affirmed their convictions.[38]

Sanger appealed these decisions to the U.S. Supreme Court in 1919. Her Supreme Court brief included a supplement "The Case for Birth Control" (from medical and sociological viewpoints) and argued that the state's suppression of contraceptive devices and birth control information was a severe and unacceptable intrusion into a married woman's personal liberty to plan her family size. *"The State has no more right to compel 'motherhood' than the individual to compel [sexual] relations."* Invoking the recent constitutional recognition of married women's property and contract rights, Sanger argued: "In this enlightened age, when we are accustomed to listen to the discussion of the rights of women to economic freedom and independence, does it not appear most unreasonable that she be deprived of the freedom of her person?" The brief also powerfully argued that the breadth of the state's prohibition was often a deprivation of life as well as liberty, because pregnancy for many women was life threatening. By barring even dissemination of information that could be life saving to these women, the state was placing their lives at risk. Because the state's bar served no legitimate state interest and, indeed, undermined many legitimate ones, such as the health and safety of women, families, and children, it was arbitrary under the Due Process Clause. Without opinion, the Supreme Court rejected these arguments.[39]

On the Large "C" Constitutional front, therefore, *Sanger v. People* fizzled, but it begat a small "c" constitutional firecracker. In *Sanger*, the New York Court of Appeals construed its state anticontraception law as authorizing physicians to prescribe contraceptives for their patients to treat "disease," which the Court broadly defined to include "any alteration in the state of body which caused or threatened pain or sickness." This liberal construction of the statute was presumably inspired by the judges' acceptance of the medical evidence proffered by Sanger and their willingness to allow some flexibility in implementing a statute that had been pressed upon the legislature by the medical profession. The Court's interpretation created an opportunity for extended administrative constitutionalism, as medical personnel and health administrators were empowered to liberate the potential mother from the contraception ban based upon their "expert" (and inevitably normative) evaluation of her mental as well as physical well-being.[40]

As a practical matter, the statutory interpretation holding in *Sanger* opened up a strategy by which birth control clinics could operate in New York. Under a theory that doctors should be available to diagnose mental as well as physical complications that pregnancies would present to particular women, doctors could then give advice and materials to prevent pregnancies. Sanger created a clinic run by doctors in New York City and in 1922 founded the American Birth Control League. Harassment by authorities, including a raid by the police in 1929, only fueled public support for the birth control movement. This was a movement broadly responsive to social needs, specifically, the refocusing of marriage around its "companionate" features, with less emphasis on its procreation function. More than was the case for married women's property laws, the nonenforcement of anticontraception statutes saw the law follow public opinion, and judges played a key role. Responding to complaints by birth control activists Mary Dennett and Margaret Sanger, federal judges in New York rendered the Comstock Act a dead letter as applied to contraceptives, by interpreting the law not to cover useful medical information and devices. The American Medical Association followed suit by grudgingly accepting contraception as a medically acceptable and even useful practice. With toleration from both the medical profession and the state, the birth control movement flourished. By 1937, birth control clinics existed in forty-one states.[41]

The new agenda for the birth control social movement in the 1930s was the use of state-funded public health clinics to supply birth control information and guidance. (The Depression left Sanger's and other birth control organizations short of money.) As before, local circumstances determined which states acted early. North Carolina in 1937–38 was the first state to fund birth control programs, motivated in large part by the state's embarrassment at its relatively high maternal and infant mortality rates. Following the experts, the state instructed its thirty-six new county health and welfare departments to provide family planning information and specific advice about contraceptive medicines and devices. Other southern states followed North Carolina for similar reasons, as did states outside the South. These programs were not always effective, however; some of the information dispensed by North Carolina's clinics was flat wrong, and some of the anticontraceptive drugs worthless to their users. Because most programs were not well publicized, women did not know about them—and social stigma discouraged most women from consulting even those whose existence was known to them. Nonetheless, by the time the United States entered World War II, 77 percent of Americans favored the distribution of contraceptives through public health clinics, thirty-six states had medically supervised birth control clinics supported at least in part by public funds, and another ten allowed such clinics to operate privately.[42]

By 1941, therefore, there were some state-supported programs as well as many private birth control clinics. A natural question was whether federal money would augment the state and private funds available for family planning. Title V of the Social Security Act of 1935 provided almost four million dollars for state maternal and children's health services. Because infant and maternal mortality were tied to unwanted pregnancies, these funds were a natural target for birth control advocates, but the program was administered by the Children's Bureau, whose head, Katherine Lenroot, was firmly opposed to any cooperation between her agency and the birth control movement. The Venereal Disease Control Act of 1939 was administered by the Public Health Service, several of whose officials cooperated closely with the birth control movement. The First Lady, Eleanor Roosevelt, pressured Surgeon General Dr. Thomas Parran Jr. (1936–48) to open up these funds to state "planned parenthood programs" by early 1942. Under pressure during wartime to give working women freedom to avoid pregnancies that would interfere with weapons and other production, even Lenroot allowed Title V moneys to be freed up for state programs as well. Although federal funds presumably found their way into some programs, it is doubtful that the flow of resources for family planning purposes was significant, and it may not have survived Mrs. Roosevelt's tenure as First Lady.[43]

The foregoing developments—administrative and judicial nullification of the Comstock statutes, the cooperation of doctors and the establishment of birth control clinics, and the fledgling movement for public family planning clinics—contributed to a revolution in the constitution of the family. Not only was marital intercourse no longer, even symbolically, just about procreation, the new constitutional vision of the "family" was one where a lot of married parents timed the birth of their children and had no more than they could capably raise. This constitutional vision, and the availability of pessaries as well as other birth control devices, contributed to the long-term trend in the United States toward smaller households: white women's birthrate plummeted from 4.2 children in 1880 to 2.1 children in 1940; women of color saw a steeper decline from 7.0 to 3.2. Another likely effect of the birth control movement was to foster an understanding of companionate marriage that was explicitly sexual. Sanger and her allies hailed sexual intercourse as the glue that bound husbands and wives together and enriched their marital lives. Contraception enabled spouses to engage in penile-vaginal intercourse without the likelihood of children, and this probably contributed to Dr. Alfred Kinsey's findings that most American husbands and wives enjoyed rich and diverse sexual relationships. The availability of contraception also probably contributed to Dr. Kinsey's findings that most Americans had engaged in penile-vaginal sex outside marriage.[44]

There were two notable holdouts against the birth control revolution— Roman Catholic Connecticut and Massachusetts, whose judiciaries refused to construe their anticontraceptive statutes to allow a broad medical-needs exception; Connecticut had the most restrictive law in the nation, barring the private *use* as well as the public *distribution* of contraceptives. Thwarted in the political and administrative process, Planned Parenthood (as Sanger's birth control organization was renamed in 1942) of Connecticut brought several Constitutional challenges, the last of which culminated in a Supreme Court decision invalidating the obsolete law in *Griswold v. Connecticut* (1965). Justice Douglas's opinion for the Court carved a "zone of privacy" for married couples out of the "penumbras" of various guarantees in the Bill of Rights. Even the Court's most conservative jurist, John Harlan, took as constitutionally axiomatic that marriage involves sexual intimacy and that the freedom to enjoy a sexual relationship without increasing the size of the family is fundamental rather than peripheral to the constitution of the family. In spite of its offbeat reasoning, *Griswold* was a Constitutional success. It not only killed the Connecticut and Massachusetts anticontraception laws but also led to the entrenchment of a new Constitutional right of sexual privacy.[45]

MUNICIPAL CONSTITUTIONALISM, THE MODEL PENAL CODE, AND SEX OUTSIDE MARRIAGE

At the same time Planned Parenthood was leading a revolution in American contraceptive practices, Americans themselves were engaging in a quieter sexual revolution. Most people had never conformed their sexual activities to the strict laws on the books, which limited sex to procreative acts within marriage, but those "lawbreakers" were generally left alone by law enforcement officials, so long as their sexual activities were with consenting adults and did not raise a public scandal. In a process of administrative constitutionalism that preceded the modern regulatory state, police officers, prosecutors, local magistrates, and city councils in the nineteenth century left people alone if they were having consensual relations in private places. The patterns of enforcement changed in America's largest cities between 1880 and 1920, when notions of "consent" and "private" evolved through a like process of administrative constitutionalism. An expanding array of state and local agencies and expanded police forces focused enforcement attention on public sexual solicitation, sexual interaction with minors, and sexual activities by unmarried adults in quasi-public places, ranging from parks to restrooms to automobiles. Reflecting the common law unity theory of marriage, married couples were left alone, even when husbands were forcing unwanted sexual activities on their wives.[46]

The extent of Americans' sexual nonconformity was a matter of clear public record only after World War II, when the Kinsey Institute published its heavily documented surveys of sexual practices for American men (1948) and women (1953). Speaking with more certainty than his (nonrandom) sample permitted, Dr. Alfred Kinsey reported that 85 percent of American white males had engaged in fornication, between 30 and 45 percent had committed adultery, 59 percent had engaged in oral sex, 70 percent had patronized sex workers, and

17 percent had engaged in sex with animals—all against the law. Kinsey concluded that sex felons "constitute more than 95 percent of the total male population." By the age of forty, 50 percent of the women in Kinsey's sample had violated fornication laws, 26 percent had committed adultery, 19 percent had had homosexual contact with other women, around one-fifth had received oral stimulation (cunnilingus), while another one-fifth had given it to a man (fellatio). The generation that came of age after World War I routinely engaged in "petting" (kissing, oral sex, stimulation of the breast) before marriage.[47]

The Kinsey reports were a national sensation, giving scientific credibility and surprisingly high numbers to a phenomenon many people suspected was the case: whatever the legal rules might be, Americans did not limit their sexual outlets to marriage. Even within marriage, sex for procreation was *not* the norm, as married couples used contraceptives, engaged in oral and anal sex and not just penile-vaginal sex, and sometimes secured abortions when all else failed. Perhaps most fundamentally, sexual relationships focused on mutual pleasure had to take account of what made women happy; "procreative" intercourse had the sexist feature of assuring an orgasm to the male partner, but usually not the female. Our social mores had already moved away from the common law, biblical ideal of sex exclusively for procreation within marriage, and toward the notion that sex for social and companionate relations was a human good and that sex for pleasure was acceptable as well. What Dr. Kinsey did not report was that administrative constitutionalism at the local level had already effectively deregulated fornication, oral sex between consenting men and women, and even adultery (to a surprising extent). Nor did he report that when sex crimes were enforced, the police usually targeted racial minorities, poor people, "homosexuals," cross-dressers, and "prostitutes," society's social outcasts.[48]

The disconnect between America's administrative constitution and state sex crime codes, together with the likelihood of arbitrariness when such laws were applied, generated demands for wholesale reform. Like most of the fundamental normative changes detailed in this book, reform was understood in small "c" constitutional rather than Large "C" Constitutional terms. Among the most dedicated students of the Kinsey reports, and adherents to the social utilitarian morality underlying those reports, were law professors Herbert Wechsler (Columbia), Louis Schwartz (Pennsylvania), and Francis Allen (Northwestern), who were advisers in a massive project conducted by the American Law Institute to develop a "Model Penal Code" that could be the basis for simplification and revision of outmoded state criminal codes. This was an approach to state-based constitutionalism different from the married women's property law approach, which had been followed for the contraception issue. Rather than starting with a focal state (such as New York) and then developing a best practices approach from that state's statute, its judicial implementation, and its elaborating or expanding amendments, the Model Penal Code project proposed to develop a best practices model through extensive consultation with legal experts, including defense attorneys, prosecutors, and judges. An integrated statute whose details were thoroughly considered would then be presented to the states for adoption. This approach to state statutory convergence was very popular in the middle part of the twentieth century; the Model Penal Code and, even more, the Uniform Commercial Code (presented to the states at about the same time) were its great success stories.[49]

In his 1953 report on sex crimes to the Illinois legislature, Professor Allen relied heavily on the Kinsey data about Americans' sexual practices and on his colleagues' understanding of how sex crime laws were actually enforced. For classic constitutional reasons, Allen's committee recommended that the state decriminalize private sexual relations between consenting adults. The argument was social utilitarian: making adult consensual activities a crime imposed hardship and penalties on people who were not harming anyone else; rather than advancing "morals," their apparent aim, the practical effect of such laws was to engender police corruption and private blackmail. Not least important, as Dr. Kinsey insisted, it was constitutional insanity to criminalize conduct that almost everyone engaged in. Kinsey's and Allen's reports were a frontal assault on the notion that the state should criminalize activities solely on the basis of their (supposed) immorality. Their normative baseline was social utility: the criminal sanction should only be deployed against *harmful* conduct. Implicitly, their normative baseline returned to the kinds of first principles we explore in chapters 1 and 2: the role of the state is to provide *security* for *all* its citizens against threats to their lives, their health, their property and livelihoods, and their basic freedoms. There was room for moral judgment in such a polity, especially as regards public conduct, but a strong presumption ought to be followed against state regulation of private and personal activities that are fulfilling to some citizens and that do not harm others.[50]

Although the Illinois legislature did not immediately act upon Allen's recommendation, his and Kinsey's libertarian idea was one whose time had come. Another booster of Kinsey's data and recommendations, Professor Schwartz deployed the idea as the conceptual foundation when he drafted the Model Penal Code's sex crime provisions. With the tacit blessing of the American Law Institute's board, Schwartz's draft of the sex crimes section focused on sexual assault and public indecency but omitted criminal prohibitions for fornication, adultery, and sodomy between consenting adults in private places. Interestingly, it was only the omission of consensual sodomy that generated a heated debate within the institute. Traditionalists, led by Judge John Parker, were unwilling to decriminalize sodomy because of its association with homosexuality, but raised no recorded objection to decriminalizing fornication and adultery. In the end, the traditionalist stance did not even prevail on consensual sodomy, which the final draft of the Model Penal Code did not include as a crime. Promulgated by the Institute in 1962, the code followed the Kinsey philosophy as regards sex crimes. The question then became whether the states would follow the lead of the legal and scientific experts.[51]

Between 1955 and 1970, most states established bar-sponsored criminal code revision commissions, almost all of which started with the Model Penal Code as their templates. The reporter and workhorse for the Illinois criminal law reform commission, Professor Allen successfully pressed the code's libertarian philosophy. His commission's draft code, completed in November 1960, reserved the criminal sanction for sexual conduct that was forcible, was imposed upon minors, or "openly flout[ed] accepted standards of morality in the community," including open and notorious sexual cohabitation. (The last precept was a stretch for the libertarian presumption.) The Illinois legislature went along with the experts' recommendations, after the Roman Catholic Church made a deal with the sponsors: in return for the commission's agreement to delete various health-of-the-mother exceptions to the criminal abortion provision, the church agreed not to oppose the decriminalization of consensual fornication, adultery, and sodomy (all serious sins, according to Catholic theology).[52]

Like the Married Women's Property Act of 1848, the Illinois Criminal Code of 1961 was a modest and compromised starting point for a small "c" constitutional revolution. The extent of the revolution would be determined by the practical and normative feedback generated by Illinois's enactment of the Model Penal Code's libertarian presumption with regard to sexual behaviors. Would the new norm hold in Illinois? Would it be picked up in other states, and perhaps liberalized to allow sexual cohabitation? Would the debate expand beyond the insiders in state capitals and become a more genuine public debate? As in Illinois, the primary mechanism for sex crime reform in other states was law reform commissions consisting of state legislators, prosecutors, defense attorneys, and criminal law professors. In most but not all states, prosecutors were agreeable to decriminalizing consensual activities, because that was already their policy or because they understood the possibilities for corruption when widely followed activities were crimes. But the administrative constitutionalism of these commissions was then subject to a political check, namely, deliberation in the state's legislature, which was often the occasion for mobilization by interested citizens and groups.[53]

Consider the operation of this kind of constitutional change in New York. Chaired by Republican assemblyman Richard Bartlett and advised by Professor

Wechsler, New York's law revision commission followed the Model Penal Code to recommend that private fornication, adultery, and sodomy between consenting adults not be crimes. Unlike in Illinois, the New York proposal generated a public debate. The Catholic Welfare Committee vigorously opposed some of the commission's liberalizations. If consensual adultery and sodomy were decriminalized, the church argued, the state would be understood as accepting and even encouraging immoral conduct. Surprisingly, the church did not insist that either fornication or sexual cohabitation be criminal offenses, even misdemeanors. Assemblyman Bartlett, a devout Catholic, did not waver in his position: criminal sodomy and adultery laws were neither humane nor socially productive. The commission backed him, over the dissents of Assemblyman Julius Volker and Senator John Hughes, both Catholic Republicans serving on the commission. Representing moral and communitarian concerns, Volker and Hughes carried their fight to the New York legislature, which adopted Bartlett and Wechsler's proposed code, but with amendments recriminalizing adultery and consensual sodomy. Although the adultery and sodomy amendments passed by massive margins in both chambers of the legislature, it is significant that no one publicly proposed to recriminalize fornication or sexual cohabitation.[54]

By the time New York partially liberalized its sex crime laws in 1965, a new sexual revolution was sweeping the country. Whereas their parents had confided their extramarital sexual practices only in the strictest confidence to Dr. Kinsey, the "baby boom" children (born 1946–1961) announced their practices to anyone who would listen. A lot of baby boomers openly lived in sexually cohabiting relationships outside marriage. They embraced the sexual freedom opened up by the combination of reliable birth control (especially the pill, which became available in 1960) and middle-class prosperity. Although many boomers also flaunted adultery proscriptions, this was neither as widespread nor so universally approved. (In *The Graduate*, a classic sixties movie, Dustin Hoffman fornicated freely with Katharine Ross and briefly entered into an adulterous affair with her mother, Mrs. Robinson [Anne Bancroft], which he ultimately regretted as he eloped with the more age-appropriate Ross.) The larger theme of the sixties' sexual revolution was the conceptual delinkage of sex from marriage and procreation. Sex was good because of its social function or, even more radically, because of its sheer pleasure.[55]

State law kept up with swiftly changing public mores, in part because the Model Penal Code was an accessible best practices template whose adoption, even with amendments, would instantly modernize the state's sexual practices code to accommodate the new social developments. Following the Illinois and New York approach, state law reform commissions developed proposed codes that legislatures edited with an eye to public opinion. Although a number of states followed New York in shying away from "legalizing homosexuality," almost all of them deregulated fornication, starting with Pennsylvania (1972) and followed by Ohio (1972), Texas (1973), Florida (1974), Kentucky (1974), Michigan (1974), California (1975), Washington (1975), Indiana (1976), Iowa (1976), Maryland (1976), Missouri (1977), Wisconsin (1977), New Jersey (1978), and various smaller states. In some jurisdictions, such as Florida and Michigan, legislatures left in place misdemeanor offenses for "open and notorious" sexual cohabitation outside marriage, but this compromise lost its appeal after 1975. Moreover, such laws were a dead letter outside the South (where they were enforced against couples of color or interracial couples). In contrast, a majority of states retained their laws making adultery a crime, though the general practice was to reduce the crime to misdemeanor status.[56]

These changes in state law reflected the small "c" constitutional change modeled earlier in this chapter, with the variation we have discussed: a law reform organization (here, the American Law Institute) developed a comprehensive reform code that reflected a new regulatory principle responsive to perceived socioeconomic needs; the reform code was adopted by a few focal states (Illinois and New York); the new principle stimulated public law debates in other states, pitting reform groups against traditionalist defenders of the status quo; in state after state, reformers prevailed in the legislature, with voters accepting or supportive of the reform. A variation in the model occurred for an area where the Model Penal Code was too libertarian: sexual assault. Although the code liberalized the traditional definition of rape, which imposed a "resistance" and mens rea requirement upon the *victim* (unusual in the criminal law), it required the use of force or serious threat to secure a conviction. This requirement was at odds with the consent-based definition of sex crimes in the code and with women's experiences. Especially after 1969, state criminal codes adopted increasingly liberal, and nuanced, definitions of sexual assault against adults and, especially, minors. During the same period, states started to repeal or ameliorate the marital rape exception in the law.[57]

The level of popular engagement varied widely as the criminal law was liberalized in these ways. California was significant in the importance of elections and popular participation in the state's approach to sex crime reform. During the governorship of Ronald Reagan (1967–75), who presided over major liberalizations of both abortion and divorce law, sex crime reform was not possible, because of the opposition of Republicans representing traditionalist rural and small town voters. The election of 1974 swept the Republicans from office at all levels of government and made sex crime reform possible—but only over strong, well-publicized opposition from traditionalist pastors and legislators. After an intense debate in public hearings, in the media, and among legislators, the California legislature enacted the Sex Crime Reform Act of 1975, which decriminalized consensual sodomy, fornication, sexual cohabitation, and adultery. A 1976 grass-roots effort to revoke the sex crime reform law through a referendum fizzled because the proposal failed to attract enough voter signatures; few religious Californians wanted to pursue the issue, and it was settled that private activities between consenting adults was not a criminal offense.[58]

Hence, it is unsurprising that California took leadership in pursuing the corollary of the foregoing criminal code reforms. Within a year of the state's sex crime reform revision, the California Supreme Court revolutionized the law of marriage, in *Marvin v. Marvin* (1976). Oscar-winning actor Lee Marvin lived in a sexually cohabiting relationship with Michelle Marvin for seven years; when he left her, she sued for support and for half of Lee's property accrued during their cohabitation. Michelle's theory was that Lee had orally promised to pool their property and to support her. Lee's attorneys responded that she needed a written contract and, in any event, could not rely on promises made in the context of a "meretricious" relationship that had been in violation of California's adulterous cohabitation prohibition (until repealed in 1975). The California Supreme Court, surprisingly, rejected both theories and recharacterized previous cases as reflecting the principle that sexual favors cannot be the sole consideration for Lee's contractual promises. The Court ruled not only that Michelle could press her contract claims but also that she could amend her complaint to add theories of implied promise and equitable relief (she had helped Lee earn his millions and so was equitably entitled to some share).[59]

Marvin v. Marvin was a national sensation. We shall not explore all its ramifications here, but the most obvious consequence was that some of the core benefits and duties long associated with marriage—community property and support obligations—were now available to unmarried couples whose conduct would have been a crime in earlier years. (In the Marvins' case, the sexual cohabitation *had* been a crime for the duration of their relationship.) Most states followed California in recognizing contract-based rights for parties in cohabiting nonmarital relationships, but without the kind of democratic deliberation that accompanied sex crime deregulation. As in California, these moves were usually made by state judges, with legislatures typically entering the picture in response to judicial decisions applying *Marvin*. Perhaps for this reason, judges even in California have been very cautious: most *Marvin* lawsuits, including Michelle's, have not been successful, and the main effect of the decision has been to apportion property accumulated during relationships in a fair way to the parties. More democratically legitimate have been even newer forms of family recognition, namely, domestic partnership ordinances adopted by municipalities and state laws recognizing civil unions, reciprocal beneficiaries, and domestic partnerships with rights and duties similar to marriage, but afforded same-sex couples (chapter 8).[60]

Traditionalist critics of *Marvin* and sex crime reform feared that these legal changes would contribute to the erosion of marriage as the metanorm in America's republic of statutes. That is, Americans would be more likely to marry if sexual cohabitation outside marriage were a crime or, at least, were not the basis for legal recognition and protection. As in many matters, traditionalists were probably right about this prediction. Although there is no definitive empirical analysis for this issue, it is reasonable to believe that criminal deregulation and civil recognition of cohabiting unions have contributed to an erosion of the national marriage rate. In 1970, there were half a million sexually cohabiting couples in the United States; by 2000, there were 5.5 million, a tenfold increase in a generation. In the past thirty years, the percentage of never-married middle-aged men and women has doubled, to almost one in ten. Nearly half of today's single mothers have never married, and the number of children living with unmarried couples has gone up more than fourfold. According to the 2000 Census, only one-quarter of American households reflect the old-fashioned marriage norm of children raised by a mother and father who are married to one another. The United States is now a country where marriage is no longer the practiced norm, and most relationships are governed by the law of contract and not the law of marriage. On the other hand, marriage retains much of its normative power: most cohabiting couples do eventually marry, and the romantic aspiration of marriage remains powerful even for those (including lesbian and gay couples) who cannot or will not ever marry.[61]

AFFIRMATIVE STATE SUPPORT FOR FAMILY PLANNING OUTSIDE MARRIAGE

The pioneering North Carolina program providing women with family planning advice illustrated the limitations of the early state programs: only married women could receive its services; women of color were segregated and treated more condescendingly than white women were; much of the counseling was incomplete or dead wrong. Although there was a huge potential demand for state-provided family counseling, few women were able to take advantage of North Carolina's relatively progressive program. After World War II, most states had no programs, and some still had laws making the distribution of contraceptives or educational materials a crime. The 1960s created an entirely new context that created strong pressure for a dramatic expansion of state-supported family planning programs. Specifically, the new context included the availability of novel birth control technologies, the birth control pill and the intrauterine device; the sexual revolution and an open embrace of sex outside marriage and without procreation; serious normative concerns about the population explosion and the pressure that placed on the environment and scarce resources; and the skyrocketing cost of welfare programs, especially the Aid to Families with Dependent Children (AFDC) program, which was perceived as subsidizing large families with single mothers, often mothers of color.[62]

Different concerns motivated different political groups: baby boomers and liberals favored government programs that made family planning materials and devices available to poor as well as middle-class Americans; feminists favored technologies and education that gave women greater control of their own bodies; many racist whites and eugenicists favored programs that reduced the birthrate for women of color; and fiscal conservatives favored efforts to contain the high costs of AFDC and other social programs affected by large welfare families. Although family planning, even for unmarried women, was accepted by growing numbers of Americans, it was initially opposed by the Roman Catholic Church and other traditionalist (and antiracist) groups. Thus, when the Illinois Public Aid Commission voted in 1962 to provide family planning services to "any recipient with a spouse or child who requests such assistance," the Catholic Church strongly opposed the move as "abet[ting] and subsidiz[ing] illicit extramarital relations." The legislature created the Illinois Birth Control Commission to study the matter. Dominated by Catholics, the commission seemed poised to kill the administrative initiative, but a coalition of "the dollar-conscious, the anti-Negro, and the humanitarians" combined to save the initiative. The commission ultimately voted 14–1 to make family planning services available to all mothers over the age of fifteen. Similar administrative initiatives, followed by religion-based criticism and usually by a political ratification or compromise, came in California, New York, and other states.[63]

The impact of administrative constitutionalism on issues such as this one— the availability of state-supported family planning to poor women, including unmarried ones—depended on public funding more than on public pronouncements. Even as these state programs proliferated, by the end of the decade it was estimated that no more than eight hundred thousand low-income women were receiving family planning services, out of 5.4 million such women of childbearing age. Both Presidents Lyndon Johnson and Richard Nixon openly advocated family planning, without any marriage limitation. As Nixon put it in a special message to Congress in July 1969, "no American woman should be denied access to family planning assistance because of her economic condition." With bipartisan support, Congress responded with the Family Planning Services and Population Research Act of 1970, which sought to make "family planning services available to all persons desiring such services" and provided $382 million for the initial three years, an amount of money that dwarfed the combined budgets of the existing state programs. By 2008, five million Americans were taking advantage of these services each year, with about a third of the women being counseled at clinics operated by Planned Parenthood. President Nixon's and Congress's delinking family planning from marriage is important normative context for the Supreme Court's otherwise surprising decision in *Eisenstadt v. Baird* (1972), which extended *Griswold's* marital privacy right to unmarried couples denied access to contraceptives.[64]

The 1970 act added a new section 1008 to the Public Health Service Act that said: "None of the funds appropriated under this Act shall be used in programs where abortion is a method of family planning." Adopted just as several states were starting to reform their laws to legalize abortions under specified circumstances, this statutory provision reflected the consensus distinction between contraception-based and abortion-based family planning. In *Roe v. Wade* (1973), the Supreme Court recognized a woman's Constitutional right to control her own body and dismissed any state interest in "potential" human life until the third trimester. Would *Roe* necessitate a change in Title X programs? Quite the contrary: Title X's precept that the state should tolerate but should not push for abortion as a method for family planning has proven to be more robust than the liberal reading of *Roe* favoring abortion as a good thing the state should be encouraging. *Roe's* Large "C" Constitutional resolution of the state's interest in the life or potential life of the fetus did not represent a small "c" constitutional settlement. Pro-life traditionalists mobilized as a normative social movement seeking to preserve not only human life but also a traditionalist ethic of family values and women's domestic role. They criticized *Roe v. Wade* because it took the most moral of issues away from family and state decision making, represented arrogant judicial legislation, and marginalized the interests of the fetus, or the unborn human child, without a solid theory or support in Americans' moral intuitions. Through organs such as the National Right to Life Committee (1973), the movement sought to amend the Constitution to overrule *Roe* and, failing that, to adopt new state laws regulating abortion in a variety of ways.[65]

In *Planned Parenthood v. Casey* (1992), a partially chastened Court upheld all but one of Pennsylvania's process-based burdens on the right to choose an abortion but reaffirmed the essential holding of *Roe*, that women have a liberty interest in controlling the terms of their pregnancies. *Casey*, of course, has not settled the contentious abortion debate, but it has had the virtue (a virtue of constitutional necessity we might add) of returning the big normative features of the debate to small "c" constitutional discussion and deliberation. Title X was an important forum for that discussion. In 1988, the Reagan administration's secretary of health and human services, Dr. Louis Sullivan, issued a rule barring Title X medical personnel from referring women to abortion clinics even if they sought expert advice specifically for that purpose. After the Supreme Court upheld this "gag rule" in 1991, it was repudiated in the election of 1992, when the gender gap was decisive in turning out the mildly pro-life President George H. W. Bush and electing pro-choice Governor William Clinton. One of Clinton's first acts as president was to suspend the gag rule, and the Department of Health and Human Services formally revoked it in July 2000, after rule-making proceedings. The administrations of George W. Bush and Barack Obama have left this original Nixonian compromise in place: the federal government's family planning funds will not be openly used to support abortion, still a controversial method for family planning, but neither will the government stand in the way of medical personnel providing accurate information to women considering abortion as a method of family planning.[66]

UNILATERAL NO-FAULT DIVORCE

Elizabeth Cady Stanton and other nineteenth-century feminists argued for liberal divorce laws, because the statute-based fault regime left wives trapped in marriages to abusive husbands. Consistent with her general philosophy that wives ought to be considered autonomous decision makers capable of managing property and entering into contracts, Stanton maintained that civil marriage ought to be considered a contract and treated like other contracts. Fueled by the married women's property and contracting laws adopted all over the United States at Stanton's urging, wives were emerging in the twentieth century as autonomous decision makers. They not only gained the right to vote but also earned money outside the home in unprecedented numbers, accounting for almost 20 percent of the work force by 1960. At the same time, they steadily reduced the number of children they were willing to bear and raise, so that by 1960 the American household size was at a historical low point.[67]

As women's economic opportunities outside the home expanded and the number of children per household slowly declined, America's divorce rate increased slowly but steadily—from an estimated 2.8 divorces per one hundred marriages after the Civil War, to 8.8 in 1910, to 17.4 in 1930, to 25.1 right after World War II. This development was pretty surprising, in light of the law's stringent requirement that divorce was only available when one party had committed a crime, such as adultery. As was the case with abortion, however, Americans who had made choices they later felt were bad for them found ways to deal with legal restrictions. One way was by obtaining a divorce in a state with a liberal law, which the Supreme Court required all other states to recognize under the Full Faith and Credit Clause of the Constitution. After Nevada in 1931 started granting divorces without a showing of fault, it became a magnet for couples who wanted quickie divorces. For couples who found a trip to Reno, Nevada, too inconvenient or expensive, there was a local alternative: a collusive process by which one spouse would ask for a divorce, the other spouse would "confess" to a crime that was no longer seriously prosecuted (usually, adultery), and the judge would end a marriage that had become unhappy for both parties.[68]

Between 1967 and 1985, American states ended this charade and, without exception, adopted statutes allowing divorce without a showing of fault or crime. We shall call this *no-fault divorce*. During the same period, thirty-four of the fifty states also allowed one spouse to force a divorce, without the consent or over the objections of the other spouse. We shall call this *unilateral divorce*. All states allowing unilateral divorce also permit divorce without fault, so the category of *unilateral no-fault divorce* states merges with the second category.[69]

The process by which this revolution occurred followed the general pattern of state-based administrative constitutionalism, whereby public demand inspired proposals adopted in a leading state and then copied by other states (*stare de statute*). Like sex crime reform laws, no-fault divorce statutes were proposed and supported by commissions consisting of administrators, academic experts, and lawyers. But unlike the Model Penal Code, for example, no-fault divorce laws departed from the regulatory structure proposed by the experts and created an even simpler approach—and one that has probably had effects on the constitution of the family. No-fault laws may have fueled an increase in the divorce rate (a matter of some debate), and they certainly revolutionized the balance of power within marriage and the expectations of couples when they consider whether to get married. The collateral consequences of the no-fault divorce revolution have appalled some of the original proponents and would have shocked Elizabeth Cady Stanton, for the main losers have, apparently, been abandoned wives and children.

THE CALIFORNIA FAMILY ACT OF 1969

Following the eastern states' marriage laws, the California Civil Code of 1872 presumed marriage for life and recognized only six grounds for divorce: one spouse's adultery, extreme cruelty, willful desertion, willful neglect, habitual intemperance, and conviction of a felony; in 1941, the legislature added incurable insanity as another ground for divorce. By 1963, when the California General Assembly's Committee on the Judiciary turned its attention to a more systematic approach to the topic, there were numerous complaints about divorce as it operated in the state. Lawyers complained that fault-based divorce forced their clients into perjury in order to end marriages that were satisfactory to neither party. (Worse from the lawyers' perspective, a lot of couples drove across the state border to Nevada, where they could secure a quick-and-easy divorce.) Husbands complained that judges were partial to wives and handed down divorce decrees that impoverished husbands. Some citizens bemoaned the escalating divorce rate and called for programs that would facilitate spousal reconciliation and strengthen marriages through educational films and counseling. Responding to all of these concerns, law professors Aidan Gough and Herma Hill Kay urged systematic reforms: adoption of rules allowing divorce at the behest of one spouse and without a showing of fault, together with the creation of a special family court to handle marriage-related disputes in a nonadversarial manner. The Judiciary Committee appointed a special advisory committee on family life, but the special committee never rendered meaningful advice.[70]

After the assembly's efforts collapsed, an association of divorced husbands sought to place a divorce reform initiative on the 1966 ballot. Although the initiative failed to collect enough signatures, it did mobilize the California Bar Association to pressure Governor Edmund Brown to appoint a Commission on the Family. Like other constitutional commissions explored in this book, the Commission on the Family consisted of administrators, academics, and legislators. Its charge was to devise legal rules and institutions that would address the foregoing problems in a practical and politically acceptable way; this is the process described in chapter 2 as deep compromise. Following Professor Kay's ideas, the commission proposed a new family court, where expert counselors and judges would work with spouses to fix broken marriages, without the traditional focus on fault. If the judge found that "the legitimate objects of matrimony have been destroyed" and no "reasonable likelihood that the marriage can be saved," an order would be entered dissolving the marriage. Upon the dissolution of the marriage, the judge would also enter a decree making financial awards, dividing property, and rendering child custody determinations based upon needs and equities, not upon the traditional criterion of fault.[71]

The proposals made by the commission were radical, as they combined three nontraditional ideas: a specialized court system to handle divorces through a nonadversarial process, the abandonment of fault as a ground for divorce or for a judicial decree settling the affairs of a failed marriage, and the allowance of divorce at the behest of one spouse and over the objections of the other spouse. Legislators introduced the commission's draft legislation in the 1967 session of the California legislature—but it immediately ran into trouble when the California Bar Association balked at the details of its proposal. Upon further study by a special committee of its own experts, the bar association developed a proposed Family Court Act that jettisoned the nonadversarial features of the commission's proposal. Senator Don Grunsky introduced the revised bill in the 1969 session of the legislature.[72]

Assemblyman James Hayes introduced a rival bill in the lower chamber; its main feature was to make unilateral divorce available without fault, but it omitted the centerpiece of both the commission's and the bar association's proposals, namely, the specialized family court. With the state bar association supporting the Grunsky bill and the Los Angeles bar supporting the Hayes bill, the legislature might have been expected to postpone the matter again, but there was bipartisan support for action in the 1969 session, and once-divorced Governor Ronald Reagan was prepared to sign a reasonable measure. So the legislators opted for a compromise, largely following the Hayes bill. The Family Law Act of 1969 permitted the dissolution of a marriage at the petition of one or both spouses, on grounds of either "irreconcilable differences which have caused the irremediable breakdown of the marriage" or "incurable insanity." The act substantially removed fault-based concerns from the terms of the divorce decree as well; spouses would presumptively share the marital property equally, spousal support was to depend on the ability of the spouse to engage in gainful employment as well as the length of the marriage and the sacrifices the dependent spouse had made for the benefit of the family; and custody was to be based on the "best interests of the child." In a subsequent assembly report explaining the legislation, language inserted by Assemblyman Hayes noted the increasing numbers of women in the workplace and their "approaching equality" with men.[73]

UNILATERAL NO-FAULT DIVORCE AND THE DELIBERATIVE IDEAL

At the same time California was studying divorce reform, the National Conference of Commissioners on Uniform State Laws (an organization that paralleled the American Law Institute as a body supporting state statutory convergences as a means for reforming the law) was engaged in the same enterprise. Influenced by the report of the Governor's Commission and the Family Law Act, the commissioners largely followed the California approach when they promulgated the Uniform Marriage and Divorce Act in August 1970. The core reform of the uniform act was to abandon crime or fault as the basis for dissolving marriages (as well as property settlement and spousal support in the wake of the divorce) and to adopt the concept of marital breakdown. The uniform act differed in many ways from the California law, but the underlying legal principle was the same. As a result of criticism from the American Bar Association, the conference promulgated a revised uniform act in 1973 that was less clearly wedded to the no-fault standard. Like the California law, the uniform law did not create a special institution to administer the new regime.[74]

State statutory convergence on the no-fault divorce norm followed a best practices path that was a hybrid of the ones followed for married women's property and for sex crime reform. As with New York's Married Women's Property Act of 1848, a number of states had already reformed their divorce laws before California acted—but the simplicity and pro-choice appeal of the California law enabled it to dominate the debate. Today, fourteen states and the District of Columbia allow divorce upon a showing of either the spouses' separation for a period of time or their "irreconcilable differences." As with the Model Penal Code, twenty-one states have followed an eclectic approach, most based upon the 1970 or the 1973 uniform law; statutory eclecticism in most of these jurisdictions allows divorce upon the basis of *either* fault/crime by one of the spouses *or* marital breakdown/irreconcilable differences. Thirty-one states allow unilateral divorce. The states are even more heterogeneous as regards the rules governing property settlement and spousal support in the wake of divorce—but homogeneous in following the best interests of the child standard to determine custody of any children.[75]

Diversity among the states with regard to the precise mix of fault and no-fault grounds for divorce and the rules accompanying marriage dissolution ought not to obscure the fact that by 1985 every state had adopted the principle that spouses ought to be able to dissolve marriages on grounds of "irreconcilable differences" or something similar, with no necessary showing of fault. Most of those states also allowed divorce upon the petition of only one spouse. A large majority of the states by 1985 were also applying the no-fault principle to the terms of the spouses' divorce agreement, including property settlements, spousal support, and child custody. This was an amazing constitutional revolution— but one beclouded with normative qualms. The unilateral no-fault divorce laws of the late twentieth century reflected a national convergence that has been sharply criticized. The states are still trying to figure out what would be the "best practice" for divorce law, and there is concern that the states have engaged in more of a race to the bottom than in an exercise of selecting the best policy.[76]

An important feminist criticism surfaced before the statutory convergence had closed; this criticism highlights the problem we encounter often in this book, that judges are typically suboptimal implementers of superstatutory schemes. In 1976, Betty Friedan warned feminists that no-fault divorce was harming women and children in households where only the husband worked outside the home; the reason was that (male) judges were approving stingy settlements that left dependent wives and children without sufficient resources, and they were not insisting that deadbeat dads make even support payments imposed by agreement or decree. In a pathbreaking study of California's experience under the 1969 Family Law Act, Lenore Weitzman reported that the ease of unilateral divorce had bad consequences for wives: the postdivorce income of the average wife plummeted, while that of the typical husband went up significantly. According to Weitzman, the main reason was that judges were not entering economically fair decrees in divorce cases: they were not valuing wives' contributions to husbands' careers, were often apportioning property in mechanical rather than realistic ways, and were even kicking mothers and children out of family homes in order to effect a 50–50 division of property. Economists such as Elizabeth Peters have suggested a more cogent reason: the availability of *unilateral* no-fault divorce meant that husbands no longer had to make side payments to dependent wives in order to secure their cooperation in a consensual divorce settlement. Whatever the precise causation, subsequent scholars have confirmed a significant postdivorce gender gap, albeit not as large as Weitzman's original estimate. For example, Professors Eleanor Maccoby and Robert Mnookin found that within three years of a divorce the typical wife's income had fallen by 35 percent, while the typical husband's was up 15 percent.[77]

That a regime has significant problems does not undermine its legitimacy, however, if the legislative and implementational processes are responsive to the problems. Indeed, legislators, judges, and other officials have been tackling the gender gap and neglect of children's interests. The best example is Wisconsin, a state which acted later in the process of convergence and so had access to the feminist doubts that would later be documented more completely by Weitzman. In 1975, the state senate rejected a unilateral no-fault bill on the ground that it did not provide sufficient postdivorce protection for dependent spouses and children. When the Wisconsin legislature did adopt a unilateral no-fault divorce statute in 1977, the law required judges to presume that marital property analogous to community property be distributed equally between the spouses and to give "appropriate economic value to each party's contribution in homemaking and child care services." In 1984, the legislature adopted a community property regime that kicked in at the beginning of the marriage. Family law scholar Martha Albertson Fineman praises the Wisconsin approach along best practices lines, but we have not seen systematic evidence demonstrating that this law has worked better than the California statute.[78]

California has revisited its unilateral, no-fault divorce regime since these problems came to light. For example, appellate courts early on admonished trial judges to enter realistic support and property decrees that reflected a truly fair economic settlement. In 1970, the California General Assembly's Judiciary Committee issued a supplemental report urging judges to protect the family home for the use of dependent spouses and children "where economic circumstances warrant." In 1984, the legislature encoded that notion as an amendment to the Family Law Act. Judges, in turn, have made some progress in taking an expansive view of the dependent spouse's contributions to the family's welfare and the needs of dependents after divorce.[79]

New York and other states have created task forces on the treatment of women in court generally, and those task forces have focused on divorce cases as a situs where women are treated unequally. Specifically, the New York task force reported in 1986 that state judges did not treat divorcing wives as equal partners in the family enterprise and, hence, received short shrift in property settlements and even spousal support. In response, some New York judges are taking a more realistic view of the "dependent" spouse's contribution to the family's net worth and apportioning more of the assets to that spouse. The larger point suggested by the various task force reports is that no-fault divorce, alone, is not responsible for unfair awards upon divorce; much of the responsibility must be shared by lawyers and judges who do not appropriately value wives' contributions to the family.[80]

One problem with these judge-based reforms is that they are a post hoc band-aid for the structural problem Elizabeth Peters identified. Under the old regime requiring both spouses to cooperate in a divorce, dependent spouses (usually wives) had much greater bargaining power, for their vetoes prevented their partners (usually husbands) from exiting the marriage. Dependent spouses could exercise their veto power to ensure not only their own financial future but also that of their dependent children—and apparently much more effectively than judges could after the fact. It is plausible to suppose that predivorce bargaining by the dependent spouse is much more effective than post hoc estimates by judges, especially if the nondependent spouse has a better legal team than the dependent spouse. Another problem has been documented in the past twenty years: divorce may be very harmful to children, not just because of the financial distress, but probably more because of the emotional distress children suffer. Has unilateral no-fault divorce caused more children to suffer in this way? If so, that is a cost much harder to fix without another constitutional revolution.[81]

RAMIFICATIONS OF UNILATERAL NO-FAULT DIVORCE FOR THE CONSTITUTION OF THE FAMILY

The unilateral no-fault divorce revolution provides us with an opportunity to identify and reflect on an important puzzle: Does legal constitutional change merely *reflect* or does it *influence* the lives, identities, and values of Americans? In our view, the typical answer is the one suggested by the unilateral no-fault divorce revolution, which was a legal constitutional development that *both* reflected *and* has molded American lives, identities, and perhaps even values.

(Married women's property laws and sex crime reform have probably enjoyed a similarly mutual relationship with social practices.)

On the one hand, unilateral no-fault divorce statutes reflected the steady post-1860 upward progress of divorce rates in the United States. The social, economic, and legal phenomena that generated ever-higher divorce rates rendered the country receptive to an understanding of marriage that was deeply consensual, and a correlative understanding that divorce ought to be available when either party withdraws his or her consent because he or she finds the relationship unsustainable. Contributing to Americans' new understanding of marriage as companionate and imbued with a need for ongoing consent were increasing economic opportunities for women outside the home, declining birth rates and family sizes within the home, and the expansion of America's consumerist society. All of these trends pressed increasing numbers of American couples to reject or modify the norm of marriage for life, especially when their own marriages turned out to be unsatisfactory. Emboldened to escape unhappy marriages, ever-higher numbers of couples seeking divorce created a hydraulic force supporting some kind of reform along no-fault lines. These are local phenomena that help explain why unilateral no-fault divorce swept the nation after the sexual revolution of the 1960s.[82]

Unilateral no-fault divorce is also consistent with, and reflects, deeper features of American culture that transcend the sixties. Even in the nineteenth century, the American family was different from families in Europe: marriage in this country was more "companionate," or grounded in mutual affection between the spouses; wives here were more autonomous than their European counterparts, even before the married women's property laws; and the focus of the family was child rearing and development. No-fault divorce is more consistent with the companionate philosophy of marriage than with traditional religious conceptions that still held sway in Europe. Perhaps most important, the voluntaristic concept of divorce on demand (even by just one spouse) is broadly consistent with libertarian strains in American culture—strains that also supported feminist demands for economic rights for wives in the nineteenth century as well as decriminalization of birth control and out-of-wedlock sex between consenting adults in the mid-twentieth century. The emergence of a conception of marriage as companionate and not "till death do us part" drove divorce rates up as economic circumstances permitted, even under the fault regimes in place everywhere before 1969. Thus, one might say that no-fault divorce reflects the aspirations and lives of Americans in the post–World War II era.[83]

An increasing number of scholars believe that unilateral divorce has *also* had an effect on the durability of marriages because it makes divorce much easier and therefore more likely. Under traditional marriage law, unilateral divorce was only possible when the wronged spouse opted to terminate the marriage; under a unilateral no-fault regime, either spouse can usually terminate the marriage, often by initiating proceedings in a quickie-divorce jurisdiction, whose judgment must be recognized in the domicile state as a matter of the Supreme Court's full faith and credit jurisprudence. It strikes us as logical that divorce rates would be higher under the new regime of unilateral no-fault divorce, than under the traditional regime. There is evidence to the contrary, however. The leading critic is Elizabeth Peters, who argued that the main effect of unilateral divorce was on the financial terms of the dissolution, as discussed above, and that the new regime had no statistically significant effect on overall divorce rates. More recent studies by family law experts such as Professor Margaret Brinig support the hypothesis that the existence of unilateral no-fault divorce statutes (especially the pure ones such as California's) are causally related to higher divorce rates, although the nature and longevity of the impact remain unclear. The best study we have seen is that of Jonathan Gruber for the National Bureau of Economic Research. Controlling for other variables, Professor Gruber found a statistically significant but small effect of unilateral divorce laws on the overall divorce rate.[84]

Professor Allen Parkman makes an even bolder claim. Because no-fault divorce makes marriages easier to exit, he argues that it has contributed to the steadily increasing rate of sexual cohabitation rather than marriage, has caused women to seek education and enter the work force in greater numbers (enabling them to avoid marriage or have more options at the end of failed marriages), has led to more antisocial behaviors among men (either because they do not marry or do not expect their marriages to last), and has impelled married couples to invest less in the relationship and in the children reared within it. Unfortunately, Professor Parkman presents no empirical evidence substantiating these claims, but Professor Gruber's analysis provides empirical support for the claims that children reared under unilateral divorce regimes are less well educated, have lower family incomes, marry earlier but separate more often, and have higher odds of adult suicide. Gruber cautions that the "causal pathways" for these results are complicated and may affect one another, but these preliminary findings are significant and provide support for some of the Parkman concerns.[85]

If these concerns are as significant as Parkman and Gruber suggest, there is a deep constitutional problem with this particular operation of our best practices model of state statutory convergences. Legislatures in states like California, New York, and Wisconsin have been highly responsive to Americans' new preferences regarding marriage and other committed relationships, and moderately responsive to the allocational problems that have arisen from unilateral no-fault divorce regimes. Although we should be concerned about the effectiveness of judicial remedies for the resource-allocation problem, we are reassured that it has become a matter for serious public deliberation. But what if the new regime has long-term psychological and other consequences that are harmful to children? Are their best interests being sacrificed to the preferences of their parents? (Of course, only the latter can vote and be heard directly in the political process; the former can only be heard or represented by surrogates.) Most discouraging, from our point of view, is that traditionalists who most devoutly believe that the well-being of children is sacrificed by divorce or even cohabitation outside of marriage have been sidetracked from best practices reform by the same-sex marriage debate. That is, rather than provoking public deliberation to revisit the issue of unilateral divorce or to advance the new "covenant marriage" idea, traditionalist groups have lent their money and their political energies to closing off marriage from lesbian and gay couples (many of whom are raising children of their own who would probably benefit from marriage).[86]

Consider a broader hypothesis that assimilates the possible consequences of unilateral no-fault divorce with those of feminism and the sexual revolution. The way Americans understand the family has dramatically shifted away from a *communitarian* conception, where moral and legal obligations bound everyone together into a mini-community, toward a *libertarian* conception, where each family member is understood as a separate utility-maximizing participant and the adult members enjoy a wide range of choices, including economic choices, sexual and family-planning choices, and exit options. To paraphrase Sir Henry Maine, the history of family law has been a transition from community obligations to liberty of contract for adults. The American constitution of the family is a microcosm of the larger constitutional evolution of our polity and our public values.

There is another way of understanding the constitutional shift. Overall, we should expect that the subjective experience and even the "joy" of marriage have become more *consumerist*. By consumerist, we mean that participants today are more likely to understand marriage as a utility-optimizing choice, like a contract, than participants would have in 1840 or even 1970. The consumerist turn in marriage reflects larger socioeconomic trends, especially urbanization, greater economic opportunities for women, and the availability of reliable birth control. Notice how the consumerist turn in America's constitution of the family is probably related to a similar turn, and at roughly the same time, in America's constitution of the workplace, voting, the market, and old age (chapters 1–4).

Americans' expectations from government have evolved toward an understanding of government as guaranteeing institutions, practices, and rules that provide us all breathing space within which to exercise *choice* as regards sexual practices, marital and other relationships, having a family and pursuing a career, voting, and engaging in business.

THE GREEN CONSTITUTION AND
JUDICIAL DEFERENCE TO
AGENCY DYNAMISM

John and Judith Rapanos have lived the American dream. The parents of six children, they are a family of developers and philanthropists who have helped remake Midland, Michigan, from a dying factory town into a "City of Science and Culture," as it now dubs itself. Their land holdings have been significant. One parcel, called the "Salzburg site" and located across from Midland's closed Dow Corning plant, contains 230 acres of land, fifty-four acres of which have soil that is semisaturated much of the year. The Salzburg site is connected to a man-made drain, which in turn drains into Hoppler Creek, flowing into the Kawkawlin River, which empties into Saginaw Bay and Lake Huron. It is also the home to dozens of species of wild animals, presumably including some species in danger of extinction. To prepare the Salzburg site for development as a shopping center, the Rapanoses filled the soggy areas with dirt in 1989.[1]

Under the constitutional regime in place during the founding era and the nineteenth century, the Rapanoses' entrepreneurial activity would have been legally unimpeachable. Like the common law of contract (chapter 3), the common law of property emphasized the rights of owners such as the Rapanoses to deploy their land as they saw fit. Their free use was limited only by preexisting liens that flowed against their land, by contractual promises they made, and by the common law of nuisance, which regulated land use that imposed harm on the neighbors or the surrounding community. America's constitution of property was linked with larger public norms. Classical liberal theories of the state, such as those espoused by John Locke and Sir William Blackstone, say that a critically important role of government is to preserve and protect private property, namely, "[t]he free use, enjoyment, and disposal of all his acquisitions, without any control or diminution save only by the laws of the land." James Madison and other theorists of the founding era believed that property rights were an important foundation for citizenship; all of the founders assumed that property rules would be the primary province of state law. Although the Supreme Court recognized early on that Congress's Commerce Clause authority gave it primacy in regulating the "navigable waters" of the United States, because of their relationship to commerce, Congress's jurisdiction was limited, and this limited authority was understood by the framers as a structural protection afforded private property by the Constitution. Adding an individual rights dimension was the Fifth Amendment in Madison's Bill of Rights (1791): "nor shall private property be taken for public use, without just compensation," which protects private property rights but also warns that they are subject to deployment for the common good.[2]

A country's legal regime of property rights mediates its people's individual liberties and the needs of the community. A largely libertarian constitution of property met the needs of a frontier society that had only six cities with more than ten thousand people, as the United States had in 1800. As the United States expanded both in size and in population, and as cities swelled with immigration from abroad as well as emigration from the American countryside, government land regulations grew like weeds in a vacant lot. With burgeoning populations, American cities aggressively regulated various deployments of property that had third-party effects, ranging from health regulations to rules suppressing stench and manure within city limits; municipalities developed licensing regimes further limiting their residents' use of land. State common law judges developed doctrines of nuisance to head off third-party effects of certain uses of private property; state statutes regulated matters of water rights. Even the United States government (the largest landowner in North America) regulated water and property. Established by statute in 1802, the Army Corps of Engineers became a powerhouse of both water projects and regulation of private deposits in navigable rivers. Throughout the nineteenth century, the federal government pursued active (albeit often ineffectual) policies of land management. After the turn of the new century, President Theodore Roosevelt and Gifford Pinchot, the first chief of the National Forest Service (1905–10), committed the country to significant long-term planning that would conserve the nation's natural resources.[3]

The twentieth century was a golden age of property regulation, through zoning and urban planning rules, broader common law understandings of what might constitute nuisances, and a steadily rising tide of environmental regulations at the local, state, and national levels. The explosion of property regulations reflected not only demographic urbanization (and suburbanization) but also a new ideology for human beings' relationship to the environment. Pioneering thinkers such as the Forest Service's Gifford Pinchot and author Aldo Leopold asserted an organic relationship between humans and the environment and argued that we have responsibilities not only to one another but also to the physical world and biosphere, which we were polluting and despoiling at ruinous levels. The celebration of Earth Day by twenty million Americans on April 22, 1970, marked the dramatic public emergence of what we now call *green thinking* as a mass social movement, whereby large numbers of Americans believe that industrialization and economic development have severely damaged the environment and threaten disastrous consequences if not halted and reversed. Green thinking understands the environment as a holistic and interdependent system, whereby damage to one part of the ecosystem has ripple effects on other parts of the system and, specifically, on human health, plant and animal life, and even the climate. Green politics demands that citizens accept responsibility for harming the environment, demand preservative and remedial measures from the state, and engage in a deliberative process to determine how the costs of the preservation and renewal should be shared.[4]

Green thinking has fundamentally changed America's constitution of property, specifically the trade-offs between individual or corporate freedom to use land and water as people wish in order to carry out their private projects, and the public health, safety, and welfare, now defined very broadly to include "natural" ecological balance or organic evolution. Alarming natural disasters in the late 1960s and early 1970s galvanized green citizens to press for national superstatutes that would not only protect against further environmental degradation but also return the environment to an earlier, healthier state. Responding to green demands, Congress enacted the Clean Air Act of 1970, the Clean Water Act of 1972, the Endangered Species Act of 1973, and subsequent statutes to head off further harm to the environment and to reverse some of the prior harm. By executive order in 1970, President Richard Nixon created a special agency to administer environmental laws (the Environmental Protection Agency, or EPA) and named a bold administrator to head it, William Ruckelshaus. Under Ruckelshaus, the EPA pioneered a number of regulatory principles that have remained lodestars in the field for the past generation. Perhaps the most famous is the *precautionary principle*, which presumes in favor of state intervention when there is a danger of harm to humans. In an early application of such a principle, Ruckelshaus took DDT off the market in 1972, well before there was a scientific consensus that the useful pesticide was actually harmful.[5]

Like Susan Deller Ross, Burke Marshall, William Baxter, Arthur Altmeyer, and Thomas Parran, introduced in earlier chapters, EPA Administrator Ruckelshaus was an exemplar of administrative constitutionalism. Similar to the others, Ruckelshaus aggressively applied broad superstatutory purposes with an eye to larger constitutional goals and values. Thus, he believed that the federal government has the ultimate responsibility to protect the public health by reversing environmental degradation, an understanding that was a narrow reading of property-protection clauses in the Constitution and a broad reading of the government's constitutional duty to protect public health and security. Like most of the other social movements discussed in this book, the Earth Day environmental movement was intimately connected to the federal government; even before there was aggressive regulation, many leaders of the green social movement were federal officials. For example, Rachel Carson, the author of *Silent Spring* (1962), the international best seller that condemned DDT and popularized green thinking, was a longtime employee of the old U.S. Bureau of Fisheries and its successor, the Fish and Wildlife Service (FWS). In turn, Carson's agency literally invented and named "wetlands" as a natural category; the FWS's Circular No. 39 defined the term in 1956 as "lowlands covered with shallow and sometimes temporary or intermittent waters."[6]

Americans have been filling in wetlands since the colonial era; it is estimated that more than 50 percent of our wetlands have been filled in during the past two hundred years. FWS's Circular No. 39 reflected the then-emerging scientific consensus that wetlands are key parts of the ecosystem that purify water, sustain varieties of life, and even protect against hurricane and other climate forces; their widespread erasure would cause immeasurable damage to the entire ecosystem. Growing numbers of citizens seized upon this fact and, inspired by green thinking about our interconnection with nature, agitated for ever-stronger regulatory responses. In 1963, Massachusetts responded with the nation's first wetlands-protection statute; Michigan (where the Rapanos property is located) passed a wetlands-protection law in 1970. By 1975, fourteen of the fifteen states with substantial wetlands had enacted similar statutes. At the national level, the Army Corps of Engineers, which had long regulated discharges into navigable waters, committed itself to a national permit program before discharges could be made into the nation's "navigable waters" and their tributaries.[7]

The Corps issued final regulations implementing this order in 1972. The permit requirement only applied to waters already used in commerce, susceptible to such use with reasonable improvement, and subject to the ebb and flow of the tide. (Under those and previous regulations, the Rapanoses's Salzburg site was not covered.) Filled with green-thinking staff and legislators such as Senator Edmund Muskie and Representative Morris Udall, Congress responded in 1972 with the Clean Water Act (CWA), enacted with large bipartisan majorities overriding President Nixon's cost-conscious veto. One purpose of the new statute was to extend national regulation beyond the Corps' traditional definition. Section 404 required a Corps permit to "discharge dredged or fill material into the navigable waters." (Imposing permit requirements for discharging pollutants into "navigable rivers," section 402 was administered by the EPA.) The law defined "navigable waters" as "the waters of the United States," without further elaboration on the face of the statute. Following what they considered an emerging scientific consensus, the sponsors and relevant committees worked from the premise of an interconnected hydrological ecosystem; aggressive national regulation was needed because polluting activities in one state would have ripple effects in other states. The Conference Committee directed administrators to give "navigable waters" the "broadest possible [C]onstitutional interpretation." Thus, the CWA's regulatory authority over "navigable waters" went somewhat beyond the Corps' traditional understanding of the term—but in 1972 it was doubtful that "waters of the United States" covered the Rapanoses's Salzburg site, for the site was not adjacent to a navigable body of water *or* its tributary. In any event, the CWA was an invitation, not just an allowance, for an administrative approach to *navigable waters* that was grounded in public health and safety, not in commerce.[8]

Consistent with his precautionary approach to regulation of DDT and other pollutants, EPA Administrator Ruckelshaus interpreted the regulatory term "navigable waters" broadly, to include not only traditional navigable waters and their tributaries but also interstate waters and a variety of intrastate waters connected to interstate commerce. The EPA's approach unmoored federal regulatory authority from the traditional basis, namely, Congress's authority to regulate interstate commerce via navigable rivers and streams, and resituated it into a different kind of federal authority to protect public health and safety. Even though the old term, "navigable waters," continued to be the basis for jurisdiction, Ruckelshaus was rethinking the government's authority through the new lens of green philosophy. According to Russell Train, who was chair of President Nixon's Council for Environmental Quality (1970–73) and then Ruckelshaus's successor at EPA (1973–77), the agency was motivated by the notion that "aquatic systems are . . . interrelated and interdependent. We cannot expect to preserve the remaining qualities of our water resources without providing appropriate protection for the entire resource."[9]

The Army Corps of Engineers initially followed a narrower understanding of "navigable waters," because its conceptual starting point was the federal authority to regulate water-based commerce and transportation. Both the EPA and the federal courts rejected the Corps' understanding as inconsistent with the new regulatory philosophy reflected in the 1972 statute, and in 1975 the Corps revised its earlier definition to give the term its "broadest possible [C]onstitutional interpretation"—but a Constitutional interpretation that was grounded in a nontraditional concept, that the federal government has broad authority to coordinate efforts to protect the public health and safety from pollution. The Corps' new definition, finalized in interim form a few months later, included "[a]ll tributaries of navigable waters of the United States up to their headwaters and landward to their ordinary high water mark," as well as wetlands that are "contiguous or adjacent to other navigable waters." Even with this wider definition, it is doubtful that the Rapanos property was covered, because its connection to a tributary of a navigable river was a man-made drain.[10]

The environment was a major issue in the 1976 presidential election, with former governor Jimmy Carter prevailing on a thoroughly green platform. In 1977, President Carter issued Executive Order 11,990 directing all federal agencies to respect existing wetlands, to consider the effect on wetlands of federal projects they were undertaking, and to preserve wetlands in the course of their projects and land management. Following the lead of President Carter and EPA Administrator Douglas Costle (1977–81), Congress passed the Clean Water Act Amendments of 1977, with a confirmation of the broad jurisdiction then asserted by EPA and the Corps. Conservation did, however, embroil the Carter administration in controversy early on. When President Carter and his Council on Environmental Quality targeted nineteen congressional water projects for termination on environmental grounds, at the same time he was issuing Executive Order 11,990, legislators fought like tigresses protecting their cubs and were able to preserve almost all of the arguably wasteful projects. This was the Carter administration's first stinging defeat on Capitol Hill. Although there were many green legislators, local pork trumped the environment in Congress, when push came to shove.[11]

Consistent with the Carter administration's emphasis on expansive wetlands protection, the Corps in 1977 sought to clarify its wetlands definitions with amended regulations, asserting that its jurisdiction extended to wetlands "adjacent" to navigable waters or their tributaries, as well as other waters "the degradation or destruction of which could affect interstate commerce." The Corps was reconceptualizing wetlands in functional terms: properties that were soaked with water at least part of the year and had a connection with the regional hydrological system. This functional thinking was reflected in the Corps' *Wetland Delineation Manual* (1987); it and EPA developed an even broader, and more controversial, set of criteria in their *Manual for Identifying and Delineating Jurisdictional Wetlands* (1989). No later than 1987, the Salzburg site became, for the first time, a regulable "wetlands," because of the amount of water in its soil and its connection to bodies of water. Consistent with this ever-broader conception, Michigan state regulators (administering the national program in that state) told the Rapanoses that their Salzburg site could not be filled without a section 404 permit. Such permits, by the way, are not like marching down to the Department of Motor Vehicles and getting a driver's license. The Corps and the EPA require documentation of the landowner's need to adjust her land and the steps she will follow to avoid or mitigate wetlands damage. This process can cost several hundred thousand dollars and can take several years before a permit is issued.[12]

As if this headache was not enough for the Rapanos family, another one loomed as a potential problem: What if filling in the wetlands destroyed the habitat for an endangered animal species? Section 9 of the Endangered Species Act (ESA) says that no person may "take" an endangered species within the United States. The statute defines "take" to mean "harass, harm, pursue, hunt, shoot, wound, kill, trap, capture, or collect." In its implementing regulations issued in 1975, the Department of the Interior's Fish and Wildlife Service defined "harm" to include "significant habitat modification or degradation where it actually kills or injures wildlife by significantly impairing essential behavioral patterns, including breeding, feeding, or sheltering." If draining and filling the Rapanoses' wetlands disrupted the breeding patterns of the endangered red-cockaded woodpecker, for example, that too would have subjected the property owners to potential criminal as well as civil liability. The Carter administration spent several years struggling with the ESA, which the Supreme Court said required the termination of the Tellico Dam project in the Tennessee Valley because it would have deprived the endangered snail darter of its last known habitat. (Ultimately, both the dam and the darter survived the bureaucratic wrangling.)[13]

John and Judith Rapanos were outraged by the dynamic, and increasingly intrusive, applications of the CWA and ESA by their implementing agencies. They and thousands of other owners are dumbfounded that their development of property connected to bodies of water only by a man-made drain can be considered "navigable waters," and that any interruption of the breeding patterns of a woodpecker would be considered a "taking" of an endangered species. The son of Greek immigrants, John Rapanos had stood up to people he considered bullies all his life—and in 1989 he ignored the state administrative warnings, disregarded both an EPA and a judicial cease-and-desist order, and filled the wetlands with sand so that the Salzburg site could be developed. If Rapanos had developed his property in 1982, rather than 1989, it is very likely he would have gotten away with violating the CWA, even as expansively interpreted. In 1980, former governor Ronald Reagan unseated President Carter; the Reagan administration was publicly committed to easing the burdens of environmental regulation on property owners and developers such as the Rapanoses. EPA Administrator Anne Burford (1981–83) refused to enforce some of the green canon and proposed to roll back existing regulations. The public uproar over her deregulatory overtures led to her ouster, however, and President Reagan felt constrained by public opinion to bring back Bill Ruckelshaus for a second term as EPA administrator (1983–85). The mild-mannered administrator with the Clark Kent look was a Green Superman who repudiated Burford and returned the agency to its activist stance of the 1970s. President Reagan remained hostile to Ruckelshaus's efforts and in 1988 issued an executive order endorsing the property rights movement and its goals, an order that the EPA essentially ignored for the last year of Reagan's term in office.[14]

Internalizing the lessons of the Burford disaster and following Ruckelshaus, Vice President George H. W. Bush won the 1988 presidential election on a platform that called for "no net loss" of wetlands. President Bush carried out his campaign pledge by appointing as EPA administrator William Reilly (1989–93), who as president of the Conservation Foundation had vigorously criticized the Reagan administration's mixed environmental record and hosted a conference publicizing the need to stop wetlands conversion of exactly the sort that John and Judith Rapanos were carrying out. The Bush administration (1989–93) made wetlands conservation a national priority and directed all federal agencies to do nothing that would destroy existing wetlands, and to do what they could to recover lost wetlands. Presidents William Clinton (1993–2001) and George W. Bush (2001–09) also directed federal agencies to *restore* lost wetlands and *create* new ones, so that there would be net gains in wetlands areas. Under our model of superstatutory norm entrenchment, broad wetlands protection seemed to have become entrenched by 1989: a puissant and lasting social movement called attention to the problem, Congress had enacted a landmark statute addressing the problem and broadly empowering agencies to deal with it, agency entrepreneurs such as Ruckelshaus and Reilly had aggressively implemented their authority, and skeptics had been rebuffed through public outrage and electoral support for green positions.[15]

But the entrenchment of a statutory norm does not tell us how far that norm should be pressed, and with what regulatory tools. As to these matters, there was a lot of regulatory play. Under Reilly's leadership, the EPA sought prompt and sharp enforcement of the wetlands regulations against violators such as the Rapanoses. Hence, the George H. W. Bush administration's Department of Justice criminally prosecuted John Rapanos for violating the CWA. This would have been unthinkable earlier in the 1980s. The sharper enforcement teeth of green constitutionalism generated a popular pushback, however. The Bush administration's aggressive wetlands-protection policy generally, and the Rapanos case as a particular cause célèbre, ramped up the *property rights movement* that had been percolating on the ground level since the 1960s. By the early 1990s, thousands of angry property owners had formed scores of local associations aimed at rolling back what they considered environmental regulatory excesses. Today, the Alliance for America is an umbrella group for more than six hundred property rights organizations. Nancie Marzulla's Defenders of Property Rights is the primary organization bringing lawsuits specifically to protect property rights, but several older litigation groups also contribute to the cause. Dozens of blogs and newsletters carry stories such as that of the Rapanoses' tussle with the green bureaucracy.[16]

The property rights movement is an intellectual as well as self-interested response to green constitutionalism. Its premise is Madisonian, the notion that private property is a human right, and that ever-increasing land regulation by the green bureaucracy poses unfair costs on some citizens; green thinking is a fundamental challenge to entrenched American values of individual free choice in managing and using one's land. Indeed, new property rights thinkers assail green bureaucrats as imposing a "new feudalism" upon an unwilling citizenry, a charge that aligns property rights with modern liberal democracy and associates environmentalism with baronial fiat as well as socialist inequities and inefficiencies. Under this competing ideology, environmentalists' romantic, almost anthropomorphic, understanding of nature is either too creepy or too abstract to justify the significant retrenchment in private property rights we have seen in the past generation. Private property is not only a cherished personal right, according to this movement, but also the foundation of the nation's flourishing economy, as well as a potential source of genuine conservation efforts. Moreover, We the People have never given our permission for the green bureaucracy to go so far, and the bureaucracy threatens not only individual choice but also the entrepreneurial spirit that made America great and unique. As a small "c" constitutional countermovement originating earlier but galvanized by the George H. W. Bush administration's new policies, the property rights activists challenged the wetlands-protection norm at least as applied and were able to trim back EPA and Corps enforcement activities in 1991—but that was two years too late for the Rapanoses.[17]

With almost comical predictability, the dueling social movements and their academic allies have Constitutionalized the various positions. Property rights advocates believe that the green feudal manor (the environmental bureaucracy) violates the Takings Clause when it deprives landowners of the most profitable use of their land without just compensation. From a Lockean understanding of state legitimacy, law professor Richard Epstein argues that excessive regulation of private property reflecting the green agenda is *theft* that must at the very least be accompanied by proper compensation. Green thinkers respond that the Takings Clause was not originally intended to cover "regulatory takings" and should not be dynamically interpreted to cover them now, in part because judges cannot develop appropriate standards for determining when regulation goes "too far." Charles Reich seeks to turn the Constitutional tables on the antifeudalists, as he argues that the Fifth Amendment creates a Constitutional right of the community to a clean environment. These arguments occupy law professors who otherwise might engage in mischief—but they have no traction in the real world, where the Supreme Court has, for the time being, given up on enforcing the Takings Clause one way or the other. But, as we have argued throughout this book, arguments that fail to be Constitutionalized by the Court often have a productive constitutional life as inspirations for agencies and judges when they apply and interpret superstatutes. Reich's vision of an affirmative duty of administrators to assure citizens a clean community is surely one that has had small "c" constitutional traction under EPA Administrators William Ruckelshaus (1970–73, 1983–85), Russell Train (1973–77), Douglas Costle (1977–81), William Reilly (1989–93), Carol Browner (1993–2001), Christine Todd Whitman (2001–03), and perhaps to a lesser extent Stephen Johnson, the first scientist to head the agency (2005–09).[18]

Thus, the effective debate between green and libertarian understandings of property has, for most practical purposes, been carried out at the small "c" constitutional level, and at that level it has been foundationally important. The theme of this chapter is the dynamics of constitutional evolution in this area of law and policy. Our main point is descriptive: the small "c" constitution of superstatutes has evolved from the get-go, and much of the evolution has gone beyond and even against the original congressional expectations. We have seen this phenomenon in earlier chapters. Over the decades, for example, the Sherman Act changed dramatically, from a law protecting small businesses as well as consumers, to one whose main goal was consumer protection through the assurance of an efficient market (chapter 3). Environmental superstatutes such as the CWA and the ESA changed just as dramatically and even more swiftly through agency regulations. We shall explore the systemic reasons why statutes generally, and superstatutes in particular, will inevitably be interpreted dynamically over time, given the structure of lawmaking and the separation of powers in our polity.

Our further themes are normative, and they cut in somewhat different directions. On the one hand, the fact that dynamic interpretation of superstatutes is usually driven by agencies renders constitutionalism more supple and adaptive in applying foundational norms and frameworks to new circumstances in our ever-changing world. Staffed with experts, capable of developing a holistic understanding of the problem, and attentive to congressional and presidential pressure or signals, the Corps and EPA have applied the Clean Water Act to a broad array of new situations and have arguably prevented significant new wetlands losses. This is a distinct advantage that small "c" constitutionalism has over its Large "C" sibling, where evolution proceeds more slowly and incompletely. On the other hand, this agency-driven dynamism can be problematic along several dimensions, and this was John and Judith Rapanos's view about the CWA's rapid evolution. They believe that the agency constructions have been deeply illegitimate, even autocratic. Property rights activists also believe that green feudalism threatens to ossify the property-driven entrepreneurial republicanism that made America great. Notice that the Rapanoses' normative stance finds support in the *consumerist constitution* we detected in the earlier chapters: Americans ought to have substantial freedom of choice in the workplace (chapter 1), the polling booth (chapter 2), among products (chapter 3), at retirement (chapter 4), and in selection and unselection of a spouse (chapter 5). But even the consumerist constitution allows, indeed demands, government attention to the lasting effects of one person's choice on the community.

Under our theory, the best way to mediate this tension between problem-solving agency dynamism and democratic accountability—and between the freedom of landowners to use their property and the needs of the community and the environment—is for Congress to revisit the superstatute and either ratify or trim back the agency's aggressive interpretation; we shall provide an example of this process under the Endangered Species Act. This optimal process has worked pretty well for the voting and antidiscrimination statutes discussed in chapters 1 and 2, as well as the social security law that was the focus of chapter 4. But it has not worked as well for the Sherman Act (chapter 3) or for the CWA and most other environmental laws. The reason Congress is an uneven check on many agencies is, again, structural. It is hard to enact legislation, and so many issues go unresolved because there is not sufficient consensus to resolve them—but this structure also reinforces the notion that when Congress can bestir itself to ratify or adjust an agency rule, the congressional response is both significant and legitimate. This is *not* to say that dynamic agency interpretations of the Sherman Act and the Clean Water Act are therefore illegitimate; it is only to say that the further removed agency rule making is from formal congressional deliberations, the greater is the burden on the agency to secure grassroots support from some other source, including direct appeals to We the People, Ourselves.

Traditionally, lawyers have assumed that the second-best institution for checking agency dynamism is judges, who can trump agency interpretations that transgress statutory deals or undermine the statute's purpose. Recently, scholars and some judges have invoked the president as a better check, for he often has the capacity to override agency dynamism and to provide some legitimacy that comes with his national accountability. The Supreme Court's agency deference decision in *Chevron U.S.A., Inc. v. National Resources Defense Council* (1984) appeared (but only appeared) to accept this latter point of view, a notion that we criticize in this chapter. On the one hand, we question the Supreme Court's commitment to a strongly deferential approach to dynamic agency interpretations, a point nicely illustrated by the Court's undeferential decision in *Rapanos v. United States* (2006). On the other hand, we emphasize the Court's important role, even under an expansive view of *Chevron*, to enforce procedural limitations on lawless or arbitrary agency action. For example, federal judges engage in "hard look" review of agency regulations and sometimes impose additional process requirements on agencies. Indeed, the Supreme Court in practice affords (and ought to afford) more deferential review of agency interpretations that are accompanied by an open process of public input and agency response.[19]

Consistent with this last suggestion, we argue that the best role for judicial review to play in the modern administrative state is to be *deliberation-inducing* as to normative agency judgments, such as the EPA's and the Corps' broad understanding of their wetlands jurisdiction. This was a point made by both Chief Justice John Roberts and Justice Stephen Breyer in their separate concurring and dissenting opinions in *Rapanos*: an earlier Supreme Court opinion had rejected the agencies' application of the permit requirement to isolated wetlands protected simply because they were habitats for migrating birds, yet neither the EPA nor the Corps had revised their regulations; both Roberts and Breyer suggested that new regulations would be appropriate after John and Judith Rapanos won their case. Whether drawing from *Chevron* (the Court's official approach) or more eclectic sources (what the Court actually does in the run of cases), judicial review of agency interpretations of law ought to be especially deferential when the agency has engaged in model deliberation, that is, addressing problems and resolving disputes in a manner that (1) is open and public, (2) considers inputs from a variety of sources and provides reasons that are factually based and linked to the superstatutory purpose, and (3) accommodates larger public norms. Conversely, when an agency has adopted an interpretation that (1) is secret and comes out of nowhere, (2) ignores inputs from other sources and is not persuasively connected to the statutory purposes, or (3) is inconsistent with larger public norms, then federal judges should be less deferential. Reflecting its current practice, the Supreme Court should openly announce deliberation as a plus factor in judicial review.[20]

Another normative suggestion developed in this chapter is that judicial review ought to understand the statutory scheme from the perspective of Congress and the agency, and this requires careful study of the statute's legislative history, its ongoing statutory and administrative evolution, and the success of the agency's implementation. Thus, we reject the primary normative lesson of the new textualism advanced by Justice Antonin Scalia, both in general and in *Rapanos*, where Scalia wrote the plurality opinion. Judicial review should be deliberation-respecting—which it cannot easily be if judges refuse to consider the deliberative materials, as Justice Scalia did in *Rapanos*. A majority of the *Rapanos* Court did consider the statutory materials and evolution, a move that we endorse. Justice Scalia's effort to reduce statutory interpretation to a semantic exercise is a bad idea: it allows activist judges to disrupt administrative constitutionalism that is on the right track, while allowing do-nothing judges to tolerate constitutionalism that is seriously off-track but within the letter of vague statutory directives.[21]

Judges do and probably should play a critical role in the administrative state. As we suggest in the next part of this book, administrative constitutionalism can go wrong in a lot of ways, including partisan or interest group capture, bad theoretical assumptions, and getting too far ahead of legitimating legislative views or public opinion. Much more than Constitutional review, small "c" constitutional judicial review of agency action can reverse the burden of inertia by overturning a properly controversial agency interpretation. A question that shall hover over the remainder of this book and that remains a central question for America's republic of statutes is: What ought to be the criteria by which judges play their important role?

THE INEVITABILITY OF DYNAMIC STATUTORY INTERPRETATION

Assume with the Rapanoses (and with us) that the Congress enacting the CWA would not have expected the section 404 permit requirement to apply to their Salzburg site *and* that the ESA Congress would not have expected the law to prohibit wetlands development that disrupts the breeding patterns of an endangered bird. One lesson that must be drawn from our constitution of statutes is that agencies will be the primary interpreters of superstatutes *and* that their interpretations will be dynamic. Traditionally, dynamic statutory interpretation has been justified as applying the statutory purpose to new circumstances—but we join political philosopher Henry Richardson in saying that dynamic applications tend to change the fundamental statutory purpose, the priority among multiple purposes, and the trade-offs between purpose and cost that were foundational to the original enactment. Moreover, agencies are more likely than judges to interpret statutes *against* as well as *beyond* congressional expectations.[22]

PRAGMATIC DYNAMISM: APPLICATION TO CARRY OUT
AND TRANSFORM STATUTORY PURPOSES

Because they are aimed at big problems and must last a long time, superstatutes tend to be relatively general, abstract, and theoretical. Although detailed in many respects, both the CWA and the ESA had this feature, as they set forth broad definitions of key terms such as "navigable waters" and "take" as applied to an endangered species. Agencies must apply these general terms to specific factual settings or problems, and in so doing will render those terms relatively particular, concrete, and practical. Because Congress usually does not focus so specifically, the agency's immediate application of general terms to specific facts will typically go beyond the expectations, or even the imagination, of the enacting Congress. In addition, Congress will sometimes deliberately choose vague terminology, as a means of postponing normative choices that potentially divide our elected representatives.[23]

Congress's expectations for regulatory jurisdiction and coverage under the 1972 CWA were vague in many respects. The report of the House Public Works Committee cautioned against reading "navigable waters" too narrowly and expressed its intent that the term "be given the broadest possible constitutional interpretation unencumbered by agency determinations which have been made or may be made for administrative purposes." The Senate Committee on Public Works also rejected "narrow" interpretations, because "[w]ater moves in hydrologic cycles and it is essential that discharges of pollutants be controlled at the source." The Conference Report followed the House Report, and the House sponsor explained that its purpose was to jettison the traditional understanding of "navigable waters" that the Corps of Engineers had been following and to adopt something much broader, so as to carry out the congressional goal of assuring "water quality" and "restor[ing] and maintain[ing] the chemical, physical and biological integrity of the Nation's waters."[24]

What does all this mean as regards wetlands? Because they are usually not navigable in the traditional sense, wetlands were generally not regulated under older statutes aimed at navigable waters. Applying the new congressional goal with increasing aggressiveness, the Corps of Engineers addressed the wetlands issue in separate regulations issued in 1973, 1975, and 1977. The 1977 regulations defined "navigable waters" for purposes of the CWA to include wetlands that are adjacent to or "are in reasonable proximity to other waters of the United States, as these wetlands are part of this aquatic system." This definition was not only way beyond the traditional (pre-CWA) jurisdiction employed by the

Corps, it was a very liberal interpretation of "waters," as the Corps included as wetlands land that was not "inundated" most of the year but nonetheless supported "vegetation typically adapted for life in saturated soil conditions." What motivated this broad reading was the Corps' effort to interpret Congress's elastic definition of "navigable waters" in light of Congress's equally elastic purpose of assuring the "integrity of the Nation's waters." Drawing upon scientific studies probably not available to Congress, the Corps concluded that allowing developers to deposit fill and other matter in wetlands adjacent to streams and the like would contribute to downstream pollution and affect the entire ecosystem.[25]

It is doubtful that the 1977 regulations encompassed the Rapanoses' Salzburg site, because that land was connected to traditionally navigable waters only by a man-made drainage system flowing into a creek that flowed into the navigable Kawkawlin River. After the Supreme Court upheld the 1977 regulations, in *United States v. Riverside Bayview Homes, Inc.* (1985), the Corps became even bolder, however. In 1986, the Corps announced that its jurisdiction extended to intrastate waters "which are or would be used as habitat by migratory birds," what became known as the Migratory Bird Rule. In 1989, the Corps and the EPA clarified the 1977 and 1986 regulations in the compliance manual discussed above; although the Corps bowed to congressional objections to the broad and elastic definition in the manual, it generally reflected the Corps' practice (and the EPA has continued to embrace the manual). In 2000, the Corps interpreted its longstanding regulations—the ones upheld in *Riverside Bayview*—to include "ephemeral streams" and "drainage ditches" as "tributaries" that are "waters of the United States," so long as they have a perceptible "high water mark." This interpretation made clear the application of the wetlands permit program to the Rapanoses' Salzburg site, as the Corps had insisted in the 1980s and afterward. The property rights movement considers this progression of regulatory jurisdiction a classic example of lawless agency turf grabbing.[26]

John and Judith Rapanos might be right to think that the Corps' ever-expanding application of section 404 to the wetlands portion of their Salzburg site was not only beyond but also against the expectations of the enacting (1972) Congress. They would have thought the same thing if the Fish and Wildlife Service of the Department of the Interior had told them that its 1975 regulations defining "take" to include habitat destruction prevented them from filling their wetlands because it would disrupt breeding patterns of a bird or other animal. Indeed, the ESA's expansion by the FWS was contrary to understandings explicitly announced by both House and Senate sponsors. Each described the

ESA's operation in the following way: section 5 protected endangered species by providing money to acquire "critical habitat" that would otherwise be destroyed by private owners, while section 9 (the do not "take" provision) protected such species against "those who would capture or kill them for pleasure or profit."[27]

Although many property owners viewed these agencies' dynamic interpretations as ill motivated (the turf-grabbing agencies were either evil or greedy), this kind of statutory evolution is inevitable if the implementing agency takes its mission seriously. To take the mission seriously, the agency would, as the Corps and the Service both did, focus on the statutory purpose as it applied the statute to circumstances not foreseen by the legislators. For a superstatute especially, the purpose will be a grand one—and the grander the purpose the more apparent it will be that statutory application not only gives the statute concrete meaning it had not previously enjoyed but also changes the statutory purpose or the balance of purposes. It was fair for the Corps to read the CWA's overall purpose to treat as much of the country's aquatic environment as an interconnected ecosystem that Congress could Constitutionally regulate. Under such a reading, the Corps was open to and embraced arguments that pollution of the Salzburg parcel would have ripple effects throughout the aquatic ecosystem, not only possible pollution, but also damage to wildlife and a flood danger. Because Congress explicitly delegated authority to the Corps and the EPA to elaborate on its potentially broad definition of navigable waters to extend to all "waters of the United States," the purposive expansion of the statute beyond, and probably against, original congressional expectations was not only likely but also legitimate.

By the way, the Corps' engagement with the statutory purpose also changed the nature of the Corps as an institution. Recall that the Corps was traditionally concerned with navigable rivers and streams, as traditionally understood, but its new statutory duties and partner (the EPA) pulled the Corps well beyond that focus. Relatedly, the pre-1972 Corps had usually sought local consensus before asserting its effective jurisdiction, so normally its officials would not engage in a project until local conflicts were resolved. To implement the CWA, however, the Corps had to be more assertive, through coercive rules, and less accommodating to local interests. Once the CWA was adopted, local land use decisions were understood to have external effects on nonlocals, and so local decision making could not possibly produce an efficient outcome. Congress's meta-purpose in enacting and amending the CWA was to transform American property regulation to serve preservationist goals—and fidelity to that meta-purpose obligated the agencies to be more aggressive as regards local interests.

This regulatory aggressiveness not only changed the nature of the Army Corps of Engineers, it created political complications for the overall statutory project by sapping the Corps of needed political support.[28]

HERMENEUTICAL DYNAMISM: INTERPRETER'S
DIFFERENT PERSPECTIVE

There is another, complementary, way to understand dynamic statutory interpretation. Under our system of separated powers, the statutory interpreters (agency officials and judges) are a set of persons different from those enacting the statute (legislators). The interpreter's perspective makes a difference in any kind of interpretation; two different people acting in good faith often interpret the same text in two different ways. Because of different professional or role-based perspectives, dynamic interpretation can occur early on in the statute's evolution, especially if the statute submerges or fails to resolve controversial issues. As time passes, the interpreter's perspective is likely to diverge in an increasing number of ways from the perspective of the statute's authors, and the changing societal and legal contexts press her to interpret the statute in ways not anticipated by its authors. To the extent that people rely upon official interpretations to structure their conduct and expectations, their reliance interests (which might themselves evolve) are a practical barrier to efforts by subsequent interpreters to retrieve the statute's original meaning. For the Rapanos family, however, reliance interests cut the other way. The price they paid for the Salzburg site probably carried the assumption that it could be developed for economic gain—an assumption and a reliance interest that they felt were threatened by the Corps' assertion of wetlands jurisdiction.

For superstatutes, the big point is that Congress after much political pulling and hauling announces a major policy or principle—and then turns over its implementation to an institution that is populated with different kinds of people (experts rather than politicians) who have different audiences or constituencies, as well as different professional perspectives and ethical duties. This book has already provided examples where such "expert agencies" have transformed superstatutes from the beginning of the statute's life: the EEOC transformed Title VII of the Civil Rights Act; the Department of Justice, both the Voting Rights Act and the Sherman Antitrust Act; and the Social Security Administration, the Social Security Act. One may tell an interest-group story for some of these agencies. Thus, critics of the EEOC say that it is captured by civil rights interests and ignores economic arguments that cautious interpretations of the statute better serve the common good. Or one may tell a public interest account. Fans of the EEOC say that its officials and staff (such as Sonia Pressman Fuentes) gave life to Title VII and prevented it from becoming a dead letter. Likewise, critics of the Department of Justice's recent efforts to trim back the Sherman Act might see the department as captured by big business, while fans of the department say that it has served consumers who were being harmed by previous overenforcement of the statute.[29]

The agencies implementing the Clean Water Act—the EPA as well as the Corps of Engineers—are different from the earlier-discussed agencies, because their expertise is science rather than civil rights or economics. Enacting the CWA in 1972, Congress was aware of the scientific consensus that America's waters were degraded, its wetlands vanishing, and consequences dire, but it is doubtful that any legislator understood the science deeply. Agencies such as the Corps and the EPA developed more experience with the ecology of the nation's waterways and had access to experts who were steeped in the science of ecosystems, such as the EPA's Richard A. Liroff. While the scientists were not the only voices important in these agencies' interpretations of the statute, they were much more important in that process than they were in the legislative process. It was easy for Congress to conclude that the nation's aquatic resources were an interconnected ecosystem—but it was the hydrological experts who pressed that principle to scientific conclusions that politicians would have quailed at, like including the Rapanoses' Salzburg site as "waters of the United States."[30]

More important, scientific knowledge (like economics and workplace justice) is itself dynamic. What the cutting-edge scientists "know" changes over time. What is scientific common knowledge today is different from what was scientific common knowledge in 1972. With regard to wetlands, certain ideas are much more widely held today within the community of biologists and naturalists than a generation ago, including the following:

- There is no such thing as a truly "isolated wetlands," because all (or almost all) wetlands are connected to rivers and other traditionally navigable waters through tributaries or, at least, groundwater flows. Hence, degradation of a seemingly isolated swamp or marsh will *inevitably* contribute to degradation of rivers and other bodies of water.
- Wetlands pollution or filling contributes not only to problems of water quality throughout the aquatic ecosystem (the traditional CWA concern), but also (1) leads to accumulations of sediment downstream; (2) harms wildlife by destroying their habitat; and (3) increases risks of flooding. There is a strong science literature documenting these processes, and experts such as Dr. Daniel Willard (who testified in the Rapanos case) are able to trace some of these effects with certainty, others with varying probabilities.
- The long-term costs of wetlands degradation are, from a scientific point of view, vaster than previously recognized. To take a dramatic example, a key

reason Hurricane Katrina approached New Orleans with such force was that the metropolitan area had lost almost all of its surrounding wetlands, which had previously slowed approaching hurricanes. From a science-based cost-benefit point of view, the hundreds of millions of dollars in economic development that resulted from filling in wetlands were not only outweighed by the astronomical costs of Hurricane Katrina (even discounted by the odds against a wind of such force moving in the path followed by Katrina) but also outweighed by the non-Katrina costs of such development on the Mississippi River ecosystem.

We do not know precisely when each of these ideas achieved scientific acceptance, but none of them was part of the regulatory discourse in 1972. Law professors Dan Tarlock and Fred Bosselman have documented the dramatic shift in ecological thinking (including core assumptions) between 1972, when the CWA was enacted, and the 1990s.[31]

If you combine Congress's broad statutory language ("waters of the United States") *plus* the congressional purpose of preventing and reversing the degradation of the nation's aquatic ecosystem *plus* this scientific understanding of the critical role played by even "isolated" wetlands in that ecosystem, *then* the Rapanos property begins to sound like something that should be regulated under the act. Congress did not say in 1972 that it wanted to slow down the transformation of wetlands to make way for shopping centers. What legislator would stand up to shopping center development? But the logic of the statute, when understood from a science perspective, suggests precisely that.

INSTITUTIONAL DYNAMISM: THE HYDRAULICS OF
AGENCY-COURT-CONGRESS INTERACTIONS

There is a third structural reason why superstatutes, especially, will evolve over time, perhaps rather quickly. Statutory interpretation is hierarchical and sequential. Statutory interpretations by private parties (like the Rapanoses) can be corrected by administrators (such as the Corps and the EPA), who can be reversed by judges, who in turn can be overridden by the legislature. Even if agencies seriously sought to enforce original intent, text, or purpose, they would not be able to do so, because of an often unpredictable hydraulic process of feedback and anticipation that occurs as the system works out statutory meaning for issues that arise after enactment. Thus it is that agencies are constantly pressed from below—by private communities of interpretation, by interest groups, by ground-level implementers of the statute, by public as well as private resistance to the statutory norm—to interpret the statute to be responsive to new facts, new needs, new ideas. They are also pressed from above—by judges, by congressional committees, by other agencies, by the White House—to interpret the statute to be responsive to current rather than historical political preferences. (Of course, social movement forces that pressure an agency from below also influence institutions that pressure the agency from above.) We focus here on the different ways that political feedback affected the dynamic interpretation of the CWA and ESA that we have described.[32]

The Corps' increasingly expansive assertions of jurisdiction over wetlands between 1974 and 1977 owed much to pressure from the EPA and from judges, who insisted that the Corps depart from its traditional focus on navigation by ships and boats. The broad EPA-Corps interpretation of the statutory term "waters of the United States" triggered intense congressional interest and was one focus when Congress amended the act in 1977. Reflecting concerns of farmers and other property owners (people like the Rapanoses), the House bill would have limited the Corps' jurisdiction to wetlands contiguous or adjacent to traditional navigable waters, a significant cutback from the Corps' then-existing regulations, *and* would have excepted a variety of farming and forestry land uses from the section 404 permit requirement. The Senate bill also would have excepted specified farming and forestry uses from section 404 but would have reaffirmed the Corps' broad jurisdiction over wetlands, including those adjacent to "tributaries" as well as those adjacent to navigable waters as traditionally defined. On the Senate floor, Senator Lloyd Bentsen of Texas proposed an amendment to the bill that would have restricted Corps wetlands jurisdiction along the lines the House was proposing. A bipartisan coalition led by Senators Edmund Muskie of Maine and Howard Baker of Tennessee narrowly defeated the amendment, on the ground that it would have impaired the ability of the Corps to protect the nation's waters as an interconnected ecosystem. The Conference Committee opted for the Senate's affirmation of the Corps' broad jurisdiction, subject to the farming and forestry exceptions in both bills, as well as a provision allowing state programs to substitute for the Corps' permit program (as Michigan did in the Rapanos case).

The Senate in particular was much more pro-environment in 1977 than it had been in 1972, partly because liberal Democrats had swept out conservative Republicans in the 1974 elections and partly because extensive networks of environmental organizations were plying Congress with green information. In addition, the Carter administration was strongly committed to an aggressive environmental policy that in 1977 seemed in sync with public opinion. Thus, in the 1970s environmental groups prevailed over traditional property interests in the political process, as evidenced by the Senate vote. This new political balance directly affected judges' willingness to give the agencies discretion to apply the wetlands law expansively. In *Riverside Bayview*, the Supreme Court sustained the Corps' expansive interpretation because the justices were persuaded that Congress in 1977 had ratified the Corps' 1977 regulations—which were probably broader than Congress's expectations had been in 1972.[33]

A similar legislative reaction followed the Department of the Interior's 1975 habitat-protection interpretation of the ESA's antitake provision. Farmers, ranchers, foresters, and property owners like the Rapanoses objected that the FWS's 1975 regulation subjected their businesses to burdens that were excessive and urged Congress to override the regulation. The Department of the Interior and environmental groups responded that habitat protection was essential to fulfill the statutory biodiversity goal of protecting endangered species against extinction. (As with the CWA, the science perspective gave depth to the ESA's goal and demonstrated that biodiversity had a wide array of benefits for humankind as well as animals.) In the 1982 ESA amendments, Congress adopted a compromise similar to that adopted in 1977 for the CWA. The 1982 amendments left the habitat regulation alone but authorized the secretary of the interior to issue permits allowing section 9 takings that were "incidental to, and not the purpose of, the carrying out of an otherwise lawful activity," if the applicant presented an acceptable "conservation plan" showing how he would "minimize and mitigate" the "impact of the activity on endangered species." The committee reports explaining the new permit program used as their paradigm a regulatory response to a California case where a development project threatened the habitat of an endangered butterfly. (Significantly, this compromise was bipartisan, accepted by the Democrat-controlled House of Representatives, the GOP-controlled Senate, and the Reagan White House.) Invoking this postenactment legislative history, the Supreme Court upheld the FWS 1975 habitat regulations in *Sweet Home*.[34]

Third, and most important for the CWA, the Corps' ever-expanding wetlands regulations ran into an increasingly conservative Supreme Court after *Riverside Bayview*. In *Solid Waste Agency v. Army Corps of Engineers* (2001), the Rehnquist Court struck down the Corps' Migratory Bird Rule, on the ground that it went beyond the statutory authority over "navigable waters" (the general statutory term, which Congress had defined as "waters of the United States"). The Court ruled that "waters of the United States" must have a "significant nexus" to waters that were or can reasonably be made navigable in the traditional sense. Four dissenters would have affirmed the Corps' interpretation following the reasoning of *Riverside Bayview*. In *Rapanos v. United States* (2006), an even more fractured Roberts Court, with no majority opinion, applied *Solid Waste* to rule that the CWA did not give the Corps jurisdiction over the Rapanoses' Salzburg site. The controlling opinion, by Justice Kennedy (concurring in the judgment of the Court), ruled that the matter should be remanded to a lower court to determine whether pollution of the Rapanoses' wetlands would actually affect the traditionally navigable Kawkawlin River. Four justices joined a narrower plurality opinion, by Justice Scalia, that would limit the Corps to permanent standing bodies of water, a limitation urged upon the Court by organizations representing the Farm Bureau, the Petroleum Institute, and the Pacific Legal Foundation, a public interest firm supporting property rights and other libertarian causes.[35]

Both Chief Justice Roberts (concurring) and Justice Breyer (dissenting) wrote opinions in *Rapanos* urging the Corps and the EPA to engage in legislative rule making to clarify the ambit of their wetlands jurisdiction and to justify it by reference to the statutory language and legislative compromises. In June 2007, the agencies promulgated a guidance document outlining their assumptions about wetlands jurisdiction after *Rapanos*, and solicited public comments with rule making in mind. Responsive to the controlling opinion by Justice Kennedy (who was following *Solid Waste*) that there must be some reasonable "nexus" between the statutory jurisdiction and traditional navigable waters, the Corps and EPA indicated that they had jurisdiction over (1) traditional navigable waters and wetlands adjacent to them; (2) "non-navigable tributaries of traditional navigable waters that are relatively permanent" in that they have continuous water flows at least seasonally (e.g., three months) and wetlands that have a "continuous surface connection" to such tributaries; and (3) nonnavigable tributaries that have nonpermanent (i.e., episodic) water flows and their adjacent wetlands, but only where they have a "significant nexus to a traditional navigable water." It is uncertain whether the Rapanoses' Salzburg site would meet that new definition of wetlands, although the agencies did not concede that point on remand from the Supreme Court. Environmentalists complain that the new guidance denies the Corps and the EPA jurisdiction over most of the wetlands in this country and thereby undermines any regulation aimed at the integrated hydrological system.[36]

Step back to 1972 and imagine what rules Congress would have expected the Corps of Engineers and the EPA to come up with to protect against the further loss of "wetlands." Even the greenest legislators would not have expected their regulatory category to include episodically soaked lands "in proximity to" traditional navigable waters, yet these lands were embraced within the Corps' 1977 regulations upheld in *Riverside Bayview*. Even legislators prescient enough to foresee the 1977 regulations would never have predicted the "nexus" rule the Supreme Court devised in *Solid Waste* and applied in Justice Kennedy's controlling opinion in *Rapanos*. (Indeed, Justice Scalia's narrower interpretation would have been unfathomable to the Congress of 1972.) Whatever the judicial interpretive methodology, the only predictable result is dynamic interpretation. Today, the "law" regulating wetlands is a crazy quilt of bright-line rules and a vague (nexus) standard that has diminishing connection to the original expectations of the enacting (1972) Congress or of the (1977) Congress that reaffirmed and expanded the original statutory ambit. Our suggestion is that this dynamic, purposive, institutionally interactive process is typical for any statute that has an important effect in our society.

JUDICIAL REVIEW AND THE LEGITIMATING ROLE OF AGENCY DELIBERATION

The first federal environmental superstatute adopted in the wake of Earth Day was the Clean Air Act Amendments of 1970. It represented a coalition of presidential-aspiring and green-thinking Democrats such as Senator Edmund Muskie and Representative Morris Udall, together with moderate Republicans, including Senator Howard Baker and President Richard Nixon, who in the same year had created the EPA by executive order. Because they relied on state implementation and relatively weak air quality standards, the 1970 amendments made only a minor dent in the nation's polluted atmosphere. Although replete with compromises (such as allowance for coal use) needed to secure legislative support, the Carter administration's Clean Air Act Amendments of 1977 greatly toughened air quality standards. For example, the 1977 amendments capped pollution-emissions levels at new or modified "major stationary sources."[37]

Western smelters objected to the potential costliness of the major stationary source rule and lobbied the EPA to treat an entire cluster of buildings within an industrial plant as a single stationary source. Such a "bubble concept" would allow firms flexibility to offset increased emissions from one building by reducing them elsewhere within the single plant. After notice-and-comment rule making, the EPA adopted the bubble concept—but the U.S. Court of Appeals for the District of Columbia Circuit twice rejected the bubble concept for "nonattainment" states where the 1977 amendments required improved emissions levels. The second case, *Chevron, U.S.A., Inc. v. Natural Resources Defense Council* (1984), reached the Supreme Court, where the bubble concept got an important analytical boost from Deputy Solicitor General Paul Bator. Representing the EPA, Bator argued that Congress's purpose was complex—to clean up the nation's air (the lower court's focus), but at a reasonable cost to industry (the EPA's additional concern). Because the statute was fairly open ended, the EPA had considerable discretion in setting this policy balance, and federal judges should not upset that balance unless the EPA's view was contrary to the statute.[38]

Bator's brief was a hit with the justices. The shakiest conference vote to reverse the lower court, Justice John Paul Stevens explained his willingness to side with the EPA: "When I am so confused, I go with the agency." In his opinion for a unanimous Court, Justice Stevens not only accepted Bator's argument from complex statutory purpose but went further to say that agencies delegated lawmaking authority from Congress and responsible to the president are more legitimate gap-filling organs in our democracy than are unelected federal judges. The Court announced a two-step inquiry for cases where an agency has been delegated lawmaking authority: First, has Congress "spoken to the precise question at issue"? If so, Congress's directive is controlling. If not, a second inquiry is "whether the agency's interpretation is based upon a permissible," or reasonable, "construction of the statute."[39]

Almost immediately after the Supreme Court handed down this decision, some judges and scholars proclaimed a "*Chevron* Revolution." In 1986, Judge Kenneth Starr (later solicitor general) announced that *Chevron* was a Magna Carta, requiring judicial acquiescence in agency deregulatory initiatives. Lower court judges have made it one of the most cited Supreme Court decisions in history, and the Court has applied the *Chevron* two-step regime in a number of high-visibility environmental cases—including *Bayview, Sweet Home, Solid Waste,* and *Rapanos*. Between *Chevron* and *Rapanos*, the Supreme Court decided 68.4 percent of its environmental law cases in favor of agency views—following the *Chevron* framework in a quarter of the cases and the more flexible *Skidmore* framework in another quarter. From our perspective, the most important feature of *Chevron* is its open recognition that agencies, not courts, are the primary statutory interpreters in the modern administrative state. But in other respects, *Chevron* as it has been aggressively interpreted by some of its biggest fans is misleading or misguided.[40]

The primacy of agencies in our republic of statutes rests upon several features of their role in statutory implementation. The reason emphasized during the New Deal was that agencies are the repositories of expert knowledge and experience. In the case of environmental superstatutes, agencies understand the science much better than courts can, and that ought to count for a lot. As former EPA General Counsel Donald Elliott has argued, *Chevron* initially empowered scientists and reduced the sway of lawyers within the EPA, on the whole a boon to administrative constitutionalism. What *Chevron* added to the New Deal account was a legitimacy argument: agencies ultimately accountable to the president are more democratically legitimate than judges accountable to no one. On the one hand, this overstates presidential authority. Although the president appoints agency heads and exercises some review authority over agency rule making through the Office of Management and Budget, he does not have the authority to impose his own preferred rules upon an agency and is subject to the first-mover advantage that the agency's professional staff have even when the president is aggressively seeking a particular policy slant.[41]

On the other hand, linking the legitimacy of agency dynamism to the president potentially undermines administrative constitutionalism in some instances. While *Chevron* potentially frees up agencies to update superstatutes in light of what experience and new science- or economics-based thinking teaches them about the best way to carry out congressional purposes, it also exposes agencies to raw political pressure, as well as the often dramatic shifts occasioned by presidential elections. As we have emphasized here, the political pressure is just as much a part of the evolution of the statutory constitution as the science- or economics-based teachings. Indeed, *Chevron* was decided at a point in our political history when partisan politics was becoming more intensely polarized, and presidents of both parties were more single-minded in seeking to control or influence "expert" agency policymaking through ideological appointments and White House review of agency rule making. The Supreme Court has been moderately responsive to this problem. Shortly before *Chevron*, the Court in *Motor Vehicle Manufacturers Association v. State Farm Mutual Automobile Insurance Co.* (1983) had overruled another Reagan administration deregulatory move, on the ground that the agency deregulation was "arbitrary and capricious" because the administrators did not explain how the essentially political judgment could be factually tied to the statutory purpose, the protection of public safety.[42]

Chevron has coexisted with *State Farm*, and it is not surprising that *Chevron* has not been quite as "revolutionary" as some of its fans claim. For starters, it is not likely that the Supreme Court is going to give up its important normative role in statutory interpretation. Although agency interpretations prevail about 70 percent of the time among the justices, they have been happy to intervene and trump bold administrative initiatives that they view as insufficiently justified, as in *State Farm*. For a recent example, the Court in *Massachusetts v. EPA* (2007) ruled that the EPA's refusal to assume jurisdiction over carbon emissions contributing to global warming violated the Clean Air Act's requirement that the agency regulate "air pollutants" that can "reasonably be anticipated to endanger public health or welfare." *Massachusetts* is one of the few post-*Chevron* Supreme Court cases where an agency interpretation can be traced to White House pressure—in this case, suppressing scientific conclusions about global warming and its causes. Yet the Supreme Court rebuked the agency, surely in part because the majority justices felt it was bowing to presidential pressure rather than carrying out its statutory mission. Although following *Chevron*, the Supreme Court was not in the least deferential to the EPA's interpretation of the 1977 Clean Air Act Amendments. And the Court went beyond *State Farm* to hold, further, that the agency's failure to provide cogent reasons for not regulating greenhouse gases was "arbitrary and capricious."[43]

The Court's more liberal justices rebuked the EPA in *Massachusetts*—but the more conservative justices were just as undeferential in *Solid Waste* and *Rapanos*, where Court majorities ruled that the expansive understanding of wetlands jurisdiction by the Corps and the EPA went beyond what Congress had authorized. Relatedly, the agencies' understanding represented an insufficiently justified incursion into private property, the theme of the property rights countermovement. In *Rapanos*, two justices made a suggestion that fits particularly well with our theory of administrative constitutionalism: to deal with the thorny normative issues surrounding the identification of "isolated" wetlands, the agencies needed a more open and inclusive process, such as rule making. Our own primary suggestion is that judges' willingness to defer to agency interpretations of superstatutes should depend, in part, on the quality of deliberation that has accompanied that decision. Put another way, judicial deference doctrine should be *deliberation-encouraging.* That was the direct lesson of *State Farm* and is the practical lesson we have drawn from the Supreme Court's deference jurisprudence as applied in the past twenty-five years.

PROPER FOUNDATIONS FOR JUDICIAL DEFERENCE TO DYNAMIC AGENCY INTERPRETATIONS

Justice Stevens's opinion in *Chevron* briefly suggested that statutory gap-filling or policy elaboration by agencies is more legitimate than similar gap-filling or elaboration by federal judges, because agencies are accountable to the president, a nationally elected official. Some judges and professors have invoked presidential accountability as the primary justification for strong judicial deference to agency interpretations. This stance strikes us as both a misreading of *Chevron* and an unwise precept. As a matter of legitimacy, Justice Stevens's opinion was primarily grounded upon the notion that *Congress* is the primary source of an agency's legitimacy as a lawmaker, for Stevens repeatedly emphasized congressional delegation as the main source of an agency's lawmaking legitimacy. The Constitution vests Congress, not the president, with all lawmaking authority, and only Congress can legitimately delegate gap-filling lawmaking authority to agencies. Also, Justice Stevens's discussion of presidential accountability was more modest than some academics have assumed. *Only* after exhausting sources of congressional expectations (including the legislative history of the statute) should a judge defer to agency interpretations. An underemphasized lesson of *Chevron* is that the Court is an agent of Congress's purposes when it interprets statutes and responds to agency constructions. As a corollary, another reason agencies might be entitled to deference is that they are likely to reflect current *congressional* preferences, pressed upon them by oversight and budget subcommittees in particular.[44]

A fundamental problem with resting agency deference primarily or exclusively on presidential accountability is that such a justification is at odds with the other justifications for deference—namely, congressional accountability and the application of expertise to advance congressional purposes. As we have seen in this book, presidential norm entrepreneurship has been critical to statutory evolution, but it has had its greatest constitutional bite when confirmed by Congress. Thus, President Lyndon Johnson and Congress worked together to create the Civil Rights Act of 1964 and the Voting Rights Act of 1965, two of our classic superstatutes (chapters 1–2). Congress ratified and expanded the antitrust activism of Presidents Theodore Roosevelt, William Howard Taft, and Woodrow Wilson when it adopted the Clayton Act of 1914 (chapter 3). Although President Franklin Roosevelt and his advisers were the primary architects of the Social Security Act of 1935, Congress working with expert administrators was responsible for its critical expansions and ultimate entrenchment (chapter 4). The Nixon White House and the remains of the Great Society Congress came together to create a federally funded program for family planning, for single as well as married women, in 1970 (chapter 5). In all these instances, the Supreme Court was highly deferential to congressional-presidential partnerships—even when agencies applied the superstatutes very dynamically. The key justification for such superdeference was that these partnerships reflected a tentative settlement of important constitutional issues, and a settlement that We the People could be said to support. Important indicators of public support were the presidential elections of 1912, 1936, 1964, and 1972, where these issues were salient and where the candidate openly supporting the new superstatute either prevailed decisively over an open critic (1936, 1964) or prevailed in a field where all the candidates openly supported the constitutional norm (1912, 1972). These are examples where presidential (national electorate) accountability reinforces congressional (aggregation of state and local races) accountability.

On the other hand, the president and the legislature are frequently at loggerheads; divided government has been the practice for at least a generation. When the Supreme Court first evaluated the agencies' wetlands regulations in *Riverside Bayview* (two terms after *Chevron*), the Court deferred, unanimously, even though President Nixon had vetoed the 1972 CWA and President Reagan had been elected on a deregulationist platform that was inconsistent with the expansive understanding of wetlands jurisdiction by the EPA and Corps of Engineers. To be sure, President Reagan had just been constrained to bring back green hero Bill Ruckelshaus to repair EPA, and his solicitor general supported the Corps in *Riverside Bayview*. But the Court would, properly, have gone along with the agency even if the White House had disavowed those agency regulations. (The White House, of course, had no authority to revoke the regulations.) The reason is that not only had the EPA and the Corps deliberated when they issued the original regulations, Congress had itself deliberated that regulatory policy when it enacted the CWA Amendments of 1977. Encouraged by the congressional confirmation and relying on the consensus of scientific experts, the agencies had expanded the regulations after further postenactment deliberations, with public feedback and criticism. The legitimacy of that deliberative sequence ratification trumped the more general lessons of the Reagan Revolution, a point the solicitor general fully internalized. Unlike federal legislators, the president can only be reelected once, a fact that diminishes his theoretical accountability advantage.[45]

The Corps and the EPA issued a comprehensive guidance the year after *Rapanos*. Neither green property nor classical property boosters are happy with the nuanced policy in the guidance, which leaves millions of acres of wetlands unregulated but theoretically limits the development options of many property owners like the Rapanoses. The guidance links CWA assertions of jurisdiction to the points made in Justice Kennedy's controlling opinion for the Court, which demanded a "nexus" between a proposed wetlands and a traditionally navigable body of water. Although the guidance did not contain as many bright-line rules as property owners would want for planning purposes, it does lay out a comprehensive scheme for preserving wetlands, within the limitations imposed by our public (constitutional) culture. As Chief Justice Roberts and Justice Breyer suggested in *Rapanos*, the Corps and the EPA have a potential *first-mover advantage*: they can frame and set the terms of the debate by issuing regulations, a fait accompli that shifts the burden of justification away from the agency and onto the critics. By the way, the first-mover advantage echoes that enjoyed by the president vis-à-vis Congress—but in this case, the agencies' first-mover advantage sometimes gives its experts leverage in fending off attacks from the White House as well as Congress and the Supreme Court. Although the president can appoint agency heads who can press his point of view and can influence the agency's agenda, there are bureaucratic and substantive limits on presidential power to overturn entrenched agency policies. Perhaps mindful of President Reagan's comeuppance in the early 1980s, the antiregulatory George W. Bush administration felt constrained to appoint Ruckelshausian moderates to run EPA rather than Burford-like leaders of the property rights countermovement. Also, a primary source of legitimacy for the EPA/Corps position is that it reflects a well-informed, scientifically grounded judgment as to the implementation of Congress's charge to preserve and protect the nation's hydro-logical ecosystem. To the extent the White House has applied backdoor pres-sure on the Corps and EPA to adjust the guidance or subsequent regulations, their legitimacy is *diminished* if the pressure required the agency to provide a dishonest account of the science and the judgment of the experts, as the ad-ministration learned in *Massachusetts v. EPA*.[46]

There is a deeper legitimacy point to be made, and here we shall borrow the FWS's experience with the ESA to speculate about the future of wetlands regu-lation. The ability of the wetlands guidance to stick in the public culture is de-termined not by the precise pressure brought to bear on the agencies by either Congress or the White House but rather by political and social reactions in thousands of localities. Does the citizenry assimilate the agency-elaborated norm, or do we resist it? One possibility suggested by the Rapanos litigation is that large swaths of the American landowning public does not, on the whole, endorse the application of green protections when a property owner loses the primary economic use of her land because of a lengthy chain of environmental effects that people consider speculative. This phenomenon has special norma-tive bite when Americans like John and Judith Rapanos purchase property with the expectation of developing it, and then find (to their surprise) that "evolv-ing" EPA/Corps rules have claimed their property as wetlands, thereby greatly reducing its value.

This is also an important lesson of *Sweet Home*. One might read the Supreme Court's opinion for the proposition that all three branches—the Congress that adopted the 1982 ESA Amendments; the FWS, whose green philosophy sur-vived the Reagan Revolution; and a deferential Court—were in agreement that the ESA is a superstatute whose biodiversity norm trumps classical property norms. Justice Scalia's lament about the plight of loggers and farmers becomes an arcadian fantasy under such a reading. In truth, however, Justice Scalia had a bigger audience than some of the commentators recognized. Editorial writers all over the West decried the Court's decision in *Sweet Home*. The executive director of the American Land Rights Association, Chuck Cushman, spoke for many westerners when he responded to *Sweet Home*. "A private-property owner is thinking to himself, 'I find a spotted owl on my property, I'm going to lose everything I've worked for all my life.'" What would Cushman recommend? "The best solution under current law is to 'shoot, shovel and shut up.'"[47]

Academics can wring their green hands at Cushman's blunt challenge to the rule of law, but the hand-wringing does nothing to persuade Chuck Cushman and John Rapanos that they and thousands of other property owners ought to fol-low the new green rules. The Clinton administration understood that. Secretary of the Interior Bruce Babbitt responded to his agency's victory in *Sweet Home*

with nothing but conciliation for Betty Orem and the other landowning plaintiffs. Secretary Babbitt pledged to "work to make this law more flexible and user-
friendly for landowners. . . . We will continue to aggressively pursue a variety of
reforms to make the Endangered Species Act less onerous on private landowners." In June 1995, a month after *Sweet Home*, the FWS started to implement
Babbitt's pledge by proposing to exempt nearly all small and residential landhold-
ers from its section 9 requirements for protecting the habitat of threatened plants
and animals. This came as no surprise to Orem, who told the media that her
property had already been completely logged, without any regard to the ESA; unlike Cushman, she did not openly defy the statute, but she did ignore it.[48]

THE PARADOX OF DEFERENCE, AND A SMALL "C" CONSTITUTIONAL LIMIT TO AGENCY DYNAMISM

We add our distinctive theory to others that support some degree of judicial
deference to agency interpretations. But we also recognize a paradox. The
Supreme Court has strong reasons, both practical and principled, to defer to
agency interpretations of superstatutes and other laws, but institutional self-
interest prevents the Court from handing over all important law-interpretation
authority to agencies. If the Court read *Chevron* broadly and genuinely internalized its deferential attitude, the justices would run the risk of rendering
themselves irrelevant—and that is *not* something we expect of important institutions in our or any other governance structure. Indeed, this does not happen.
When important normative issues of constitutional (or quasi-Constitutional)
significance are involved in an agency interpretation case, the justices may talk
deference, but they perform their normative role to the hilt. Consider the interesting way this process occurs.

Step 1 of *Chevron* asks whether Congress has directly addressed the issue. If
so, the judge should follow the congressional directive, which will often support the agency. Most of the agency interpretation cases are resolved in favor of
the agency, either because its position coincides with congressional directives
(step 1) *or* because there is no clear directive and the agency interpretation is
reasonable (step 2). When interpreting environmental superstatutes, the Supreme Court rarely trumps dynamic agency interpretations with legislative
history suggesting that the agency is going against original congressional expectations. *Sweet Home* is instructive in this regard. It was *legislative-history-hating*
Justice Scalia, in dissent, who relied on sponsors' statements to argue that Congress expected to protect habitat through section 5 government purchases, not
through the section 9 prohibitions applicable to property owners. The majority
rejected those legislative history arguments, for reasons explored below.[49]

When it trumps agency interpretations of the statutory green constitution, the Supreme Court usually relies on statutory plain meaning. Thus, Justice Scalia's plurality opinion in *Rapanos* engaged in a detailed linguistic and dictionary examination of "waters" to conclude that Corps jurisdiction extended *only* to "continuously present, fixed bodies of water, as opposed to ordinarily dry channels through which water occasionally or intermittently flows." Although Justice Kennedy opined that the plurality's reading of "waters" was too narrow, he rejected the Corps' broad understanding, largely because it would delete half of the term of art chosen by Congress—"*navigable* waters." These are fine arguments, but they do not exhaust the possible meanings of "waters of the United States," the precise definition given by Congress to the statutory term. There is no dispute that *wet*lands contain *waters*, at least part of the year, and so it is not immediately clear why not all wetlands fall within the plain meaning of the statute. The majority justices sarcastically dismissed the possibility that "wetlands" as defined by the Corps included properties that were dry much of the year. As Justice Stevens argued in his *Rapanos* dissent, the Supreme Court itself has used terms such as "stream" and "channel" to include seasonal or ephemeral flows of water.[50]

Much of the debate in *Rapanos* about the meaning of "waters of the United States" sounded like a word game—and a word game in which the justices did *not* take a very deferential attitude toward the Corps' interpretation of the statute, even though all of the justices conceded that *Chevron* was fully applicable. Indeed, the justices' concession should have been even broader. Beyond (and preexisting) *Chevron*, the Supreme Court has repeatedly held that an agency's interpretation of its own valid regulation can only be overturned if "plainly erroneous or inconsistent with the regulation." Because the Corps was interpreting a longstanding regulation (the one upheld in *Riverside Bayview*) asserting jurisdiction over wetlands adjacent to "tributaries," its application in *Rapanos* was entitled to what is called *Auer* superdeference as well as *Chevron* deference. Although Justice Scalia is the Court's most aggressive watchdog for *Auer* superdeference for agency interpretations of their own regulations, his plurality opinion in *Rapanos* not only showed no deference to the agency's interpretation but also completely ignored the *Auer* line of cases.[51]

Nor do we find Justice Scalia's position in *Sweet Home* and *Rapanos* cogently justified by syntax, dictionaries, and the statutory texts. "Waters of the United States" and "take"/"harm" are elastic terms: they can be interpreted narrowly (Scalia), or they can be interpreted broadly (Stevens), or they can be interpreted somewhere in between (Kennedy). Although Justice Scalia refused to admit any elasticity in this plainly elastic language, his opinions dripped with sarcastic references to what he seems to consider green feudalism. In his *Sweet Home* dissent, Justice Scalia chided the majority for imposing "unfairness to the point of financial ruin—not just upon the rich" agribusinesses "but upon the simplest farmer who finds his land conscripted to national zoological use," referring to the ESA's biodiversity purpose. In *Rapanos,* his plurality opinion bewailed the expense John Rapanos had sacrificed to defend his land against a permit scheme administered by the Corps exercising "the discretion of an enlightened despot."[52]

The rhetorical sarcasm reveals the normative (small "c" constitutional) reasons why Justice Scalia read the statutes more narrowly than the agencies did. For Scalia, a critical norm is the Locke-Blackstone-Madison view of private property as foundational to liberty in all the ways we used the term in chapter 2: liberty as noninterference (the simplest farmer can use his land as he wants, so long as he is not simply creating a nuisance); liberty as security (the farmer's land sustains him and his family and enables him to pursue his simple life projects); and even liberty as participation (the primary stakeholders in a democracy are those simplest farmers). Neither Locke nor the recent property rights movement denies that the government has an obligation to regulate land use that imposes externalities (costs not borne by the owner) upon the larger community, but they believe that such regulations need to be local and fair. As reflected in Justice Scalia's opinions in both *Sweet Home* and *Rapanos,* the constitutional objections to federally imposed green feudalism are that it goes beyond the proper authority of the federal government *and* unfairly denies property owners the full economic use of their land. One reason the Rapanos case gained great notoriety was that the agencies were applying an aggressive and dynamic regulatory jurisdiction to a family that had bought the property well before such regulation was conceivable. Set aside the sarcastic rhetoric of Justice Scalia's opinions and focus on the serious constitutional issues he is raising. Those issues resolved the case for John and Judith Rapanos.

As a matter of the public record, the justices might bristle at our suggestion that small "c" constitutional norms would affect their constructions of statutes. Their official line is that judges should strive for objectivity, the ability for people of all values to reach the same answer under the proper methodology. Perhaps that is one feature of judging that sets it apart from administration, but another feature of judging is integration of particular areas of law into larger public norms. And that feature assures that constitutional assumptions are going to influence textual constructions. In a recent empirical examination of 1,014 Supreme Court cases involving an agency statutory interpretation (1984–2006), we found that textual plain meaning was the dominant mode of judicial

Table 6. Justices' agreement with agency interpretations, 1,014 cases (1984–2006)

Justice	Overall agreement rate	Agreement with liberal agency interpretations	Agreement with conservative agency interpretations	Ideological differential, conservative minus liberal win rates
Stephen Breyer	72.0%	79.5%	64.9%	(14.6%)
Ruth Bader Ginsburg	69.5%	77.1%	61.9%	(15.2%)
Anthony Kennedy	69.3%	61.8%	74.0%	12.2%
David Souter	68.7%	75.6%	62.5%	(13.1%)
Antonin Scalia	64.5%	53.8%	71.6%	17.8%
Clarence Thomas	63.1%	46.8%	75.8%	29.0%
John Paul Stevens	60.9%	79.2%	49.6%	(29.6%)

Source: William N. Eskridge Jr. and Lauren E. Baer, "The Continuum of Deference: Supreme Court Treatment of Agency Statutory Interpretations from *Chevron* to *Hamdan*," *Georgetown Law Journal* 96 (2008): 1154–56 (tables 20–21).

reasoning—but this did not guarantee political neutrality in the justices' voting patterns. Table 6 summarizes those patterns for the justices voting in both *Sweet Home* (1995) and *Rapanos* (2006).

As the table reveals, all of the justices reveal a significant amount of "ideological" voting, agreeing with agency textual readings much more often in cases where those readings line up with a justice's partisan preferences as to debated constitutional issues. Note that the gap between their votes in liberal and conservative agency interpretations is particularly high for the Court's most textualist judges, namely, 17.8 percent for Justice Scalia and 29.0 percent for Justice Thomas. Justice Kennedy, the only sitting justice who was in the majority for both *Sweet Home* and *Rapanos*, has the lowest differential, 12.2 percent. Using smaller datasets, other scholars have made similar findings for Supreme Court justices and judges on the D.C. Circuit when deciding agency interpretation cases in general and environmental cases in particular.[53]

We do not necessarily read this as evidence that textualist justices are trying to smuggle right-wing values into liberal statutes, but we do view this as evidence of a more banal proposition: how judges read open-textured terms like "take," "harm," "waters," and the like will be influenced by the normative priors that they bring to the interpretive enterprise. The hearts of Justices Scalia and Thomas (who, ironically, have relatively little property of their own) bleed for John and Judith Rapanos. They are sympathetic to the property owners' lament that evolving zoning and other land use rules deprive them of economic uses they assumed when they purchased land, although they also understand that ongoing and often surprising impairment of property rights is an inevitable feature of modern government. But such regulation is most legitimate when accomplished by local and state legislatures, where property owners have a great deal of political sway. What especially irks these justices about the wetlands cases is that increasingly intrusive regulation is imposed by an unelected national green bureaucracy, acting without discernible congressional authorization. Their policy vision is connected with their Constitutional vision: property is a personal right (Fifth Amendment) that is presumptively left to state rather than federal regulation (Article I and the Tenth Amendment), and certainly not to unsupervised bureaucrats, whom property rights enthusiasts sarcastically deem "enlightened despots" (separation of powers in Articles I–III). Starting from very different normative baselines, Justices Ginsburg and Breyer (loaded with property, compared with their conservative brethren) view the federal government's regulatory authority much more expansively and understand environmental regulation to be one of the central constitutional duties of modern government. Thus, they read the ecological science materials avidly and have internalized that point of view. So they are going to be more sympathetic to the agency's mission and less patient with the Rapanoses, who ignored agency notices and even a judicial cease-and-desist order.

In our view, deference is still doing a lot of work for both sets of constitutionalists: even skeptics of the green constitution have internalized its entrenchment in America's republic of statutes. In *Rapanos*, it is notable that green-baiting Justice Scalia cheerfully announced that the CWA's term "navigable waters" *cannot* be limited to waters that are actually "navigable" because the statute defines the term more broadly, a literal reading would be inconsistent with the CWA's structure, and *Solid Waste* had squarely rejected such a reading. Himself a property-respecting conservative, Justice Kennedy, who like Justice Scalia was appointed by President Reagan, was even more deferential, chiding his fellow Reagan appointee for being "unduly dismissive of the interests asserted by the United States," including the important environmental role of wetlands.[54]

DELIBERATION-INDUCING THEORY FOR JUDICIAL REVIEW OF AGENCY DYNAMISM

The small "c" constitutional concerns motivating Justice Scalia's opinions in *Rapanos* and *Sweet Home* suggest a normative justification for aggressive judicial review, especially in *Rapanos*. Both scholars and judges believe that the primary (and for many the only) justification for judges' trumping agency interpretations is the rule of law, whether enforced through plain meaning analysis or resort to legislative history. For important constitutional issues, we suggest that the more robust justification for judicial overrides of agency interpretations is more institutional and dialectic than legal and interpretive.

Consider the rule of lenity, which says that ambiguous criminal statutes should be construed against the government. The rule of lenity could justify Justice Scalia's narrow construction of the CWA in *Rapanos*, which involved an actual criminal prosecution, and of the ESA in *Sweet Home*, where the statute's civil and criminal liability provisions are in pari materia (so a broad interpretation of the civil provisions probably carries over to the criminal ones). The rule of lenity is liberty protecting, in both the liberal and civic republican senses. It protects the average citizen against prosecution where the statute is ambiguous; We the People deserve clear notice of criminal conduct so that we can, potentially, plan our affairs to avoid government interference and possible jail time. But the rule of lenity also serves a democratic purpose: the community's moral judgment associated with criminal liability will not be visited upon conduct that has not been the subject of legislative deliberation and a targeted statute. Put another way, the rule of lenity cautions *against* dynamic interpretations of criminal statutes by prosecutors, juries, and judges.[55]

This latter justification of the rule of lenity is a *deliberation-inducing* justification for an undeferential approach to agency interpretations of an open-textured statute. Libertarian and civic republican concerns might trump deference in those cases. If an agency or a social movement strongly believes that more regulation is needed, deliberation-inducing review signals that it must petition the legislature for such regulation. This is a possible defense of *Rapanos* and a reason for the Court not to defer entirely to the Corps under the *Chevron* or the superdeference regime for agency interpretations of its own regulations. The Corps had taken the CWA far beyond the green expectations of the 1972 Congress, and even of the 1977 Congress—and the agency's expansive view of its own jurisdiction raised more red flags when it treaded heavily on local property uses that had very tangential connections to the traditional jurisdictional hook for congressional regulation, namely, "navigable waters." At the very least, as Chief Justice Roberts and Justices Kennedy and Breyer emphasized, the Corps needed to justify its jurisdictional expansions by reference to the statute and ought to do so through the rule-making process that echoes the legislative process (citizen petitions and feedback, deliberation, and a published rule that is binding as a matter of law). Contrast *Sweet Home*, where the FWS's controversial habitat regulations had been the source of specific congressional attention.

In 1982, a divided Congress (Democratic House, GOP Senate) responded to the regulations not by overriding them but by creating an exemption process within the Department of the Interior for ordinary land use proposals affecting habitat of endangered species, so long as the landowner minimized the harm. In terms of congressional deliberations, *Sweet Home* and *Riverside Bayview* were much stronger cases for the environmentalists than *Rapanos.*

The 1977 CWA Amendments, the 1982 ESA Amendments, and the administration of both statutes reflect the sociopolitical fact that the full weight of green thinking has *not* become an entrenched part of America's statutory constitution. Green property has transformed land use regulation at the national, state, and local levels—but reliance interests remain a concern in periods of swiftly expanding regulations. The Clinton administration's response to *Sweet Home* and the George W. Bush administration's response to *Rapanos* are strikingly similar in that respect. Even though the FWS prevailed in *Sweet Home,* the Interior Department immediately recognized regulatory exceptions for small businesses and ordinary property owners. After its loss in *Rapanos,* the Army Corps and the EPA not only retreated from a broad assertion of jurisdiction in their 2007 guidance but according to environmentalists all but ceased to enforce the wetlands rules. As a side note, John Rapanos's own criminal prosecution was the result of his stubborn refusal to obey a lawful court order and what even the most ardent property rights advocates conceded was "mulish" behavior. One of the most important rules for a conservative rule of law jurist is the *absolute* duty to obey a court injunction, even if it is grounded in an incorrect application of law; hence, even if the Rapanoses were right to object to the agencies' dynamic statutory interpretation, they were wrong to violate a judicial order. We should have thought this feature of the case worth mentioning when the Supreme Court evaluated Rapanos's criminal conviction, but none of the justices even threw a footnote at this rule of law point.[56]

Deliberation-inducing judicial review rests upon the idea that important shifts of a constitutional magnitude ought not to be made without deliberation that is open and public; reasoned and factual; and legitimate. Small "c" constitutional moves ought to be publicly justified and debated, at least through agency rule making and perhaps through formal congressional action. Thus, judges should not defer and should be skeptical of agency norm entrepreneurship that pushes superstatutory evolution into significant collision with other fundamental norms, *unless* Congress after deliberation and public feedback has authorized such entrepreneurship. This antideference precept helps explain why the Court in the pregnancy discrimination cases was unwilling to go along with the EEOC's expansion of Title VII to include a huge new area of employment rules (chapter 1). The Supreme Court has encoded this idea in what one of our students calls the *critter canons*, namely, the rules of thumb that Congress does not "hide elephants in mouseholes" and that when Congress is making a big change in the statutory constitution it says so (the "dog doesn't bark" canon).[57]

This antideference precept reveals an important connection between Large "C" Constitutionalism and small "c" constitutionalism. In *Solid Waste*, Chief Justice Rehnquist's opinion for the Court invoked another version of our antideference precept, namely, the "avoidance canon," whereby judges are supposed to interpret ambiguous statutes to avoid difficult Constitutional problems. The chief justice found two interconnected Constitutional problems with the Corps' Migratory Bird Rule. One was that it was unclear whether Congress had authority under the Commerce Clause to regulate property having no connection to interstate commerce beyond the protection of migratory birds. The Court had long recognized Congress's authority to regulate navigable waters as an example of its Commerce Clause authority, but the Migratory Bird Rule had an attenuated connection with navigable waters. A related concern was that the Corps' expansive interpretation of the CWA would "result in a significant impingement of the States' traditional and primary power over land and water use," a potential concern given the Constitution's federalist structure generally and the Tenth Amendment in particular. These Constitutional concerns not only provided the chief justice with a reason to read the CWA cautiously but also justified his undeferential attitude toward the Corps' dynamic interpretation of the statute.[58]

Like the rule of lenity and the critter canons, the avoidance canon is an example of our antideference precept, but it also illustrates a new connection between Large "C" Constitutionalism and small "c" constitutionalism. We have repeatedly seen how the Supreme Court has interpreted the Constitution to accommodate important constitutional initiatives, from the Sherman Act of 1890 (chapter 3) to the Social Security Act of 1935 (chapter 4) to the Voting Rights Act of 1965 (chapter 2). *Solid Waste* and *Rapanos* illustrate how superstatutory constitutional law might be influenced by shadow Constitutional law. We emphasize "shadow," because if Congress enacted the Migratory Bird Rule after deliberation and findings, it is very probable that the Court would sustain such a law under the Commerce Clause, notwithstanding the lengthy chain between traditional navigable waters and the rule. As our general antideference precept suggests, this is a deliberation-forcing move on the part of the Court: Congress, and not just an agency (or the president), must deliberate and make this important constitutional move. Note that deliberation-forcing rules such as this one have strong substantive effects, because Congress will usually not be able to muster the energy and supermajorities needed to work an override bill through the many veto gates.[59]

RETHINKING STATUTORY INTERPRETATION DOCTRINE

The conventional wisdom is that statutory interpretation is governed by rules somewhat different from those governing Constitutional interpretation, to wit: (1) The plain meaning rule—apply ordinary meaning unless it would generate absurd results—remains the primary rule for statutory interpretation, and it actually plays a decisive role in most of the cases, as in *Sweet Home* and *Rapanos*. Large "C" Constitutional interpreters rarely even quote the provision they are interpreting, and when it is relevant it is usually not dispositive. (2) Legislative materials play very different roles. Many Constitutional interpreters will *not* consider the deliberations of the Philadelphia Convention or Congress (proposing amendments); most interpreters will consider state ratifying deliberations as evidence of original meaning, but typically they are used to determine Constitutional purposes and principles, not specific expectations. Statutory interpreters typically use legislative history to determine whether legislators had a specific intent when they adopted particular texts; some interpreters will not consider any legislative materials. (3) The Supreme Court says that *stare decisis* is superstrong for statutory precedents, but relaxed for Constitutional ones.[60]

Consider another contrast, announced by administrative law scholar Jerry Mashaw. Professor Mashaw says that agencies follow, and on the whole should follow, approaches to statutory interpretation different from those that judges follow, to wit: (1) Agencies should not be strictly bound by the plain meaning rule, as judges are in statutory cases, and should be more instrumental: apply statutes to carry out their purposes. (2) Agencies should be very interested in all kinds of legislative materials, not only the original legislative history, but also "subsequent" legislative history, which judges should generally not examine too closely (according to Mashaw). (3) As *Chevron* acknowledged, agencies are not bound by *stare decisis*, at least when they are engaged in legislative rule making. In perhaps the strongest contrast with precedent-following courts, agencies should feel free to change their interpretations, as the EPA did in *Chevron* (allowing the bubble concept that the agency had earlier abandoned) and the Corps of Engineers did in the Migratory Bird Rule (which carried its jurisdiction much further than earlier rules had done). Although Mashaw's theory has been a matter of debate among administrative law professors, it is a thoughtful and important statement of sharp distinctions between agency and judicial modes of interpreting the same statutory materials.[61]

As a positive matter, our theory of statutory constitutionalism maintains that these sharp divisions, mapped out in table 7, do not and should not reflect practice, at least as regards superstatutes. Statutory interpretation, whether by judges or by agencies, is and ought to be purposive and dynamic. Larger

Table 7. Contrasting doctrines of interpretation (conventional wisdom)

	Agency interpretation of statutes (Mashaw)	*Judicial interpretation of statutes*	*Judicial interpretation of Constitution*
Textual materials	Read statutory text in light of purpose	Plain meaning rule: unambiguous text governs	Read Constitutional text in light of its purpose and Constitutional principles
Original meaning materials	Consult legislative history; including "subsequent" legislative materials	Focus on original legislative history to understand specific intent of legislature	Consult original materials, but mainly to determine Constitutional principles and purposes
Stare decisis	Little or no *stare decisis* for agency precedents	Superstrong presumption of correctness for statutory precedents	Relaxed *stare decisis* for Constitutional precedents

principles play a big role, as they did in *Sweet Home* and *Rapanos*. And the Supreme Court overrules or narrows superstatutory precedents as often as it does Constitutional precedents, well illustrated in the Court's Sherman Act jurisprudence (chapter 3). When construing superstatutes, the justices may write opinions that devote more pages to textual analysis and legislative history, but the driving methodology is not much different from that which they follow when interpreting the Constitution. And given the fundamental nature of small "c" constitutionalism, this is what the justices ought to be doing.

Likewise, some of the distinctions drawn by Professor Mashaw should not be pressed too hard. Agencies ignore clear statutory texts at their peril, and judges do not feel themselves bound by arguably clear texts when constitutional values are at stake, as in the green cases discussed here. Judges do, and ought to, consult legislative history. We are inclined to agree with Mashaw that agencies should overrule their own precedents more easily than courts do. But we dissent from Mashaw's skepticism about agency engagement with larger normative frames. Thus, we maintain that agencies play an important constitutional role in our governance—more important than judges in fact. Given this critically important role, agencies interpreting statutes often behave like judges interpreting the Constitution: they devise from the superstatutory text, legislative history, and statutory evolution a grand design and purpose, and then apply the superstatute to carry out that design and purpose. The main difference, in our view, derives from institutional structure: agencies can and should be more pushy when applying superstatutes than the Court is when applying the Constitution, because it is easier for the governmental process to override the agency (the president, judges, legislators can do so).[62]

In the balance of this chapter, we shall suggest some ways in which judicial statutory interpretation ought to adapt practices from agency statutory interpretation. Supreme Court justices are already doing this when constitutional issues are at stake, and our recommendation is that judges at all levels be more open (or perhaps just self-aware) that they are behaving like agencies—but without the legitimacy, judgment, or expertise. It is this kind of modest and helpful judicial attitude that underlies the notion of "deference" to agency interpretations.

THE NORMATIVITY OF PLAIN MEANING

Agencies read statutory language purposively, and this ought to be a model for all statutory interpreters. Agency-like purposivism ought to be an antidote to the dictionary and grammar fetishism judges often engage in. We urge judges to avoid excessively dogmatic statutory readings and to return to a modified version of the Hart and Sacks approach of allowing agencies to read statutes to carry out their purposes, unless the agency interpretation imposes a meaning on the statute its words "will not bear." Judges can and perhaps ought to hew closely to text and give it stingy readings for ordinary statutes, but for superstatutes judges ought to be attentive to small "c" constitutional purposes, as well as competing constitutional norms.[63]

Does a wetland connected to a navigable river by a drainage ditch and a creek fall within the CWA's asserted jurisdiction over "waters of the United States"? The EPA and the Corps of Engineers understood the statutory language in light of the overall statutory purposes of assuring clean water and protecting the aquatic ecosystem against degradation. In the Rapanos proceedings, they applied that analysis to assert jurisdiction over the Salzburg site and other wetlands. The government's brief to the Supreme Court approached the statutory term historically, functionally, and purposively. "Waters of the United States" included the Salzburg site because environmental science demonstrated that degradation of such wetlands contributed directly to the degradation of other parts of the ecosystem. Indeed, viewed cumulatively, wetlands constitute the overwhelming majority of acres contained within the nation's aquatic ecosystem. To edit out Corps jurisdiction over the Salzburg wetlands would, as a functional matter, revise the CWA to cover "a fraction of the waters of the United States." This functional analysis of the statutory text was seconded by an *amicus* brief filed by four former EPA Administrators in support of the Corps' interpretation. A further *amicus* brief filed by thirty-three states asserted that for three decades the states have *relied* on the Corps' broad functional jurisdiction in structuring their own regulatory efforts. In its first Supreme Court brief, an association of state regulators put it this way: "Continued federal protection of intrastate nonnavigable tributaries and adjacent wetlands is necessary to prevent devastating injury to downstream States, such as pollution and flooding, which would threaten lives and harm economic resources, including our nation's traditional navigable waters."[64]

The Corps' legal argument was closely connected to its policy argument: it literally understood "waters of the United States" to be our interconnected aquatic ecosystem. The purposive approach is the right one for any interpreter to take, in our view. Everyone understands that meaning depends on context, but what lawyers do not always appreciate is that context is thoroughly normative. If we were at the beach and told young Penelope, "Don't go into the water," the child would know she was not supposed to wander into the ocean but could take a shower at the beach. The reason Penelope, a very discerning kid, could make this distinction is that she understands the shared normative context of the directive: youngsters should avoid danger, but cleanliness is encouraged. In this instance, context very much *narrows* the meaning of "water." Consider another usage: "I just waxed the floor—keep the living room free of water(s)!" Here, normative context *broadens* the meaning of "water(s)"—not just the gale-force storm that is now raging (so close the windows) but also liquid dripping off your raincoat and shoes as well as a glass of soda pop, which of course is not exactly "water" but falls within the directive nonetheless. When viewed in light of the directive's purpose (avoid staining the waxed floor) and the shared normative context (we all need to cooperate with Dad's effort to keep the house shiny-clean), "waters" means more than pure H_2O. It may include any liquid that could damage the freshly waxed floor. This is precisely the kind of normative thinking that the Corps and the EPA were engaged in—and should have been engaged in. By the way, this is not the *only* kind of norm the Corps and EPA should have considered. Like the FWS and the Department of the Interior after *Sweet Home*, the Corps and the EPA do need to consider the localism issues raised by pushing too hard on the statutory purpose. If pushing too hard for the right thing creates local political resistance, then the best is the enemy of the good and the agencies ought to proceed more cautiously.

Judges can learn from this—and it is clear that they already have. The plurality opinion in *Rapanos*, reflecting the narrowest understanding any justice has rendered for the Corps' jurisdiction, justified its interpretation in the right way. Its conclusion was that the statutory terms "cannot bear the expansive meaning the Corps would give it" (a pointed reference to Professors Hart and Sacks, who were Justice Scalia's instructors in law school). Justice Scalia justified that assertion through a variety of analyses, the least successful was his resort to *Webster's Second*, the Scalia dictionary of choice since 1994. *Webster's* defines "waters" (the plural form used in the CWA) as "the flowing or moving masses, as of waves or floods, making up such streams or bodies" including oceans, rivers, and lakes. But *Webster's* also defines "waters" as connoting a "flood or inundation; as the *waters* have fallen." Justice Scalia rejected this broader definition on the ground that it is too "poetic" for Congress to have followed—but how does he know that? He cited no evidence for his observation, and there was plenty of evidence to the contrary. An *amicus* brief from the key Republican and Democrat legislators involved in the 1977 CWA Amendments argued that the broader, more poetic meaning is exactly what they had in mind, and they supported their characterization with detailed references from the public record. This kind of arbitrary definition-shopping by the plurality opinion reveals a risk of textualist interpretation: it can easily become a process of looking out over the crowd (of dictionary meanings) and picking out your friends.[65]

Justice Scalia's arguments from dictionary meaning and common usage make out a case for a narrower definition of "waters of the United States" but do not establish that his is the *only* meaning the words will bear (his stated test). The arguments that close off other meanings rest on a normative context different from the Corps' protect-the-ecosystem understanding of the CWA's purpose. Both the CWA and the Constitution reserve primary responsibility for intrastate land and water regulation to the states, and Justice Scalia objected that the Corps' comprehensive understanding of its jurisdiction would "authorize the Corps to function as a *de facto* regulator of immense stretches of intrastate land—an authority the agency has shown its willingness to exercise with the scope of discretion that would befit a local zoning board." In our view, it was this *normative* context that conclusively narrowed the meaning of "waters of the United States" for four justices. Essentially, Justice Scalia's word game boiled down to a normative argument: Congress had not spoken clearly enough to justify agency jurisdiction to the extent demanded by the Salzburg site.[66]

Note the irony. *Chevron* required the Court to affirm the Corps' interpretation unless Congress had directly addressed the issue and decided otherwise. At the Supreme Court level, the *Chevron* tiebreaker has the effect of polarizing the justices' discussions. If you want to reverse the agency, for whatever reason, you have to eliminate ambiguity. Given the broad language used in most superstatutes such as the CWA, this is often hard to do. Some justices, such as Scalia, resort to normative canons of statutory construction to solve this problem. We consider this to be a core judicial role in modern constitutionalism—but it must not be confused with statutory plain meaning. It is judicial activism, in the sense that judges are making substantive judgments. Other justices, such as Stevens, resort to legislative context to resolve (or to generate) statutory ambiguity. We now turn to that topic.

STATUTORY AND LEGISLATIVE HISTORY

Agencies read legislative history to understand the evolution of the statute and current political alignments. This ought to be an antidote to the practice some judges follow of ignoring legislative materials *and* to the practice other judges follow of seeking out original deals and enforcing them even after circumstances have changed. We urge judges to read statutory history to understand the values and choices made by the legislature and how legislators have responded to dynamic agency interpretations.[67]

Traditionally, judges and scholars have justified resort to legislative history as a means of discerning the "intent" of the legislators who enacted the statute. The intent might be the specific meaning the legislators expected their statute to carry with it, the more general purposes the legislators were trying to accomplish with the statute, or even the original meaning of the words chosen by the legislators. From all these perspectives, legislative history is archaeological: it enables the interpreter to understand the statute as its drafters and enacters understood it at the time of enactment. Because they are often involved in statutory drafting and congressional deliberations, agencies know the legislative history very well, and their briefs typically provide the legislative archaeologist with excellent material, albeit slanted in favor of the agency's interpretation. Agency briefs also deploy legislative history in a dynamic manner, to recount the life of the statute and not just its birth.

Recall *Babbitt v. Sweet Home,* where the Court upheld the Department of the Interior's interpretation that the ESA's bar to "harming" endangered species included destruction of a species' habitat. As in *Rapanos,* Justices Stevens (writing for the *Sweet Home* majority) and Scalia (writing for its three dissenters) heatedly debated whether there was one single meaning of "harm" that the statutory words would bear, for both recognized that the agency prevailed under *Chevron* if there were statutory ambiguity. To say that "harm" can *never* mean destruction of an animal's habitat is a hard case to make, however. Realizing that, the challengers relied on the legislative history of the 1973 ESA, which had been persuasive in the lower court. Their evidence was so good that legislative-history-hating Justice Scalia smuggled it into his dissenting opinion (bracketed with disclaimers but relied on nonetheless). Both the Senate and House managers of the bill explained that it was section 5 of the proposed act would deal with the huge threat "to animals stem[ming] from the destruction of their habitat" by "providing [federal] funds for acquisition of critical habitat." In contrast, section 9, the no-take provision, addressed "[a]nother hazard to endangered species," namely, "those who would capture or kill them for pleasure or profit."[68]

End of case? No, because 1973 was not the last time Congress visited the issue. Solicitor General Drew Days's brief for the government was a classic example of how agencies approach legislative materials—and how judges ought to as well. The solicitor general conceded some force to the sponsors' statements but pointed out that their brief discussion never represented that section 9's "harm" standard gave no protection to individual animals whose species was endangered. He argued that there was room in the statute for the department's 1975 regulation, which did indeed trigger legislative discussion. In 1977–78, Congress deliberated ESA amendments responding to the Supreme Court's decision condemning the one hundred million dollar Tellico Dam in order to save the snail darter's habitat. Congress rethought its absolute prohibitions but rejected Utah senator Jake Garn's proposal to override the department's 1975 harm-to-habitat regulation. Instead, in the 1978 ESA Amendments, Congress established an Endangered Species Committee to grant exceptions for ESA applications that imposed excessive costs. After 1978, developers, ranchers, and farmers continued to object that the committee was inaccessible to their complaints. When a more property-friendly Congress revisited the issue in 1982, it again rejected proposals to revoke or override the 1975 harm-to-habitat regulation. By that point, it appeared that the regulations were accepted in both the House (controlled by the Democrats) and the Senate (under GOP control), but also that there was bipartisan support for a process that would allow farmers, developers, and ranchers to use their land for valid economic purposes notwithstanding habitat threats. Accordingly, the 1982 ESA Amendments authorized the secretary of the interior to grant permits for section 9 takings that were incidental to lawful activities and that minimized impact on endangered species. The Conference Report established that the 1982 permit program was a direct response to the complaints against the 1975 harm-to-habitat regulation.[69]

Like the CWA, whose ongoing history was the subject of solicitor general briefing in *Riverside Bayview*, *Solid Waste*, and *Rapanos*, the ESA is a law whose aggressive implementation created an ongoing policy and political discourse within Congress as well as the agency. *Sweet Home* reflects the fact that this ongoing discourse—what is often pejoratively referred to as "subsequent legislative history"—is relevant to judicial evaluations of expansive, purposive agency applications of broad statutory directives. For the green constitution, which necessarily limits the rights of property owners and businesses, the Rehnquist and Roberts Courts are filled with skeptical voices, and so the Department of the Interior's triumph in *Sweet Home* is remarkable. That the Corps did as well as it did in *Rapanos* is also remarkable. Its defeat in *Solid Waste* is understandable, for Congress's 1977 deliberations had little if any bearing on the Corps' post-1977 Migratory Bird Rule.

In *Rapanos*, Justice Scalia treated the subsequent legislative history with skepticism reflecting his formalist position that such history is irrelevant unless it explains the meaning of statutory language adopted by Congress in a subsequent amendment. (In *Sweet Home*, however, the legislative deliberations were preenactment legislative history for the 1982 ESA Amendments and provided useful information about the meaning of the ESA text, as amended in 1982, yet this is the only legislative history that Justice Scalia refused to consider in *Sweet Home*.) In our view, the Scalia approach is not only too limited, it is also not the approach judges actually follow, and indeed is not the approach Justice Scalia actually followed in *Sweet Home* and other cases. Attention to the ongoing legislative history of a statute is often going to be useful information for courts evaluating agency rules and interpretations. At the very least, such evidence provides the Court with valuable information about public and sometimes private *reliance* on or *acquiescence* in agency interpretations. It also provides the Court with useful information about the possible political consequences of disagreeing with the agency. The Supreme Court suffered needless humiliation when it dismissed serious agency views about the proper meaning of the nation's civil rights laws in pregnancy discrimination cases of the 1970s (chapter 1) and race discrimination cases of the 1980s.[70]

One lesson we draw from the recent examples of angry congressional overrides is that the sources of legitimacy and power are not completely different for courts and agencies. If either institution advances policy initiatives We the People strongly dislike *or* reneges on existing policies that We the People like or have relied on, that body risks losing public face if Congress rebukes it and risks congressional rage if it is considered uncooperative or hostile to popular projects. It is in the interest of both courts and agencies not to be perceived as too *activist*. But what people perceive as "activist" depends on political consensus: a decision contrary to a normative equilibrium will be rebuked immediately, while one contrary to a majority view will be criticized as wild and activist.

RELAXED *STARE DECISIS* IN STATUTORY CASES

Agencies do not consider themselves strictly bound by existing rules, but do consider reliance interests before changing their rules. This ought to be an antidote to judicial proclamations that statutory precedents are entitled to a superstrong presumption of correctness and ought rarely to be overruled. Following *Chevron*, we urge courts to give breathing room for agency interpretations to evolve and to write and interpret their own precedents to allow agency flexibility.[71]

The implication of *Chevron* is that a Supreme Court decision deferring to an agency interpretation is *not* creating a *stare decisis* effect for that interpretation. When there is a zone of indeterminacy in the statutory command, any reasonable agency interpretation within that zone ought to be acceptable, and so the effect of the Supreme Court's decision is minimized. (That is, the *stare decisis* effect is really the specification of the zone, not the particular agency interpretation.) In *National Cable & Telecommunications Association v. Brand X Internet Services* (2005), the Supreme Court held that a prior lower court construction of an ambiguous statute was not a bar to the agency's formulation of a rule to the contrary. "A court's prior judicial construction of a statute trumps an agency construction otherwise entitled to *Chevron* deference only if the prior court decision holds that its construction follows from the unambiguous terms of the statute and thus leaves no room for agency discretion." Justice Clarence Thomas's opinion for the Court justified such an approach by reference to *Chevron* and its aversion to "ossification" of the law if court decisions always sealed a statutory interpretation in stone. Consistent with *Brand X*, Chief Justice Roberts and Justices Kennedy and Breyer asserted in *Rapanos* that the Corps had ample policy room to elaborate on the controlling standard for wetlands regulation, so long as it respected the *Solid Waste* requirement that degradation of a wetlands must have a "significant nexus" to traditionally navigable waters.[72]

Brand X represents an understanding of *stare decisis* as a process of ongoing elaboration *or* experimentation that we should extend beyond the Court's *Chevron* jurisprudence. As we saw in chapter 3, the Court periodically revisits and overrules its Sherman Act precedents with rarely a mention of the superstrong presumption of correctness of statutory precedents. The reason for the periodic overrulings is that expert evaluation of many of the older precedents suggests that they burden market decisions without any discernible benefit for consumers, the Court's current understanding of the Sherman Act's purpose. The Court does not lightly cast aside these precedents; in the past generation it has only done so when the FTC and the Department of Justice's Antitrust Division formally suggest an overruling in an *amicus* brief.[73]

We urge the Court to generalize its Sherman Act jurisprudence, at least somewhat. Typically, when the Court has overruled a Sherman Act precedent, it has rejected an interpretation that originated in a Justice Department or FTC prosecution during the 1950s and 1960s—and the overruling comes at the behest of the same agencies, which have now concluded that the earlier, more aggressive approach to the Sherman Act did not subserve its consumer welfare purpose. (We emphasize that neither the agencies nor the Court comes to such conclusions lightly; the process of reconsideration and then overruling usually proceeds over ten years or more.) Likewise, the Supreme Court should be willing to revisit other kinds of precedents when the agency that helped persuade the Court of the cogency of one reading has come to a new and deeply considered conclusion that is at odds with the old precedent. Such a pattern of experience and critique/agency proposal/judicial response is a model for how our legal system is to evolve in a manner that is responsive to learning and experience yet is also orderly and respects reliance interests.

The green constitution perfectly reflects the phenomena we have been exploring in this book: the recognition of critically important values and principles in superstatutes that displace common law baselines, perhaps only in part; elaboration of those values by agencies applying bold green principles to revamp public law; and popular and legislative feedback ratifying agency boldness and entrenching green values in our statutory constitution. That this process entails dynamic agency interpretations of green superstatutes is merely an obvious corollary of what we have been describing.

The evolution of wetlands regulatory policy that has been the focus of this chapter adds an interesting twist to our account. In prior chapters, we have seen the Constitution bend in the face of superstatutory forces. Thus, Congress's spending power was expanded to accommodate the safety net constitution during the New Deal, just as the commerce power and the coinage power were expanded to accommodate the monetary constitution during the founding era and Reconstruction. In this chapter, we have seen the judicially enforced Constitution assert itself, albeit through dynamic statutory interpretations interposed at the margins, though important margins where much is at stake. It is remarkable how much liberal agency dynamism the very conservative Rehnquist and Roberts Courts have accommodated, and even assimilated into their own thinking about statutory interpretation. But it is also notable that the Court has rolled back some of the agency dynamism and has forced the agency to justify the significant regulation it has imposed upon traditional property rights. This, too, can be justified under our theory. Dynamic agency interpretations that run up against entrenched constitutional norms without popular or at least legislative deliberation are headed for trouble, the legal point of Justice Scalia's opinions in both *Sweet Home* and *Rapanos*.

The larger point that emerges from our history of wetlands regulation and the contentious Rapanos litigation is that the green constitution is revolutionizing not only the relationship of Americans and their environment but also the notion of what is "property" and its relationship to liberty, the normatively charged but dynamic concept explored in chapter 2. Classic theories of property emphasize liberty as noninterference and as security: the land is a family's source of income, identity, and flourishing, and government regulation was largely limited to preventing your use of land from harming me. Some classical theorists, such as Madison, also found a republican theme and viewed land through the prism of liberty as civic engagement. Green property deemphasizes land as the source of personal and family security and settles on the land more civic obligations than many Americans are willing to absorb. But in a genuinely republican moment, Earth Day, April 22, 1970, green property has seized the imagination of millions of Americans and has earned their loyalty for decades to come.[74]

The Clean Air Act and the Clean Water Act are now entrenched superstatutes: We the People have internalized their norms of environmental nondegradation and renewal, and any institution of government that openly renounced those norms would be subject to a popular firestorm. Moreover, these superstatutes are backed up by determined administrators having the weight of state as well as federal governments on their side. John and Judith Rapanos learned this the hard way. Although they won their Supreme Court case, the government on remand was prepared to establish the wetlands eligibility of their Salzburg site under Justice Kennedy's controlling "nexus" approach—and at that point the Rapanoses settled with the government. According to the Rapanos blog, the family agreed to pay "fines and mitigation fees approaching $1 million."[75]

The government's ability to squash the Rapanos family is not necessarily a green victory and ought to be understood as a cautionary tale. Like social security (chapter 4) and unilateral divorce (chapter 5), the wetlands-regulatory policy in our republic of statutes is far from perfect, and the endangered species policy is widely considered an expensive policy failure. A central problem with both policies is that evolving visions of a green future are clashing with particular land use decisions by private landowners who made investments before regulators decided that certain land development plans would in fact impose externalities, when viewed from a holistic green perspective. This clash between private reliance on property rights and the evolving regulatory judgments about what is an externality is probably an inevitable feature of the green constitution, but the conflict is deepened when regulators have created new rules without sufficient public deliberation and consensus. The wetlands policy is probably more successful because it has received more targeted congressional deliberation, evasion is more difficult (filling in bogs is a more visible activity than knocking off woodpeckers), and more resources are devoted to education and enforcement. But both the wetlands and the endangered species habitat policies suffer from a mismatch between problem and regulatory solution. That is, command-and-control permit regimes with broad prohibitions and cumbersome exemption processes are probably not the best mechanism for preserving wetlands and protecting species from extinction. To the extent that the wetlands-preservation and biodiversity norms are worth pursuing, the challenge for the next generation of administrative constitutionalists is to come up with more effective regulatory tools that minimize public-private showdowns such as we saw in the Rapanos case.[76]

Part III

CYCLES OF CONSTITUTIONAL ENTRENCHMENT AND DIS-ENTRENCHMENT

Administrative constitutionalism is central to the republic of statutes. It is inevitable. And it is experimental. One of the great virtues of statute-based constitutionalism over a large "C" Constitution is that the former is more adaptable. There are many commitments that are fundamental to us today, but will not be so fundamental fifty years from now. And commitments whose importance holds up over time might be hard to implement exactly right. Institutions as well as rules have to be tried and discarded. This is usually easier to accomplish for statutory commitments, even entrenched ones, than for Constitutional commitments.

Chapter 7, on the monetary constitution, illustrates this point wonderfully. The Constitution of 1789 said precious little about monetary policy or public finance, which is a virtue. Indeed, the document might have been a better charter if it had said less than it does. The Coinage Clauses of Article I, Sections 8 and 10, are an obvious (source of) power if read broadly or a mistake if read narrowly (as leading historians say the framers expected) to bar Congress from issuing paper currency not backed up by specie. Monetary policy is tricky. Not only did the framers have no brilliant ideas about how it should work, it is also a policy area that is particularly dynamic. The monetary needs of the internationally connected United States are very different from those of colonial America, and war puts a particularly strong strain on monetary policy (as the framers would have known from their own experience). Institutions such as the Federal Reserve Board would have been inconceivable to the framing generation, and its policy instruments appropriate for the twenty-first century might not have been appropriate for the eighteenth.

The same point could be made for the constitution of sexual morality (chapter 8) and national security (chapter 9). The Constitution of 1789, as amended, wisely says nothing definitive about these topics; the most that it does is to establish a deliberative institutional framework for these issues to be dealt with over time. Like the monetary constitution, the constitutions of sexual morality (chapter 8) and national security (chapter 9) have witnessed sea changes in the last generation alone. For sexual morality, the constitutional changes have been responsive to socioeconomic developments giving rise to a visible gay rights movement. With regard to homosexuality, America's constitution of morality went through a significant regime shift in the late twentieth century, mostly under the aegis of municipal and state law. From a regime where homosexuality was considered predatory and malignant, most states and localities had by 2000 moved toward a regime of tolerance. The gay rights agenda for the new millennium is to effect another shift, from a tolerance regime, where heterosexuality is preferred in state policy, to a regime of "homo equality," where gay people are treated as full and equal citizens.

Chapters 7 and 8 trace a long history where entrenched regimes (such as the United States Banks, 1791–1832, and the antihomosexual constitution, 1921–2003) are subjected to critique because they are inconsistent with grand constitutional themes, such as democratic governance (the Jacksonian critique of the bank) or equal protection (the gay critique of the antihomosexual constitution). Thus, both chapters present accounts of successful *dis-entrenchment.* As with entrenchment, the key governmental actors for dis-entrenchment are *not* judges enforcing the Constitution but are instead nonjudicial officials, including the chief executive, cabinet-level officials, legislators and advisory commissions, and ordinary enforcement personnel. The monetary constitution presents a particularly interesting case, because "entrenched" national policy has gone through further convulsive changes since the fall of the United States Bank. The currently entrenched Federal Reserve System has had its own ups and downs and may be morphing into a new kind of institution as our book goes to press.

The national security constitution, explored in chapter 9, presents another variation on the cycles of entrenchment, namely, bold administrative experiments that *failed,* on the whole, to dis-entrench the established regime. Specifically, we provide an account of several innovative approaches designed by the Bush-Cheney administration to fight the war against terror; the different approaches have suffered different fates. On the one hand, Vice President Richard Cheney's notion that wiretapping restrictions should be loosened so that the executive branch can farm for data potentially relevant to terrorist activities is an idea that has attained significant bipartisan traction, modifying and perhaps eventually displacing a superstatute that reflected an earlier libertarian consensus. On the other hand, the vice president's view that waterboarding and other forms of coercive interrogation are acceptable means for gathering intelligence has suffered rebukes from every quarter and has given way to the traditional norm forbidding official torture of suspects.

A related theme of this part is that administrative constitutionalism often goes off track. The primary challenge to administrative constitutionalism is that administrators may be easily derailed from their statutory mission by *agency capture*, when an agency pursues rent-seeking policies benefiting special interests and not the common good. Capture that throws an agency off its public mission can be achieved not only by (1) businesses regulated by the statute (the traditional capture scenario, epitomized by the Interstate Commerce Commission), but also by (2) the statutory beneficiaries and (3) political parties. These different forms of capture do not have the same normative valence. Thus, the worst form of capture is when private interests hijack a public agency for private gains. While partisan capture may also have that feature, it usually entails the adoption of a different (partisan) theory of the public interest purposes of the agency. When the Reagan administration took over the Environmental Protection Agency (EPA) and the Department of the Interior in 1981, there was something of both forms of capture: Anne Gorsuch (EPA) and James Watt (Interior) sought to cut what they considered overregulation, but they also arguably broke the law and rewarded their friends with public goodies. Often the agency capture debate is really a debate about whether the public project is structured correctly or is pursing the right goals. Such debates have saturated the rocky history of America's monetary constitution (chapter 7). Did Nicholas Biddle and the United States Bank represent the capture and exploitation of farmers by eastern financial interests, as the Jacksonians claimed in the 1830s, or were they the prudent managers of a stable economy, as the Whigs asserted? We think more the latter, and ironically better examples of capture are episodes where the supposedly incorruptible Federal Reserve Board of Marriner Eccles, Arthur Burns, and Alan Greenspan was sometimes a partisan pawn of presidential politics.

Another challenge is substantive: administrative constitutionalism, even when not captured by a special or partisan interest, can go wrong when officials vigorously enforce a regulatory regime's least productive or its seriously mistaken directives. Recall from chapter 3 that many economists criticize the pre-1969 Department of Justice and the Warren Court for an overzealous application of the big-is-bad themes of the Sherman, Clayton, and Celler-Kefauver Acts. Whatever one's views about that, it's even harder to deny that Earl Warren revealed lamentable judgment when he was governor of California (1943–53) and presided over the most vigorous antihomosexual *Kulturkampf* in American history (chapter 8). Warren and his allies pushed for or supported powerful punitive and rehabilitative legislation under the aegis of protecting children against child molesters (heterosexual as well as homosexual), but the legislation was so sweeping that it applied to lesbians and gay men who sought to date or cohabit with adults of the same sex. The legislation rested upon antihomosexual prejudices and false stereotypes, and the Warren-era enforcement amplified the worst features of a regime that considered decent people outlaws. In the hands of bigoted police officers, militant school boards, and hospital administrators that would serve as models for *One Flew Over the Cuckoo's Nest*, the prejudice-based and punitive features of the legislation were frequently applied in grotesque and inhumane ways. As we explore in chapter 9, the Federal Reserve Board (the darling of agency fans such as ourselves) provides many examples of bad substantive theory leading to disastrous consequences.

A final challenge to administrative constitutionalism is tunnel vision. Agencies can go too far when they engage in what they consider necessary and democratically approved actions that violate deeper constitutional commitments of our polity. The administrators and legislators who defiantly defended American apartheid suffered from this vice; certainly by the 1960s, diehard southern defiance of national equality values was not only substantively mistaken but also strongly inconsistent with both small "c" and Large "C" Constitutions. Another example of this problem is more recent (chapter 9). Secretary of Defense Donald Rumsfeld, Vice President Richard Cheney, and lower-level administrators and legal advisers interpreted the hard-to-calibrate external threat to national security to sanction "torture" of detained persons. Many soldiers, agents, and other on-the-ground personnel carried the policy even further, perhaps believing that extreme activities were appropriate under the circumstances and even sanctioned by their superiors.

Earl Warren, Richard Cheney, and Alan Greenspan were visionaries pressing a constitutional vision, just as were Susan Deller Ross, William Baxter, and Robert Ball, visionaries discussed admiringly in earlier chapters. In retrospect, the visions of Warren, Cheney, and Greenspan were administrative constitutionalism gone wrong, and this is a price the United States pays for small "c" constitutionalism where the important implementation comes from administrators vested with great discretion. Another theme of this part, however, is that the checks and balances—most of them outside the Large "C" Constitution— provide ways to manage renegade constitutionalism and have operated to reverse the worst mistakes. Indeed, an important theme of this final part of the book is the ways in which bad or obsolete constitutional regimes can be slowed down, halted, or even dis-entrenched.

The most common method of regulating renegade administrative constitutionalism is the internal checks and balances within the executive branch. One kind of internal check is a requirement for cooperation of different officials or agencies before the government can act. The classic example of this check is operation of the criminal justice system, which requires the concurrence of the police making the arrest *plus* the prosecutor bringing the charge *plus* the grand and petit juries, whose assent is needed to bring the indictment and then to convict. During the height of the antihomosexual Kulturkampf, state and local prosecutors as well as state law reform commissions took the lead in softening the impact of aggressive legislation and police brutality. A second internal check is duplication of responsibilities among agencies; if one agency is captured or operating under deluded policy assumptions, an agency with overlapping jurisdiction can register a dissent. Pockets of resistance to the Bush-Cheney administration's culture of torture emerged in the State Department, the Justice Department, and ultimately within the Office of Legal Counsel. The critics not only resisted the legal arguments for immunizing torture but also leaked key documents to the press, where they generated tremendous public debate and criticism. A third internal check is White House review, which we have not found to have been as puissant as these other checks.

A second potential check against administrative constitutionalism gone wrong is Congress. Senator Nelson Aldrich and Representative Carter Glass were the leading government actors responsible for advancing proposals that were the basis for the Federal Reserve Act of 1914, which replaced the nation's unsatisfactory experience with the National Banking System (chapter 7). But Congress has typically been a sluggish responder. Even more than the president, Congress can get carried away with ill-considered policies that are temporarily popular. For example, Congress and state legislatures followed the lead of Governor Warren's antihomosexual policies and innovated a few aggressive ones of their own (chapter 8). More important, it is harder for Congress to get its act together sufficiently to respond to administrative abuses and monitor the "agency problems" outlined above. Led by legislators such as Senator John McCain, Congress pushed back some against the Bush-Cheney administration's culture of torture, but most of the push back was after the fact and may have been ineffectual (chapter 9).

We find the judiciary to be a third, and exceedingly important, check against administrative constitutionalism gone wrong. Given the life tenure of federal judges, those courts are hard to capture by one interest group or ideology-driven political party. Moreover, the professional culture of the judiciary and the adversarial structure of adjudication provide a useful second look at the rationality of agency policies and their consistency with larger legal commitments (a judicial specialty). Thus, state and federal judges, most of them personally as homophobic as Governor Warren, set limits on aggressive antihomosexual policies even at the height of the terror. (And when Governor Warren became Chief

Justice Warren, he was stalwart in setting limits on the administration of apartheid, the exemplar of squalid constitutionalism.) The California Supreme Court, in fact, insisted upon tolerant and lawful treatment of sexual and gender minorities by aggressive police and school boards well before such tolerance was politically imaginable. The U.S. Supreme Court indirectly set limits on the administrative culture of torture when it ruled that the Geneva Conventions are self-executing treaties that are the law of the land.

THE MONETARY CONSTITUTION AND ADMINISTRATIVE EXPERIMENTATION

Thomas Hobbes argued that the fundamental protection that a state, any state, must provide is for the security of the lives of its citizens. Without that, life would be an unending competition among the predatory and the vulnerable, accompanied by a high level of violence. If government could not guarantee against this hopeless situation, life would be no better than in the state of nature. Under these circumstances, government could command neither obedience nor respect and probably would not endure for long. It certainly would not deserve to. This is well accepted. It is often forgotten that Hobbes also said that the state of nature is miserable not only because people are liable to be killed but also because it perpetuates unending poverty and a generally precarious existence. Indeed, to be unbearable, life in the state of nature need not be marked by much actual fighting; its violence might well be of a more insidious kind. As Hobbes remarked in a famous passage, people so insecure would be afraid to invest in the future at all, knowing that the fruits of their investments could easily be taken from them, perhaps even at the cost of their lives. "In such condition there is no place for industry, because the fruit thereof is uncertain: and consequently no culture of the earth; no navigation, nor use of the commodities that may be imported by sea; no commodious building; no instruments of moving and removing such things as require much force; no knowledge of the face of the earth; no account of time; no arts; no letters; no society; and which is worst of all, continual fear, and danger of violent death." Only in concluding did Hobbes lament that the state of nature finds "the life of man, solitary, poor, nasty, brutish, and short."[1]

We can agree with Hobbes that the primary obligation of the state is to provide a stable structure for society so that its citizens can be secure in their persons but also have secure enough hold of their possessions to undertake vital cooperative projects. In this respect, Hobbes anticipated Locke's more explicit focus on property rights. This was a focus that was daily in evidence in the English legal tradition as well. Hobbes's argument was framed in a highly simplified world of isolated individual deciding in conditions of terror to authorize a sovereign to stand above them and regulate their interactions. In actual fact, rights to personal security and property emerged more gradually out of more complex historical and social conditions. The world was made up not merely of people but included all kinds of communities, institutions, and groups, including families, within which individuals themselves were formed.

Social security (chapter 4) and family law (chapter 5) are examples of legal structures that are security-enhancing in a direct way: the government creates a structure of mutual obligation and forced savings to enable the average citizen to have a strong assurance that her or his needs are met in sickness, disability, and old age. Other legal structures are security-enhancing in an indirect, but no less important, way. America's colonial and early common law constitution recognized and enforced rights to own and develop property and to enter into commercial obligations. Without these guarantees, a viable economy might not have been possible. In this respect, the common law of property and contracts, as well as family law, were fundamental to early American economic security and the operation of a market economy. One could write an entire book about the constitutional importance of property and contract law and the ways American property and contracts law has changed over the past two centuries. In this chapter, we want to focus on an often overlooked feature of the constitution of the market: the state's control of money and its regulation of banking.[2]

State actors may wish to protect property rights, but states will themselves be tempted to erode their value in many ways—not merely through confiscation and taxation but also by undermining the value of the currency, which is both the medium of exchange and the store of value. Consider an example. On June 20, 1860, Susan P. Hepburn of Louisville, Kentucky, borrowed money from Henry Griswold and agreed to repay him $11,250 on February 20, 1862. Hepburn was slow to repay her debt, and Griswold turned to state courts for an order directing that he be paid. Hepburn was directed to repay her debt, with interest, and she did so in March 1864, depositing $12,270 with the court. But there was a twist. In 1860, the only national legal tender that would have satisfied Hepburn's debt was gold and silver coin—but on February 25, 1862, Congress enacted a law authorizing the Treasury Department to issue $150 million in paper notes and directed that these notes had be accepted as "legal tender" for debts and other obligations in the United States. Hepburn repaid her debt in these paper notes, even though her original agreement to pay was entered into when only specie would have been acceptable, and the same was true when her debt was due to be repaid (five days before the legal tender statute was enacted). Because the federal government had run up a large debt during the Civil War, these notes were heavily discounted and therefore not redeemable in $12,270 worth of gold or silver, a boon to Hepburn. Griswold cried foul and demanded payment in hard currency. Would a sound government allow Hepburn to pay in the manner she did? In *Hepburn v. Griswold* (1870), the Supreme Court agreed with Griswold.[3]

The monetary constitution tackles questions like this; it describes the state's structures and policies for creating, monitoring, and regulating the nation's money. Establishing and maintaining a stable and readily available currency is tricky. From the first days of the republic, no issue has been more difficult and politically fraught for the national government than the establishment, disestablishment, or regulation of institutions of banking, currency, and national finance. Hepburn's case, for example, became a national cause célèbre, dividing both political parties and becoming the occasion for the swiftest volte-face in the history of the U.S. Supreme Court. This chapter shows how these issues deeply implicate our national values of *liberty* and *democracy*. Irresponsible monetary policy implicates liberty as noninterference because it can destroy citizens' contractual expectations and even their valuable property, and liberty as security because it can undermine people's past plans and their willingness to engage in future plans. Henry Griswold certainly felt his liberty was undermined in both of these ways by Susan Hepburn's exploiting the 1862 legal tender statute. (Future Griswolds might be more cautious in agreeing to contractual terms, and future Hepburns would find it harder to borrow and plan.) For Hobbesian and Lockean reasons, monetary and banking policy is one of the most important things a government does—and, realizing that, We the People have made it a matter of heated political deliberation, with regulation a matter of national identity and democratic accountability, and not just economic efficiency. Hence, such policy implicates liberty as civic engagement as well. Indeed, as we shall show, social movements have arisen around the particular matter of public finance, the way they have focused on antidiscrimination legislation (chapters 1 and 2), married women's property and contracts statutes (chapter 5), and even social security (chapter 4). And the government has been responsive to popular opinion in devising public financial institutions and processes. We the People have been eager to repudiate legislatures and chief executives who have presided over financial crises.

No policies in our history have been more politically galvanizing or consistently divisive than those regulating money. Think of it. The first political parties arose mostly to support or oppose Treasury Secretary Alexander Hamilton's economic program, the centerpiece of which was his proposal to charter the First Bank of the United States. The Jeffersonian Republicans identified themselves in large part as opponents of the First Bank, and (after President Madison, following the 1812 war, acquiesced in the re-creating of a national bank) their critique was transformed into a Democratic crusade against the Second Bank led by President Andrew Jackson. The Whig Party formed in part in opposition to "King Andrew's" crusade and was politically sustained by the bank issue until the party fractured over slavery. (When the Whigs first won the presidency in 1840, it was political payback for the economic woes following Jackson's antibank vendetta.) The inability of the Whigs to break Democratic Party dominance in the 1840s and 1850s can be largely traced to their own failed banking policies. The Civil War raised the stakes of public finance and created a whole new system of national banks. For a generation after Reconstruction, the most divisive ideological debate in American politics involved currency issues. Greenbackers, bimetallists (silver and gold), and populists viewed *Hepburn v. Griswold* as the worst Supreme Court decision since *Dred Scott* and celebrated its overruling a year later. Goldbugs and bankers celebrated *Hepburn* as exemplary Constitutionalism, where steady Chief Justice Salmon Chase (who as treasury secretary had supported the legal tender law over his private reservations) set forth limits on irresponsible monetary policy. Although the goldbugs ultimately prevailed in this debate, a new generation of American corporate capitalists demanded structural changes, and their popular movement yielded the Federal Reserve Act of 1913.

The Federal Reserve System was itself the consequence of several social movements, including one flying under the banner of corporate capitalism. The Fed of course was not the end of debate, nor the end of monetary problems. If monetary historians are right that misguided monetary policies in 1928–32 are what made the Depression of 1929 "Great," we might plausibly attribute the rise of mid-century Democratic dominance substantially to failures of monetary management under the Republicans. In the wake of the depression, President Franklin D. Roosevelt took the nation off the gold standard—perhaps the most radical and important constitutional move in America's history, and a move that was confirmed by the Banking Act of 1935. One might say that the most lasting feature of our monetary constitution was the gold standard, and some believe the regime of the gold standard was codified in the Coinage Clauses of the Constitution of 1789. Nonetheless, this was a feature wholly unsuited for modern governance, and its dis-entrenchment in 1935 came none too soon.

The deep issues of money supply and management have always been political: banking policy in every period produced or reproduced the deepest cleavages of party politics. And it has been republican: people of all stations get involved in the politics of public finance, both because it affects the lives of everyone and because the issues involve activated deep-seated and resilient conflicts of interest within the electorate and, perhaps as important, conflicting visions as to what the United States is and ought to become. The gross outlines of these cleavages are clear to anyone with a passing knowledge of American history: regional divisions either between the industrial and financial centers and the hinterlands, or between the North and South or the East and West; localized class conflicts of various kinds, including divisions between creditors like Griswold and debtors like Hepburn; as well as emergent conflicts within the banking class itself (many of which were themselves products of banking legislation and policy). The constitutional issues, the issues of deep political principle, played themselves out dramatically in our history. Who can forget the imagery of William Jennings Bryan's Cross of Gold speech? Or President Andrew Jackson's denunciations of Mr. Biddle's Bank? Or President Franklin Delano Roosevelt's (FDR) biblical condemnation of "unscrupulous money changers" in his first Inaugural Address? And the venom directed against FDR when he took the nation off the gold standard in 1935? How about Fed Chair Alan Greenspan's confession that "we were wrong" in downplaying the housing bubble that broke the American economy in 2008? Each dramatic episode invoked a republican vision of America. These sharply drawn visions of good and evil make it clear that the struggle to create a set of institutions that could sustain a relatively stable currency (which may properly be called a central bank) was about more than mere material gains and losses.

Our argument in this chapter is that an independent central bank presiding over a national paper currency emerged as a superstatutory framework regime only in fits and starts. The path to an independent central bank and a national paper currency was anything but linear and took years of experimentation and struggle, including a struggle against Large "C" Constitutional understandings. Central banking functions were exercised by different institutions—sometimes chartered national banks, sometimes the Treasury Department, and sometimes marketlike institutions—or by the operation of the international gold standard. Importantly, the role of the central banking institution changed over time, shifting from acting as a traditional banker (holding depositions, making loans), to being a special customer (that is, the government), to behaving like a large but still traditional bank open to all kinds of customers but with some important privileges relative to its competitors, to operating as a bank to other banks, to being a regulator of the financial and banking systems, to becoming what would now be understood as a central bank by exercising control over the money supply. And its degree of independence varied greatly over time as functions were exercised by a publically chartered private institution, to a department of the federal government, to decentralized markets, and back again. At the same time, the nature of legal currency in the United States varied from era to era. Much of the experimentation here was driven by wars and crises—the War of 1812 and the ensuing deflation, the panics of 1837–39 and 1893, the Civil War (which created Susan Hepburn's opportunity to repay her debt in devalued notes), World Wars I and II (which were followed by significant contractions), the Great Depression after 1929, the Vietnam War (which contributed to the terrible stagflation of the 1970s), and the Great Financial Meltdown of 2008. The recent economic crisis offers the novel phenomenon where bubble-producing policies were not generated by a war or crisis but came about for some other reason, which the experts are still trying to decipher.

As a matter of constitutional design, the foregoing features of public finance— its importance to the state's core functioning, the deep tension between expert management and democratic accountability, the need for institutions of public finance to operate under drastically varying conditions (war, popular unrest, prosperity), and the utter impossibility of predicting future challenges—render it uniquely *unsuited* to be governed by superentrenched Large "C" Constitutional rules. There are a surprising array of relatively bright-line rules or original understandings about public finance in the Constitution of 1789, and all of them have been fudged or jettisoned when the governing coalition has believed the nation's economic stability and growth depended upon institutional innovation (and cheap money), whether it be the United States Bank or the legal tender rules that benefited Susan Hepburn and infuriated Henry Griswold. As the *Hepburn* case reflects, many Americans would like to have fixed universal rules for the monetary constitution—from the goldbugs of the nineteenth century to the free silver enthusiasts of the late nineteenth century to the monetarists of the twentieth. But, for public finance, the greatest virtue of administrative constitutionalism is its relative flexibility: the basic design of the system can be abandoned if it does not work, and when it does more or less work administrators can learn from past mistakes and update the design or its operational principles.

Accordingly, the monetary constitution offers good examples of administrative constitutionalism gone wrong, and it has gone wrong in a variety of different ways—the United States Bank's design was inconsistent with democratic premises that became overwhelming in the 1830s; the National Bank System was poorly designed to meet the central goals of public finance, namely, the provision of liquid capital for business needs and the smoothing over of financial adjustments; the gold standard America followed for most of its history created unpredictable and destabilizing flows of specie; and even the widely admired Federal Reserve System has committed a variety of regulatory faux-pas that were the results of partisan influence or bad economic theory. When administrative constitutionalism has veered off course, the primary institutional mechanism for correction would presumably be the president, who has strong electoral and legacy incentives to prevent economic meltdowns and has the ability to respond quickly and decisively (and with advice from experts) to both short-term crises and longer-term dilemmas. Perhaps the best example of presidential initiative was Franklin Roosevelt's abandonment of the gold standard through executive order (authorized by Congress), which set the stage for a pure fiat-based money system. As we show in the following historical study, however, presidents have performed their correctional role unevenly. President Andrew Jackson may have had a point that the Second Bank was arrogant, aristocratic, and not accountable to the public interest, but his hysterical campaign to destroy the bank also crushed the country's economy for almost a decade. And, ironically, his reforms pushed the key central banking functions onto new privately run clearinghouses that were even less responsive to public opinion than the Second Bank was. Since the creation of the Federal Reserve System, presidents have worked closely with the ministers of public finance, but presidents from Nixon and Johnson to Clinton and Bush have not influenced the Fed in particularly beneficent ways.

The Supreme Court is virtually worthless as a checking mechanism, because judges are not experts in financial markets, their backward-looking sources of law are precisely the wrong sources for guidance, and the case-by-case means of adjudication moves too slowly. These limitations are illustrated by the Court's poor performance in *Hepburn v. Griswold*, the most swiftly renounced Constitutional decision in the Court's history. (The best feature of the Court's performance in monetary constitution cases is that *Hepburn* was a temporary departure from the Court's accustomed role of acquiescing in whatever the political branches and the bankers decide to do.) Like the Court, Congress moves too slowly to address immediate crises but, unlike the Court, is essential for ratifying any long-term mechanism. The impetus for congressional action has come from social movements; within government the representatives for those social movements have included executive officials such as Secretaries of the Treasury Alexander Hamilton, Roger Taney, and Salmon Chase; as well as legislators such as Senator Nelson Aldrich and Representative Carter Glass, and their advisers such as Paul Warburg.

In the end, the most effective checks on the monetary bureaucracy are economists and the electorate. Economists are ex ante checks. Our system of public finance has for almost one hundred years been managed by an agency heavily staffed with economists. If economists speak with one voice—as they sometimes do—that is a significant internal check on the willingness of the Fed to press particular policies. Unfortunately, there are many issues on which the economists do not speak in one voice, there are some issues as to which the economists are wrong or not far-sighted enough, and there are some issues as to which the Fed is bent by the president toward poor decisions. So mistakes are made, and the electorate emerges as a post hoc check. Nothing outrages the voters more than an economic crisis that turns them out of jobs and ruins their investments, and nothing energizes the political system more than outraged voters.

THE ROLLER-COASTER HISTORY OF
THE UNITED STATES BANK, 1791–1836

The euphoria Americans felt at Independence soon gave way to the sober realization that it would be hard to establish the country on a sound financial footing. "Continentals" issued during the Revolution were worthless, and the states had assumed staggering debts. For example, if Susan Hepburn had re-paid her debt to Henry Griswold in notes issued by the Continental Congress in 1782 rather than in the 1862 greenbacks, the creditor would have felt even more cheated than he did in the 1860s. The phrase "not worth a Continental" arose out of the low value of this currency by war's end. To establish reliable credit and currency and to manage the nation's money supply were tasks be-yond the capacity of the Articles of Confederation and constituted one impor-tant reason the northern states led the way in abandoning the articles as our framework for governance. Although the Constitution of 1789 was surprisingly restrictive with regard to national finance and currency, the framers-turned-governors escaped its apparent restrictions with a boldly dynamic interpretation that has repeatedly trumped original meaning with practical necessity in every Supreme Court opinion on these issues, with the exception (treated in the next section) of the First Legal Tender Case involving Hepburn and Griswold.

THE FIRST BANK OF THE UNITED STATES, 1791–1811

The law creating the First Bank of the United States was adopted only after a great Constitutional debate—one that occurred within President George Wash-ington's cabinet and the First Congress, not within the Supreme Court or the federal judiciary. Secretary of the Treasury Alexander Hamilton proposed the First Bank on the Lockean ground that the government has an affirmative responsibility to create structures that would facilitate a flourishing national market and economy. Hamilton could assume the operation of state contract and property common law—the basis for most of the small "c" constitutional that the United States had during the founding era—but he worried that there would not be a stable currency and ready availability of credit for business expansion. During the Revolution, credit was scarce, and after Independence there was a shortage of specie and confidence in paper currency then in circulation. Hence in 1789 Hamilton proposed that the federal government assume all public debts in the country *and* that a national bank be established. The two proposals were intertwined, with the goal being to create a stable currency that would allow business expansion through easier credit. Business expansion, in turn, would fuel a national civic identity that would enrich the United States socially and politically as well as economically.[4]

Within Washington's cabinet, Secretary of State Thomas Jefferson and Attorney General Edmund Randolph opposed Hamilton's proposal. Philosophically, they did not favor policies favoring the interests of traders and industrialists over farmers and shopkeepers, which they believed the bank represented; they felt that our national flourishing would be driven by the republican ardor of the farmer and the shopkeeper, not the capitalist entrepreneurs and bankers. (Jefferson even failed to understand that farmers needed credit, something that became clear to his heirs twenty years later when Madisonians in the South and West supported creation of the Second Bank.) Constitutionally, they maintained that creation of a United States Bank was beyond the limited authority granted Congress in Article I. Because a federally chartered bank would go well beyond the common law and would be inconsistent with state statutes, such a power needed to be explicitly named in Article I, Section 8's comprehensive listing of national powers, which of course it was not. Such an authority was well beyond the ambit of the Coinage Clause, and there was no other obvious basis for the bank in Article I, Section 8's list of delegated powers. Indeed, the Philadelphia Convention's Committee of Style had rejected proposals by James Madison and Charles Pinckney that Congress be empowered to charter corporations. During the Convention debates, Madison pressed this proposal as a part of Ben Franklin's motion to give Congress the authority to build canals; most of the speakers opposed Madison's proposal, and one of them specifically warned that it could create discord in the incorporation of a national bank. In 1791, Madison assured his close ally Jefferson that the Constitution affirmatively withheld authority from Congress to adopt Hamilton's proposal.[5]

Arguably the ablest lawyer in America, the secretary of the treasury started from a different, and more aggressive, baseline. A fundamental project of the Constitution was to create institutions that facilitated the operation of national commerce, banking, and economy. To this end, Article I not only granted Congress particular powers, such as the coinage authority denied to the states, but in Clause 18, the final provision, of Section 8, Article I also gave Congress explicit authority to "make all Laws which shall be necessary and proper for carrying into Execution the foregoing powers, and all other Powers vested by this Constitution in the Government of the United States, or in any Department or Officer thereof." The bank was "necessary and proper" to enable Congress to exercise its explicitly authorized powers to "pay the Debts . . . of the United States" (Article I, Section 8, Clause 1); to "borrow Money on the credit of the United States" (Clause 2); to "regulate Commerce" (Clause 3); and to "regulate the Value" of domestic coinage, "and of foreign Coin" (Clause 5). Based upon his ambitious vision for an economically thriving America, intimately tied to this enabling interpretation of the Constitution, Hamilton persuaded President Washington that his proposal was in the long-term interest of the country, and the president signed the bank bill into law on February 25, 1791.[6]

The bank was an odd creature from our modern vantage point: a private institution in which the federal government provided 20 percent of the capital (ten million dollars), held 20 percent of the stock, and named five of its twenty-five directors. This may have reflected both a desire to regulate credit outside the pressures of politics and a philosophy of few federal government employees and departments that the Washington administration followed. In any event, the public-private hybrid was perhaps the most important institution created during the Washington presidency. It served as both a depository of some government receipts as well as a lender to the government. Its capital would consist partly of gold and partly of government debt. While it could maintain branches wherever it wished and could issue notes, there was little explicit awareness of its capacity to regulate the supply of money (a core central banking notion today), even though it certainly did regulate money as part of its normal operations. Part of the reason is that, under a specie standard, such regulation was thought to be automatically achieved by market-driven movements of gold and silver. There was still a refusal, grounded in current understandings of the Constitution, to see bank notes, whether issued by state banks or the Bank of the United States, as money. Still, the bank used its regulatory powers cautiously and did not much exploit its competitive advantages relative to state banks. Although there were not many state banks around at the start, they immediately proliferated.[7]

The operation of the Bank of the United States was never as smooth as Hamilton had hoped it would be, but it was a qualified success. The nation's money supply relied mostly on the operation of the traditional specie standard (gold and silver were part of the coinage at a statutory fixed price ratio) under which banks were required to convert currency into gold. The bank generally maintained a conservative (high) ratio of specie to notes and was able, and usually willing, to finance species shortfalls in the states, thereby limiting financial crises. Yet in 1811 the Senate defeated a bill to recharter the Bank of the United

States, upon the tiebreaking vote of Vice President George Clinton, President James Madison's second in command. Why? Apparently, the main reason was partisan politics. Although the rechartering was an initiative pressed by Madison's esteemed Treasury Secretary Albert Gallatin, Madison's Democrat-Republican Party viewed the bank though the lens of the political struggles of the founding generation: as a part of the Federalists' political program that was a common threat to interfere with state banks. But by this time, the expanding and powerful banks in New England (the core region of Federalist strength) had stopped buying up federal debt, and had no interest in recreating a powerful competitor for business or in empowering a new regulatory institution— whereas the weaker southern and western banks needed the boost that that a central bank could provide. So the configuration of financial interests had turned topsy-turvy. Moreover, the end of the First Bank left the national government without a fiscal intermediary to hold and disburse its funds, and Secretary Gallatin entered into a series of agreements with private banks that could receive deposits and make payments for the federal government. This jerry-rigged system of public finance did not work well when the nation went to war.[8]

SECOND BANK OF THE UNITED STATES, 1816–36

The War of 1812 with Great Britain produced a financial crisis. The federal government was unable to secure enough loans to finance this ill-conceived war and, as an alternative, funded the war through issuing interest-bearing Treasury notes, which were acceptable by the government as payment for taxes and therefore immediately became a quasi-currency. At the same time, states were issuing new paper notes. The effect of this uncoordinated and massive issuance of notes was a terrible inflation combined with a shortage of commercially acceptable currency (either specie or creditworthy paper). This crisis generated demands for a new Bank of the United States and disrupted the ideological split (Republicans against, the fading Federalists in favor of the Bank) that had sunk the bank in 1811.[9]

Reflecting the new terms of debate, President Madison himself, in his annual message to Congress, admitted the need for a central monetary authority:

> It is, however, essential to every modification of the finances that the benefits of an uniform national currency should be restored to the community. The absence of the precious metals will, it is believed, be a temporary evil, but until they can again be rendered the general medium of exchange it devolves on the wisdom of Congress to provide a substitute which shall equally engage the confidence and accommodate the wants of the citizens throughout the Union. If the operation of the State banks can not produce this result, the

probable operation of a national bank will merit consideration; and if neither of these expedients be deemed effectual it may become necessary to ascertain the terms upon which the notes of the Government (no longer required as an instrument of credit) shall be issued upon motives of general policy as a common medium of circulation.

The political question was whether or not Congress would agree to a charter that provided for a large enough bank to fund governmental needs, that would also be able to manage the currency (now that it was untethered from specie), and that regulated the growing system of state banks. On January 30, 1815, President Madison vetoed Congress's first bill, on the ground that it did not invest the bank with a sufficiently clear public mandate to restore a stable currency. This first proposal seemed to Madison no more than a private bank, and an undercapitalized one at that. If there had to be a Bank of the United States, he wanted one large enough to manage the war debt, powerful enough to regulate the nation's credit, and public enough to expect it would do all this in the public interest. Despite the opposition of New England financial institutions, Congress in April 1816 agreed to a bill that Madison could sign.[10]

More than its predecessor, the Second Bank was forced from the beginning to behave as a regulatory agency and to make controversial policy choices. During the War of 1812, banks had extended credit widely, resulting in a general price rise, and banks in the South and West were forced to suspend convertibility into gold. The result was a gold drain toward places where gold was more valuable, namely, to Europe and to the New England banks that maintained convertibility throughout the war. Once these Treasury notes were withdrawn, banks would be forced to withdraw credit. So the first job of the Second Bank was to help Treasury to reign in the postwar inflation by restoring gold convertibility at prewar rates, essentially by retiring government debt. At the same time, it was expected to bail out southern and western banks or at least cushion the blow to them that would come from retiring the Treasury notes that were at the base of their credit (by not demanding specie for state notes and providing new loans). The first task contradicted the second and was bound to nullify it in fairly short order. The resulting deflation, which was fundamentally the result of Treasury policy of buying and retiring government notes, and the ensuing depression in 1819 did nothing for the bank's popularity. While it is clear to historians that it was Treasury and not the bank that was doing the dirty work of contracting the money supply—indeed, the bank actually tried to offset Treasury policy by extending credit to banks even while Treasury was buying up the debt—the bank was widely blamed for the resulting depression. And this blame was to haunt the Second Bank when it needed a new charter.

Bitter conflicts with state banks surfaced because the Second Bank established branches (eighteen by the end of 1817) that competed actively with state banks. (In the previous decades, state-chartered banks had proliferated, and the states themselves viewed those banks as important to local finance and growth.) One such conflict arose when Maryland imposed a tax on the Baltimore branch of the Second Bank. James McCulloch, the cashier of the branch, refused to pay, on the ground that the federally chartered institution was immune from state taxation. Maryland responded by arguing, first, that Congress had no authority to charter a bank and, second, that even a federally chartered institution was liable to state taxes. The controversy reached the Supreme Court, more than a generation after a similar Constitutional debate had been resolved in Washington's Cabinet, when the president agreed to support Hamilton's proposal for the First Bank. In *McCulloch v. Maryland* (1819), Chief Justice John Marshall was able to start his opinion with the observation that decades of experience with and acquiescence in the Bank(s) of the United States gave them a strong presumption of Constitutionality. Not only did Marshall then proceed to sustain the Second Bank against Constitutional objections, he set forth one of the most expansive theories for interpreting the Constitution ever penned by a U.S. Supreme Court justice.[11]

After noting Maryland's argument that Article I nowhere explicitly gave Congress the authority to establish a bank or charter a corporation, Chief Justice Marshall responded that such level of detailed authorization would be utterly inconsistent with the nature of a written Constitution. "Its nature, therefore, requires that only its great outlines be marked, its important objects designated, and the minor ingredients which compose those objects be deduced from the nature of the objects themselves." By giving Congress explicit authority to collect taxes, borrow money, issue currency, regulate commerce, and raise and maintain the armed forces, Article I implicitly but unmistakably also gave Congress authority to adopt measures appropriate to carry out those massive projects. This logic was confirmed by the Necessary and Proper Clause, which closes and sums up the powers granted in Article I, Section 8. Marshall interpreted that provision to give Congress broad "discretion, with respect to the means by which the powers it confers are to be carried into execution." Summing up his approach to the Constitution, Marshall said: "Let the end be legitimate, let it be within the scope of the [C]onstitution, and all means which are appropriate, which are plainly adapted to that end, which are not prohibited, but consistent with the letter and spirit of the [C]onstitution, are [C]onstitutional."[12]

The Marshall Court's broadly nationalist jurisprudence also opened up the federal courts as a forum for the bank to protect its interests. In *Osborn v. Bank of the United States* (1824), Chief Justice Marshall created out of the Second Bank's authorizing statute an implied grant of federal jurisdiction over any lawsuit in which the bank was a party. This construction was motivated by concerns that state judges would attack the bank in order to protect their local banks. *Osborn* was not only a dynamic construction of the statute, which just said that the Second Bank could "sue or be sued" in state or federal circuit courts, but also a preface to another breathtaking interpretation of the Constitution. Marshall construed Article III's "arising under" grant of jurisdiction to extend so far as to include cases where federal law is "an ingredient" of the cause of action. His extraordinary opinion amounted to a dramatic judicial extension of both the statute and the Constitution. Yet, as Justice Johnson's (legally cogent) dissent wearily observed, "I have very little doubt that the public mind will be easily reconciled to the decision of the Court here rendered . . . . The Bank of the United States, is now identified with the administration of the national government. . . . [S]erious and very weighty doubts have been entertained of its constitutionality, but they have been abandoned."[13]

The era of good feeling in the 1820s was a golden age for the Second Bank. Not only did the bank triumph over its state critics, its president Nicholas Biddle played an increasingly assertive role in national politics as well as finance. Under Biddle, the Second Bank began for the first time explicitly to embrace its central banking functions, actively regulating the currency in a countercyclical manner, influencing the conduct of state banks, and serving as a lender of last resort. Some historians have suggested that the Second Bank was created to do exactly this and that it did so fairly successfully until it was destroyed by President Andrew Jackson. Indeed, the Bank of the United States, widely reviled in high school history courses as "undemocratic," may have been our country's most successful system of money and finance until the twentieth century.[14]

THE DEMISE OF THE SECOND BANK, 1832–36

The debates between the Jeffersonians and Hamiltonians over the United States Bank were updated and broadened during the presidency of Andrew Jackson (1829–37). Both the sectional schism and the philosophical disagreement had deepened by the time Jackson assumed office. New England merchants as well as manufacturers felt the Second Bank was doing an excellent job assuring a ready supply of credit at affordable prices. But farmers and small businesses in the West and South complained that the price of credit was high in their regions, and that the profits of banking dominated by eastern banks. The balance of power had also shifted, as new western and southern states had joined the union since 1791 (or 1816) and greatly outnumbered the eastern states by 1829.

The ideological debate was fanned by occasionally aggressive behavior by the Second Bank, rewarding allies and disciplining small businesses and banks.[15]

Lulled into complacency during the era of good feeling, President Biddle openly asserted regulatory authority over state banks, an assertion that brought trouble for the Second Bank. In addition, Biddle's responses to complaints about the bank's abuse of power were needlessly provocative, given the anxiety the bank generated, thanks to the enormous public power vested in an institution controlled by private financial interests concentrated in the East. For example, Biddle protested to a congressional committee that his bank had not oppressed the state banks. "There are very few banks which might not have been destroyed by the exertion of the power of the Bank. None have ever been injured. Many have been saved." Senator Thomas Hart Benton of Missouri, a close ally of Andrew Jackson, retorted that such statements were "proof enough" of "a moneyed oligarchy established in this land. . . . The power to destroy all other banks is admitted and declared," a power that could be exercised anywhere at any time, a lurking threat to both prosperity and democracy. As a populist, President Jackson distrusted the Bank of the United States philosophically, and he personally despised Nicholas Biddle. The president resolved to destroy them both, which he did, at the price of financial chaos for much of the next generation.[16]

The democratic critique of the Second Bank produced a prolonged and wrenching constitutional struggle. Hoping to use the bank to defeat Jackson in the 1832 presidential election, leaders of the new Whig Party in Congress (Senators Henry Clay and Daniel Webster) secured passage of a bill to recharter the bank in 1832, four years before its charter expired. Jackson vetoed the legislation. His famous veto message seized upon *McCulloch*'s reasoning and turned it against the bank: "Under the decision of the Supreme Court, therefore, it is the exclusive province of Congress and of the President to decide whether the particular features of this Act are *necessary* and *proper* to enable the bank to perform conveniently and efficiently the public duties assigned to it as fiscal agent." Jackson's answer was no, and for that reason he concluded that it was his Constitutional duty to veto the legislation. The apoplectic Whigs did not have the votes to overturn the veto, and so the Second Bank's charter was set to expire in 1836.[17]

Next, President Jackson withdrew all federal funds from the bank. This was more legally complicated than the recharter veto, for the 1816 statute authorized the Secretary of the Treasury to remove federal funds, but only with a public explanation to Congress. Jackson went through two treasury secretaries before he was able to secure one (Roger Taney) who was willing to carry out his bidding. The Whigs in Congress howled at this imperious action of "King Andrew." Notwithstanding the controversy, Secretary Taney withdrew the funds, forcing the Bank of the United States to restrain its countercyclical operations at the peril of bankrupting itself. After the federal charter expired in 1836, Biddle tried to reinvent the bank under a state charter, but this foundered after a few years. Like the First, the Second Bank expired after a sharp political conflict over rechartering; and until 1913, there was no national bank at all.

THE INDEPENDENT TREASURY AND NATIONAL BANKING SYSTEMS, 1840–1913

With the demise, once and for all, of the Bank of the United States, this country engaged in a series of institutional experiments, played out along partisan lines in a highly polarized era. To the extent there was national leadership, it came from the Treasury Department, in which the Democratic Party vested responsibilities falling out of the bank wars and later the Republican Party turned to for financing the Civil War (1861–65). It was during the Civil War that the Treasury Department issued the paper notes that Susan Hepburn used to repay her debt, precipitating a series of Supreme Court opinions ultimately confirming the *McCulloch* idea that the Constitution would not stand in the way of the pragmatic needs of national financial policy.

POLITICS + STATUTORY RIGIDITY = PUBLIC FINANCE DISASTER, 1837–46

President Jackson's destruction of the United States Bank had many downsides. As it had done following the War of 1812, the Treasury Department assumed many of the central banking functions that had been performed by the Second Bank, first by creating a system of "pet" (state deposit) banks to hold federal deposits, and it intervened actively in monetary decisions through them and separately. These interventions were, arguably, quite disastrous. Filled with federal money, the pet banks issued thousands of dollars in state notes, which fueled a speculative bubble in public land sales and resales. To slow it down, the Treasury Department issued the "specie circular," which required payment in gold or silver for all public lands; Congress then enacted legislation distributing federal deposits to the states in proportion to their populations. Treasury's action pushed gold toward the West, and away from banks in the East, which created a liquidity crisis for the latter. At more or less the same time, British banks raised their discount rate, thereby increasing the flow of specie overseas. The results were financially calamitous. Eastern banks were forced to suspend specie payments and, under federal law, were no longer eligible to remain in the pet bank scheme. Federal statutory law also prevented Treasury from correcting these imbalances by moving funds east to solve the crisis.

Most economic historians believe that this sequence of events caused banks to call in their loans, which triggered debtor defaults by the cartload and thereby created a deeper liquidity crisis and dramatically burst the land bubble. By this account, the Panic of 1837 was the result, and after a mild rebound the economy fell into a severe depression that lasted from 1839 to 1843. The lesson usually drawn from this experience is that when monetary policy gets mixed up in politics, there is a risk of disaster. Another lesson is that institutional rigidity is just as fatal as politics when it comes to public finance; indeed, partisan politics is often intertwined with too much institutional rigidity. Whatever its intrinsic problems might have been, the pet bank system was sunk by rigid statutory requirements and unforeseen circumstances. The country needs experts to manage monetary policy, and a flexible statutory framework that gives them room to exercise judgment without undue political pressure. This was a lesson the Hamiltonians had understood but the Jacksonians forgot.[18]

Having retired after two exhausting terms, President Jackson missed the Panic of 1837. The consequences of his populist monetary policy were enjoyed by his handpicked successor, President Martin Van Buren (1837–41). The Democrats suffered large election losses in 1838; this was really the first time in American history that business conditions had caused such a large mid-term setback for the president's party, giving the Whigs a majority in Congress. Many of Jackson's antibank loyalists were defeated, and congressional Democrats were anxious to repair the damage. For their part, the Whigs smelled blood in the water and anticipated rising to power over the repercussions of the Democrats' catastrophic banking policies. President Van Buren's response was to create a structure of public finance that kept federal money under the control of the Treasury Department—but Whig control of Congress thwarted his efforts until 1840, when Congress at his behest created an independent subdepartment within Treasury to handle all of the federal government's financial transactions. The same year, however, Van Buren was defeated for reelection by General William Henry Harrison. Whig majorities in Congress forthwith repealed Van Buren's subtreasury law.[19]

Senator Henry Clay of Kentucky, the Whig leader in Congress, had planned to charter a Third United States Bank, along Hamiltonian lines. Clay and his colleagues were thwarted, however, by President John Tyler, a pseudo-Whig who inherited the presidency when President Harrison died after only a month in office (the new president was the tail end of "Tippecanoe and Tyler too," the first American political campaign slogan to earn great and enduring popularity). Tyler vetoed the Third Bank bill and made his own very intriguing proposal to separate monetary policy from politics. Tyler's bill would have established an independent Board of Exchequer, with exclusive authority to receive, hold, and distribute public monies. The president would appoint the five members of the board, with Senate approval, but could not remove them except for physical inability, incompetence, or neglect of duty. Unfortunately, this proposal never received serious consideration, because President Tyler was an isolated figure for most of his tenure, reviled by the Whigs for betraying their platform and shunned by the Democrats for leaving their party to run with Old Tippecanoe.[20]

When the Democrats regained power in the 1844 election, President James Knox Polk (1845–49) made it a priority to revive the Van Buren platform, and he won congressional adoption of the Independent Treasury Act of 1846. The statute established subtreasuries located in six different cities (later expanded), which would handle tax collections and federal disbursements without assistance from private financial institutions. This law established permanent governmental control over public funds, and so was a repudiation of the Bank of the United States, but entrusted those funds to financial experts. Politically, therefore, Jacksonian democracy triumphed, at least in part. But because the operation of the independent Treasury was too rigid (surpluses simply accumulated when the economy expanded, and payments had to be made in specie), the subtreasuries were able to play little role in monetary policy. Instead, a system of bank-created clearinghouse associations emerged, patterned after the innovative Suffolk Bank system of the 1820s that regulated northeastern banks. This development permitted some of the features of a national currency to be pieced together under the auspices of associations of banks. In effect, the clearinghouse system played the crucial role of currency regulation, even creating fiat money in times of crisis. Ironically, the function of controlling the currency was even further removed from the control of responsible elected officials than it had been under the Second Bank. (In this sense, the Jacksonians lost. Control of money and monetary policy shifted away from government and toward the eastern banks that President Jackson hated.) It seems fair to say that private banks had become far more independent and collectively more powerful in influencing monetary phenomena even if they could not always coordinate to exercise that power in ways that served their collective aims. While the period was one of booms and busts and sometimes unstable banking practices, it was also a period of the most dramatic economic expansion the country had ever seen. The clearinghouses and the Treasury Department generally managed to maintain a specie-based currency with only occasional breakdowns.[21]

The Independent Treasury Act created a huge new problem, however. It required Treasury officers to deal *only* in Treasury notes or specie. In effect, national financial transactions had to be done in gold coin, which created increasingly odd scenarios of subtreasury vaults bursting with bullion and guarded by sleepless officials, watching over their vaults with shotguns, pitchforks, and glass bottles to repel thieves. "To keep relations between the government and the economy 'pure' and wholesome, tons of gold had to be hauled to and fro in dray-loads, with horses and heavers doing by the hour what bookkeepers could do in a moment." This system worked inefficiently in peacetime—and not at all once the nation fell into Civil War.[22]

THE CIVIL WAR AND THE CREATION
OF A NATIONAL CURRENCY, 1861–73

Before the Civil War, "currency" in the United States consisted of coins issued by the federal government and paper notes issued by state banks. The former were subject to unpredictable bouts of hoarding, while the latter were subject to fraud and hard-to-predict solvency of the issuer. To ameliorate the second problem, an elaborate system of discounting the different currencies evolved. Tackling the second problem directly, President Lincoln's Treasury Department, under the leadership of Secretary Salmon Chase, proposed that state bank notes be displaced with federal ones. The National Banking Act of 1863 created national banks that could issue notes secured by federal reserves. When state notes continued to flourish, Congress adopted a series of statutes taxing new state bank notes. The effect of the latter laws was to induce state banks to give up their currency-generating role and become deposit-and-loan institutions. This was a major rearrangement of the federal system with regard to financial institutions and currency. Like so many other money controversies of the nineteenth century, this one reached the Supreme Court. Writing for the Court, Chief Justice Salmon Chase (the former treasury secretary) upheld this major revision in *Veazie Bank v. Fenno* (1869). Against the federalism objection, Chase blithely relied on the power of Congress to establish the terms of our nation's currency; once Congress (following Secretary Chase's leadership) took responsibility for a unified national currency, it followed that Congress could preempt competing state government, state bank, or foreign notes.[23]

At the same time the Lincoln administration was creating and empowering national banks, it was borrowing money hand over fist to finance the Civil War. At first, Treasury's demand notes were repayable in specie (gold), but by August 1861 Treasury Secretary Chase started issuing interest-bearing securities to pay for the escalating war. This placed enough strain on the financial system—yet the next year demanded even larger sums of money beyond what taxes were expected to yield. At the behest of Secretary Chase (over his own private reservations), Congress in 1862 authorized the Treasury Department to issue interest-bearing demand notes that were *not* redeemable in specie and that were to be "lawful money and a legal tender in payment of all debts, public and private, within the United States." These notes were called *greenbacks*. Thus, there were by 1865 two national fiat currencies—greenbacks and national bank notes, discussed above.[24]

Greenbacks amounted to the explicit creation of a federal paper currency considered legal tender for everything and not just for debts to the government, of a kind that many experts believed would have been unConstitutional in peacetime. The most cogent Constitutional objection to greenbacks was *not* that they were irredeemable in specie. The objection was that the 1862 law required creditors like Henry Griswold to take greenbacks from debtors without a premium; by 1864, when a state judge directed Susan Hepburn to pay Griswold what she owed him (plus interest), the market premium for gold had reached 185 percent. Could a creditor owed $100 have demanded $185 in greenbacks? The statute said no. Griswold cried Constitutional foul, and the Kentucky state courts agreed.

In a Constitutional surprise, the Supreme Court affirmed the lower courts and ruled for the creditor in *Hepburn v. Griswold* (1870), the First Legal Tender Case. Chief Justice Chase, who had publicly supported the 1862 statute but had become disenchanted with Republican financial policies, wrote for four of the eight participating justices that Congress had no Constitutional authority to require people to take paper money as legal tender for preexisting debts. Consider the Constitutional text and structure. The concern that coins would be debased by profligate state legislatures was entrenched in the Constitution's rule that no state may "coin Money; emit Bills of Credit; [or] make any Thing but gold and silver Coin a Tender in Payment of Debts" (Article I, Section 10, Clause 1). Complementing the No State Coinage Clause, the Constitution empowers Congress to "coin Money, regulate the Value thereof, and of foreign Coin" (Article I, Section 8, Clause 5). The Coinage Clause gives Congress the authority not only to establish a national currency but also to regulate its supply, value, and other features. Does the Coinage Clause authorize Congress to require Americans like Henry Griswold to treat paper money the same as gold coins? And can Congress impose this legal tender requirement upon contracts previously entered, as Susan Hepburn's agreement was?

The chief justice concluded that the original meaning of the Coinage Clauses did not authorize Congress to go that far. The Philadelphia Convention had originally debated a Coinage Clause that authorized Congress to "emit bills on the credit of the United States" (a power explicitly denied the states). With the horrors of debased paper currency still fresh in their minds, framer after framer rose to object that the federal government ought *not* have this power either. James Madison, the vigilant note taker, and Gouverneur Morris, perhaps the most financially sophisticated Philadelphia participant, opined that the federal government ought to have authority to issue interest-bearing notes under the Borrowing Clause but *not* the authority to impose such notes or any other instrument as a "legal tender," or mandatory currency. Nine states voted to strike the bills of credit authority. Chief Justice Chase reasoned that this background history of the Coinage Clause was dispositive of the Constitutional question. (In his classic study of the legal tender issue, Kenneth Dam believes that Chase was right, as a matter of original Constitutional meaning.) Although he was off the Court by the time the decision was announced, Justice Robert Grier expressed agreement with the chief justice on the Constitutional issue after reading the opinion before he left the Court; at the end of his opinion, therefore, Chase claimed five votes. Three justices dissented.[25]

The First Legal Tender Case was more of a sensation than *Veazie Bank* had been. The majority opinion was authored by Lincoln's disaffected Treasury Secretary, who was openly flirting with the Democratic Party to receive its nomination for president in 1872, and it was joined by the remaining Democrats on the Court. The three dissenters were Republicans appointed by President Lincoln (Samuel Miller, David Davis, and Noah Swayne), and they took the majority's approach as a rebuke to the Republicans' conduct and financing of the Civil War. *Hepburn v. Griswold* was the first time the Supreme Court had invalidated a federal statute based upon the expectations of the delegates at the Philadelphia Convention. Pragmatists assailed the opinion for a formalism that promised to obstruct the federal government's ability to deal with economic emergencies and fund expensive wars; even originalists have sometimes disrespected the opinion for relying on the secret deliberations at Philadelphia rather than the public deliberations of the state ratifying conventions. We add our own criticism here. Recall the facts of the case: Susan Hepburn and Henry Griswold entered into the contract in 1860; payment was due February 20, 1862; Congress passed the legal tender statute in March 1862, *after* payment was due. Did Congress intend the legal tender law to apply to contracts entered, and payment owed, before its enactment? Nothing in the statutory text or legislative history suggests that it did, and such a reading would certainly have undermined Griswold's reliance interests. As a matter of legal craft and constitutional wisdom, judges ought to choose a narrow statutory construction rather than a strained reading of the statute that presents serious Constitutional problems. Ironically, this (obvious) point was only raised by senile Justice Grier, whose views were noted, second hand, at the end of the plurality opinion.[26]

On the day the First Legal Tender Case was announced, President Ulysses Grant named two new justices to the Court—one to replace Justice Grier and one to fill a spot that had been previously created by Congress. Given the partisan voting patterns on this issue, the legal tender question immediately returned to the Court, and a new majority (the two new Grant justices plus the three *Hepburn* dissenters) overruled *Hepburn* in the Second Legal Tender Case, *Knox v. Lee* (1871). As if to underscore the essentially political nature of the volte-face, the opinion for the Court was delivered by Justice William Strong (Grant's first nominee), with an elaborate concurring opinion written by Justice Joseph Bradley (Grant's second). The new Court majority quoted or paraphrased line after line from *McCulloch v. Maryland*: Debtors and creditors alike had relied on the 1862 act, and the Court should be loathe to unsettle such reliance interests; "decent respect for a co-ordinate branch of the government" establishes a presumption that "there has been no transgression of power"; the Constitution "prescribes outlines," leaving the details to be filled in by reference to the great purposes of the document; and the Necessary and Proper Clause gives Congress wide berth in meeting the challenges facing the country. After pages of broad principles, the Court brushed aside the stingy text of the Constitution, the Philadelphia debates, and the recent *Hepburn* precedent, essentially, because they were inconsistent with the spirit of *McCulloch*.[27]

Neither the 1862 legal tender law nor the Legal Tender Cases resolved the currency issue for small "c" constitutional purposes, as the nation remained closely divided between greenbackers and goldbugs for a generation. Reflecting the views of eastern workers, southern and western farmers, and small businesses, the greenbackers understood money as a political instrument accountable to the democratic process. The greenbackers saw themselves as the populist heirs to Andrew Jackson, even though Jackson had in fact been a hard-money man at least in the political context of his opposition to the bank. Nonetheless, the greenback movement represented itself as neo-Jacksonian in its insistence that public finance and money supply be governed by democratic processes rather than by the decisions of eastern bankers. Reflecting the views of those eastern banks and their allied corporate concentrations, goldbugs understood money economically, as a mechanism in the complicated national economy, governed by the bloodless rules of the market; theirs was an extension of the old Hamiltonian position. The goldbugs supported the National Banking System (NBS) as well as strict convertibility of all currency into specie, while the greenbackers maintained that the NBS represented an unconstitutional delegation of public power to private interests, the bankers. Because they felt that the NBS concentrated in eastern bankers the privilege of making a profit from money, the greenbackers believed the NBS violated the Jeffersonian/Jacksonian precepts favoring equal citizenship and disfavoring "class legislation." Concentration of financial power in the eastern banks not only redistributed economic power away from the West and South but also undermined democracy in all regions. As business historian Gretchen Ritter put it, "[t]he greenbackers saw in the NBS a threat to the republic itself." To guarantee both economic flourishing and genuine democracy, the greenbackers argued for government-assured bonds and low interest rates for all areas of the country.[28]

The decades-long debate between the greenbackers and the goldbugs framed issues of public finance and currency in civic republican and constitutional terms. Because Americans remained intensely but evenly divided on these issues, the political process did not decisively address them. After the Civil War, the Republicans followed a monetary policy that vacillated between promises to stabilize money by guaranteeing it against specie reserves (which risked deflation) and the practical needs of the monetary system for greenbacks. So Congress basically kept deferring resumption of specie convertibility, effectively allowing the economic expansion to catch up with the money supply, and this finally permitted a gradual resumption in 1879. But while greenbacks could now be converted, they were not actually removed from circulation. As no one wanted to impose the pain of withdrawing the vast quantities of greenbacks, they simply remained a permanent part of the money supply but were now backed by specie.[29]

The legal tender issue returned to the Supreme Court in the wake of an 1878 statute that ended resumption, reversed the prior policy of withdrawing greenbacks, and (according to the Treasury Department's interpretation) permitted "the reissuance of greenbacks in notes of different denominations from those redeemed." In *Juilliard v. Greenman* (1884), the Third Legal Tender Case, the Supreme Court, with only one dissenter, held that Congress's authority to create greenback legal tender, without specie redemption rights, persevered in peacetime and was not limited to the "self-preservation" language in the Second Legal Tender Case. Citing *McCulloch*, Justice Horace Gray's opinion the Court said that the wisdom and need for a paper currency "is a political question to be determined by Congress when the question of exigency arises, and not a judicial question, to be afterwards passed upon by the courts." Picking up on some language in the Second Legal Tender Case, the Court further concluded that the power to issue paper money and regulate currency was an authority "inherent" in all governments and, therefore, would be read into the Constitution as well.[30]

Juilliard epitomizes the small "c" nature of the monetary constitution, and the gravitational force it can exert on the Large "C" Constitution. Justice Gray perceived that an important Lockean justification for the state is the regulation of the currency to assure conditions for economic flourishing—available credit at reasonable rates and little inflation. This is an important positive obligation of government, and not one that the judiciary ought to enforce through finding hard-wired rights and limitations in the Constitution. Presumably, the Court understood that the American political system had not come to rest upon the precise shape the monetary constitution would have, but the Court certainly had no better answers and was in no position to second-guess Congress. The larger lesson of *Juilliard* and the other Legal Tender Cases is that institutions and rules for the monetary constitution are ones particularly inapt for placement in the Large "C" Constitution—not only because they are positive obligations that judges are not competent to enforce but also because different economic and sociopolitical circumstances call for different structures.

THE INADEQUACY OF THE CIVIL WAR FRAMEWORK, 1893–1907

After *Juilliard*, the United States had a relatively coherent national monetary policy: legal tender would consist of coins issued by the federal government, greenbacks, and, increasingly, notes issued by national banks, with state notes on their way to extinction. Unfortunately, this was not a successful monetary policy. Because the United States remained on the gold standard (by formal statute in 1900, by policy before that), the value of the currency fluctuated with currency movements in other gold standard nations. Even though the Treasury Department continued to exercise some control over the money supply and therefore over the value of the currency, and private financial clearinghouses could cushion the effect of moderate shocks on the growing and dispersed banking system, the postwar system had no definite lender of last resort that could provide any real shelter from a strong blow of external events, including those triggered from abroad. Moreover, the system suffered from an inflexible level of circulating currency and from immobile reserves. Because the national bank note currency fluctuated in response to the bond market, and not always in response to the credit needs, business planning was subject to unpredictable disruptions and business decisions were influenced by inefficient considerations. Making matters worse was the fact that bank reserves were dispersed throughout the country and were largely immobile, for regulatory reasons. Consequently, there were mismatches between areas of the country needing credit and availability of funds.[31]

The regulatory framework of the National Banking System concentrated banking services and reserves in the eastern banks, which both raised the cost of capital in the South and West and contributed to periodic panics, where a New York bank failure would trigger a chain reaction of withdrawals from other banks, thereby drying up credit everywhere. There was one such serious panic each decade after the Civil War. The biggest such panic yielded the Depression of 1893, which greenbackers blamed on the concentration of money in eastern banks and goldbugs blamed on the inability of the NBS to generate countercyclical lending or infusions of money to offset temporary shortages. (Both critiques were probably correct.) The Depression of 1893 generated serious thinking about monetary reform by a social group that business historian James Livingston calls the new "corporate capitalists." While the goldbugs of the 1870s reflexively defended the NBS against greenback critiques, their analogues in the 1890s both vanquished the neogreenbackers (the free silver populists) in the 1896 election *and* came to the conclusion that the NBS was an inadequate system. The new corporate capitalists represented a fresh consciousness, and their internal discussions formed the basis for a social as well as intellectual movement that ultimately transformed America's monetary constitution.[32]

Between 1906 and 1908, the new corporate capitalists deliberated about what to do under the auspices of the New York Chamber of Commerce's currency committee, the American Banking Association's currency commission, and other private groups. Their leading theorist was Paul Warburg, a German immigrant whose experience in European public finance made him an invaluable partner at Kuhn, Loeb & Co. and an acute analyst of America's financial travails. In 1906, Warburg published "A Plan for a Modified Central Bank," which identified the dispersal of reserves and the immobilization of commercial paper as "evils" in our nation's public finance. To remedy these ills, Warburg proposed the creation of European-style commercial paper guaranteed by the federal government and a central bank that could hold the reserve funds of members banks, thereby improving liquidity and providing funds for banks in need. Warburg's paper "The Discount System in Europe" reported that European central banks helped stave off panics by concentrating cash reserves and then deploying them in areas of greatest capital need during a crisis. Warburg's ideas had a receptive audience among the new corporate capitalists, who were determined to remake this country's system of public finance in a manner that would sustain the powerful economic growth, without ruinous panics, that they intended to spearhead in the new century.[33]

THE FEDERAL RESERVE SYSTEM, 1913 ONWARD

By the turn of the twentieth century, the notion of federal government responsibility for currency and the availability of credit was entrenched in America's monetary constitution. No one seriously debated this issue anymore. That settlement did not tell our leaders precisely what the federal government's actual policy should be, but the nation's various experiments in public finance did suggest some policies to avoid. That public finance should *not* turn over significant public power entirely to private bankers was suggested by the successful Jacksonian attack on the Bank of the United States and the continuing greenback resentment against a system dominated by eastern bankers. That public finance should *not* be set by rigid, excessively specific legislation interfering with regulatory flexibility was suggested by the failure of the pet bank approach. That public finance should *not* leave banks and their customers vulnerable to cyclical variations in demand for money and episodic panics was suggested by the periodic crises under the National Banking System. Avoiding these problems, Congress created the Federal Reserve System, which was a national regulatory body designed to smooth over temporary variances and panics with monetary powers. Conceptually, the Federal Reserve System is touted for combining financial expertise and independence from politics. Although neither of these aspirations has been fully realized, the trial and error of earlier generations has contributed to an institutional mechanism that is superior to those developed and implemented by Treasury Secretaries Alexander Hamilton, Roger Taney, and Salmon Chase. And certainly the system we have now, a system that is being tested as we go to press, is vastly superior to anything that the Philadelphia Convention could have devised in 1787–89. This is one of the central normative themes of our study of the republic of statutes: it is a bad idea to hard-wire most small "c" constitutional mechanisms into a hard-to-change Large "C" Constitution, and it is a good idea to entrench those mechanisms in superstatutes that can be adapted to new circumstances by legislation or administrative construction. Nowhere is this theme more apt than in public finance.

Accordingly, the Federal Reserve System is a mechanism that had roots in what came before and is evolving decade by decade into a new regulatory institution. The pre-1913 system was a mix of public agencies like the Treasury Department; private regulated entities such as state-or federal-chartered banks; and mostly unregulated entities, especially the clearinghouses. The new system created a new private-public administrative entity (the Federal Reserve System, or FRS) and added new regulations to previously unregulated activities. That new system had the tremendous virtue of a learning curve, which allowed financial administrators to meet new challenges with immediate and potentially inventive regulatory responses. The flip side, of course, is that the administrators of the monetary system can also make mistakes, and some of the Federal Reserve System's mistakes have been doozies, contributing significantly to the recession of 1920–21, to the Great Depression of 1929 and the recession of 1937–38, to inflation between 1965 and 1975, and to the Great Financial Meltdown of 2008. That the system has survived its biggest blunders is testimony to its political entrenchment, which in turn owes much to widespread agreement that this is a structure that combines the expertise of economics with political responsiveness. These features guarantee that the FRS learns from its previous mistakes and that future mistakes will tend to be those where there is shared responsibility.

In 1907, there were in place serious economic criticisms of the nation's hodge-podge monetary network (the NBS, Treasury, international gold markets, and private clearinghouses), which threatened to hold back America's growth; Warburg's and other well-considered policy proposals for replacing the NBS with a central bank; and political support for a central bank proposal from the new corporate capitalists, economists, bankers from all areas of the country, and leaders in both political parties. The crisis of 1907 provided confirmation that the hodge-podge network was unworkable and an incentive to experiment with a new system. The economy had grown at a rapid clip between 1905 and 1907, too rapid a clip. When contraction occurred, it triggered a domino effect, starting in New York and spreading all over the country. As one bank after another ran out of money or hoarded its funds, businesses good and bad failed. Warburg and other theorists maintained that the crisis would have been contained if there had been a central bank. By their account, Europe experienced a much milder downturn because its central banks had slowed down the earlier boom and then supplied needed liquidity when private banks nervously stopped lending.[34]

After 1907, there was a consensus among the experts that a federally chartered institution was needed that would perform central banking functions—specifically, providing an "elastic" currency that could be used to ameliorate the drying up of credit during seasonal variations and during bank panics—and this required coordinating the activities of the diverse multitude of state and federal banks. Such an institution, if it was workable, would be able to respond more actively to international or domestic shocks, though today's economists would think that it had a poor basis for identifying the conditions that should trigger action or for deciding what action it should take. Still, if one thinks there is no little chance to learn without the capacity to act, it seems possible that bad beliefs would eventually start to correct themselves. And by this time it seems that most of the Constitutional issues had been resolved in a way that would make room for such a new and powerful creature (a remarkable development in itself). One issue that had not been formally resolved was whether Congress could create a public "executive" agency (the central bank) but deny the president effective control over its operations and its policy decisions (a key plank in Warburg's and related proposals). An arresting feature of the ensuing debates is that this issue never surfaced as an important concern, and the independent agency that emerged has never been seriously challenged on Constitutional grounds.[35]

The new corporate capitalists and their institutional outlets engaged in a public education campaign to effectuate their plans through a new statute. As a first step, Congress in 1908 adopted the Aldrich-Vreeland Act, which sought to make the money supply more elastic in periods of artificial currency short-falls. This was a band-aid at best for a flawed system, but the act also created the National Monetary Commission to make a comprehensive study of the nation's monetary system and to make recommendations for reform. Senator Nelson Aldrich, the powerful Rhode Island Republican and father-in-law of John D. Rockefeller, chaired the commission. Leading the commission on a European tour, Aldrich learned a great deal about comparative practice and, under the influence of Paul Warburg, was persuaded that America needed a European-style central bank, a national board of commercial bankers who would operate outside of politics, serving as fiscal agent for the federal government, a lender of last resort for private banks, and manager of the nation's currency. Aldrich unveiled his plan for a "national reserve association" in January 1911, and the National Monetary Commission endorsed it in 1912. The Aldrich plan would have created fifteen districts where branches of the national reserve association would be located; central authority would be with the national reserve board, whose membership would be determined by the member banks; only six of forty-five board members were federal officials or nominated by a federal official.[36]

Unfortunately for the Aldrich plan, stalwart Republicans had been routed in the 1910 election, and they lost the presidency to Governor Woodrow Wilson in 1912. The Democrats were skeptical of any plan, like Aldrich's, that vested responsibility for monetary policy with private bankers, the so-called "money trust" distrusted by progressives and latter-day populists (such as William Jennings Bryan, who was instrumental in Wilson's nomination and election and served as his first secretary of state). The Democrats and some Republicans insisted that the government play a bigger role in the central bank. Although the new corporate capitalists and Wilson's New Freedom seemed, superficially, to replicate the old debates between Hamilton and Jefferson, Biddle and Jackson, McKinley and Bryan, in fact there was much more common ground than in the polarized debates of the past. Both sides favored a central bank that would smooth over the financial roller coasters that prevailed under the National Banking System, and both sides relied on economists and serious policy analysts in crafting and refining their own positions. This shared purpose and reliance on economic expertise created room for compromise—but compromise that would probably tilt toward the bankers' preferences, because both sides also recognized that corporate capitalism was the new foundation for American economic growth. In short, public finance was moving toward a focus on the needs of J. P. Morgan and John D. Rockefeller (capitalists who were the objects of early Sherman Act prosecutions), rather than those of Henry Griswold and small businesses such as Manion & Company discussed in chapter 3.[37]

That Paul Warburg was an adviser to both Republican bankers and Virginia Representative Carter Glass, the primary sponsor of President Wilson's Federal Reserve bill, illustrates the amount of political consensus that surrounded the congressional debates in 1913. After a great deal of internecine congressional wrangling and partisan debate, Congress enacted the Federal Reserve Act of 1913. The new statute created a national currency, Federal Reserve notes, and a decentralized central bank system, the core elements of which were private banks organized into twelve Federal Reserve Districts, presided over by a Federal Reserve Board (or the "Fed"). The districts were dominated by private banks, but they were formally subject to the central policymaking body (the board) consisting of public officials who sat in Washington. The primary goal of the act was to prevent the seasonal credit shortages and periodic panics characteristic of the post–Civil War regime, but the drafters gave little guidance as to the means the system was supposed to follow to achieve this goal or as to other goals and how they should interact with the primary goal.[38]

The Federal Reserve Act created an agency that was, at the beginning, weak and confused. That its infancy coincided with World War I was particularly unfortunate, because Federal Reserve System policy was subordinated to the finance-the-war imperatives of Treasury Secretaries William McAdoo (1914–18) and Carter Glass (1918–20). Because the administrators were in a weak position politically and had no accurate theory for calibrating monetary policy more generally, they fell into a series of misadventures. For example, hyperinflation was tolerated in order to finance the war, and the system was sluggish in responding. When administrators did respond after the war had ended, their adherence to an old-fashioned gold standard motivated an overreaction—and the resulting deflationary moves drove the country into a recession in 1920–21. (Because few Americans understood the proper role of monetary policy and because the prime directive was the war effort, the Federal Reserve System was not widely blamed for this faux-pas.)[39]

The act's compromise structure also generated regular conflict between what the central government wanted (cheap loans and protection against bank failures) and what the regional banks wanted, especially the powerful New York banks (a stable gold-based currency that could meet international and local obligations). The regional banks retained a great deal of authority for policy initiatives, and that authority was aggressively pressed by Benjamin Strong, the governor of the New York Federal Reserve Bank (1914–28). Strong was an exemplar of administrative constitutionalism, for he had a vision of the proper operation of public finance and pursued this vision aggressively and relentlessly.

Unfortunately, Strong also exemplified the challenges to successful constitutionalism of this sort. To begin with, the structure of the system undermined coherent policy formation. Although his support from New York's banking community commanded followership from the other federal reserve regions, Strong constantly butted heads with Governor Adolf Miller of the Federal Reserve Board, and the first fourteen years of the agency's operation was a series of battles between Strong and Miller over the content and timing of public policy. More important, both Strong and his rivals operated under incorrect assumptions about public finance, at least until 1922. They assumed that finance would operate under gold standard rules, where money and interest rates would rise and fall with the movement of specie, and that the federal reserve discount rate was a "penalty rate that changed in response to market rates," rather than one that pushed the market in countercyclical directions. Following Governor Strong, the Federal Reserve Board increased the discount rate in 1920 in order to bolster the gold reserve ratio—but because that rate hike came at the beginning of a downturn in prices and production, the board's action pushed the downturn into a recession.[40]

A virtue of administrative constitutionalism is that, even under challenging circumstances, there is usually a learning curve. Governor Benjamin Strong was a rather apt student. After the disastrous consequences flowing from the discount rate increases in 1920, Strong and others concluded that financial interventions should not be driven by mechanical adherence to gold reserve targets and should develop new mechanisms for regulatory intervention. At Strong's behest, the regional governors created the Committee of Governors on the Centralized Execution of Purchases and Sales of Government Securities in 1922. The committee's "open market" operations (buying and selling short-term Treasury notes) represented a powerful new tool that could operate on a much larger scale than the discount rate and that could greatly enhance the capacity of the new system to smooth out disruptions. Predictably, the board resisted and then, in 1923, assumed nominal control of Strong's committee by reconstituting it as a board-regulated but Strong-operated Open Market Investment Committee. Economists at the time, and even now, dispute whether this tool was used in a way having this desirable effect—but under Strong's influence, open market operations were applied deftly during the 1920s, arguably preventing a major recession in 1923 and helping fuel a decade of low inflation and steady growth. Governor Strong died of tuberculosis in 1928, and the result was a system without an experienced leader. George Harrison, Strong's successor as governor of the New York Bank, was unable to command the respect (or fear) of the board in Washington, which sought to reassert its authority. It did so in the most disastrous way possible—just as Congress in the McFadden Act of 1927 was removing the sunset for the Federal Reserve System that had been part of the 1913 act and was recognizing (perhaps prematurely) that the Fed was an entrenched keystone of America's constitution of public finance.[41]

THE FEDERAL RESERVE SYSTEM, THE GOLD STANDARD, AND THE GREAT DEPRESSION, 1929–35

Starting with Irving Fisher's *The Stock Market Crash and After* (1930), continuing with Milton Friedman and Anna Schwartz's *Monetary History of the United States* (1963), and carried forward by more recent scholars such as current Federal Reserve Board Chairman Ben Bernanke, the conventional wisdom among monetary historians has been that Federal Reserve System blunders pushed the stock market crisis of 1929 into the Great Depression, and made our Depression much Greater than those of other countries with defter monetary policies. Some historians believe the blunders would have been avoided had Benjamin Strong continued to dominate Federal Reserve policy, but illness had taken Strong out of the policymaking loop in 1927. Led by Harrison and Miller, the board tightened money supply to reign in rampant Wall Street speculation that some financial experts considered unproductive. Such a tightening was unwise, as there was no discernible inflationary pressure, and money was *already* tight. The result of the Fed's policy was a sharp deflation and an economic downturn—a downturn that became a nosedive when the stock market crashed in October 1929. Remarkably, the Fed did not respond appropriately (with infusions of liquidity) to the downward spiral until Congress in early 1932 put pressure on it to expand the money supply, which the Fed did through open market purchases of securities. According to Friedman and Schwartz, the 1932 monetary expansion revived the economy somewhat—until Congress recessed and the Fed ended its purchase program. Between Franklin Roosevelt's election in November 1932 and his assumption of office in March 1933, the economy reached new lows, in part because of continued scarcity of credit. While there is much dispute on this, most monetary historians believe that the actions of the Fed, which tended to be contractionary even in the face of successive waves of bank failures, probably prolonged and deepened the Depression of 1929. The Wilsonian solution to the problem of panics may have contributed to the greatest depression in American history.[42]

The onset of the Depression, and especially its unprecedented length and depth, changed the political environment in important ways, both domestically and internationally. Most of our major trading partners were forced off the gold standard almost immediately. Unlike earlier suspensions of convertibility into gold, this time the shift seemed permanent. Guaranteed redemption of paper currency in gold (or silver) was too restrictive of the need for an expanded money supply for modern industrial countries, and they demonstrated that countries unencumbered by the gold standard suffered a less severe depression than those (like the United States) cleaving to it. The day he assumed office, President Franklin Roosevelt declared a bank holiday and secured from Congress the Emergency Banking Relief Act of 1933, which confirmed the president's authority to close all banks and authorized him to call in all gold and specie in private possession and convert it into paper currency. Presidential executive orders effectively nationalized the nation's gold stock at its current price (a bit more than twenty dollars) and immediately revalued the gold price at thirty-five dollars, achieving a massive windfall for the federal government. By its Joint Resolution of June 5, 1933, Congress nullified any and all contractual obligations giving the obligee a right to require payment in gold or specie or in currency measured against a gold standard. Susan Hepburn would have been pleased and Henry Griswold appalled, for Congress was relying on the Supreme Court's broad authorization in the Second Legal Tender Case.[43]

Much of the business community was alarmed by these measures, and many firms refused to go along with them. Several lawsuits reached the Supreme Court in 1935, before the switch in time that paved the way for massive judicial accommodation of the New Deal. Given the Legal Tender Cases, the Constitutional challenge did not focus on Congress's authority to control the money supply or to impose paper money as the standard currency. The challenge was, instead, that Congress could not exercise this authority to retroactively nullify private contracts and, essentially, confiscate private property. As Justice James McReynolds put it in *United States v. Bankers Trust Co.* (1935), the issue was whether the Joint Resolution and other statutes "were designed to attain a legitimate end" or, "under the guise of pursuing a monetary policy, Congress really has inaugurated a plan primarily designed to destroy private obligations." Speaking for four justices in dissent, McReynolds found the latter: "Valid contracts to repay money cannot be destroyed by exercising power under the coinage provision." The rule of law, McReynolds reasoned, requires the government to honor promises made to investors, and the Supreme Court must enforce this duty when Congress and President Roosevelt tried to sacrifice it. The alternative: "moral and legal chaos." This reasoning is reminiscent of Chief Justice Chase's thinking in *Hepburn v. Griswold*, the First Legal Tender Case.[44]

Chief Justice Charles Evans Hughes, the Republican presidential candidate whom Wilson had defeated in 1916, had spent his post-1916 career as a corporate attorney steeped in the precepts Justice McReynolds was emphasizing. Yet Hughes spoke for a Court majority in *Bankers Trust* and a companion case, and his judgment was that Congress's goal was "legitimate," reminiscent of the Second Legal Tender Case (also a 5–4 decision). In language that made the skin of his former corporate clients crawl, Hughes began with the proposition that private contractual obligations were always subject to public policy, so long as Congress was announcing a public policy within its Constitutional authority. The question was "whether the gold clauses do constitute an actual interference with the monetary policy of the Congress," in light of the circumstances faced by the country (citing *McCulloch* of course). Hughes quoted extensively from the House Banking Committee report, which had reliably found that the government could not even begin to turn back the depression without reinvigorating the money supply, and that required calling in the gold and removing the convertibility constraint from the money supply. The Chief Justice's analysis consciously recalled *McCulloch*'s notion that so long as Congress was pursuing a legitimate public-regarding goal, it had wide leeway in choosing the means for achieving the goal. Notice that this decisive rebuke to the Old Court came three years before the famous Court-packing controversy.[45]

Notice also that the big Constitutional showdown in the arena of monetary policy came in a case that raised fairness claims of the sort that Henry Griswold had pressed in the First Legal Tender Case—and not structural Constitutional claims, such as the power of Congress to abandon the gold standard or, for that matter, to create a law-executing agency outside the control of the president. Indeed, at the same time the Supreme Court was deliberating about the Constitutionality of the gold clause abrogation, Congress was considering legislation that would strengthen the structure of the Federal Reserve System. Even more than had been the case with the Federal Reserve Act of 1913, there was significant public interest in the Banking Act of 1935, in part because it made permanent the popular Federal Deposit Insurance Corporation, which had been created by the Banking (Glass-Steagall) Act of 1933, to insure people's deposits and stanch the flow of bank closures. The 1935 act reaffirmed, expanded, and improved the precepts of the 1913 act and cemented that regime as an entrenched framework in our national constitution of statutes.[46]

This was a major constitutional moment in the nation's history. The regime cemented by the 1935 act was very different from the monetary constitution in place after the 1913 act. The old regime was based on the gold standard, and financial liquidity was influenced by international markets and the price of gold. The new regime was based on fiat money (not gold) and therefore required active regulation because the gold market would no longer regulate monetary value. This was really a pretty important Large "C" Constitutional adjustment as well, if it is correct to say that the Coinage Clause had committed the nation to the gold standard. Of course, the new monetary constitution was not articulated in any detail in 1935. Subsequent policymakers debated how to regulate fiat money so as to optimize the economic opportunities of citizens. Monetarists like Milton Friedman, Ed Prescott, Bob Lucas, Tom Sargent, and John Taylor on the right have jousted with fiscal policy Keynesians like Paul Krugman and John Kenneth Galbraith on the left in public debates over the best policy in the new era. Noneconomists have weighed in with other socioeconomic goals (mainly, full employment) that the monetary constitution ought to be pursuing.

Aiming to avoid the uncoordinated policy drift that occurred in 1929–32, the Banking Act of 1935 centralized and expanded the authority of the Board of Governors in Washington. For example, the board was given the power to set and adjust reserve requirements against which member banks could make loans. The act directed the board to periodically approve discount rates, which affected the cost of money for the member banks. The Federal Open Market Committee was statutorily sanctioned, relocated in Washington, and reconstituted to include the seven governors of the board, who were joined by (but could outvote) the presidents of the New York and four other regional banks. Centralization of authority with the board also permitted much more governmental influence in monetary decisions than had been likely under the previous system. With power allegedly came increased freedom from political pressure. The 1935 act provided that the president, with Senate approval, should appoint board members for fourteen-year terms. The theoretical consolidation of authority in Washington was confirmed by President Roosevelt's appointment of Marriner Eccles as chairman of the Federal Reserve Board (1934–48). Unlike previous chairmen, Eccles dominated Fed policy. Ironically, because he was a proto-Keynesian and not a monetarist, Eccles's dominance did not result in an aggressive use of its new monetary powers by the board. In fact, Eccles's tenure was erratic. Monetarist historians believe that the Fed's restrictive response to inflation fears threw the nation into the severe recession of 1937–38. Eccles's chairmanship was marked by passivity on the part of the Federal Reserve System and dominance of Treasury Secretaries Henry Morgenthau (1934–45) and John Snyder (1945–53) on matters of interest rates. During and after World War II, the prime directive was maintaining low interest rates so that the enormous federal deficit could be serviced at a reasonable price. And after the war, political leaders were reluctant to allow the Fed to reverse the previous monetary expansion, for they did not want to suffer political consequences of a contraction in the economy.[47]

THE MODERN FEDERAL RESERVE SYSTEM, 1951—PRESENT

Tension between the Federal Reserve Board and the Treasury Department came to a head in late 1950, when Fed Chairman Thomas McCabe and New York Regional Bank Governor Allan Sproul objected to the assumption that the Federal Reserve Board continued to be bound by the "pegged rates" Treasury set as optimal for financing yet another international conflict, the Korean War. Treasury insisted that interest rates remain low and announced that the government (including the Fed) supported that policy, notwithstanding serious inflation concerns. Supported by the financial press, legislators such as Senator Paul Douglas of Illinois (a former professor of economics), and some experts within the Truman administration, McCabe and Sproul ultimately stood up to President Truman and Secretary Snyder—and the latter blinked. The two agencies agreed, in the Treasury–Federal Reserve Accord of March 4, 1951, to proceed along separate tracks, a public announcement that the Federal Reserve System "independence" promised in the 1935 act was, for the first time, being given effect. President Eisenhower's treasury secretary, George Humphrey, and deputy secretary, W. Randolph Burgess, were opposed to pegged rates, and they consolidated Fed independence in 1953.[48]

The post-1951 Federal Reserve System little resembled the original agency contemplated by President Wilson, Representative Glass, and early Fed Governor Warburg (1914–18), the immediate parents of the 1913 act. Not only was the board clearly in charge of the system and freed from domination by the Treasury Department, the regulatory mechanisms had been transformed. A system that was expected to be a mechanical fix for the liquidity crunches of the earlier era had become a complicated system that vested expert administrators with significant discretion affecting not only money supply and credit availability but also inflation, production, and the overall economy. The gold standard was gone as an assumption of monetary policy, and the discount rate was supplemented and overshadowed by open market operations as mechanisms for the Federal Reserve System to affect credit and money supply. Pro-cyclical policies were replaced by countercyclical ones.[49]

A central feature of the post-1951 Federal Reserve System is that it is dominated by economic analysis and is relatively nonpartisan (though it is dominated by economic conservatives drawn from both parties). Presidents have been under tremendous pressure to name as board members, and especially as the chairman of the board, only bankers and academics who have shown both deep knowledge and mature judgment about American banking. Almost half of the board members have been economists, and the staff is dominated by professional economists representing a variety of theoretical schools. Only men acceptable to the banking community have been appointed chairmen, and all of the chairmen since 1951 have been distinguished financial analysts: William McChesney Martin Jr. (1951–70), Arthur Burns (1970–78), Paul Volcker (1978–87), Alan Greenspan (1987–2006), and Ben Bernanke (appointed 2006).[50]

That is not to say that the Fed has been unaffected by politics. While the Federal Reserve System has been one that Congress has reaffirmed periodically, legislators have also sought to influence the board's administrative constitution-alism. For example, in the Employment Act of 1946, Congress attempted to articulate some of the Fed's duties, and effectively to add new ones. Congress was tackling some hard questions. Was the board to stabilize prices or to smooth interest rate fluctuations? Or was it to maintain high employment or to promote growth? These goals could easily be in conflict, and Congress was tempted to press the Fed to focus on full employment, arguably to the neglect of its monetary policy duties. (The original 1945 bill would have imposed full employment as a statutory right, but that language was withdrawn in the final statute.) To this day there remains disagreement as to the precise balance that the national government should be seeking and as to the steps that could help create an optimal balance. In any case, the majority behind the cautiously worded 1946 act was temporary. Despite the attempts of political leaders to bend the Fed to political purposes, there remained some breathing space for a central bank to operate independently. Although the Fed continued to accommodate governmental policies, William McChesney Martin Jr. brought a more restrained approach to the board in the 1950s. He was able to establish, for a decade or so, a policy of moderate monetary expansion and stable price levels.[51]

This process broke down in the mid-sixties. As we have seen before, a foreign war created hard-to-manage problems for public finance. The Great Society financed the Vietnam War through large budget deficits rather than higher taxes. The Federal Reserve Board obligingly pursued accommodative policies, permitting a vast expansion in public debt, with eventual inflationary consequences. Beginning in 1970, the Nixon administration and Federal Reserve Chairman Arthur Burns sought to restrain inflation, but haphazardly because of the necessity to finance expanding governmental operations. President Nixon imposed wage and price controls and other unsuccessful experiments. At first, the Fed manipulated reserve requirements and used open market operations to tighten credit—but in 1972 Chairman Burns cooperated with the Nixon administration to give the sluggish economy an election-year booster shot. None of these short-term gyrations did the economy much good, and their baleful effect was exacerbated by the first OPEC oil price increase in 1973–74. The result was a Keynesian surprise: stagflation, where the country suffered from both high unemployment and significant inflation. Just as monetary mismanagement under the Democrats contributed to Nixon's election in 1968, mismanagement under the Republicans contributed to Democratic electoral victories in 1974 and 1976.[52]

The Democrats had their own agenda for the Fed. The Humphrey-Hawkins Full Employment Act of 1978 required the president, the Federal Reserve Board, and other organs of government to cooperate in pursuit of four goals: full employment, low inflation, high production, and balanced budgets and trade.

Responding to the stagflation of the Nixon-Ford era, the sponsors intended to create a statutory commitment to full employment as well as low inflation. By the time Humphrey-Hawkins was enacted, however, inflation was increasing, and the Federal Reserve was in no position to try to implement its goal of full employment. In 1980–81, Fed Chairman Paul Volcker felt that he had a window of opportunity to clamp down on endemic inflation by sharply restricting money growth. This sharp contraction, and sky-high interest rates, contributed to the electoral defeat of President Carter in the 1980 election, but Fed policy also sent the inflation rate plummeting even as unemployment increased, peaking during the 1981–82 recession.[53]

The experts' retrospective verdict on Volcker's policies has been generally pretty favorable. The jury is still out on his successor as chair, Alan Greenspan. Like Volcker, Greenspan was an announced monetarist, unwilling to apply the Keynesian overlay of Humphrey-Hawkins. (Unlike orthodox monetarists, however, Greenspan was unwilling to commit to a policy of keeping money expansion on a steady path through thick and thin; instead, he seemed to have an inflation-target policy which strict monetarists like Friedman oppose.) Greenspan, moreover, handled his first big crisis, the stock market crash on Black Friday in 1987, with skill and confidence. The market not only recovered but remained strongly bullish, with only a few blips, for the next two decades. Not only did the economy boom, with low unemployment, inflation remained at modest levels. In contrast to the stagflation of the early 1970s, the Greenspan era was boom without inflation, and the Fed was a primary cheerleader, even when many economists were warning that the boom rested upon unrealistic speculation in internet industries (1990s) and real estate speculation as well as derivatives (the 2000s). In retrospect, it appears that Greenspan was less single-minded in pursuing monetary objectives than he had advertized. In effect, the Fed pursued a multi-objective policy that it usually criticizes when Congress tries to impose it, as in Humphrey-Hawkins. Even from a Keynesian, much less a Friedmanite, point of view, Greenspan's cheerleading an economy whose expansion was built on real estate and other bubbles is subject to harsh criticism. Indeed, the Fed could have raised interest rates and dampened the demand for home loans that fueled the real estate bubble and very probably could have prevented or forestalled many of the financial practices that led to the meltdown in September and October 2008. Put critically, the Federal Reserve Board under Greenspan was driving the economic train too fast, *and* the conductor was asleep at the wheel. More mildly, regulators may not have had the authority to stop all of the disastrous lending policies—but had interest rates been higher, many of those policies would not have been nearly as attractive to lending and financial institutions.[54]

When Greenspan retired, and his reputation was at its peak, there was bipartisan support for naming Federal Reserve Governor (formerly a professor at Stanford and Princeton Universities) Ben Bernanke to succeed him. When the real estate and other bubbles burst in 2008, the Fed under Bernanke teamed up with Treasury Secretary Henry Paulsen to devise a series of rescue operations for the sinking stock market and teetering financial institutions. History will assess Bernanke's record along several dimensions. Could he have changed monetary policy before the financial crisis in a way that might have slowly deflated the housing bubble? Or was it too late by 2006 to do that? The nature of bubbles is that they are built of self-reinforcing expectations, so a change in money policy might have destabilized interlocked expectations and simply produced an earlier crash. Even if an earlier crash might have been less destructive of the economy, could any political leader actually explain such a policy? This is one set of questions. Another line of inquiry would be whether Bernanke adopted or supported good policies after the bubble burst. The jury is still out on this question, in part because there is no consensus as to what should have been the policy response, but it is clear that Bernanke exercised his authority as Fed chair aggressively. Not only did the Fed lower the discount rate to zero percent by the end of 2008, its purchase of longer-term notes (the policy called quantitative easing) had the effect of injecting a huge amount of new liquidity after interest rates had bottomed out. Should the Fed have done more? And what will be the longer-term consequences of these policies? Did Bernanke have leverage over banks to ensure that they made loans rather than deleveraging their own portfolios? And, if he did, would he have been wise to use it or did he think that massive deleveraging of bank balance sheets was a necessary first step to recovery even if many consumers and businesses remained credit starved? We have no answers to these questions.

Clearly, though, Bernanke and Paulsen spearheaded an aggressive, inventive, and massively expensive administrative constitutionalism that not only deployed the Fed's traditional mechanisms (engaging in open market operations to drive interest rates down) more aggressively than ever before but also arranged federal loan guarantees to bail out some financial institutions (such as American International Group and Bank of America) but not others (poor Bear Stearns and Lehmann Brothers) and secured from Congress a $700 billion slush fund for ailing banks, businesses, and (as it turned out) automakers. Largely on the sidelines were a bewildered small-government president (George W. Bush) and a deeply suspicious Democrat-controlled Congress that went along with lavish bailouts because it had no better alternative. As we go to press in September 2009, it remains to be seen how well Bernanke and Paulsen did. They may have saved the country from another Great Depression. Or they may have squandered hundreds of billions of dollars in taxpayer money, much of it wasted on failing banks and auto companies, lavish corporate parties, and bonuses and golden parachutes to executives. Or they may have done both. Fed Chair Bernanke is reportedly seeking legislation that would expand the Fed's role in directly monitoring financial institutions, a role that the Fed has not performed well in the recent past.[55]

We do not have a comprehensive theory for what caused the Great Financial Meltdown of 2008, but it seems clear that administrative constitutionalism was both contributing cause and possible cure for it. Bubbles are well known to economists and policymakers (at least after the fact), and the law of bubbles is that they will burst, with catastrophic consequences. The last decade was a period of several classic bubbles: the Internet bubble (which popped in 2000–01), the real estate and derivatives bubble (popping in 2008). To be sure, some economists, like Chairman Greenspan himself, misunderstood or underestimated those bubbles, but other economists (only a minority, and they were thought of as being like Chicken Little by the majority) did see them rather clearly, and the regulatory agencies did not heed their warnings. Although Congress unwisely freed financial institutions from some of their regulatory limitations, much of what drove the bubbles was subject to regulation by the Securities and Exchange Commission, state banking regulators, or the Fed—none of which was doing their jobs very aggressively. As regards the Federal Reserve System, some lessons we draw from the meltdown are that (1) administrative constitutionalism can go really wrong when the administrators are lethargic and ignore their statutory mandates, and this may be the most common pathology of administrative constitutionalism; (2) the Fed's comparative advantage is its command of monetary policy, and it might be useful to provide the agency with more instruments to influence long-term interest rates, but it seems like a mistake to pile too many regulatory responsibilities on the agency; and (3) the Fed is not independent of politics (though it may be more independent than other regulatory institutions). This last point is no news to anyone who has studied the history of the Federal Reserve Board, whose close and constant contacts with the executive department render it vulnerable to political bullying and manipulation.[56]

On the other hand, even the blunders of the Greenspan era do not seem to imperil the entrenchment of the Federal Reserve System, though they probably will affect the nature of the Fed's authority and responsibilities. (An educated guess is that the Fed will gain new tools for use in a financial crisis.) The reasons are not too mysterious. The Fed retains the confidence and serves the interests of corporate banking and capitalism, now more concentrated than ever before. But also the Fed deserves a great deal of respect for its central mission, the application of countercyclical monetary measures during potential panics and crises. We the People have come to accept the quasi-independence of the Fed as needed to manage unruly and hard-to-predict financial markets and currency flows. Note, too, that the Fed's mistakes do become large public issues rather quickly, because they contribute to financial crises—and nothing (short of a big war) commands the attention of the President, Congress, and We the People more dramatically than a financial crisis.

THE ANTIHOMOSEXUAL CONSTITUTION AND ITS DIS-ENTRENCHMENT

The son of a Dominican mother (Maria Dolores Maldonado) and Nicaraguan father (Julio Sarria), José Sarria was the first of his family to be born in the United States. His birth certificate says he was born on December 12, 1923, but Sarria thinks his mother had it postdated by a year, to deflect attention from the fact that she was unmarried when he was born. In any event, the young Sarria was raised in northern California by his extended family, with special attention from his mother and godmother, Jesserina Millen. In most respects, Sarria was exemplary of America's "Greatest Generation": he was a clean-cut young man with a dazzling smile, was devoted to his family, achieved a good education, and proudly served his country in the army during World War II. In one respect, however, José Sarria was set apart from his age cohort: he was a barely concealed homosexual and cross-dresser.[1]

Dolores Maldonado was, apparently, unfazed by her son's sexual and gender orientation, but it was a matter of *constitutional* concern for the city government in San Francisco, the California state government, and even the federal government in Washington, D.C., in the mid-twentieth century. American society in that period viewed people like José Sarria with alarm, as sick and disgusting "degenerates" who were threats to children and to public order. Normatively, Americans viewed any kind of sexual or gender variation as *malignant*, namely, bad and dangerous. This norm gave rise to a regulatory regime that criminalized their characteristic conduct and excluded known homosexuals and cross-dressers from most of the normal trappings of citizenship. Police protection against violence and blackmail was not available to most Americans like José Sarria; instead, the police were sources of antigay violence and blackmail. In addition, the antihomosexual state sought to exclude people like Sarria from public service, professional careers requiring state licenses, voting, and jury service. The state harassed them, subjecting them to arrest for innocent activities, opening their letters, spying on their political activities, and even disrupting their efforts to socialize. In a process where San Francisco and California led the way, and other cities and states followed their initiatives, our constitution by 1961 had become one of *compulsory heterosexuality*: if you were not heterosexual, or would not pretend to be, you were an outlaw, an enemy of the state.

Like the constitution of racial apartheid before it, the constitution of compulsory heterosexuality illustrates the fact that small "c" constitutionalism can be and often is a brutal and unjustified state of affairs for many Americans. The gentle reader might marvel: thank God we have Large "C" Constitutionalism to correct processes like this one. As we have repeatedly shown in this book, however, judges interpreting the Large "C" Constitution will almost never directly challenge an entrenched small "c" constitutional consensus, and the Supreme Court's adherence to the constitution of compulsory heterosexuality was a parody of that point. Thus, the liberal Warren Court (1953–69) delivered one of the most homophobic decisions in the Court's history, not only rejecting a modest rights claim but aggressively interpreting a medical exclusion to include anyone the government thought was a "homosexual or sex pervert." The less liberal Burger Court (1969–86) in one of its last cases broadly ratified the antihomosexual constitution, where sexual and gender minorities whose love that dared not speak its name was a crime the law could consider worse than rape.

It is true that the very conservative Rehnquist Court (1986–2005) set forth some Constitutional limits on the state's ability to treat sexual minorities as outlaws—but that Large "C" Constitutional development followed the small "c" constitutional dis-entrenchment of the old norm. And the small "c" dis-entrenchment started at the level of private social mores before it affected positive law. Married women's property laws came only after larger numbers of women were beginning to accrue property, and increasing numbers of men viewed the rights of wives through their roles as fathers and not as husbands (chapter 5). Rules against pregnancy "discrimination" became possible in the civil rights era only because more women were entering the workplace and were proving to be productive workers who needed to be accommodated (chapter 1). The notion of old-age insurance started with family and employer anxieties about the new phenomenon whereby many workers lived beyond their years of employability and apart from family members who could care for them (chapter 4). Outrage by farmers, small businesses, and ordinary consumers at the abuses of "robber barons" and cartels was a social precondition for state and later federal antitrust laws (chapter 3). And who can imagine the vast array of environmental laws without Earth Day, April 22, 1970 (chapter 6)?

In the same way, the long process for dis-entrenchment of the norm of homosexuality as a malignant variation started with social interactions, then proceeded at the state and municipal levels, and finally appeared in Supreme Court decisions at the national level. California led the way, in part because it had flourishing lesbian and gay subcultures and in part because the excesses of the antihomosexual Kulturkampf drove thousands of gays out of their closets and into politics, as well as more private conversations with neighbors, friends, and relatives. When its legislature decriminalized consensual sodomy in 1975, California was endorsing a new norm of *tolerable sexual variation*: lesbian, gay, bisexual, and transgendered (LGBT) persons such as José Sarria pose no threat to public order and ought to be treated with tolerance and respect, but the state can still prefer heterosexuality as the norm. Civil marriage, brimming with moral significance as well as state-enforced benefits and duties, can be limited to different-sex couples, as California also did in a 1977 statute and in a 2000 initiative. Between 1975 and 2003, states in a fitful and uneven process converged upon the norm propounded by California, just as they had done in the matter of no-fault divorce (chapter 5). The Supreme Court's decision sweeping away the few enforceable consensual sodomy laws (ghettoized in the South, the old bastion of segregation) confirmed and deepened a normative realignment that had already occurred. Elaboration of the new norm, of tolerable sexual variation, is being played out mainly in the context of antidiscrimination laws, which originated at the municipal level, have been successfully developed at the state level (with California again the pioneer), and are now on the verge of adoption at the national level.

The current debate, in California and elsewhere, is in response to a norm first openly professed by José Sarria, who in 1961 ran for a seat on the San Francisco Board of Supervisors on this platform: "Gay is Good," and not just tolerable. In the language we are using, the new norm is that homosexuality is a *benign sexual variation*, and the state ought to treat LGBT people like Sarria the same as it treats straight people. The best-known battleground for this proposition is full state recognition of lesbian and gay families and marriages. As our book goes to press, the norm that marriage *must* be different-sex is entrenched in America's constitution of tolerable sexual variation. LGBT people and their supporters seek to dis-entrench this norm as well. We support this effort but do not believe that the Constitution, interpreted and enforced by federal judges, will deliver this norm to a population that supports the existing consensus. The primary audience for same-sex marriage discourse is municipal councils and mayors, state legislators and governors, and state judges—not the United States Supreme Court. This chapter closes with some thoughts about the modest role that Constitutional litigation can play in the same-sex marriage debate. The main role, and it is significant, of Constitutional litigation is to empower judges, if they choose, to *reverse the burden of inertia* as to a small "c" constitutional issue that is in political play. The burden-shifting power of the Court has its most powerful and productive effect when a new norm has already achieved general support, and the Court sweeps away the last vestiges of the old norm. Working from this benchmark, we shall lay out the probable trajectory of same-sex marriage in the United States.

THE REGIME OF COMPULSORY HETEROSEXUALITY (MALIGNANT SEXUAL VARIATION)

When José Sarria was born in San Francisco, the city's Board of Supervisors and the California legislature had already pioneered a constitutional regime for sexual and gender variation: homosexual sodomites and cross-dressers were outlaws, enemies of the state. Other states with urban populations of gender-benders and "fairies" (as effeminate gay men were then often called) were adopting the same regime at about the same time, and after 1923 the states focused more sharply and more pervasively on "homosexuals and other sex perverts" as objects for state concern, exposure, and discipline or expulsion from civil society. The period after World War II witnessed an antihomosexual terror that was vicious but not unprecedented in world history; it was a carbon copy of a similar regime developed by Nazi Germany between 1933 and 1945. Unlike the Nazis, however, antihomosexual Americans such as California governor Earl Warren (1943–53) operated in a constitutional system where the harshest rules were hard to enforce and generated some public opposition.[2]

CONSTRUCTING THE ANTIHOMOSEXUAL CONSTITUTION, 1860–1935

Following the statutory precedent set by almost all its sibling states, California's first legislature in 1850 outlawed "the infamous crime against nature." Neither the state sodomy law nor any other statute had anything to say about "homosexuality," however, for that concept did not enter our public culture for another generation. Neither the California sodomy law nor the law in any other American state covered oral sex; only anal penetration by a penis was regulated. Hence, sex between women was legal, as were most consensual activities between men. Before 1900, almost all persons convicted of the crime against nature were men accused of anal rape, sex with a minor, or public sex. In fact, few were prosecuted for sodomy in the nineteenth century, and crime against nature laws had no broader public law significance.[3]

In the early twentieth century, middle-class communities grew alarmed by the increasing public visibility of fairies and their subcultures in rapidly growing urban centers such as New York City, Boston, Chicago, St. Louis, Portland, Seattle, Los Angeles, and San Francisco (dubbed "Sodom by the Sea"). Some citizens objected to *sodomites* who violated natural law and biblical admonitions against nonprocreative sexuality; others expressed disgust with people that medical experts termed *inverts* or *degenerates* who had reverted to a more primitive evolutionary condition. Degenerates were considered threats to the fabric of society, corrupting the young. Racist medics linked "degenerate races" (people of color) with gender and sexual inversion. Sodomites, inverts, perverts, and degenerates were all considered predatory threats against children, the family, and the social fabric.[4]

Reflecting new social attitudes, law enforcement officials began to target inverts and degenerates and invested more resources to flush them out of their sexual closets. In 1914, for an important example, the Long Beach, California, police arrested thirty-one men for being part of a consensual oral sex ring. Because the crime against nature did not include oral sex, most of the defendants went free. Responding to public outrage, the California legislature added to the penal code's list of serious felonies "fellatio" (oral sex on a man) and "cunnilingus" (oral sex on a woman), later recharacterized as "oral copulation." Authorities in this same period created an array of other crimes to suppress same-sex intimacy and gender nonconformity. Thus, San Francisco made it a crime for anyone to appear in public "in a dress not belonging to his or her sex" in 1866, followed by Oakland in 1879 and Los Angeles in 1889. By 1930, most large California cities had laws criminalizing gender disguise or cross-gender attire. In 1903, the California legislature made it a crime to be an "idle, lewd, or dissolute person." Local authorities used this "lewd vagrancy" statute to harass and arrest cross-dressing women, female impersonators, and effeminate male inverts looking for partners. In 1921, the legislature made it a misdemeanor to engage in "any act . . . which openly outrages public decency," another vaguely worded law that was applied against gender and sexual nonconformists.[5]

Under these open-ended laws, almost any kind of activity deviating from standard sexual intercourse or gender presentation could be a crime in California. These crimes were enforced with increasing vigor after World War I, when Sarria was born. The pattern of arrests also took a turn, away from the focus on rape and abuse of minors, and toward greater enforcement against consenting adults of the same sex, "homosexuals." To enforce the emerging antihomosexual norms against consenting adults, police engaged in undercover stakeouts, posing as decoys in public restrooms and parks, and spying on people in their own homes. The consequences of being apprehended were potentially severe. In 1921, a man convicted of sodomy in California could go to jail for ten years, and a man or woman convicted of oral copulation could be imprisoned for fifteen years. Inspired by degeneracy theorists, the legislature in 1909 provided for the sterilization of any person convicted of two or more sexual offenses if he showed evidence that he was a "moral or sexual pervert." In the next twenty years, the state sterilized almost seven thousand "homosexuals" and "perverts"; the numbers went up after the legislature expanded the law to apply also to anyone committed to a state hospital and afflicted with "perversion."[6]

The constitution outlined by California's regulatory regime was one where "homosexuals and other sex perverts" were outlaws, excluded from the ordinary privileges of citizenship. Similar regimes were established in other states with large cities having noticeable communities of sexual and gender minorities: New York (New York City), Massachusetts (Boston), Illinois (Chicago), Ohio (Cleveland), Maryland (Baltimore), Oregon (Portland), and Washington (Seattle). Southern states and the District of Columbia generally did not have visible subcultures of this sort and did not adopt explicit regimes before World War II. Although it did not regulate sex crimes as the states did, the federal government targeted sexual and gender "perverts" as well, banning homosexual literature from entering the country from abroad or being carried by the U.S. mail service and excluding degenerates from military service and from immigration into this country from abroad.[7]

THE ANTIHOMOSEXUAL TERROR, 1935–69

By the time Earl Warren became governor of California in 1943, twenty-year-old José Sarria was serving his country as a barely closeted gay soldier, accepted by his colleagues and essentially left alone by the authorities. Indeed, Sarria may have owed his ability to serve in the military to his homosexuality. Rejected by the navy and marines because he was too short, but fired up by the attack on Pearl Harbor, Sarria allegedly seduced an army recruiter in return for sneaking him into that branch, where he served with distinction in the European theater. Little did Sarria realize that he and the country he was serving were on the verge of a major change after the war. Reflecting both a nostalgia for old-fashioned gender roles that had been suspended during the war and new fears of corrupting alien political, racial, and sexual influences, both state and national governments feverishly embraced the notion of compulsory heterosexuality, complete with marriage and 2.2 children, as the norm after the war. Gays were not just collateral damage of this renewed national priority, they were scapegoats sacrificed to reassure America that it was morally straight. State and federal governments adopted an unprecedented (outside Nazi Germany) array of antihomosexual regulatory measures, including harsh criminal and civil sanctions for consensual activities.[8]

The ostensible justification for these new regulatory measures was the public's panicked belief that sex criminals, who were epitomized by "homosexuals and other sex perverts," were molesting children at unheard-of levels. In 1939, the California legislature adopted a sexual psychopath law providing a process for civil commitment of defendants predisposed "to the commission of sexual offenses against children." In 1945, the legislature and Governor Warren removed the requirement that the sex crime be against children, freeing the state to send ordinary "inverts" convicted of consensual homosexual activities to mental hospitals for indefinite periods of time. Subsequently, the legislature made failure to register as a sex offender one of the grounds for initiating a psychopathic offender proceeding and provided that a sexual psychopath found not amenable to "treatment" could still be held indefinitely by the state. After 1954, sexual psychopaths were committed to Governor Warren's crowning achievement, Atascadero Hospital. There, inmates were subjected to inhumane "therapies" (lobotomies, electrical shocks, experimental drugs) to "cure" them of "perversion." Later, Atascadero pioneered a pharmacological version of waterboarding, where injection of a drug into the victim replicated the feeling of suffocation. The hospital was colloquially known as the "Dachau for Queers."[9]

Notwithstanding the public focus on protecting children, California's enforcement of criminal sanctions against activities between consenting adults also soared in the period after 1945. The San Francisco and Los Angeles police recorded unprecedented levels of consensual sodomy and solicitation arrests after the war, because they assigned hundreds of police officers to stake out homosexual cruising areas to observe illegal behavior or to present themselves for possible solicitation. One such area was the public restrooms at the St. Francis Hotel, the tony Nob Hill establishment. There, the police arrested José Sarria for homosexual solicitation of an undercover vice cop during his last year in college, where he had matriculated after he was honorably discharged from the army in 1945. Although he had to sell some property to pay the fine, Sarria was relatively fortunate (and not just because he did not qualify for the state sterilization program). For soliciting another adult male, he could have been charged with attempted sodomy or oral copulation; conviction of such a crime could not only have subjected him to commitment as a sexual psychopath, it would have consigned him to lifetime state surveillance. In 1947, Governor Warren and the California legislature required convicted sex offenders (including people convicted of consensual oral or anal sex) to register with the police in their home jurisdictions. In 1950, the legislature adopted statutes increasing the penalties for sodomy; creating a new crime for loitering around a public toilet; and requiring registration of toilet loiterers and "lewd vagrants" (the statutory charge usually leveled against men soliciting sex from other men). In 1952, the legislature and the governor eliminated the maximum sentence for consensual sodomy, thereby making it a potential life sentence.[10]

Engaging in either one-time homosexual liaisons or long-term homosexual relationships was not just a serious crime in California; such activity excluded the suspected homosexual from a variety of rights and benefits. People who engaged in "immoral conduct," including sodomy and oral copulation, stood to lose teaching positions and state civil service jobs. The California legislature in 1952 expanded the bases for revoking teaching certificates to include any conviction for "lewd vagrancy" and loitering at a public toilet, misdemeanor sex crimes enforced almost entirely against homosexuals; these were the crimes that Sarria committed at the St. Francis. "Gross immorality" was a statutory basis for disciplinary action against a host of other licensed professionals, including lawyers, doctors, dentists, pharmacists, and embalmers and funeral directors. Many homosexual persons lost or left their teaching and other professional jobs because of these policies. José Sarria was one of them; his aspiration to become a public school teacher ended with his arrest for solicitation; the arrest also impelled him to leave college.[11]

With his potential teaching career foreclosed by state law, Sarria had to explore other options. Within several years of his arrest, he was able to transform his job as a waiter at the Black Cat bar in the North Beach section of San Francisco, into a career as an entertainer and celebrity. With a pleasing tenor voice, Sarria began serenading the customers, then performed for them, and by the mid-fifties was putting on full-dress comic operas every Sunday. *Carmen* was his favorite. Would Sarria suffer the tragic fate of Bizet's heroine at the hands of the state's terrorist campaign against perverts? After Prohibition ended, the California legislature allowed alcohol sales at licensed establishments such as the Black Cat, with a statutory exclusion for bars and restaurants that regulators considered "disorderly" establishments. Warren-era California considered homosexual hangouts *per se* "disorderly" and invested significant resources in monitoring such establishments, typically by sending undercover investigators to report excessive affection, sexual expression, and cross-dressing in places with liquor licenses. Based upon reports of homosexual dancing, kissing, and hand-holding inside the premises as well as solicitation for sexual activities outside, the state authorities could close down a bar by taking away its liquor license, which is exactly what happened to the Black Cat in 1949, before Sarria's operatic career had unfolded. Fortunately for Sarria, Sol Stoumen, the owner, challenged the agency's revocation of his liquor license and won it back through the courts. In 1955, the legislature enacted a law allowing regulators to close down bars that had become a "resort for sex perverts," and regulators went after the Black Cat again and again, with Stoumen fighting them each time. The famous gay bar eventually gave up the last of its nine lives and closed in 1963. By then, José Sarria was the most famous homosexual in America.[12]

At the same time California was declaring war against homosexuals, the federal government was following a similar aggressive philosophy at the national level. Both the armed forces and the federal civil service promulgated new and tougher rules against military service or federal employment by "homosexuals and other sex perverts," rules that were enforced by periodic witch hunts and purges of suspected homosexuals. (Thus, it would have been much harder for an effeminate, cross-dressing gay man such as Sarria to serve his country in the army than it had been before and during World War II.) Although known for its anticommunist witch hunts, the McCarthy era actually identified and disciplined very few Communists, but it disrupted the careers of thousands of lesbian or gay civil service employees and loyal soldiers each year in the 1950s. More vicious versions of California's Earl Warren conducted their own state-supported vendettas against homosexuality. The most famous of the antihomosexual crusaders were FBI Director J. Edgar Hoover (himself a closeted cross-dresser) and former Florida governor Charlie Johns, whose legislative investigating commission hounded lesbian and gay persons from the state's high schools and colleges, purged the civil service, and published a hysterical purple booklet called "Homosexuality and Citizenship" (1965). Political leaders and police chiefs all over America made names for themselves by conducting costly campaigns to purge local culture of homosexual cruisers, bars, and literature: New York mayors Fiorello LaGuardia, Robert Wagner, and John Lindsay; Chicago mayor Richard Daley and his corrupt police chiefs; Atlanta police commissioner Herbert Walker; Dade County sheriff Tom Kelly; Dallas County (Texas) district attorney Henry Wade; and Harris County (Texas) district attorney Carol Vance are among the most famous.[13]

RESISTANCE TO THE CONSTITUTION OF COMPULSORY HETEROSEXUALITY, 1950–69

By 1961, the antihomosexual constitution was entrenched at every level of American government: municipal, state, and federal governments were committed to the constitutional norm that "homosexuals" such as José Sarria were criminals and outlaws. Like apartheid's constitution of white supremacy, the antihomosexual constitution was encoded in a variety of interconnected regulatory forms, including:

- state sodomy laws, which made gay people's characteristic conduct felonious, as well as a wide array of solicitation, vagrancy, and indecency laws that were widely but erratically deployed to harass and arrest homosexuals for solicitation and cross-dressing;

- federal, state, and municipal administrative policies excluding known or even suspected homosexuals from civil and military service, as well as any role in public education;
- federal immigration laws and administrative policies excluding homosexual "aliens" from entering the United States or becoming citizens;
- state licensing requirements excluding persons convicted of crimes of moral turpitude (sodomy, solicitation) from securing or retaining professional licenses;
- federal and state obscenity laws that administrators construed to criminalize virtually all homoerotic and transgendered materials and a great deal of homophile literature;
- state liquor licensing requirements and administrative regulations barring establishments from serving drinks to homosexuals or serving as homosexual gathering places;
- state laws and municipal ordinances barring movies or plays depicting "sexual perversion."

The antihomosexual constitution was most fully elaborated in states like California and New York and in the District of Columbia, but its precepts saturated American public culture.[14]

Not a single public figure openly dissented from or questioned this consensus until Dr. Alfred Kinsey published his landmark studies on male (1948) and female (1953) sexual practices. Himself a closeted bisexual, Dr. Kinsey demonstrated to a shocked America that homosexual behaviors (and indeed noncomforming sexual activities of all sorts) were a lot more common than anyone had guessed. The normative message of the Kinsey reports was that there was a tolerable range of sexual variation and that state efforts to suppress or punish noncomforming sexuality were both cruel and wasteful. Some thoughtful Americans were persuaded by Kinsey's facts and arguments.[15]

Dissent also grew directly from the terror. The antihomosexual constitution and its heavy-handed enforcement were costly expenditures of scarce state resources; pragmatic officials such as New York governor Thomas Dewey believed that the terror corrupted police departments and diverted attention away from malefactors who were actually harming other people. Unknown to Dewey and other officials, this regime also inspired increasing numbers of homosexuals to see their group as an unjustly persecuted minority. The "homophile" movement, originating in California around 1950, directly challenged the constitution of compulsory heterosexuality, maintaining that homosexuality was a "tolerable" variation from and posed no threat to the accepted norm, heterosexuality. Tiny and mysteriously named organizations such as the Mattachine Society (mostly gay men) and the Daughters of Bilitis (lesbians) implored the state to decriminalize homosexual intimacy and allow homosexuals to form organizations, socialize in gay bars, and publish gay-friendly tracts and literature.[16]

In the 1960s, as more lesbians and gay men lived openly in big cities such as San Francisco and Los Angeles, the original homophile organizations were joined by larger grass-roots associations, and their message of tolerance began to have wider currency. José Sarria was a key figure. His increasingly flamboyant costumes and opera performances had transformed the Black Cat into the most gay-affirming space in America; for homosexuals, it was the bar where everybody knew your real name and called you "girlfriend." At the end of Sarria's Sunday operas, he would lead everyone in a rendition of "God Save Us Nellie Queens" (to the tune of "God Save the Queen"). "I sang the song as a kind of anthem, to get them realizing that we had to work together, that we were responsible for our lives." The Black Cat became a place where queer was the norm, and straight had to defend his intrusion. Before almost anyone else, Sarria recognized the political as well as social necessity of safe spaces like the Black Cat; it was social shame that enabled oppressive laws to go essentially unchallenged. "We could change the laws if we weren't always hiding."[17]

In 1960, Sarria and his friends organized the League for Civil Education to conduct programs of public education to refute untruthful stereotypes about gay people, to educate gays about police practices, and to provide support for lesbians and gay men who were victims of discrimination and violence. In 1961, his candidacy for the Board of Supervisors garnered 5,613 votes. After the state closed down the Black Cat for good, Sarria and other activists in 1963 founded the Society for Individual Rights (SIR), which was the largest grass-roots homophile group of the era. SIR reflected a new model for gay activism, whereby "homosexuals" publicly and noisily protested police oppression and demanded dignified treatment by the government. Similar models were adopted in Washington, D.C., New York City, and Philadelphia in the 1960s. Activists in these cities had some success in discouraging police aggression.[18]

Although homophile theorists such as Sarria understood their group as a persecuted minority, very much like African and Latino Americans, they did not follow the lead of the NAACP's Legal Education and Defense Fund and seek Constitutional remedies against their state oppression. Instead, they supported legislative and administrative reform advanced by allies such as Dr. Kinsey. In 1955, the American Law Institute (ALI) followed Kinsey to exclude consensual sodomy from its Model Penal Code (MPC), because criminalizing such conduct served no public interest and engendered police corruption. The homophile press celebrated and publicized this important proposal, as well as

Illinois' decriminalization of consensual sodomy along MPC lines in 1961. Between 1964 and 1967, the California legislature's Penal Code Revision Project drafted new sex crime provisions. Following the ALI's reasoning, Project Director Arthur Sherry proposed to deregulate consensual sodomy and oral copulation. Police officers later told the legislature that these laws did not contribute to the public good. But legislators did nothing, fearing that sodomy reform would be understood as "promoting homosexuality." The legislature was also unwilling to reexamine the state's vague laws against public indecency, lewd vagrancy, and the immoral practices disqualification for teaching certificates.[19]

California homophile groups were able to protect the publication of their bland informational magazine, *One, Inc.*, against ridiculous Post Office censorship, but otherwise the Constitution was as antihomosexual as the public culture. In *Boutilier v. Immigration and Naturalization Service* (1967), the Supreme Court upheld the deportation of a bisexual Canadian based upon a McCarthy-era law's exclusion of aliens who were "afflicted with psychopathic personality" disorder. The only evidence against Clive Michael Boutilier was his admission that he had enjoyed sexual relations with men as well as women, and all of the medical evidence in the record concluded that this did *not* render the man clinically "psychopathic." At conference, even Chief Justice Warren, the sponsor of California's antihomosexual terror, conceded that "a homo immigrant might not be psychotic," but he joined the Court majority in concluding that admitted "homosexuality" was, standing alone, sufficient evidence of "psychopathic personality" to allow the agency to deport someone or exclude him from entering the country, even when all of the expert medical evidence was to the contrary. Not only did the Supreme Court reject all of Boutilier's Constitutional claims, the justices went out of their way to rewrite the statute to violate the Fifth Amendment's requirements that punitive laws must clearly identify prohibited conduct, that arbitrary classifications must not be used by the state, and that state action depriving persons of liberties must be based upon evidence meeting statutory criteria.[20]

THE REGIME OF TOLERATION AND NO PROMO HOMO
(TOLERABLE SEXUAL VARIATION)

America's antihomosexual constitution was normatively vulnerable, for it rested upon inaccurate beliefs about gay people, was wasteful and corrupting in practice, and scapegoated a minority group for social ills to which it did not contribute. In short, it was a bad regime—and really bad if you were an uncloseted homosexual cross-dresser like José Sarria. The process of dis-entrenching that constitutional regime is the project of this part of the chapter, which reveals the process to be a difficult and lengthy one. That is a feature of constitutionalism: like Rome, a constitutional regime cannot be built in a day—nor can it be unbuilt in a day (also like Rome). And it certainly cannot be unbuilt by making abstract Constitutional appeals to judges, although Large "C" Constitutional appeals can ultimately have bite if they are backed up by small "c" constitutional developments in the trenches.

Is it easier to dis-entrench small "c" constitutional norms than Large "C" norms? Usually it is. Norms involving gender and sexuality provide several examples. The small "c" constitution had substantially accepted women's equal citizenship by the time the Constitution was amended to give women the right to vote (1920), had endorsed equal treatment for women by the time the Supreme Court subjected sex discriminations to heightened scrutiny (1976), and had moved toward the norm of tolerable sexual variation well before the Supreme Court ruled that gay people could not be considered presumptive criminals (2003). The perseverance of de facto racial segregation is (we think) a counterexample, but for the most part Constitutional norms are not only formally harder to dis-entrench through Article V but also functionally harder to dis-entrench through Supreme Court decisions. But a Constitutional dis-entrenchment has a big advantage over a constitutional dis-entrenchment: it is usually more thoroughgoing. Most states allowed women to vote in 1920, a constitutional revolution, but after the Nineteenth Amendment was added to the Constitution *all* states gave the vote to women. (Again, race is the exception that proves the rule. The Fifteenth Amendment was nullified by the small "c" constitution and only grew teeth when federal statutory changes dis-entrenched the state evasions [chapter 2].)

GAY RIGHTS AND SODOMY REFORM, 1961–86

Like José Sarria's groups in San Francisco, other gay rights groups became more assertive in the 1960s. Thousands of lesbians, gay men, bisexuals, and transgendered people streamed out of their closets after the Stonewall riots of June 1969 in New York City. The myriad gay rights groups that rose and fell in this period were dedicated to dis-entrenching the small "c" anti-homosexual constitution. They realized that the first and most essential steps were challenging abusive police practices and decriminalizing consensual sodomy. Steady political pressure on police chiefs, district attorneys, and mayors in cities like San Francisco, New York, Los Angeles, Philadelphia, and Washington, D.C., made great headway toward the former goal.[21] Although one-quarter of the states decriminalized consensual sodomy between 1961 and 1975, those actions did not significantly advance the latter goal as a constitutional matter, because sodomy reform generally occurred without public debate.[22]

In most states, the association of consensual sodomy with homosexuality rendered sodomy reform radioactive, as it was in California during the 1960s. New York (1965), Pennsylvania (1972), and Michigan (1974)—liberal states with visible lesbian and gay populations—adopted the MPC but left consensual sodomy a crime. Indeed, when the citizens of Idaho learned that their legislators had decriminalized "homosexuality" upon adoption of the MPC in 1971, the public uproar was so fierce that the Idaho legislature repealed the MPC and reinstated the prior, obsolete criminal code in 1972. Kansas (1969), Texas (1973), and Montana (1973) took the next logical step: when legislatures in those states adopted a version of the MPC, they left criminal *only* "deviate sexual intercourse" (the MPC's creepy term for sodomy) between persons of the same sex. As the experience of these states illustrates, the increasing public presence of open LGBT people was just as likely to generate an antihomosexual backlash as to persuade folks to remove the social stigma created by consensual sodomy laws.[23]

The initial backlash was reversible, however, once a critical mass of openly gay people revealed this group to consist of responsible citizens who were no longer willing to accept their outlaw status. This process occurred in the large California cities between 1965 and 1975. With increased visibility and electoral cohesiveness on issues of concern to them, the LGBT community attracted mainstream allies. In the legislature, Assemblyman Willie Brown and Senator George Moscone (both representing San Francisco and responsive to its gay voters) pledged their support for state sodomy reform, which legislators from rural and suburban districts strongly opposed. The 1974 election saw liberal Democrats win the governorship and large majorities in the legislature. After a full-fledged public and legislative debate, Brown and Moscone in 1975 won enactment of a sex crime reform statute that decriminalized consensual sodomy (the first time that had happened in the United States). The debate was notable in three ways. First, the sponsors of the Brown-Moscone bill openly engaged opponents on the small "c" constitutional issue of the status of LGBT people in California. While opponents assailed sodomy reform on the ground that it would pollute public culture with shameless and predatory homosexuals, Brown and Moscone calmly defended it on the ground that gays were decent people who did not deserve to be made into criminals. Second, the public was aware of the debate and joined it; legislators were flooded with letters, groups of all sorts engaged in lobbying, and the matter was hotly debated in the newspapers.[24]

Third, and most important, there were plenty of opportunities for We the People to respond to the legislature's action. As in many other states, California allows the voters to veto statutes adopted by the legislature (referendum) and to initiate statutes or constitutional provisions of their own. After sodomy repeal, opponents sought a referendum—but were, significantly, unable to gather enough signatures. By their silence, the people had sent a message of tolerance. That message was confirmed in 1978, when the voters overwhelmingly rejected the Briggs Initiative, which would have barred public schoolteachers from engaging in private homosexual activities or even for supporting toleration of homosexuals generally. These events confirmed that California's own constitution had abandoned compulsory heterosexuality in favor of homo tolerance. Tolerance, by the way, did not mean full equality. In 1977, two years after sodomy reform, and after a few lesbian and gay couples asked the state to provide them with marriage licenses under the state's gender-neutral family code, the California legislature overwhelmingly reaffirmed the limitation of civil marriage to straight couples. A constitution of tolerance still allowed the state to favor heterosexuality, whose link with treasured marriage was reaffirmed.[25]

That California altered its constitution to provide tolerance rather than persecution for LGBT people did *not* mean the whole country was prepared to do so. After California, sodomy reform was impossible without accepting the notion that homosexuality was a tolerable variation from the norm—and very few states were willing to accept that idea. The Supreme Court certainly was not. In 1976, the justices summarily rejected gay people's efforts to expand the *Roe v. Wade* privacy right to strike down consensual sodomy laws. When the justices did consider the issue with the benefit of full briefing and oral argument, in *Bowers v. Hardwick* (1986), they held that there was no Constitutional right to engage in "homosexual sodomy," because it was condemned by "millennia of moral teaching" and by an Anglo-American legal tradition dating back to King Henry VIII, who considered the "crime against nature" even more reprehensible than rape. Writing for four dissenters, Justice Harry Blackmun (the author of *Roe v. Wade*) argued that consensual sodomy was protected by the privacy right; also dissenting, Justice John Paul Stevens argued that the state could not single out "homosexual sodomy" for unique criminal disapproval.[26]

Lawyers and academics assailed the Court's opinion in *Bowers v. Hardwick*, because it made elementary factual errors and went out of its way to express antihomosexual sentiments (arguably out of place for a statute that criminalized all sodomy by anyone). We have made these criticisms ourselves, but this book's theory of statutory constitutionalism suggests a gentler reading of the Supreme Court's decision. *Bowers* was a "negative" Large "C" Constitutional pronouncement: the Court was not saying that the Constitution requires states to criminalize homosexual sodomy; stripped of its crude rhetoric, *Bowers* should be read as a statement that the nation's small "c" constitution had *not* accepted the norm of tolerable sexual variation in 1986. Because twenty-four states still had such laws in 1986, it was premature to say there was a state statutory consensus that homosexual sodomy should not be a crime. In 1981, the District of Columbia repealed its consensual sodomy law as part of a sex crime reform statute. The House of Representatives, the most liberal branch of the federal government in 1981, voted 281–119 to override the District, on the ground that sodomy reform would "promote homosexuality" and thereby corrupt public culture. Representative Al Gore voted to denigrate homosexuality as corrupt. So did Representative Geraldine Ferraro. And Representatives Richard Gephardt and Richard Cheney, both parents of lesbian daughters. The list is a long one, filled with liberal Democrats voting with conservative Republicans. Can the Supreme Court be faulted for misreading the constitutional culture in light of this public event, which transpired across the street from the justices' chambers? The majority justices can certainly be criticized for their errors of fact and injudicious rhetoric; also, the Court could have struck down the Georgia law on narrow due process grounds, as one of us has argued.[27]

Although California had already signed on to a constitution of toleration for gay people in 1975, and New York joined it by action of its Court of Appeals, the nation as a whole had not gone nearly that far. Indeed, state sodomy reform had stalled after 1977, when celebrity Anita Bryant and other supporters of traditional family values had been able to overturn an antidiscrimination law in Dade County, Florida. Most Americans still found homosexuals disgusting because of their gender-deviant and purportedly avaricious behaviors and feared them as predatory threats to their own children. The politics of disgust and contagion that Anita Bryant mobilized claimed even more space in public culture after 1981, as Reagan Republicans assumed national office and news reports repeatedly associated homosexual conduct (the historic crime against nature, anal sex) with transmission of the virus causing AIDS. Once AIDS became associated with homosexual sodomy, opinion polls demonstrated that Reagan-era Americans grew even less willing to decriminalize such conduct.[28]

Could the Supreme Court, through a brave Constitutional decision, have transformed this homo-hostile constitutional climate in 1986? The braver the Supreme Court's opinion, the lower the odds that it would have transformed the constitution in a productive way. Public opinion was much more supportive of a woman's right to choose abortion in 1973 (the year of *Roe*) than of a homosexual's right to engage in intimate sexual activities in 1986 (*Bowers*). The Court's Constitutional protection of women's choice did not persuade pro-life Americans that abortion was acceptable; instead, it made them angrier and more frustrated, because the normal political process seemed closed off to their heartfelt moral views. Even some moderates were opposed to *Roe* for this reason. If an abortion-protective Court opinion stirred such controversy, as *Roe* did, is it not likely that a sodomy-protective opinion would have been at least as contentious? Because a great deal of the nation's homophobia was irrational but deeply felt for religious and even psychosexual reasons, people would have reacted emotionally to any Supreme Court opinion "protecting" homosexuals. The emotional power of homophobia that confronted the Court in 1986 may have been even more powerful than we are depicting it. Since the 1950s, most Americans incorrectly but devoutly considered homosexuals a Fifth Column or a Trojan Horse, undermining America's moral fiber from within, and therefore a worse threat to national security than Communism. This metaphor of contagion got a boost when the media and the government portrayed "promiscuous homosexuals" as Trojan horses who sneaked the HIV virus into the United States, and thereby wreaked havoc on the nation's public health. (The HIV virus itself operated like a Trojan horse, sneaking into the body as a harmless visitor and then taking over white blood cells.) For the Supreme Court to announce that the Constitution protected AIDS-spreading sexual conduct would have subjected the justices to the charge that they were the fools who brought the Trojan horse into the citadel and celebrated it. The majority justices were correct in perceiving that a broad Constitutional protection for homosexual sodomy carried peril for the Court's own legitimacy in a still antihomosexual democracy.

Large "C" Constitutional dynamics also suggest the perils of deciding *Bowers* with a strong pro-privacy opinion (again, the Georgia law could have fallen under a more narrowly focused Constitutional analysis). President Reagan was elected twice, by large margins, on a pro-life platform. By 1986, traditionalists were making headway against *Roe v. Wade,* which meant that an expansion of *Roe's* privacy right to include homosexual intercourse, at the height of AIDS hysteria, might have undermined the privacy right in a very concrete way. When the Senate Judiciary Committee grilled Judge Robert Bork (Reagan's nominee to replace moderate Justice Powell on the Supreme Court) on the privacy right in 1987, the focus was *Griswold v. Connecticut* (1965), the marital contraception case that Judge Bork unwisely lampooned. The American people were both unpersuaded and alarmed; their lopsidedly negative reaction doomed the Bork nomination and helped save *Roe v. Wade* from being overruled. (Justice Anthony Kennedy, who inherited the Powell seat, was the critical fifth vote saving *Roe* in 1992.) Isn't it likely that Judge Bork would have had a better case against the privacy right if the focus of his testimony had been a denunciation of a Supreme Court decision extending *Roe* to protect homosexual sodomy? (Because of his own concerns about homosexuality, Judge Bork would certainly have focused on a pro-gay *Bowers* opinion.) Would Senator Joseph Biden, the chair of the Judiciary Committee, and his Democratic and moderate Republican colleagues have been as bold in their defense of the privacy right if the most recent decision had been one protecting homosexual sodomy at the height of its connection with AIDS?[29]

Not only did the *Bowers* dissenters overstate the Constitutional case for seeking to impose a homo-tolerant constitution on the entire nation in 1986, the gay-bashing *Bowers* majority did more than its share to advance a gay-friendly constitution. When law students read Justice Byron White's brusque opinion for the Court—and they all did, for *Bowers* immediately became required reading at every law school in America—they were often outraged at the Court. Justice White and his elderly colleagues were substantially ignorant about the lives of gay people and harbored the traditional array of erroneous stereotypes about them, but younger Americans were more likely to know openly LGBT friends, relatives, and teachers and so tended to read *Bowers* from a gay-friendlier point of view. Many law students found the *Bowers* class discussion an occasion for them to "come out" to their classmates, and for the first time in history thousands of practicing attorneys (and former law clerks) came out as lesbian or gay. *Bowers* was the lawyers' Stonewall, a display of antihomosexual spleen that fueled public responses from gay law students and lawyers, and the growing number of gay-friendly allies. Many of those allies in the press brought unprecedented publicity to the facts that the litigants had presented to an unresponsive Court: LGBT Americans are normal and not defective from a medical or scientific point of view and are important leaders in a variety of fields as well as neighbors and relatives all across America; they are not carriers of disease, and in fact lesbians suffer much lower rates of sexually transmitted diseases and abuse than do straight men or women; LGBT people form meaningful relationships, and lesbians in particular were bearing and rearing children within committed homosexual unions. For millions of Americans, the focal image of the predatory and diseased child molester faded and was replaced with an image of lesbians raising children, gay couples keeping house, and homosexual neighbors, teachers, and civic leaders.[30]

By 1993, the coming-out-of-the-closet backlash against *Bowers*, the efflorescence of family-affirming stories about lesbian and gay families, and the abatement of the AIDS epidemic and its disassociation with gay sex all contributed to a modest sea change in Americans' attitudes about homosexuals and homosexual sodomy laws. Opinion polls in the 1990s revealed that Americans still disapproved of homosexual activities (albeit at much lower rates), but no longer thought they should be illegal. Large and growing majorities of Americans told pollsters that gay people should not be subject to job discrimination, even in such traditional bastions of homo exclusion as police forces, school teaching, and the armed forces. More Americans than before considered themselves liberals on matters of personal choice, but Americans who disapproved of sex outside a committed relationship now found the situation more complicated, with the lesbian baby boom, the gay marriage movement, and the many stories of dedicated AIDS caregivers. Many thoughtful traditionalists rejected, for pragmatic reasons, the notion that an increasingly visible part of the community must be considered presumptive criminals.[31]

In this new social climate, constitutional discourse about sodomy laws changed—and the changes were not limited to the salons of academia or the editorial room of the *New York Times*. An early signal of the new discourse came out of Lexington, Kentucky, in the Baptist heartland. In 1992, the Kentucky Supreme Court rejected and disrespected the Supreme Court's opinion in *Bowers* and ruled that Kentucky's misdemeanor sodomy law violated the state constitution's rights to privacy and equal protection. State Senator Ernesto Scorsone, the gay legislator-lawyer representing the defendants in *Commonwealth v. Wasson* (1992), had confronted the AIDS issue and other substantive issues head on and had presented extensive evidence to the trial judge. Following the evidence, which was not disputed by the state, the lower courts had ruled that gay people were decent citizens who ought not be singled out as presumptive criminals, and Kentucky's highest court agreed. The state's homosexual-only sodomy law was a violation of both privacy and equal protection guarantees in the state constitution. In the wake of the court's decision, traditionalists petitioned the Kentucky legislature to place a measure on the ballot to amend the state constitution to override *Wasson*. Senator Scorsone, of course, was central to that debate, as he was an active member of the Democratic Party caucus that controlled the Senate. Heeding his words of caution and respecting his argument that *Wasson* was a salutary development for all citizens, legislators agreed to leave the issue to the courts, and the state moved on to matters of more pressing public concern.[32]

Wasson was a harbinger, and the election of 1992 suggested that a gay-tolerant constitution was in the works. Republican Pat Buchanan's aggressively homophobic speech at the GOP National Convention in August appalled President George H. W. Bush, who said not a word about homosexuals during the campaign, and it modestly contributed to William Clinton's election as president on a gay-friendly platform. Although Congress rejected President Clinton's initiative to allow LGBT people to serve openly in the armed forces, the 1993 Don't Ask, Don't Tell statute was an effort at reaching a tolerant compromise whereby lesbian and gay persons could serve their country, as José Sarria had done during World War II, so long as they remained discreet about their sexual orientation (as Sarria had). Soon after Don't Ask, Don't Tell, in fact, the District of Columbia repealed its consensual sodomy law for a second time, and no one in Congress tried to override the District (and this was a Congress where vocally antihomosexual Senators Jesse Helms and Trent Lott held positions of power). In the next decade, one state after another decriminalized consensual sodomy either through legislation (as in Rhode Island and Arizona) or through court decisions accepted by the political process (as in Montana, Tennessee, Georgia, Arkansas, Minnesota, and Maryland). In every instance of sodomy repeal, opponents' predictions of rampant AIDS and other sexually transmitted diseases, child molestation, and other forms of homo aggression failed to appear—and the mounting evidence that sodomy laws contributed nothing to public health and a lot to blackmail and police corruption chipped away at traditionalist enthusiasm for such measures. The overwhelming medical consensus was that sodomy laws undermined anti-AIDS campaigns and actually contributed to the spread of HIV, the virus that causes AIDS.[33]

By the time the Constitutional issue returned to the U.S. Supreme Court in 2003, not only had public opinion changed but thirty-seven states and the District of Columbia had decriminalized consensual sodomy. As in chapter 3, this convergence of state norms across all parts of the country represented a shift in America's small "c" constitution. These new-repealing states had abandoned the antihomosexual constitution, rejecting the notion that "homosexuals" were presumptive outlaws. What is more, many of these jurisdictions had gone considerably further, concluding that sexual orientation was not a valid basis for allocating employment opportunities. California was a pioneer here as well, as the first state to prohibit private sexual orientation employment discrimination, explained below. Twelve other states and the District of Columbia had by 2003 also adopted statutes barring sexual orientation discrimination by private employers, and the Employment Non-Discrimination Act (barring private employment discrimination nationwide) came within one vote of passing the Senate in 1996. Twenty-two states and the District of Columbia had statutes or executive orders prohibiting sexual orientation discrimination in state employment; a presidential executive order barred sexual orientation discrimination in federal employment. Not a single antidiscrimination law or order had produced significant complaints from employers or even religious organizations, and most of the laws and orders had been greeted with approval by economists, humanitarians, and corporate executives.[34]

As we argued in chapter 5, one state can propound a constitutional change, which can become nationally entrenched if other states follow its lead after a process of public deliberation and elaboration. To be sure, sodomy reform, following California's 1975 statute, was not as universally followed as no-fault divorce, following California's 1969 statute. But in both cases a normative statutory change was understood to be revolutionary by its supporters, faced down public opposition, and worked so well that other jurisdictions followed. (Indeed, we think California's sodomy reform was a much more successful experiment than unilateral no-fault divorce was, because it did not have a downside effect on its intended beneficiaries.) By the time a Large "C" Constitutional challenge to consensual sodomy laws returned to the Supreme Court, in *Lawrence v. Texas* (2003), the small "c" constitutional landscape had been transformed, as evidenced by state statutes and judicial opinions, as well as opinion polls. The extent of its transformation was vividly illustrated by the briefs filed in *Lawrence*: Who really felt the country needed sodomy laws? Supporting the challengers to the Texas Homosexual Conduct Law were not just the usual liberal suspects (the ACLU, gay rights and feminist groups, the NAACP) but also a rainbow coalition of moderate and traditionalist perspectives. The conservative Cato Institute filed a powerful *amicus* brief urging the Court to overturn all consensual sodomy laws, as did the Republican Unity Coalition, former Wyoming senator (1979–97) and Senate Republican whip Alan Simpson, and the Log Cabin Republicans. There were no briefs supporting the law from the family-values-saturated Bush-Cheney administration or even from the Texas attorney general, a conservative Republican who declined the Court's request for a brief. Whereas twenty-nine churches and faith groups filed a brief supporting the challengers, no denomination filed in support of the Texas Homosexual Conduct Law—not the Roman Catholic Church, not the Southern Baptist Convention, not the Church of Jesus Christ of Latter-Day Saints.[35]

When the Court handed down its Constitutional landmark in *Lawrence v. Texas* on June 26, 2003, few tears were shed for the Texas Homosexual Conduct Law. The decision was a reaffirmation of the constitution of tolerance that religious moderates as well as gay activists and liberals had long advocated. Importantly, *Lawrence* made tolerance a Constitutional floor that swept up laggard southern states and imposed upon them the constitutional norm that California had pioneered. But if LGBT people were no longer outlaws, were they completely the same as straight people in the eyes of the law? Not quite. The law did not treat LGBT people exactly the same as straight people. The primary issue that has defined the parameters of the gay-tolerant constitution was same-sex marriage.

THE CONSTITUTION OF TOLERATION: NO GAY MARRIAGE, 1989–2003

Toleration of a practice or an idea is different from approval of it. If you are tolerant of my religious practices, you are not going to interfere with those practices, and implicitly you do not believe that they will harm innocent third parties. Also implicit in the concept of tolerance is that you do not find my religious practices completely acceptable for yourself and others, and you may think them not the best for me, but they are within the realm of acceptable ("tolerable") choices I can make. (Thus, you might not tolerate religious disagreement from your six-year-old daughter that you tolerate in your adult friends and co-workers.) In short, tolerance connotes disapproval as well as allowance or acquiescence. The disapproval can be mild or even empty, but it might also be severe. You find my religion disgusting, but for practical reasons you believe there is nothing to be done to stop me from practicing it. Some of my best friends are (fill in a religion you do not like), but I don't want my daughter to marry one.

By 1986, an increasing number of Americans were gay tolerant in this way. One of the many embarrassments of *Bowers* was that the Supreme Court reaffirmed and seemed to celebrate *intolerance* for homosexuality at a time when Western Europe, Canada, and other industrial nations were filling in the details of a gay-tolerant regime, which was the next logical step for most American states as well. In addition to laws barring antigay discrimination, violence, and hate speech, some European states seriously considered legislative petitions for recognition of lesbian and gay marriage. In 1987, Sweden recognized same-sex cohabitation by law. In 1989, Denmark created "registered partnerships" for lesbian and gay couples and vested them with almost all the same legal rights, benefits, and duties pertaining to married couples. Denmark's registered partnership law created a mild sensation among LGBT people in this country. Lesbian and gay couples who had assumed that the state would never recognize their relationships, and who were happy the state was not trying to put them in jail or take away their beloved children, suddenly realized that same-sex marriage was a possibility.[36]

It was, of course, a possibility America was not ready for. In the shadow of AIDS and *Bowers*, not even the California legislature was prepared to follow Denmark, and Governors George Deukmejian (1983–91) and Pete Wilson (1991–99) were firmly opposed to any relationship rights for "homosexuals." Weren't those people satisfied now that the state was no longer trying to put them in jail? LGBT people were themselves ambivalent about marriage equality, but one of the loopy things about Large "C" Constitutional law enforced by judges is that *anyone* can march into court and demand a decision on the merits. Once the larger community had assimilated the fact that gays were normal, functioning citizens and that many of them formed committed relationships and raised children, it was hardly illogical to wonder whether the Equal Protection Clause is not violated when the state provides hundreds of legal rights and duties to heterosexual married couples, but not a single one to similarly situated lesbian and gay couples.

So a handful of couples did present courts with Constitutional arguments for same-sex marriage. The two primary lawsuits were *Dean v. District of Columbia* (1995) and *Baehr v. Lewin* (Hawaii, 1993). The *Dean* lawsuit lost in the District's Court of Appeals by a 2–1 vote, with the deciding vote coming from an unmarried judge whom insiders believed was a closeted homosexual. On a court filled with heterosexuals, the marriage plaintiffs in *Baehr* prevailed on a 2–1–1 vote. Writing for a plurality, Justice Steven Levinson interpreted the Hawaii Constitution as subjecting the exclusion of same-sex couples to strict scrutiny: on remand, the state would have to show a compelling public interest in excluding Ninia Baehr and Genora Dancel from civil marriage. On remand, Judge Kevin Chang found all the state's arguments unsupported by factual evidence and in December 1996 ruled the discriminatory treatment unconstitutional.[37]

Baehr v. Lewin fueled the kind of Constitutional moment that gives Bruce Ackerman nightmares and delights Antonin Scalia. When We the People learned about the Hawaii decision, many were appalled and alarmed. Associating line-crossing homosexual sodomy with the cherished institution of marriage disgusted many Americans. Their disgust was exacerbated by the prospect of contagion—indeed, gay marriage activists themselves suggested that other states would have to recognize potential Hawaiian gay marriages (a misunderstanding of the Full Faith and Credit Clause). A reenergized Republican Party seized upon this as an issue it could use to cement its status as America's new majority coalition, except that the Democrats showed almost as much zeal in rebuking the Hawaii Supreme Court. Between 1995 and 2005, forty-three states adopted statutes or state constitutional amendments barring their judges from recognizing same-sex marriages in their jurisdictions; one of those states was California, whose citizens in 2000 voted by a big majority for the Knight Amendment, which prohibited out-of-state marriage recognition. States have a fair amount of discretion to refuse to recognize out-of-state marriages, but a bipartisan supermajority in Congress (85–14 in the Senate, 342–67 in the House) enacted the Defense of Marriage Act (DOMA) in 1996 to assure the states that they would not have to recognize such marriages. Moreover, DOMA mandated that more than eleven hundred federal statutory and regulatory provisions using the term "marriage" or "spouse" could never include same-sex couples married under state law. Heading off same-sex marriage and overriding the trial judge's injunction, gay-tolerant Hawaii in 1998 adopted a state constitutional amendment allowing the state to limit marriage to different-sex couples.[38]

The rejection of same-sex marriage was no stealth constitutionalism. Voters were aware of the issue and overwhelmingly agreed that the traditional constitutional understanding that marriage is between one man and one woman should be reaffirmed. Marriage had *always* been different-sex and logically did not apply to couples who could not bear children through their own intercourse. Also, there was a normative exhaustion with the liberalization of marriage through cohabitation and no-fault divorce. Fewer people were getting married, and the marriages didn't last. Would same-sex marriage be a liberalization that would exacerbate those trends? The evidence was thin, but few Americans were willing to give gay marriage the benefit of the doubt. And they had doubt about the benefit.

Justice Scalia seized upon this constitutional consensus in *Lawrence v. Texas.* Strenuously dissenting from the Court's Constitutional decision, he had little to say in defense of consensual sodomy laws, but a lot to say about same-sex marriage. Scalia felt that the majority opinion in *Lawrence* spelled the end of morals-based legislation—not just sodomy laws but also laws against fornication, adultery, bigamy, adult incest, bestiality, obscenity, and masturbation(!). All of these regulations abridge someone's *liberty* to seek sexual satisfaction. Why shouldn't their gratification be entitled to the same level of Constitutional protection as "homosexual sodomy"? Moreover, he argued, precedents like *Lawrence* Constitutionalize the entire "homosexual agenda," which entails invalidation of all state discriminations against homosexuals, including state and national bars to same-sex marriage. The majority said it was not addressing marriage, which entails very different considerations, but Scalia's point retains its analytical power. If the ancient crime against nature violates the Constitutional privacy right, why doesn't the equally ancient marriage discrimination against same-sex couples? Indeed, as Scalia pointed out, Canadian courts had, on the eve of *Lawrence*, followed that kind of Constitutional reasoning to invalidate provincial marriage exclusions.[39]

Although Justice Scalia's parade of homo horribles was unpersuasive to the Court majority in *Lawrence*, its audience was also Congress, which had before it a proposed Federal Marriage Amendment (FMA). The FMA would have prohibited courts from imposing same-sex marriage through interpretation of the U.S. Constitution or of a state constitution. In the wake of *Lawrence*, the Massachusetts Supreme Judicial Court ruled that the state could not bar same-sex marriage under the state constitution. Not too long after *Lawrence*, President George W. Bush endorsed the FMA, and the Republican Party made it a centerpiece of Bush's successful reelection campaign in 2004. Thirteen states amended their constitutions to bar same-sex marriage through voter initiatives in the 2004 election, and in the next several years no state followed Massachusetts in requiring *marriage* for same-sex couples. In 2006–07, the highest courts of New York, Washington, and Maryland completely rejected lesbian and gay couples' state constitutional marriage claims, and the New Jersey Supreme Court ruled that civil union but not marriage was required (itself a significant development). So the FMA never passed Congress, but the public debate confirmed the DOMA norm: America's homo-tolerant constitution does not recognize same-sex marriage.[40]

THE PROPOSED REGIME OF EQUAL CITIZENSHIP FOR LGBT AMERICANS (BENIGN SEXUAL VARIATION)

The post-*Lawrence* treatment of the marriage issue suggests a larger point about the Supreme Court's landmark decision overruling *Bowers v. Hardwick*. Although most Constitutional law professors (especially those who are not lesbian or gay) joined Justice Scalia in viewing *Lawrence* as a Constitutional revolution that swept away state regulations of private sexual activities and antigay discriminations, our analysis suggests that this view is premature. The constitutional regime now in place (both before and after *Lawrence*) is one of tolerance, but a "tolerant" regime still allows a lot of state regulation and preference for heterosexuality, as the marriage litigation reveals. Thus, in the wake of *Lawrence*, lower courts have ruled that the government can criminalize the sale of sex toys for private use, severely police same-sex fraternization in the armed forces, bar LGBT people from adopting children, and exclude lesbian and gay couples from civil marriage. While we agree with the Constitutional specialists that some of these lower court decisions are debatable (especially the Florida Adoption Case), we dissent from their belief that *Lawrence* requires different results in most or all of those cases. To the contrary, Constitutional landmarks like *Lawrence* and *Brown* are no more than starting points in a larger public law debate that occurs largely outside the courts. How accepting should the state be of homosexuality? Should lesbian and gay citizens, and couples, be treated exactly the same as straight couples? Can the tolerant state still discriminate?

On the other hand, we agree with Justice Scalia that there is a slippery slope "problem" (from his perspective) or "opportunity" (a lesbian or gay perspective) after *Lawrence*. A regime of tolerance is an unstable one if the distinguishing trait, like religion, sexual orientation, or ethnicity, proves to be an arbitrary basis for evaluating people's humanity and their ability to be engaged in civic projects, including marriage. The experience of LGBT Americans has in fact been precisely this kind of *equality practice*: even small rights advances encourage more gay persons to come out of their closets and engage their families, neighbors, and associates as openly gay; that engagement undermines stereotypes and counters continuing prejudice with other feelings (friendship, gratitude, and the like) and thereby makes it possible for another rights advance.[41]

The current constitutional discourse revolves around precisely how gay-accepting the constitution of homo tolerance is. Traditionalists by and large maintain that the tolerant constitution relieves homosexuals of their previous outlaw status but leaves many other exclusions in place. Gay rights supporters recall José Sarria's slogan, Gay is Good, and maintain that LGBT people should have rights of full and equal citizenship. There should be no discrimination between gay and straight in the law, including the law of marriage. These claims can and should be made in Large "C" Constitutional terms, but advocates ought to be aware that the U.S. Supreme Court is unlikely to accept such Constitutional claims until the small "c" constitution has (decisively) shifted toward a regime of full homo equality. Such a shift, we maintain, best occurs through a public statute-focused dialogue involving legislatures, administrators, judges, and We the People. A successful constitutional transformation along precisely these lines is occurring in California.

THE STATUTORY MODEL FOR HOMO EQUALITY:
CALIFORNIA, 1975–2008

Return to the norm pioneered by Alfred Kinsey and José Sarria: homosexuality is one of several benign sexual variations, and there is typically no rational basis for treating gay people differently from straights. Although we agree with Kinsey and Sarria on this point, most Americans do not (though this traditional stance is in the process of collapsing). For that reason, the law continues to discriminate against LGBT persons, and the homo-tolerant constitution permits some different treatment. Any constitutional change is going to be socially driven and legally incremental, along the lines suggested in the Introduction and in chapters 1–3 of this book. The impetus for change must, in that sense, come from the people themselves, typically through social movements persuading mainstream citizens that old-fashioned stereotypes and fears are no longer acceptable in civil society. The primary audience for the social movement is, therefore, citizens, voters, and legislators, not judges; the primary mechanism for pressing such constitutional change ought to be statutes, not court decisions. For a new norm to stick, the putative superstatute must be workable, must generate an enthusiastic constituency, and must operate at an acceptable cost. Consider how such an incremental step-by-step approach has led California all the way to the threshold of gay marriage.[42]

Gay marriage was, of course, inconceivable under the old regime where homosexuals were outlaws, and so a needed first step was repeal of the consensual sodomy law, accomplished after serious public debate by the California legislature in 1975. The repeal not only imposed no tangible costs on anyone, it was a symbolic move that liberated more gay people to come out of their closets and seek rights of equal treatment. The most necessary equality right was protection against job discrimination; most LGBT people feared retaliation from their employers more than from the police, and employment discrimination probably kept more gays in the closet than police harassment did. Following the "San Francisco Model," reflected in the work of José Sarria and Willie Brown, gay rights leaders focused not on the state or federal courts but on neighborhoods, social interactions, administrators, and municipal councils. In the wake of sodomy reform, activists initiated local conversations all over the state and procured ordinances barring private job discrimination based on sexual orientation from the city councils of Berkeley (1978), San Francisco (1978), Los Angeles (1979), Oakland (1984), Santa Monica (1984), West Hollywood (1984), Sacramento (1986), Long Beach (1987), and San Diego (1990). Each of these cities also prohibited discrimination in municipal employment, a policy adopted for state employees in 1979 by an executive order issued from Governor Jerry Brown. In *Gay Law Students v. Pacific Telephone & Telegraph* (*PT&T*) (1979), the California Supreme Court interpreted the Labor Code's antidiscrimination provision as prohibiting private job discrimination against LGBT employees, a result the legislature codified in a 1992 statute.[43]

As *PT&T* suggests, courts were highly relevant to the gay-is-good campaign for equal rights. Significantly, however, *PT&T* was an exercise in statutory, not just Constitutional, interpretation. In statutory interpretation cases, the court is applying a preexisting law, sometimes in the policy-aggressive ways that agencies routinely do; their application can be overridden by the legislature or, in states like California, by popular referendums. Indeed, the 1978 Briggs Initiative was a popular response to California Supreme Court opinions ruling that school boards could not discharge teachers simply for engaging in private homosexual activities and needed to show a nexus between the teacher's private life and his or her ability to perform teaching responsibilities. In a like manner, lower courts construed California's Unruh Act to bar discrimination against LGBT people by "public accommodations," another principle the legislature embraced and codified after experience with that principle.[44]

The gay-is-good norm received a tremendous boost from legislative, administrative, and judicial prohibition of sexual orientation as a permissible classification for employment or access to public accommodations. Although antihomosexual violence and discrimination still occurred in California, the public culture was by the 1980s set against it and provided gay people remedies. There was still not complete legal equality, of course, because lesbian and gay relationships were not treated the same as straight ones. Many LGBT persons aspired to committed relationships, and increasing numbers of them wanted to raise children within such unions. Given the legislature's 1977 rebuff to same-sex marriage, Matt Coles and other gay activists in San Francisco devised an alternate institution, "domestic partnership," that would provide both recognition and some benefits for same-sex couples. They originally propounded this idea at the municipal level, whose councils were more likely to recognize that homosexuality was a completely benign sexual variation. In 1985, the Berkeley City Council adopted the first operative municipal domestic partnership ordinance, which ultimately allowed city employees to obtain health benefits for their same-sex partners. Similar laws were adopted by municipal legislatures in West Hollywood (1985), Santa Cruz (1986), Los Angeles (1988), San Francisco (1989 [revoked by referendum], 1990), Sacramento (1992), San Diego (1994), Oakland (1996), and Long Beach (1997). At the same time city councils were creating a new partnership institution for lesbian and gay couples, state judges were creating a new parenting institution: "second-parent adoptions," whereby the female partner of a lesbian mother would become the second mother to her child, without the first mother's having to give up parental rights (as is typical in adoption cases).[45]

As before, critics who assailed legal rights for gays as antifamily or promoting an unhealthy lifestyle found their claims undermined when rights were extended to LGBT people. The lesbian or gay employee did her or his job diligently, the bisexual high school guidance counselor could be quite effective if she or he were not persecuted by the bureaucracy, the gay couple buying a house next door were good neighbors, and the lesbians raising children together as committed partners and joint parents became valued members of the PTA and sometimes role models for other households. These normal Americans were the typical beneficiaries of pro-gay legislation, and its most important effect was to provide everyday evidence that LGBT people shared most of the values— family, hard work, neighborliness, caregiving, charity—of their straight neighbors and, in many cases, were eager to learn from those neighbors and share their own comparative advantages. The Williams Institute at UCLA is steadily compiling statistical evidence of this process, but its ethnography remains to be written. So our account involves some guesswork and speculation.

How could this social process not have constitutional ripple effects? The normalization of homosexuality generated more pressure for equal treatment from the state—as before, primarily through legislation and *not* litigation. In 1999, the California legislature passed a modest statewide domestic partnership law. A feared voter backlash never materialized, presumably for the reasons suggested above; instead, in 2000 the voters ratified the Knight Initiative, providing that out-of-state same-sex "marriages" should not be recognized in the state. In 2003, the legislature extended the benefits of statewide domestic partnership to include almost all the legal benefits and most of the legal obligations accorded civil marriage. Thousands of lesbian and gay couples registered as partners, many of them because the new law automatically rendered both partners the joint parents of the children they were raising within the partnership. The closer domestic partnership got to marriage, the less opposition there seemed to be; there was no popular initiative to overturn the revolutionary 2003 statute, and Senator Pete Knight (the author of the 2000 initiative) took the position that domestic partnership, with almost all the same rights and duties of marriage, was fine. The proposed Marriage License Nondiscrimination Act of 2005, passed by the California legislature but vetoed by Governor Arnold Schwarzenegger, announced a constitutional obligation to treat lesbian and gay couples exactly the same as straight couples. That aspiration was not met by the domestic partnership law, which "den[ied] them the unique public recognition and affirmation that marriage confers on heterosexual couples."[46]

While the legislature and governator were sparring over how far the state should go, the California Supreme Court ruled in the *California Marriage Cases* (2008) that the state's regime of domestic partnerships for same-sex couples and marriage for different-sex couples violated the equality guarantee of the California Constitution. Chief Justice Ronald George's opinion for a closely divided Court not only rejected Attorney General Jerry Brown's argument that the domestic partnership provided roughly equal treatment for lesbian and gay couples, it relied on the legislature's steady progress right up to the threshold of same-sex marriage as evidence that there was no compelling state interest in denying the full dignitary rights that go with the name (marriage) and the same institution. In a less-remarked but even more important feature of his opinion, the chief justice ruled that sexual orientation classifications are inherently *suspect*, and thus subjected to the most skeptical judicial scrutiny, like race, ethnicity, religion, and sex. More than eighteen thousand lesbian and gay couples were married in California between June and November 2008, a process that was halted when the voters adopted Proposition 8, amending the California Constitution to recognize only unions of one man and one woman as "marriages" in that state.[47]

LARGE "C" CONSTITUTIONAL LAW AND GAY MARRIAGE

The account above demonstrates that California's constitution has evolved from an antihomosexual one (roughly 1921–75) to a gay-tolerant one (1975–2008) and now rests on the border of a constitution of full equality for lesbian, gay, and bisexual citizens. A handful of other jurisdictions—New Jersey, the District of Columbia and possibly Hawaii, Oregon, and Washington—have made a similar constitutional transition. We decline to say that California's public culture has embraced the notion of homosexuality as a benign variation, because the successful electoral campaign for Proposition 8 relied on the argument that schoolchildren would be taught that "gay marriage" was as good as what was considered "real marriage." A bare majority of voters accepted this tolerance script. As of June 2009, three states—Massachusetts (2003–04), Connecticut (2008), and Iowa (2009)—have recognized same-sex marriages through court decisions, and the political response in all three states has thus far been acquiescent. Three other states—Vermont (2009), Maine (2009), and New Hampshire (2009)—have recognized same-sex marriages by legislation. (The voters in Maine revoked marriage equality in November 2009.)[48]

The remainder of the country is at various points in stage 2, the gay-tolerant constitution, with several states gay tolerant only because they are not prepared to resist *Lawrence* (the way they resisted *Brown*) and because they believe that *Lawrence* requires as little of them as *Brown* did. Because we are persuaded that full equality for gay people is good for the country, we think that more states will move from stage 2 (gay-tolerant) to stage 3 (gay is okay or even good). But not all states will make this transition in the near future; the country operated under vastly different state regimes as regards different-race marriage for decades, and it is quite possible that the states will remain divided on issues of homo equality and gay marriage for some time to come.

Will the Large "C" Constitution and the U.S. Supreme Court require that the remainder of the country follow Massachusetts, Connecticut, and Iowa? Some legal academics, including one of us (with the enthusiastic concurrence of the other), have argued that, as a matter of Constitutional principle, the Equal Protection Clause requires same-sex marriage. The exclusion of same-sex couples is a sexual orientation discrimination that ought to be subjected to heightened scrutiny *and* denies lesbian and gay couples a fundamental right, independently justifying strict scrutiny. Although we think Justice Scalia overreads *Lawrence* to logically require same-sex marriage recognition, we think he is onto the same idea, although he finds it repugnant to the proper Constitution. And the foregoing Constitutional arguments were the exact grounds for the state constitutional rulings in the *California Marriage Cases*.[49]

Notwithstanding the possible cogency of these arguments, our theory of statutory constitutionalism firmly insists that the Large "C" Constitution has nothing to add at present and should stay out of the same-sex marriage debate for a while longer. On the one hand, the Court should avoid the mistake of *Roe v. Wade*, which was to announce a Constitutional right prematurely, before the small "c" constitution had come to rest on an important norm (choice). Indeed, announcing a Constitutional right to same-sex marriage today would be more aggressive and daring than *Roe* was in 1973. In 2010, there are five states recognizing same-sex marriages, while in 1973 there were a dozen or more states that had recognized a woman's right to choose abortion. Even judges who agree with us, that there is a good Constitutional argument for same-sex marriage, ought also to agree that the issue is premature. The Warren Court was right to avoid the issue of different-race marriage right after *Brown*, when thirty states barred such marriages. By the time the Warren Court reached the issue, in *Loving v. Virginia* (1967), half of those states had repealed their antimiscegenation laws in the wake of *Brown*. In our view, the Warren Court between 1954 and 1967 was underenforcing the Equal Protection Clause with regard to the issue of different-race marriage, and that such underenforcement was justified so that the small "c" constitution could prepare the way for full enforcement. We think the same is true for same-sex marriage: the Equal Protection Clause should remain underenforced, for now, as the issue continues to be deliberated at the state level.[50]

The same argument applies to the Constitutional strategy suggested by the Supreme Courts of Vermont (1999) and New Jersey (2006). Both courts ruled that it was a violation of equal protection norms for the state to provide hundreds of automatic rights and duties for different-sex couples through marriage laws, and nothing comparable to lesbian and gay couples, but they further ruled that it was up to their legislatures to determine a remedy. In both instances, legislatures adopted civil union statutes, providing all the legal rights and benefits those states provided to married couples. As we go to press in January 2010, five states have recognized same-sex marriages; three states (California, New Jersey, Oregon) and the District of Columbia have civil union or domestic partnership laws providing all or almost all the rights and duties of marriage to same-sex couples; three states (Hawaii, Maine, Washington) have more limited statewide domestic partnership laws. Although eleven states do *not* a constitutional revolution make, if this pattern continues, the Supreme Court ought at some future time to Constitutionalize the Vermont civil union or Massachusetts marriage experience: states cannot provide a wide array of legal benefits to different-sex couples and nothing to same-sex couples. The choice between the Vermont and Massachusetts approaches is that the former would leave the choice of constitutional remedy—marriage, civil union, or domestic partnership—to the legislature, while the latter would not. In the *Marriage Cases*, the California Supreme Court essentially synthesized the two: the court followed Massachusetts in requiring same-sex *marriage*, but the chief justice's opinion recognized that the voters could override their result in the next election, as indeed they did, with Proposition 8. (The California Supreme Court subsequently upheld Proposition 8 as a valid amendment to the state Constitution.)[51]

If the U.S. Supreme Court should avoid the *Roe* mistake of premature Constitutionalization of a right, it should also avoid the *Bowers* mistake of premature rejection of a Constitutional right. Although formally entrenched in America's statutory constitution (DOMA and the like), the norm of one man, one woman marriage is under siege, and with good reason: the state should be respecting and supporting committed lesbian and gay couples, including those raising children. Thus, the Court should be reluctant to say that the Equal Protection Clause has no relevance to gay marriage. As Alex Bickel argued in the race context, a Supreme Court opinion rejecting a Constitutional claim does legitimate the state policy being challenged, and so the Court was right *not* to reaffirm antimiscegenation laws after *Brown*, just as it was right not to overturn them immediately. As with different-race marriage, the Court should steer clear of the same-sex marriage debate until there is small "c" constitutional clarity.[52]

There are collateral legal issues that might reach the Court. One set of issues relates to interstate recognition. Article IV, Section 1, of the Constitution requires that "Full Faith and Credit shall be given in each State to the public Acts, Records, and judicial Proceedings of every other State." Section 1 gives Congress a specific role in giving "Effect" to this norm, and there is a full and credit statute essentially repeating the clause. Does the Full Faith and Credit Clause or statute require Alabama to recognize California gay marriages if a partnered couple moves there? No, the Supreme Court allows each state much latitude to follow its own statutory constitution and not those of its sibling states. As the divorce revolution taught us, however, the Court has repeatedly ruled that state court *judgments* must be given interstate recognition. Hence, a California judgment terminating a domestic partnership and apportioning community property, including property in Alabama, must be recognized by Alabama authorities, even if they disrespect the underlying homosexual relationship. This is settled Constitutional law, which we'd hope the U.S. Supreme Court would not unsettle by creating exceptions for civil union or domestic partnership divorce judgments that are genuine adversary proceedings.[53]

The most contentious issues in divorce proceedings are typically those involving child custody and visitation. The interstate features of those issues are now governed by a detailed federal statute, the Parental Kidnapping Prevention Act of 1980 (PKPA). Under the act, if a California court has jurisdiction over a partnered couple and its children and renders a judgment or even preliminary order adjudicating child custody and visitation, an Alabama court cannot reject that judgment even if one of the partners and the children move to that state. Has this PKPA rule been overridden by DOMA, which relieves the Alabama court of any duty to give effect to a "judicial proceeding of any other State . . . respecting a relationship between persons of the same sex that is treated as a marriage under the laws of such other State, . . . or a right or claim arising from such relationship"? Informed by the Constitutional full faith and credit rule for judgments, state courts have generally held that Congress did not intend DOMA to override the PKPA, at least as regards civil union divorces. To hold that DOMA overrides the PKPA, the Court would probably have to say that DOMA applies to civil unions, that an adjudicated child custody/visitation order is one "respecting . . . a right or claim arising from such relationship," and that Congress has the authority under the "prescribe Effect" sentence of the Full Faith and Credit Clause to override the Court's longstanding jurisprudence on interstate judgments. If the Supreme Court wants to continue its tiresome ideological warfare related to the evolving constitution of homosexuality, the justices can squabble over these issues.[54]

In our view, the better path for *all* the justices (gay friendly or not) would be *not* to read the ambiguous DOMA language broadly. Small "c" constitutional as well as Large "C" Constitutional norms provide strong justification for a nonexpansive reading. While only a handful of states have recognized same-sex marriages, unions, or partnerships, all the states except Florida, Mississippi, Utah, and Arkansas allow lesbian and gay adults to adopt and raise children; bizarrely, Florida allows lesbians and gay men to be foster parents but not adoptive parents. Seventeen states (ten by statute) formally recognize "second parent adoptions," where a child has two legal parents of the same sex; in thirteen other states, lower courts have gone on record as authorizing such adoptions. The emerging norm is that lesbians and gay men are capable parents, that the state should recognize their parenting relationships, and that recognition should extend to coparents who are in a committed relationship (like a marriage!). Should a conservative Supreme Court justice liberally interpret the DOMA language to cover civil union divorces, when such an aggressive reading would be inconsistent with the PKPA's text (and would require the justices to overcome their rule against implied repeals), with the PKPA's core purpose, with the Court's own longstanding judgments jurisprudence, and with the emerging state consensus that lesbian and gay parenting rules ought to be the same as those for straight parents? We actually think that the most conservative justices ought to agree with us, as indeed the Virginia Court of Appeals (not a hotbed of gay-friendly jurisprudence) has recently done.[55]

THE PRODUCTIVE JUDICIAL ROLE IN A REPUBLIC OF STATUTES

Under our theory of a constitution of statutes, is there a productive role for the judiciary to play? The Conclusion to this book explores the role of the U.S. Supreme Court and Large "C" Constitutional judicial review, but here we focus instead on the California Supreme Court, which played a mighty productive role in the evolution of that state's sexual constitution. First, the court blunted the hardest edges of the antihomosexual constitution regnant for most of the twentieth century. Here is a dramatic way of putting the matter. California's antihomosexual constitution (1935–61) resembled that developed by Nazi Germany (1933–45), from draconian laws to human experimentation. With regard to sexual variation, American progressives such as Earl Warren were responding to eugenics-loving and sex-negative impulses similar to those Chancellor Hitler and his associates responded to. But California's antihomosexual terror was much less effective in practice than Germany's was, and a key reason it was less effective was the rights that state and federal judges assured even despised homosexuals. Process rights recognized under either the California or the United States Constitution played a tangible role in taming the excesses of the gay bashers in government. When José Sarria was arrested at the St. Francis in the late 1940s, local prosecutors could have charged him with attempted oral copulation, a felony. Yet even the most vicious prosecutor would *not* have done so under the circumstances, because the Bill of Rights required the state to persuade a local jury, beyond a reasonable doubt, that Sarria was attempting this felony. The odds of success for that enterprise were low, and the cost of such a prosecution prohibitive. The California and U.S. Supreme Courts expanded those protections, such that such a prosecution in 1965 was even less likely, because the indigent Sarria would have been entitled to a free lawyer, *Miranda* warnings that anything he said would be used against him, and a jury not obviously stacked against him as a Latino. He also would have had a plausible entrapment defense and, under the state constitution, a privacy right to occupy a closed toilet stall. Homosexuals of that era became very knowledgeable about the Bill of Rights, which literally saved thousands of lives from ruination at the hands of the terror. Armed with due process, American homosexuals after World War II could evade Atascadero in ways that German homosexuals could not avoid Dachau.[56]

Second, the California Supreme Court protected the rights of all citizens to political engagement without harassment by the state. Once some sexual and gender minorities were emboldened to come out of the closet and organize politically, to resist and dis-entrench this constitution, other provisions of the Constitution were silent background norms that prevented the state from stopping them (another big difference between this country and Nazi Germany). Thus, even dedicated persecutors never considered denying gay and transgendered people the right to vote, which gave this minority some leverage in some big cities by the end of the 1960s. Some persecutors, such as the FBI's J. Edgar Hoover, wanted to squash homophile organizations such as the Daughters of Bilitis and the Mattachine Society, but the California Supreme Court firmly interpreted the First Amendment as protecting minority groups' freedom of association, their right to protest through marches and other public spectacles, and their freedom to publish minority-affirming and critical articles and books. By the time Sarria and his colleagues established SIR, these Constitutional rights were entrenched, and even the homophobic Warren Court had sometimes protected explicitly homophile publications from state censorship. For gay people, the big payoff came after Stonewall (1969), when thousands of LGBT people poured out of their closets and into the streets, formed hundreds of rights-claiming associations, and published up a storm. Much of this activity would have been a lot harder if strong and entrenched First Amendment protections had not been in place. In its landmark opinion in *PT&T*, still an amazingly prescient opinion, the California Supreme Court ruled that LGBT people's "coming out of the closet" constituted political activities that could not be the basis for employment discrimination.[57]

Third, the California Supreme Court has on various occasions provided gentle nudges toward a more gay-friendly statutory constitution in the state. It accomplished this through its common law power or through liberty-protecting statutory interpretations. For example, in *Stoumen v. Reilly* (1951), the California Supreme Court ruled that state law did not allow liquor regulators to close down the Black Cat bar simply because it was a place where "persons of known homosexual tendencies" congregated. The California Supreme Court, literally, saved the venue that not only became José Sarria's platform for stardom within the gay community but also served as a unique situs for homo community and pride that was the basis for increasingly assertive activism in the 1960s. In *Pryor v. Municipal Court* (1979), the court revisited the "lewd vagrancy" antisolicitation law that ensnared Sarria in the 1940s. Finding that the law was applied in a discriminatory manner against "male homosexuals," the majority interpreted the misdemeanor to be applicable only to solicitation of sexual conduct that would occur in a public place *and* to sexual touching the actor has good reason to believe would be offensive to the other person. After *Pryor*, the lewdness law could not be applied to offers to go home with another man for consensual activities. Coupled with the legislature's repeal of the consensual sodomy law, this theoretically removed homosexuals from the state criminal code and confirmed their status as "outlaws no more."[58]

Other California Supreme Court opinions deployed the court's common law or statutory interpretation authority to create windows of equality for lesbian and gay Californians. The court's 1979 opinion in *PT&T* created the first statewide rule against sexual orientation workplace discrimination in the United States, a truly daring statutory decision. In recent years, the court's equality-generating decisions have been in the arena of family law. In *Sharon S. v. Superior*

Court (2003), the court recognized adoptions, whereby the same-sex partner of a parent can become the "second parent" without the first parent's giving up her legal rights. The court reasoned that lesbian and gay families served the fundamental purpose of adoption law: the best interests of children. In *Elisa B. v. Superior Court* (2005), the court interpreted the Uniform Parentage Act to allow for two mothers. These were harbingers to the *California Marriage Cases* (2008).[59]

In the foregoing cases, the California Supreme Court was extending liberty protections to a social group that was unfairly despised and affording equality practice to that group once there was political space for toleration. Yet the court's rulings were not necessarily the final word on these matters of state policy. Like most other states, California has a process by which We the People can initiate an amendment to the state constitution, and traditionalists placed on the November 2008 ballot an initiative to override the court. Proposition 8 sought to add a new section 7.5 to Article I of the California Constitution: "Only marriage between a man and a woman is valid or recognized in California." The traditionalist campaign for Proposition 8 was itself a remarkable constitutional moment for California. To begin with, traditionalists not only conceded the desirability of the state domestic partnership law, giving almost all marital rights and benefits to same-sex couples, but their campaign relied on and celebrated the substantial equality afforded these couples by state law. Gone were the arguments made in the Briggs Initiative of 1978, that "homosexuals" are child molesters and other hysterical appeals to prejudice and erroneous stereotypes. The discourse of toleration replaced the discourse of homophobia among the *opponents* of gay rights and among many religious fundamentalists.[60]

A discourse of toleration is not a discourse of complete equality, however, and that was the focus of the 2008 electoral debate. Opponents of Proposition 8 argued that the time had come to grant full civil equality for lesbian and gay citizens, the promise of the *Marriage Cases.* Supporters of Proposition 8 responded that the state *should* be reserving "traditional marriage" for heterosexual unions, as they were in fact *better* than lesbian and gay unions from the perspective of parents. Several specific arguments for Proposition 8 were based upon misleading or erroneous characterizations of state law. For the best example, Yes-on-Eight television and Internet ads claimed that the *Marriage Cases* would force public schools to specifically teach that gay marriage was as good as straight marriage. Many opponents believed that was true, but neither the *Marriage Cases* nor state law required schools to say anything specific about lesbian and gay marriages, and California law gives parents a right to opt out of sex and family education programs in the public schools. At worst, the argument was a revival of the old trope that gay people are antifamily and their agenda is predatory, seeking the conversion of innocent children (your children!) to homosexuality. At best, though, the argument was a legalistic way of putting the central normative issues: Were lesbian and gay citizens entitled to full equality? Was California ready to go beyond the tolerance regime and endorse José Sarria's Gay is Good regime?[61]

Proposition 8 passed, 52–48 percent, in November 2008. Opponents immediately challenged it as a violation of Article XVIII of the California Constitution, which requires that fundamental "revisions" to the Constitution go through a more deliberative process, where two-thirds of each chamber of the legislature must support a measure before it is submitted to the voters for majority approval. The Proposition 8 litigation posed these questions: What is the Large "C" Constitution for? What is its relationship to the small "c" constitution? Proponents of Prop 8 updated Aristotle through the lens of democratic theory: the small "c" constitution, expressed through a popular vote, trumps the Large "C" Constitution. Opponents followed the standard account of Large "C" Constitutionalism outlined in chapter 1 of this book: a foundational document, applied by judges, ought to be hard to amend. Following from our analysis in chapter 1, the stance of the Proposition 8 opponents would empower judges too much by rendering Constitutional push backs too hard to achieve, while the stance of Proposition 8 proponents made Constitutional push backs too easy to accomplish and undermined deliberation. From our theoretical perspective, the chief problem in the Proposition 8 litigation was that Article XVIII makes Constitutional amendments too easy and revisions too hard. A better structure would be that in the Massachusetts, Vermont, and Iowa Constitutions, all of which allow simple majorities of two successive legislative sessions to place a Constitutional amendment on the ballot for majority approval. Such a structure would give majorities opportunity to respond to judicial decisions, but only after public deliberation and feedback.

In the end, the California Supreme Court had little difficulty coming up with a Solomonic compromise: the justices ruled in *Strauss v. Horton* (2009) that Proposition 8 was a valid Constitutional amendment but did not apply retroactively to invalidate the eighteen thousand lesbian and gay marriages that were performed between June and November 2008. This was a good second-best resolution. The court had *reversed the burden of inertia*, but the traditional understanding of marriage had reasserted itself, and the justices acquiesced in that constitutional decision. But they also helped create *conditions for falsification of stereotypes* by guaranteeing the legality of thousands of marriages that could serve as an educational opportunity for future voters. What the voters put into the California Constitution through Proposition 8 can be removed from the Constitution in a subsequent initiative. As we understand it, some traditionalists are now proposing supermajority rules to remove something from the

California Constitution—and if that occurs one might expect the California Supreme Court to enforce the deliberative requirements of Article XVIII more forcefully.

Like the previous chapter on the monetary constitution, this chapter on the constitution of homosexuality is an account of constitutional change, where previously settled institutions and practices were overturned because they no longer met the fundamental needs of the democratic polity. Although the problems addressed and the mechanisms of dis-entrenchment in these chapters are very different, we also find some commonalities. It is very important for a polity to get the small "c" constitutional arrangements right, and this is a job courts cannot perform. The heavy lifting is done by private norm entrepreneurs, administrators, and legislators, not by judges. In addition, a constitutional regime that worked for the country in the 1860s (such as the national bank system regime and that of criminal sodomy laws) will probably not work for the country in the 1960s.

Dis-entrenchment of the old regime to make way for a new one is an important public project that has got to involve popular opinion, experienced administrators, wise legislators; it can be abetted by inertia-reversing judges. These two chapters suggest two different models for official dis-entrenchment. Dis-entrenchment of the national antihomosexual constitution, the story of this chapter, was accomplished through state statutory and constitutional convergence around the new norm of a gay-tolerant constitution. Dis-entrenchment of the national banking system, one story in chapter 7, was accomplished through congressional convergence around a new institution, the Federal Reserve System. The next chapter presents a third model, where the federal executive branch spearheaded proposed constitutional realignments, some successful and others not.

THE NATIONAL SECURITY
CONSTITUTION

By some accounts, Abdul Razzaq Hekmati was an Afghan hero. Cooperating with American advisers and Afghan nationalists, Hekmati fought the Russians who occupied Afghanistan in the 1980s and, after the Russian withdrawal, resisted the terrorist Taliban government. In 1999, he orchestrated a daring operation that liberated three opposition leaders from the Taliban's highest security prison, located in Kandahar. After the prison breakout, Hekmati left Afghanistan, fearing retaliation from the merciless Taliban. By other accounts, however, this man was a trained al Qaeda terrorist and a security guard for Osama bin Laden (the al Qaeda leader who planned the 9/11 attacks on the United States), a Taliban commander during its reign of terror, and after the 2001 American occupation a Taliban loyalist plotting to assassinate members of the American-backed government in his home country.[1]

Supporting the latter account was Sher Mohammed Akhundzada, the post-Taliban governor of Helmand Province, Afghanistan. Based upon his tip, American forces apprehended Hekmati in early 2003 and transported him to Camp X-Ray, a detention center for "unlawful enemy combatants" in Guantánamo Bay, Cuba. There, he was held without legal representation or a hearing to determine whether he was an unlawful combatant, until the Supreme Court in *Hamdi v. Rumsfeld* (2004) ruled that the president could not indefinitely hold men like Hekmati without providing some kind of hearing. After *Hamdi*, such a hearing was held. Still denied legal representation and not allowed to examine evidence against him, Hekmati maintained that he was an opponent of the Taliban and had nothing to do with al Qaeda. He challenged the hearsay account of Governor Akhundzada, partly on the ground that it was given to the Americans as retaliation against him for reporting the governor's corruption and his protection of Taliban leaders in Helmand Province. Also, Hekmati implored the tribunal to secure statements from two of the anti-Taliban leaders he helped break out of prison in 1999: Ismail Khan, the minister of energy for the pro-American government of Afghan president Hamid Karzai, and Hajji Zaher, a general in the Karzai government's Border Guards. The tribunal head told Hekmati that neither witness was available and that neither had responded to American requests for their evidence. Both Khan and Zaher have told independent observers that the Americans never contacted them. In any event, Hekmati remained in detention at Guantánamo.[2]

Although his interaction with American authorities is an unusual case in several respects, Hekmati's story reflects the many points at which the lives of people who are not U.S. citizens (and have never entered this country) are affected by America's constitutional values. For example, our Civil War experience gave rise to important theorizing about the rules governing treatment of prisoners of war. These precepts had an international audience. Under American leadership, the nations of the world entered into the Geneva Conventions after World Wars I and II, with the goal being to establish international norms for treatment of prisoners of war, civilians, and others caught up in transnational conflicts. The assumption of most provisions of the Geneva Conventions—indeed, the assumption of modern international law—is that they would govern conflicts between *nations*. That assumption is becoming exceptional rather than normal, as Abdul Razzaq Hekmati's case reveals. Everyone knows the world has shrunk, and we are more interdependent than ever before. What is less noted is that state actors no longer dominate the world stage; they are joined and sometimes overshadowed by multinational corporations, nongovernmental organizations (NGOs), and chains of terrorist groups. Hekmati was detained not because he was an Afghan patriot but because he was allegedly an operative of al Qaeda, a nonstate actor that is a primary object of America's "war on terrorism." Just as our country's republic of statutes is being enriched by bilateral treaties and multilateral conventions enacted into law through transnational superstatutes, earlier treaties and conventions (such as the Geneva ones) are being applied to the new circumstances of an interdependent world where allies and enemies are often not nations or governments.[3]

A related question is institutional. In American history, the executive branch has been the primary organ for updating and applying traditional understandings to new circumstances. The presidency of George W. Bush (2001–09) classically exemplified the administrative constitutionalism we have been exploring in this book. The driving force was Vice President Richard Cheney, probably the most influential second in command in our nation's history. He and his executive department allies believed that America's national security was at risk and that decisive, intrusive, and brutal response was needed to head off further immediate attacks. Within four months of the terrorist attacks on 9/11/2001, Vice President Cheney and his allies had finalized decisions to wiretap domestic conversations with possible links to suspected terrorists; to round up suspects (such as Hekmati) and detain them indefinitely at our naval prison in Guantánamo; to subject some of those suspects to enhanced interrogation techniques, including psychological and physical abuse such as waterboarding (in which water is poured over the suspect's hooded face, creating the sensation that he is drowning); and to try some of the suspects for war crimes in ad hoc military commissions where convictions would be all but certain, in part because the defendants would not have meaningful access to lawyers and exculpatory evidence. These were bold actions.[4]

Were they wise actions smartly advancing national security that is a core responsibility of the state—or were they examples of administrative constitutionalism gone bad? Critics of these policies argue that they were (1) bad ideas in practice, (2) illegitimate because not the product of genuine public deliberation, and (3) inconsistent with larger norms. Consider the last objection. None of the policies was explicitly authorized by statute, and some of the actions were arguably contrary to statutory limits. How much leeway does the president have to go beyond or against congressional directives? These were questions that had arisen when the Franklin Roosevelt administration (1933–45) detained Japanese Americans during World War II. In both instances, administrative entrepreneurs were responding to emergency circumstances in light of three kinds of constitutional norms:

- *Preconstitutional norms,* namely, the fundamental presuppositions (those that go without saying) of a constitutional polity; as Hobbes and Locke would have understood the matter, the most fundamental goal of government is to protect the security of the people against enemy attack, and this prime directive does not have to be encoded in a legal text to have normative political bite.
- *Constitutional norms,* namely, those encoded in or derived from the U.S. Constitution, including separation of powers and equal protection, each of which provides both authorization and limitation for the executive department.
- *Statutory norms,* namely, those encoded in or derived from federal superstatutes, including framework laws that authorize, structure, or limit executive responses to foreign-based emergencies.

As we have seen elsewhere in this book, these different norms interact in the process of administrative deliberation—but not always seamlessly. During Franklin Roosevelt's administration, for example, the preconstitutional norm of self-defense motivated a narrow reading of the Constitutional equal protection norm and a broad reading of Congress's statutory authorization for the president's order detaining Japanese Americans.

The same array of norms reappeared when the Supreme Court considered the legality of the detention program in *Korematsu v. United States* (1944). Writing for the Court, Justice Hugo Black ruled that Congress had authorized a temporary detention and that this did not violate the Constitution, even though citizens were targeted simply because of their Japanese ethnicity. Reading the Constitution as well as the statute in the light of the preconstitutional self-defense norm, Justice Black argued that the wartime emergency justified this extraordinary action. In a concurring opinion, Justice Felix Frankfurter argued that congressional and executive exercise of military powers during wartime could be justified even if the same actions were "lawless" if performed in time of peace; this was an open admission that the preconstitutional self-defense norm was actually trumping the Constitutional and perhaps also the statutory norms.[5]

Pressing Frankfurter's idea in a different direction, Justice Robert Jackson dissented. He agreed that the generals could do what they felt they had to do during the emergency. "It would be impracticable and dangerous idealism to expect or insist that each specific military command in an area of probable operations will conform to conventional tests of constitutionality. When an area is so beset that it must be put under military control at all, the paramount consideration is that its measures be successful, rather than legal. The armed services must protect a society, not merely its Constitution." Thus, Jackson recognized the preconstitutional argument from necessity—but he refused to bend the Constitution to accommodate it. "But if we cannot confine military expedients by the Constitution, neither would I distort the Constitution to approve all that the military may deem expedient. This is what the Court appears to be doing, whether consciously or not." Justice Jackson, a staunch law-and-order conservative (and the late Chief Justice William Rehnquist's mentor), announced that any government action targeting and penalizing citizens solely because of their birth ancestry was unConstitutional and ought not be enforced by the judiciary. For this reason, the Court should not give post hoc authorization for instrumentally valid military actions that were nonetheless inconsistent with the Constitution. Also dissenting, Justices Frank Murphy and Wiley Rutledge made the simpler point that race-based classifications are odious distinctions that had not been shown to serve the self-defense goal asserted by the administration.[6]

On the same day the justices announced their decision in *Korematsu*, they handed down a companion decision that balanced these norms in a different way. In *Ex parte Endo* (1944), a unanimous Supreme Court granted the habeas corpus petition of Mitsuye Endo and directed the federal authorities to release her from wartime detention. The authorities had conceded that Endo was a loyal citizen, and from that concession Justice William Douglas's opinion for the Court reasoned that her continued detention could not serve the wartime purpose the Roosevelt administration posited in *Korematsu*, namely, the weeding out of disloyal Japanese Americans. The holding of Douglas's opinion was that there was no statutory authority for the extraordinary *continued* detention of Mitsuye Endo. Because Endo's case was not such a direct challenge to the validity of the government's internment program and because the emergency had passed, the Constitutional equality concerns trumped weaker preconstitutional security concerns and demanded a narrower reading of the open-textured statute.[7]

One way of thinking about the *Korematsu* debate is to imagine a Dual Constitution, one governing in normal times, and another governing during emergencies. Because of parallels with the Roman Republic's willingness to vest extraordinary powers in a dictator during times of emergency, we call this the *Roman* approach for Constitutional treatment of national security issues. Examples of such an approach in modern governance include Article 48 of the Weimar (German) Constitution and, perhaps, Article 16 in the Constitution of the French Fifth Republic. As these examples illustrate, the Roman approach has a shaky record: Weimar used Article 48 too much (repeatedly to deal with budgetary impasses, and ultimately to justify Nazi measures), while the Fifth Republic used Article 16 only once, during the Algerian crisis of 1962, to equally ill effect. Justice Jackson's fear, and what separated him from Justice Frankfurter, was that the emergency half of the Dual Constitution runs the risk of polluting the other half and even supplanting it entirely through a proliferation of "emergencies." Weimar political philosopher Carl Schmitt offered a broader critique, that liberal democracies were incapable of crafting preexisting rules that could realistically constrain the conditions under which a dictator would be appointed or that could effectively set limitations upon his authority.[8]

Illustrating Schmitt's observation were the actions taken by President Abraham Lincoln soon after he assumed office in 1861. As southern states left the Union and initiated hostilities, Lincoln on his own authority mobilized the armed forces, blockaded southern ports, and suspended habeas corpus. There was no statutory authority for these actions, and Congress was not in session to grant the president such authority in time for an effective response. As in *Korematsu*, the preconstitutional norm of national security trumped Constitutional objections. As a practical matter, however, Lincoln was asserting only temporary "dictatorial" authority. When Congress returned to Washington, D.C., it granted Lincoln statutory authority for his unilateral actions, except for habeas (which was later settled by a president-congressional compromise). As in *Endo*, the participants recognized the need for statutory authority to impose restrictions on citizens' physical as well as economic liberty. A *Lincolnian* approach is similar to the Roman approach in its temporary accommodation of preconstitutional security concerns; it is different in that Lincoln appointed himself temporary dictator, and his actions set the stage for a war that lasted more than four years. A *modified Lincolnian* approach would be the one Lincoln said he would have followed had Congress been in session: the president seeks congressional authorization before engaging in extraordinary responses to security threats.[9]

Responding to the terror attacks of 9/11/2001, the Bush-Cheney administration on its own authority issued directives to detain some American citizens and many noncitizens like Hekmati without formal charges or trials, to interrogate those detainees through "special" and "extraordinary" interrogation techniques, including various forms of psychological and physical abuse, and to eavesdrop on private conversations between Americans and foreigners without warrants or any judicial allowance. The internal debates within the administration suggest that the prime movers were not following either a Roman or a Lincolnian approach. These and other extraordinary measures were based upon a *presidential* approach long embraced by Vice President Cheney. They combined (1) a powerful regard for preconstitutional security concerns with (2) an instrumental belief that security required extensive intelligence and prophylactic and preemptive measures, and with (3) a Constitutional theory of broad presidential authority free of congressional restraints. Like Lincoln and perhaps like Black in *Korematsu*, Cheney and his allies believed that the nation's chief executive has an *obligation* as well as the discretion to aggressively protect the integrity of the union and its security. These administrative constitutionalists were also serious Schmittians: external rules of law could not and should not constrain their exercise of sovereign authority to respond to such security threats. Their Large "C" Constitutional theory raised the Schmittian stakes: his Article II authority as commander in chief empowered the president to respond in any way necessary to protect the country against terrorist attacks, and Congress has no authority to establish preexisting rules that legally constrain the executive.[10]

The presidential approach was legally rationalized in internal executive department memoranda by Cheney's allies, namely, his chief of staff David Addington, William J. Haynes II of the Defense Department, Timothy Flanigan in the White House, and John Yoo in the Office of Legal Counsel of the Department of Justice. Ironically, the view that the president's executive and commander-in-chief powers cannot be limited by statute is inconsistent with the original meaning of the Constitution of 1789 and subsequent presidential as well as congressional practice. It is also a politically risky strategy, because the president then bears the entire blame if his emergency response is a failure. Not least important, such a strategy is at odds with *Youngstown Sheet & Tube Co. v. Sawyer* (1952), the famous Steel Seizure Case, where the Court invalidated President Harry Truman's wartime seizure of domestic steel production. Congress had provided several statutory mechanisms by which President Truman could have handled the steel strike that threatened wartime production, but Truman followed none of those processes and acted on his own authority. Writing for the Court, Justice Black invalidated the president's action because it was "legislative" in nature. Concurring, Justice Jackson faulted the president for not following the procedures lawfully prescribed by Congress.[11]

The lesson of the Steel Seizure Case is that when extraordinary circumstances confront the nation, the terms of our response ought to be guided by the normative commitments reflected in high-profile statutes that have been adopted by Congress and the president after sober deliberation before the fact. (Such high-profile statutes represent a congressional-presidential bargain, for they must pass both chambers of Congress *and* are subject to the president's veto, which gives him significant leverage to influence the final compromise.) This approach reveals several important connections between the Large "C" Constitution and its small "c" sibling. The Court's holding in the Steel Seizure Case was that the president may usually not exercise rights-shifting authority without congressional statutory delegation. The Steel Seizure Case has become black letter law for both the Large "C" Constitution and our constitution of statutes. That also means that Constitutional issues involving presidential authority are typically resolved through statutory rather than purely Constitutional interpretation, so long as Congress is acting within its Constitutional authority. If superstatute X authorizes the president to detain American citizens under specified circumstances, the separation of powers issues are usually resolved by determining whether X, as a matter of interpretation, applies to the case at hand. Conversely, such resolution will not be a matter of ordinary statutory interpretation and will be brigaded with explicit normative trappings—as in *Endo*, where Justice Douglas assumed that "the Chief Executive and members of Congress . . . are sensitive to and respectful of the liberties of the citizen. In interpreting a war-time measure we must assume that their purpose was to allow for the greatest possible accommodation between those liberties and the exigencies of war. We must assume, when asked to find implied powers in a grant of legislative or executive authority, that the law makers intended to place no greater restraint on the citizen than was clearly and unmistakably indicated by the language they used." As we argued in chapters 6 and 7, this is an explicit statement of the normative debate that is always occurring when superstatutes evolve to meet new problems under new understandings about our polity and the world.[12]

Grounded in executive-legislative bargains, Jackson's *Youngstown* approach has been the dominant one for both the United States and its European and North American allies in responding to emergencies. European prime ministers have secured from their parliaments carefully defined powers to deal with anticipated emergencies. Politically, this makes a great deal of sense, because it provides the chief executive with some guidance as to what is acceptable in that society, and he or she can share the blame if things go wrong. Although the Jacksonian (*Youngstown*) approach has virtues of institutional cooperation and public deliberation, with the possibility of popular feedback, it also has significant difficulties. To begin with, this strategy runs the risk of sacrificing Constitutional values in ordinary as well as extraordinary times. Starting in 1974, Great Britain adopted a series of Defense against Terrorism Acts that have gradually expanded the powers of the police to hold people without charging them. Concerned observers believe that these new powers have been creeping into ordinary police actions, precisely the fear that Justice Jackson harbored. Also, what Jackson's approach gains in democratic legitimacy and potential respect for human rights, it might lose in terms of efficacy. The technology of terrorism and the nature of its organization render any national security superstatute vulnerable to a more rapid obsolescence than we have seen for other landmark laws in the course of this book—and the Schmittian claim that the rule of law cannot constrain executive response to emergencies takes on added force.

The Bush-Cheney administration sought to synthesize these considerations in an interesting way: executive officials took decisive action and adopted tough prophylactic measures based upon their assumption that the presidential approach was correct, but in public and judicial defenses of their actions they wrapped themselves in the Jacksonian (*Youngstown*) or the Lincolnian approach. (In common parlance, this is called having your cake and eating it, too.) Thus, immediately after 9/11, the administration secured from Congress an Authorization for the Use of Military Force Act of 2001 (AUMF), vesting the president with broad authority to act against nations, organizations, and persons that had contributed to the attacks on 9/11/2001. The Bush-Cheney administration relied on the AUMF as a legal basis for detaining citizens and noncitizens suspected of involvement with al Qaeda and other terrorist groups and for its wiretapping and surveillance of international communications. These were controversial claims, but they powerfully illustrate that fundamental issues of America's national security constitution have gradually migrated away from Large "C" Constitutional claims to practices of statutory interpretation. And Carl Schmitt's theory may retain its power here as well: landmark national security statutes like the AUMF are often open-textured, what American Schmittians call "gray holes" that in practice leave the executive unchecked by the rule of law. Is the AUMF such a gray hole?

The account that follows in this chapter suggests that legal rules and constitutional norms did exercise a constraining influence on Vice President Cheney's agenda, partly through administrative counterpressure within the executive department and partly through publicity and congressional and judicial push back. Under the theory of our book, what defeated much of the Cheney agenda was the perception that it violated small "c" constitutional commitments— longstanding rules and practices that were considered workable and represented a just balance between rights and security. Indeed, and contrary to most American Schmittians, even the Rehnquist and Roberts Courts pushed back against the Cheney constitutional agenda.[13]

To be sure, *Korematsu* is evidence that the Supreme Court is not a reliable bulwark against abuses of the Roman or Lincolnian approach in times of perceived crisis or emergency. But how does the Schmittian critique explain *Endo*? One explanation is that by the time the Court decided both *Korematsu* and *Endo*, the government had already decided to close down the detention centers; the fever of anti-Japanese sentiment had passed, though the war was far from over. *Endo* allowed the Court to announce a small "c" constitutional norm as a baseline against which future presidents and Congresses could act; it is also a warning to future executives that the judiciary is not entirely passive even during wartime. Consistent with *Endo*, any activism is probably going to be through statutory interpretations rather than Constitutional trumps. Indeed, the most important judicial interventions will occur when the country is working on a Jacksonian bargain involving all the relevant institutional actors. Indeed, as the primary voice for liberty and equality concerns, the Court will often want to place its stamp upon the bargain, especially if the new framework statute reflects public fear and executive power grabs, as one might expect under conditions of emergency and crisis. (If the framework statute runs into unforeseen circumstances, we are back to the Roman or the Lincolnian approach for all practical purposes.) An overall point of this chapter is that the national security constitution is most productively seen as a constitutional bargain: a product of institutional interaction that spurs public debate about the best approach for protecting both security and liberty in an era where the challenges to both are changing.[14]

Apparently, Vice President Cheney and his legal allies devoutly believed that the traditional bargain represented by the Steel Seizure Case was outdated under the new circumstances and threats posed by mobile, well-funded, anti-American terrorist groups such as al Qaeda. The reigning Jacksonian (*Youngstown*)

approach, they thought, was too slow and deliberative to meet the swiftly changing demands of terrorist threats. So the Cheneyites substituted the more mobile
and responsive presidential approach within the executive branch and then
tried to sell it to legislators and judges after the fact. As we urged in earlier chapters, and shall urge in the Conclusion, public deliberation is key. Our self-
defense policies are as constitutive of our national identity, our constitution, as
our civil rights, electoral, market-regulatory, social insurance, family, and environmental policies are, and for that reason they require public deliberation—a
public process of problem solving, trade-offs, and feedback. As Heidi Kitrosser
has argued, we can engage in secret processes at the micro level if the overall
macro-level policy is transparent and acceptable to the body politic. And, as
Justice Kennedy established in the most recent war on terror decision by the
Supreme Court, the habeas corpus superstatute and its corresponding Constitutional guarantee mean that the judiciary will continue to play a role in the
national balance between security and liberty.[15]

Consider the following deep dilemma. On the one hand, the Roman and
the presidential approaches are most susceptible to extreme and damaging responses to perceived emergencies, as the Cheney-Addington response has turned
out to be. Supporting what we are calling a Jacksonian approach, Stephen Holmes
argues that it is usually a better way to respond to emergencies if one follows
experience-tested rules and protocols than if one engages in ad hoc spur-of-the-
moment solutions. Thus, paramedics, air-traffic controllers, and military commanders faced with unexpected emergency circumstances do better by following
professional procedures than by following their guts. Philip Bobbitt makes a
broader point, that this process of requiring the executive to follow statutory
law, soberly interpreted, is as important as ever, even as the nature of national
security challenge has changed. Robert Jackson's stand against internment of
Japanese American citizens was an important defense of the democratic ideal
that America was, literally, fighting for against Imperial Japan, Nazi Germany,
and Fascist Italy in the Great War. The meta-war was Democracy versus Totali-
tarianism; today it is the Rule of Law versus Terror. (It is important that the United
States not accept the false and internationally polarizing view that the conflict is
between the West and Islam.) What states of consent such as the United States
offer to the world is the notion that government provides security for We the
People, which includes security against arbitrary government action. Terror
wins when states of consent stoop to the level America reached in Abu Ghraib,
where our personnel engaged in torture, degradation, and sacrilege against
Muslim prisoners.[16]

Here is the theme of this chapter. Before 9/11, America's constitution of national security consisted of rules, practices, and understandings that reflected

presidential-congressional bargains (Jackson's opinion in *Youngstown*). As a substantive matter, the constitution authorized the president to respond to and head off enemy attacks, but did not allow the president to detain suspected enemies indefinitely, to try them in tribunals where they did not have basic due process rights, and to torture them. Nor did the constitution allow the president to intercept domestic conversations except through a process protecting citizens' privacy. Administrative constitutionalists allied with Cheney challenged both the procedural structure of the national security constitution and its particular rules. By their account, the national security constitution consists of presidential decisions about what is best to protect the country against a novel and dynamic threat. In the new world order where nonstate terrorism is the biggest threat, the national security constitution empowers the president to respond to and head off enemy attacks, and that power included discretion to detain suspected enemies indefinitely, to create tribunals to try them as war criminals, and to secure intelligence from them, using enhanced interrogation techniques when necessary.

Generally, the presidential approach has not supplanted the presidential-congressional bargain approach. Even the Bush-Cheney administration felt compelled to seek or rely upon congressional authorization for its innovations, and the Supreme Court repeatedly reaffirmed the Steel Seizure framework for the national security constitution. Within that framework, however, there was some movement toward Cheneyite security values. This was especially true for the balance between privacy and security in electronic surveillance; the pre-Cheney superstatute was significantly amended in 2007–08, and it appears the amended regime will stick. Thus far, practices of indefinite detention, summary proceedings for suspected enemies, and brutal interrogation techniques have gained little traction, but the perseverance of the traditional rules may weaken if there are further attacks on American soil.[17]

THE BILL OF RIGHTS AND MILITARY COMMISSIONS

We start our study of the national security constitution with the Bush-Cheney administration's policy of detaining suspected terrorists without charges and trying some of them in ad hoc military commissions not seen in this country for sixty years. Largely the product of the vice president's office, this administrative constitutionalism was beset by all the difficulties we described in the introduction to this third part of the book: critics argued that it was the result of fiat within the executive department, was inconsistent with legal and Constitutional limits, and was a bad idea. Our account will focus on the first two criticisms. The nation's experience with military commissions illustrates the difficulty of finding limits in the old and impossible-to-amend Constitution, but the possibilities for legal bite in the small "c" constitutional world of statutes and (as we explore later in the chapter) treaties.

The Bill of Rights, the first ten amendments to the U.S. Constitution, protect freedom of expression, press, assembly, and religion (First Amendment) and require just compensation for governmental takings of property (Fifth). These are important substantive protections, but much of the Bill of Rights is procedural. Thus, the Fourth Amendment protects people against "unreasonable searches and seizures" of their "persons, houses, papers, and effects"; the Fifth protects "any person" against double jeopardy or self-incrimination in criminal cases and bars the federal government from depriving "any person" of life, liberty, or property "without due process of law"; applying only to criminal prosecutions, the Sixth guarantees accused persons notice of the charges against them, a speedy trial by an impartial jury, the right to confront accusers, compulsory process to secure testimony of witnesses, and the assistance of counsel for their defense; the Seventh preserves trial by jury in civil "[s]uits at common law"; and the Eighth bars "[e]xcessive bail," "excessive fines," and infliction of "cruel and unusual punishments." The process protections of the Bill of Rights are fundamental to our Large "C" as well as our small "c" constitutional democracy.[18]

Yet when Abdul Razzaq Hekmati fell into the custody of the American government, his jailers did not believe their treatment of him was governed by the Bill of Rights. Contrary to the broad and unqualified language of the Fifth Amendment, the military sought self-incriminating statements from the prisoner, and they may have deployed torture that could violate the broad text of the Eighth Amendment. For several years, Hekmati was detained without formal charges, was denied the assistance of counsel and the right to see the evidence against him, and had no speedy trial before an impartial jury—all contrary to the Sixth Amendment, if you read nothing but its text. If Hekmati had gone to trial on the charges that he had violated the law of war, the executive order governing that process would have allowed for exclusion of the defendant from portions of the proceedings, permitted secret and hearsay evidence, and established as presiding judges personnel who could be removed by the Department of Defense; this is not a process that would ordinarily satisfy the Due Process Clause of the Fifth Amendment. Yet the Bush-Cheney administration took the position that these guarantees of the Bill of Rights do not apply to an "unlawful enemy combatant," namely, an enemy combatant violating the law of war. If you compare the Bush-Cheney position with the text of the Constitution, you will immediately be struck by their inconsistency: the Fourth, Fifth, Sixth, and Eighth Amendments by their terms apply to all "people" or "persons" without regard to citizenship, and without any territorial limitation either (unlike the Thirteenth Amendment); likewise, those amendments contain no limitation in matters of national security, nor does the Commander-in-Chief Clause of Article II authorize the president to set aside the protections of the Bill of Rights.

Yet the Bush-Cheney administration's interpretation did not come out of thin air; indeed, it reflected a sophisticated process by which the preconstitutional norm of national self-defense interacts with Constitutional rights and even framework statutes (a process outlined above). The administration's lawyers maintained that the Constitution, including the Bill of Rights, had to be read against the background of international law, which recognizes nations' entitlement to self-preservation. The self-preservation precept inspires the international law norm that "enemy combatants" violating the law of war need not be accorded the normal process protections of either international law or positive law. Alleging that Hekmati was a terrorist, the government maintained that he fell outside the normal range of due process protections. The administration also argued that the general language of the Constitution should be read in the light of a longstanding constitutional consensus authorizing the president as commander in chief to try unlawful combatants by a summary process. Even in light of what we have demonstrated in the course of this book, the reader might be surprised by the boldness of such an argument, but the vice president's general mode of argument has a Constitutional grounding. As Carl Schmitt would have predicted, the protections of the Bill of Rights are open-textured and subject to debate, so that when the nation's security is at stake there is plenty of maneuvering room for the executive branch to do what it wants. But Schmitt's theory does not account for what actually happened to Vice President Cheney's aggressive constitutionalism of national defense: the small "c" constitutional precepts invoked by Cheney and his legal allies were met by others that were better grounded in America's republic of statutes.[19]

INDETERMINACY IN THE BILL OF RIGHTS

The Bill of Rights contains some of the more determinate and easy-to-apply rules of our Constitutional lexicon. The Sixth Amendment's requirements of notice, speedy public trial by jury, the right of confrontation, compulsory process for obtaining witnesses, and assistance of counsel provide an irreducible floor of process in ordinary criminal trials. The legal terms of art used in this amendment give it a fairly clear meaning as regards criminal trials in normal circumstances. Thus, were Abdul Razzaq Hekmati a New York resident charged with a federal crime, it is clear from the text of the Sixth Amendment that the federal government would have to inform Hekmati of the statute he allegedly violated and of the acts he allegedly committed, could not detain him indefinitely without bringing him to trial, and would have to allow him access to an attorney of his choice, who would be able to cross-examine witnesses and dispute evidence against the accused. But even the Sixth Amendment contains fuzzy edges: How "speedy" must the trial be? When is a jury not "impartial"? Does the government have to provide Hekmati an attorney if he cannot afford one? Other Bill of Rights guarantees are even less determinate. The Eighth Amendment bars "excessive" bail and fines, as well as "cruel and unusual punishments." The adjectives suggest a comparative judgment but provide no guidance as to how to exercise such a judgment. Excessive compared to what norm? Cruel in what way? How unusual does the punishment have to be?[20]

Does the Bill of Rights therefore consist of nothing but gray holes that American Schmittians can understand as leaving no usable "law" to constrain the executive? No, in large part because of our common law constitutionalism. During the twentieth century, the indeterminacy of the Bill of Rights was ameliorated through hundreds of Supreme Court decisions interpreting and applying its protections in particular cases and controversies. Those Supreme Court precedents give specificity to the amendments' open texture, although each precedent creates new fuzzy edges. In Hekmati's case, almost all of the precedents were inapplicable, according to the government's lawyers. Hekmati was not prosecuted for ordinary federal crimes but was held as an "unlawful enemy combatant." This is a term of art under international law and now codified by federal statute. An *enemy combatant* is a person who serves openly in the armed forces of a state engaged in hostilities with the United States. An *unlawful enemy combatant* is a person who has engaged or assisted in hostilities against the United States but not openly as a member of a hostile state's armed forces. Under traditional international law, persons engaged in nonstate terrorism are considered unlawful enemy combatants; this was the claim against Hekmati. Thus, a common law constitutionalism can buttress as well as limit executive power.[21]

The Supreme Court ruled in *Ex parte Quirin* (1942) that the president has authority to establish military tribunals to try and to sentence (to death) foreign agents provocateurs who were unlawful enemy combatants violating the law of war. The agents provocateurs challenged their convictions on the ground that the government failed to follow the procedures required by the Fifth and Sixth Amendments. The Court unanimously rejected that argument, on the ground that American practice, consistent with the law of nations, had since the founding era considered unlawful enemy combatants, especially but not limited to "aliens," outside the protections of the Bill of Rights. The Bush-Cheney administration maintained that Hekmati and other suspected terrorists fell within the *Quirin* rule and, therefore, that the government did not need to follow the ordinary Constitutional process. This was an aggressive expansion of *Quirin*, where the agents provocateurs were caught red-handed. In contrast, most post-9/11 detainees maintained that they were neither combatants nor enemies; Hekmati and many others plausibly claimed that they had been turned over to the Americans by opportunists seeking bounties or vengeance. Unlike the prisoners in *Quirin*, they were denied due process without reliable evidence that they were enemies of any sort or that they were enemies who had violated the law of war.[22]

FILLING IN THE DETAILS OF THE BILL OF RIGHTS BY STATUTE

One might be alarmed that *Quirin* rendered irrelevant the finely wrought protections of the Bill of Rights, based upon statutory codifications of international law. Alarmed one might be, but exceptional this is not. Although the point of Constitutional protections is supposed to be judicially enforced limits against arbitrary statutory policy, in practice statutory convergences typically frame and mold the contours of Constitutional rights. Perhaps surprisingly, this idea helps explain both the origin and the evolution of many Bill of Rights guarantees. Often, statutory convergences have encouraged judges to read the criminal process amendments expansively. Sometimes, they have encouraged expansive readings and then set limits. Sometimes, they have carved out exceptions to apparent Constitutional protections.

Consider the Sixth Amendment's requirement that an accused person have "the Assistance of Counsel for his defence." The original purpose of the Assistance of Counsel Clause was to abolish the English common law bar to counsel's representing an accused at the indictment stage of felony prosecutions and all stages of misdemeanor ones. The principle was that it was unfair to assail a criminal defendant with serious federal charges without allowing him or her, from the beginning of the process, a right to representation by someone who understood the law and could speak the language of the law. Thus, judges did not understand the Assistance of Counsel Clause to require the state to provide counsel. In the first half of the twentieth century, however, most states adopted statutory or (in a few states) judicial policies requiring appointment of counsel in capital and serious felony cases if the defendant could not afford one. Federal prosecutors followed those policies, even though they were not technically binding on them, and this became the quasi-official position of the Department of Justice. In *Johnson v. Zerbst* (1938), the New Deal Court followed the departmental practice to reinterpret the Sixth Amendment to require appointment of counsel in federal cases. Citing the diversity of state policies, the Court in *Brady v. Betts* (1942) declined to extend *Johnson* to the states under the Due Process Clause.[23]

Although *Betts* rejected a blanket extension of the federal standard to all the states, the Court did impose on the states a requirement that counsel must be appointed when the defendant is unable to secure a fair trial without counsel, under the circumstances. Writing for three dissenters, Justice Hugo Black argued that it was fundamentally unfair, and therefore in violation of the Due Process Clause, for the state to convict a poor person of a felony unless he were represented by counsel. His primary evidence for that proposition was state statutory practice, which he documented in an appendix to his dissent. According to Justice Black, thirty-five states required, generally by statute, that counsel be appointed for indigent defendants in capital and serious felony cases; thirteen states had no such requirement. Twenty-one years later, only five of fifty states—all in the Deep South, where the criminal process was used to terrorize African American males—failed to require counsel. Motivated by this new consensus, and the racial injustice undergirding the outlier position, the Court in *Gideon v. Wainwright* (1963) overruled *Betts* and required appointed counsel in all state felony cases.[24]

Something of the same phenomenon has driven the Supreme Court's Eighth Amendment death penalty jurisprudence, but with a twist. The Eighth Amendment's bar to cruel and unusual punishments was not originally intended to regulate the death penalty, but the Court's evolutive approach to that Constitutional bar invited litigation that tracked state statutory and administrative practice. By the time the Court ruled in *Furman v. Georgia* (1972) that the death penalty could not be imposed without powerful guidance to juries exercising discretion in such cases, almost all the states had abandoned enforcement of the extreme form of punishment. Hence, state practice supported an expansion of the Constitutional language. To everyone's surprise, however, thirty-five states responded to *Furman* with new death penalty statutes, more limited than the old ones, but also more often invoked. Following this new state statutory convergence, the Court ruled in *Gregg v. Georgia* (1976) that the death penalty was not a *per se* violation of the Eighth Amendment, so long as jury discretion was appropriately channeled by state law and judicial instructions. In *Coker v. Georgia* (1977), however, the Court ruled that the death penalty could not be Constitutionally applied in rape cases, also perfectly reflecting state statutory convergence (only three of the new laws applied to rape). The Court's subsequent limitations have repeatedly been informed by explicit surveys of state statutory law and administrative practice.[25]

As the Court's Eighth Amendment jurisprudence suggests, statutory convergences are not a one-way ratchet; they can constrict as well as expand the protections of the Bill of Rights. For example, Chief Justice John Roberts relied on widespread state and federal endorsement of lethal injections as the most humane way to carry out the death penalty in his opinion upholding this method in *Baze v. Dees* (2008). This, indeed, was the dilemma faced by Abdul Razzaq

Hekmati: federal statutes framed the Constitutional inquiry as to what procedural rights applied to trials of accused enemy combatants. Holding that the literal requirements of the Fifth and Sixth Amendments did not end the inquiry, the *Quirin* Court invoked an 1806 statute imposing the death penalty on alien spies violating the law of nations. "This enactment must be regarded as a contemporary construction of both Article III, §2 and the Amendments as not foreclosing trial by military tribunals, without a jury" and the other procedures required by the Bill of Rights. Because that construction had been followed since the founding era, the Court gave it "the greatest respect." The Articles of War that Congress adopted in 1916 carried forward, in Article 15, this international common law precept, and the *Quirin* Court ruled that the saboteurs had only those rights set forth in the statute, not those in the Bill of Rights. In short, longstanding statutory practice was evidence of a preconstitutional norm that set limits on plain Constitutional text.[26]

On the other hand, *Quirin* itself was not a great constitutional success: the justices who decided the case had second thoughts after the men had been executed, as the opinion justifying their execution (after the fact) was embarrassingly hard to write; commentators, including law-and-order conservatives such as Justice Scalia, have been sharply critical; and subsequent administrations declined to create ad hoc tribunals such as the one allowed in *Quirin*. Nonetheless, immediately after 9/11, Vice President Cheney and David Addington revived the idea, dormant for two generations, as an effective way to deal with suspected terrorists. Before 9/11, there was an interagency process for handling such proposals, with input from the Departments of Defense, Intelligence, and Justice, and from the National Security Council. The vice president was able to circumvent that process and sell the idea directly to the White House. Relying on a few key allies—Secretary of Defense Donald Rumsfeld, Deputy White House Counsel Timothy Flanigan, and Office of Legal Counsel attorney John Yoo (who wrote an opinion supporting the legality of the proposed commissions)— Cheney and Addington secured President Bush's approval of an executive order issued November 13, 2001, just days after American forces invaded Afghanistan to overthrow the terrorist-supporting Taliban government. Relying on Cheney-allied lawyers' expansive reading of *Quirin*, the Commander-in-Chief Clause, and the 2001 AUMF, the executive order authorized the detention of and the use of ad hoc military commissions against any noncitizen whom the executive determined "there is reason to believe" was a member of al Qaeda or "engaged in, aided or abetted, or conspired to commit acts of international terrorism." Secretary of State Colin Powell and the judge advocate generals of the armed forces only learned of the idea after the executive order was issued, and their objections were too late. Meanwhile, the Department of Defense developed procedures for the commissions to follow. In trials for terrorism, hearsay evidence would be admissible, as were confessions, including those secured through extraordinary means; the presiding officials would be military judges who could be removed during the case and had discretion to limit evidence the accused may present or may even have access to; there would be no jury trial right, and the accused could be convicted and sentenced to death if the evidence was thought by the presiding judge to be of "probative value to a reasonable person." It was unclear what access to counsel prisoners like Hekmati would have. The procedures were inconsistent with the Bill of Rights, with traditional practices in the armed forces, and with the framework statute on point, the Uniform Code of Military Justice of 1950 (UCMJ). Were those legal guidelines completely irrelevant under *Quirin*? The Schmittian answer was that they were.[27]

THE SUPREME COURT ENFORCES HEKMATI'S PROCESS RIGHTS

Carl Schmitt's theory that the liberal rule of law would exercise no constraining power on the executive in times of emergency provides a possible explanation for why the Cheney-Addington innovations (indefinite detention of mere suspects and trial of possible enemies by ad hoc tribunals) might have smooth sledding immediately after 9/11. But would these innovations stick in the American constitution? Would these innovations, renouncing the old constitutional bargain, be accepted by other branches and thereby create a new constitutional (and thereby Constitutional) bargain? Would the Supreme Court go along, for example? Some of the American Schmittians are disdainful of the possibility that unelected federal judges would stand in the way of emergency-driven responses: they won't stand in the way, and they should not. The strongest version of such claims are not consistent with the complicated institutional response to the Cheney-Addington policies, and weaker versions of the Schmittian claim add nothing to the longstanding conventional wisdom that judges are reluctant to intervene in national security matters.[28]

The first set of Supreme Court decisions involved challenges to the administration's indefinite detention of persons such as Hekmati, men suspected of terror activity but often without hard evidence to that effect. In *Hamdi v. Rumsfeld* (2004), eight justices ruled that the administration could not, consistent with the Due Process Clause, detain suspected terrorists without some process for them to present evidence to a neutral decision maker challenging the factual basis for their detention. On the same day, the Court ruled in *Rasul v. Bush* (2004) that Guantánamo prisoners such as Hekmati had access to the federal courts through a writ of habeas corpus to challenge their detention and the terms of their confinement at Camp X-Ray. These pronouncements are at odds with the American Schmittians' view that judges will not stand up to executive responses to emergencies, but the Schmittians confidently respond that the Supreme Court's pronouncements mean next to nothing as applied. Is that the case? Following *Hamdi*, the Bush-Cheney administration not only established tribunals allowing more due process but also released almost a hundred detainees, largely because the government admitted that it had never possessed hard evidence to detain them. On the other hand, Hekmati and many other detainees remained in confinement at Guantánamo, with the possibility of trial for war crimes, with convictions expected from the Article II military commissions established by the November 2001 executive order.[29]

A Yemeni national also held at Guantánamo upon accusations of assisting bin Laden, Salim Ahmed Hamdan challenged the military commissions. From a Constitutional point of view, his case seemed like a long shot: *Quirin* had carved his situation out of the Bill of Rights, Congress in the UCMJ had knowingly reaffirmed and ratified the president's *Quirin* authority, and it was doubtful that a Supreme Court with seven justices named by conservative Republican presidents would want to overrule or even narrow *Quirin*. Nonetheless, Hamdan had various legal arguments that would allow him to escape the fate of the World War II saboteurs. Thus, he maintained that trial of alleged unlawful enemy combatants could only proceed in tribunals or mechanisms authorized by Congress, namely, those provided for in Article 21 of the UCMJ. Like the prior framework law, Article 21 authorized military commissions to try "offenders or offenses" that "by statute or by the law of war may be tried by" such commissions. The administration had a hard time coming up with a plausible story that Hamdan had violated the law of war. Unlike the *Quirin* saboteurs, Hamdan had never set foot in the United States, and the most the government could say was that he was guilty of an international "conspiracy" to harm the United States. But conspiracy, without something more, is not a traditional violation of the law of war; any soldier fighting a war can be said to conspire with his fellow soldiers to bring down the other side. Four of the eight participating justices agreed with Hamdan on this point, but that did not constitute the majority Hamdan needed to overturn his conviction.[30]

Hamdan also argued, however, that even if he were properly tried by an Article 21 military commission, the president was mistaken about what process was required by the framework statute. A Supreme Court majority sustained this objection. Justice John Paul Stevens's opinion for the Court in *Hamdan v. Rumsfeld* (2006) started with the "background assumption" of military law, that punitive trials presumptively follow the well-established procedures followed in military courts-martial, which roughly track the framework for criminal processes contained in the Bill of Rights, analyzed above. (Court-martial defendants have rights of notice, representation by counsel, confrontation of adverse evidence and witnesses, and impartial decision makers; their jury is members of the armed forces, as is the presiding judge.) Article 36(a) of the UCMJ authorizes the president to promulgate rules of "procedure, including modes of proof, in cases before courts-martial, courts of inquiry, military commissions, and other military tribunals," in "regulations which shall, so far as he considers practicable, apply the principles of law and the rules of evidence generally recognized in the trial of criminal cases in the United States district courts, but which may not be contrary to or inconsistent with this chapter." Article 36(b) then says: "All rules and regulations made under this article shall be uniform insofar as practicable and shall be reported to Congress." Because these provisions require a deliberative process and reasons for establishing ad hoc procedures, neither of which could be found in the executive order, the Court ruled that the military commissions were contrary to the statute. Although the president has considerable discretion under Article 36(a) to depart from the process used in civil trials, he has much less discretion to announce rules in military trials that are not "uniform." Court-martial trials allow rights of confrontation, jury verdicts, and impartial judging that the tribunals did not, and that was fatal to their legality, the Court ruled.[31]

The Supreme Court's *Hamdan* judgment is an anti-Schmittian moment in the evolution of America's statutory constitution. An impoverished Yemeni caught up in the war on terrorism prevailed against the Bush-Cheney administration—saved by the UCMJ and our nation's long tradition of due process even in military trials under wartime conditions. But the Supreme Court's opinion was not quite the triumph that the *New York Times* and its readers thought it to be. It was simply one stage in an ongoing tug of war regarding the content of our country's national security constitution. In the wake of *Hamdan*, the administration returned to Congress and secured important framework legislation that, again, triggered modest judicial push back. We shall return to this in due course.

THE WAR AGAINST TERRORISM AND THE NATIONAL SECURITY CONSTITUTION

Even at the apex of its popularity, the Bush-Cheney administration ran into determined, and partially successful, opposition to the mechanisms it deployed to fight the war against international terrorists. We shall briefly trace two other issues where political as well as moral opposition forced the administration to back away from remarkable constitutional (and Constitutional) claims, but the other lesson from these case studies is that the national security constitution is in the process of changing in the wake of 9/11. The interdependent world in which the United States is the undisputed superpower is one posing new and greater risks than those posed during the Cold War era. The preconstitutional notion that the core role of the republican state is to provide security for its citizens has been mobilized in new ways that are still unfolding.

ELECTRONIC SURVEILLANCE: UPDATING AN OBSOLETE FRAMEWORK STATUTE

The National Security Act of 1947 formally established an "intelligence community" within the national government, originally under the leadership of the CIA director and now under the authority of the director of national intelligence. Today, there are at least seventeen agencies or portions of agencies within that community, and they perform one of the key tasks of the modern era: providing ahead-of-the-curve information about matters that others are trying to keep secret. When the intelligence community is doing its job, the president and other officials can make well-informed decisions about matters of foreign affairs and can head off many potential disasters. We the People are more secure. When the community is not doing its job, bad decisions result. Some of the nation's greatest disasters, from the Bay of Pigs debacle in 1961 to the Iraq War launched in 2003, have relied on inaccurate "facts" and poor intelligence judgments.[32]

Conversely, the intelligence community itself poses risks to Americans' liberties. Consider the National Security Agency (NSA), created by executive order in 1952 "to conduct 'signals intelligence,' including the interception and analysis of messages transmitted by electronic means." Obviously, this is an important safeguard for national security: most plots to harm American citizens or to attack this country are going to generate electronic chatter, and technologies detecting and translating these messages can provide invaluable early warning to officials. To do its job, the NSA monitors communications between points in this country and those abroad, and probably internal American communications as well; the jurisdictional line between foreign and domestic surveillance is permeable. What Congress found in the mid-1970s, however, was that NSA surveillance routinely focused on internal American political activities, especially the civil rights movement and "racial matters," "student agitation," and asserted "foreign influence" on the antiwar movement. This was not only an apparent waste of the agency's resources, it also threatened to chill people's exercise of their civil liberties.[33]

Did this activity violate the Fourth Amendment's bar to "unreasonable searches and seizures"? Although the Supreme Court has ruled that domestic wiretaps fall under the Fourth Amendment, it has never firmly ruled as to international wiretaps. After extensive public hearings, the committee chaired by Senator Frank Church concluded in 1976 that these unauthorized and invasive activities of the

NSA and other agencies raised Constitutional concerns: they invaded what the committee believed were Constitutional rights of American citizens, without any effective monitoring by neutral officials. The committee distinguished between what Heidi Kitrosser calls *micro-secrecy*, where agencies like the NSA kept new information secret in order to protect sources and confirm or elaborate on it, and *macro-secrecy*, where agencies like the NSA shielded whole programs from any kind of monitoring from legislators as well as other executive officials. The former is often necessary, while the latter is in tension with the constitutional norm of checks and balances and poses a threat to the conditions of democracy. The normative punch line of the Church Committee was that micro-secrecy is tolerable so long as there is *macro-transparency*, or democratically determined limits and some assurance of monitoring. The executive branch has, episodically, gone along with this norm, but in practice it has not been well monitored by Congress or agencies to which Congress has delegated monitoring responsibilities. Indeed, wiretapping may be an area where a modest version of the Schmittian thesis is most appropriate: because the activity itself must be secret, the possibility of reliable outside monitoring is small. But even as to this kind of hard-to-monitor activity, there has been a surprising amount of public deliberation, more than the Schmittian hypothesis would suggest.[34]

Responding to the Church Committee's report, Congress enacted the Foreign Intelligence Surveillance Act of 1978 (FISA). FISA regulates electronic surveillance of communications to or from any person in the United States; the statute authorizes electronic surveillance, with few exceptions, only pursuant to a warrant from a special surveillance court. (The FISA court consists of Article III judges appointed by the chief justice.) Otherwise, the wiretap is illegal, even if authorized by the president, a major change from prior law. The USA Patriot Act of 2001 amended FISA to liberalize the showing that must be made to secure a warrant for specified surveillance. FISA also requires periodic review and certification by the attorney general that the secret NSA wiretapping is following the statutory requirements and adhering to its limitations.[35]

On the day that terrorists launched their attacks on American soil, 9/11 itself, Vice President Cheney discussed an immediate intelligence-gathering operation to head off another attack, which he thought imminent. A week later, Michael Hayden, the NSA director, reported to the vice president the technological possibilities for intelligence gathering, both with and without the constraints of FISA. The vice president gave Hayden, Addington, and CIA Director George Tenet a green light to develop new internal guidelines for a wiretap and surveillance program outside FISA's strict limitations. Setting a pattern that would be repeated on the issues of military commissions (discussed above) and interrogation (below), Cheney and Addington sold the program directly to President

Bush, without allowing other intelligence and diplomatic officials know that such a program was even being considered. The president secretly authorized the NSA to intercept telephone calls where one party was outside the United States; his authorization was not even known by most intelligence officials. On October 25, Cheney and Addington briefed four members of Congress on the Terrorist Surveillance Program (TSP). In December, Justice Department official James Baker and FISA Chief Judge Royce Lamberth were told about the program, and Office of Legal Counsel attorney John Yoo briefed those officials on the legal justifications for it. Yoo argued that FISA did not even apply to the new program, and that if it did the statute would violate the Commander-in-Chief Clause. These were the Constitutional arguments that the vice president and his lawyer (Addington) devoutly believed to be true as well as useful for protecting the country.[36]

In this case, however, there was resistance within the executive branch. Although State Department officials were not in the loop, a few Justice Department officials were, because the attorney general was required periodically to certify to FISA Court Chief Judge Lamberth that the administration's wiretapping program was consistent with FISA. In late 2003, Assistant Attorney General Jay Bybee, head of the Office of Legal Counsel (OLC), was promoted to the Ninth Circuit, and Attorney General John Ashcroft vetoed Cheney ally John Yoo to replace Bybee. The new head of the OLC was Jack Goldsmith, a friend of Yoo's from law school, but not someone who was willing to follow Yoo's lead uncritically, as Bybee had been. Goldsmith was surprised to learn of TSP and troubled when he could not justify its consistency with FISA. In December, he approached Attorney General Ashcroft and his deputy, James Comey. Both agreed with Goldsmith's assessment that the program would have to be modified in order to receive the attorney general's approval. Addington and his allies, however, were unwilling to make the needed changes. A battle royal ensued within the executive branch, pitting the vice president's office and the NSA against the Justice Department and the FBI. (The high, or low, point of the struggle occurred in an intensive care hospital room, where Addington tried to bully a deathly ill Ashcroft into recertifying the NSA program, with Ashcroft and Comey standing up to the vice president's men.) Although Cheney persuaded the almost comically clueless president to reauthorize the program on his own authority on March 11, 2004, the president withdrew the authorization when threatened with mass resignations within the Justice Department and FBI. The program was adjusted to meet Goldsmith's legal objections and reauthorized as amended.[37]

Early in 2005, administrative resistance surfaced again, this time through leaks about the program to the press. Newspaper reports of a secret wiretap program, later confirmed by the administration, fueled a public debate. Critics argued that the program was unauthorized by FISA and was indeed unConstitutional. In addition to its standard argument based upon the president's commander-in-chief power, the administration also argued that Congress had implicitly authorized the program (as allowed by FISA) when it adopted the AUMF authorizing the president "to use all necessary and appropriate *force*" against those responsible for the 9/11 attacks. Critics responded that the president was applying the 2001 statute and his commander-in-chief powers way beyond their textual and historical meaning and contrary to judicial and other precedents. Senator Tom Daschle, the majority leader when the AUMF was adopted, testified that the Bush-Cheney administration had specifically asked for authority to engage in domestic as well as extraterritorial actions responding to al Qaeda, and that the Senate leadership had refused.[38]

Under tremendous fire in the media, the president ultimately backed away from the proposition that his wiretapping authority was unlimited by congressional statutes; in a Lincolnian move, President Bush submitted proposed legislation authorizing the NSA program. In 2007, a Congress controlled by the Democrats enacted emergency legislation authorizing the NSA to continue national security wiretaps for the time being, without FISA's warrant requirement. After debating the substance of permanent framework legislation in this area, and balancing the incommensurable values of national security and individual liberties, Congress adopted the FISA Amendments of 2008. The revised framework statute makes it much easier for NSA to conduct warrantless surveillance of communications with an international component. It reflects Heidi Kitrosser's notion that macro-transparency is all we can expect in this arena.[39]

After 2005, the debate over wiretapping was deliberative as we have been using that term. The debate was carried on in public forums—congressional hearings, legislative debates, executive department meetings, the media—and approached the issue in a factual and problem-solving manner. Participants from a variety of perspectives recognized that the warrant requirement does not make sense for wiretaps that are seeking evidence about who the terrorists are and what their next plot might be, namely, present- and future-oriented facts. Hence, the NSA needs broad authority to engage in electronic surveillance, but with post hoc protections against the use of such data for domestic political purposes. The FISA amendments of 2007 and 2008 are experiments along these lines, which is the point of administrative constitutionalism.[40]

ENHANCED INTERROGATION AND WATERBOARDING

In addition to the NSA wiretapping program, the Bush-Cheney administration was engaging in a secret program of aggressive interrogation practices in the wake of 9/11. During the administration of President William Clinton (1993–2001), the CIA had developed a "rendition" program whereby the agency would kidnap suspected foreign enemies and turn them over to other foreign governments for aggressive interrogation, including human torture in an indefinite number of cases. Furthermore, the CIA's own interrogations were often rougher than those authorized by the FBI and the army's regularized (and highly successful) processes. As early as the 1980s, Vice President Cheney had been impressed with the power of aggressive interrogation, and after 9/11 he had a ready ally in CIA Director George Tenet. Their view was that aggressive interrogation should be used to gather intelligence about al Qaeda, but that the administration should distance itself from "torture." Indeed, President Bush's first formal public statement, issued on February 7, 2002, committed the country to the proposition that persons detained by the armed forces must be treated "humanely and, to the extent appropriate and consistent with military necessity, in a manner consistent with the principles" of the Geneva Conventions.[41]

The February 7 statement did not apply to the CIA, which was actively rounding up suspected terrorists and on March 28 captured Abu Zubaida, believed to be a top al Qaeda operative. Always concerned with potential criminal liability, Director Tenet asked how aggressive he could be in interrogating Zubaida, and the matter was referred to John Yoo in the OLC. Yoo reportedly consulted with David Addington, Tim Flanigan, and Alberto Gonzales (White House counsel) and advised the CIA, on an interim basis, that it could engage in various forms of psychological stress and physical abuse; the only method Yoo specifically rejected was burying the suspect alive, even if the agency planned to dig him up before he actually died. Yoo considered that to be "torture," and he was mindful that the United States had signed and ratified the United Nations Convention Against Torture and Other Cruel, Inhuman, or Degrading Punishment, and that Congress had codified the torture prohibitions as crimes in the U.S. Code. During the summer, Abu Zubaida became the first human being subjected to waterboarding (an excruciating process whereby the victim's hooded face is doused with enough water to simulate the sensation of drowning) with the knowledge and acquiescence of the White House, relevant cabinet officials, and the executive department's chief legal office.[42]

On August 1, 2002, Assistant Attorney General Jay Bybee, the head of the OLC, signed off on a memorandum providing a legal basis for the CIA's use of rough tactics. (A similar memorandum was addressed to the Defense Department on March 14, 2003.) Substantially written by John Yoo, the OLC memorandum interpreted the torture convention and the accompanying criminal statute to regulate a very narrow range of conduct. "Torture" by their reading only included the intentional infliction of "severe pain and suffering" of "an extreme nature" and "equivalent in intensity to the pain accompanying serious physical injury, such as organ failure, impairment of bodily function, or death." Would floggings, brutal beatings, genital abuse, or even rape of prisoners be torture *only* if they led to organ failure, permanent functional impairment, or death? The official answer seemed to be that rape was ordinarily not legal torture; "certain acts may be cruel, inhuman, or degrading, but still not produce pain and suffering of the requisite intensity to fall within [the statutory] proscription against torture." Moreover, Bybee and Yoo concluded that officials who tortured detainees such as Salim Hamdan and Abdul Hekmati under a good faith belief that such abuses were needed to protect the country would be immune from legal prosecution for violating the law. Finally, they maintained that the criminal statute did not apply to conduct authorized by the chief executive, because Congress could not Constitutionally abridge the president's powers under the Commander-in-Chief Clause. Bybee and Yoo read that clause to vest in the president "the primary responsibility, and therefore the power, to ensure the security of the United States in situations of grave and unforeseen emergencies." That clause also vests the president with ultimate and untrumpable power to capture, detain, and interrogate enemy personnel.[43]

Even within the stop-terrorists-at-all-costs corridors of the Bush-Cheney administration, Jay Bybee's torture memorandum raised eyebrows, but its conclusions had a receptive audience in the White House, the office of Vice President Richard Cheney, and the Department of Defense. The CIA and Defense Department had already become aggressive in their techniques, and officials were more than a little worried about potential criminal liability. Issued by the OLC, which was then considered the gold standard for executive department legal advice, the memorandum reassured intelligence officers that techniques such as waterboarding, considered torture under customary international law, were not "torture" under American domestic law; that the few techniques falling under the Bybee-Yoo definition of torture were immune from prosecution; and that Congress didn't even have the authority to regulate such activities. The torture memorandum was a partial allowance for intelligence (and later defense) personnel to engage in aggressive interrogation techniques. Immediately after the OLC go-ahead, the CIA waterboarded Abu Zubaida eighty-three times in August 2002.[44]

The enhanced interrogation techniques used by the CIA rapidly became known to some of the Defense Department officials at Guantánamo. On October 11, 2002, those officials asked Secretary Rumsfeld for permission to use eighteen harsh interrogation techniques, including prolonged isolation, forced nakedness, hooding, shackling in stressed positions, forced standing for long periods, religious and sexual humiliation, playing on people's phobias (such as a fear of dogs), threats of harm to the prisoner or his family, mock executions, and waterboarding. Although the Department of the Army was not in favor of these techniques, as a matter of law or policy, William J. Haynes II, general counsel for the department and another Cheney-Addington ally, advised Rumsfeld that all of the techniques were legal but suggested that waterboarding and mock executions were "not warranted at this time." Rumsfeld signed onto Haynes's advice. In the wake of this authorization, the interrogation teams at Guantánamo used all the weapons at their disposal, especially against Mohammed al-Qahtani, a Saudi citizen who may have been the twentieth hijacker on 9/11. For weeks, Qahtani was subjected to extreme psychological and physical intimidation, including long periods of sleep deprivation, blaring loud Western rock music, sexual insults toward his mother and sister, threats to his family, and fraternity-style hazing. Suicidal, Qahtani filled in the details of his original confession, but independent observers believe that none of the new details was reliable, and it remains unclear whether the enhanced interrogation techniques provided any useful information. Extraordinary interrogation techniques continued to migrate from place to place, until a media disaster overtook the Bybee-Yoo legal advice.[45]

On April 28, 2004, Solicitor General Paul Clement defended the administration's indefinite detention policy before the Supreme Court, in the oral argument for *Hamdi*. In a companion case argued the same morning, one of the justices wondered what institution protected the human rights of detained persons. Weren't judges the only officials who would have the political ability to protect against human rights abuses? The solicitor general responded: "You have to recognize that in situations where there is a war—where the Government is on a war footing, that you just have to trust the executive to make the kind of quintessential military judgments that are involved in things like that." That night, CBS News ran the first of dozens of media reports on the sexual abuse, humiliation, and severe punishment of prisoners at Abu Ghraib prison in Iraq. Naked prisoners were stacked in a human pyramid. One prisoner was photographed with a hood on his head and electrodes attached to his fingers. American guards posed proudly, some smirking, as they displayed their degraded human trophies. None of the photographs revealed evidence that the administration conceded to be torture, under the Bybee-Yoo interpretation, yet every one of the photographs demeaned American national pride and enraged Iraqis and Muslims in the region. Their cumulative effect on world opinion was immediately and overwhelmingly negative. America's self-image as an honorable country took hits domestically as well as internationally. Trust the executive?[46]

Two months later, the Supreme Court revealed less than complete trust when it handed down its decisions in *Hamdi* and *Rasul*. The country was also skeptical, as revelations of serious abuse continued to pour out. The Red Cross reported that physical and psychological coercion were routine techniques deployed at Abu Ghraib and Guantánamo and concluded that many of these techniques violated norms of international law. The media discovered details about the secret CIA interrogation facilities and the "alternative interrogation techniques," with reports of waterboarding gaining particular prominence. The administration blamed these assertedly isolated abuses on individual soldiers and created a few scapegoats, but other soldiers testified to Human Rights Watch that the abuse of prisoners grew out of an attitude that came from the Pentagon and the White House: "No blood, no foul," the punch line that the Defense Department drew from the Bybee-Yoo memorandum. Revelations of widespread abuse, degradation, near-torture, and clear torture of detainees, many of them adolescents and all of them merely accused and not convicted terrorists, have continued to pour forth.[47]

That these abuses occurred on a significant scale indicates that our nation's constitutional consensus against torture was in play after 9/11. The Bybee-Yoo memorandum was an opening move in the administration's bid to recalibrate the nation's national security constitution in the wake of 9/11. It is significant, however, that within the Bush-Cheney administration there was push back, based upon the rule of law that the Schmittians denigrate. Starting in December 2002, Alberto Mora, the general counsel of the navy, mounted an insistent campaign to halt the aggressive techniques used at Guantánamo; ultimately the judge advocate generals of all the branches joined Mora. Although Haynes and Rumsfeld reaffirmed aggressive interrogation, their view collapsed under sustained legal attack. Jack Goldsmith, Bybee's successor as OLC chief, withdrew the Bybee-Yoo torture memorandum. It fell to Dan Levin, Goldsmith's OLC successor, to devise new standards for interrogation, and Levin decided to subject himself to most of the techniques that Bybee, Yoo, and Haynes had sanctioned. It took only one waterboarding session for Levin to conclude that this was serious torture. As the revelations continued to come forth, the administration publicly backed away from most of the conclusions of the torture memorandum.[48]

A Congress controlled by the Republican Party, fresh from President Bush's decisive reelection in November 2004, responded as well. Senator John McCain, a former prisoner of war in Vietnam, introduced an amendment to the defense budget bill to prohibit "inhumane treatment" (not only "torture") of prisoners held by the United States anywhere in the world. On October 5, 2005, the Senate voted 90–9 in favor of the McCain Amendment. Shortly after that, Vice President Cheney implored McCain to exempt the CIA from the strictures of his amendment—right on the eve of new revelations. The *Washington*

Post on November 2 reported that the CIA had after 9/11 been operating secret prisons in eight countries and Guantánamo. At those so-called black sites, CIA interrogators were authorized to use waterboarding and other methods condemned by international law and the torture convention. McCain refused to back away from the full force of his amendment, and Congress passed the Detainee Treatment Act of 2005, which the president signed into law on December 30. The statute confines interrogation techniques to those identified in the *Army Field Manual* and specifically prohibits "cruel, inhuman, or degrading treatment" of detained persons. Although David Addington sought to neutralize the effect of the McCain Amendment through a (secret) narrowing interpretation from OLC attorney Steven Bradbury, the rule of law representing traditional American practice was swallowing up the Cheney-Addington innovations.[49]

As the foregoing account suggests, even determined administrative constitutionalists responding to a serious national emergency face checks and balances when their innovations go too far. No one institution can always be counted on to check executive misadventures. The Supreme Court is well situated to slow down aggressive actions and sometimes reverse the burden of inertia, but it takes a long time for issues to reach the Court, and its real authority is limited. Congress can respond more quickly, has more powerful weapons at its disposal (such as funding limits or cutoffs), and is the most legitimate agency of correction. But it is often easy for a determined executive branch to block congressional action. In the case of human rights violations, the most effective checks were within the executive branch itself. Although the internal checks provided by legal advisers, other departments, and ground-level personnel did not trigger significant public dialogue, they did head off many abusive practices and probably discouraged initiatives that would have been even more harmful.

NATIONAL SECURITY: THE RELATIONSHIP BETWEEN LARGE "C" AND SMALL "c" CONSTITUTIONALISM

The military commission, wiretapping, and torture controversies all illustrate the constitutive as well as governance issues raised by the national security constitution. Although the bulk of the legal discussion focused on the authority of the president to ignore congressional directives (the separation of powers issue) and the ability of statutes to constrain executive actions (the Schmitt thesis and the rule of law issue), the big stakes in these debates were small "c" constitutional in the purest Aristotelian sense: What are our national values? How do we behave toward suspected enemies? What rules do we play by when we suspect people of participation in terrorist groups? These larger normative questions are bound up in the governance questions as well, including what are the limits to the president's authority to protect us against suspected terrorists?

In the matter of separation of powers, the Constitutional and constitutional limits end up being part of the same *statutory* inquiry, as illustrated by the leading Supreme Court decision, the Steel Seizure Case (1952), discussed above. In his influential concurring opinion, Justice Robert Jackson identified three contexts for separation of powers analysis: zone 1, where the president acts pursuant to a congressional authorization, such that the only Constitutional limits are those applicable to the entire federal government (such as the Bill of Rights); zone 2, where the president acts under his own inherent powers, which Jackson opined may be defined to include areas where Congress has ceded to the president practical authority by default (what he called a "zone of twilight"); and zone 3, where the president acts contrary to congressional directives and can only succeed when his inherent powers trump those of Congress.[50]

Justice Jackson's Steel Seizure concurrence has been the most influential statement of separation of powers doctrine in the past century. The lawyers for both Salim Hamdan and Secretary of Defense Rumsfeld in the Military Commissions Case invoked the Jackson framework. Justice Stevens's majority opinion in *Hamdan v. Rumsfeld* (2006) followed it closely, as did Justice Thomas's dissenting opinion; their disagreement lay in their conflicting views about how much inherent power the president had and what limits the UCMJ placed on the president's discretion. In memoranda presented to Congress regarding the Constitutionality of the secret NSA wiretapping program, both scholars questioning the program and administration lawyers defending it explicitly argued within the Jackson framework. Even the Bybee-Yoo memorandum, which did not mention the Jackson opinion (and was universally criticized for that omission), seems to have approached the issues within that framework. Because there was a relevant statute, the authors started with the argument that almost all aggressive interrogation techniques met the terms of the statute as they understood it and, at the Constitutional stage of their analysis, recognized that there would be some cases falling under Jackson's zone 3. Thus, they had to argue, and did argue, that the president's commander-in-chief authority trumped Congress's regulatory authority in those cases. Unhappily, their broad view that the Commander-in-Chief Clause allows the president to supplant domestic statutes enacted by Congress has no support in the original meaning of Article II and virtually no support in the pre-2001 understanding of Article II. As David Barron and Martin Lederman have demonstrated in detail, no pre-twentieth-century president even asserted a commander-in-chief authority that could not be guided by statute, and such presidential assertions were quite rare even in the last century.[51]

The Jackson framework is a perfect fit for our view that America's statutory constitution is where the normative action is in the modern regulatory state, and our thesis has implications for Jackson's framework. The growth of the administrative state, grounded in statutes, has not neglected the fields of military affairs, international relations, and foreign policy. As Congress has legislated in these areas, with increasing specificity, Jackson's zone 2, the "zone of twilight," is disappearing, becoming ever dimmer if you will. Unless the Roberts Court is more willing to accept the broad commander-in-chief claims of the Bush-Cheney administration, Jackson's zone 3 is also on the wane.[52]

In the arena of foreign affairs and national security, the entrenchment of the Jackson framework is by no means a disaster for presidential power, for as we have repeatedly noted in this book the president has big first-mover advantages in pressing policy initiatives. This advantage is particularly keen in matters of national security and foreign affairs, where speedy response to fast-changing circumstances is essential. For this reason, we believe that President Bush left his successor, President Barack Obama, with greater authority to deal with suspected terrorists like Abdul Razzaq Hekmati than he inherited from Presidents George H. W. Bush and William Clinton. Consider three recent statutes adopted by Congress at the president's request. First, as noted above, Congress in 2007 and 2008 granted the NSA extensive authority to engage in warrantless wiretaps of international communications with persons in the United States. Thus, the president has been able to persuade even the opposing party that he needs extraordinary authority to intercept international communications, without the delays and extra costs that a warrant requirement would usually entail. The Cheney-Addington administrative constitutionalism has had some successes in America's statutory constitution, and expanded wiretapping authority, with fewer protections for individual privacy, is probably its most important legacy.[53]

The administration probably did not tap into Abdul Hekmati's conversations, but as we have seen the executive department detained him for several years and may have engaged in coercive interrogation techniques with him. One would expect that the 2005 Detainee Treatment Act would have ended such techniques, for it reaffirmed the antitorture norm whose entrenchment in American constitutionalism has been repeatedly confirmed by administrative, statutory, and treaty deliberations. That is pretty much true, and we unaware of evidence that the government tortured Hekmati after the 2005 statute, but it is worth noting that the DTA provided interrogators who torture detained aliens with a good faith defense to criminal charges: if the interrogators believed, both reasonably and in good faith, that they were not violating antitorture law when they waterboarded, electroshocked, and otherwise mistreated their victims, then they would be immune from prosecution. The statute provides that advice of counsel—the Bybee-Yoo memorandum and its progeny—is relevant to a determination of good faith. Generally, we do opine that the antitorture norm has

been reaffirmed, but less sweepingly than it would have been understood before 9/11.[54]

The DTA also took away the detainees' habeas corpus right to challenge the
process by which their status as illegal combatants and war criminals would
be adjudicated. The Supreme Court in *Hamdan* interpreted this provision to
be inapplicable to detainees like Salim Hamdan who had already, as of December 30, 2005, filed their habeas petitions, but of course that left other detainees
with only a very limited judicial review the DTA provided for them in the D.C.
Circuit. *Hamdan* did require the president to create tribunals that gave normal
due process, something much closer to the Bill of Rights (which we describe
above) than to the 2001 executive order. The president was loath to do that and
returned to the GOP-controlled Congress after *Hamdan* to secure legislation
placing no-process military commissions on a better legal footing.[55]

After extensive hearings where military lawyers defended the Supreme Court's
decision and advocated procedural protections for detainees like Hamdan and
Hekmati, Congress responded with a bipartisan compromise statute, the Military Commissions Act of 2006 (MCA). The new law expanded the crimes for
which an enemy combatant could be tried as a war criminal and authorized
Combatant Status Review Tribunals (CSRTs) to determine guilt, with more of
the traditional Bill of Rights protections than the 2001 executive order had allowed. On the one hand, the new law accorded accused terrorists a presumption of innocence and qualified rights to counsel, against self-incrimination, and
confrontation of adverse evidence and witnesses. On the other hand, it limited
judicial review of tribunal guilty verdicts. (We particularize the procedures below.) There is much to criticize in the statute, from both human rights and
national security points of view, but the MCA does reaffirm the norm that even
suspected enemies of the worst sort—accused terrorists—are entitled to procedural protections and cannot be adjudicated by the summary process that the
Nazi saboteurs suffered during World War II (*Quirin*).[56]

Although the MCA revoked his right to habeas corpus, the new statute gave
Abdul Razzaq Hekmati some hope. He was certain that, if he could get a fair
hearing, he would be released. This was no delusion on his part; British journalist Andy Worthington has independently verified most of Hekmati's claims
through personal interviews and investigations in Iraq. The administration's
charges that Hekmati worked with al Qaeda have never had any evidentiary
basis, which defense counsel could press as a basis for dismissal of those charges.
The act would allow the hearsay statements of his accuser (Sher Akhundzada) to
be admitted into evidence, but Hekmati's attorney could impeach and perhaps
discredit that accusation as the product of a corrupt pro-Taliban scoundrel re-
taliating against him; this same official was allegedly responsible for the deaths

of Hekmati's father, his two brothers, his sister, and two of his sons, according to independent reports from Iraq. Counsel could secure statements and perhaps the live or video testimony of Hajji Zahar and Ismail Khan, who would testify that Hekmati orchestrated the 1999 prison break that humiliated the Taliban government and helped fuel the indigenous rebellion against them. Other Iraqis have told independent observers that Hekmati did work as a truck driver for the Taliban, but only because such duties were imposed on all able-bodied men, and that after the prison break the Taliban would have executed him if they could have found him. In short, even the government-friendly procedures established by the MCA gave the accused opportunities to uncover and present relevant factual defenses, and it seems as though much of the international humanitarian and journalist community has been uncovering precisely these kinds of exculpatory materials.[57]

THE GENEVA CONVENTIONS

Our account of the national security constitution is yet more complicated. One of the central legal issues confronted by the Bush-Cheney administration's response to 9/11 was whether the president was bound by international law or treaty to accord rights to suspected terrorists. In 1949, the United States signed the Geneva Conventions, which codified rules followed by the United States itself after the Civil War. In 1955, the Senate voted unanimously to ratify these conventions, and since then they have been the law of the land. Strongly internalized by the armed forces, the Geneva Conventions have become a fundamental feature of the national security constitution.[58]

Human rights lawyers argued that the administration's treatment of Abdul Hekmati and Salim Hamdan violated the Third Geneva Convention (1949). The Third Convention guarantees humane treatment and wartime due process to prisoners of war, civilians, and others caught in the crossfire of international conflicts. Article 5 provides that captured persons must be treated as "prisoners of war" (POWs) protected by the Geneva Conventions "until such time as their status has been determined by a competent tribunal." Independent of the Article 5 protections, Common Article 3 prohibits "the passing of sentences and the carrying out of executions without previous judgment pronounced by a regularly constituted court affording all the judicial guarantees which are recognized as indispensable by civilized peoples" in the course of an "armed conflict not of an international character." In his lawsuit, Hamdan argued that his detention violated both Article 5 and Common Article 3: he was a POW taken in connection with the United States' invasion of Afghanistan and therefore fell under Article 5, as both warring countries had ratified Geneva III; if the invasion were not considered an international conflict, he was then covered by Common Article 3. Detaining him without charges violated Common Article 3, because the military commissions were not "regularly constituted courts" and did not afford the needed "judicial guarantees" of fairness in adjudication. Although not at issue in Hamdan's case, the Geneva Conventions also prohibit torture and abusive and humiliating treatment of POWs and other detained persons.[59]

The Geneva Conventions were an early but not permanent casualty of the war against terror. In a speech to the Chamber of Commerce on November 14, 2001, Vice President Cheney said that suspected terrorists were not legitimate POWs. Following the lead of Under Secretary Douglas Feith, Defense Secretary Rumsfeld confirmed that Afghans captured during the conflict in that country were unlawful enemy combatants who were not protected by the Geneva Conventions. Within the executive department, there was some urgency to determine the status of the captured suspects, lest their detention and enhanced interrogation later be held to violate international law. Secretly, Vice President Cheney secured President Bush's agreement that the Geneva Conventions did not apply to suspected terrorists on January 8, 2002. Unaware that the president had already signed off on the issue, the State Department's legal adviser, William H. Taft IV, submitted a lengthy memorandum arguing that Afghan fighters were clearly covered by the Geneva Conventions (a submission to which John Yoo responded with his own lengthy memorandum days later). David Addington drafted a memorandum to the president arguing that the war on terrorism was "a new kind of war" that rendered the Geneva Conventions "quaint" and "obsolete." If they were bound by the Geneva rules, American service personnel would have to coddle suspected terrorists, which would be both absurd and counterproductive. The memorandum of January 25, 2002, was signed by White House Counsel Alberto Gonzales and represented the administration's official but secret viewpoint for the next three years.[60]

Vice President Cheney and many administration lawyers took the position that the Geneva Conventions are not legally enforceable as the "law of the land" to benefit anyone, much less suspected terrorists. Within the Bush-Cheney administration, however, Secretary of State Condoleezza Rice (who replaced Colin Powell in January 2005) and her legal advisers argued for application of Common Article 3 to detained persons, at least as a matter of U.S. self-interest, to stanch the diplomatic bleeding that had occurred in the wake of Abu Ghraib. Although Rice's position was still blocked by the vice president, the Detainee Treatment Act of 2005 and the Military Commissions Act of 2006 assumed the validity of the Geneva Conventions. In *Hamdan v. Rumsfeld*, the Supreme Court ruled that Common Article 3 was legally enforceable to assure Hamdan due process in the criminal proceedings to which he was subject. Following up on *Hamdan*, the Defense Department in Directive 2310.01E (issued in September 2006) relied on Common Article 3 as "a minimum standard of care and treatment of all detainees." In short, the Cheney-Bush administration was compelled to acquiesce in the authority of the Geneva Conventions, at least in its public discourse. The election of 2008, in which both Republican (John McCain) and Democratic (Barack Obama) candidates were strong supporters of the Geneva Conventions, represented a public repudiation of Vice President Cheney's constitutional campaign against them.[61]

TREATIES, CONVENTIONS, AND CONGRESSIONAL-EXECUTIVE AGREEMENTS AS POTENTIAL SUPERSTATUTES

What we call superstatutes are not limited to laws passing through the channels of Article I, Section 7, but can include treaties and conventions that are negotiated by the president and ratified by two-thirds of the voting Senate, the process identified in Article II, Section 2. Indeed, this "Treaty Clause" stands somewhere between Article I, Section 7, and Article V (amending the Constitution) as a way fundamental national commitments can be formalized in our polity. Generally, it is much harder for the president to procure treaty ratification through two-thirds of the Senate than to secure statutes adopted by majorities in both House and Senate; that result holds up even when one considers that controversial statutes can be filibustered, which requires sixty votes in the Senate to terminate. For this reason, many international commitments that were once ratified as treaties are now enacted into law as executive-congressional agreements. The Law of the Sea Convention, for example, languished for decades as a signed treaty that the president was unable to get ratified by two-thirds of the Senate; abandoning the Article II, Section 2, process, President Bush asked Congress to enact the convention into law under the Article I, Section 7, process.[62]

As international law scholar Oona Hathaway has documented, the fate of the Law of the Sea Convention reflects the typical means by which the United States now secures international obligations: rather than submitting treaties and conventions to the Senate for two-thirds approval, presidents typically negotiate treaties and conventions and submit them as statutes. Increasingly, presidents are negotiating such international agreements pursuant to congressional authorization in framework statutes such as the Trade Agreement Act of 1974. Does this violate the Constitution? Eminent Constitutional scholar Laurence Tribe maintains that Constitutional text, original meaning, and early precedent require, even today, the president to follow the Treaty Clause when securing our international commitments; in many instances, congressional-executive agreements violate the Constitution and ought to be nullified by the Supreme Court, he suggests rather more tentatively. We think Tribe makes out an excellent original meaning and text-based case for preserving the central role of treaties, but, perhaps unfortunately, it is a case that has long since been overtaken by America's constitution of statutes. Indeed, from the beginning of our republic, officials objected to presidential-senatorial hijacking of the normal legislative process through treaty commitments. Reflecting the lessons experience taught President Washington, Chief Justice Jay, and Representative Madison, our small "c" constitution has embraced congressional-executive agreements as a substitute for treaties not just because they are easier to procure but also because a treaty's effectiveness often requires action by Congress as a whole. If treaty supporters need the support of the House in any event, why not go the congressional-executive agreement route? And so we have.[63]

An 1890 tariff statute authorized the president to negotiate reciprocal trade agreements with other countries, which would then supersede existing tariff duties for that country. This was an unprecedented delegation of treaty-based lawmaking to the president and therefore Constitutionally objectionable as in derogation of both the nondelegation doctrine or, under Tribe's theory, the Treaty Clause itself. Yet the Supreme Court upheld the delegation in *Field v. Clark* (1892). In the next century, the practice allowed by the Court in *Field* expanded to include what are now calling congressional-executive agreements, where the president negotiates and signs an international agreement pursuant to a general congressional authorization, and Congress then enacts the agreement as a statute. Indeed, congressional-executive agreements were the *dominant* form of international agreements in the twentieth century and have been the overwhelmingly dominant form after the New Deal.[64]

Accordingly, the Geneva Conventions of 1949 would have been just as much the law of the land if they had been adopted as congressional-executive agreements and not treaties. Indeed, they would have been more clearly law of the land trumping state law and having the force of federal law if the Eisenhower administration had followed the congressional-executive agreement route, because treaties do not have such effect unless they are "self-executing," a malleable concept that sharply divided federal judges in the *Hamdan* appeals. Moreover, the point of our book is that deep entrenchment is not the product of mere enactment, even enactment by acclamation or by a dramatic political showdown. Instead, entrenchment of treaties as well as congressional-executive agreements and domestic superstatutes is a product of administrative implementation, popular feedback, and congressional reaffirmation and elaboration over time (chapters 2 and 5).

In the *Hamdan* appeals, the Bush-Cheney administration took the position that the Geneva Conventions were anything *but* entrenched; they were not even self-executing, and if self-executing they were superseded by congressional authorizations for the president to use "appropriate force" in responding to 9/11 and the ongoing terrorist threats to national security. If entrenched, the conventions should be given the narrowest construction and not be allowed to interfere with the president's central mission of dealing with enemy aliens in any way that he deems appropriate. Conversely, Hamdan's attorneys and the dozens of *amici* supporting him maintained that the Geneva Conventions were entrenched both as a matter of law and as a matter of institutional practice and public opinion. In that event, the Third Geneva Convention had to be vigorously enforced by judges as well as administrators. Having read the dozens of briefs in the case (one of us filed an *amicus* brief on the statutory issues), we turn to that topic, which is deeply interesting to the project of this book.[65]

THE ENTRENCHMENT OF THE GENEVA CONVENTIONS' NORMS

There can be little doubt that the humane treatment norm of the Geneva Conventions is an admirable norm in the abstract, or that this is a widely accepted norm in the international community. Sixty-one nations negotiated the terms of the convention in the wake of revelations about the horrors committed by Nazi and other war criminals during World War II. The protections of the 1929 Geneva Convention were considered too vague and weak, and the delegates were determined to come up with more specific protections. By 2005, almost two hundred nations, including Afghanistan and the United States, had ratified the conventions. Subsequent international conventions, such as the International Convention on Civil and Political Rights (ICCPR), have confirmed and reiterated the humane treatment and due process norms of Geneva. As such, the Geneva Conventions have become firmly entrenched in "customary international law" as well as specific treaty-based international commitments. Like the Bill of Rights, moveover, the Geneva Conventions entail both negative and positive duties on the part of the state. On the one hand, they bar the state from engaging in prohibited activities, such as torture. On the other hand, and more important, they commit the state to positive processes, including humane treatment of POWs and detainees and the establishment of just procedures before trying such persons for war crimes.[66]

Our analysis has legal bite as well. If self-executing, the Geneva Conventions provide a basis for habeas corpus to detained persons like Hamdan and Hekmati, subject of course to subsequent statutes and treaties. Our judges have long followed the dictum that ambiguous statutes and even the Constitution should be interpreted to be consistent with customary international law and specific treaties. Hence, ambiguities in our country's habeas law or in the UCMJ are supposed to be resolved to make these laws consistent with such international obligations. Indeed, because the UCMJ by its terms refers to the "law of war," namely, customary international law, the Geneva Conventions and other similar sources are formally incorporated into America's positive law even if they were not self-executing.[67]

Notwithstanding these legal precepts, our view is that constitutional entrenchment makes a difference in how treaties, conventions, and the like interact with domestic law and with the range of discretion afforded the president and other executive actors. And entrenchment into *America's* statutory constitution requires something more than treaty commitment and international consensus—though both features can play a role in constitutional entrenchment, because following those treaty norms has network effects that informally but powerfully reinforce those norms. As a general matter, entrenchment requires a deliberative as well as popular process. By and large, we find that the Geneva norms of humane treatment and due process have been so entrenched.

One feature of the entrenchment has been the moral consensus that inhumane treatment of detained persons is wrong, but practical concerns have probably dominated moral ones. As a practical matter, mistreatment of detained persons and prisoners raises the stakes of war and other forms of conflict. Raising the stakes is a "game of chicken" that is bad for all sides. Thus, if the United States abuses soldiers or civilians from a foreign enemy (whether it be a nation like Afghanistan or a group like al Qaeda), the abuse triggers anger and retaliation on the other side and among persons sympathetic or even relatively neutral. Conversely, if the United States credibly promises humane treatment of prisoners and can cite an international consensus for it, one might expect better treatment for captured Americans than the enemy would otherwise provide. Thus, when the Eisenhower administration proposed ratification of the Geneva Conventions in 1955, Secretary of State John Foster Dulles said this: "America's participation [in the conventions] is needed to . . . enable us to invoke them for the protection of our nationals." Senator Mike Mansfield, a leading Democrat, concurred: "Without any real cost to us, acceptance of the standards provided for prisoners of war, civilians, and wounded and sick will insure improvement of the condition of our own people as compared with what had been their previous treatment."[68]

The notion of practical reciprocity created a tremendous ongoing constituency for the moral norm among Defense Department administrators because soldiers and their commanders strongly supported it, from the very beginning.

As the commander of all allied forces during World War II, General Eisenhower agreed with the Red Cross that the Germans treated American POWs more humanely than Soviet prisoners, assertedly because the United States and Germany (but not Russia) were parties to the 1929 Geneva Convention. As soon as the United States formally ratified the 1949 Geneva Conventions, the army updated its *Field Manual* to adopt Article 5 almost verbatim, and gave it a most liberal gloss. The humane treatment and due process norms of the Third Geneva Convention "appl[y] to any person not appearing to be entitled to prisoner-of-war status . . . who asserts that he is entitled to treatment as a prisoner of war." The Judge Advocate General's Handbook was similarly revised, and army regulations to this day treat the norms of the Geneva Conventions as entrenched and entitled to the broadest application. "All persons taken into custody by U.S. forces will be provided with the protections of the [Geneva Conventions] until some other legal status is determined by competent legal authority." Navy regulations have been even more liberal, directing that "individuals captured as spies or illegal combatants have the right to assert their claim of entitlement to prisoner-of-war status before a judicial tribunal and to have the question adjudicated."[69]

During the hostilities in Vietnam, the Nixon administration announced that it would treat North Vietnamese and Vietcong soldiers as entitled to the protections of the Geneva Conventions, in order to secure reciprocal protections from the other side, who considered the American soldiers to be "war criminals" because they were (from Vietnam's point of view) violating the international law of war. Among military officers, there is substantial consensus that reciprocity had a significant effect. Speaking on the fiftieth anniversary of the Geneva Conventions, Senator John McCain, a POW whose treatment violated these standards, said: "I am certain we all would have been a lot worse off if there had not been the Geneva Conventions around which an international consensus formed about some very basic standards of decency that should apply even amid the cruel excesses of war." Milt Bearden, who commanded the CIA's war in Afghanistan, reported unspeakable brutality in the way the Afghans and Russians treated each other's prisoners. When the United States entered the conflict, we insistently followed the Geneva Conventions, which in Bearden's judgment materially affected the treatment the Afghans and Russians accorded all their prisoners. As late as 2002, the State Department believed that the Geneva protections applied fully to persons such as Hekmati who were captured or detained in connection with the American invasion of Afghanistan.[70]

The negative reaction voiced publicly by military lawyers from all branches of the armed forces to the Bush-Cheney administration's position on interrogation of CIA prisoners indicates how strongly the Geneva Conventions are entrenched within the U.S. military. The judge advocate generals dissented from the administration's position that Common Article 3 does not apply to enemy combatants and that aggressive interrogation techniques are compatible with the Conventions. Their position was supported in Senate hearing testimony by both current and former military lawyers. In both cases, the military lawyers asserted that the administration's interpretation of the Geneva Conventions was fundamentally at odds with its core principles. They argued that downgrading American compliance with the Conventions exposes our service members to the grave threat of inhumane treatment at the hands of enemies, and they urged the Senate to make it clear in the Military Commissions Act of 2006 that the United States would adhere to the Geneva Conventions, in particular Common Article 3.[71]

The American people seem to agree with the approach long held by the State Department and the army, not the novel approach adopted by the Bush-Cheney administration. Opinion polls suggest approval of the humane treatment standard of the Geneva Conventions, and most people are also sympathetic to the notion that someone cannot be held forever upon the say-so of an executive department official alone. (We understand that polling results depend critically on how a question is posed, but these generalizations seem the most robust from the data described in the margin.) It is a notable irony that President Bush's Republican Party nominated as his successor a former POW who felt he benefited from the Geneva Conventions—former Captain John McCain, the senior senator from Arizona who stood up to the president and vice president and insisted on making universal the antitorture provisions of the Detainee Treatment Act of 2005. While McCain was not so vocal in defense of the Geneva Conventions during the campaign, the disappearance of the Cheney-Addington viewpoint in public discourse is evidence of the robustness of the Geneva Convention norms even in emergency times.[72]

THE ONGOING PROCESS OF PARTICULARIZING AND ENFORCING THESE COMMITMENTS

The reaffirmation of antitorture and humane treatment norms for suspected unlawful enemy combatants does not end the constitutional conversation, for the devil is always in the details. What do these norms mean in practice? In *Hamdan v. Rumsfeld*, the Supreme Court majority fractured on precisely what the Geneva Conventions require, with Justice Kennedy, the critical fifth vote, declining to particularize those requirements as applied to the original Cheney-Addington military commissions. For example, the Court majority did not say whether Common Article 3 denies the presiding officer significant discretion to remove the accused from parts of his trial. Nor did the Court say whether Common Article 3 requires the exclusion of evidence and confessions secured through torture and other illegal methods. There are dozens of questions about the process for proper military commissions that the Court did not address. Some of them are specified in Article 75 of Protocol I to the Geneva Conventions (1977), but the United States did not ratify Protocol I, and there was not a Court majority in *Hamdan* for the proposition that military commissions must (presumptively) follow the procedures set forth in Article 75.[73]

The Military Commissions Act of 2006 is, at this point, the most complete articulation of the trial process that the national security constitution affords accused unlawful enemy combatants. Both the legislative deliberations, which took extensive testimony from military lawyers (one of whom, Senator Lindsay Graham, was a sponsor of the statute), and the statutory text took account of the Third Geneva Convention in crafting the procedures owed these accused persons. The MCA explicitly negates some court-martial procedures, such as the guarantee of a speedy trial and the discovery rights an accused has for the evidence the prosecutor has in her possession (including exculpatory evidence), but does afford much more process than the 2001 executive order did. Among the procedures guaranteed by the MCA are the following:

- notice to the accused of charges against him "as soon as practicable";
- right to counsel, either a qualified civilian attorney or a military lawyer appointed to represent the accused;
- a military judge presiding over the trial, with guilt determined by a military tribunal, where conviction would require assent of two-thirds of the members;
- a right against self-incrimination and the exclusion of statements obtained by torture, but statements obtained through techniques short of torture and pre-DTA statements could be admitted if the presiding judge felt they would serve the "interests of justice";
- rights of the accused and his counsel to compulsory process to secure evidence and witnesses, to present evidence at trial, to cross-examine witnesses;
- discretion of the presiding judge to admit evidence if it has "probative value to a reasonable person," specifically including some hearsay evidence and evidence secured without a warrant;
- conviction by vote of two-thirds of the members of the tribunal; and
- limited judicial review of tribunal verdicts by the D.C. Circuit.

Congress believed these procedures met the requirements of Common Article 3 of the Geneva Conventions.[74]

It is hard to evaluate these procedures in the abstract, for their ultimate fairness will depend on how well they are implemented in actual trials, a point Justice Kennedy made in *Hamdan*. Dozens of detainees were released after the MCA, usually because the administration preferred release to the embarrassment of a hearing without admissible evidence. Although there were some hearings, with releases as well as decisions not to release, many procedural questions remained unanswered. Among them was the circumstances under which torture-induced confessions would taint prosecutions.[75]

While reaffirming our nation's commitment to the Geneva norms in general and Common Article 3 in particular, the MCA also directed the president to reevaluate the interrogation methods used by the CIA and other agencies. On July 20, 2007, President Bush issued such an order, concluding that the CIA's interrogation program "fully complies" with the standards of Common Article 3, which the administration interpreted to allow humiliating and degrading treatment of prisoners so long as it is not done in a manner "so serious that any reasonable person, considering the circumstances, would deem the acts to be beyond the bounds of human decency." This strikes us as a vague and lenient standard that does not live up to the Geneva norms, but again the devil is in the details, and in this case there is already a lot of evidence that the CIA interrogation program in action flunks International Law 101. CIA Director Michael Hayden admitted to Congress in February 2008 that the agency used waterboarding on Khalid Mohammed and other prisoners—a technique that Louise Arbour, the U.N. high commissioner for human rights, immediately condemned as torture in violation of the U.N. Convention. We now know that Mohammed was waterboarded on 183 separate occasions in March 2003, and that new evidence provides additional support for Arbour's assessment. If not torture, these are probably inhumane methods disapproved by the Geneva Conventions and the U.N. Torture Convention. As our book goes to press in January 2010, the Obama administration is revising the standards the CIA can use in interrogations.[76]

In the wake of the Detainee Treatment Act, *Hamdan*, and the Military Commissions Act, the army also returned to the drawing board, with more positive results. In September 2006, the army issued a new *Field Manual on Intelligence Operations*, which unequivocally embraced the Geneva norm of humane treatment. Explaining the new document's repudiation of the CIA's approach, Lieutenant John Kimmons said: "No good intelligence is going to come from abusive practices." Former military personnel have favorably contrasted the army's manual with the vague and lenient standards announced for the CIA. The army has also stood by its longstanding position that any enemy combatants it captures should be accorded presumptive POW status and the protections of Article 5 of the Geneva Convention, until a competent tribunal has decided otherwise. A product of long experience as well as thoughtful deliberation from many different perspectives, the army's field manual has guided the Obama administration as it has been setting new standards for the CIA and other agencies.[77]

It is notable that the highly Schmittian Bush-Cheney administration had to bow to the rule of law during a period of emergency and fear, at some odds with Schmittian theory. This is a remarkable achievement, and one coupled with serious public deliberation suggesting new processes (often balancing away some privacy protections) for better defenses against terrorism. Not only is the strong version of Carl Schmitt's hypothesis wrong, even more modest versions of it turn out to be overstated. Mass detentions without careful attention to danger and culpability were repudiated, and determined officials were forced by the rule of law to release men they deeply feared. Outright torture was generally avoided even by the most determined Cheneyites, and abusive interrogation techniques embraced by the administration were rolled back, again thanks to the rule of law. Illegal wiretapping probably had a more rational purpose than detention and torture, but it too was brought within the rule of law in the right way—after public and congressional deliberation that was problem solving in focus, open and largely transparent, and seriously considered the larger constitutional issues of privacy as well as national security.

So is this a happy constitutional ending? Not quite.

As a result of being subjected to aggressive interrogation techniques and then solitary confinement since 2006, Salim Ahmed Hamdan deteriorated both physically and mentally. He was virtually driven out of his mind by the conditions of his confinement. In 2007, his lawyers indicated that Hamdan was no longer capable of cooperating in his own defense, but in 2008 he was tried for various war crimes by a tribunal constituted under the MCA. Defense counsel objected to secret evidence, to evidence they claimed had been procured by torture, and to other procedural shortcuts. The jury of military officers acquitted Hamdan of the most serious war crime charges but convicted him of conspiracy, which is not a war crime under international law but is a crime under the MCA. The presiding judge imposed a sentence of sixty months for the crime. Salim Hamdan had already been imprisoned, under brutal conditions, for more than sixty months. In *Boumediene v. Bush* (2008), the Supreme Court struck down that part of the MCA denying persons in Hamdan's situation the right of habeas corpus, and Hamdan then sought release on habeas, after serving a period of torture-laced detention that exceeded his sentence. Although the Bush-Cheney administration persisted in its claim that Hamdan was an illegal enemy combatant, the Department of Defense transferred him to his native country (Yemen) in November 2008 and released him on January 8, 2009.

It remains unclear how much the detention process has harmed this man, physically, emotionally, and spiritually.[78]

For his part, Abdul Razzaq Hekmati was unable to benefit from the Supreme Court's decision in *Hamdan*, from the new procedures afforded by Congress's 2006 statutory response, or from the Supreme Court's decision in *Boumediene*. On December 30, 2007, Hekmati died in Guantánamo. Unlike Hamdan, he was of sound mind. Unlike the detainees human rights groups claim have died from torture while in American custody, Hekmati died of what appear to be natural causes, namely, cancer. Yet it remains tragic that a man independent sources have shown to be an Afghan hero, an ally of democracy, and precisely the kind of leader that America should want to support in the Middle East, spent the last five years of his life in captivity, hemmed in by fabricated charges, unhelpful procedures, and a bureaucracy of fear. The government shipped Hekmati's body back to Afghanistan, where it was buried in Kandahar. In a final chapter that only Kafka could have imagined, neither his widow nor his surviving son, Hekmatullah, attended Abdul Razzaq Hekmati's funeral. The son was in hiding. "He is scared of the Taliban and scared of the government and the Americans, because the Americans took his innocent father and they could take him, too."[79]

CONCLUSION: CONSTITUTIONAL HORTICULTURE: DELIBERATION-RESPECTING JUDICIAL REVIEW

Engineering and architectural metaphors dominate discussion of Large "C" Constitutionalism by both political scientists and law professors. The dominant image is one of architects who design a Constitution, which is then constructed or built according to the design and is supposed to be interpreted to carry out that design. These metaphors have largely supplanted the older Aristotelian metaphor of a constitution as "the life of the city," a pragmatic description of social norms and practices that have become entrenched in a society. The newer architectural metaphors have more bite for modern political problems, which assume that by creating a well-designed written Constitution some important social project (such as liberal rights, markets, or democracy) can be realized or encouraged.

There is more than one way of thinking about Constitutional "design," however. One can take an engineering perspective, where the designer hardwires the system to proceed in a certain way and then turns it loose, like a well-made watch or machine. An engineering perspective focuses on the moment of design; whether that moment is when the Constitutional text was formulated (as in Philadelphia, 1787) or is ratified (by the states in 1787–89), it is usually a period of time confined to months or a few years. Another perspective, suggested to us by political theorist Peter Ordeshook, is *horticultural*, where the designer plants a garden, whose plan changes as the plants develop and receive further attention from the gardener, her agents, and her successors. Thus the Constitution plants institutions, gives them powers or duties, and announces rights. The general purposes, powers, and rights sprout and grow, taking form as they are cultivated by the implementing persons and institutions. The full-grown Constitutional trees adapt to climatic changes (or not) and if successful flourish and reproduce. In contrast to the engineering perspective where the designer can be a stranger—a clockmaker who designs the mechanism and leaves it to function as planned—the horticultural perspective requires that the designer and her successors be stakeholders with an ongoing relationship to the design.[1]

The horticultural perspective emphasizes what is patently true in political life—that deliberation about what we should do is open ended and never definitively ends. As one of us said long ago, "there is no last word in politics." And that's not only a fact but a good thing. This implies that the set of legitimate deliberative participants is also open ended and that there is no moral priority among them. The framers had much to say about our Constitution, as did the ratifiers, but so have all the intervening generations. And so will our children and others yet to come. The small "c" constitution is, as Jed Rubenfeld has reminded us, a kind of compact extended through time.[2]

The horticulture metaphor is one that potentially captures the imagination of many American citizens, including Augustina (Sally) Durán Armendáriz. She was born (1942) and raised in Gilroy, California, the garlic capital of America, and so an appropriate (redolent) spot for the horticulture metaphor. The daughter of Mexican American field workers, Durán Armendáriz has worked as a paralegal assistant for most of her adult life. When she suffered complications with her first pregnancy in 1970, she took time off from work—but the state unemployment compensation fund refused to cover her disability because it involved *pregnancy*, which it did not cover. Durán Armendáriz was one of the plaintiffs in *Geduldig v. Aiello* (1973), discussed in chapter 1. She was dismayed by the Supreme Court opinion dismissing her Constitutional claim in a rather mechanical fashion, on the ground that her discrimination did not strictly rest upon a sex-based classification. How could nine elderly men say that discrimination on the basis of *pregnancy* was not a *sex* discrimination? At least Congress got it right, in the Pregnancy Discrimination Act of 1978, and the California legislature did, too, as it repealed the pregnancy exclusion soon after *Geduldig*.[3]

From the perspective of Americans like Sally Durán Armendáriz, the Constitution ought to be viewed horticulturally, as planting a garden that she and other Americans have been tending and revising for more than two centuries. As women have become stakeholders in the modern American garden, the plan needs to accommodate this fact—and the state needs to accommodate pregnancy lest it denigrate and mistreat half of the gardeners in our polity. Moreover, this was precisely the conclusion reached by the Equal Employment Opportunity Commission (EEOC), which deliberated about the issue for several years before issuing its Sex Discrimination Guidelines in 1972, which treated pregnancy discrimination as illegal sex discrimination. On the other hand, the horticultural perspective helps explain and perhaps even justify the Supreme Court's reluctance to Constitutionalize the EEOC's stance. Making pregnancy discrimination illegal was a major step for the polity. Congress had never deliberated about the matter, and most states in 1973 did discriminate in some way or another. There was a great deal of uncertainty as to the costs and consequences of a broad rule, and the Court declined to cut off democratic deliberation on this important topic in *Geduldig*. Large "C" Constitutional law, as announced by the Supreme Court, almost never trumps entrenched constitutional arrangements, rarely ventures beyond public consensus, and seldom corrects injustices that the political system wants to preserve. This makes some horticultural sense out of *Geduldig*, though much less out of *General Electric Co. v. Gilbert* (1976), where the Court extended the Constitutional holding to Title VII and squarely rejected the EEOC's pragmatic approach to that superstatute.[4]

The horticultural point of *Geduldig* is that the fashioning of the American garden is the job of We the People and is usually entrusted to our elected officials, as well as to administrative agencies. As such, constitutional deliberation about the shape and content of that garden is never ending. Consistent with this notion, judicial review has repeatedly (re)interpreted the Large "C" Constitution to accommodate popularly accepted federal superstatutes and state statutory convergences. As we have shown in this book, the Court has upheld against Constitutional attack unprecedented and legally questionable congressional enactments such as the Voting Rights Act of 1965, which essentially placed the South into receivership for franchise purposes (chapter 2); the application of the Sherman Act of 1890 to intrastate conspiracies (chapter 3); the various titles of the Social Security Act of 1935 (chapter 5); the Army Corps of Engineers' wetlands regulations under the Clean Water Act of 1972 (chapter 6); the Bank of the United States and the creation of legal tender not backed by gold (chapter 7); the Immigration and Naturalization Service's application of a statutory "psychopathic personality" exclusion to gay and bisexual aliens (chapter 8); and the summary procedures for dealing with illegal enemy combatants permitted by the 1916 Articles of War (chapter 9). What makes *Geduldig* different from these earlier examples is that California's pregnancy-based discrimination was in 1973 an old policy under attack, rather than a new policy initiative that the country needed to experiment with.

Conversely, the never-ending constitutional deliberation we describe sometimes provides new Constitutional bite, as old practices are overtaken by new deliberated consensuses. Thus, the Supreme Court has applied open-textured Constitutional guarantees aggressively to codify state and federal statutory convergences when it has struck down outlier laws barring married couples from using contraceptives (chapter 4); criminalizing "homosexual sodomy" (chapter 8); and denying accused felons access to attorneys (chapter 9). What makes *Geduldig* different from these earlier examples is that there was no statutory convergence in 1973 around the precept that pregnancy-based discrimination was impermissible; the issue was skirted in the congressional and state debates over the Equal Rights Amendment. As it did in *Gilbert*, the Court has been willing to override agency interpretations that are more aggressive than the justices felt our legal traditions and congressional authorizations permitted; we have provided other examples of such judicial go-slow decisions in the arenas of antitrust (chapter 3), environmental law (chapter 6), and national security (chapter 9).

Thus, our study of the statutory constitution adds further support, across a number of subject areas, to the political science account of a Supreme Court that gets along by going along with the public consensus reflected in popular, long-term statutory regimes. Our account also renders us less alarmed than critics such as Dean Larry Kramer, who assails the Court's rhetoric and its occasional activism as a challenge to popular sovereignty. "We the Court," Kramer warns, seeks to replace "We the People" as the Constitutional sovereign. It is true that the Court frequently strikes down outlying state rules and sometimes strikes down federal statutes on technical proceduralist grounds, as illustrated in the federalism cases of the Rehnquist Court (1986–2005). Also, the Court's reasoning in both the strike downs and the upholdings has a channeling effect on political discourse and sometimes even on public policy. We think the Court's effect comes as much from restrictive statutory interpretations as from its Constitutional activism.[5]

We also disagree with Mark Tushnet's argument that there is some urgent need to *take* the Constitution away from the Court. Like our response to Dean Kramer, we'd say to Professor Tushnet that the Court's Constitutional activism can easily be overstated and that most of the justices' activist moves find support in congressional enactments and popular opinion. We provide a few examples of unjustified activism in this Conclusion, but our larger project illustrates how exceptional these activist moments have been. More important, even if the Court lost its authority to engage in Constitutional review, its residual authority to review agency regulations would have much the same effect. Under the aegis of statutory review, the Court would enforce its understanding of small "c" constitutional values, including Large "C" Constitutional rules and notions.[6]

Even if there is no value added by judicial review, We the People are not going to take it away, à la Tushnet, nor is the Supreme Court going to give it up. In that event, is there a conceptual payoff that a statute-based horticultural understanding offers Constitutional theory? We think there is. A central dilemma is that the outdated Constitution is almost impossible to change through the Article V process, leaving Constitutional evolution to the potentially countermajoritarian and out-of-touch discretion of unelected judges. We the People are therefore caught between the Scylla of Constitutional ossification and the Charybdis of Court tyranny. In a very American (that is to say, *practical*) way, the Supreme Court has steered the Constitution between Scylla and Charybdis by confining most of its activism to aggressive statutory interpretations that can be overridden by legislation and by paying careful attention to America's constitution of statutes when the justices exercise their judicial review power. As to the latter point, statutory convergences and success stories provide excellent guideposts for judges because they are *legal* sources of the sort that judges are skilled at analyzing and integrating; because they are relatively *democratic* in the accountability their authors and agents have to the citizenry; and because they are *robust* in light of deliberative inputs from multiple institutional sources over a period of time. In other words, statute-based constitutionalism enables judge-based Constitutionalism to do its job without harm to our constitutional democracy.

Indeed, it is high time for otherwise competing theories of judicial review to converge on the axiom that legislative and administrative constitutionalism does play *and* ought to play a critical role in the operation of judicial Constitutionalism. Our primary thesis is that Constitutional judicial review ought to be *deliberation-respecting*. Deliberation-respecting review takes the state as well as national deliberative process seriously, as having significant normative force when judges evaluate the Constitutionality of its products (laws and policies). Thus, the Court ought to give the benefit of every Constitutional doubt to a superstatute, such as the Social Security Act of 1935, a thoughtful response to an important social problem adopted after intense public debate and congressional deliberation. When applying the open-textured provisions of the Constitution—those protecting free speech, equal protection, due process, and the like—the Court should consider the deliberated responses of Congress and state legislatures over time before striking down outlying municipal or state measures. One form of deliberation-respecting judicial review occurs when the Court essentially remands an issue to Congress because it has apparently not focused on Constitutional norms and duties, but we should sharply distinguish deliberation-respecting review from that which is deliberation-*forcing*, where the Court treats the legislative process like a lower court and imposes fact finding and other requirements. Like John Hart Ely's representation-reinforcing theory, our approach is reluctant to enforce hard substantive limits on the political process.[7]

A deliberation-respecting role is most consistent with the institutional and civic republicanism with which we started this book. In most instances, that means the Court should defer to laws and policies that reflect the deliberated views of Congress and the president, the balance of state legislatures, or the people themselves, when they have spoken clearly enough. We are not prepared to say that the Court should never enforce hard Constitutional limits on the political process, but our theory does suggest that the Court ought generally to enforce hard limits in a soft way. If the Court believes it should be pushing back against congressional, presidential, or (most likely) agency initiatives, its best strategy is to do so in a way that allows and even invites further congressional, presidential, or agency deliberation. Such review can be accomplished through narrow interpretations of statutes, Constitution-based canons of construction, or Constitutional review that leaves the political branches options for responding. This form of judicial review also preserves the possibility of efficacious popular feedback, and for that reason is more consistent with democratic premises. To be sure, such a deliberation-*inducing* mode of judicial review protects the status quo against innovations, for it reverses the burden of political inertia: a narrow statutory interpretation will be hard to override if supported by either political party, the chief executive, or powerful interest groups.

Although we reject Professor Tushnet's provocative notion of denying the Supreme Court and the judiciary any power of judicial review, the deliberation-respecting theory that we derive from legislative and administrative constitutionalism is broadly consistent with the concerns of popular constitutionalism, although our theory rests upon a longer back-and-forth process involving popular and expert proposals, statutory enactments, administrative implementation, and popular responses. Deliberation-respecting judicial review most consistent with theories of judicial review that emphasize institutional dialogue, such as those posed by Bruce Ackerman, Robert Burt, Michael Dorf and Barry Friedman, Oona Hathaway, Martha Minow, Victoria Nourse, Robert Post and Reva Siegel, and other theorists mentioned in chapter 1.[8]

Moreover, deliberation-respecting theory helps plug large normative holes in the older and more established theories of judicial review. Original meaning theories, for example, are popular justifications for judicial review but are hard to implement as a practical matter. As we demonstrate below, statutory constitutionalism provides a more objective and democratically responsive method for judges to apply ambiguous original Constitutional meaning to modern problems. Other theories of judicial review apply common law precepts, which judges are adept at using but which raise legitimacy problems. Superstatutes and state statutory convergences provide useful and democratically accountable precedents to guide judges applying Constitutional common law. Under a common law approach to Constitutional rights, judges should be highly reluctant to strike down laws reflecting constitutional consensus, and less reluctant to strike down laws that have become constitutional outliers. Finally, critical theories celebrate the Court's countermajoritarian role, but such a role is one fraught with institutional risk for the "least dangerous branch." Our suggestion is that the Court's power to challenge majoritarian policies is best played out through deliberation-*inducing* moves, namely, decisions that invite or require Congress and the political process to respond after further deliberation and popular feedback—and not through deliberation-*ending* moves, namely, judicial vetoes on what Congress and the states can do in response to important public problems.

DELIBERATION-RESPECTING ORIGINAL MEANING REVIEW

From the perspective of most Americans, judicial review is important because it guarantees rights and the governance structure laid out in the U.S. Constitution. Consistent with this value, the most accessible theory of Constitutional interpretation is that judges should apply the text and principles of the sacred text of our civic religion. Its central aspirations are easy to apprehend and have proven quite workable. For example, the Constitution assures that state statutes will be the default regulation for most Americans (Article I; Amendments IX–X) and demands that each state have a "Republican Form of Government" (Article IV, Section 4). It requires states to accord comity to each another's judgments (Article IV) and implicitly bars the states from disrupting interstate trade or commerce (Article I, Sections 8, 10). The Constitution also creates the primary organs of national governance and the famous system of checks and balances to prevent any branch from monopolizing governance (Articles I–III). It defines the process by which federal statutes are adopted (Article I, Section 7), enforced (Articles II, Sections 1, 3; III, Section 1), and amended or repealed (Article I, Section 7). Not least important, the Constitution defines a wide range of individual rights that state and federal governments must respect (Article I, Section 9; the Bill of Rights and other amendments). Responsibility for respecting these rights is vested in all federal officials; federal and state courts are vested with judicial review authority to give most Constitutional rights and some responsibilities enforcement bite (Articles III and VI). The main requirements of the Constitution are apparent from reading its text, and many ambiguities can be cleared up by reading the document as a whole and by reference to historical circumstances. Constitutional rules and structure pervasively influence and affect constitutional politics and, perhaps, create optimal conditions for its flourishing.[9]

Many of the greatest judges in American history, from Chief Justice John Marshall to Justices Joseph Story, Joseph Bradley, Oliver Wendell Holmes Jr., Louis Brandeis, Harlan Stone, Hugo Black, Robert Jackson, and John Harlan, have followed such a text-based or structural approach to Constitutional interpretation.

Even legal academics, unfairly stereotyped as woolly headed zealots seeking to read *New York Times* values into the Constitution, typically advocate theories of interpretation that are grounded primarily in the document's text, structure, and principles. Recent scholars advancing such theories are ideologically diverse, including Akhil Reed Amar, Curtis Bradley, Steven Calabresi, Vicki Jackson, John Manning, Victoria Nourse, Michael Stokes Paulsen, Saikrishna Prakash, Suzanna Sherry, William Michael Treanor, Carlos Vázquez, Robin West, John Yoo, and Ernest Young. But how should the Constitution's text and structure be read? Ambiguities resolved? Text- and structure-oriented scholars pose a variety of answers, often framed in the engineering mode described earlier. What we argue here is that the horticultural mode is a more useful way of understanding and applying text-based Constitutional precepts and principles.[10]

Original meaning theories face a dilemma nicely documented in the recent empirical volume published by political scientist Nathan Persily and his colleagues. Across a number of subject areas, Professor Persily's group found that Americans are committed to two notions that seem to be in conflict: they want judges to enforce the Constitution according to the plain meaning of its text and, when the text is vague, according to original meaning or some other majoritarian criterion—but they also want judges to enforce Constitutional values that We the People *today* find admirable and useful. As Judge Robert Bork learned in his Supreme Court confirmation hearings, dogmatic original meaning theories can be vulnerable under the terms of this paradox. Statutory constitutionalism as we have presented it in this book offers a workable way for original meaning and other textual theories of Constitutionalism to address this paradox: judges should read and understand the text, structure, and history of the Constitution against the public law landscape shaped by state statutory convergences and, especially, federal superstatutes. This kind of deliberation-respecting judicial review is the best way to carry out original meaning or structural jurisprudence in a republic of statutes. And it is not unusual for the most dogmatic originalist to justify his understanding of original design through the dynamic prism of statutory constitutionalism.[11]

Consider a hot-off-the-presses example of our point. Since 1976, District of Columbia gun control laws have not only required that handguns be registered but have essentially barred the possession of loaded handguns in the home. A police officer challenged this regulation as inconsistent with the Second Amendment, which says: "A well regulated Militia, being necessary to the security of a free State, *the right of the people to keep and bear Arms, shall not be infringed.*" The District argued that the Second Amendment's Constitutional protections extend no further than the militia context; that is, the operative clause (*italicized*) is limited by the purpose clause that precedes it. The District's argument was supported by Supreme Court precedent and by the interpretive presumption that every phrase or word in the Constitution should be read to add something. (If the operative clause were read broadly, the purpose clause would be surplusage; the Second Amendment would mean exactly the same thing if it were dropped out.) Yet in an opinion by über-textualist Justice Antonin Scalia, the Supreme Court in *District of Columbia v. Heller* (2008) read the operative clause to recognize a judicially enforceable right for law-abiding citizens to possess firearms within the home for self-defense. Under that reading, the District's restriction violated the Constitution.[12]

To escape the force of the rule against surplusage and the weight of precedent, Justice Scalia relied heavily on original meaning. His main argument was that Englishmen of the eighteenth century, including the colonists, understood that a central protection against tyranny was the existence of an armed citizenry and that the Second Amendment should be read to codify that understanding. Although his *Heller* opinion is the most detailed display of originalist jurisprudence by a majority opinion in the Court's history, it is an incomplete analysis of the meaning the Second Amendment's language actually carried with it for eighteenth-century Americans. According to most professional linguists and historians familiar with that period, "bear arms" was almost always used in the eighteenth century to mean use of weapons in a military context; hence, the Second Amendment's original linguistic or political meaning was to allow citizens to "keep" military weapons insofar as needed to "bear" them in military service. This reading has the virtue of being consistent with the purpose clause's emphasis on a citizen militia. And it is consistent with, even if a narrower reading of, the armed-citizens-as-bulwark-of-liberty tradition described in Justice Scalia's opinion. Moreover, such a reading is supported by the drafting history of the Second Amendment and by the contrast with the broader language of the Revolutionary-era Pennsylvania and Vermont Declarations of Rights, which protected the people's "right to bear arms for the defence of themselves and the state," without any mention of militia service.[13]

Finally, it is striking that Scalia's opinion for the Court said, in dicta, that the federal government can impose registration requirements, regulate interstate shipment and public displays or concealment of guns, bar convicted felons from owning guns, and prohibit the use of particularly dangerous firearms. Ironically, Scalia rewrote the Second Amendment *both* to render the purpose clause surplusage *and* to weaken the operative clause, for the federal government is, on his account, authorized to "infringe" on the right to "keep" or "bear" arms in lots of ways. Written under the strictures of Ockham's Razor, here is how the Second Amendment would have to read in order to fit the *Heller* opinion: "The right of law-abiding people to keep small Arms in their homes, for self-defense purposes, shall not be subjected to unreasonable regulation." Notice how different the *virtual* Second Amendment is from the *actual* Second Amendment. Notice also how the Second Amendment has morphed into a privacy right remarkably similar to the one the Supreme Court recognized in *Griswold v. Connecticut* (1965), an opinion that Justice Scalia considers the antithesis of original meaning.[14]

If you focus on the original eighteenth-century Second Amendment, *Heller* is hard to defend—a point Scalia himself realized, for much of his opinion was devoted to much more recent nineteenth- and some twentieth-century evidence of "original meaning." That discussion suggests that something horticultural was influencing the majority justices. Justice Stevens, in dissent, chided the majority for relying heavily on what he calls "post-enactment history," but we offer the following defense that Justice Scalia can—and ought—to draw from the theory in this book. America's small "c" constitution has long given special recognition to a citizen's right to keep a gun to protect family and home. In 1765, Blackstone said that "the right of having and using arms for self-preservation and defence" in the English Bill of Rights of 1689 was one of the fundamental rights of Englishmen, and this point was widely recognized in early state constitutions as well as the debates over the ratification of the U.S. Constitution. Although it is *not* clear that this guarantee of America's eighteenth-century common law constitution applied rigidly outside the militia context, that issue was not posed to America's founders, because of the close connection among citizenship, service in the militia, and protection of the home (in an era before municipal police forces and when almost everyone lived in small towns or rural areas). How did America's small "c" constitution change once this close connection faded? After municipal police forces and the federal standing armed forces supplanted the militia, did We the People abandon the notion of an individual right to keep guns in the home for self-protection? These are relevant questions from a horticultural point of view.[15]

We have no dogmatic view on how to answer these questions, which were posed and cogently analyzed in the separate dissenting opinion by Justice Breyer. But we observe that there is not only much small "c" constitutional support for Justice Scalia's resolution, but that such support probably influenced the Justices who constituted the Court majority. As an *amicus* brief from Members of Congress (including the vice president in his capacity as president of the Senate) documented, the Reconstruction Congress as well as Congresses throughout the twentieth century explicitly recognized a fundamental right to gun ownership to protect home and family, at the same time Congress was imposing a wide array of regulations under its authority over the District of Columbia or its Commerce Clause power. America's small "c" constitution has evolved in its stance toward gun ownership and regulation, and it has evolved through a democratic process that has repeatedly affirmed that there is a modest arena, the home, where state regulatory interests are outweighed by our tradition of individual rights.[16]

In 1892, after municipal police forces had replaced state militias, Congress made it a crime in the District of Columbia (over which Congress has plenary jurisdiction) to carry a concealed pistol, except in one's business and "dwelling house." Permits for carrying concealed weapons in public were available for "necessary self-defense." A brief legislative discussion suggested that senators were sensitive to a citizen's "natural right to carry the arms which are necessary to secure their persons and their lives." In 1932, Congress imposed extensive regulations on gun use and ownership in the District but explicitly left possession of handguns in the home unregulated. The committee reports noted that "the right of an individual to possess a pistol in his home or on land belonging to him would not be disturbed by this bill."[17]

Although Congress enacted important national gun control legislation in 1927 and 1934, legislators apparently did not believe they were violating the core protections of the Second Amendment. The legislators' balance between public safety and private sanctuary was explicit in the Property Requisition Act of 1941, enacted on the eve of our entry into World War II. The act authorized the president to requisition private property for national defense purposes, but Congress stipulated that the act not be construed "to authorize the requisitioning or require the registration of any firearms possessed by any individual for his personal protection or sport" or "to impair or infringe in any manner the right of any individual to keep and bear arms." In the extensive debate over requisitioning or registration of firearms, members of Congress insisted upon these caveats for Second Amendment reasons. Although hunting was repeatedly mentioned, the primary justification was that a hallmark of totalitarian (Nazi and Communist) regimes was disarming citizens. Accordingly, to distinguish our liberty-protecting constitutionalism from theirs, Congress reaffirmed the individual's right to "the private ownership of firearms and the right to use weapons in the protection of his home, and thereby his country."[18]

The Gun Control Act of 1968 creates Congress's primary national regime for firearm regulation. This is a broad and "infringing" regime, but Congress rejected proposals for nationwide registration of handguns, and the 1968 act is notable for *not* regulating gun ownership by law-abiding citizens for self-defense or home use. Section 101 of the statute says that "it is not the purpose of this title to place any undue or unnecessary Federal restrictions or burdens on law-abiding citizens with respect to the acquisition, possession, or use of firearms appropriate to the purpose of hunting, trapshooting, target shooting, personal protection, or any other lawful activity." Although this is the sort of cheap talk Congress often engages in for political purposes, it does help explain the regulatory choices made in the statute Congress enacted. Indeed, in the Firearms Owners' Protection Act of 1986, Congress amended the 1968 act in minor ways to further protect "the rights of citizens to keep and bear arms under the second amendment."[19]

Accordingly, Justice Scalia's "original meaning" is a meaning that has, horticulturally, been teased out over time and accepted by a succession of Congresses. The best defense of *Heller* is statutory constitutionalism of the sort we are defending. We are still inclined to dissent from the majority's activism, however, and the reason is that the nation is still experimenting with gun regulation. Much of the regulation is probably inefficacious and may even be counterproductive, but the fact is that we do not know exactly what works and what does not work. Local experiments are a good way to test hypotheses and gauge public reactions. In this respect, there is a significant *deliberation-ending* feature to *Heller* that justifies the dissenters' position. Thus, we applaud Justice Scalia's dynamic, horticultural approach to original meaning but regret that he still insisted on cutting off the District's effort to regulate guns in the home as well as on the street.

Consider another gun-related issue where the Supreme Court has applied original meaning theory aggressively. The framers of the Constitution probably contemplated that firearms regulations, if any, would be concentrated at the state level, yet Congress has long regulated gun ownership and use pursuant to its Article I Commerce Clause authority. After decades of ever-expanding firearms laws, Congress enacted the Gun-Free School Zones Act of 1990, which made it a federal crime "knowingly to possess a firearm" in a "school zone," defined to include spaces within one thousand feet of a school. Did Congress have authority to enact such a law? In a Constitutional Surprise, the Supreme Court said it did not. Chief Justice Rehnquist's opinion for the Court in *United States v. Lopez* (1995) emphasized the fact that Congress made no effort, either on the face of the statute or in committee reports explaining its purpose, to tie the school zone bar to interstate commerce or any other national interest. Although Justice Breyer, in dissent, did an excellent job filling that legal gap, the Court's response was that judges have been doing too much of Congress's explanatory work already. So much that by 1990 Congress was behaving as though it had unlimited jurisdiction, which is not just arguably beyond its Commerce Clause power (the usual objection) but seems like a denial of the Constitutional structure. From a horticultural point of view, *Lopez* reflects a distinction between a statute where Congress could have invoked a Constitutional justification but ignored the Constitution, and a statute where Congress attended to its Constitutional duty. Thus, we would read *Lopez* as an example of deliberation-inducing review, an interpretation explicitly pressed by two concurring justices.[20]

Even our most generous reading of *Lopez* does not support the Court's decision striking down part of the Violence against Women Act of 1994 (VAWA) in *United States v. Morrison* (2000). The statute itself was a model of legislative deliberation. After four years of hearings and consultation with dozens of leading experts and task force reports on gender bias in twenty-one states, Congress found that gender-motivated violence was a serious nationwide phenomenon and had profound and growing effects on the public as well as private lives of many American citizens, especially female citizens. The costs of gender-motivated violence are borne not just by its individual victims but by society as a whole, in the form of the costs of victim treatment, lost productivity, disruption of economic activity. Estimates of the costs of gender-motivated violence ranged from three to ten *billion* dollars per year. Even though the VAWA was enacted before *Lopez*, Congress had engaged in much more deliberation than it had in the Gun-Free School Zones Act—including extensive hearings documenting the national scope of the problem of gender-motivated violence, the economic (commercial) effects of the problem, and the costs and benefits of various solutions. Although this case was therefore materially different from *Lopez*, the Supreme Court read the earlier precedent to establish a substantive rather than procedural limit on Congress's Commerce Clause authority: it could not be used to regulate "noneconomic" activities such as sexual assault. Justice David Souter's dissenting opinion lamented that this new effort to find a substantive line between conduct Congress could and could not regulate under the Commerce Clause was no more likely to succeed than earlier line-drawing tests periodically developed and periodically abandoned by previous Courts. Our account suggests that Justice Souter is right.[21]

Indeed, our theory of deliberative constitutionalism adds this argument to Justice Souter's dissent. In VAWA, Congress adhered to the Constitutional limitations on its authority and did so in a deliberative way. Chief Justice William Rehnquist's opinion for the Court imposed a new Constitutional requirement on Congress and was therefore *deliberation-forcing*—but it was deliberation-forcing in a way that Congress is ill equipped to implement. As Professors Philip Frickey and Stephen Smith have cogently argued, legislation is usually a deliberatively messy process. Where the stakes are high, as they are for most important constitutional matters, the legislative record will rarely look like the kind of judicial record *Morrison* seems to require. Evidence will be argued at a high level of generality, for attention to specifics will threaten the sponsoring coalition. Compromises and vague delegations are necessary for most such statutes to get through the legislative process. As we have argued throughout this book, the making of a superstatute only commences with its enactment; the fate of the statutory principle or policy critically rests on the implementers and the decisions they make. It is a political decision for the Supreme Court to veto VAWA for the reasons given in the chief justice's opinion. Given the lengthy record of congressional deliberations, the urgency of the problem, and the support shown VAWA by the large majority of states during the congressional hearings and in *amicus* briefs to the Court, the shift in the chief justice's reasoning from *Lopez* to *Morrison* is constitutionally lamentable.[22]

It remains to be seen how far the Supreme Court will press the aggressively substantive judicial review deployed by the *Morrison* majority. As a prescriptive matter, America's statutory constitution augurs against a substance-based stingy understanding of Congress's regulatory jurisdiction under Article I and other power-conferring provisions of the Constitution, including Section 5 of the Fourteenth Amendment (also an unsuccessfully asserted basis for Congress's regulation in *Morrison*). Likewise, our view of constitutionalism is consistent with the Court's lenient review of Congress's decisions to apply general labor, civil rights, and other laws to the states pursuant to Section 5 of the Fourteenth Amendment. Indeed, the leading case is one that upheld a family medical leave statute that is a continuing legacy of Sally Durán Armendáriz's unsuccessful Constitutional litigation and the successful statute (PDA) that emerged from that litigation. But before examining that law, we want to relate statutory constitutionalism to another set of theories about the utility and proper method for judicial review.

COMMON LAW CONSTITUTIONALISM AND STATUTES AS PRECEDENTS

Many Constitutional rights recognized by the Supreme Court are not as easily susceptible to the kind of textual and structural analysis that one might apply to Article I or (much of) the Bill of Rights. The Equal Protection and Due Process Clauses of the Fourteenth Amendment are quite open textured, and the Court has committed itself to evolutive readings of both provisions that long ago rendered Fourteenth Amendment original meaning largely irrelevant except as a potential limiting principle. Relatedly, some of the Court's structural jurisprudence has an attenuated foundation in particular provisions of the Constitution: a "dormant" or "negative" implication from the Commerce Clause that state regulation interfering with interstate commerce must be regulated; a rule against federal "commandeering" of state legislatures or executive officers (but not judicial officers) to carry out Congress's projects directly, loosely associated with the Tenth Amendment; and state immunities from lawsuits, sometimes associated with the Eleventh Amendment (which by its terms only applies to lawsuits against states by citizens of other states or foreign countries) but more properly understood as a gloss on Article III's "judicial Power." Each of these Constitutional protections, if judicially enforced, is vulnerable to the points we made in the first part of this chapter: each would be an instance of aggressive judicial review not obviously supported by the Constitutional text, original meaning, or republican deliberation. As such, our theory would suggest that the Court should be more cautious and should step back from its previous activism in some or all of these arenas.[23]

Professor Henry Paul Monaghan observes that most of the Supreme Court's Constitutional jurisprudence is old-fashioned common lawmaking. Rather than reasoning from the language of a text and its legislative history (or original meaning), the Court's opinions in equal protection, due process, dormant commerce clause, and federalism cases typically start with a review of the principles and precepts announced in precedents of the Court and then apply those principles and precepts to decide the case at hand, usually reasoning by analogy to previous judicial decisions rather than reasoning deductively from original meaning or even purpose. Professor Ernest Young has expanded this idea into a general theory of Constitutional interpretation. Such an approach "would interpret foundational texts in an incremental common-law manner, respecting without fetishizing original intent, majority decisionmaking, and bright-line rules," with precedents being both the anchors and the driving force of case-by-case Constitutional evolution. (Again, we have a standing objection to the Court's activism when there is no "foundational text," as is the case with the Dormant Commerce Clause and commandeering lines of Supreme Court decisions.)[24]

Common law Constitutionalism is an excellent example of a horticultural rather than an engineering approach to Constitutional design. Like our horticultural gloss on original meaning and structure theories above, a common law approach has the advantage of allowing Constitutional updating in a slow-but-sure incremental process that judges are skilled at performing and that reveals stability over long periods of time. As we are arguing in this book, entrenchment of a norm or framework can proceed, and perhaps best proceeds, through the interaction of institutions and the public over long periods of time. Common law Constitutionalism is, however, potentially unconnected to public feedback and therefore runs the risk of alienating fundamental law from popular sources of legitimacy. The gardeners in our horticultural metaphor are *not* only judges but also legislators, agencies, private groups, and the public at large. A substantial solution to this dilemma is obvious: America's constitution of statutes provides a mechanism for the common law Constitutionalist to solve or ameliorate this problem, for it provides practically useful, and *legal*, guideposts for the common law Constitutional judge. Indeed, we now suggest that a workable and legitimate common law Constitutionalism ought to be, and usually is in practice, deliberation-respecting.

Specifically, common law Constitutionalism ought to consider state statutory convergences, federal superstatutes, and some executive directives as *precedents* to be studied and presumptively followed in deciding how to apply open-textured Constitutional provisions or doctrines with loose textual associations. This idea is an old one. As Justice Harlan Fiske Stone put it three generations ago, there is "no adequate reason for our failure to treat a statute much more as we treat a judicial precedent, as both a declaration and source of law, and as a premise for legal reasoning." Stone was thinking about how statutes ought to guide state common law decisions, but we think the concept is even more useful in Constitutional common law, which has bigger legitimacy challenges to meet. Another reason for treating statutory convergences and superstatutes as precedents is that such judicial review is usefully deliberation-inducing in the most republican sense of that term. Because the fruits of legislative deliberation are, themselves, evidence of Constitutional meaning, that is an incentive for social movements *not* to bypass legislatures, and it is an incentive for legislatures to get involved with important normative issues rather than leaving them for judicial resolution.[25]

Under such an approach, the Court in Constitutional cases ought to pay attention to and defer to exemplary deliberations where they have occurred, as in federal superstatutes and, perhaps more weakly, state statutory convergences. In most instances, such attention will provide a reason for the justices to be cautious before they override the political process. *Heller* helps us see how this works both ways, though. Public deliberation by the Reconstruction Congress and by Congress regulating guns throughout the twentieth century repeatedly reaffirmed the norm that citizens have a fundamental right to possess handguns in the home for self-defense, and that deliberation gave support to the Court's interpretation of the ambiguous Second Amendment to recognize an individual right outside the militia context. On the other hand, decades of deliberation by Congress and the large majority of states persuaded even Justice Scalia that almost all other forms of gun regulation were valid under the Second Amendment, as revised by the Court. We believe Justice Scalia was wise to trim his judicial review in this way, for in the end it is up to We the People and our representatives to decide. Conversely, our theory contains a negative or dormant notion: where We the People have not reached a consensus one way or the other, the Court is entitled to craft its deference in more mundane ways, through passive virtues, the application of neutral principles, and the like. Thus, our bottom line in *Heller* would be to overturn the District's law through

statutory interpretation that Congress could override, rather than by announcing a bright-line rule that binds Congress as well as the District.[26]

We have already seen examples of common law Constitutionalism in this
book. The right of privacy, for example, rests upon a broad reading of the Due
Process Clause of the Fifth and Fourteenth Amendments that finds only general support in original meaning and American history. As we demonstrated in
chapter 5, the Supreme Court's leading statement of this right came in the
safest of cases, *Griswold v. Connecticut* (1965), where the justices struck down
the nation's only state law barring the private use of contraceptives by married
couples. In the wake of national deliberation and bipartisan approval of state-
supported family planning by unmarried as well as married women, the Court
expanded the *Griswold* right to unmarried couples in *Eisenstadt v. Baird* (1972).
This common law Constitutional right formed a partially cogent basis for *Roe v.
Wade* (1973): consistent with state statutory developments, nineteenth-century
abortion laws were ripe for reconsideration, but neither state nor national deliberations suggested a consensus in favor of abortion on demand. The Supreme
Court realigned the privacy right with state and federal deliberations in *Planned
Parenthood v. Casey* (1992), which reaffirmed a woman's liberty interest in pregnancy and its termination but also recognized state interests with wide deliberative support, including waiting periods, educational materials for pregnant
women, and notification requirements for minors.[27]

Chapter 8 presents an even more detailed examination of the way in which
famous Constitutional decisions depend strongly on small "c" constitutional
deliberations at the state as well as the national level. Few Supreme Court decisions have inspired more vigorous criticism and denunciation than *Bowers v.
Hardwick* (1986), but our account suggests a surprisingly cogent reason for the
Court's reluctance to expand the privacy right to include "homosexual sodomy" between consenting adults: public deliberation was not at rest on the issue. Although half the states had repealed their consensual sodomy laws, most
of the repeals were adoptions of the Model Penal Code, with no deliberation
on sodomy. Once "homosexuality" became the focal point for public deliberation about sodomy reform, even liberal states like New York and Massachusetts
were reluctant to repeal their laws, and the House of Representatives voted 281–119
to override sodomy reform in the District of Columbia (1981). With AIDS phobia at its apex, deliberation-respecting justices ought to have thought twice before overturning all sodomy laws in 1986. As in *Roe*, there was a lower-stakes
basis for Constitutional review, namely, invalidation of broad laws as void for
vagueness; such review would not have taken contentious moral issues out of
the public deliberative process but would have reversed the burden of inertia.
In any event, once AIDS phobia had peaked and gay people gained greater

acceptance, public support for consensual sodomy laws evanesced—and the Supreme Court swept the remaining laws away in *Lawrence v. Texas* (2003). As we argue in chapter 8, *Lawrence* established a regime of gay tolerance, not full equality for lesbian and gay citizens, who are continuing their equality campaign primarily around the issue of gay marriage.[28]

As illustrated by the race and sex discrimination discussion in the Introduction and chapters 1 and 2, the common law methodology is tailor-made for the Equal Protection Clause, which is open textured but clearly entails comparative judgments. If the state singles out Latino American students for humiliating treatment and even physical abuse because of their ethnicity, as Sally Durán was a generation ago, a judge's judgment about the arbitrariness of this practice or policy will be, and ought to be, influenced by the framing deliberations surrounding the Fourteenth Amendment, the anticaste purpose of the amendment, the relevance or not of this trait to legitimate educational functions, the prevalence of such policies as "official" and their success or failure, and statutory debates, amendments, and practices. *Brown* is a success story for common law Constitutionalism, as the NAACP's desegregation litigation followed the common law model to establish that race and ethnicity were *never* reliable regulatory categories connected with legitimate state interests. Its campaign persuaded the Truman and Eisenhower administrations, the President's Commission on Civil Rights, congressional committees, social scientists in this country and around the world, and state legislators outside the South, who not only abandoned the segregated schools policy but often adopted statutes positively forbidding such segregation. That institutional support, in turn, made it easier for the Supreme Court to overturn generations of de jure school segregation in *Brown*.[29]

Brown did not hold that race can never be a state classification, for the justices knew that the next big issue would be laws forbidding different-race marriages—and thirty states had such laws in 1954. This is the reason the Supreme Court properly ducked the miscegenation issue in *Naim v. Naim* (1956). But *Brown* proved to be deliberation-inducing, because it put the issue of race discrimination on the public law agenda all over the nation and also because it encouraged the efforts of civil rights groups and their allies. State legislatures everywhere outside the South revisited the marriage issue. By 1967, all but sixteen states (pretty much the same states that in 1954 had required school segregation) had repealed their miscegenation laws. Legislature after legislature decided such laws reflected unacceptable racist views or served no valid social purpose. At that point, the Warren Court unanimously struck down such laws. *Loving v. Virginia* (1967) is also the first case where the Court struck down a state law on the ground that race is a suspect classification requiring a compelling state interest.[30]

Relying on similar statutory and deliberative guideposts, feminist ACLU lawyers shortly after *Loving* argued that sex, too, is an irrational and therefore suspect classification under the Equal Protection Clause. This was a harder argument to make from the original meaning and structure of the Constitution, as the Fourteenth Amendment itself reflects a gendered understanding of citizenship and the drafters and ratifiers rejected feminist demands that sex as well as race discrimination be targeted for Constitutional disapproval. Instead, feminist litigators relied on the increasing number of state laws to that effect, and landmark sex discrimination legislation adopted by Congress between 1963 and 1972, including the Equal Pay Act of 1963, Title VII of the Civil Rights Act of 1964, and Title IX of the Education Amendments of 1972. The Court also cited Congress's overwhelming vote in favor of the Equal Rights Amendment. The Supreme Court might well have ruled that sex is a suspect classification, based upon this emerging statutory consensus, if the ERA had not been pending. Several justices believed that the Article V process should be allowed to run its course before the Court ruled. Although the ERA failed to be ratified, it achieved a remarkable vote of popular confidence: more than two-thirds of the members of Congress and state legislatures took the position that sex is a suspect classification. In a classic common law move, the Court then internalized the failed ERA's central principle into the Equal Protection Clause, while at the same time internalizing the most cogent reservations advanced by ERA opponents such as Mrs. Phyllis Schlafly.[31]

The ERA debate taught the justices that large majorities of Americans endorsed the central lesson of the proposed amendment, that sex was irrelevant to most state policies and that women should not be discriminated against based on stereotypes. So in *Craig v. Boren* (1976), the Court ruled that sex-discriminatory statutes reflecting "traditional attitudes and prejudices about the expected behavior and roles of the two sexes in our society" violated the Equal Protection Clause. Hedging its bets, in classic common law style, the Court did *not* declare sex to be a suspect classification like race, for that would have been immediately fatal to numerous sex-discriminatory policies that most Americans were not prepared to disturb and that was the basis for Mrs. Schlafly's successful STOP ERA movement. Among them were state refusals to recognize same-sex marriage (arguably a sex discrimination); the exclusion of women from combat and other positions in the armed forces; and various federal and state laws that compensated women for perceived disadvantages. Race-based marriage and military exclusions were unConstitutional in the 1970s, as were many affirmative action programs—but between 1972 and 1981 the Supreme Court explicitly upheld analogous sex-based discriminations.[32]

Legislative deliberation at both national and state levels guided the Court's common law Constitutionalism in these cases. Unlike *Brown* and *Loving*, where states everywhere but the South had repealed previous race discriminations, cases where the Court denied sex discrimination claims involved issues as to which federal and state legislative deliberation provided no basis for disapproval. Accordingly, the Supreme Court rejected sex discrimination arguments challenging (1) state bars to same-sex marriage, an easy call in a decade when not a single state recognized such marriages; (2) women's exclusion from draft registration, in light of federal statutes barring women from serving in combat, a policy military officials supported; and (3) government policies providing remedial benefits for women, in light of the endorsement of sex-conscious remediation in the Social Security Act of 1935 and many other federal and state laws. In contrast, federal and state governments had by 1976 repealed virtually all the laws excluding women from certain occupations, attendance at state colleges and universities, service on juries, and other fundamental public rights. These statutes reflected deliberate judgments by legislators and, to a certain extent, their constituents across regions and at both the state and the federal level. The Supreme Court Constitutionalized these judgments in *Craig* and subsequent cases, precedents that established a new Constitutional floor, applicable nationwide; after *Craig*, the state needed more than ordinary justifications when using sex-based classifications. Like *Loving*, this line of cases was deliberation-ending, very aggressive judicial review. For the Court's Constitutional move to work, the issues must really be ones where We the People have deliberated extensively and where public views have largely stabilized. We doubt this had occurred on the issue at stake in *Craig*; indeed, our theory provides a basis for challenging the result in *Craig* itself. The state barred men (but not women) aged eighteen to twenty-one from purchasing 2 percent beer. Although this was a sex discrimination resting on gender stereotypes, the discrimination was rationally related to the much higher accident rate of young men compared with young women.

Recall Sally Durán Armendáriz's case, *Geduldig v. Aiello* (1974). Scholars today tend to view the case as an example of nine old gentlemen who could not understand how pregnancy-based exclusions were rank sex discriminations having no place in democratic governance. That perspective does insufficient justice to the realities that common law Constitutionalism confronts. Under the perspective of this book, the pregnancy discrimination claims in the case had three Constitutional strikes against them. First, the case came to the Court just after the ERA went to the states for ratification and several years before *Craig*. Hence, the argument that the pregnancy-based exclusion bore only on women and was thereby Constitutionally suspect lacked firm support for its premise, that sex discriminations themselves are Constitutionally suspect. Second, even if *Geduldig* had come to the Court after *Craig*, California demonstrated that its program in practice paid out more compensation to female than male claimants even with the pregnancy exclusion. In our view, this does not refute the core sex discrimination argument, but most of the Burger Court justices felt it took the edge off such a claim, because it was not clear to them that women as a group were disadvantaged by the program. Third, there was no statutory consensus that pregnancy discrimination was a form of illegitimate or baseless discrimination. This was a wide-ranging policy issue, for countless employers, banks, and other institutions did consider pregnancy when they made hires, promotions, loans, and other decisions. State legislatures had not addressed these issues, nor had Congress. Although the EEOC had issued a pregnancy discrimination guideline under Title VII, employers claimed that guideline was inconsistent with Congress's own deliberations in 1964 and with advice the EEOC was giving before 1972.[33]

As chapter 1 recounted, the Court followed *Geduldig* in the subsequent Title VII case of *General Electric Co. v. Gilbert* (1976). In light of the EEOC's thoughtful guideline, *Gilbert* strikes us as a misguided statutory interpretation decision. That is, however defensible *Geduldig* was under a cautious and deliberation-respecting theory of judicial review, *Gilbert* was less defensible, because the EEOC had engaged in a thoughtful deliberative process in its role implementing Title VII. In any event, *Gilbert* proved to be deliberation-inducing, as it galvanized the women's movement to press for national pregnancy-protective legislation; the ensuing public debate yielded the Pregnancy Discrimination Act of 1978 (PDA). The statute responded to the unfair hardships pregnancy discriminations imposed upon working mothers, but had a broader agenda. Congress in the PDA recognized that workplace pregnancy discriminations often reflected gender stereotypes, whereby employers assumed that women would quit work after they had children. The PDA's goal was to assure female employees genuinely equal workplace treatment and opportunities and to create conditions and mindsets more conducive to women's equal citizenship. The stakes of workplace pregnancy discrimination were quite high. With support cutting across party, regional, and ideological lines, Congress overrode the Court with the PDA, and the Court has sometimes given the statute a broad reading. States have amended their antidiscrimination laws to follow the PDA. California also repealed its pregnancy exclusion from the unemployment compensation law, but assume that California were to revive such a law. The California law in Durán Armendáriz's case would not violate the precise terms of the PDA, which applies only to employment decisions, not state programs.

Would it now violate the Constitution? Or would the Court for *stare decisis* reasons follow *Geduldig*?

Common law courts will overrule precedents that have grown out of sync with the broad fabric of the modernizing common law, and we think such a fate ought to befall *Geduldig*. California revoked its pregnancy discrimination soon after winning the Constitutional case, and the large majority of state compensation plans no longer exclude pregnant women. Both federal and state workplace discrimination laws consider pregnancy a largely inadmissible criterion, as a sex discrimination. The normative case against pregnancy discrimination made out to Congress by Sue Ross, Wendy Williams, and other leaders of the Campaign to End Discrimination against Pregnant Workers remains fresh and persuasive today. Indeed, the Supreme Court has implicitly recognized its force. When Congress included state employers in the Family Medical Leave Act of 1993 (FMLA), it was acting under its Fourteenth Amendment authority to "enforce" the Equal Protection Clause. The Supreme Court has ruled that Congress can only enforce the Fourteenth Amendment against violations as defined by the Court's precedents. (In light of that requirement, it is noteworthy that the PDA's Constitutionality as applied to state employers has not been seriously disputed.) Nevada argued that Congress was not remedying equality violations as defined by *Geduldig*. Although ignoring *Geduldig*, Solicitor General Ted Olson rested the government's case on evidence that state as well as private workplaces still presented unequal conditions for men and women, with women still stereotyped as less reliable employees because they would devote relatively more time to bearing and raising children. The PDA, Olson argued, was an incomplete *Constitutional* remedy—and six justices agreed. Ironically, the opinion for the Court in *Nevada Department of Human Resources v. Hibbs* (2002) was written by Chief Justice William Rehnquist, who had written *Gilbert* a generation earlier.[34]

Chief Justice Rehnquist accepted Congress's constitutional rationale for the FMLA and treated it as a Constitutional rationale as well: "Historically, denial or curtailment of women's employment opportunities has been traceable directly to the pervasive presumption that women are mothers first, and workers second. This prevailing ideology about women's roles has in turn justified discrimination against women when they are mothers or mothers-to-be." This Constitutional concern motivated the PDA, which addressed only half the problem, direct discrimination against pregnant workers, without addressing the broader problem, stigmatizing female workers as the only ones who have to be accommodated. "By creating an across-the-board, routine employment benefit for all eligible employees [in the FLMA], Congress sought to ensure that family-care leave would no longer be stigmatized as an inordinate drain on the workplace caused by female employees [protected by the PDA], and that employers could not evade leave obligations simply by hiring men." To hold that the FLMA was an exercise of Congress's Section 5 power, the Court had to be saying that all these concerns were of a Constitutional, not just constitutional magnitude. In short, *Geduldig*, which Rehnquist did not discuss or cite, was deeply and not just technically wrong: California violated the Equal Protection Clause not only because it denied an important benefit to female workers, Sally Durán Armendáriz's original gripe, but also because it reinforced traditional stereotypes about male and female workers: if a man was injured in a barroom brawl, his resulting unemployment was compensable because he was expected to come back to work, while a pregnant woman's unemployment was not compensable because she might not return to work. This was Wendy Williams's big point when she represented Armendáriz, and was the big point made to Congress by the Campaign to End Discrimination against Pregnant Workers.[35]

Justice Anthony Kennedy's sharply reasoned dissenting opinion revealed some other remarkable features about the majority. Kennedy pointed out that thirty states and the District of Columbia had, before 1993, required employers to give medical leaves. From the perspective of our theory, this suggests that it would have been appropriate for the Court to concede that *Geduldig* had been wrongly decided, and that state and federal legislative embrace of Durán Armendáriz's constitutional arguments was the occasion for overruling *Geduldig*. But the solicitor general was not prepared to renounce *Geduldig*, nor was the chief justice—and that failure gave Justice Kennedy ammunition for his position, that Congress was not remedying Large "C" Constitutional violations. Even discriminatory parental leaves did not violate the Constitution—as the associate solicitor general conceded at oral argument, minutes after he had mistaken Justice Ruth Bader Ginsburg for Justice Sandra Day O'Connor, the only women to have served as Supreme Court justices at that time—and so it went without saying that neither did a state's failure to provide parental leaves *or* its provision of such leaves to all employees (as most states were then doing). Recognizing this conundrum, Justice John Paul Stevens declined to join the chief justice's opinion, but joined its result because he did not think Congress needed a Fourteenth Amendment basis for legislating. The other justices in the majority were surely nervous but held their tongues so that the FMLA could be ratified by an opinion for the Court authored by the chief justice.[36]

So Sally Durán Armendáriz can take consolation in the fact that her loss in *Geduldig* is now in a Constitutional Closet. For all practical purposes, it has been superseded by the PDA. That the late chief justice had to pretend it did not exist for him to uphold the FMLA surely has constitutional significance but does not amount to a formal Constitutional overruling. The matter is further complicated by the fact that two of the six *Hibbs* majority are now off the Court, replaced by two jurists who would be even more reluctant to overrule *Geduldig*; a third majority justice has been replaced by a jurist who would be open to reconsidering *Geduldig*. So there it sits, in Constitutional limbo. Under the common law Constitutionalism we are exploring here, *Geduldig* should not be followed or applied by the Court. It is, at best, a Constitutional appendix, the remnant of an earlier regime that is left in place so long as it does no harm.

As the foregoing discussion reveals, common law Constitutionalism can be a mechanism by which statutory convergences as to personal rights and liberties become Constitutional floors. The creation of new Constitutional floors is a tricky business for our polity: Constitutional litigation is expensive and can be divisive; when the Court creates a new floor prematurely (as in *Roe v. Wade*) it creates great anger, but it also creates anger when it denies rights that Americans consider fundamental for us all (as in *Bowers v. Hardwick*). Against these costs, what benefits do Constitutional floors provide Us the People? Probably the primary benefit is symbolic. *Brown*, *Loving*, *Craig*, *Hibbs*, and *Lawrence* are big splashy recognitions that racial and ethnic minorities, women, and gay people are equal citizens who must be given the same dignified treatment as the racial majority, men, and straight people. That the nation's highest Court announces that the Constitution does not tolerate discriminatory treatment gives great hope to these groups and is educative for traditionally entitled groups.

But we immediately caution that the symbolic benefits of these Supreme Court decisions can be better achieved through national legislation. The enactment of the FMLA was a more important public event than the Supreme Court's decision in *Hibbs*, and the political campaigns for the Civil Rights Act of 1964 and the Voting Rights Act of 1965 overshadow the litigation campaign in *Brown* and were much bigger news than the *Loving* litigation. One reason that landmark legislation has more significance than a landmark court decision that announces the same new normative commitment is that the former requires larger-scale popular mobilization, bringing in more groups and perspectives, and in the end represents a more direct and explicit "buy-in" by We the People. Even the presentation makes a difference. A Supreme Court decision offers the norm as a kind of "deduction" or implication of normative commitments, which is useful but not as politically deep as a norm that Americans unite behind as a national commitment.

To say that superstatutes are more permanent markers of national commitment is not to say that superprecedents are not terribly important. Quite the opposite, for norms are entrenched through *institutional interaction*. The antidiscrimination norm has become entrenched in this way. State legislatures and governors (such as Earl Warren of California) were the legal pioneers, followed by both state and federal judges who developed hearing records that laid out the wrongs and harms of apartheid. And *Brown* really did transform and enrich the debate, in complicated ways that historians have argued over. From our theoretical point of view, *Brown*'s greatest contribution was that it was deliberation-inducing. Although Congress was not in a position to respond until the 1960s, *Brown* put desegregation on the national agenda and rendered civil rights a critical issue in the 1960 presidential election. Responding to invigorated social activism as well as unworthy southern responses, Congress did enact landmark statutes that the Supreme Court interpreted aggressively in response to executive petitions. The institutional interaction was different for issues of women's rights (Congress was an earlier leader) and gay rights (state judges were the heroes here), but our point is that entrenchment came because some key institution was able to put the pressing matter on the public agenda, to articulate a principle that resonated with the national conscience, and to apply the principle in a way that generated feedback. The Supreme Court exercising a power of judicial review is often that key institution.

DELIBERATION-INDUCING REVIEW AND CONSTITUTIONAL CANONS

Should Constitutionalism *never* stand against federal superstatutes, state statutory convergences, and executive-congressional agreements? At the ground level of social movements, of course, countermajoritarian politics is precisely what Constitutionalism *ought* to do. Even when local school boards everywhere segregated Mexican American children and treated them in other discriminatory ways, as Sally Durán was treated in Gilroy's public schools, it was right for people of conscience to object that this was wrong under the Constitution. In our view, segregation of and discrimination against Mexican American or African American schoolchildren were properly considered unConstitutional well before *Brown v. Board of Education* (1954), but it was not possible for the Supreme Court to recognize that right until there had been legislative and executive deliberation on the matter around the time of *Brown*. We do not have any strong view as to *when* the federal courts should have intervened, though it astounds us that continued segregation of Mexican American schoolchildren was accepted by many school districts and some judges as late as 1971, almost two decades after *Brown*.[37]

Some constitutionally entrenched values are squalid values, and a virtue of Constitutionalism is to criticize those values before judges. Recall our horticultural perspective. The Constitution vests its own cultivation ultimately in We the People, but if social elites deny or denigrate citizens' participation in the political process of tending the garden, constitutional horticulture is stymied, and input from judges a step removed from day-to-day politics is most needed. This is really the best defense of *Brown*. Although the Court's dis-entrenchment of apartheid might be defended on the basis of original meaning or common law Constitutionalism, as we have done above, the most convincing justification for the extraordinary investment of judicial and national resources following from *Brown* remains some version of Dean John Hart Ely's *representation-reinforcing* judicial review. As Ely argued, apartheid harmed a "discrete and insular minority" that was an object of irrational stereotypes and vicious prejudice. We'd tie the prejudice against minorities problem with the political lock-in problem, also described by Ely's overall theory. Apartheid was a system designed to deny the citizenship and democratic participation of people of color, and it did so successfully. Given the representation defects flowing from apartheid, neither state legislatures nor Congress (paralyzed by southern fillibuster-prone senators) was able to deliberate successfully. What *Brown* did was to *reverse the burden of inertia*, from the defenders of segregation to its critics. But for the highly unusual circumstances of apartheid, our theory would be more skeptical of *Brown* because it was deliberation-forcing rather than deliberation-respecting—but the deliberative process was so flawed that there was too little to respect. Indeed, we view *Brown* as an example of *deliberation-liberating* judicial review. When normal politics has broken down, there are some instances where the Court is justified in jump-starting it, liberating deliberation from local blockages.[38]

There is no constitutional structure today as malign as pre–World War II apartheid, but there are serious critics who maintain that one or more entrenched features of America's statutory constitution ought to be dis-entrenched the way that *Brown*, the Civil Rights Act, and subsequent statutes accomplished against apartheid. Thoughtful Americans believe that the Voting Rights Act has pushed us toward a race-based system of proportional representation (chapter 2), that the Sherman Act ought to be junked and the market allowed to operate without much regulation (chapter 3), that the Social Security Act has been an inefficient mechanism for retirement benefits (chapter 4), that the California (No-Fault) Divorce Act has been a disaster for wives and children (chapter 5), that the Clean Water and Endangered Species Acts have denied Americans the rightful and efficient use of their property (chapter 6), that the Defense of Marriage Act denies worthy lesbian and gay couples the federal rights and recognition their committed marriages and unions deserve (chapter 8), and that statutory requirements for some due process to accused terrorists, bars to coercive interrogation techniques, and limits on government wiretaps are rendering the country vulnerable to further terrorist attacks (chapter 9). We agree with some of these criticisms. An important theme of this book is that these constitutional critics ought to address their arguments primarily to their fellow citizens, legislators, and agencies—not to federal judges, at least not primarily. Thus, we are skeptical of the Supreme Court's campaign against race-based considerations in local and state programs seeking to desegregate public education. As Justice Breyer has argued most eloquently, the political process is working well in most instances, and the Court is on shaky ground in criticizing school districts' efforts to diversify.[39]

Ironically, our thesis is a plausible one in part because of the Large "C" Constitutionalism we have been critiquing. That is, for democratic constitutionalism to operate effectively, especially in the horticultural sense we have been stressing, We the People must be able to push back against governmental frameworks and norms, including entrenched ones. The greatest strength of our Constitution is that it guarantees multiple institutional forums where popular voices can criticize and resist—from juries adjudicating criminal and civil statutory claims to private associations and media outlets to accountable representatives (including elected legislators and executive officials at various levels). The Court's most constructive contribution to democratic constitutionalism is guaranteeing opportunities for widespread critical engagement through deliberation-protecting judicial review that assures citizens basic participatory rights of voting, jury service, and political association. For basic deliberation-protecting rights, the Supreme Court should face down popular criticism. Beyond that, the Court should proceed cautiously in pressing its own critiques of entrenched norms; the justices might be persuaded that their critiques are required by the Constitution, but our book suggests the need for judicial humility in light of history. If the justices are determined to protect Constitutional structure and individual rights beyond participatory ones, our theory suggests that they should channel their review in a deliberation-inducing manner. The best mechanism for deliberation-inducing review is through statutory interpretations openly informed by normative canons, described at the end of this Conclusion.

DELIBERATION-PROTECTING JUDICIAL REVIEW

The Constitution establishes a framework that protects democratic participation in its ongoing horticulture. Article I and the Seventeenth Amendment assure that members of Congress will be elected according to popular vote. Although the Constitution builds on state franchise rules, it bars voting discrimination based upon race (Amendment XV), sex (Amendment XIX), ability to pay a poll tax (Amendment XXIV), and age unless under eighteen (Amendment XXVI). The First Amendment protects political discussion—speech, press, and assembly in its text and marches, parades, and associations by precedent reasoning from that text. The Constitution's due process (Amendments V and XIV) and jury trial (Amendments VI and VII) rights are also deliberation-protecting, for they assure individuals that the state will not penalize them without giving them a chance to state their case before an impartial decision maker and, sometimes, a jury of their peers.[40]

Strict enforcement of these fundamental Constitutional protections is probably the most productive thing that judges can realistically do to enrich democracy and assure conditions for republican deliberation. Such enforcement is work judges are well trained to do, and they usually do it neutrally and sometimes enthusiastically. And enforcement of the foregoing Constitutional rights does contribute to—albeit does not guarantee—the responsiveness of government to new problems and the needs of emerging groups. Legislators and chief executives, and through their influence agencies as well, are more responsive when voters and not just citizens are concerned about a particular policy. Even a small minority of the population can swing close elections. The right to protest and make arguments in newspapers, public addresses, protests, parades, normative associations, and personal testimony also enhances democracy. Criminal process protections, especially the jury trial right, stand in the way of excessive state penalties against nonconforming but otherwise harmless (or even potentially helpful) citizens. And the Supreme Court has repeatedly declared that the rights to vote, to dissent, and to enjoy fair jury trials are *fundamental* rights that the state can only abridge with narrowly tailored statutes serving compelling policies.[41]

Thus, justices with no particular sympathy for people of color were willing to enforce Constitutional voting and criminal process protections for racial minorities in the decades before *Brown*. The Court's pre-*Brown* decisions imposed new Constitutional rules against segregation in voting, unfair trials for black defendants accused of serious crimes, and arbitrary efforts to impose apartheid rules on private property transactions. Few of these Supreme Court decisions were clearly supported by state statutory convergences or federal congressional or executive acts, and all went against the grain of southern apartheid. But judicial pronouncements protecting people of color in criminal prosecutions, exercise of the franchise, and property ownership were Constitutionally robust because those decisions (1) were grounded in the text and traditions of the Constitution, the Bill of Rights, and the Reconstruction Amendments; (2) were essentially procedural, slowing down abusive processes and opening up the political process somewhat, but without requiring dramatic reallocations of resources; and, in retrospect certainly, (3) contributed to a thoughtful constitutionalism, where public values remained within the control of popular majorities, legislatures, and executive norm entrepreneurs. Although the immediate political and social effect of these Constitutional decisions is subject to debate, they were in the longer term a positive contribution to American democracy and laid the Constitutional groundwork for both *Brown* and the Civil Rights Act of 1964.[42]

"Homosexuals," the most despised group in America during the 1950s, found some security in judicial review of state and federal terror campaigns. Judges who were far from gay friendly performed heroically when they enforced simple rules against police coercion and entrapment, prosecutions based upon ridiculous inferences or even fabricated evidence, illegal searches and seizures, politically motivated censorship of gay literature and political materials, disruption of ordinary socializing, and so forth. Chapter 8 of this book demonstrates how the California Supreme Court slowed down that state's antihomosexual *Kulturkampf* during the 1950s and 1960s through a soft-spoken insistence upon Constitutional rights for lesbians, gay men, and bisexuals to free association, privacy, and speech. As one of us has argued elsewhere, the antihomosexual Warren Court sometimes went out of its way to *deny* ordinary rights for gay people, but its strong and broadly applicable Constitutional protections for criminal defendants, protesters, and potential voters had direct and positive effects on gay rights, because they opened up the democratic process in ways that gay people could use to persuade their neighbors of the injustice of the antihomosexual constitution. During the 1960s, it was much harder for the state to persecute and imprison gay people for consensual relationships or even "cruising," because of the Warren Court's revolution in criminal procedure. After the Stonewall riots of 1969, when thousands of gay people came out of the closet and became politically active, antigay police knew they were not allowed to close down gay rights organizations and censor their literature. By destroying the rural domination of state legislatures, the Court's one-person, one-vote decisions gave urban-centered pro-gay legislators greater voice and facilitated sodomy reform and antidiscrimination laws in California and other states.[43]

The democracy-liberating features of Constitutionalism have not been as dramatic for Latinos such as Sally Durán Armendáriz and her family. Like gay people, Latinos have benefited from the Court's longstanding Constitutional protection of speech, press, political association, and other forms of dissent, but have found the Supreme Court traditionally unreceptive to their specific claims of state discrimination. Also like gay people, state discrimination against Latinos has been justified on the basis of "conduct"—gay people's sodomy, and language abilities or accent for Latinos—that judges have been reluctant to second-guess. Recall, from chapter 1, the point that the Supreme Court has long been reluctant to police state exclusions that have discriminatory race- or ethnicity-based effects. Thus, in *San Antonio Independent School District v. Rodriguez*

(1974), the Court declined to strike down Texas's educational funding system that denied decent educational opportunities to most Latino American and African American children in the state. Texas also sought to deprive Latino Americans of their right to vote, and got away with it long after the Supreme Court attacked its exclusion of African American voters. It was not until the Voting Rights Act Amendments of 1975 that minority-language voters, most of whom are Latino Americans, enjoyed antidiscrimination protections with bite. The 1975 act requires voting districts with nontrivial language-minority populations to provide voters not proficient in English with materials in their own language.[44]

Unlike the literacy test provision examined in chapter 2, the language-assistance provision (section 203) of the Voting Rights Act remains contested. When the act came up for renewal in 2006, Representative Peter King proposed that section 203 be deleted, on the grounds that it was no longer needed to protect Latino American voters against discrimination and that English-speaking ability ought to be a requisite for voting. The House defeated the King Amendment by a vote of 238–185, a decisive but not overwhelming majority. The modest margin of defeat and the relationship of language *assistance* to concern about illegal immigration suggest that there may be a Constitutional challenge to section 203. The argument would be that denying the vote to citizens who are not proficient in English does not violate the Fourteenth or Fifteenth Amendment, and Congress's authority under the Enforcement Clauses of those amendments does not reach any further. This is a serious argument grounded in recent precedent, but ought to be rejected. In 1975, Congress found pervasive and serious evidence of ethnicity-based discrimination under the pretext of language deficiencies, and Congress in 2006 heard evidence that such discrimination had not ended and would return with a vengeance if section 203 were not renewed. This ought to be sufficient under the Fifteenth Amendment, which reflects strong constitutional as well as Constitutional commitment to an open and available franchise to as many citizens as possible. Our view enjoys support in Supreme Court precedents upholding the voting-assistance provision for non-English-speaking citizens who had completed primary schools in Puerto Rico in the original Voting Rights Act of 1965, and the nationwide literacy test ban in the 1970 amendments. Even though the Supreme Court itself had never found that literacy tests violated the Fourteenth or Fifteenth Amendment, the Court was open to Congress's fact-based judgment that such tests were often pretexts for Constitutional violations.[45]

Few Constitutional principles are as entrenched in American law and society as the notion that juries must be drawn from a cross-section of society; a corollary is that prosecutors cannot exclude potential jurors because of their race. Can Sally Durán Armendáriz be excluded because she is Mexican American? The Supreme Court long ago said *no* to that question, but what if a prosecutor excludes her because she is bilingual? Some prosecutors have defended the practice on the ground that bilingual jurors will substitute their translations for those rendered by the official government translator. While reaffirming the rule against exclusion based on Latino ethnicity, a divided Supreme Court allowed such exclusion for this practical reason in *Hernandez v. New York* (1991). The Court did not rule out all Constitutional challenges to such exclusions, but Justice Kennedy's plurality opinion gave them a narrow berth. This issue will recur if future prosecutors follow the practice allowed in *Hernandez*. Between 1940 and 2000, the number of Spanish-speaking Americans increased tenfold, from about 1.8 million to more than eighteen million persons. About two-thirds of Americans with Latino ancestry are bilingual. Some do not speak English proficiently, and if they become criminal defendants, their testimony and usually the testimony of other witnesses will have to be rendered with the aid of an official interpreter.[46]

As Justice Kennedy observed in *Hernandez*, it is not irrational for a prosecutor to worry that bilingual jurors will second-guess the rendering of the official translator. But neither is it irrational for a prosecutor to think that men will second-guess the testimony of women in rape cases—yet the Equal Protection Clause does not allow prosecutors to strike males from juries for that reason, because it would be a sex discrimination. In cases where the bilingual jurors struck by a prosecutor are all Latinos, the Equal Protection Clause *ought* not allow the strikes because they are tantamount to discrimination based on ethnicity or race. It is not enough to say, as Justice Kennedy did, that the jurors were being struck because they were bilingual, not because they were Latino. This is the same kind of argument the Court made in *Geduldig* (Sally Durán Armendáriz was discriminated against because of pregnancy, not sex). Ethnicity and bilingual abilities are often practically inseparable; that is, the only bilinguals that typically concern the prosecutor in a Latino-defendant case will be jurors with Latino names. For example, we bet that a lot of prosecutors do not even ask non-Latino jurors whether they can speak Spanish. And we bet that most bilingual Latino Americans would be perfectly willing to follow the judge's instructions to stick to the official translation. As our wagers suggest, we are skeptical that *Hernandez* represents the last Constitutional word on the issue. Some strikes of bilingual jurors represent Constitutionally questionable race or ethnicity discrimination, and therefore ought to be invalidated under *Hernandez*. The Court ought to remain open-minded on this issue, and attentive to experience in states with large bilingual populations. In such states, Latino American groups ought to seek state recognition of a norm against discrimination on the basis of bilingualism, through rules of procedure or perhaps legislation. At some point, the *Hernandez* rule might become irrelevant, but if not irrelevant the Court should sustain ethnicity-based challenges in the space left open in Justice Kennedy's opinion.

DELIBERATION-INDUCING JUDICIAL REVIEW
AND THE AVOIDANCE CANON

As the foregoing analysis indicates, even substantive judicial review is usually better characterized as *deliberation-inducing* rather than as an absolute *veto* or *trump*. In bridge, my trump card, properly displayed, overrides any card from another suit—but that is not the way judicial review usually works. Instead of trumping all the cards in other suits, the judicial review card usually requires Congress to play a higher-value card (that is, more deliberation or a more explicit statement in the statute) in the suit it has chosen. To be clear, playing the judicial review card has substantive effects. After *Morrison*, it is harder for Congress to protect citizens against private violence, but there remain acceptable channels for Congress to do so, including its power to condition federal funds under the Spending Clause of Article I. The primary effect of deliberation-inducing review is to channel the political process. Certain goals such as categorizing everybody by race for its own sake are off-limits. If a legislature wants to adopt a race- or sex-based classification, it must have good reason to believe that those measures will serve legitimate state policies and must consider less restrictive means of achieving the same goal. A similar analytic structure governs First Amendment rights of speech and press, also erroneously understood as trumps. If the state restricts speech or publication, it (1) must have a goal unrelated to the suppression of expression or dissent; (2) must have good reason to believe that the speech-suppressing measure will advance that goal; and (3) must consider other means to achieve that goal and have good reason to reject them. Professor Alec Stone Sweet demonstrates that this analytical structure, which Germany's Constitutional Court calls "proportionality review," is the dominant approach to Constitutionalism in the global community. Professor Stone Sweet has suggested to us that parliaments all over the world are receptive to what we are calling deliberation-inducing Constitutional review, because it helps them do their own constitutional jobs more thoughtfully.[47]

The connection between Constitutionalism and constitutionalism has another dimension. When the Supreme Court interprets statutes, it does so against background principles of statutory interpretation that are grounded in the Constitution. If a Mexican family such as the turn-of-the-century Duráns came into the United States today, they would be met by detailed statutory barriers to entry, limitations on one's ability to stay in this country, and procedures for securing entry or resisting deportation. Few issues have captivated American politics in the past one hundred years more than immigration, and an array of increasingly detailed framework statutes have been enacted. The Supreme Court never strikes down significant provisions of these statutes on Constitutional grounds; the justices say that the Constitution vests in Congress "plenary power" to regulate immigration and naturalization. Notwithstanding this plenary powers doctrine, the Constitution pervasively affects the way these superstatutes are applied against Mexican and other immigrants. Professor Hiroshi Motomura has documented this rich history of statutory interpretation in the shadow of the Constitution.[48]

For example, the Immigration and Naturalization Service (INS) once followed a practice whereby investigating officers later served as judges in deportation cases. Such a conflation of prosecutorial and judicial duties in the same official is not Constitutionally tolerated in ordinary criminal cases. Under the plenary powers doctrine, however, it appeared that this would be tolerated in deportation cases—but the Court invalidated the practice on statutory grounds in *Wong Yang Sung v. McGrath* (1950). Invoking the Administrative Procedure Act of 1946, which reflected a separation of prosecutorial and judicial functions in administrative proceedings as a presumptive rule, the Court interpreted the 1917 act as requiring this separation. The text of the statute was not decisive, which usually means that the agency has discretion, but in *Wong Yang Sung* that discretion went against the grain of administrative due process values—both the small "c" constitutional rule of the APA as well as the neutrality norm in the Due Process Clauses of the Large "C" Constitution. Professor Motomura has documented dozens of similar cases where the Supreme Court applied what he calls *phantom norms* inspired by Constitutional or constitutional baselines to soften the edges of immigration statutes. Under the phantom norms approach, Constitutional values influence the evolution of immigration law, subject to Congress's override with clearer language. When Congress does override the Court's quasi-Constitutional construction, the Court generally goes along.[49]

The pervasive influence of Constitutional baselines in Supreme Court statutory interpretation can be generalized beyond the immigration context. Literally dozens of the Court's standard canons of statutory construction explicitly reflect Constitutional norms, and hundreds of Supreme Court cases have applied Constitution-based canons in the past generation. This is what Professor Philip Frickey and one of us have called "quasi-Constitutional law." The best example of such a rule of construction is the *avoidance canon*, which says that when one interpretation of an ambiguous statute raises "serious [C]onstitutional difficulties," courts ought to choose another plausible construction that avoids those problems. The avoidance canon is famously malleable: How ambiguous does the statute have to be? How serious the Constitutional difficulty?[50]

We agree with the malleability criticism but offer a defense of the avoidance canon inspired by Professor Frickey's work. The avoidance canon can and should lower the stakes of Constitutional litigation, by providing a mechanism whereby the Supreme Court can articulate Constitutional concerns but without seeking to end public deliberation about an issue of concern to the body politic. (Various Large "C" Constitutional doctrines also function as remands rather than vetoes, including the void for vagueness doctrine that could have been invoked in *Roe* and *Bowers* and the federalism-deliberation requirement articulated by the concurring opinions in *Lopez*.) In short, the avoidance canon functions as a *deliberation-inducing* form of judicial review.[51]

Consider a useful example where the avoidance canon would have been more appropriate than aggressive judicial review. Recall *Heller v. District of Columbia* (2008), the case where a narrow Supreme Court majority revived and revised the Second Amendment to strike down the District's regulation of handguns in the home. Handguns remain an unresolved focus of important public deliberation, and the Court's Constitutional analysis was not a cogent intervention. (For the deliberation-respecting reasons Justice Scalia smuggled into his original meaning opinion, we do not think *Heller* was a great Constitutional calamity, however.) Clearly, though, gun rights are a big normative concern for five justices. In that event, a more appropriate, and more lawlike, intervention would have been through statutory rather than Constitutional interpretation.

In 1906, Congress authorized the District to enact "all such usual and reasonable police regulations . . . as [the District] may deem necessary for the regulation of firearms." This law remains in effect and trumps any local regulation to the contrary, as a matter of ordinary law. Given Congress's own actions respecting a homeowner's self-defense interest in home handguns, recounted above, the District's 1976 statute barring operative handguns in the home might be construed as not "usual and reasonable." While the statutory terminology is susceptible to different interpretations, this is where the avoidance canon comes into play. The five *Heller* justices (or any one of them) ought to have applied the 1906 statute to preempt the District's 1976 regulation, on the ground that the broad federal law should be interpreted to avoid the serious Second Amendment difficulties (from their point of view) that would attend a narrower construction. By interpreting the 1906 statute to preempt the District's law, the Court would have provisionally ended the District's experiment, but not the public debate, for Congress could revisit the issue in fresh authorizing legislation.[52]

NORMATIVE META-CANONS FOR THE REPUBLIC OF STATUTES

The well-established avoidance canon is an important formal link between Large "C" and small "c" constitutionalism. Another well-established canon is foundational to small "c" constitutionalism: statutes should be interpreted to carry out their public-regarding purposes, unless the purposive construction imposes upon the text a meaning it will not bear. This was the canon the EEOC was applying when it opined in 1972 that employer pregnancy-discrimination policies constituted unlawful discrimination because of sex under Title VII. The purpose of Title VII was to integrate women and men into workplaces where they had been excluded or burdened with unnecessary qualifications. Because the EEOC believed that pregnancy-discriminating policies burdened female employees (and only those employees) and as a practical matter limited their job options, the agency concluded that "discrimination because of sex" included pregnancy-based discriminations. We maintain that the EEOC's approach was the right one, and that the Supreme Court interpreted the statute incorrectly in *Gilbert*.[53]

In our republic of statutes, we'd take the purposive approach one step further. In the spirit of the avoidance canon, we suggest that statutory interpreters never forget that they are carrying out the core meta-purposes of government, including those announced by Thomas Hobbes and John Locke and explored in chapter 2. While the statutory text, its purpose and legislative history, and its context within particular statutory schemes remain the critical tools for figuring out how to apply statutes, the fact remains that those sources will not always yield interpretive closure, especially with regard to big issues. In the event of ambiguity, we urge interpreters to consider those meta-purposes suggested by small "c" constitutional goals and norms. Consider three meta-canons that are suggested by the nation's core commitment to unobstructed markets, national security, and equal citizenship—substantive themes that have pervaded this book (as we explained in the Introduction).

1. *Market meta-canon.* Our history of federal assurance of the market in chapters 3 and 7 supports an *anti-bottleneck canon*. State contract law, federal antitrust statutes, and various international trade conventions converge on the notion of an unobstructed market, a market without what Thurman Arnold called "bottlenecks," as a foundational role for the state. The notoriously open-textured Sherman Act has through its history been interpreted with this meta-canon in mind, although different periods of our history entertained different conceptions of what market structures impeded full and fair competition. Today, the prevailing norm is maximization of consumer welfare, a norm consistent with the constitutional developments traced in this volume. The anti-bottleneck meta-canon also has traction in Large "C" Constitutional interpretation, with specific reference to the "Dormant" Commerce Clause. If history or rational choice logic is any guide, individual states pursuing their self-interests would tend to hoard resources, impose tariffs, and shift regulatory costs onto out-of-staters; once one

state adopts such piggy policies, its neighbors are likely to follow, and pretty soon there is a trade war. Congress has the power to regulate such activities, but it would be very difficult for the slow-moving legislature to monitor and then preempt the many and evolving ways states seek rents at the expense of outsiders. Congress might create a federal agency with authority to monitor interstate externalities and enter orders barring them. In our view, this is probably the best institutional solution, but few such statutes have been enacted thus far. In the absence of an administrative solution, federal judges are best suited to case-by-case adjudication of claims that a state is discriminating or otherwise imposing excessive burdens on other states' interstate commerce, and an abundant Dormant Commerce Clause jurisprudence monitors such clashes.[54]

America's statutory constitution, therefore, provides an explanation for the rise of the Dormant Commerce Clause, as well as statute-based *legal* criteria for guiding the Court when applying this line of common law Constitutionalism. Our theory is simple: the Court ought, primarily, to be guided by federal statutory policy in determining what areas to apply sharper-eyed scrutiny to and, secondarily, to consider state statutory convergences when evaluating asserted state interests. Under our deliberation-respecting theory, if Congress has enacted legislation recognizing state regulatory interests, the Court ought to be more cautious in applying its Dormant Commerce Clause jurisprudence. Conversely, where legislation reflects a congressional judgment that local interests must be more tightly monitored, the Court should be more scrutinizing. Finally, when evaluating the legitimacy and weight of the state's regulatory interest, the Court should consider congressional preferences reflected in statutes, as well as widely held state policies. This is precisely the approach the Roberts Court has followed in recent cases, most notably *United Haulers Association, Inc. v. Oneida-Herkimer Solid Waste Management Authority* (2007), and we endorse it.[55]

2. Security meta-canon. Our history of the national security constitution in chapter 9 supports what we call the *Endo meta-canon.* It is accepted in our constitutional culture that individual liberty against state intrusion is an important value, but that it can sometimes be compromised when necessary to protect national security. The executive branch is the initial actor when security is threatened, and such officials need leeway to respond to unanticipated problems and threats, but within the rule of law. In *Ex parte Endo* (1944), where the Supreme Court ruled that the president was not authorized to detain concededly loyal Japanese Americans indefinitely, the opinion for the Court started with the baseline assumption that "the Chief Executive and members of Congress . . . are sensitive to and respectful of the liberties of the citizen. In interpreting a wartime measure we must assume that their purpose was to allow for the greatest possible accommodation between those liberties and the exigencies of war. We must assume, when asked to find implied powers in a grant of legislative or executive authority, that the law makers intended to place no greater restraint on the citizen than was clearly and unmistakably indicated by the language they used." This *Endo* meta-canon suggests a presumption against reading exceptions into framework statutes Congress has enacted, after full deliberation, to provide a structure for the security-protecting state. This meta-canon provided important protection for persons the Bush-Cheney administration wanted to try as war criminals in tribunals rigged to assure convictions, as the Supreme Court applied a presumption against presidential innovation beyond the requirements of the Uniform Code of Military Justice in *Hamdan v. Rumsfeld* (2006).[56]

In *Hamdi v. Rumsfeld* (2004), the *Endo* meta-canon supported the approach taken by Justices Souter, Ginsburg, Scalia, and Stevens, who insisted that the Authorization of Military Force Act of 2002 did not allow the president to detain suspected terrorists indefinitely—but they were in the minority. On the other hand, four other justices joined Justice O'Connor's plurality opinion, which interpreted the Due Process Clause to require some kind of hearing for the detained persons. *Hamdi* was a flip of the avoidance canon as well as the *Endo* meta-canon but ended up with the same point: the rule of law protected even suspected terrorists against arbitrary detentions. This point was hammered home emphatically in *Boumediene v. Bush* (2008), which overturned a statutory effort to deny habeas corpus to the detainees. Like the anti-bottleneck meta-canon, the *Endo* meta-canon has traction in Constitutional cases as well as statutory ones.[57]

3. *Equality meta-canon.* The foregoing discussion supports what we call the *Carolene meta-canon*, which stipulates that truly ambiguous statutes should be construed in favor of politically marginalized minorities (if applicable). We have defended this idea in earlier work, on the Elysian ground that such a meta-canon offsets a political process defect and on the republic-of-statutes ground that such a meta-canon offers Congress an opportunity to revisit the statute under conditions where there is probably political support for doing so (because the losing group in the statutory case is not the *Carolene* group). The California Supreme Court was following the *Carolene* meta-canon when it persistently interpreted antihomosexual laws narrowly and sometimes invalidated such laws, given their operation on a group that was reviled by the state and marginalized politically for generations.[58]

Consider the application of the *Carolene* meta-canon to a current issue. Forty-eight states deny the franchise to prisoners convicted of felonies, and most of those states extend the disenfranchisement beyond the time of incarceration. The state and federal prison population increased from 300,024 persons in 1977 to 2,319,258 persons by 2008; for the first time in our history, the ratio of Americans behind bars is more than one to one hundred. A majority of these prisoners are African American or Latino American. The total disenfranchised population has more than doubled in the last generation, creating our nation's most dramatic "democratic contraction" since the early apartheid period. Do these laws violate the Constitution? The Supreme Court ruled in *Richardson v. Ramirez* (1974) that such laws are not per se unConstitutional infringements on the fundamental right to vote. A deliberation-respecting theory such as ours augurs against overruling *Ramirez*, in part because recent federal statutes have relied on its precept.[59]

The Voting Rights Act, however, provides that "no voting qualification or prerequisite" can be applied "in a manner which results in a denial or abridgment of the right of any citizen of the United States to vote on account of race or color." Although it appears that Congress in 1965 and 1982 (when section 2 was amended to monitor voting rules with racially discriminatory effects) was not targeting felon disenfranchisement laws, Congress was targeting *any* law that had a disproportionate race effect. Today, felon disenfranchisement laws not only have that effect but have them on a much larger scale than could have been imagined in 1982, significantly affecting the ability of voters of color to protect their interests. Read literally, the Voting Rights Act calls at least some of the felon-disenfranchisement laws into question—and the *Carolene* meta-canon reinforces the notion that the statute should be read to protect against race- or ethnicity-based voting deprivations.[60]

NOTES

INTRODUCTION

1. *Brown v. Board of Education*, 347 U.S. 483 (U.S. Supreme Court, 1954); Ronald Dworkin, *Taking Rights Seriously* (Cambridge, MA: Harvard University Press, 1977), 147 (quotation in text); see ibid., 147–49, 208, 215. For other leading statements of the notion that Constitutionalism and public morality tend to merge, see Ronald Dworkin, *Law's Empire* (Cambridge, MA: Harvard University Press, 1986); Owen M. Fiss, "Objectivity and Interpretation," *Stanford Law Review* 34 (1982): 749–50. See also Robin West, "Unenumerated Duties," *University of Pennsylvania Journal of Constitutional Law* 9 (2006): 243–49, suggesting that this idea has wide acceptance among Constitutionalists and criticizing its cogency.
2. John Rawls, *Political Liberalism* (New York: Columbia University Press, 1993).
3. Some legal academics maintain that federal judges have prophetic wisdom and have educated America in its proper public values. E.g., Owen M. Fiss, "The Supreme Court 1978 Term—Foreword: The Forms of Justice," *Harvard Law Review* 93 (1979): 1–58.
4. See generally John A. Ferejohn and Larry D. Kramer, "Independent Judges, Dependent Judiciary: Institutionalizing Judicial Restraint," *New York University Law Review* 77 (2002): 962–1039. The state action doctrine has some foundation in the Constitution's text, but also in the nature of the judicial power. The Supreme Court has a powerful incentive to maintain its political support/legitimacy by limiting its intrusions into divisive political issues. As a result, the history of federal jurisdiction is, to an extent, a history of self-imposed jurisdictional limitations. The fundamental one was, of course the Court's insistence on strict interpretation of Article III's Cases and Controversies Clause. E.g., Letter from John Jay and the Associate Justices of the Supreme Court to George Washington (August 8, 1793), explaining that the Article III judicial power does not include the authority to issue purely advisory opinions. But it is also evident in the Court's repeated refusals to give wide readings to various open-textured clauses such as the Guarantee Clause of Article IV and the Privileges

and Immunities Clause of the Fourteenth Amendment. E.g., *The Slaughterhouse Cases*, 83 U.S. 36 (U.S. Supreme Court, 1873). There are many other examples restricting federal courts from removing cases from state courts and giving a narrow interpretation of "federal questions" for the purposes of asserting jurisdiction. Thus, we see the state action doctrine as another example—arguably the most important one—of a self-limiting doctrine imposed by the Court.

5. Lawrence G. Sager, "Fair Measure: The Legal Status of Underenforced Constitutional Norms," *Harvard Law Review* 91 (1978): 1212–64, as well as Sager, "Justice in Plain Clothes: Reflections on the Thinness of Constitutional Law," *Northwestern University Law Review* 88 (1993): 410–35.

6. Civil Rights Act of 1964, Public Law No. 88-352, tit. VI (1964); Elementary and Secondary Education Amendments of 1965, Public Law No. 89-10, 79 Stat. 27 (1965); *Green v. New Kent County School Board*, 391 U.S. 430 (U.S. Supreme Court, 1968) (requiring unitary school districts); James Dunn, "Title VI, the Guidelines and School Desegregation in the South," *Virginia Law Review* 53 (1967): 42ff. (tracing the dramatic impact of the 1964 and 1965 Acts on school integration). For an account of the many failures of *Brown*, see Gerald Rosenberg, *The Hollow Hope: Can Courts Bring About Social Change?* (Chicago: University of Chicago Press, 1991, revised edition, 2008).

7. *Brown v. Board of Education*, 139 F.Supp. 468 (U.S. District Court for the District of Kansas, 1955) (finding that Topeka satisfied the *Brown* mandate); *Brown v. Board of Education*, 84 F.R.D. 383 (U.S. District Court for the District of Kansas, 1979) (ruling that HEW could not collaterally challenge the 1955 decree). For subsequent decisions in the case, see *Brown v. Board of Education*, 892 F.2d 851 (U.S. Court of Appeals for the Tenth Circuit, 1989), vacated and remanded, 503 U.S. 978 (U.S. Supreme Court, 1992), reinstating prior opinion on remand, 978 F.2d 585 (U.S. Court of Appeals for the Tenth Circuit, 1992); *Brown v. Unified School District No. 501*, 56 F.Supp.2d 1212 (U.S. District Court for the District of Kansas, 1999) (holding that Topeka's system was unitary and satisfied the Equal Protection Clause).

8. Civil Rights Act of 1964, Public Law No. 88-352, titles VI and VII, 78 Stat. 241 (1964), codified at 42 U.S.C. §§ 2000e et seq. (prohibiting federally funded programs from discriminating because of race, etc., and prohibiting private workplace discrimination because of race, sex, etc.); Public Law No. 92-261, 86 Stat. 103 (1972) (expanding Title VII to cover public employers); Pregnancy Discrimination Act of 1978, Public Law No. 95-555, 92 Stat. 2076 (1978), codified at 42 U.S.C. § 2000a(k) (amending Title VII to include pregnancy-based discrimination as a species of sex discrimination).

9. For an excellent account of the evolution of the antidiscrimination principle found in the 1964 act, see Hugh Davis Graham, *The Civil Rights Era: Origins and Development of National Policy, 1960–1972* (New York: Oxford University Press, 1989).

10. Max Weber, *Economy and Society: An Outline of Interpretive Sociology*, Guenther Roth and Claus Wittich, editors, and Ephraim Fischoff, translator (Berkeley: University of California Press, 1978), 941–48; see generally David Singh Grewal, *Network Power: The Social Dynamics of Globalization* (New Haven: Yale University Press, 2008), 116–22.

11. *Green v. New Kent County School Board*, 391 U.S. 430 (U.S. Supreme Court, 1968), requiring formerly segregated-by-law jurisdictions to take immediate steps toward creating a "unitary school system"; *Loving v. Virginia*, 388 U.S. 1 (U.S. Supreme Court, 1967), following the state statutory consensus (outside the South) to strike down a law barring different-race marriages. On the national political consensus (outside the South) reflected in *Brown*, see Mary L. Dudziak, *Cold War Civil Rights: Race and the Image of American Democracy* (Princeton: Princeton University Press, 2000).

12. For an important theory that state legitimacy rests today (and we think has long rested) on the state's ability to provide security, see Philip Bobbitt, *Terror and Consent: The Wars for the Twenty-First Century* (New York: Alfred A. Knopf, 2008).

13. The account that follows is adapted from William N. Eskridge Jr., "America's Statutory 'constitution,'" *UC Davis Law Review* 41 (2007): 1–44. For a parallel account, see Ernest Young, "The Constitution Outside the Constitution," *Yale Law Journal* 117 (2007): 408–73. For a classic account of the rich lessons that can be derived from the text of the Constitution and its amendments, see Akhil Reed Amar, *America's Constitution: A Biography* (New York: Random House, 2005).

14. Administrative Procedure Act of June 11, 1946, chap. 324, 60 Stat. 237 (1946), codified at 5 U.S.C. §§ 551–55, 701–06, et al.; Thomas A. Merrill, "Rethinking Article I, Section 1: From Nondelegation to Exclusive Delegation," *Columbia Law Review* 104 (2004): 2097–2181. For the normative debate over agencies, compare David Schoenbrod, *Power Without Responsibility: How Congress Abuses the People Through Delegation* (New Haven: Yale University Press, 1993), and Gary Lawson, "Delegation and Original Meaning," *Virginia Law Review* 88 (2002): 327–404 (both authors arguing that administrative lawmaking and adjudication go against the Constitution's structure and original meaning), with Peter Strauss, "The Place of Agencies in Government: Separation of Powers and the Fourth Branch," *Columbia Law Review* 84 (1984): 573–669 (arguing that independent agencies, with delegated lawmaking authority, fit comfortably within the Constitution's framework).

15. Daniel A. Farber, William N. Eskridge Jr., and Philip P. Frickey, *Cases and Materials on Constitutional Law: Themes for the Constitution's Third Century* (St. Paul: West, third edition, 2003), 1191–1206 (Supreme Court's refusal to enforce the Republican Form of Government Clause, Article IV, § 4); ibid., 448–81 (Supreme Court's unsuccessful effort to protect private contracting and property against excessive state regulation); ibid., 1000–1047 (Supreme Court's aggressive review of state regulations discriminating against, or sometimes just affecting, interstate commerce and imposing costs on the national market); ibid., 181–90, 348–83, 517–82 (Supreme Court's aggressive review of state regulations of the family that pose problems of race discrimination, sex discrimination, or privacy concerns). On the regulatory and structuring role played by municipal ordinances in the nineteenth century, see William Novak, *People's Welfare: Law and Regulation in Nineteenth-Century America* (Chapel Hill: University of North Carolina Press, 1996).

16. For an excellent introduction to the relative inclusiveness of the Constitution of 1789, see Amar, *America's Constitution*, 64–76. On the history of state, and therefore national, voting rules, see Alexander Keyssar, *The Right to Vote: The Contested History of Democracy in the United States* (New Haven: Yale University Press, 2000). On the

democratizing amendments, see Amar, *America's Constitution*, 395–401 (Fifteenth, racial minorities); ibid., 421–25 (Nineteenth, women); ibid., 443 (Twenty-third, no poll taxes); ibid., 445–47 (Twenty-sixth, eighteen-year-olds). On closing off the franchise in the post-Reconstruction South, see J. Morgan Kousser, *The Shaping of Southern Politics: Suffrage Restriction and the Establishment of the One-Party South, 1880–1910* (New Haven: Yale University Press, 1974), 239 (table 9.1, cataloguing the precise new voting restrictions adopted by southern states, 1871–1908), a process reversed by the Voting Rights Act of 1965, Public Law No. 89-110, 79 Stat. 437 (1965), codified at 42 U.S.C. §§ 1971, 1973, et al. (discussed in chapter 2).

17. Civil Rights Act of 1964, Public Law No. 88-352, tit. VII, 78 Stat. 241 (1964), codified at 42 U.S.C. §§ 2000e et seq. (prohibiting private workplace discrimination "because of sex"); Public Law No. 92-261, 86 Stat. 103 (1972) (expanding Title VII to cover public employers); Education Amendments of 1972, Public Law No. 92-318, tit. IX, 86 Stat. 373–75 (1972), codified at 20 U.S.C. §§ 1681 et seq. (prohibiting educational programs that receive federal money from discriminating on the basis of sex); Pregnancy Discrimination Act of 1978, Public Law No. 95-555, 92 Stat. 2076 (1978), codified at 42 U.S.C. § 2000a(k) (amending Title VII to include pregnancy-based discrimination as "discrimination on the basis of sex").

18. Age Discrimination in Employment Act of 1967, Public Law No. 90-202, 81 Stat. 602 (1967), codified at 29 U.S.C. §§ 621 et seq.; Americans with Disabilities Act of 1990, Public Law No. 101-336, 104 Stat. 327 (1990), codified at 42 U.S.C. §§ 12101 et seq.; (proposed) Employment Non-Discrimination Act, Appendix 6 to William N. Eskridge Jr. and Nan D. Hunter, *Sexuality, Gender, and the Law* (Mineola, NY: Foundation Press, second edition, 2003).

19. Sherman Anti-Trust Act of July 2, 1890, chap. 647, 26 Stat. 209 (1890), codified at 15 U.S.C. §§ 1 et seq., expanded by the Clayton Act of 1914, Act of October 15, 1914, chap. 323, 38 Stat. 73 (1914); Social Security Act of August 14, 1935, chap. 531, 49 Stat. 620 (1935), codified at 42 U.S.C. §§ 301 et seq., and repeatedly expanded by statutory amendment; Employee Retirement Insurance Security Act of 1974, Public Law No. 93-406, 88 Stat. 829 (1974), codified at various parts of 26 U.S.C. and 29 U.S.C.

20. The purposive features of deliberation are especially well developed in Henry M. Hart Jr. and Albert M. Sacks, *The Legal Process: Basic Problems in the Making and Application of Law*, William N. Eskridge Jr. and Philip P. Frickey, editors (Westbury, NY: Foundation Press, 1994 [1958 tentative edition]); Henry S. Richardson, *Democratic Autonomy* (Oxford: Oxford University Press, 2002), 85–93.

21. The distinction in text between political *will* and administrative or judicial *judgment* is taken from *The Federalist* No. 78 (Hamilton), in *The Federalist Papers*, Clinton Rossiter, editor (New York: New American Library, 1961).

22. We are treating state constitutional rules as part of America's small "c" constitution when they converge on a particular norm. Of course, within the state itself, these would be Large "C" Constitutional norms. Because every state constitution is much easier to amend than the U.S. Constitution, every state constitution is a lot longer and encodes more institutions, rules, and norms. See Donald S. Lutz, "Toward a Theory of Constitutional Amendment," in Sanford Levinson, editor, *Responding to*

Imperfection: The Theory and Practice of Constitutional Amendment (Princeton: Princeton University Press, 1995). For that reason, there is much greater overlap between the Large "C" and small "c" constitutions at the state level than at the national level.

23. William N. Eskridge Jr. and John Ferejohn, "Super-Statutes," *Duke Law Journal* 50 (2001): 1215–76, articulated the idea in the text as our theory of *superstatutes*, namely, a "series of laws that (1) seeks to establish a new normative or institutional framework for state policy and (2) over time does 'stick' in the public culture such that (3) the super-statute and its institutional or normative principles have a broad effect on the law—including an effect beyond the four corners of the statute." Ibid., 1216. On the president's first-mover advantage in making policy initiatives, see Terry M. Moe and William G. Howell, "The Presidential Power of Unilateral Action," *Journal of Law, Economics, and Organization* 15 (1999): 132–79; William G. Howell, *Power and Persuasion: The Politics of Direct Presidential Action* (Princeton: Princeton University Press, 2003).

24. For important statements of the superstatutory significance of transnational commitments, see, e.g., Daniel J. Elazar, *Constitutionalizing Globalization: The Postmodern Revival of Conferal Arrangements* (Lanham, MD: Rowman & Littlefield, 1998); Oona Hathaway, "Treaties' End: The Past, Present, and Future of International Lawmaking in the United States," *Yale Law Journal* 117 (2008): 1236–1362; Peter J. Spiro, "Globalization and the (Foreign Affairs) Constitution," *Ohio State Law Journal* 63 (2002): 649–730.

25. For wonderful but differently focused understandings of what *deliberation* properly entails, but united around the idea that deliberation is *not* the Supreme Court, see Philip Bobbitt, *Shield of Achilles: War, Peace, and the Course of History* (New York: Alfred A. Knopf, 2002); Amy Gutmann and Dennis Thompson, *Democracy and Disagreement* (Cambridge, MA: Harvard University Press, 1996), and *Why Deliberative Democracy?* (Princeton: Princeton University Press, 2004); Jeremy Waldron, *Law and Disagreement* (New York: Oxford University Press, 1999), and *Dignity of Legislation* (Cambridge: Cambridge University Press, 1999).

26. For an argument that state legitimacy has recently changed from a welfarist understanding to a consumerist one, see Bobbitt, *Shield of Achilles* and *Terror and Consent*. We agree with Bobbitt about the shift but situate it much earlier, starting in the New Deal.

27. *Naim v. Naim*, 350 U.S. 985 (U.S. Supreme Court, 1956) (dismissing the Constitutional appeal challenging Virginia's antimiscegenation law, when thirty of forty-eight states had similar laws); *Loving v. Virginia*, 388 U.S. 1 (U.S. Supreme Court, 1967) (striking down Virginia's antimiscegenation law, when only sixteen of fifty states had such laws). For a brief account of the state-by-state repeals of such laws, see Randall Kennedy, *Interracial Intimacies: Sex, Marriage, Identity, and Adoption* (New York: Pantheon, 2003), 244–80.

28. Philip P. Frickey, "Getting from Joe to Gene (McCarthy): The Avoidance Canon, Legal Process Theory, and Narrowing Statutory Interpretation in the Early Warren Court," *California Law Review* 93 (2005): 397–464.

CHAPTER 1. THE CONSTITUTION OF EQUALITY
AND ADMINISTRATIVE CONSTITUTIONALISM

1. California Unemployment Insurance Code § 2626 (1972). Aiello's history is taken from the Complaint filed in _Aiello v. Hansen_, reprinted in Record on Appeal, 1–15, _Geduldig v. Aiello_, 417 U.S. 484 (U.S. Supreme Court, 1974) (Docket No. 73-640).

2. O'Steen's history is taken from Record on Appeal, _General Electric Co. v. Gilbert_, 429 U.S. 125 (U.S. Supreme Court, 1976) (Docket No. 74-1589); Telephone Interview by Kevin Schwartz with Sherrie O'Steen, fall 2005.

3. _DeShaney v. Winnebago County Department of Social Services_, 489 U.S. 189 (U.S. Supreme Court, 1989); Paul Brest and Sanford Levinson, _Processes of Constitutional Decisionmaking: Cases and Materials_ (Boston: Little Brown, third edition, 1992), 1111–20, discussing _DeShaney_ and the Court's unwillingness to apply the Constitution to protect "affirmative" rights.

4. _Geduldig v. Aiello_, 417 U.S. 484 (U.S. Supreme Court, 1974), rejecting the claim that pregnancy-based exclusion from the state unemployment compensation program violated the Equal Protection Clause.

5. Interview of Sonia Pressman Fuentes by William N. Eskridge Jr., New Haven, CT, November 1, 2008.

6. For important work arguing for aggressive agency and executive construction of the Constitution, see Stephen M. Griffin, _American Constitutionalism: From Theory to Politics_ (Princeton: Princeton University Press, 1996); William N. Eskridge Jr. and Kevin Schwartz, "_Chevron_ and Agency Norm Entrepreneurship," _Yale Law Journal_ 115 (2006): 2623–32; Jill Elaine Hasday, "Fighting Women: The Military, Sex, and Extrajudicial Constitutional Change," _Minnesota Law Review_ 93 (2008): 96–164; Sophia Z. Lee, "Race, Sex, and Rulemaking, 1964–1977: Revising Equal Protection History, Recovering Administrative Constitutionalism" (draft 2007); Trevor W. Morrison, "Constitutional Avoidance in the Executive Branch," _Columbia Law Review_ 106 (2006): 1189–1259; Keith E. Whittington, "Extrajudicial Constitutional Interpretation: Three Objections and Responses," _North Carolina Law Review_ 80 (2001): 773–851. An earlier use of the term is in Elizabeth Fisher and Ronnie Harding, "The Precautionary Principle and Administrative Constitutionalism: The Development of Frameworks for Applying the Precautionary Principle," in Elizabeth Fisher et al., editors, _Implementing the Precautionary Principle: Perspectives and Prospects_ (Cheltenham, U.K.: Edward Elgar, 2006).

7. Pregnancy Discrimination Act of 1978, Public Law No. 95-555, 92 Stat. 2076 (1978), codified at 42 U.S.C. § 2000e(k); Family and Medical Leave Act of 1993, Public Law No. 103-3, 107 Stat. 6 (1993), codified at 29 U.S.C. §§ 2601 et seq.

8. U.S. Constitution, XIV Amendment, § 1 (Equal Protection Clause). Our account of the documentary premise and its implications is drawn from _The Federalist_ No. 78 (Alexander Hamilton), in _The Federalist Papers_, Clinton Rossiter, editor (New York: New American Library, 1961).

9. William Michael Treanor, "Judicial Review before _Marbury_," _Stanford Law Review_ 58 (2005): 455–562; _Marbury v. Madison_, 5 U.S. 137 (U.S. Supreme Court, 1803);

McCulloch v. Maryland, 17 U.S. 316 (U.S. Supreme Court, 1819). On the foundational importance of the Marshall Court in creating a judge-governed rule of Constitutional law, see Brest and Levinson, *Processes of Constitutional Decisionmaking*,
69–140; G. Edward White, with the aid of Gerald Gunther, *The Marshall Court and
Cultural Change, 1815–1835* (volume 3 of *The Oliver Wendell Holmes Devise History
of the Supreme Court of the United States* [New York: Macmillan, 1988]).

10. U.S. Constitution, Article VI, Clause 2 (Supremacy Clause, quoted in text); Judiciary
Act of September 24, 1789, ch. 20, 1 Stat. 73 (defining the Supreme Court's powers of
appellate review as well as its original jurisdiction); Henry J. Bourguignon, "The
Federal Key to the Judiciary Act of 1789," *South Carolina Law Review* 46 (1995): 647,
700 (1995) (background of Judiciary Act of 1789, with focus on creating national
uniformity of federal law).

11. On the general proposition that the Supreme Court's Constitutional interpretations
bind the other institutions of government, for practical rule of law reasons, see Larry
Alexander and Frederick Schauer, "On Extrajudicial Constitutional Interpretation,"
Harvard Law Review 110 (1997): 1359–87.

12. Complaint, Record, 10–12, *Geduldig* (Docket No. 73-640) (all three Constitutional
claims rest upon the arbitrariness of state sex discrimination); Brief for Appellees,
48–52, *Geduldig* (Docket No. 73-640) (arguing that sex discriminations must be subjected to strict scrutiny); Wendy Webster Williams, "Equality's Riddle: Pregnancy
and the Equal Treatment/Special Treatment Debate," NYU *Review of Law & Social
Change* 13 (1984–85): 325–31 (demonstrating how pregnancy discrimination is sex
discrimination). For the historical context of the analogy between race and sex discrimination, see Serena Mayeri, "Constitutional Choices: Legal Feminism and the
Historical Dynamics of Change," *California Law Review* 92 (2004): 755–839.

13. Brief for Appellant, 10–37, *Geduldig* (Docket No. 73-640), explaining the state's rationale; Affidavit of Charles E. Sevick, Record, 35–36, *Geduldig* (Docket No. 73-640)
(pregnancy benefits would increase state costs by 36.4 percent); Affidavit of William
D. Smith, 47–50, *Geduldig* (Docket No. 73-640) (female employees draw much
more than their pro rata share from the unemployment compensation program).

14. Robert H. Bork, *The Tempting of America: The Political Seduction of the Law* (New
York: Free Press, 1989) (leading statement of original meaning as the only legitimate
basis for constitutional interpretation); Adam Winkler, "A Revolution Too Soon?
Woman Suffragists and the 'Living Constitution,'" *New York University Law Review*
76 (2001): 1456–1526 (examining the rejection of women's equality in the Reconstruction Amendments and early Supreme Court opinions).

15. U.S. Constitution, Article VII (original terms under which the Constitution would
come into effect); ibid., Article V (two processes by which the Constitution can be
amended; the first process is noted in text). See generally Sanford Levinson, editor,
Responding to Imperfection: The Theory and Practice of Constitutional Amendment
(Princeton: Princeton University Press, 1995).

16. For a thorough examination of the Constitution as it has evolved through the amendment process, see Akhil Reed Amar, *America's Constitution: A Biography* (New York:
Random House, 2005).

17. For an argument that our Constitutional system should have more big showdowns, see Eric A. Posner and Adrian Vermeule, "Constitutional Showdowns," *University of Pennsylvania Law Review* 156 (2008): 991–1048.

18. On the feminist ambivalence toward the ERA, see Cynthia Harrison, *On Account of Sex: The Politics of Women's Issues, 1945–1968* (Berkeley: University of California Press, 1988). On the law side, Barbara A. Brown et al., "The Equal Rights Amendment: A Constitutional Basis for Equal Rights for Women," *Yale Law Journal* 80 (1971): 871–930.

19. James Madison, *The Virginia Report of 1799–1800, Touching the Alien and Sedition Laws* (New York: Da Capo Press, 1970) (reprint of original *Report*, as well as Virginia and Kentucky Resolutions); Brest and Levinson, *Processes of Constitutional Decisionmaking*, 62–68 (excerpts and discussion).

20. Brief for Appellant, 14, *Geduldig* (Docket No. 73-640) (quotation in text). On the liberty-protecting features of the Constitution, see Randy Barnett, *Restoring the Lost Constitution: The Presumption of Liberty* (Princeton: Princeton University Press, 2004); Akhil Reed Amar, "The Bill of Rights as a Constitution," *Yale Law Journal* 100 (1991): 1131–1210.

21. *Roe v. Wade*, 410 U.S. 1 (U.S. Supreme Court, 1973); *Maher v. Doe*, 432 U.S. 464 (U.S. Supreme Court, 1977) (upholding, against equal protection challenge, state exclusion of abortion from Medicaid program for the poor); *Poelker v. Doe*, 432 U.S. 529 (U.S. Supreme Court, 1977) (municipal hospital can refuse to perform abortions).

22. *San Antonio Independent School District v. Rodriguez*, 411 U.S. 1 (U.S. Supreme Court, 1973), holding that there is no "fundamental right" to a public school education. For academic arguments for affirmative Constitutional duties, see Frank Michelman, "States' Rights and States' Roles: Permutations of 'Sovereignty' in *National League of Cities v. Usery*," *Yale Law Journal* 86 (1978): 1165–95; Laurence H. Tribe, "Unraveling *National League of Cities*: The New Federalism and Affirmative Rights to Essential Governmental Services," *Harvard Law Review* 90 (1977): 1065–1104. These are brilliant articles, but ones that have had no traction among judges and very little among law professors.

23. Complaint, Section X, ¶ 1 (quotation in text), Record, 12, *Geduldig* (Docket No. 73-640); Brief for Appellees, 28–52, *Geduldig* (Docket No. 73-640).

24. See Robert A. Dahl, *Pluralist Democracy in the United States: Conflict and Consent* (Chicago: Rand McNally, 1967); Adam Przeworski, *Democracy and the Market: Political and Economic Reforms in Eastern Europe and Latin America* (Cambridge: Cambridge University Press, 1991).

25. Thomas Hobbes, *Leviathan* (1651), Review and Conclusion, modern edition by Richard Tuck, editor (Cambridge: Cambridge University Press 1996), 491 (quotation in text); Hobbes, *The Elements of Law Natural and Politic* (1650), ¶ 20.5, modern edition by Ferdinand Tonnies, editor (London: M. M. Goldsmith, 1969), 110. See generally Kinch Hoekstra, "The *De Facto* Turn in Hobbes's Political Philosophy," in Tom Sorell and Luc Foisneau, editors, *Leviathan after 350 Years* (Oxford: Oxford University Press, 2004), 33–73.

26. See John Locke, *A Second Treatise of Government* (1689), ¶ 147, reprinted in *Two Treatises of Government and A Letter Concerning Toleration*, Ian Shapiro, editor

(New Haven: Yale University Press, 2003), where Locke lays out the distinction between "executive" and "federative" powers:

> These two powers, executive and federative, though they be really distinct in them-
> selves, yet one comprehending the execution of the municipal laws of the society
> within its self, upon all that are parts of it; the other the management of the security
> and interest of the public without, with all those that it may receive benefit or damage
> from, yet they are always almost united. And though this federative power in the well
> or ill management of it be of great moment to the common-wealth, yet it is much
> less capable to be directed by antecedent, standing, positive laws, than the executive;
> and so must necessarily be left to the prudence and wisdom of those, whose hands it
> is in, to be managed for the public good: for the laws that concern subjects one
> amongst another, being to direct their actions, may well enough precede them. But
> what is to be done in reference to foreigners, depending much upon their actions,
> and the variation of designs and interests, must be left in great part to the prudence
> of those, who have this power committed to them, to be managed by the best of their
> skill, for the advantage of the common-wealth.

27. Locke, *Second Treatise*, ¶ 222, reprinted in *Two Treatises of Government*, Shapiro edition, 197–98 (quotation in text); see ibid., 136, 155, 178 (various points where Locke
makes it clear that "property" includes people's "lives, liberties, and estates"). See
generally Ian Shapiro, "John Locke's Democratic Theory," in ibid., 309–40; Richard
Ashcraft, "Locke's Political Philosophy," in Vere Chappell, editor, *The Cambridge
Companion to Locke* (Cambridge: Cambridge University Press, 1994), 226–51.

28. *The Federalist* No. 1 (Hamilton), Rossiter edition, 33 (first quotation in text, with
emphasis added); ibid., 36 (second quotation, emphasis in original); *The Federalist*
No. 78 (Hamilton) (advantages of a national judiciary; key role of federal judges was
to take the edge off of "partial and unjust laws"). See generally David Epstein, *The
Political Theory of* The Federalist (Chicago: University of Chicago Press, 1984), 35–
58, 162–92.

29. See William J. Novak, "*Salus Populi*: The Roots of Regulation in America, 1787–
1873" (Ph.D. dissertation, Brandeis University, 1992), and *The People's Welfare: Law
and Regulation in Nineteenth Century America* (Chapel Hill: University of North
Carolina Press, 1996); Bray Hammond, *Banks and Politics in America from the
Revolution to the Civil War* (Princeton: Princeton University Press, 1957) (Bank of
the United States); Jerry L. Mashaw, "Administration and 'The Democracy': Administrative Law From Jackson to Lincoln, 1829–1861," *Yale Law Journal* 117 (2008),
1598, 1628–66 (steamship regulation).

30. See generally Daniel A. Farber, *Lincoln's Constitution* (Chicago: University of Chicago Press, 2003); Novak, *The People's Welfare*, 1–50; Stephen Skowronek, *Building a
New American State: The Expansion of National Administrative Capacities, 1877–
1920* (Cambridge: Cambridge University Press, 1982). National regulation of morals
was not as successful; consider the Mann Act of 1910, which was applied in a highly
discriminatory manner; Prohibition, which was repealed in 1933; and the Child Labor Act, which was invalidated in *Hammer v. Dagenhart*, 247 U.S. 251 (U.S. Supreme
Court, 1918).

31. Address of Governor Franklin D. Roosevelt to the Commonwealth Club, San Francisco, September 22, 1932, excerpted in *Our Democracy in Action: The Philosophy of Franklin D. Roosevelt* (Washington: National Home Library Foundation, 1940), 80–81 (quotations in text). On Hoover and the Great Flood of 1927, see John M. Barry, *Rising Tide: The Great Mississippi Flood of 1927 and How It Changed America* (New York: Simon & Schuster, 1997), 261–377.

32. President Franklin D. Roosevelt, Message to the Congress on the State of the Union (January 11, 1944), in Samuel I. Rosenman, editor, *The Public Papers and Addresses of Franklin D. Roosevelt: Victory and the Threshold of Peace, 1944–45* (New York: Random House, 1950), 13:41 (FDR's Second Bill of Rights). See generally William Edward Leuchtenberg, *The FDR Years: On Roosevelt and His Legacy* (New York: Columbia University Press, 1995); Cass R. Sunstein, *The Second Bill of Rights: FDR's Unfinished Revolution and Why We Need It More Than Ever* (New York: Basic Books, 2004).

33. *Brown v. Board of Education*, 347 U.S. 483, 493 (U.S. Supreme Court, 1954) (quotations in text). Accounts of the statutes mentioned in text are provided in chapter 3 (Sherman Act), chapter 4 (Social Security and Medicare Acts), and chapter 7 (Federal Reserve Act and its 1935 amendment).

34. John Locke, *A Letter Concerning Toleration* (1689), in *Two Treatises*, Shapiro edition, 211–54 (Locke's political philosophy arguments for religious toleration); William N. Eskridge Jr., "Pluralism and Distrust: How Courts Can Support Democracy by Lowering the Stakes of Politics," *Yale Law Journal* 114 (2005): 1279–1328, drawing from Przeworski, *Democracy and the Market*, 36–37.

35. See William N. Eskridge Jr. and Sanford Levinson, editors, *Constitutional Stupidities, Constitutional Tragedies* (New York: New York University Press, 1998), assembling an impressive roll call of "stupidities" in the Constitution that make no sense today but are entrenched in the founding document by Article V.

36. G. Allan Tarr, "Introduction," in Tarr and Robert F. Williams, editors, *State Constitutions for the Twenty-First Century: The Politics of State Constitutional Reform* (Albany, NY: State University of New York Press, 2006), 1–5. For an excellent older survey, see Donald S. Lutz, "Toward a Theory of Constitutional Amendment," in Levinson, editor, *Responding to Imperfection*, 247–49 and table 1.

37. Tarr and Williams, editors, *State Constitutions for the Twenty-First Century*, appendix, 197–203 (processes for state constitutional amendments, state by state); Lutz, "Theory of Constitutional Amendment," 263 (our Constitutional amendment rate would triple if we reduced the ratification requirement to two-thirds); ibid., 261 and table 11 (comparison of amendment rate in the United States and other countries).

38. John Hart Ely, *Democracy and Distrust: A Theory of Judicial Review* (Cambridge, MA: Harvard University Press, 1980).

39. For an argument that the Nineteenth Amendment does go further, see Reva B. Siegel, "She the People: The Nineteenth Amendment, Sex Equality, and the Family," *Harvard Law Review* 113 (2002): 947–1046.

40. On the failure of the ERA, see Carol Felsenthal, *The Sweetheart of the Silent Majority: The Biography of Phyllis Schlafly* (Garden City, NY: Doubleday, 1981), 232–42 (Schlafly's reaction to the ERA); Jane J. Mansbridge, *Why We Lost the ERA* (Chicago: University of Chicago Press, 1986).

The post–New Deal amendments have involved term-limiting the president (Amendment XXII), allowing the citizens of the District of Columbia to vote for president (XXIII), abolishing poll taxes in federal elections (XXIV), adjusting conditions for the vice president to take over the president's duties upon the latter's incapacity (XXV), giving eighteen-year-olds the right to vote (XXVI), and regulating congressional pay raises (XXVII).

41. On feminist critiques of the Constitution's insensitivity to private sources of violence against women and minorities, and episodic state efforts to do something about it, see Catharine A. MacKinnon, *Toward a Feminist Theory of the State* (Cambridge, MA: Harvard University Press, 1989); Robin West, *Progressive Constitutionalism: Reconstructing the Fourteenth Amendment* (Durham, NC: Duke University Press, 1994); Ruth Gavison, "Feminism and the Public/Private Distinction," *Stanford Law Review* 45 (1992): 1–45; Catharine A. MacKinnon, "Reflections on Sex Equality Under the Law," *Yale Law Journal* 100 (1991): 1281–1328; Mari J. Matsuda, "Public Response to Racist Speech: Considering the Victim's Story," *Michigan Law Review* 87 (1989): 2320–81.

42. U.S. Constitution, Preamble (quotation in text); ibid., art. IV (Protection Clause); ibid., XIV Amendment, § 1 (Equal Protection Clause). For a strongly affirmative, Lockean reading of the Equal Protection Clause, see Robin West, *Re-Imagining Justice: Progressive Interpretations of Formal Equality, Rights, and the Rule of Law* (Burlington, VT: Ashgate, 2003).

43. House Committee on Labor, Seventy-first Congress, *Hearings on Old Age Pensions* (1930), 166 (testimony of James A. Emery, general counsel of the National Association of Manufacturers) (first quotation in text); U.S. Constitution, Article I, § 3 (Taxing Clause, quoted in text); *Old Age Pensions, 1930*, 246 (supplemental statement of Abraham Epstein) (third quotation in text). For other arguments supporting the Constitutionality of the proposed Social Security Act, see ibid., 127 (statement of Representative Fiorello LaGuardia, New York); H. C. Gilbert, Library of Congress, Legislative Research Service, "Constitutionality of Old Age Pension Legislation" (February 12, 1930), ibid., 114–18.

44. The argument in text is adapted from West, *Progressive Constitutionalism.* For the dilemma faced by progressives arguing for more expansive rights protections the Supreme Court declines to find, see Robin West, "Constitutional Skepticism," *Boston University Law Review* 72 (1992): 765–98.

45. These institutionally driven readings, by the way, cut across ideological boundaries. While judicial conservatives insist upon federalism limits on Congress's authority, the right to bear arms, the free exercise right for religions, judicial progressives push for separation of powers limits on the president's authority, the right to privacy, and the antiestablishment of religion. And the social movements petitioning the Court for rights that advance their agendas tend to frame their Constitutional claims in terms of negative liberty and structural limits.

46. *Federalist* No.78 (Hamilton), Rossiter edition, 465–66, 469 (quotations in text). Much of our analysis updating Hamilton's argument is inspired by Neil K. Komesar, *Imperfect Alternatives: Choosing Institutions in Law, Economics, and Public Policy* (Chicago: University of Chicago Press, 1994), 123–50, who suggests that legal theorists

must evaluate judicial review in terms of the roles that the judiciary, as an institution, can most competently perform. For other dim appraisals of the federal judiciary's competence to perform more than the most elementary rule of law functions, see Larry D. Kramer, "The Supreme Court, 2000 Term—Foreword: We the Court," *Harvard Law Review* 115 (2001): 4–108; Bork, *The Tempting of America.*

47. On the Supreme Court's tendency to underenforce Constitutional norms and principles, see Lawrence G. Sager, "Fair Measure: The Legal Status of Underenforced Constitutional Norms," *Harvard Law Review* 91 (1978): 1212–64, as well as Sager, "Justice in Plain Clothes: Reflections on the Thinness of Constitutional Law," *Northwestern University Law Review* 88 (1993): 410–35.

48. See, e.g., Joan C. Williams and Stephanie Bornstein, "Symposium: The Evolution of 'FreD': Family Responsibilities Discrimination and Developments in the Law of Stereotyping and Implicit Bias," *Hastings Law Journal* 59 (2008): 1311–58; Joan C. Williams and Nancy Segal, "Beyond the Maternal Wall: Relief for Family Caregivers Who Are Discriminated Against on the Job," *Harvard Women's Law Journal* 26 (2003): 77–162. See also Nancy E. Dowd, "Work and Family: The Gender Paradox and the Limitations of Discrimination Analysis in Restructuring the Workplace," *Harvard Civil Rights–Civil Liberties Law Review* 24 (1989): 79–172; Rosalind Chait Barnett, "Preface: Women and Word: Where We Are, Where Did We Come From, and Where Are We Going?" *Journal of Social Issues* 60 (2006): 667–74.

49. On standing, compare *Allen v. Wright*, 468 U.S. 737, 740, 766 (U.S. Supreme Court, 1984) (denying standing to parents of color suing the federal government for continuing to fund segregated academies, because the parents had no "particularized" injury), with *Massachusetts v. EPA*, 549 U.S. 497, 505–06 (U.S. Supreme Court, 2007) (allowing a state plus some environmentalists to sue EPA for failing to enforce environmental directives), with ibid., 535 (Roberts, C.J., dissenting) (persuasively demonstrating that standing in this case was very unusual in light of traditional Supreme Court practice).

On political questions, compare *Boumediene v. Bush*, 128 S.Ct. 2229, 2240 (U.S. Supreme Court, 2008) (adjudicating claim by accused enemy combatants, notwithstanding congressional and presidential determination that administrative procedures and limited judicial review were sufficient), with ibid., 2279–93 (Roberts, C.J., dissenting) (arguing that detainees' claims were nonjusticiable and, at best, premature).

50. *Geduldig v. Aiello*, 417 U.S. 484 (U.S. Supreme Court, 1974) (upholding California's exclusion of pregnancy claims from its disability-unemployment law); Pregnancy Discrimination Act of 1978, Public Law No. 95-555, 92 Stat. 2076 (1978), codified at 42 U.S.C. § 2000e(k); EEOC, "Employment Policies Relating to Pregnancy and Childbirth," *Federal Register* 44 (April 20, 1979): 23805–12 (codified at 29 C.F.R. § 1604.10) (EEOC regulations and explanatory materials implementing PDA). The normative history of the PDA is recounted in William N. Eskridge Jr., "America's Statutory Constitution," *University of California, Davis, Law Review* 41 (2007): 1–44.

51. Americans with Disabilities Act of 1990, Public Law No. 101-336, 104 Stat. 327 (1990), codified at 42 U.S.C. § 12101 et seq. For a detailed analysis of the Supreme Court's narrowing of the ADA, see Michael Selmi, "Interpreting the Americans with Dis-

abilities Act: Why the Supreme Court Rewrote the Statute, and Why Congress Doesn't Care," *George Washington Law Review* 76 (2008): 522–75. Most of the Court's opinions have been modified or overridden by the ADA Amendments Act of 2008, Public Law No. 110-325 (effective January 1, 2009).

52. For feminist analysis supporting affirmative protections, see, e.g., Lise Vogel, *Mothers on the Job: Maternity Policy in the U.S. Workplace* (New Brunswick, NJ: Rutgers University Press, 1993); Wendy Webster Williams, "Notes from a First Generation," *University of Chicago Legal Forum* 99 (1989): 99–113.

53. *Nevada Department of Human Resources v. Hibbs*, 538 U.S. 721, 737 (U.S. Supreme Court, 2002) (quotation in text).

54. U.S. Department of Labor, *Family and Medical Leave Surveys, 2000* (Washington, DC: GPO, 2001). For critiques of the FMLA's limitations, see Amy Armenia and Naomi Gerstel, "Family Leaves, the FMLA, and Gender Neutrality: The Intersection of Race and Gender," *Social Science Research* 35 (2006): 872–86; Wen-Jui Han and Jane Waldfogel, "Parental Leave: The Impact of Recent Legislation on Parents' Leave Taking," *Demography* 40 (2003): 198ff.

55. Noah D. Zatz, "Managing the Macaw: Third-Party Harassers, Accommodation, and the Disaggregation of Discriminatory Intent," *Columbia Law Review* 209 (2009).

56. For an exemplar of the excellence the standard account still calls forth, see, e.g., Amar, *America's Constitution*. Ironically, Professor Amar is now a coeditor of the Constitutional law casebook that most systematically questions the standard account. See Paul Brest, Sanford Levinson, Jack Balkin, Akhil Reed Amar, and Reva B. Siegel, *Processes of Constitutional Decisionmaking: Cases and Materials* (New York: Aspen, fifth edition, 2006).

57. Mark V. Tushnet, *Taking the Constitution Away from the Courts* (Princeton: Princeton University Press, 1999). Since Tushnet's book, there has developed a virtual cottage industry of legal academics urging an abolition or drastic curtailment of the Supreme Court's role in interpreting the Constitution. E.g., Mark Graber, *Dred Scott and the Problem of Constitutional Evil* (Cambridge: Cambridge University Press, 2006) (drastic curtailment); Larry D. Kramer, *The People Themselves: Popular Constitutionalism and Judicial Review* (Oxford: Oxford University Press, 2004) (drastic curtailment); Jeremy Waldron, *Democracy and Disagreement* (Oxford: Oxford University Press, 1999) (abolition); Keith Whittington, *Political Foundations of Judicial Supremacy: The Presidency, the Supreme Court, and Constitutional Leadership in U.S. History* (Princeton: Princeton University Press, 2007) (significant curtailment); Christopher L. Eisgruber, "Judicial Supremacy and Constitutional Distortion," in Sotirios Barber and Robert P. George, editors, *Constitutional Politics: Essays on Constitutional Making, Maintenance, and Change* (Princeton: Princeton University Press, 2001), 70–90 (significant curtailment); George Thomas, "Recovering the Political Constitution: The Madisonian Vision," *Review of Politics* 66 (2004); 233–56 (significant curtailment).

58. Philip Bobbitt, *Terror and Consent: The Wars for the Twenty-First Century* (New York: Alfred A. Knopf, 2008). For early discussions of the new public law, see William N. Eskridge Jr. and Gary Peller, "The New Public Law Movement: Moderation as a Postmodern Cultural Form," *Michigan Law Review* 89 (1991): 707–91; Edward

Rubin, "The Concept of Law and the New Public Law Scholarship," *Michigan Law Review* 89 (1991): 792–836.

59. Alexander M. Bickel, *The Least Dangerous Branch: The Supreme Court at the Bar of Politics* (New Haven: Yale University Press, 1962), popularized the term "countermajoritarian difficulty." Our leading historian of this concept is Professor Barry Friedman. See, e.g., Friedman, "The Birth of an Obsession: The History of the Countermajoritarian Difficulty (Part Five)," *Yale Law Journal* 112 (2002): 153–259.

60. Bruce Ackerman, *We the People 2: Transformations* (New Haven: Yale University Press, 1998), 32–68 (unconventional politics of the Philadelphia Framers and the Federalist proponents of the new Constitution), 99–119 (unconventional politics of Reconstruction Amendments).

61. Bruce Ackerman, *We the People 1: Foundations* (New Haven: Yale University Press, 1991), 49–50. See also Ackerman, *We the People 2*, 359–60, which maps out a more comprehensive pattern of events for the New Deal transformation: Triggering election, 1936 → Unconventional threat by FDR, 1937 → Court's switch in time, 1937–38 → Transformative FDR appointments to the Court, 1937–38 → Consolidating elections, 1938 and 1940 → More transformative appointments, 1939–42 → Final consolidation of new Constitutional order by the reformed Court. For a formalization of this more complicated process for amending the Constitution, see ibid., 403–18; Bruce Ackerman, *The Failure of the Founding Fathers* (Cambridge, MA: Harvard University Press, 2005), 7–11.

62. Compare Bruce Ackerman, "Constitutional Politics/Constitutional Law," *Yale Law Journal* 99 (1989): 531–36, which provides a rigorous logic-based critique of *Plessy* in light of the New Deal Moment, with Mark Tushnet, "Following the Rules Laid Down: A Critique of Interpretivism and Neutral Principles," *Harvard Law Review* 96 (1983): 781–827, which defends *Brown* as an exercise in Constitutional translation. Accord, Lawrence Lessig, "Fidelity in Translation," *Texas Law Review* (1993): 1165, 1171–72. Although most originalists consider translation too dynamic to qualify as a good theory of original meaning, e.g., Steven Calabresi, "The Tradition of the Written Constitution: A Comment on Professor Lessig's Theory of Translation," *Fordham Law Review* 65 (1997): 1435–56, conservatives defending *Brown* have generally fallen back on a theory of "we have learned a lot about why southern apartheid is bad since 1933." E.g., Bork, *The Tempting of America*, 81–82; Richard A. Posner, *The Problems of Jurisprudence* (Cambridge, MA: Harvard University Press, 1990), 302–09.

63. Ackerman, *We the People 1*, 272–77 ("depth," "breadth," and "decisiveness"), 285–90 ("mobilized deliberation" and "codification"); Bruce Ackerman, "The Living Constitution," *Harvard Law Review* 120 (2007): 1737–1812 (published version of the 2006 Oliver Wendell Holmes Lectures). Critics taking Ackerman to task for posing an unadministrable "moments" test include Richard A. Posner, *Overcoming Law* (Cambridge, MA: Harvard University Press, 1995); Michael J. Gerhardt, "Ackermania: The Quest for a Common Law of Higher Lawmaking," *William & Mary Law Review* 40 (1999): 1731–94; Suzanna Sherry, "The Ghost of Liberalism Past," *Harvard Law Review* 105 (1992): 918–34.

64. On the FMLA as a key issue, perhaps the biggest single issue, in the 1992 election, see Martha Fitzsimmons, editor, *The Finish Line: Covering the Campaign's Final Days* (New York: Freedom Forum Media Studies Center, 1993); Lauren J. Asher and

Donna R. Lenhoff, "Reports from the Field: Family and Medical Leave: Making Time for Family Is Everyone's Business," *Caring for Infants and Toddlers* 11 (2001), available at www.futureofchildren.org/information2827/information_show.htm?doc_id=79389 (viewed February 7, 2009).

65. The treatment of the Civil Rights Act of 1964 in Ackerman, "Living Constitution" (2007), sounds a lot like its treatment in William N. Eskridge Jr. and John Ferejohn, "Super-Statutes," *Duke Law Journal* 50 (2000): 1215–76, a point Ackerman acknowledges, "Living Constitution," 1753 note 38, with the further observation (which we share) that the main difference is whether "landmark statutes . . . deserve *full* admission into the [C]onstitutional canon." Ibid. (emphasis in original).

66. One way to view the Ackermanian position is to say that the PDA as a Constitutional Amendment (or Mini-Moment) overruled *Geduldig* as a matter of *authoritative command*, the same way that the Fourteenth Amendment overruled *Dred Scott*. Yet the two Constitutional experiences are markedly different: Reconstruction Republicans announced to the country that they wanted *Dred Scott* expunged from the Constitution, and We the People responded with approval, while PDA feminists were only publicly attacking *Gilbert*.

67. John Yoo, *The Powers of War and Peace: The Constitution and Foreign Affairs After 9/11* (Chicago: University of Chicago Press, 2005). For some thoughtful efforts to elbow judicial review out of the National Security Constitution, see Eric A. Posner and Adrian Vermeule, *Terror in the Balance: Security, Liberty, and the Courts* (Oxford: Oxford University Press, 2007); John Yoo, *War by Other Means: An Insider's Account of the War on Terror* (New York: Atlantic Monthly Press, 2006).

68. Yoo, *Powers of War and Peace*; John Choon Yoo, "The Continuation of Politics by Other Means: The Original Understanding of War Powers," *California Law Review* 84 (1996): 167–305. Yoo's use of historical materials is sharply criticized by William Michael Treanor, "Fame, the Founding, and the Power to Declare War," *Cornell Law Review* 82 (1997): 695–772, as well as Jane Stromseth, "Understanding Constitutional War Powers Today: Why Methodology Matters," *Yale Law Journal* 106 (1996): 860–61; David Cole, "What Bush Wants to Hear," *New York Review of Books*, November 17, 2006, 8–11. See also Martin S. Flaherty, "History Right? Historical Scholarship, Original Understanding, and Treaties as 'Supreme Law of the Land,'" *Columbia Law Review* 99 (1999): 2095–2153, for a more general indictment of Yoo's historical methodology.

69. Yoo, *Powers of War and Peace*, 9–10; *Dames & Moore v. Regan*, 453 U.S. 654 (U.S. Supreme Court, 1981) (upholding presidential Iranian Hostages Agreement and applying it to require that valid American lawsuits against Iran be "suspended").

70. Yoo, *Powers of War and Peace*, 17 (the "dynamic manner" in which the Constitution creates foreign affairs powers "can be read to permit existing practice"); ibid., 299–302 (globalization as the new engine expanding Constitutional limits); ibid., 250–92 (detailed examination of executive-legislative agreements); Oona A. Hathaway, "Treaties' End: The Past, Present, and Future of International Lawmaking in the United States," *Yale Law Journal* 117 (2008): 1236–1362.

71. Compare Bruce Ackerman and David Golove, "Is NAFTA Constitutional?" *Harvard Law Review* 108 (1998): 799, 861–96, arguing that the New Deal Constitutional

Moment rendered congressional-executive agreements interchangeable with treaties, with Yoo, *Powers of War and Peace*, 259–64, which rejects that theory.

72. On the new threats exposed by 9/11, and the expansive understanding of Article II
those threats call forth, see Yoo, *Powers of War and Peace*, 1–24; Posner and Vermeule, *Terror in the Balance*. On the adverse possession argument for the unitary
executive, see Steven G. Calabresi and Christopher S. Yoo (no relation to John Yoo),
The Unitary Executive: Presidential Power from Washington to Bush (New Haven:
Yale University Press, 2008), a president-by-president survey of unitary executive assertions and mini-showdowns with Congress and the Court over issues included in
that concept.

73. EEOC, "Guidelines on Discrimination Because of Sex," *Federal Register* 37 (April 5,
1972): 6835–37 (EEOC's original sex discrimination guidelines, including a bar to
discrimination against pregnant workers). For an excellent account of the debates
within the EEOC, see Kevin Schwartz, "Equalizing Pregnancy: The Birth of a
Super-Statute" (Yale Law School Supervised Analytic Writing paper, 2005).

74. Attorney General Edwin Meese, "The Law of the Constitution," *Tulane Law Review*
61 (1987): 985–86 (quotations in text). For political science support for Meese's positive
thesis, see, e.g., Stephen M. Griffin, *American Constitutionalism: From Theory to Politics* (Princeton: Princeton University Press, 1996); Mark A. Graber, *Rethinking Abortion: Equal Choice, the Constitution, and Reproductive Politics* (Princeton: Princeton
University Press, 1996); Whittington, *Political Foundations of Judicial Supremacy*.

75. Among the leading appreciations of General Meese's view that Constitutionalism is
institutionally polycentric rather than exclusively judicial are Sanford Levinson,
"Can Meese Be Right This Time?" *Tulane Law Review* 61 (1987): 1071–78; Michael
Stokes Paulsen, "The Most Dangerous Branch: Executive Power to Say What the
Law Is," *Georgetown Law Journal* 83 (1994): 217–345. An expansion of Attorney General Meese's point is systematically defended in Saikrishna Banglaore Prakash, "The
Executive's Duty to Disregard Unconstitutional Laws," *Georgetown Law Journal* 96
(2008): 1613–83. The term *polycentric Constitutionalism* is inspired by Robert C. Post
and Reva B. Siegel, "Legislative Constitutionalism and Section 5 Power: Policentric
Interpretation of the Family and Medical Leave Act," *Yale Law Journal* 112 (2003):
1943–2059. Our work is represented in William N. Eskridge Jr. and John Ferejohn,
"Virtual Logrolling: How the Court, Congress, and the States Multiply Rights,"
Southern California Law Review 68 (1995): 1545–64, and "The Article I, Section 7
Game," *Georgetown Law Journal* 80 (1992): 523–64.

76. Leading sources for the notion of public values as the product of a dialogue among
institutions include Henry M. Hart Jr. and Albert M. Sacks, *The Legal Process: Basic
Problems in the Making and Application of Law*, William N. Eskridge Jr. and Philip
P. Frickey, editors (Westbury, NY: Foundation Press, 1994 [1958 tentative edition]),
1209–10; Barry Friedman, "Dialogue and Judicial Review," *Michigan Law Review* 91
(1993): 577–697; ibid., 581 (first quotation in text); Michael C. Dorf and Barry Friedman, "Shared Constitutional Interpretation," *Supreme Court Review* 2000: 61–107.

77. President's Commission on the Status of Women, *American Women* (Washington,
DC: 1963), 44–45 (quotation in text); Harrison, *On Account of Sex* (NOW); Jo Ann
Freeman, *The Politics of Women's Liberation: A Case Study of an Emerging Social*

Movement and Its Relation to the Policy Process (New York: MacKay, 1975), 202–04 (anti-sex-discrimination statutes, 1971–72). For the statutes described in text, see Equal Employment Opportunity Act of 1972, Public Law No. 92-261, 86 Stat. 103 (1972); Education Amendments of 1972, Public Law No. 92-318, § 901, 86 Stat. 235, 373–74 (1972); Act of October 14, 1972, Public Law No. 92-496, § 3, 86 Stat. 813–14 (1972) (expanding mission of Civil Rights Commission to include sex discrimination); State and Local Fiscal Assistance Act of 1972, Public Law No. 92-512, § 122, 86 Stat. 919, 932 (1972) (sex discrimination bar for funds used by state and local governments).

78. *Frontiero v. Richardson*, 411 U.S. 677 (U.S. Supreme Court, 1973) (striking down a federal statutory discrimination against the spouses of women serving in the armed forces); *Geduldig v. Aiello*, 417 U.S. 484 (U.S. Supreme Court, 1974) (upholding California's exclusion of pregnancy-based disability from its unemployment compensation fund).

79. Our generalizations are largely taken from House Committee on Education and Labor, Ninety-fifth Congress, First Session, *Hearings on Legislation to Prohibit Sex Discrimination on the Basis of Pregnancy* (1977); e.g., ibid., 50–52 (testimony of Sherrie O'Steen). There was similar testimony in Senate Committee on Human Resources, Ninety-fifth Congress, First Session, *Hearings on Pregnancy Discrimination* (1977).

80. *1977 House Pregnancy Hearings*, 11–20 (statement of Professor Wendy Webster Williams, Georgetown University Law Center, and lawyer in *Geduldig*); ibid., 30–42 (statement of Susan Deller Ross, Campaign to End Discrimination against Pregnant Workers); ibid., 173–89 (statement and testimony of Alexis Herman, director, Women's Bureau of Employment Standards Administration, U.S. Department of Labor). Director Herman also responded to the argument that the PDA would be costly to employers. See ibid., 180–86 (letter from Alexis Herman, director, Women's Bureau of Employment Standards Administration, U.S. Department of Labor, to Rep. Augustus Hawkins, subcommittee chair).

81. For an excellent treatment of the PDA Coalition, see Kevin Schwartz, "Equalizing Pregnancy."

82. EEOC, "Employment Policies Relating to Pregnancy and Childbirth," *Federal Register* 44 (April 20, 1979): 23805–12 (codified at 29 C.F.R. § 1604.10 [2007]); Family and Medical Leave Act of 1993, Public Law No. 103-3 (1993), upheld in *Nevada Department of Human Resources v. Hibbs*, 538 U.S. 721 (U.S. Supreme Court, 2003), discussed in the Conclusion to this book.

83. Reva B. Siegel, "You've Come a Long Way, Baby: Rehnquist's New Approach to Pregnancy Discrimination in *Hibbs*," *Stanford Law Review* 58 (2006): 1871–98. See also Post and Siegel, "Policentric Interpretation of the Family and Medical Leave Act."

CHAPTER 2. THE DEMOCRATIC CONSTITUTION
AND OUR EPISODIC REPUBLIC

1. The account in text is taken from the Record on Appeal, 7–8, *Lassiter v. Northampton County Board of Elections*, 360 U.S. 45 (U.S. Supreme Court, 1961) (1958 Term, Docket No. 589).

2. Brief of Appellant, 27–33, *Lassiter* (1958 Term, Docket No. 589) (Lassiter's argument that the state literacy requirement violated the Fourteenth Amendment), unanimously

rejected in *Lassiter v. Northampton County Board of Elections*, 360 U.S. 45 (U.S. Supreme Court, 1961). On the origins of the North Carolina law, as part of a systematic campaign to exclude people of color from the franchise, see J. Morgan Kousser, *The Shaping of Southern Politics: Suffrage Restriction and the Establishment of the One-Party South, 1880–1910* (New Haven: Yale University Press, 1974), 11–44, 56–62, 183–95.

3. Sean Wilentz, *The Shaping of American Democracy, 1789–1865* (Princeton: Princeton University Press, 2004), 116–25 (expansion of the franchise during the Jefferson presidency), 177–78 (same, Madison), 181–202 (same, Monroe); Akhil Reed Amar, *America's Constitution: A Biography* (New York: Random House, 2005), 395–401 (Fifteenth Amendment, no race discrimination in the franchise); ibid., 421–25 (Nineteenth Amendment, no sex discrimination); ibid., 443 (Twenty-fourth, no poll taxes in federal elections); ibid., 445–47 (Twenty-sixth, eighteen-year-olds can vote). See generally Alexander Keyssar, *The Right to Vote: The Contested History of Democracy in the United States* (New Haven: Yale University Press, 2000).

4. Voting Rights Act of 1965, Public Law No. 89–110, § 4, 79 Stat. 445 (1965) (suspension of literacy tests in selected jurisdictions); ibid., § 5 (requiring southern jurisdictions to obtain DOJ or D.C. Circuit "preclearance" for any change in voting rules or districts). On the inefficacy of case-by-case enforcement of Constitutional voting rights, see David J. Garrow, *Protest at Selma: Martin Luther King Jr. and the Voting Rights Act of 1965* (New Haven: Yale University Press, 1978), 11–30. On the ways in which the litigation informed the drafting of the new statute, see Brian K. Landsberg, *Free at Last to Vote: The Alabama Origins of the 1965 Voting Rights Act* (Lawrence: University Press of Kansas, 2007).

5. Our thinking about "democratic constitutionalism" has been influenced by a variety of important works, among them being Henry S. Richardson, *Democratic Autonomy: Public Reasoning About the Ends of Policy* (New York: Oxford University Press, 2002); Iris Marion Young, *Inclusion and Democracy* (Oxford: Oxford University Press, 2000); Bruce Ackerman, "The Living Constitution," *Harvard Law Review* 120 (2007): 1737–1812 (published version of the 2006 Oliver Wendell Holmes Lectures).

6. Our views about "liberty" are informed by Philip Pettit, *Republicanism: A Theory of Freedom and Government* (Oxford: Clarendon Press, 1997), as critically appreciated in John Ferejohn, "Pettit's Republic," *Monist* 84 (2001): 77–95; Frank I. Michelman, "The Supreme Court, 1985 Term—Foreword: Traces of Self-Government," *Harvard Law Review* 100 (1986): 4–77.

7. Among the theoretical work that has influenced our thinking about institutional deliberation in the modern administrative state, these have been the most important: Richardson, *Democratic Autonomy*; Barry Friedman, "Dialogue and Judicial Review," *Michigan Law Review* 91 (1993): 577–697; Mark C. Suchman and Lauren B. Edelman, "Legal Rational Myths: The New Institutionalism and the Law and Society Tradition," *Law and Social Inquiry* 21 (1996): 903–41.

8. U.S. Const. art. I, § 1, cl. 2 (following state voting rules for House elections); ibid., art. II, § 1, cl. 2 (state legislatures to determine voting rules for selection of presidential electors); ibid., XVII Am., § 1 (following state voting rules for Senate elections). The

Supreme Court upheld a blatantly exclusionary literacy test in *Williams v. Mississippi*, 170 U.S. 213 (1898), and followed *Williams* in subsequent cases.

9. See Aristotle, *Politics* (ca. 330 B.C.), book III, in Jonathan Barnes, editor, *The Complete Works of Aristotle* (Princeton: Princeton University Press, 1984), 2:2023–45; Polybius, *The Rise of the Roman Empire* (ca. 146 B.C.), book VI, modern edition, F. W. Walbank, editor, and Ian Scott-Kilvert, translator (New York: Penguin, 1979), 302–52; Charles de Secondat, baron de Montesquieu, *The Spirit of the Laws* (1748), book XI, modern edition, Anne E. Cohler, editor and translator (New York: Cambridge University Press, 1989), 149–82; Alexis de Tocqueville, *Democracy in America* (1835), modern edition, Isaac Kramnick, editor, and Gerald E. Bevan, translator (New York: Penguin, 2003).

10. On the end of the Roman Republic, see Michael Grant, "Introduction," in Cicero, *On Government*, modern edition, Michael Grant, translator (New York: Penguin, 1993), 1–12.

11. On the Athenian constitution and its evolution, see Mogens Herman Hansen, *The Athenian Democracy in the Age of Demosthenes* (Norman: University of Oklahoma Press, 1991); Josiah Ober, *Mass and Elite in Democratic Athens* (Princeton: Princeton University Press, 1989), 53–103; Martin Ostwald, *From Popular Sovereignty to the Sovereignty of Law* (Berkeley: University of California Press, 1986).

12. Plato, *Crito*, in Eric H. Warmington and Philip G. Rouse, editors, *The Great Dialogues of Plato*, W. H. D. Rouse, translator (New York: New American Library, 1956), 447, 454–59 (Socrates' concluding speech accepting the judgment of the jury and refusing to defy the laws of Athens by fleeing). See also Ober, *Democratic Athens*, for an account of Pericles and Demosthenes.

13. Aristotle, *Politics*, book III, § 4, in Barnes, editor, *Complete Works*, 2:2026 (first quotation in text, emphasis supplied); ibid., book IV, § 11, in Barnes, editor, *Complete Works*, 2:2056 (second quotation); book IV, § 1, in Barnes, editor, *Complete Works*, 2:2046 (third quotation); see ibid., book II, in Barnes, editor, *Complete Works*, 2:2000–2023 (analyzing various constitutions of different Greek city states, including Athens and Sparta).

14. Aristotle, *Politics*, book IV, § 1, in Barnes, editor, *Complete Works*, 2:2046 (quotation in text). On the British constitution, see, e.g., Barry R. Weingast, "The Economic Role of Political Institutions: Federalism, Markets, and Economic Development," *Journal of Law, Economics, and Organization* 11, no. 1 (1995): 1–31.

15. Aristotle, *Constitution of Athens*, in Barnes, editor, *Complete Works*, 2:2341–83 (history and critique of the Athenian constitution); Aristotle, *Politics*, book IV, §§ 11–12 (the "best political community" and the most stable government is one "formed by citizens of the middle class").

16. Polybius, *Rise of Roman Empire*, book VI, §§ 3–10, in Walbank edition, 303–11 (following Aristotle in supporting the superiority of a mixed constitution), §§ 11–18, in Walbank edition, 311–18 (applying this notion to explain the power of the Roman constitution); Montesquieu, *Spirit of the Laws*, book XI, §§ 12–19, in Cohler edition, 165–81 (developing Aristotle-Polybius defense of mixed government); ibid., book XI, § 6, in Cohler edition, 151–52 (separation of powers).

17. Aristotle, *Constitution of Athens*, §§ 12–23, in Barnes, editor, *Complete Works*, 2:2346–56 (with fits and starts, Athens's constitution became more democratic); Polybius, *Rise of Roman Empire*, book VI, §§ 51–56, in Walbank edition, 344–49.

18. See generally J. G. A. Pocock, *The Machiavellian Moment: Florentine Political Thought and the Atlantic Republican Tradition* (Princeton: Princeton University Press, 1975), 506–52; Bernard Bailyn, *The Ideological Origins of the American Revolution* (Cambridge, MA: Harvard University Press, 1967; enlarged edition, 1992); Larry D. Kramer, *The People Themselves: Popular Constitutionalism and Judicial Review* (Oxford: Oxford University Press, 2004). On the Washington administration and its creation of statutory and practical frameworks for governance, see Forrest McDonald, *The Presidency of George Washington* (Lawrence: University Press of Kansas, 1974); Leonard Dupee White, *Federalists: A Study in Administrative History* (New York: Macmillan, 1948 [revised edition, 1956]); Gerhard Casper, "An Essay in Separation of Powers: Some Early Versions and Practices," *William & Mary Law Review* 30 (1989): 211–61. We include state common law because it constituted a fundamental regulatory and normative regime for family formation, economic transactions, and property ownership. Classic constitutionalists considered the distribution of property a key feature of a society's constitution. E.g., Polybius, *Rise of Roman Empire*, book VI, §§ 47–50, in Walbank edition, 341–44; Eric Nelson, *The Greek Tradition in Republican Thought* (Cambridge: Cambridge University Press, 2004).

19. *The Federalist* Nos. 62–63 (Alexander Hamilton), in Clinton Rossiter, editor, *The Federalist Papers* (New York: New American Library, 1961), praising representative democracy; ibid., Nos. 10 (James Madison) and 49 (Hamilton), cautioning against direct democracy; Amar, *America's Constitution*, 64–76 (excellent discussion of the franchise provisions of the Constitution of 1789). The statements in text are not so true for Thomas Jefferson, who had much greater faith in We the People than his political contemporaries (Presidents Washington and Adams, Chief Justice Jay, Secretary Hamilton, and even Jefferson's ally, Representative Madison).

20. de Toqueville, *Democracy in America*, vol. 1, part 2, chap. 5, in Kramnick edition, 228 (quotation in text); Gordon Wood, *The Radicalism of the American Revolution* (New York: Vintage, 1991); Sean Wilentz, *The Rise of American Democracy: Jefferson to Lincoln* (New York: Norton, 2005), 116–25 (democratization under Jefferson), 177–78 (Madison), 181–202 (Monroe). On the history of state, and therefore national, voting rules, see Keyssar, *The Right to Vote*.

21. Wilentz, *Rise of American Democracy*, 312–455 (Jackson's presidency), 483–89 (transformation of the Whig Party). For recent contrasting explorations of this period, see Daniel Walker Howe, *What God Hath Wrought: The Transformation of America, 1815–1848* (Oxford: Oxford University Press, 2006); Walter A. McDougall, *Throes of Democracy: The American Civil War Era, 1829–1877* (New York: Harper, 2005); David S. Reynolds, *Waking Giant: America in the Age of Jackson* (New York: Harper, 2008).

22. On the Constitutional expansion of the franchise, see Ellen DuBois, *Feminism and Suffrage: The Emergence of an Independent Women's Movement in America, 1848–1869* (Ithaca, NY: Cornell University Press, 1978); Aileen S. Kraditor, *The Ideas of the Woman Suffrage Movement, 1890–1920* (New York: Columbia University Press, 1965); David A. J. Richards, *Conscience and the Constitution: History, Theory, and*

Law of the Reconstruction Amendments (Lawrence: University Press of Kansas, 1993). On direct democracy, see Initiative and Referendum Institute, *Overview of Initiative Use, 1904–2006* (November 2006); Elisabeth R. Gerber, *The Populist Paradox: Interest Group Influence and the Promise of Direct Democracy* (Princeton: Princeton University Press, 1999); John G. Matsusaka, *For the Many or the Few: The Initiative, Public Policy, and American Democracy* (Chicago: University of Chicago Press, 2004).

23. Keyssar, *Right to Vote*, 141–46; Kousser, *Shaping of Southern Politics*, 239 (table 9.1, cataloguing the precise new voting restrictions adopted by southern states, 1871–1908); Jeff Manza and Christopher Uggen, *Locked Out: Felon Disenfranchisement and American Democracy* (New York: Oxford University Press, 2006), 41–68 (felon disenfranchisement laws in North, 1840s–50s, and South, 1870s–1900s).

24. On America's democracy-enhancing response to Nazi Germany and Communist Russia, see Mary Dudziak, *Cold War and Civil Rights: Race and the Image of American Democracy* (Chicago: University of Chicago Press, 2000); Richard Primus, *The American Language of Rights* (Cambridge: Cambridge University Press, 1999).

25. Voting Rights Act of 1965, §§ 4–5, 10; *Harper v. Virginia Board of Elections*, 383 U.S. 663 (U.S. Supreme Court, 1966) (accepting the Department of Justice's petition to overturn all state poll taxes as unConstitutional); David L. Epstein et al., *The Future of the Voting Rights Act* (New York: Russell Sage, 2006). On the pressures, including judicial pressure, undermining the exclusion of blacks as early as the 1930s, and escalating after World War II, see Michael J. Klarman, *From Jim Crow to Civil Rights: The Supreme Court and the Struggle for Racial Equality* (Oxford: Oxford University Press, 2004).

26. *South Carolina v. Katzenbach*, 383 U.S. 301 (U.S. Supreme Court, 1966), upholding the VRA § 4's suspension of literacy tests and § 5's preclearance requirement; *Katzenbach v. Morgan*, 384 U.S. 641 (U.S. Supreme Court, 1966), upholding the VRA § 4(e)'s special voting rules for Spanish-language voters who had completed sixth grade in Puerto Rican schools; *City of Rome v. United States*, 446 U.S. 156 (U.S. Supreme Court, 1980), upholding refusal to preclear voting changes having a disparate impact on racial minorities; Voting Rights Act Reauthorization in 1982, Public Law 97-205, § 3, 96 Stat. 134 (1982), amending the VRA § 2 to cover voting rules that have a racial effect. For an excellent history of VRA § 5, see J. Morgan Kousser, "The Strange and Ironic Career of Section 5 of the Voting Rights Act, 1965–2002," *Texas Law Review* 86 (2008): 667–775.

27. On the pervasive importance of the two-party system, see Daryl J. Levinson and Richard H. Pildes, "Separation of Parties, Not Powers," *Harvard Law Review* 119 (2006): 2311–86; Samuel Issacharoff and Richard H. Pildes, "Politics as Markets: Partisan Lockups of the Democratic Process," *Stanford Law Review* 50 (1998): 643–717.

28. We do not have Lassiter's testimony for this point, but documentation of discriminatory treatment and, at best, paternalistic attitudes toward black voters in Alabama is recounted in *United States v. Cartwright*, 230 F. Supp. 873 (U.S. District Court for the Middle District of Alabama, 1964) (Frank Johnson, J.); Landsberg, *Free at Last to Vote*, 44–72, 95–99. For a horrific literary parallel from South Carolina, see Sue Monk Kidd, *The Secret Life of Bees* (New York: Viking, 2002), which recounts the

story of a black woman whose effort to vote triggers white violence against her and lands her in jail when she fights back.

29. Pettit, *Republicanism*, 22–23, 35–36, critically appreciated in Ferejohn, "Pettit's Republic." See also, Pettit, *A Theory of Freedom: From the Psychology to the Politics of Agency* (Oxford: Oxford University Press, 2001), 152–74.

30. Aristotle, *Constitution of Athens*, § 16, in Barnes, editor, *Complete Works*, 2:2350–51 (first quotation in text); Plato, *Republic*, book II, ¶ 561c–d, Allan Bloom, editor and translator (New York: Basic Books, second edition, 1991) (second quotation); ibid., ¶ 563d (third quotation); Maurizio Viroli, *Machiavelli* (New York: Oxford University Press, 1998), 119 (summarizing the Roman understanding of liberty).

31. Leonardo Bruni, *Oratio in Funere Nanni Strozzae* (1428) (quotations in text), translated and quoted in Hans Baron, *The Crisis of the Early Renaissance: Civic Humanism and Republican Liberty in an Age of Classicism and Tyranny* (Princeton: Princeton University Press, 1966), 419.

32. Niccolò Machiavelli, *Discourses on the First Ten Books of Titus Livy* (1531), book II, discourse 16, Bernard Crick, editor, Leslie J. Walker, translator, with revisions by Brian Richardson (New York: Penguin, 1983), 154–57 (first two quotations in text); ibid., discourse 58, Crick edition, 252–57 (third quotation). For important, albeit differently focused, background to Machaivelli's *Discorsi*, see Baron, *The Crisis of the Early Renaissance*, 412–40; Pocock, *Machiavellian Moment*, 83–218; Quentin Skinner, *The Foundations of Modern Political Thought: The Renaissance* (Cambridge: Cambridge University Press, 1978).

33. Niccolò Machiavelli, *The Art of War* (1521), book 1, Neal Wood editor, Ellis Farneworth translator (New York: De Capo Press, 1965); Neal Wood, "Introduction," ibid., liii–lix (discussion of *virtù* in Machiavelli's thought). On the citizen who drops his plow, serves to defend the polity, and then returns to his plow, see Machiavelli, *Discourses*, book III, chaps. 25 (Cincinnatus) and 47; Machiavelli, *Art of War*, book 1, Wood edition, 15–17.

34. James Harrington, *The Commonwealth of Oceana*, Henry Morley, editor (London: G. Routledge & Sons, 1887) (1656), 27 (emphases added). For discussions of Harrington, see Fergus Millar, *The Roman Republic in Political Thought* (Hanover, NH: University Press of New England, 2002), 86–96; Pocock, *Machiavellian Moment*; Pettit, *Republicanism*, 39–40.

35. Montesquieu, *Spirit of the Laws*, book XI, § 6, in Cohler edition, 155–57 (first two quotations in text); ibid., book XII, in Cohler edition, 188 (third quotation); ibid., book III.3, in Cohler edition, 21 (fourth quotation). See also Jean-Jacques Rousseau, *On the Social Contract* (1762), in Donald A. Cress, editor and translator, *Basic Political Writings* (Indianapolis: Hackett, 1987), 150–51 (distinguishing between "natural liberty," as noninterference, and "civil liberty" as nondomination).

36. Pocock, *Machiavellian Moment*, 506–26.

37. Thomas Hobbes, *Leviathan* (1651), chaps. 21 and 47, Richard Tuck revised student edition (Cambridge: Cambridge University Press, 1996); ibid., chap. 21, in Tuck edition, 151 (quotation in text); Quentin Skinner, *Hobbes and Republican Liberty* (Cambridge: Cambridge University Press, 2008), arguing that Hobbes was the first to pose the notion of liberty as noninterference, in opposition to the republican conception

of liberty. See also Sir William Blackstone, *Commentaries on the Laws of England* (Oxford: Clarendon Press, 1765), 1:123–24, 125–29 (common law rights of all Englishmen included personal security, or "a person's legal and uninterrupted enjoyment of his life, his limbs, his body, his health and his reputation"; liberty to move about; and property, including "[t]he free use, enjoyment, and disposal of all his acquisitions, without any control or diminution save only by the laws of the land").

38. *Federalist* No. 1 (Alexander Hamilton), in *The Federalist Papers*, Clinton Rossiter, editor (New York: New American Library, 1961), 35 (first quotation in text); *Federalist* No. 51 (Madison), Rossiter edition, 323 (second quotation in text); *Federalist* No. 37 (James Madison), Rossiter edition, 231 (third quotation); *Federalist* No. 51 (Madison), Rossiter edition, 322 (fourth quotation); *Federalist* No. 78 (Hamilton), Rossiter edition, 470 (fifth quotation). On the Constitution as a hybrid of liberal and republican features, see John P. Diggins, *The Lost Soul of American Politics: Virtue, Self-Interest, and the Foundations of Liberalism* (Chicago: University of Chicago Press, 1986); Cass R. Sunstein, "Interest Groups in American Public Law," *Stanford Law Review* 38 (1985): 29–87.

39. Francis Lieber, *Manual of Political Ethics* (Philadelphia: J. P. Lippincott, second edition, 1890), 1:383–84 (first and second quotations in text); ibid., 401–02 (emphasizing the duties of helpfulness morally owed by the citizen even when not required by law); *Dred Scott v. Sandford*, 60 U.S. 393, 420–21 (U.S. Supreme Court, 1857) (third quotation).

40. The account of the reconstruction amendments, and their debt to the antislavery ideology, draws from Jacobus tenBroek, *The Antislavery Origins of the Fourteenth Amendment* (Berkeley: University of California Press, 1951); Robert Kaczorowski, "Revolutionary Constitutionalism in the Era of the Civil War and Reconstruction," *New York University Law Review* 61 (1986): 863–940; Melissa Lamb Saunders, "Equal Protection, Class Legislation, and Color-Blindness," *Michigan Law Review* 96 (1997): 245, 271–93. On the judicial retreat from the republicanism of the Reconstruction Amendments, see William E. Nelson, *The Fourteenth Amendment: From Political Principle to Judicial Doctrine* (Cambridge, MA: Harvard University Press, 1988), 148–200; Arnold M. Paul, *Conservative Crisis and the Rule of Law: Attitudes of the Bar and Bench, 1887–1895* (Gloucester, MA: Peter Smith, 1976).

41. Walt Whitman, *Democratic Vistas* (1870), in Justin Kaplan, editor, *Walt Whitman: Complete Poetry and Collected Prose* (New York: Library of America, 1982), 949 (first two quotations in text); House of Representatives, Forty-sixth Congress, Second Session, Miscellaneous Document No. 46-20 (Washington, DC: GPO 1880), 18–22 (testimony of Susan B. Anthony, third quotation); Elizabeth Cady Stanton et al., *History of Woman Suffrage* (New York: Fowler and Wells, 1881–1922) (6 volumes of documentary history of the feminist campaign for a Constitutional right to vote).

42. Jane Addams, "The Social Necessity for Social Settlements" published as "A New Impulse to An Old Gospel," *Forum* 14 (November 1892): 345–58, discussed in Victoria Bissell Brown, *The Education of Jane Addams* (Philadelphia: University of Pennsylvania Press, 2004), 263–70; Adolf A. Berle and Gardiner C. Means, *Modern Corporation and Private Property* (Chicago: Commerce Clearing House, 1932); National Resources Comm. (Gardiner C. Means), *The Structure of the American Economy* (Washington, DC: GPO, 1939–40).

43. Address of Governor Franklin D. Roosevelt to the Commonwealth Club, San Francisco, September 22, 1932, excerpted in *Our Democracy in Action: The Philosophy of Franklin D. Roosevelt* (Washington, DC: National Home Library Foundation, 1940), 80–81 (first quotation in text); Radio Address of President Franklin D. Roosevelt, November 4, 1938, excerpted in *Democracy in Action*, 167 (second quotation); Commonwealth Club Speech, 80–81 (third and fourth quotations); Address of President Franklin D. Roosevelt at Marietta, Ohio, July 8, 1938, excerpted in *Democracy in Action*, 134–36.

44. Marietta Address, 135 (first quotation in text); Address of President Franklin D. Roosevelt to the Democratic Convention at Philadelphia, July 1936, discussed in Cass R. Sunstein, *The Second Bill of Rights: FDR's Unfinished Revolution and Why We Need It More Than Ever* (New York: Basic Books, 2004), 75–77.

45. See generally David J. Garrow, *Bearing the Cross: Martin Luther King, Jr. and the Southern Christian Leadership Conference* (London: W. Morrow, 1986); Aldon D. Morris, *The Origins of the Civil Rights Movement: Black Communities Organizing for Change* (New York: Free Press, 1984). For a briefer account, see Adam Fairclough, *Better Day Coming: Blacks and Equality, 1890–2000* (New York: Viking, 2001).

46. John Hart Ely, *Democracy and Distrust: A Theory of Judicial Review* (Cambridge, MA: Harvard University Press, 1980) (elaborating on the Rooseveltian ideal of a passive Constitutionalism for socioeconomic legislation and more skeptical "representation-reinforcing" judicial review when channels of political change are being blocked); William N. Eskridge Jr., "Some Effects of Identity-Based Social Movements on Constitutional Law in the Twentieth Century," *Michigan Law Review* 100 (2002): 2194–2226 (New Deal and Warren Court's revolution in criminal procedure and habeas corpus, responding to racist applications of criminal sanction); ibid., 2299–2334 (broad application of Constitutional protections against some private actors, to open up political process); Reva B. Siegel, Comment, "Dead or Alive: Originalism as Popular Constitutionalism in *Heller*," *Harvard Law Review* 122 (2008): 191–245 (understanding the Supreme Court's recent Second Amendment activism as a response to the puissant gun rights social movement).

47. On the ferocious southern backlash against *Brown*, see Numan V. Bartley, *Rise of Massive Resistance: Race and Politics in the South During the 1950s* (Baton Rouge: Louisiana State University Press, 1969). On the Harvard Law School's critical approach to the Warren Court, see William N. Eskridge Jr. and Philip P. Frickey, "Historical and Critical Introduction," in Henry M. Hart Jr. and Albert M. Sacks, *The Legal Process: Basic Problems in the Making and Application of Law*, Eskridge and Frickey, editors (Westbury, NY: Foundation Press, 1994 [1958 tentative edition]), lix–lxii. For the March on Washington, see Garrow, *Bearing the Cross*, 231–86.

48. The quotations in text are taken from Dr. Martin Luther King Jr., "I Have a Dream" (Washington, DC, August 23, 1963), reproduced in audio and written transcript at http://www.americanrhetoric.com/speeches/mlkihaveadream.htm (viewed June 5, 2008).

49. Dr. King, "I Have a Dream" (quotations in text, emphasis added); ibid., quoting Amos 5:24.

50. On the primary importance of grass-roots mass mobilization by people of color for the success of the civil rights movement, see Fairclough, *Better Day Coming;* Garrow, *Bearing the Cross.* On the pioneering findings of the Civil Rights Commission, see Subcommittee No. 5, the House Committee on the Judiciary, Eighty-ninth Congress, First Session, *Hearings on Voting Rights* (1965), 123–311 (testimony of Reverend Theodore Hesburgh, for the U.S. Commission on Civil Rights).

51. The story of the SCLC's Selma campaign, Bloody Sunday, and their relationship to the VRA's enactment is told in magisterial detail by Garrow, *Protest at Selma*, 31–132. For the drafting history and policy basis for the VRA, see *1965 House Voting Rights Hearings*, 2–121 (testimony of Attorney General Nicholas Katzenbach and former assistant attorney general Burke Marshall); Senate Committee on the Judiciary, Eighty-ninth Congress, First Session, *Hearings on Voting Rights* (1965), 1447–1534; Landsberg, *Free at Last to Vote*, 34–147 (detailed examination of three voting rights cases litigated by the department), 148–89 (pervasive influence of the three Alabama lawsuits on the content of the VRA).

52. Montesquieu, *Spirit of the Laws*, book XI, in Cohler edition, 155–57.

53. For especially thoughtful discussions of deliberation, see Amy Gutmann and Dennis Thompson, *Democratic Disagreement* (Cambridge, MA: Belknap Press of Harvard University Press, 1996), and *Why Deliberative Democracy?* (Princeton: Princeton University Press, 2004); Henry Richardson, *Democracy and Autonomy: Public Reasoning about the Ends of Policy* (Oxford: Oxford University Press, 2002); Jeremy Waldron, *Law and Disagreement* (New York: Oxford University Press, 1999); Frank I. Michelman, "The Supreme Court, 1985 Term—Foreword: Traces of Self-Government," *Harvard Law Review* 97 (1986): 9–77.

54. *The Federalist* No. 70 (Hamilton), in Rossiter edition, 426–27 (quotation in text). On classical and Renaissance theories, see Maurizio Viroli, *Republicanism*, Antony Sugaar, translator (New York: Hill & Wang, 2002), 4; Quentin Skinner, *Reason and Rhetoric in the Philosophy of Hobbes* (Cambridge: Cambridge University Press, 1996), 15–16.

55. Garrow, *Protest at Selma*, 41 (reprinting Department of Justice's proposed Twenty-fifth Amendment, quoted in text).

56. For other dialogic theories of fundamental normative commitments, see, e.g., Robert Burt, *Constitution in Conflict* (Cambridge, MA: Belknap Press of Harvard University Press, 1992); Cass R. Sunstein, *One Case at a Time: Judicial Minimalism on the Supreme Court* (Cambridge, MA: Harvard University Press, 1999); Friedman, "Dialogue and Judicial Review"; Suzanna Sherry, "Civic Virtue and the Feminine Voice in Constitutional Law," *Virginia Law Review* 72 (1986): 543–616; Suchman and Edelman, "Legal Rational Myths."

57. Henry S. Richardson, *Practical Reasoning about Final Ends* (Cambridge: Cambridge University Press, 1994). See also Daniel A. Farber and Philip P. Frickey, "Practical Reason and the First Amendment," *UCLA Law Review* 34 (1987): 1615–56; Ernest Young, "Rediscovering Conservatism: Burkean Political Theory and Constitutional Interpretation," *North Carolina Law Review* 72 (1994): 619–703.

58. Compare John Rawls, *Political Liberalism* (Cambridge, MA: Harvard University Press, 1991), and Owen Fiss, "The Supreme Court, 1978 Term—Foreword: Forms of Justice," *Harvard Law Review* 93 (1979): 1–57, both of which depict the Supreme

Court as the ideal forum for deliberation about the nation's public values, with Aristotle, *Rhetoric*, book I, § 3, in Barnes, editor, *Complete Works*, 2:2159–61 (distinguishing between deliberative rhetoric, which looks to the future and is appropriate for policymaking, and "forensic" rhetoric, which looks to the past and is appropriate for a court at law).

59. John Dewey, *The Public and Its Problems* (New York: Henry Holt, 1927), reprinted in Jo Ann Boydston, editor, *The Later Works of John Dewey, 1925–1953* (Carbondale: Southern Illinois University Press, 1981–91), 2:364–65; Robert B. Westbrook, *John Dewey and American Democracy* (Ithaca: Cornell University Press, 1991), 300–18. See also the Address of Governor Franklin D. Roosevelt, Accepting the Democratic Presidential Nomination, July 2, 1932, reprinted in Merwin W. Hunt, editor, *Public Addresses of Franklin Delano Roosevelt* [1932–34] (Los Angeles: DeVorss, 1934), 19–32, which outlines a public law agenda supported by all "common sense citizens." Ibid., 25.

60. On the relatively uncompromised path the VRA took between between introduction and enactment, see Garrow, *Protest at Selma*, 161–78; Landsberg, *Free at Last to Vote*.

61. Richardson, *Democratic Autonomy*, 214–30, urging notice-and-comment rule making as the best way to manage the need for agency norm elaboration and the risk of unaccountable or ungrounded agency opportunism; Mark Seidenfeld, "A Civic Republican Justification for the Bureaucratic State," *Harvard Law Review* 105 (1992): 1511–76, arguing that agencies are potentially the best situs in government for public-regarding policy elaboration but exploring the limitations of agencies and how to deal with those limitations. See also Jody Freeman, "Collaborative Governance in the Administrative State," *UCLA Law Review* 45 (1997): 1–98.

62. On classical adjudication, see Lon Fuller, "The Forms and Limits of Adjudication," *Harvard Law Review* 92 (1978): 353–408. On congressional response to Supreme Court VRA interpretations, see Kousser, "Strange, Ironic Career of Section 5," 685–89 (1970 reauthorization), 707–12 (1982 reauthorization), 745–63 (2006 reauthorization); Nathaniel Persily, "The Promise and Pitfalls of the New Voting Rights Act," *Yale Law Journal* 117 (2007): 174–253 (2006 reauthorization).

63. For important institutional transformations in the years leading up to the VRA, see Landsberg, *Free at Last to Vote*, 154–55, 167–68 (experience with the 1957 and 1960 acts transformed DOJ views about literacy tests and the proper goals of those statutes); *1965 VRA House Hearings*, 124–28 (evolution of the views of the U.S. Civil Rights Commission, 1959 to 1963 Reports).

64. *1965 House Voting Rights Hearings*, 541–55 (Representative Howard Callaway, Georgia, denouncing voting discrimination because of race but asserting that existing remedies are sufficient); *1965 Senate Voting Rights Hearings*, 777–98 (Senator Sam Ervin, North Carolina, assuring the committee that people of color can vote freely in his state).

65. Among the segregationists turned out in the 1966 election were Representative Howard Smith and Senator Willis Robertson of Virginia (primary defeats); segregationist Democrats lost governorships to pro–civil rights Republicans in Arkansas and Maryland (Spiro Agnew!). Virtually all the new GOP senators (such as Howard Baker in

Tennessee, Charles Percy in Illinois, and Edmund Brooke in Massachusetts, the first African American senator since Reconstruction) and governors (such as Claude Kirk in Florida, Norbert Tiemann in Nebraska, Tom McCall in Oregon, and Dewey Bartlett in Oklahoma) were relatively pro–civil rights as well. The pattern continued in the election of integrationist Republican Linwood Holton as governor of Virginia in 1967; unlike many liberal Democrats, Holton sent his daughter to an integrated public school.

66. *Gaston County, North Carolina v. United States*, 395 U.S. 285 (U.S. Supreme Court, 1969), affirming, 288 F. Supp. 678 (U.S. District Court for the District of Columbia, three judge court, 1968). On the lethargic implementation of the VRA during the 1960s, see L. Thorne McCarty and Russell B. Stevenson, Note, "The Voting Rights Act of 1965: An Evaluation," *Harvard Civil Rights—Civil Liberties Law Review* 3 (1968): 357, 372–78.

67. Voting Rights Act Amendments of 1970, Public Law No. 91-285, 84 Stat. 315 (1970); Subcommittee No. 5, House Committee on the Judiciary, Ninety-first Congress, First Session, *Hearings on Voting Rights Act Extension* (1969), 9–69 (testimony of Howard Glickstein, General Counsel of the Civil Rights Commission); ibid., 129 (Mississippi attorney general A. F. Summer) (quotation in text); ibid., 218–45 (Attorney General John Mitchell).

68. On the beneficial effect of the VRA on southern politics, see, e.g., Luis Fuentes-Rohwer and Guy-Uriel E. Charles, "Preclearance, Discrimination, and the Department of Justice: The Case of South Carolina," *South Carolina Law Review* 57 (2006): 827–58.

69. Voting Rights Act Amendments of 1975, Public Law No. 94-73, title III, 89 Stat. 402 (1975), codified as amended at 42 U.S.C. § 1973aa-1a (protecting language-minority voters against discrimination and assuring most such voters access to voting materials in their language); Voting Rights Act Reauthorization and Amendments Act of 2006, Public Law No. 109-246, 120 Stat. 577 (2006) (retaining § 203 language-assistance rules); James Thomas Tucker, "The Politics of Persuasion: Passage of the Voting Rights Act Reauthorization Act of 2006," *Journal of Legislation* 33 (2007): 238–40 (discussing the unsuccessful 2006 proposal to delete § 203 and its relationship to immigration anxieties).

70. Donald S. Lutz, "Toward a Theory of Constitutional Amendment," in Sanford Levinson, editor, *Responding to Imperfection: The Theory and Practice of Constitutional Amendment* (Princeton: Princeton University Press, 1995), 255, tables 7 and 9 (state constitutional amendment); ibid., 263, table 15 (two-legislative-session requirements for constitutional change in other countries). For a more recent survey, see G. Allan Tarr and Robert F. Williams, editors, *State Constitutions for the Twenty-First Century: The Politics of State Constitutional Reform* (Albany: State University of New York Press, 2006).

71. *Harper v. Virginia Board of Elections*, 383 U.S. 663 (U.S. Supreme Court, 1966); Garrow, *Protest at Selma*, 121–26 (excellent account of the poll tax provisions at various points in the VRA's legislative history); Bruce Ackerman and Jennifer Nou, "Canonizing the Civil Rights Revolution: The People and the Poll Tax," *Northwestern University Law Review* 123 (2008): 63–148 (excellent account of the *Harper* litigation and its relationship to the VRA).

72. Brief for the Appellant, *Northwest Austin Municipal Utility District No. 1 v. Holder,* 129 S.Ct. 2504 (U.S. Supreme Court, 2009) (Docket No. 08-322), 43, arguing that the VRA has successfully completed its mission (thereby negating the need for section 5) and citing Abigail Thernstrom, "Section 5 of the Voting Rights Act: By Now, a Murky Mess," *Georgetown Journal of Law and Public Policy* 5 (2007): 41, 44 (arguing that today's dearth of any practices as bad as "fraudulent literacy tests" is evidence that there is no need for the VRA).

73. 2006 VRA Reauthorization § 2(b)(1), (2), and (7), 120 Stat. 577–78 (quotations in text). Summarizing congressional deliberations and findings are House Report No. 109-478 (2006); Senate Report No. 109-295 (2006). For a realistic appraisal of the odd legislative history of the 2006 reauthorization, see Persily, "The Promise and Pitfalls of the New Voting Rights Act."

74. *Northwest Austin Municipal Utility District No. 1 v. Holder,* 129 S.Ct. 2504, 2513 (U.S. Supreme Court, 2009), narrowly construing the VRA to avoid the serious constitutional attack on section 5. See also *Miller v. Johnson,* 515 U.S. 900 (U.S. Supreme Court, 1995) (interpreting the VRA to avoid Constitutional problems with race-based districting).

CHAPTER 3. THE CONSTITUTION OF THE MARKET AND STATE LEGITIMACY

1. The story in text is taken from Transcript of Record, 37–43, *Addyston Pipe and Steel Company v. United States,* 175 U.S. 211 (U.S. Supreme Court, 1899) (1898 Term, Docket No. 269).

2. See *Wabash, St. Louis & Pacific Railroad Co. v. Illinois,* 118 U.S. 557 (U.S. Supreme Court, 1886) (invalidating state regulation of railroad traffic originating or ending outside the state boundaries, as inconsistent with the negative implication of the Commerce Clause); *Allgeyer v. Louisiana,* 165 U.S. 578 (U.S. Supreme Court, 1897) (striking down a state licensing law as inconsistent with substantive due process liberty of contract guarantees). Oddly, neither of these precedents relied on the Contracts Clause, U.S. Constitution Article I, § 10, clause 1.

3. Sherman Anti-Trust Act of 1890, chap. 647, §§ 1–2, 26 Stat. 209 (1890), codified at 15 U.S.C. §§ 1–7. The Manion & Company grievance was part of the government's case against the pipe and foundry cartel in the famous case of *United States v. Addyston Pipe & Steel Co.,* 85 Fed. 271 (U.S. Court of Appeals for the Sixth Circuit, 1898) (Taft, C.J.), *affirmed,* 175 U.S. 211 (U.S. Supreme Court, 1899).

4. For a general introduction to the Sherman Act in all its complexity, see Phillip E. Areeda and Herbert Hovenkamp, *Antitrust Law: An Analysis of Antitrust Principles and Their Application* (New York: Aspen, third edition, 2006). For a recent decision applying the Court's "implied antitrust exemption" jurisprudence, see *Credit Suisse Securities v. Billing,* 551 U.S. 264 (U.S. Supreme Court, 2007).

5. On the evolution of statutory purpose as agencies apply the law, see Henry S. Richardson, *Democracy and Autonomy: Public Reasoning about the Ends of Policy* (Oxford: Oxford University Press, 2002). For an explication of the consumer-welfare, economics-based understanding of the Sherman Act, see Thomas V. Vakerics and Richard A. Givens, *Antitrust Basics: An Economic Approach* (New York: Law Journal Press, 1985).

6. Alfred D. Chandler Jr., *The Visible Hand: The Managerial Revolution in American Business* (Cambridge, MA: Belknap Press of Harvard University Press, 1977), as well as *Shaping the Industrial Century: The Remarkable Story of the Evolution of the Modern Chemical and Pharmaceutical Industries* (Cambridge, MA: Harvard University Press, 2005). See also Glenn Porter, *The Rise of Big Business, 1860–1910* (New York: Crowell, 1973).

7. Henry Billings Brown, *The Twentieth Century* (New Haven: Yale University, 1895), 14 (first quotation in text); William Letwin, *Law and Economic Policy in America: The Evolution of the Sherman Antitrust Act* (Chicago: University of Chicago Press, 1965), 54–70 (second quotation); Thomas K. McCraw, *Prophets of Regulation: Charles Francis Adams, Louis D. Brandeis, James M. Landis, and Alfred E. Kahn* (Cambridge, MA: Belknap Press of Harvard University Press, 1984), 65–79 (Americans' horror at economic concentration); Hans B. Thorelli, *The Federal Antitrust Policy: Origination of an American Tradition* (Baltimore: Johns Hopkins University Press, 1954), 63.

8. Letwin, *Evolution of the Sherman Act*, 70 (quotation in text); S. 3445, Fiftieth Congress, First Session (1888) (Sherman's original bill). The documents referred to in this section are produced and discussed by the excellent legislative history in Earl W. Kintner, editor, *The Legislative History of the Federal Antitrust Laws and Related Statutes* (New York: Chelsea House Publishers, 1978), 1:7–363.

9. First Annual Message of President Benjamin Harrison, December 3, 1889, in Kintner, *Legislative History*, 1:60 (quotation in text); Report of the House Committee on Manufactures, H.R. Report No. 50-4165 (1889); Report of the Senate Select Committee on the Transportation and Sale of Meat Products, Senate Report No. 51-829 (1890).

10. *Congressional Record* 21 (March 21, 1890): 2460 (statement of Senator Sherman) (first quotation in text); ibid., 2569 (March 24, 1890) (Senator Sherman) (second quotation).

11. S.1, as reported by the Senate Committee on the Judiciary, Fifty-first Congress, First Session, April 2, 1890, reprinted in Kintner, *Legislative History*, 1:275–77; Report of the House Committee on the Judiciary, H.R. Report No. 51-1707 (April 25, 1890), reprinted in Kintner, *Legislative History*, 1:295–96 (quotation in text).

12. S. 3445, Fiftieth Congress, Second Session (August 14, 1888) (first quotation in text); *Congressional Record* 21 (March 24, 1890): 2569 (Senator Sherman) (second quotation in text). Compare Robert H. Bork, "Legislative Intent and the Policy of the Sherman Act," *Journal of Law and Economics* 9 (1966): 7, 11–19, arguing for a narrow efficiency-based intent for the Sherman Act Congress, with Areeda and Hovenkamp, *Antitrust Law*, 1:8–11, 41–63, disagreeing with the Bork account, after an extensive examination of the legislative history.

13. *Congressional Record* 21 (March 1890): 137 (Senator Edmunds) (quotation in text). For arguments that the Sherman Act's *primary* goal was protecting small business competitors, see Herbert Hovenkamp, "Antitrust's Protected Classes," *Michigan Law Review* 88 (1989): 21–30; Robert Lande, "Wealth Transfers as the Original and Primary Concern of Antitrust: The Efficiency Interpretation Challenged," *Hastings Law Journal* 34 (1982): 65–136.

14. Richard Hofstadter, *The Age of Reform: From Bryan to F.D.R.* (New York: Vintage Books, 1955), 277 (quotation in text).

15. Letwin, *Evolution of the Sherman Act*, 103–16; Arthur M. Schlesinger Jr. and Fred Israel, editors, *History of American Presidential Elections, 1789–1968* (New York: Chelsea House, 1971), 2:1733–35 (Democrats' platform for 1892 election, quotation in text); ibid., 1738–41 (GOP platform, also supportive of the antitrust law).

16. *United States v. E.C. Knight Co.*, 156 U.S. 1 (U.S. Supreme Court, 1895); *United States v. Debs*, 64 Fed. 724 (Circuit Court for the Northern District of Illinois, 1894) (application of the Sherman Act to break the Pullman strike), *affirmed on other grounds sub nom. In re Debs*, 158 U.S. 564 (U.S. Supreme Court, 1895); *United States v. Trans-Missouri Freight Association*, 166 U.S. 290 (U.S. Supreme Court, 1897); Letwin, *Evolution of the Sherman Act*, 117–30. On the legal and judicial profession's near-hysterical reaction to labor activism, see Arnold M. Paul, *Conservative Crisis and the Rule of Law: Attitudes of Bar and Bench, 1887–1895* (Ithaca, NY: Cornell University Press, 1960).

17. Letter from Attorney General Judson Harmon to U.S. Attorney James Bible, December 2, 1896, quoted in Letwin, *Evolution of the Sherman Act*, 135 (quotation in text); *United States v. Addyston Pipe & Steel Co.*, 78 Fed. 712 (Circuit Court for the Eastern District of Tennessee, 1897), *reversed*, 85 Fed. 271 (U.S. Court of Appeals for the Sixth Circuit, 1898) (Taft, C.J.), *affirmed as modified*, 175 U.S. 211 (U.S. Supreme Court, 1899).

18. Brief and Argument for Appellants, *Addyston Pipe* (U.S. Supreme Court, 1898 Term, Docket No. 269), 47–48 (cartel's Commerce Clause argument); Supplemental and Reply Brief for Appellants, ibid., 16–25 (cartel's liberty of contract argument); Points for the United States in Reply, ibid., 8 (government's response to the liberty of contract argument); *Addyston Pipe*, 175 U.S., 245 (quotation in text); *Allgeyer v. Louisiana*, 165 U.S. 78 (U.S. Supreme Court, 1897) (leading liberty of contract decision before *Lochner v. New York*, 198 U.S. 45 (1905)). Most scholars believe that *Addyston Pipe* buried the liberty of contract objection to the Sherman Act. For a more cautious view, see Alan J. Meese, "Liberty and Antitrust in the Formative Era," *Boston University Law Review* 79 (1999): 59–67.

19. [Justice] David Josiah Brewer, *The Liberty of Each Individual* (Address, July 4, 1893), in David Josiah Brewer Papers, Yale University, Document 3-133 (quotation in text). To the same effect, see [Justice] Brown, *Twentieth Century*, 14; [Judge] Horace Lurton, "Is the Trust Dangerous?" in *Proceedings of the Tenth Annual Meeting of the Bar Association of Tennessee* (1869): 144; [Judge] William Howard Taft, "Criticisms of the Federal Judiciary," *American Law Review* 29 (1895): 646–49.

20. *Northern Securities v. United States*, 193 U.S. 197 (U.S. Supreme Court, 1904); Letwin, *Evolution of the Sherman Act*, 182–239 (in-depth examination of the evolution of President Roosevelt's attitude toward the antitrust law and of the Northern Securities prosecution); Bruce Harbaugh, "Election of 1904," in Schlesinger and Israel, editors, *Presidential Elections*, 2:2023 (Democratic candidate's old-fashioned common law view of monopoly regulation).

21. Richard A. Posner, "A Statistical Study of Antitrust Enforcement," *Journal of Law & Economics* 13 (1970): 375 (table 5), documenting the boom in antitrust judgments and consent decrees during the Roosevelt and, especially, Taft administrations; Paolo Coletta, *The Presidency of William Howard Taft* (Lawrence: University Press of

Kansas, 1973), 153–65, describing Taft's vigorous antitrust policy, which drove business interests to support Roosevelt in 1912; *Standard Oil of New Jersey v. United States*, 221 U.S. 1 (U.S. Supreme Court, 1911), upholding prosecution of the Standard Oil trust but opining that the Sherman Act only outlawed "undue restraints" and that challenged conduct should be viewed under a vaguely articulated "rule of reason," ibid., 66; *United States v. American Tobacco Co.*, 221 U.S. 106 (U.S. Supreme Court, 1911) (similar to *Standard Oil*). For a future elaboration, clarifying that the rule of reason asked whether a particular practice was designed to "destroy" or undermine competition, see *Board of Trade of the City of Chicago v. United States*, 246 U.S. 231, 238 (U.S. Supreme Court, 1925) (Brandeis, J.).

22. Schlesinger and Israel, editors, *Presidential Elections*, 2:2168, noting the Democrats' attack on the antitrust issue, quoted in text.

23. *Trans-Missouri*, 166 U.S., 323–24 (quotation in text); *Northern Securities*, 193 U.S., 360–64 (Brewer, J., concurring in the judgment), upholding Sherman Act prosecution because market concentration created a coercive environment for smaller competitors; ibid., 400–411 (Holmes, J., dissenting), providing an acid critique of the majority's expansive application of the antitrust law.

24. Letter from Louis Brandeis to Woodrow Wilson, September 30, 1912, in Melvin I. Urofsky and David W. Levy, editors, *Letters of Louis D. Brandeis* (Albany: State University of New York Press, 1971–78), 2:688–94 (first quotation in text); Letter from Louis D. Brandeis to Elizabeth Brandeis Raushenbush, November 19, 1933, in ibid., 5:527 (second quotation). See also McCraw, *Prophets of Regulation*, 94–114 (detailed examination of Brandeis's anti-bigness thinking); Melvin I. Urofsky, "Wilson, Brandeis, and the Trust Issue, 1912–1914," *Mid-America* 44 (January 1967): 3–28.

25. Clayton Act of 1914, §§ 2–3, 7–8, chap. 323, 38 Stat. 730, 730–33 (1914), codified at 15 U.S.C. § 12 et seq.

26. Clayton Act §§ 4, 16, 38 Stat., 731, 737 (treble damages and injunctive relief for private parties harmed by antitrust violations). Before 1914, employers could sue unions for treble damages, e.g., *Loewe v. Lawler*, 208 U.S. 274 (U.S. Supreme Court, 1908), but it was only after 1914 that employers were authorized by statute to seek labor injunctions. See *Paine Lumber v. Neal*, 244 U.S. 459, 471 (U.S. Supreme Court, 1917).

27. Clayton Act of 1914, §§ 6, 20, 38 Stat., 731, 738–39; *Duplex Printing Press Co. v. Deering*, 254 U.S. 433 (U.S. Supreme Court, 1921). See also Daniel R. Ernst, "The Labor Exemption, 1908–1914," *Iowa Law Review* 74 (1989): 1151, 1163–72 (excellent analysis of the background and congressional consideration of the Clayton Act's labor exemptions).

28. Federal Trade Commission Act of 1914, chap. 311, 38 Stat. 717 (1914), codified at 15 U.S.C. §§ 41 et seq.; McCraw, *Prophets of Regulation*, 124–35 (emphasizing FTC's slow start and lack of an intelligent implementing strategy, as well as wartime needs, as reasons the FTC had no regulatory success).

29. Information about the assistants to the attorney general and staffing (here and elsewhere in this chapter) is taken from www.usdoj.gov/atr/timeline.htm (viewed January 2009).

30. Ellis W. Hawley, "Herbert Hoover, the Commerce Secretariat, and the Vision of an 'Associative State,' 1921–1928," *Journal of American History* 61 (June 1974): 116–40,

detailing Hoover's leadership in discouraging aggressive government regulation of business; Posner, "Statistical Study of Antitrust Enforcement," 375 (table 5), documenting the dramatic fall-off of antitrust judgments and consent decrees, 1930–34; *Board of Trade of the City of Chicago v. United States*, 246 U.S. 231, 238 (U.S. Supreme Court, 1925).

31. Act of March 23, 1932, 47 Stat. 70 (1932), codified at 29 U.S.C. § 101 (Norris—La Guardia Act), barring federal judges from issuing injunctions in controversies arising out of labor disputes; A.L.A. *Schechter Poultry Corp. v. United States*, 295 U.S. 553 (U.S. Supreme Court, 1935), unanimously striking down the NRA as a violation of the nondelegation doctrine; Ellis W. Hawley, *The New Deal and the Problem of Monopoly: A Study in Economic Ambivalence* (Princeton: Princeton University Press, 1966), 166–68; Rudolph J. R. Peritz, *Competition Policy in America 1888–1992* (Oxford: Oxford University Press, 1996), 75–89.

32. *Appalachian Coals, Inc. v. United States*, 288 U.S. 344, 359 (U.S. Supreme Court, 1933) (quotation in text). We owe the *Addyston Pipe* analogy (as well as a great deal of other analyses in this chapter) to George Priest.

33. Gardiner C. Means, "Industrial Prices and Their Relative Inflexibility," Senate Document No. 13, Seventy-fourth Congress, First Session (1935); Hawley, *New Deal and the Problem of Monopoly*, 292–301. See also Adolf A. Berle and Gardiner C. Means, *Modern Corporation and Private Property* (Chicago: Commerce Clearing House, 1932), 18; National Resources Comm. (Gardiner C. Means), *The Structure of the American Economy* (Washington, DC: GPO, 1939–40).

34. On Assistant Attorney General Arnold, see Spencer Weller Waller, *Thurman Arnold: A Biography* (New York: New York University Press, 2005). On the internal debates within the New Deal and Arnold's place in those debates, see Hawley, *New Deal and the Problem of Monopoly*, 413–19, 460–65; Alan Brinkley, "The New Deal and the Idea of the State," in Steve Fraser and Gary Gerstle, editors, *The Rise and Fall of the New Deal Order, 1930–1980* (Princeton: Princeton University Press, 1995), 85–121.

35. Hawley, *New Deal and the Problem of Monopoly*, 420–38; Posner, "Statistical Study of Antitrust Enforcement," 375 (table 5), documenting the huge increase in antitrust judgments and consent decrees for the government during the 1940s.

36. *United States v. Socony-Vacuum Oil Co.*, 310 U.S. 150 (U.S. Supreme Court, 1940), the oil cartel case; ibid., 224–25 note 59 (Justice Douglas's broad theory of per se liability for price-fixing conspiracies); *United States v. Aluminum Company of America*, 148 F.2d 416 (U.S. Court of Appeals for the Second Circuit, 1946), the Alcoa case, which Supreme Court had sent to the Second Circuit because there was not a quorum of justices who could hear the appeal; Waller, *Thurman Arnold*, 86–109, an account of Arnold's prosecutions, many of which irritated core Democratic Party constituencies; ibid., 110 (quotation in text).

37. Thurman W. Arnold, *Fair Fights and Foul: A Dissenting Lawyer's View* (New York: Harcourt, Brace & World, 1951), 129 (quotations in text). An even more starkly bimodal statement of antitrust principle (as protecting both consumers and small businesses) is Thurman W. Arnold, *Democracy and Free Enterprise* (Norman: University of Oklahoma Press, 1942).

38. *United States v. Aluminum Co. of America*, 148 F.2d 416, 428 (U.S. Court of Appeals for the Second Circuit, 1946) (quotation in text).

39. Thurman W. Arnold, *The Bottlenecks of Business* (New York: Reynal & Hitchcock, 1940), 122, 202, 211–12, and *Fair Fights and Foul*, 113–30 (Arnold's contemporary and subsequent reflections on the Sherman Act and his philosophy for applying it).

40. *South Carolina State Highway Department v. Barnwell Brothers, Inc.*, 303 U.S. 177 (U.S. Supreme Court, 1938), rejecting the arguments in Brief on Behalf of the United States as *Amicus Curiae, Barnwell Brothers* (1937 Term, Docket No. 161); *Southern Pacific Co. v. Arizona*, 325 U.S. 761 (U.S. Supreme Court, 1945), adopting the arguments in Brief for the United States as *Amicus Curiae, Southern Pacific* (1944 Term, Docket No. 56).

41. Charles Warren, "A Bulwark to State Police Power—The United States Supreme Court," *Columbia Law Review* 13 (1913): 667–95; William Novak, "Law and the State Control of American Capitalism, 1877–1932" (draft 2004).

42. See Wendell Berge, *Cartels: Challenge to a Free World* (Washington, DC: Public Affairs Press, 1944), and "Monopoly—Threat to American Democracy," *Christian Register*, November 1946 (quotation in text); accord, Arnold, *Democracy and Free Enterprise* (tying antitrust law to America's struggle against totalitarian polities like Nazi Germany); John Kenneth Galbraith, *American Capitalism: The Concept of Countervailing Power* (Boston: Houghton Mifflin, 1952). For an early report on the concentration problem, see Temporary National Economic Committee, Final Report and Recommendations, Senate Document No. 35, Seventy-seventh Congress, First Session (1941).

43. *United States v. Columbia Steel Co.*, 334 U.S. 495 (U.S. Supreme Court, 1948); ibid., 535–40 (Douglas, J., dissenting); FTC Report on the Merger Movement: A Summary Report (Washington, DC: GPO, 1948); Celler-Kefauver Act of 1950, chap. 1184, 64 Stat. 1125–28 (1950), codified at 15 U.S.C. § 18 (quotation in text). For an excellent, and skeptical, analysis of Celler-Kefauver's legislative history, see Derek C. Bok, "Section 7 of the Clayton Act and the Merging of Law and Economics," *Harvard Law Review* 74 (1960): 226, 234–49.

44. *Brown Shoe Co. v. United States*, 370 U.S. 294 (U.S. Supreme Court, 1962) (first quotation in text); Brief for the United States, *Brown Shoe* (1961 Term, Docket No. 4), 79–97 (aggressive analysis of the legislative purpose of the 1950 amendments); John Files, "Obituary: Lee Loevinger, 91, Kennedy-era Antitrust Chief," *New York Times*, May 8, 2004 (second quotation in text). Loevinger personally argued *United States v. Philadelphia National Bank*, 321 U.S. 374 (U.S. Supreme Court, 1963), which carried the *Brown Shoe* anticoncentration philosophy even further.

45. Carl Kaysen and Donald F. Turner, *Antitrust Policy: Economic and Legal Analysis* (Cambridge, MA: Harvard University Press, 1971), 44 (quotation in text); *United States v. Von's Grocery Co.*, 384 U.S. 270 (U.S. Supreme Court, 1966) (second quotation), going well beyond the economic theory in Brief for the United States, *Von's Grocery Co.* (1965 Term, Docket No. 303); Department of Justice Merger Guidelines (1968), 1 CCH Trade Regulation Reporter ¶ 4430 (1968). For an earlier institutionalist-economic argument for presumptive deconcentration, see Carl Kaysen and Donald F. Turner, *Antitrust Policy* (Cambridge, MA: Harvard University Press, 1959), 265–72.

46. *Dr. Miles Medical Co. v. John D. Park & Sons Co.*, 220 U.S. 373 (U.S. Supreme Court, 1911); *United States v. Arnold, Schwinn & Co.*, 388 U.S. 365 (U.S. Supreme Court, 1967), going somewhat beyond the economic theory in Brief for the United States, *Arnold, Schwinn & Co.* (1966 Term, Docket No. 25).

47. For early economic critique, see Bok, "Section 7 of the Clayton Act," 231–33, 238–49 (skeptical of the agencies' claim that business concentration was an increasing problem for the economy).

48. There is a debate in the literature as to which particular school of thought has most influenced the Supreme Court. For useful analyses, see Einer Elhauge, "Harvard Not Chicago: Which Antitrust School Drives Recent Supreme Court Decisions," *Competition Policy International* 3 (2007): 59–80 (Harvard School approach dominates Supreme Court antitrust analysis); Richard Schmalensee, "Thoughts on the Chicago Legacy in U.S. Antitrust," in Robert Pitofsky, editor, *How the Chicago School Overshot the Mark: The Effect of Conservative Economic Analysis on U.S. Antitrust* (Oxford: Oxford University Press, 2008), 11–23 (greater emphasis on Chicago); Herbert Hovenkamp, "The Harvard and Chicago Schools and the Dominant Firm," in ibid., 109–22 (tilt toward Harvard); Joshua D. Wright, "The Roberts Court and the Chicago School of Antitrust: The 2006 Term and Beyond," *Competition Policy International* 3 (2007): 25–58 (emphasis on Chicago).

49. Our generalizations about Professor Director's approach are based upon the account of his influence in Richard A. Posner, "The Chicago School of Antitrust Analysis," in E. Thomas Sullivan, editor, *The Political Economy of the Sherman Act: The First One Hundred Years* (New York: Oxford University Press, 1991), 193–209. We have also benefited deeply from the recollections of Professor George Priest.

　　For an early casebook based upon those materials, see Richard A. Posner, *Antitrust: Cases, Economic Notes, and Other Materials* (St. Paul: West, 1974); see ibid., 397–98, setting forth the Director-inspired economic efficiencies of mergers; ibid., 416–17, explaining how strong enforcement of anti-merger rules would harm small businesses. For an argument that Director was right to reject the view of organization theorists such as Donald Turner that increasing market concentration produced increasingly anticompetitive behaviors, see Frank H. Easterbrook, "Workable Antitrust Policy," *Michigan Law Review* 84 (1986): 1696–1713.

50. Posner, *Antitrust*, 234–38, setting forth the Director-inspired economics of resale price maintenance.

51. Compare Robert H. Bork, *The Antitrust Paradox: A Policy at War with Itself* (New York: Free Press, 1978), 154 (predatory pricing ought to be *per se* legal), with Philip Areeda and Donald F. Turner, "Predatory Pricing and Related Practices Under Section 2 of the Sherman Act," *Harvard Law Review* 88 (1975): 697–733 (arguing that such pricing ought to be illegal if the predator prices below cost).

52. Classic books applying Director's antitrust theory are Bork, *Antitrust Paradox*; Ward S. Bowman Jr., *Patent and Antitrust Law: A Legal and Economic Appraisal* (Chicago: University of Chicago Press, 1973); Richard A. Posner, *Antitrust Law: An Economic Perspective* (Chicago: University of Chicago Press, 1976), and *Antitrust*. Leading articles include Bork, "Policy of the Sherman Act," and "The Rule of Reason and the Per Se Concept: Price Fixing and Market Division," *Yale Law Journal* 75 (1966): 373–

453; Posner, "The Social Costs of Monopoly and Regulation," *Journal of Political Economy* 83 (1975): 807ff.

53. *Flood v. Kuhn*, 407 U.S. 258 (U.S. Supreme Court 1972), declining to overrule *Federal Baseball Club v. National League*, 259 U.S. 200 (U.S. Supreme Court, 1922), because it was a longstanding interpretation of the Sherman Act and Congress had, by its "positive inaction," failed to override it. For other cases where the Court ruled that Congress is the better forum to revisit arguably incorrect Sherman Act precedents, see *Square D Co. v. Niagara Frontier Tariff Bureau*, 476 U.S. 409 (U.S. Supreme Court, 1986); *Southern Motor Carriers Rate Conference, Inc. v. United States*, 471 U.S. 48, 55 and note 18 (U.S. Supreme Court, 1985); *Illinois Brick Co. v. Illinois*, 431 U.S. 720, 729–48 (U.S. Supreme Court, 1977).

54. See Thomas E. Kauper (assistant attorney general, 1972–76), "Influence of Conservative Economic Analysis on the Development of the Law of Antitrust," in Pitofsky, editor, *How the Chicago School Overshot the Mark*, 40–50. For an economic critique of the *per se* rule against vertical restraints, see Subcommittee on Commerce and Finance of the House Committee on Interstate and Foreign Commerce, Ninety-third Congress, Second Session, *Hearings on H.R. 122 etc.* (1974), 18 (testimony of Assistant Attorney General Bruce Wilson); Donald I. Baker (assistant attorney general, 1976–77), "Vertical Restraints in Times of Change: From *White* to *Schwinn* to Where?" *Antitrust Law Journal* 44 (1975): 537–49.

55. Airline Deregulation Act of 1978, Public Law No. 95–504, 92 Stat. 1705 (1978); McCraw, *Prophets of Regulation*, 261–82.

56. *Continental T.V., Inc. v. GTE Sylvania, Inc.*, 433 U.S. 36, 48 note 13 (U.S. Supreme Court, 1977) (first quotation in text, quoting Baker, "Vertical Restraints"); ibid., 51–57, following the academic literature assuming that antitrust policy should maximize economic welfare and that vertical territorial restraints are often pro-competition. The six justices in the *GTE* majority were Potter Stewart (appointed by President Eisenhower in 1958), Warren Burger (Nixon, 1969), Harry Blackmun (Nixon, 1970), William Rehnquist (Nixon, 1971), Lewis Powell (Nixon, 1971), and John Paul Stevens (Ford, 1975). One Democratic appointee, Byron White, concurred only in the judgment and objected to overruling *Schwinn*, an opinion he had authored. Ibid., 59–71. Two Democratic justices dissented, William Brennan (a Democrat appointed by President Eisenhower) and Thurgood Marshall (appointed by President Johnson).

57. *Reiter v. Sonotone*, 442 U.S. 330, 343 (1979), closely following the analysis of Brief of the United States as *Amicus Curiae, Reiter* (Docket No. 78-690), 12–15. Both the Department of Justice brief and the Court's opinion quoted and relied on Bork, *Antitrust Paradox*, 66, which endorsed the notion that the Sherman Act's purpose was "consumer welfare." For a review of subsequent cases relying on consumer welfare as the purpose, see John B. Kirkwood and Robert H. Lande, "The Chicago School's Foundation Is Flawed: Antitrust Protects Consumers, Not Efficiency," in Pitofsky, editor, *How the Chicago School Overshot the Mark*, 89–106.

58. *United States v. Western Electric Co.*, 569 F. Supp. 990 (U.S. District Court for the District of Columbia 1983), reporting the AT&T divestiture consent decree; William F. Baxter, "Conditions Creating Antitrust Concerns with Vertical Integration by

Regulated Industries—For Whom the Bell Doctrine Tolls," *Antitrust Law Journal* 52 (1983): 243–47.

59. Department of Justice, 1982 Merger Guidelines, June 14, 1982, *Federal Register* 47 (June 30, 1982): 28492ff.; Department of Justice, 1984 Merger Guidelines, June 14, 1984, *Federal Register* 49 (June 29, 1984): 26823ff.; ibid., "Purpose and Underlying Assumptions" (quotation in text); William F. Baxter, "Responding to the Reaction: The Draftsman's View," *California Law Review* 71 (1983): 618–31.

60. *Monsanto Co. v. Spray-Rite Service Corp.*, 465 U.S. 752 (U.S. Supreme Court, 1984), narrowly construing the Court's per se rule against resale price maintenance and ducking the invitation to overrule *Dr. Miles* made in Brief of the United States as *Amicus Curiae, Monsanto* (Docket No. 82-914). For descriptions of the department's *amicus* brief activities, see William F. Baxter, "Preface to a Review of Antitrust Division Briefs," *Journal of Reprints, Antitrust Law and Economics* (1985): i–ii; Richard Schmalensee, "Bill Baxter in the Antitrust Arena: An Economist's Appreciation," *Stanford Law Review* 51 (1999): 1317, 1329–30.

61. Charles F. Rule and David L. Meyer, "An Antitrust Enforcement Policy to Maximize the Economic Wealth of All Consumers," *Antitrust Bulletin* 82 (1988): 677ff., statement of post-Baxter antitrust thinking at the Antitrust Division; Speech by Assistant Attorney General James F. Rill, *Antitrust & Trade Regulation Reporter* (BNA) 57 (November 9, 1989): 671, announcing that the department was no longer challenging *Dr. Miles*; *State Oil Co. v. Khan*, 522 U.S. 3 (U.S. Supreme Court, 1997), overruling *Albrecht v. Herald Co.*, 390 U.S. 145 (U.S. Supreme Court, 1968), and closely following the arguments made by Chief Judge Posner, 93 F.3d 1358 (U.S. Court of Appeals for the Seventh Circuit, 1996), and by Brief for the United States and the Federal Trade Commission as *Amicus Curiae* Supporting Reversal, *Khan* (Docket No. 96-871).

62. *Leegin Creative Leather Products v. PSKS, Inc.*, 551 U.S. 877 (U.S. Supreme Court, 2007), overruling *Dr. Miles* and closely following the economic and legal arguments set forth in Brief for the United States as *Amicus Curiae, Leegin* (Docket No. 06-480) (signed by Solicitor General Paul Clement, counsel of record, who also presented an oral argument, as well as FTC General Counsel William Blumenthal, and Assistant Attorney General Thomas Barnett). Compare Brief of the American Antitrust Institute as *Amicus Curiae* in Support of Respondent, *Leegin* (Docket No. 06-480), presenting economic arguments for the presumptive inefficiency and potential for abuse of minimum resale price requirements; Robert Pitofsky (FTC chair, 1995–2001), "In Defense of Discounters: The No-Frills Case for a Per Se Rule Against Vertical Price-Fixing," *Georgetown Law Journal* 71 (1983): 1487ff.

63. The data in the text are adapted from the useful empirical survey in Leah Brannan and Douglas H. Ginsburg (assistant attorney general [antitrust], 1985–87), "Antitrust Decisions of the U.S. Supreme Court, 1967–2007," *Competition Policy International* 3 (2007): 3, 14–15 (figure 1).

64. *Congressional Record* 21 (1890): 2570 (Senator Sherman, first quotation in text); ibid., 2457 (Senator Sherman, second quotation). See Lande, "Wealth Transfers," 99–101 (surveying legislative debates of the Sherman Act and concluding that this neo-republican goal was fundamental to the statute).

65. *Congressional Record* 96 (1950): 16,452 (Senator Kefauver, quotation in text); Lande, "Wealth Transfers," 127–30 (Clayton Act sponsors motivated by a social theory positing that concentration of economic power was bad for democracy); ibid., 118–19 (FTC Act sponsors, same theory); ibid., 130–39 (Celler-Kefauver Act sponsors, similar theory).

66. On the Sherman Act as a common law statute, where *stare decisis* does not exercise strong constraint, see *State Oil Co. v. Khan*, 522 U.S. 3 (U.S. Supreme Court, 1997); *Leegin Creative Leather Products v. PSKS, Inc.*, 551 U.S. 877 (U.S. Supreme Court, 2007). For excellent analyses revealing deeper forms of anticompetitive threats, see Thomas G. Krattenmaker and Steven Salop, "Anticompetitive Exclusion: Raising Rivals' Costs to Achieve Power over Price," *Yale Law Journal* 96 (1986): 209–93.

67. See Henry Richardson, *Democracy and Autonomy: Public Reasoning about the Ends of Policy* (Oxford: Oxford University Press, 2002).

68. E-mail from Professor George Priest to Professor William N. Eskridge Jr., March 29, 2009. On the remarkable career of Alfred Kahn, see McCraw, *Prophets of Regulation*, 222–99.

69. Compare Philip Bobbitt, *Terror and Consent: The Wars for the Twenty-First Century* (New York: Alfred A. Knopf, 2008).

70. The data are analyzed and presented as evidence that the United States would be better run by Robert Bork and Dick Posner than by We the People in Bryan David Caplan, *The Myth of the Rational Voter: Why Democracies Choose Bad Policies* (Princeton: Princeton University Press, 2007).

71. *Appalachian Coals, Inc. v. United States*, 288 U.S. 344, 359 (U.S. Supreme Court, 1933) (quotation in text).

CHAPTER 4. THE SAFETY NET CONSTITUTION AND THE POLITICS OF ENTRENCHMENT

1. Our story of Ida May Fuller is taken from the Social Security Administration's (SSA) Web site, www.ssa.gov/history/imf.html (viewed January 2008).

2. Social Security Act of August 14, 1935, ch. 531, 49 Stat. 620 (1935), codified at 42 U.S.C. §§ 301 et seq.

3. The tension between idealistic reform and cynical skepticism in social security is captured by comparing Arthur J. Altmeyer, *The Formative Years of Social Security* (Madison: University of Wisconsin Press, 1968) (practical account of how social security helped millions of old people), with Jerry R. Cates, *Insuring Inequality: Administrative Leadership in Social Security, 1935–54* (Ann Arbor: University of Michigan Press, 1983) (cynical account of how social security reinforced economic inequalities in this country).

4. Important accounts of the patchwork evolution of American protective legislation include Michael B. Katz, *In the Shadow of the Poorhouse: A Social History of Welfare in America* (New York: Basic Books, 1986); Theda Skocpol, *Protecting Soldiers and Mothers: The Political Origins of Social Policy in the United States* (Cambridge: Harvard University Press, 1992); Social Security Administration, "Historical Background

and Development of Social Security: Pre—Social Security Period," available on the SSA's Web site, www.ssa.gov/history/briefhistory3.html (examined January 2008).

5. The idea of social insurance was popularized in Henry R. Seager, *Social Insurance: A Program of Social Reform* (New York: Macmillan, 1910). On the conservative "ideology" of the New Deal's particular brand of social security, see Cates, *Insuring Inequality*, 13–17.

6. Indeed, the insurance principle would imply that expected benefits would be equal to the expected value of contributions, when invested in long-term government bonds, net of administrative costs. This does not imply that what a recipient actually receives is related to her actual contributions in this way. She has, after all, survived long enough to receive benefits. The equality holds only in expectation.

7. Altmeyer, *Formative Years of Social Security*, 29 (first quotation in text); ibid., 31 (second quotation). See generally Martha Derthick, *Policymaking for Social Security* (Washington, DC: Brookings Institution, 1979).

8. U.S. Bureau of Labor Statistics, "Statistical Data Regarding Old-Age Dependency, Care of the Aged, Etc.," March 8, 1930, reprinted in House Committee on Labor, Seventy-first Congress, *Hearings on Old Age Pensions* (1930), 248–63. See also Abraham Epstein, *Facing Old Age, a Study of Old Age Dependency in the United States and Old Age Pensions* (New York: Alfred A. Knopf, 1922).

9. Abraham Epstein, *Insecurity, a Challenge to America: A Study of Social Insurance in the United States and Abroad* (New York: Random House, 1933) (survey of European laws); *1930 House Old Age Pensions Hearings*, 17–43 (testimony of American Association for Labor Legislation, describing state old-age support laws and making a detailed case for national legislation); ibid., 67–79 (testimony of Abraham Epstein, representing the American Association for Old-Age Security); ibid., 93–99 (American Federation of Labor); 143–47 (Roman Catholic Church). Excellent comparative law analyses include Hugh Heclo, *Modern Social Politics in Britain and Sweden: From Relief to Income Maintenance* (New Haven: Yale University Press, 1974); Arnold J. Heidenheimer et al., editors, *Comparative Public Policy: The Politics of Social Choice in America, Europe, and Japan* (New York: St. Martin's Press, 1990).

10. House Committee on Labor, Seventy-third Congress, *Hearings on Old Age Pensions* (1934), 17–43 (testimony of Abraham Epstein, representing the AAOAS and describing state legislation as of 1934); Comment of Governor Roosevelt of New York upon the Report of the New York State Old Age Security Commission of Inquiry, February 1930, reprinted in *1930 House Old Age Pensions Hearings*, 289–90 (quotations in text).

11. Edwin Amenta, *When Movements Matter: The Townsend Plan and the Rise of Social Security* (Princeton: Princeton University Press, 2006).

12. William E. Leuchtenberg, *Franklin D. Roosevelt and the New Deal* (New York: Harper & Row, 1963), 4–11 (early New Deal responses to the Depression); *A.L.A. Schechter Poultry Corp. v. United States*, 295 U.S. 495 (U.S. Supreme Court, 1935) (invalidating NIRA as an unconstitutional delegation of public authority to private cartels); *United States v. Butler*, 297 U.S. 1 (U.S. Supreme Court, 1936) (invalidating the AAA tax and conditional farm subsidies program as an effort by Congress to regulate local agricultural production constitutionally vested in the states alone).

13. The quotations in the text are taken from Message from President Franklin Delano Roosevelt to Congress, Reviewing the Broad Objectives and Accomplishments of the Administration, June 8, 1934, available on the SSA's Web site, www.ssa.gov/history/fdrstmts.hmtl#message1 (examined January 2008).

14. Executive Order No. 6,757, June 29, 1934, available on the SSA's Web site, www.ssa.gov/history/fdrstmts.hmtl#message3 (viewed January 2008); Address by President Franklin Delano Roosevelt to the Advisory Committee on Economic Security, on the Problems of Economic and Social Security, November 14, 1934, available on the SSA's Web site, www.ssa.gov/history/fdrstmts.hmtl#message5 (viewed January 2008).

15. The Report of the Committee on Economic Security and related documents can be accessed on the SSA's Web site, www.ssa.gov/history/reports/ces/cesbasic.hmtl (viewed January 2008).

16. The quotations in text are taken from a Message from President Franklin Delano Roosevelt to Congress, Transmitting the Report of the Committee on Economic Security, January 17, 1935, available on the SSA's Web site, www.ssa.gov/history/fdrstmts.hmtl#message6 (viewed January 2008).

17. David Kennedy, *Freedom from Fear: The American People in Depression and War, 1929–1945* (New York: Oxford University Press, 1999), 267 (Roosevelt quotation in text). The president's rhetoric notwithstanding, the program was not intended to be fully funded in the sense of having a dedicated account holding the accumulated contributions. This would have been resisted as either highly deflationary (if not invested in the private sector) or subversive of the private sector (if it was). The actuaries at the SSA, the members of the relevant congressional committees, and the administration understood the commitment of the government to pay benefits as a binding promise. This assumption could not be tested, however, since the program was expected to generate revenues far in excess of payouts for decades.

18. "Ex-President Hoover's Call to Republicans," *New York Times*, March 24, 1935, 32 (quotation in text). On the behind-the-scenes difficulties faced by the social security bill, especially its old-age insurance title, see Altmeyer, *Formative Years of Social Security*, 31–42; Edward Berkowitz and Larry DeWitt, "Conservatives and American Political Development: The Case of Social Security, 1934–1956," in Brian J. Glenn and Steven M. Teles, editors, *Conservatism and American Political Development* (Oxford: Oxford University Press, 2009).

19. For a neat examination of the way that New Deal administrators like Altmeyer demonized flat benefit proposals on the Left (Townsend) and the Right (Chamber of Commerce), see Cates, *Insuring Inequality*, 50–85.

20. U.S. Constitution, Article I, § 8 (granting Congress authority to provide for and regulate the national armed forces but no specific authority to provide for old-age pensions); Epstein, *Insecurity: A Challenge to America*, chap. 28 (describing early federal efforts to provide for old-age pensions, including Wilson's nutty Old Home Guard proposal).

21. *1930 Old Age Pensions House Hearings*, 228 (testimony of Thomas F. Calwalader, Sentinels of the Republic) (first quotation in text), 166 (testimony of James A. Emery, general counsel of the National Association of Manufacturers) (second quotation);

accord, ibid., 155–87 (Emery's extended testimony), 189–219 (testimony of Noel Sargent, NAM's Industrial Relations Department), 221–45 (testimony of Miss Mary G. Kilbreath, Woman Patriot Publishing Co.).

22. Ibid., 127 (statement of Representative Fiorello LaGuardia, New York); accord, H.C. Gilbert, Library of Congress, Legislative Research Service, "Constitutionality of Old Age Pension Legislation" (February 12, 1930), reprinted in ibid., 114–18.

23. Ibid., 246 (supplemental statement of Abraham Epstein) (emphasis added).

24. *Helvering v. Davis*, 301 U.S. 619 (U.S. Supreme Court, 1937) (upholding the old-age insurance program, McReynolds and Butler dissenting), closely following Brief for Petitioners, *Helvering* (1936 Term, Docket No. 910) (the attorney general's detailed brief); *Charles C. Steward Machine Co. v. Davis*, 301 U.S. 548 (U.S. Supreme Court, 1937) (upholding the unemployment compensation program, Van Devanter, McReynolds, Sutherland, and Butler dissenting). See also Marjorie Shearon, "Economic Insecurity in Old Age: Social and Economic Factors Contributing to Old-Age Dependency," attached to the Brief for Petitioners in *Helvering* (1936 Term, Docket No. 910).

25. James A. Hagerty, "Landon Condemns the Security Law: Would Amend It," *New York Times*, September 27, 1936, 1, 31; Barry Cushman, *Rethinking the New Deal Court: The Structure of a Constitutional Revolution* (New York: Oxford University Press, 1998).

26. The history of social security from 1935 to 1950 is classically rendered in Altmeyer, *Formative Years of Social Security*, 43–209. On the 1950 amendments, see Wilbur J. Cohen and Robert J. Meyers, "The Social Security Amendments of 1950: A Summary and Legislative History," *Social Security Bulletin* (1950), reprinted on the SSA's Web site, www.ssa.gov/history/1950amend.html (visited January 2008).

27. Matthew McCubbins, Roger Noll, and Barry Weingast (collectively known as "McNollGast"), "Administrative Procedures as Instruments of Political Control," *Journal of Law, Economics, and Organization* 3 (1987): 243–77; McCubbins, Noll, and Weingast, "Structure and Process, Politics and Policy," *Virginia Law Review* 75 (1989): 431–82.

28. Terry Moe, "Political Institutions: The Neglected Side of the Story," *Journal of Law, Economics, and Organization* 6 (1990): 213–53.

29. On the endogeneity of preferences, see Robert Cover, "The Supreme Court, 1982 Term—Foreword: *Nomos* and Narrative," *Harvard Law Review* 97 (1983): 4–68; Cass R. Sunstein, "Legal Interference with Private Preferences," *Chicago Law Review* 53 (1986): 1129–74.

30. Terry Moe, "Political Control and the Power of the Agent," *Journal of Law, Economics and Organization* 22 (2005): 1–29. On the survival and flourishing of social security during the Eisenhower administration, see Edward Berkowitz, *Robert Ball and the Politics of Social Security* (Madison: University of Wisconsin Press, 2003); Berkowitz and DeWitt, "Conservatives and the Case of Social Security."

31. On the cogent conservative critique of FDR's reserve fund idea, see Edward D. Berkowitz, "The Transformation of Social Security," in Steven A. Sass and Robert K. Triest, editors, *Social Security Reform: Links to Saving, Investment and Growth* (Boston: Federal Reserve Bank of Boston, 1997), 19–28.

32. Chancellor Bismarck created social insurance in Germany partly as a way of fore-stalling socialism. Motivated by the same concerns with social stability, Bismarck's idea was emulated a few years later in Austria and, after the First World War, else-where in Europe. Peter Flora and Arnold Heidenheimer, *The Development of Wel-fare States in Europe and America* (New Brunswick, NJ: Transaction Books, 1981).

33. Advisory Council on Social Security, Report (December 10, 1938), available on the SSA's Web site, www.ssa.gov/history/reports/38advise.html (viewed January 2008); Nancy Altman, *The Battle for Social Security* (Hoboken, NJ: John Wiley, 2005).

34. Martha Derthick, *Policymaking for Social Security* (Washington, DC: Brookings Institute, 1979).

35. The composition of the 1937–38 Advisory Council is available on the SSA's Web site, www.ssa.gov/history/reports/38advise.html (viewed January 2008).

36. Ida May Fuller's picture and her history as the first recipient are celebrated on the SSA's Web site, www.ssa.gov/history/briefhistory3.html and www.ssa.gov/history/imf.html (quotation in text) (viewed January 2008).

37. Because the social security program raised its own revenue through payroll taxes, Congress's powerful revenue committees (the House Ways and Means Committee and the Senate Finance Committee) became the forums for congressional decision making on social security. These were two of the most powerful and fiscally conser-vative congressional committees, led by legendary and often conservative figures like Wilbur Mills, Walter George, Arthur Vandenberg, Russell Long, and Robert Kerr, many of whom were either southern Democrats or Midwestern Republicans. While the committees' minority members were conservative and widely respected, they were also restrained in their partisanship on the committee, and most of them were willing to bargain for compromises rather than oppose the program outright. See John Man-ley, *The Politics of Finance* (Boston: Little, Brown, 1970).

38. 1948–49 Advisory Council on Social Security, Report (October 1948), described and reprinted in the SSA's Web site, www.ssa.gov/history/reports/48advisegen.html (viewed January 2008); Berkowitz, *Robert Ball and the Politics of Social Security* (de-scribing the key informational role played by SSA staff representative Robert Ball).

39. For excellent analyses of the 1950 amendments, see Altman, *Battle for Social Secu-rity*, chap. 9; Altmeyer, *Formative Years of Social Security*, 169–208; Cohen and Mey-ers, "The Social Security Amendments of 1950."

40. On the Eisenhower administration's capitulation to the social security idea, see Alt-meyer, *Formative Years of Social Security*, 209–55. Congress's practice of raising so-cial security benefits in election years was made possible by the conservative method of making the seventy-five-year projections that Robert Myers employed. His method guaranteed that actual revenues would always exceed the forecast, so that Congress could afford to use the unanticipated surplus to raise benefits. Then, following the elections, Congress would enact another bill that increased either the taxable base or the payroll tax rate. Allegedly, Robert Ball discovered this feature of Myer's projec-tions while serving as staff chief for the Advisory Council in 1947–48 and conveyed that information to Ways and Means Committee staff. See Nancy Altman and Theo-dore Marmor, "Social Security in Transition: From the Mid 1950s to the Late 1970s," in Glenn and Teles, editors, *Conservatism and American Political Development*.

41. The political appeal of the social insurance model is explored comparatively in Karl Ove Moene and Michael Wallerstein, "Inequality, Social Insurance, and Redistribution," *American Political Science Review* 95 (December 2001): 859–74.

42. President Franklin D. Roosevelt, Message to the Congress on the State of the Union (January 11, 1944), in Samuel I. Rosenman, editor, *The Public Papers and Addresses of Franklin D. Roosevelt: Victory and the Threshold of Peace, 1944–45* (New York: Random House, 1950), 13:41 (Second Bill of Rights).

43. Peter A. Corning, "The Evolution of Medicare" (Washington, DC: SSA, 1969), chaps. 2–3, available on the SSA Web site, www.ssa.gov/history/corning.html (viewed January 2008).

44. Ibid., chap. 4.

45. Ibid., chap. 4; Altman and Marmor, "Social Security in Transition" (the Goldwater quotation and anecdote in text).

46. The causes of stagflation in the 1970s were complex. The inflationary pressures of the Vietnam War certainly played a part, and many economists thought that inflationary expectations had been cemented into wage contracts as well. In 1973, moreover, OPEC unilaterally raised oil prices, sending Western economies into a collective tailspin.

47. Facing likely impeachment and left with virtually no political support in the wake of his role in the Watergate cover-up, President Nixon resigned in 1974. Six months later, Mills resigned as Ways and Means chair. Delicate sensibilities forbid us from telling the tale of Wilbur Mills and Fanne Fox, the "Argentinian Firecracker," in the text. On October 7, 1974, Mills's car, driven by a former Nixon staffer, was stopped by the police. Inside the car were an inebriated Ways and Means chairman and Ms. Fox. The latter ran from the car and jumped into the Tidal Basin, giving the media a field day. Mills resigned his chairmanship two months later after appearing at a Fanne Fox performance in a similarly inebriated condition.

48. Altman, *Battle for Social Security*, 224. A more detailed report on the changing state of public confidence in Social Security is presented in Fay Lomax Cook, Jason Barabas, and Benjamin Page, "Invoking Public Opinion: Policy Elites and Social Security," *Public Opinion Quarterly* 66 (2002): 248. Figure 4 of this article shows the drop in public confidence from 1975 to about 1983, when the bipartisan reforms were implemented, at which point confidence levels increased from roughly 30 percent saying very or somewhat confident to roughly 50 percent in 1992. After that public confidence began another decrease during the Clinton years. The basic data are from surveys conducted for the American Council of Life Insurance and conducted by several organizations.

49. Our account of the Reagan-era social security politics draws from Martha Derthick and Steven M. Teles, "Riding the Third Rail: Social Security Reform," in W. Elliott Brownlee and High Davis Graham, editors, *The Reagan Presidency: Pragmatic Conservatism and Its Legacies* (Lawrence: University Press of Kansas, 2003), 182–208.

50. Altman, *Battle over Social Security*, 230 (quoting Stockman).

51. Derthick and Teles, "Riding the Third Rail." For an explanation of why the 1981 Reconciliation Bill was much more successful in cutting programs with poor clien-

tele than those with middle-class beneficiaries, see John Ferejohn, "Congress and Redistribution," in Allen Schick, editor, *Making Economic Policy* (Washington, DC: American Enterprise Institute Press, 1984).

52. Nancy Altman, who worked for Chairman Greenspan during the proceedings, presents an "inside" account of the bipartisan commission's activities in chapter 13 of *Battle for Social Security.*

53. Steven Teles, "Conservative Mobilization Against Entrenched Liberalism," in Paul Pierson and Theda Skocpol, editors, *Transformations of the American Polity* (Princeton: Princeton University Press, 2007).

54. Derthick and Teles, "From Third Rail to Presidential Commitment—And Back? The Conservative Campaign for Social Security Privatization and the Limits of Long-Term Political Strategy," in Glenn and Teles, editors, *Conservatism and American Political Development.*

55. Employee Retirement Income Security Act (ERISA), Public Law No. 93-406, 88 Stat. 829 (1974), requires employers to vest pension rights after a certain time period, defines tax treatment of employee benefits, and imposes some minimum requirements on funding. In addition, ERISA preempts conflicting state laws. Ibid., § 514.

56. Peter Germanis, "Increase the IRA Advantage," *Heritage Foundation Backgrounder,* August 24, 1983, 11 (quotation in text).

57. Cook, Barabas, and Page, "Invoking Public Opinion: Policy Elites and Social Security," 251 (polling data discussed in text); Lawrence Jacobs and Robert Shapiro, "Myths and Misunderstandings about Public Opinion Toward Social Security" (New York: Century Foundation, 1999) (quotation in text).

58. Americans seem unsure which is the greater threat: the economy, which is hard to blame or control, or politicians, who are easy to blame (and possibly to control as well). This pattern is probably key to the "third rail" feature of social security: once a politician reveals himself as a threat to the program, the public has a convenient and plausible target to blame. And, given their history of opposition and grudging support, conservative Republicans are already under a veil of suspicion, though, in principle, any politician could be vulnerable.

59. 1994–96 Advisory Council on Social Security, Report (January 1997), available on the SSA's Web site, www.ssa.gov/history/reports/adcouncil/report.toc.html (viewed January 2008); Carolyn Weaver, "The Economics and Politics of the Emergence of Social Security: Some Implications for Reform," *Cato Journal* (Fall 1983): 361–91.

60. George W. Bush, "Address to the 2000 Republican National Convention" (August 3, 2000), available at www.cnn.com/ELECTION/2000/conventions/republican/transcripts/bush.html (viewed January 2008) (quotation in text).

61. Altman, *Battle for Social Security.*

62. Jacobs and Shapiro, "Myths and Misunderstandings about Public Opinion," show that opinion poll findings depend rather closely on precise question wordings and are likely to be over- or misinterpreted—and that this is precisely what happened to conservatives on the issue of social security.

63. Derthick and Teles, "From Third Rail to Presidential Commitment—and Back?"

64. Ibid.

CHAPTER 5. THE CONSTITUTION OF THE FAMILY
AND STATUTES AS PRECEDENTS

1. *Noel v. Ewing*, 9 Ind. 37 (Indiana Supreme Court, 1857). For an excellent explication of the constitutive role of early American marriage law, see Nancy F. Cott, *Public Vows: A History of Marriage and the Nation* (Cambridge, MA: Harvard University Press, 2000), 9–55.

2. Sir William Blackstone, *Commentaries on the Laws of England* (Oxford: Clarendon Press, 1765), 1:442–43 (first two quotations in text); James Wilson, *Works*, Robert Green McCloskey, editor (Cambridge, MA: Harvard University Press, 1967), 601; James Kent, *Commentaries on American Law* (New York: O. Halsted, 1827), 2:109 (similar description of coverture). An excellent discussion of coverture law is Hendrik Hartog, *Man and Wife in America* (Cambridge, MA: Harvard University Press, 2000), 103–22. For similar rules under the civil law in Louisiana, see Kathryn Lovio, "The Changing Concept of Family and Its Effect on Louisiana Succession Law," *Louisiana Law Review* 63 (2003): 1161ff.

3. Sir Edward Coke, *The Third Part of the Institutes of the Laws of England* (London: A. Crook, fifth edition, 1677), 58–59 (describing the detestable "crime against nature"); Jonathan Ned Katz, *Gay/Lesbian Almanac* (New York: Harper & Row, 1983), 66–133 (collecting colonial and early state common law decisions and statutes criminalizing fornication, adultery, incest, seduction, and the crime against nature).

4. *Palmer v. Palmer*, 1 Paige's Ch. 276 (New York Chancellor, 1828) (quotation in text); 1813 New York Laws chap. 102; Hartog, *Man and Wife*, 64–76; Marylynn Salmon, *Women and the Law of Property in Early America* (Chapel Hill: University of North Carolina Press, 1986).

5. See *Reynolds v. United States*, 98 U.S. 45 (U.S. Supreme Court, 1878) (disapproving of polygamy as a threat to the political as well as familial order because it would corrupt husbands), relying on Francis Lieber, *Manual of Political Ethics* (Philadelphia: A. J. Lippincott, 1838–39) (making the republican point that the good husband was the good citizen).

6. Elizabeth Cady Stanton, "Why Legislatures Should Make Precedents," discussed in Peggy A. Rabkin, *Fathers to Daughters: The Legal Foundations of Female Emancipation* (Westport, CT: Greenwood Press, 1980), 108–09. See generally Lois Banner, *Elizabeth Cady Stanton: A Radical for Women's Rights* (Boston: Little, Brown, 1980). On the thesis that declining fertility rates altered men's views, see Raquel Fernandez, "Women's Rights: Selfish Husbands and Altruistic Fathers" (draft 2008).

7. Professor Jill Hasday is engaged in a project that demonstrates various ways federal statutory policies have strongly affected the family in the post–New Deal era. See Hasday, "The Canon of Family Law," *Stanford Law Review* 57 (2004): 825–900. Our generalization in the text is for the longer period, and we think it likely (but are open to persuasion otherwise) that state statutory law remains the primary, even if not the only important, legal regime affecting the American family.

8. On nineteenth-century state statute-making to supplant the common law, see James Willard Hurst, *The Growth of American Law: The Law Makers* (Boston: Little, Brown, 1950), 199–246; Jacob Katz Cogan, "The Look Within: Property, Capacity, and Suf-

frage in Nineteenth-Century America," *Yale Law Journal* 107 (1997): 199–246. For the term *stare de statute* and the idea of statutes as precedents, see Frank E. Horack Jr., "The Common Law of Legislation," *Iowa Law Review* 23 (1937): 41–56. On the states as laboratories of experimentation, see Justice Brandeis's famous dissenting opinion in *New State Ice Co. v. Liebmann*, 285 U.S. 262 (U.S. Supreme Court, 1932).

9. Important studies of the states as laboratories of experimentation include Virginia Gray, "Innovation in the States: A Diffusion Study," *American Political Science Review* 67 (1973): 1174–85; Craig Volden, "States as Policy Laboratories: Emulating Success in the Children's Health Insurance Program," *American Journal of Political Science* 50, no. 2 (2006): 294–312; Jack L. Walker, "The Diffusion of Innovations among the States," *American Political Science Review* 63 (1969): 880–89. A cautionary note is sounded in Susan Rose-Ackerman, "Risk-Taking and Reelection: Does Federalism Promote Innovation?" *Journal of Legal Studies* 9 (1980): 593ff.

10. Carole Shammas, *A History of Household Government in America* (Charlottesville: University of Virginia Press, 2002); Fernandez, "Selfish Husbands, Altruistic Fathers."

11. See Allen Parkman, *Good Intentions Gone Awry: No-Fault Divorce and the American Family* (New York: Rowman & Littlefield, 2000), presenting strong cultural conclusions about the effect of no-fault divorce; Jonathan Gruber, "Is Making Divorce Easier Bad for Children? The Long-Run Implications of Unilateral Divorce," *Journal of Labor Economics* 22 (2004): 799–833, providing empirical evidence for a significant and broad effect of unilateral divorce, but not for no-fault divorce standing alone. Both of these excellent works provide a survey of previous literature.

12. Feminists assailed traditional state rape law and even the Model Penal Code for the obstacles to rape prosecutions, and the old legal rules were swiftly overtaken by more aggressive provisions that addressed some feminist concerns. See Martha Chamallas, "Consent, Equality, and the Legal Control of Sexual Conduct," *Southern California Law Review* 61 (1988): 777–842. On the close relationship between public opinion and judicial enforcement of abortion rights, see Samantha Luks and Michael Salamone, "Abortion," in Nathaniel Persily et al., editors, *Public Opinion and Constitutional Controversy* (Oxford: Oxford University Press, 2008), 81–107

13. On the demographics of the current American family, see Tavia Simmons and Martin O'Connell, *Married-Couple and Unmarried-Partner Households: 2000* (Washington, DC: U.S. Census Bureau, February 2003).

14. Shammas, *Household Government in America*, 108–44.

15. Mary Beth Norton, *Liberty's Daughters: The Revolutionary Experience of American Women, 1750–1830* (Boston: Little, Brown, 1980); Richard Chused, "Married Women's Property Law: 1800–1850," *Georgetown Law Journal* 71 (1983): 1359–1425.

16. Act of November 2, 1835, 1835 Arkansas Territorial Laws 34–35; Chused, "Married Women's Property Law," 1398–1400.

17. Thomas Herttell, *The Right of Married Women to Hold and Control Property Sustained by the Constitution of the State of New York* (New York, 1839), 79; see Norma Basch, *In the Eyes of the Law: Women, Marriage, and Property in Nineteenth-Century New York* (Ithaca, NY: Cornell University Press, 1982), 114–19.

18. Herttell, *Right of Married Women*, 22 (first quotation in text); ibid., 41–42 (slavery analogy); ibid., 55–57, 65–67 (married women's ownership of property would contribute to

family prosperity and harmony); Sarah Moore Grimké, *Letters on the Equality of the Sexes and the Condition of Women* (Boston: I. Knapp, 1838); see Elizabeth Bowles Warbasse, *The Changing Legal Rights of Married Women, 1800–1861* (New York: Garland, 1987), 100–108.

19. 1840 New York Laws chap. 80; 1845 New York Laws chap. 11; New York Legislature, *Assembly Documents* (1844): vol. 3, # 96 (Judiciary Committee's report); Basch, *Eyes of the Law*, 136–48.

20. Basch, *Eyes of the Law*, 136–61; Warbasse, *Legal Rights of Married Women*, 216–27.

21. Act of April 7, 1848, 1848 New York Laws chap. 200, § 1 (quotation in text); ibid., § 2 (married woman could receive and treat as her separate property a bequest or gift); *Yale v. Dederer*, 18 N.Y. 265 (New York Court of Appeals, 1858) (MWPA did not allow a wife to pledge her property without husband's consent).

22. Chused, "Married Women's Property Law," 1399–1400 and notes 205–09; Rabkin, *Fathers to Daughters*, 125–38 (surveying the post-1848 New York case law).

23. Elizabeth Cady Stanton, Susan B. Anthony, and Matilda J. Gage, *The History of Woman Suffrage* (New York: Fowler & Wells, 1881–1922), 1:99 (quotation in text); ibid., 70–73 (reprinting the Declaration); ibid., 577–83 (the 1853 Rochester convention). See generally Ellen Carol DuBois, *Feminism and Suffrage: The Emergence of an Independent Women's Movement in America, 1848–1869* (Ithaca, NY: Cornell University Press, 1978).

24. Basch, *Eyes of the Law*, 189–91; Warbasse, *Legal Rights of Married Women*, 256–61.

25. Elizabeth Cady Stanton, *Address to the Legislature of New York, Adopted by the State Woman's Rights Convention, Held at Albany, Tuesday and Wednesday, February 14 and 15, 1854* (Albany: Weed, Parsons, 1854), 3–5, 8 (quotations in text); ibid., 11–14 (examples where wives were unjust victims of coverture-based rules). The Address is excerpted in Ellen Carol DuBois, editor, *The Elizabeth Cady Stanton–Susan B. Anthony Reader* (Boston: Northeastern University Press, revised edition, 1992), 44–52.

26. Stanton et al., *History of Woman Suffrage*, 1:607 (quotation in text); Basch, *Eyes of the Law*, 190–91; Warbasse, *Legal Rights of Married Women*, 260–61.

27. 1858 New York Laws chap. 187; Basch, *Eyes of the Law*, 191–93; Warbasse, *Legal Rights of Married Women*, 261–62. See generally Kathleen Barry, *Susan B. Anthony: A Biography of a Singular Feminist* (New York: New York University Press, 1988).

28. 1860 New York Laws chap. 90; Basch, *Eyes of the Law*, 194–99; Warbasse, *Legal Rights of Married Women*, 261–64.

29. *Brooks v. Schwerin*, 54 N.Y. 343, 348 (New York Court of Appeals, 1873) (quotation in text); 1860 New York Laws chap. 90, §§ 1–2 (earnings), §§ 2–6 (conveyance of property), § 7 (lawsuits), § 9 (joint guardians), § 11 (inheritance). In 1862, the legislature made it easier for husbands to bind a child to a guardian or in an apprenticeship.

30. Basch, *Eyes of the Law*, 167 (listing of feminist leaders in various states); Warbasse, *Legal Rights of Married Women*, 265–72 (Ohio and Massachusetts); Chused, "Married Women's Property Law," 1424 note 361 (survey of married women's earnings laws).

31. *Birkbeck v. Ackroyd*, 74 N.Y. 356 (New York Court of Appeals, 1878), overridden by 1884 New York Laws chap. 381, and 1902 New York Laws chap. 289; Rabkin, *Fathers*

to Daughters, 138–46 (discussing the evolution of New York law). For an even more despairing survey of judicial decisions applying the earnings laws, see Reva B. Siegel, "The Modernization of Marital Status Law: Adjudicating Wives' Rights to Earnings, 1860–1930," *Georgetown Law Journal* 82 (1994): 2127–2211.

32. Reva B. Siegel, "'The Rule of Love': Wife Beating as Prerogative and Privacy," *Yale Law Journal* 105 (1996): 2117–2208, and "Home as Work: The First Woman's Rights Claims Concerning Wives' Household Labor, 1850–1880," *Yale Law Journal* 103 (2003): 1073–1217.

33. Stanton, *Address to the Legislature, 1854,* 11 (quotation in text). On the Nineteenth Amendment, see Aileen S. Kraditor, *The Ideas of the Woman Suffrage Movement, 1890–1920* (New York: Columbia University Press, 1965); Reva B. Siegel, "She the People: The Nineteenth Amendment, Sex, Equality, Federalism, and the Family," *Harvard Law Review* 115 (2001): 947, 960–1022.

34. Letter from Elizabeth Cady Stanton to Gerrit Smith, December 21, 1855, reprinted in Stanton et al., *History of Woman Suffrage,* 1:840–41 (quotation in text). On feminists' claims of "self-ownership," see Jill Elaine Hasday, "Contest and Consent: A Legal History of Marital Rape," *California Law Review* 88 (2000): 1417–27.

35. Act of March 2, 1873, ch. 258, 17 Stat. 598 (1973) (the Comstock Act); see Nicola Beisel, *Imperiled Innocents: Anthony Comstock and Family Reproduction in Nineteenth-Century America* (Princeton: Princeton University Press, 1997). On the new contraception and abortion laws, see Janet Farrell Brodie, *Contraception and Abortion in Nineteenth-Century America* (Ithaca, NY: Cornell University Press, 1994); James C. Mohr, *Abortion in America: The Origins and Evolution of National Policy, 1800–1900* (New York: Oxford University Press, 1978).

36. Andrea Tone, *Devices and Desires: A History of Contraceptives in America* (New York: Hill and Wang, 2002); Tone, "Black Market Birth Control: Contraceptive Entrepreneurship and Criminality in the Gilded Age," *Journal of American History* 87 (2000): 435–59.

37. Tone, "Black Market Birth Control," 435–59.

38. *People v. Sanger,* 118 N.E. 637 (New York Court of Appeals 1918), affirming Sanger's conviction for violating N.Y. Penal Code § 1142. On Sanger and the birth control movement, see Ellen Chesler, *Woman of Valor: Margaret Sanger and the Birth Control Movement in America* (New York: Simon & Schuster, 1992); Linda Gordon, *Woman's Body, Woman's Right: A Social History of Birth Control in America* (New York: Grossman, 1976).

39. Brief on Behalf of the Plaintiff in Error, 31, *Sanger v. People,* 251 U.S. 537 (U.S. Supreme Court, 1919) (1919 Term, Docket No. 75) (quotation in text; emphasis in original); see ibid., 39 ("a married woman has the fundamental right to determine whether she shall or shall not conceive and when she shall not conceive"); id. 43 (men and women have a *"natural right to say how many children they will bring into the world and when"*); ibid., 50–57 (threats to the health and even lives of pregnant women). The brief made this analogy: even a law barring abortions would violate the Due Process Clause if it did not include an exception for situations where the mother's life was at stake. Ibid., 54–55. For the Court's summary disposition, see *Sanger v. People,* 251 U.S. 537 (U.S. Supreme Court, 1919) (per curiam).

40. *Sanger*, 118 N.E., 638 (New York Court of Appeals interpretation of the law to allow prescriptions for contraceptives needed to protect the mental as well as physical health of the mother).

41. On the roller-coaster legal history of Sanger's post-1918 clinics, see David M. Kennedy, *Birth Control in America: The Career of Margaret Sanger* (New Haven: Yale University Press, 1970), 181–212. For court decisions nullifying the Comstock Act, see *United States v. Dennett*, 39 F.2d 564, 569 (U.S. Court of Appeals for the Second Circuit, 1930) (narrowly interpreting the federal Comstock Act to be inapplicable to birth control instructional materials); *United States v. One Package*, 86 F.2d 737, 739–40 (U.S. Court of Appeals for the Second Circuit, 1936) (narrowly interpreting the Comstock Act to allow a medical clinic to import contraceptives as needed to promote women's health and safety). On the increasing incidence of birth control clinics, see Joyce Ray and F. G. Gosling, "American Physicians and Birth Control, 1936–1947," *Journal of Social History* 18 (1985): 399–411; Note, "Contraceptives and the Law," *University of Chicago Law Review* 6 (1939): 260–69.

42. Johanna Schoen, "Fighting for Child Health: Race, Birth Control, and the State in the Jim Crow South," *Social Politics* 4 (1997): 90–113; Appellants' Brief, 30 (app. C), *Tileston v. Ullman*, 318 U.S. 44 (U.S. Supreme Court, 1943) (1942 Term, Docket No. 420) (map entitled "States Having Contraceptive Services Under Medical Supervision," 1942).

43. Compare Kennedy, *Birth Control in America*, 260–67, who considers the Roosevelt administration debates consequential, with Carole R. McCann, *Birth Control Politics in the United States, 1916–1945* (Ithaca, NY: Cornell University Press, 1996), 198–200, who does not.

44. The Kinsey studies (cited in note 47 below) documenting the rich and variegated sexual lives of Americans were based on thousands of in-depth interviews Dr. Kinsey conducted with adult Americans between 1938 and the early 1950s; most of those interviewed had become sexually active in the 1920s or 1930s. See Wardell B. Pomeroy, *Dr. Kinsey and the Institute for Sex Research* (New Haven: Yale University Press, 1982), describing the Kinsey methodology and his interview sample.

45. *Griswold v. Connecticut*, 381 U.S. 479, 484 (U.S. Supreme Court, 1965) (Douglas, J., for the Court); ibid., 499–507 (Harlan, J., invoking his dissenting opinion in *Poe v. Ullmann*, 367 U.S. 497 (U.S. Supreme Court, 1959)). For excellent background analysis, see David J. Garrow, *Liberty and Sexuality: The Right to Privacy and the Making of* Roe v. Wade (New York: Macmillan, 1994), 44–78 (unsuccessful litigation in Connecticut and Massachusetts seeking maternal health exceptions to contraception laws); ibid., 94–106, 152–95 (Planned Parenthood's unsuccessful Constitutional challenges to the Connecticut contraceptives use law); ibid., 196–269 (the *Griswold* litigation and the Court's decision).

46. On the massive regulation of sexual solicitation and other quasi-public crimes between 1880 and 1920, see Philip Jenkins, *Moral Panic: Changing Concepts of the Child Molester in Modern America* (New Haven: Yale University Press, 1998); Ruth Rosen, *The Lost Sisterhood: Prostitution in America, 1900–1918* (Baltimore: Johns Hopkins University Press, 1982); Judith Walkowitz, *Prostitution and Victorian Society: Women, Class, and the State* (New York: Cambridge University Press, 1980).

47. Alfred C. Kinsey, Wardell B. Pomeroy, and Clyde E. Martin, *Sexual Behavior in the Human Male* (Philadelphia: W. B. Saunders, 1948), 392 (quotation in text); Alfred C. Kinsey, Wardell B. Pomeroy, Clyde E. Martin, and Paul Gebhard, *Sexual Behavior in the Human Female* (Philadelphia: W. B. Saunders, 1953), 280–81, 286, 419, 453. For an analysis of Kinsey's studies as expressions of ideology as much as scientific reports, see David Allyn, "Private Acts/Public Policy: Alfred Kinsey, the American Law Institute and the Privatization of American Sexual Morality," *Journal of American Studies* 30 (1996): 405–28.

48. On America's new constitution of sexual relations and behavior, from the 1920s to the 1960s, see William N. Eskridge Jr., *Dishonorable Passions: Sodomy Law in America, 1861–2003* (New York: Viking, 2008), 109–65.

49. On the American Law Institute and its Model Penal Code project, see Herbert Wechsler, "The Challenge of a Model Penal Code," *Harvard Law Review* 65 (1952): 1097–1133.

50. *Report of the Illinois Commission on Sex Offenders to the 68th General Assembly of Illinois* (March 15, 1953); Telephone Interview with Francis Allen, February 27, 2004; Letter from Francis Allen to William N. Eskridge Jr., June 25, 2004.

51. Louis B. Schwartz, Book Review (Kinsey, *Human Male*), *University of Pennsylvania Law Review* 96 (1948): 914–18; ALI, Minutes of the Ninetieth Meeting of the Council, March 11–14, 1953, 11, in Papers of Learned Hand, Harvard Law Library, Box 120, Folder 7; Louis B. Schwartz, "Morals Offenses and the Model Penal Code," *Columbia Law Review* 63 (1963): 669, 675 (subsequent elaboration by the Associate Reporter).

52. Illinois State and Chicago Bar Associations' Joint Committee to Revise the Illinois Criminal Code, "Committee Foreword" to Tentative Final Draft of the Proposed Illinois Revised Criminal Code of 1961 (Chicago: Burdette Smith, 1960), 239 (quotation in text); Eskridge, *Dishonorable Passions*, 124–27 (detailed account of the history underlying Illinois's adoption of the Model Penal Code in 1961).

53. The political account of the law reform commissions is taken from Eskridge, *Dishonorable Passions*.

54. Ibid., 144–47 (archival account of New York's criminal code reform); Catholic Welfare Committee, Memorandum with Respect to the Proposed New York State Penal Code (1964), discussed in Note, "Deviate Sexual Behavior: The Desirability of Legislative Proscription?" *Albany Law Review* 30 (1966): 291–94.

55. Catherine S. Chilman, *Adolescent Sexuality in a Changing American Society* (Washington, DC: HEW Publication No. 79-1426 [NIH], 1979), as well as David Allyn, *Make Love Not War: The Sexual Revolution—An Unfettered History* (Boston: Little, Brown, 2000); Beth Bailey, *From Front Porch to Back Seat: Courtship in Twentieth-Century America* (Baltimore: Johns Hopkins University Press, 1988); John Modell, *Into One's Own: From Youth to Adulthood in the United States, 1920–1975* (Berkeley: University of California Press, 1989); Kevin White, *Sexual Liberation or Sexual License? The American Revolt against Victorianism* (Chicago: Ivan R. Dee, 2000).

56. Eskridge, *Dishonorable Passions*, 144–47, 161–65, 176–82 (work of sex crime commissions, 1961–1985); Richard A. Posner and Katharine B. Silbaugh, *A Guide to America's Sex Laws* (Chicago: University of Chicago Press, 1996), 98–102 (fornication and

open cohabitation laws circa 1996), 103–10 (adultery remained a crime in twenty-six states circa 1996).

57. Eskridge, *Dishonorable Passions*, 144–47, 163–64, 182–84 (detailed account of sex crime reform discourse in New York [1965], Texas [1969], and Idaho [1971–72]). On the evolution of sexual assault law, see Susan Estrich, *Real Rape* (Cambridge, MA: Harvard University Press, 1987); Martha Chamallas, "Consent, Equality, and the Legal Control of Sexual Conduct," *Southern California Law Review* 61 (1988): 777–842.

58. Eskridge, *Dishonorable Passions*, 197–201 (account of California's sex crime reform law and the unsuccessful popular effort to revoke it).

59. *Marvin v. Marvin*, 557 P.2d 106 (California Supreme Court, 1976).

60. Assessments of the modest effect of *Marvin* causes of action are Cynthia Grant Bowman, "Legal Treatment of Cohabitation in the United States," *Law and Policy* 26 (2004): 119–51 (surveying same-sex as well as different-sex relationship recognition and comparing American developments with those in other Western countries); Ann Laquer Estin, "Ordinary Cohabitation," *Notre Dame Law Review* 76 (2001): 1381–1408; Jana Singer, "The Privatization of Family Law," 1992 *Wisconsin Law Review* 1447–59. For Michelle Marvin's eventual loss on all her claims, see *Marvin v. Marvin*, 176 Cal. Rptr. 555 (California Supreme Court, 1981).

61. Simmons and O'Connell, *Married-Couple and Unmarried-Partner Households: 2000* (analysis of 2000 census data); Andrew Hacker, "The Case Against Kids," *New York Review of Books*, November 30, 2000, 12–16. The 2000 Census data are available online and can be viewed at www.census.gov/population/www/cen2002/briefs.html (viewed July 1, 2003).

62. C. Thomas Dienes, *Law, Politics, and Birth Control* (Urbana: University of Illinois Press, 1972), 254–66.

63. Ibid., 273–77 (Illinois debate, including the quotations in text); Subcommittee on Employment, Manpower, and Poverty of the Senate Committee on Labor and Public Welfare, Eighty-ninth Congress, Second Session, *Hearing on Family Planning Program* (1966), 104–09 (describing New York's family planning program); Subcommittee on Health of the Senate Committee on Labor and Public Welfare, Ninety-first Congress, First and Second Sessions, *Hearings on Family Planning and Population Research, 1970* (1969–70), 205–09 (describing California's program).

64. Message of the President of the United States Relative to Population Growth, House of Representatives Document No. 91-139 (July 21, 1969) (first quotation in text); Family Planning Services and Population Research Act of 1970, Public Law No. 91-572, § 2(1) 84 Stat. 1499 (1970) (second quotation); *Eisenstadt v. Baird*, 405 U.S. 438, 453 (U.S. Supreme Court, 1972) (broadening the *Griswold* marital privacy right, to assure "the *individual*, married or single," freedom from "unwarranted governmental intrusion into matters so fundamentally affecting a person as the decision whether to bear or beget a child").

65. *Roe v. Wade*, 410 U.S. 113 (U.S. Supreme Court, 1973); Garrow, *Liberty and Sexuality*, 389–599 (detailed account of the *Roe* litigation and the justices' deliberations); Dallas A. Blanchard, *The Anti-Abortion Movement and the Rise of the Religious Right: From Polite to Fiery Protest* (New York: Twayne, 1994), 22–36 (institutional history of

the pro-life movement); ibid., 37–50 (essential ideology of pro-lifers); Kristen Luker, *The Politics of Motherhood* (Berkeley: University of California Press, 1984).

66. *Planned Parenthood v. Casey*, 505 U.S. 833 (U.S. Supreme Court, 1992) (joint opinion of O'Connor, Kennedy & Souter, JJ.); *Rust v. Sullivan*, 500 U.S. 173 (U.S. Supreme Court, 1991) (narrowly upholding Dr. Sullivan's gag order imposed on Title X medical personnel providing family planning information); Memorandum from President William J. Clinton for the Secretary of Health and Human Services, Regarding the Title X "Gag Rule" (January 22, 1993) (suspending the gag rule, which in 2000 was revoked by HHS notice-and-comment rule making). For an interesting but different exploration of *Roe* and popular constitutionalism, see Robert Post and Reva B. Siegel, "*Roe* Rage: Democratic Constitutionalism and Backlash," *Harvard Civil Rights–Civil Liberties Law Review* 42 (2007): 373–433.

67. Barry, *Susan B. Anthony*; Nelson Manfred Blake, *The Road to Reno: A History of Divorce in the United States* (New York: Macmillan, 1962), 87–105. On women's and married women's participation in the work force, see U.S. Department of Labor, Women's Bureau, *Handbook on Women Workers* (Washington, DC: GAO, 1969) (Bulletin No. 294), 10 (table 1).

68. Max Rheinstein, "The Law of Divorce and the Problem of Marriage Stability," *Vanderbilt Law Review* 9 (1956): 633 and note 2 (survey of the increasing divorce rate).

69. For a list of state laws adopting the no-fault regime as well as the unilateral divorce regime, see Gruber, "Long-Run Implications of Unilateral Divorce," 803 (table 1).

70. California Civil Code of 1872, § 92 (grounds for divorce); ibid., §§ 111–21 (defenses to divorce included situations of mutual fault or collusion). Our discussion in the text draws from the first-hand account of a key participant, Herma Hill Kay, "Equality and Difference: A Perspective on No-Fault Divorce and Its Aftermath," *Cincinnati Law Review* 56 (1987): 1–6, 26–32.

71. California Governor's Commission on the Family, Report (December 1966), 10–29; ibid., 91 (quotation in text); ibid., 39–48 (no-fault regime for financial awards, property settlements, and child custody).

72. See Herbert Krom, "California's Divorce Law Reform," *Pacific Law Journal* 1 (1970): 173–74, summarizing the bar association committee's criticisms of the commission's report and the new proposal emerging from that critique.

73. Family Law Act § 8, 1969 California Statutes chap. 1608 (standards for marital dissolution, codified at California Civil Code § 4506); ibid. (standards for property division, spousal support, and custody); California Assembly Committee on the Judiciary, Report on A.B. No. 530 and S.B. No. 252 (the Family Law Act), *Assembly Journal* 4 (1969): 8062 (August 8, 1969) (subsequent committee report explaining the no-fault divorce law).

74. Max Rheinstein, *Marriage Stability, Divorce, and the Law* (Chicago: University of Chicago Press, 1972), 382–91; Kay, "Equality and Difference," 44–51 (detailed account by law professor involved in the uniform law as well as the California act).

75. The diversity of state approaches, and the numbers of states in the categories described in the text, are taken from Kay, "Equality and Difference," 5–14 (summary); ibid., 51–54 (state-by-state analysis), as well as Gruber, "Long-Run Implications of Unilateral Divorce," 803 (table 1).

76. New York has liberalized its divorce law but still does not list "irreconcilable differ-ences" as a ground for divorce. See Assembly Bill A02580, the Divorce Reform Act of 2009 (introduced January 20, 2009), proposing to add irreconcilable differences as a ground for divorce in New York.

77. Betty Friedan, *It Changed My Life: Writings on the Women's Movement* (New York: Random House, 1976), 325–26; Lenore Weitzman, *The Divorce Revolution* (New York: Free Press, 1985), 25–26 (success of the no-fault principle); ibid., 323 (after no-fault divorce, the average wife suffers a 73 percent decline in standard of living, while the husband's improves by 42 percent); H. Elizabeth Peters, "Marriage and Divorce: Informational Constraints and Private Contracting," *American Economic Review* 76 (1986): 437–54 (arguing that unilateral divorce harmed the economic interest of de-pendent wives whose consent had to be purchased in the prior regime); Eleanor E. Maccoby and Robert H. Mnookin, *Dividing the Child: Social and Legal Dilemmas of Custody* (Cambridge, MA: Harvard University Press, 1992), 260–61 (revising Weitzman's dramatic findings downward but documenting a significant gender gap after divorce).

78. 1977 Wisconsin Laws chap. 105, § 41 (no-fault law's requirements for property divi-sion in divorce proceedings); 1984 Wisconsin Laws chap. 186, § 47 (community property regime); Martha Albertson Fineman, "Implementing Equality: Ideology, Contradiction and Social Change: A Study of Rhetoric and Results in the Regula-tion of the Consequences of Divorce," *Wisconsin Law Review* 1983: 789–885 (study of the 1977 law).

79. California Assembly, Committee on the Judiciary, Report on A.B. No. 530 and S.B. No. 252 (the Family Law Act), *Assembly Journal* 1 (1970): 785–87; 1984 California Statutes chap. 463 (authorizing a "family home award" to spouse having custody of minor children).

80. Unified Court System, Office of Court Administration, Report of the New York Task Force on Women in the Courts (1986), 93–124; Kay, "Equality and Difference," 58–77.

81. For evidence that divorce has pervasive and harmful effects on children, see, e.g., Sara McLanahan and Gary D. Sandefur, *Growing Up with a Single Parent: What Hurts, What Helps* (Cambridge, MA: Harvard University Press, 1994); Judith Waller-stein et al., *The Unexpected Legacy of Divorce: A Twenty-Five-Year Landmark Study* (New York: Hyperion, 2000).

82. Victor R. Fuchs, *How We Live* (Cambridge, MA: Harvard University Press, 1983), 149–50.

83. For descriptions of unique features of American families, compared with European ones, see Carl N. Degler, *At Odds: Women and the Family in America from the Revo-lution to the Present* (New York: Oxford University Press, 1980), 8–9; Shammas, *Household Government in America*.

84. Compare Peters, "Marriage and Divorce: Informational Constraints and Private Contracting," 437–54 (finding no causal relation between no-fault statutes and higher divorce rates), with Douglas W. Allen, "Marriage and Divorce: Comment," *Ameri-can Economic Review* 82, no. 3 (June 1992): 679–85 (criticizing Peters's categoriza-tion of states and finding that the corrected data support a causal connection), and Margaret F. Brinig and Frank F. H. Buckley, "No-Fault Laws and At-Fault People,"

International Review of Law and Economics 18 (1998): 325–40 (finding a 6 percent effect), and with Justin Wolfers, "Did Unilateral Divorce Laws Raise Divorce Rates? A Reconciliation and New Results," *American Economic Review* 96 (2006): 1802–20 (finding a short-term effect but no long-term effect on divorce rates), and Gruber, "Long-Run Implications of Unilateral Divorce," 811–14 (finding a 1.4 percent effect on divorce rates).

85. Parkman, *Good Intentions Gone Awry*, 111–28; Gruber, "Long-Run Implications of Unilateral Divorce," 814–28 (empirical evidence that children reared under unilateral divorce regimes are less well educated, have lower family incomes, marry earlier but separate more often, and have higher odds of adult suicide).

86. On traditionalists' counterproductive focus on denying marriage to lesbian and gay couples, see William N. Eskridge Jr. and Darren R. Spedale, *Gay Marriage: For Better or For Worse? What We've Learned from the Evidence* (New York: Oxford University Press, 2006), 207–19.

CHAPTER 6. THE GREEN CONSTITUTION AND
JUDICIAL DEFERENCE TO AGENCY DYNAMISM

1. The Rapanoses' story is taken from the Record and Brief for Petitioners in *Rapanos v. United States*, 547 U.S. 715 (U.S. Supreme Court, 2006) (Docket No. 04-1034); Gregory T. Broderick, "The Shifting Sands of the Clean Air Act," *Liberty*, July 2005, available at http://libertyunbound.com/archive/2005_07/broderick-water.html (viewed August 2008).

2. Sir William Blackstone, *Commentaries on the Laws of England* (Oxford: Clarendon Press, 1765), 1:134 (quotation in text). Recent articulations of classic liberal understandings of property rights include James W. Ely Jr., *The Guardian of Every Other Right: A Constitutional History of Property Rights* (New York: Oxford University Press, third edition, 2007); Richard A. Epstein, *Takings: Private Property and the Power of Eminent Domain* (Cambridge, MA: Harvard University Press, 1985); Richard A. Epstein, "Property as a Fundamental Civil Right," *California Western Law Review* 29 (1992): 187–207; Carol M. Rose, "'Enough and as Good' of What?" *Northwestern University Law Review* 81 (1987): 417–42. See also Carol M. Rose, "The Guardian of Every Other Right: A Constitutional History of Property Rights," *Constitutional Commentary* 10 (1993): 238–46.

3. For increasing regulation of land and water in the nineteenth century, see William J. Novak, *The People's Welfare: Law and Regulation in Nineteenth-Century America* (Chapel Hill: University of North Carolina Press, 1996) (municipal regulations); Morton J. Horowitz, *The Transformation of American Law* (Cambridge, MA: Harvard University Press, 1977) (state common law); Jerry L. Mashaw, "Reluctant Nationalists: Federal Administration and Administrative Law in the Republican Era, 1801–1829," *Yale Law Journal* 116 (2007): 1636–1740 (early federal land regulation), and "Administration and 'The Democracy': Administrative Law From Jackson to Lincoln, 1829–1861," *Yale Law Journal* 117 (2008): 1628–66 (federal steamship regulation); W. Todd Benson, *President Theodore Roosevelt's Conservation Legacy* (West Conshohocken, PA: Infinity Publishing, 2003) (Roosevelt-era conservation policy).

4. On the *green ideology*, see Charlene Spretnak and Fritjof Capra, *Green Politics* (New York: Dutton, 1984 [revised edition, Bear Publishing, 1986]); Philip Shabecoff, *A Fierce Green Fire: The American Environmental Movement* (New York: Hill & Wang, 1993). See also Robert Gottlieb, *Forcing the Spring: The Transformation of the American Environmental Movement* (Washington, DC: Island Press, 1993). Important introductions to *green thinking* as it relates to property law start with J. Peter Byrne, "Green Property," *Constitutional Commentary* 7 (1990): 239–50, and also include Terry W. Frazier, "The Green Alternative to Classical Liberal Property Theory," *Vermont Law Review* 20 (1995): 299–372; Eric T. Freyfogle, "The Construction of Ownership," *University of Illinois Law Review* 1996: 173–82; David B. Hunter, "An Ecological Perspective on Property: A Call for Judicial Protection of the Public's Interest in Environmentally Critical Resources," *Harvard Environmental Law Review* 12 (1988): 311–84.

5. EPA, "DDT Ban Takes Effect" (press release, December 31, 1972), available at www.epa.gov/history/topics/ddt/01.htm (viewed March 6, 2009). For Ruckelshaus's oral history, see www.epa.gov/history/agency/ruckelshaus.htm (viewed March 8, 2009). On the precautionary principle, see Elizabeth Fisher et al., editors, *Implementing the Precautionary Principle: Perspectives and Prospects* (Cheltenham, UK: Edward Elgar, 2006); Douglas A. Kysar, "It Might Have Been: Risk, Precaution, and Opportunity Costs," *Journal of Land Use and Environmental Law* 22 (2006): 1–57.

6. Rachel Carson, *Silent Spring* (New York: Houghton Mifflin, 1962), a pioneering book arguing for the DDT ban because of its harm to the biosphere; Samuel P. Shaw and C. Gordon Fredine, *Wetlands of the United States: The Extent and Their Value to Waterfowl and Other Wildlife* (Fish & Wildlife Service, Circular No. 39, 1956) (quotation in text); see National Research Council, Committee on Characterization of Wetlands, *Wetlands: Characteristics and Boundaries* (Washington, DC: National Academy Press, 1995), 48 (attributing to FWS the first use of the term "wetlands").

7. See generally Robert W. Adler, Jessica C. Landman, and Diane M. Cameron, *The Clean Water Act 20 Years Later* (Washington, DC: Island Press, 1993). On the importance of wetlands preservation, see Shaw and Fredine, *Wetlands of the United States* (the 1956 FWS document); John and Mildred Teal, *Life and Death of the Salt Marsh* (Boston: Little, Brown, 1969). On early state regulation, see Jonathan H. Adler, "Wetlands, Waterfowl, and the Menace of Mr. Wilson: Commerce Clause Jurisprudence and the Limits of Federal Wetland Regulation," *Environmental Law* 29 (1999): 1–68; Brief for the American Farm Bureau Federation as *Amicus Curiae* in Support of Petitioners, 17–25, *United States v. Rapanos*, 547 U.S. 715 (U.S. Supreme Court, 2006) (Docket No. 04-1034). For the Corps of Engineers' proposed rules for regulating discharges into navigable rivers, see *Federal Register* 35 (December 31, 1970): 20005–09.

8. What is now called the CWA was originally the Federal Water Pollution Control Act Amendments, Public Law No. 92-500, 86 Stat. 816 (1972), codified at 33 U.S.C. §§ 1251–1376; see id. § 404(a), 33 U.S.C. § 1344(a) (permit requirement for dredge and fill into "navigable waters"); ibid. § 422(7), 33 U.S.C. § 1362(7) (defining "navigable waters"); cf. 33 C.F.R. § 328.3(a)(1) (traditional regulatory definition of "navigable waters"). For an excellent introduction to the CWA and its legislative history, see

Sam Kalen, "Commerce to Conservation: The Call for a National Water Policy and the Evolution of Federal Jurisdiction Over Wetlands," *North Dakota Law Review* 69 (1993): 873–90; see also Donna M. Downey et al., "Navigating Through Clean Water Act Jurisdiction: A Legal Review," *Wetlands* 23 (September 2003): 475–78.

9. *Federal Register* 38 (May 22, 1973): 13528–40 (EPA's post-CWA rule interpreting "navigable waters"); Senate Public Works Committee, Ninety-fourth Congress, Second Session, *Hearings on Section 404 of the Federal Water Pollution Control Act Amendment of 1972* (1976), 41 (testimony of EPA Administrator Russell Train) (quotation in text). This regulation did not cover wetlands, but in an earlier statement EPA had announced its policy to "preserve the wetland ecosystems and to protect them from destruction through waste water or nonpoint source discharges regarding protection of wetlands" and to "minimize alterations in the quantity or quality of the natural flow of water that nourishes wetlands and to protect wetlands from adverse dredging or filling practices." *Federal Register* 38 (May 2, 1973): 10834.

10. For the Corps' own expanded definition in the face of criticism, see *Federal Register* 40 (May 6, 1975): 19766; ibid. (July 25, 1975): 31320, 31324–25; Lance D. Wood, "Don't Be Misled: CWA Jurisdiction Extends to All Non-Navigable Waters and to Their Adjacent Wetlands," *Environmental Law Review* 34 (2004): 10187, 10211.

11. Executive Order 11,990, "Protection of Wetlands," *Federal Register* 42 (May 24, 1977): 26961; Jeffrey K. Stine, "Environmental Policy During the Carter Presidency," in Gary M. Fink and Hugh Davis Graham, editors, *The Carter Presidency: Policy Choices in the Post—New Deal Era* (Lawrence: University Press of Kansas, 1998), 179–201.

12. *Federal Register* 42 (July 19, 1977): 37122, 37144 (quotation in text). Following updated EPA regulations in 1979, the Corps issued further updated regulations in 1986. *Federal Register* 51 (November 13, 1986): 41206, 41217, codified at 40 C.F.R. § 230.3(s). The high point of the Corps' understanding is contained in the Federal Interagency Committee for Wetland Delineation, *Federal Manual for Identifying and Delineating Jurisdictional Wetlands* (1989), discussed in Mark A. Chertok and Kate Sinding, "Federal Jurisdiction over Wetlands: 'Waters of the United States,'" in Kim Diana Connolly, Stephen M. Johnson, and Douglas R. Williams, editors, *Wetlands Law and Policy: Understanding Section 404* (Chicago: American Bar Association, 2005), 59, 88–91. On the assumption of wetlands enforcement by the states in general and Michigan in particular, see Ronald Keith Gaddie and James L. Regens, *Regulating Wetlands Protection: Environmental Federalism and the States* (Albany: State University of New York Press, 2000).

13. Endangered Species Act of 1973, Public Law No. 93-205, 87 Stat. 884 (1973), codified at 16 U.S.C. §§ 1531 et seq.; see ibid., § 9(a)(1), 16 U.S.C. § 1538(a)(1), making it unlawful to "take" an endangered species; ibid., § 3(19), 16 U.S.C. § 1532(19), defining "take" (first quotation in text); *Federal Register* 40 (1975): 4416 (second quotation), currently codified at 50 C.F.R. § 17.3 (2006); William Bruce Wheeler and Michael J. McDonald, *TVA and the Tellico Dam, 1936–1979: A Bureaucratic Crisis in Post-Industrial America* (Knoxville: University of Tennessee Press, 1986). We reiterate what is implicit in the text: John Rapanos was prosecuted only for violating the CWA; the ESA problem we hypothesize is one that other wetlands owners have encountered, but not one that bedeviled the Rapanoses, to our knowledge.

14. Executive Order No. 12,630, "Government Actions and Interference with Constitutionally Protected Property Rights," *Federal Register* 53 (March 15, 1988): 8859 et seq., codified at 3 C.F.R. § 554. It appears that this executive order "has gone mostly unused." Nancy G. Marzulla, "State Private Property Rights Initiatives as a Response to 'Environmental Takings,'" *South Carolina Law Review* 46 (1995): 613, 630.

15. As president of the Conservation Foundation, Reilly convened the National Wetland Policy Forum, which recommended this policy in 1988: "No overall net loss of the nation's remaining wetland base, as defined by acreage and function, and to restore and create wetlands, where feasible, to increase the quality and quantity of the nation's wetlands resource base." Conservation Foundation, *Protecting America's Wetlands: An Action Agenda* (Washington, DC: Conservation Foundation, 1988). For subsequent articulations, after Reilly's tenure, see White House Office on Environmental Policy, "Protecting America's Wetlands: A Fair, Flexible, and Effective Approach" (August 24, 1993); Council on Environmental Quality, *Conserving America's Wetlands 2006: Two Years of Progress Implementing the President's Goal* (April 2006).

16. On the origins and early activism of the property rights movement, see Nancie G. Marzulla, "Property Rights Movement: How It Began and Where It Is Headed," in Philip D. Brick and R. McGreggor Cawley, editors, *A Wolf in the Garden: The Land Rights Movement and the New Environmental Debate* (London: Rowman & Littlefield, 1996).

17. The most thoughtful conceptual introduction to the property rights protection movement we have read is Jonathan H. Adler, "Back to the Future of Conservation: Changing Perceptions of Property Rights and Environmental Protection," *New York University Journal of Law & Liberty* 1 (2005): 987ff. For other work usefully explaining the property rights point of view, see Kirk Emerson, "Taking the Land Rights Movement Seriously," in Brick and Cawley editors, *Wolf in the Garden*, 115–34; John McClaughry, "The New Feudalism," *Environmental Law* 5 (1975): 675–702; Bruce Yandle, "Escaping Environmental Feudalism," *Harvard Journal of Law & Public Policy* 15 (1992): 517–39. Responding to the feudalism charge is Richard J. Lazarus, "Debunking Environmental Feudalism: Promoting the Individual Through the Collective Pursuit of Environmental Quality," *Iowa Law Review* 77 (1992): 1739–74, who argues that green thinking reconceptualizes the relationship between the individual and the land and is an admirable effort to protect future generations from the excesses of current consumption.

18. Compare Epstein, *Takings* (viewing property as prepolitical and requiring the government to pay when it regulates property), with Peter J. Byrne, "Ten Arguments for the Abolition of the Regulatory Takings Doctrine," *Ecology Law Quarterly* 22 (1995): 89–142, and with Charles A. Reich, "Beyond the New Property: An Ecological View of Due Process," *Brooklyn Law Review* 56 (1990): 731–46 (arguing for a Fifth Amendment right to a clean and healthy environment). On the original meaning of the Takings Clause, see William Michael Treanor, "The Original Understanding of the Takings Clause and the Political Process," *Columbia Law Review* 95 (1995): 782–887. On the property rights movement's shift from courts to legislatures as the forums for articulating their takings claim, see Alfred M. Olivetti Jr. and Jeff Worsham, *This*

Land Is Your Land, This Land Is My Land: The Property Rights Movement and Regulatory Takings (New York: LFB Scholarly Publishing, 2003).

19. *Rapanos v. United States*, 547 U.S. 715 (U.S. Supreme Court, 2006), overturning the Corps' assertion of wetlands jurisdiction over the Rapanoses' Salzburg property.

20. Compare *Wyeth v. Levine*, 129 S.Ct. 1187, 1201–03 (U.S. Supreme Court, 2009), where the Court refused to credit an agency interpretation that drug law preempts state tort claims when the agency has not provided well-informed or cogent reasons, and instead relied on the agency's previous views, supported by deliberations within the agency and inputs from science advisory committees, with *Geier v. American Honda Motor Co.*, 529 U.S. 861, 875–83 (2000), where the Court deferred to long-time agency views, which were the result of fact-based deliberations and application of the agency's expertise.

Also compare *Motor Vehicle Manufacturers Association of United States, Inc. v. State Farm Mutual Automobile Insurance Co.*, 463 U.S. 29 (U.S. Supreme Court, 1983), where the Court overturned an agency rule that failed to justify or explain the rule it was reversing, with *FCC v. Fox Television Stations, Inc.*, 129 S.Ct. 1800 (U.S. Supreme Court, 2009), where the Court upheld an agency order that fully explained why it was creating a harder line against indecent language on television.

21. Notwithstanding Justice Scalia's well-publicized attack on legislative history in statutory cases, the Court routinely relies on it to good effect. E.g., *Wyeth v. Levine*, 129 S.Ct. 1187 (U.S. Supreme Court, 2009).

22. For a structural explanation of why statutes *will* be interpreted dynamically over time, see William N. Eskridge Jr., *Dynamic Statutory Interpretation* (Cambridge, MA: Harvard University Press, 1994), chap. 2. See also ibid., chap. 5, for an argument that agencies will be the source of most dynamic interpretations. For the beyond/against distinction, see Daniel A. Farber, "Statutory Interpretation and the Principle of Legislative Supremacy," *Georgetown Law Journal* 78 (1989): 281–318.

23. Joseph A. Grundfest and A. C. Pritchard, "Statutes with Multiple Personality Disorders: The Value of Ambiguity in Statutory Design and Interpretation," *Stanford Law Review* 54 (2002): 627–736 (describing and providing examples of Congress's use of ambiguous language); Lisa Schultz Bressman, "*Chevron*'s Mistake," *Duke Law Journal* 58 (2009): 549–621, especially 566–70 (describing deliberate ambiguities as implicit congressional delegations to agencies).

24. House Report No. 92-911 (House Public Works Comm., 1972), 76–77 (first quotation in text); Senate Report No. 92-414 (Senate Comm. on Public Works, 1971), 77 (second quotation); Conference Report No. 92-1236 (Conference Comm., 1972), 144 (third quotation); *Congressional Record* 118 (October 4, 1972): 33756–57 (Representative Dingell (D-MI, House sponsor) (fourth quotation); CWA, 33 U.S.C. § 1251 (statutory purposes). The legislative history of the act is collected in Congressional Research Service, Library of Congress, *Legislative History of the Federal Water Pollution Control Act Amendments of 1972* (Washington, DC: GPO, 1973).

25. *Federal Register* 42 (1977): 37122, 37128–29. For the rather involved procedural history of the 1977 regulations, see Kalen, "Commerce to Conservation," 891–97.

26. *United States v. Riverside Bayview Homes, Inc.*, 474 U.S. 121 (U.S. Supreme Court, 1985); *Federal Register* 51 (1986): 41206–60, especially 41217 (Corps' new Migratory

Bird Rule); Federal Interagency Committee, *Federal Manual for Identifying and Delineating Jurisdictional Wetlands* (Washington, DC: GAO, 1989) (broad EPA-Corps understanding of wetlands coverage, abandoned by the Corps as a result of congressional pressure); *Federal Register* 66 (2000): 12818–99, especially 12823 (Corps' broad interpretation of "tributaries").

27. *Congressional Record* 119 (1973): 30162 (Representative Sullivan, House ESA floor manager) (quotation in text); ibid., 25669 (Senator Tunney, Senate ESA floor manager) (similar statement). As Justice Scalia later put it: "Habitat modification and takings . . . were viewed [by the enacting Congress] as different problems, addressed by different provisions of the Act." *Babbitt v. Sweet Home Chapter of Communities for a Greater Oregon*, 515 U.S. 687, 728 (U.S. Supreme Court, 1995) (dissenting opinion).

28. On the Corps of Engineers' successful adaptation to a new era of environmental sensitivity, see Jeanne Nienaber Clarke and Daniel C. McCool, *Staking Out the Terrain: Power and Performance Among Natural Resource Agencies* (Albany: State University of New York Press, 1996), 17–68. The evolving regulatory approach of the Corps may have eroded its political support. Traditionally, members of Congress could count on the fact that a Corps-supported project would not be conflictual, as local conflicts had to be resolved before the Corps would proceed. See John A. Ferejohn, *Pork Barrel Politics: Rivers and Harbors Legislation, 1947–1968* (Stanford, CA: Stanford University Press, 1974); Arthur Maass, *Muddy Waters: The Army Engineers and the Nation's Rivers* (Cambridge, MA: Harvard University Press, 1951). After the CWA, however, the Corps' more aggressive stance was likely to step on the toes of locally powerful landowners such as the Rapanoses. Episodes such as this not only fueled the new property rights movement but also might be expected to rile members of Congress and turn them against the Corps. Recall President Carter's disastrous effort to cancel water projects not environmentally justified: pork usually trumps green in the legislature.

29. Compare Hugh Davis Graham, *The Civil Rights Era* (New York: Oxford University Press, 1990), arguing that the EEOC was gradually "captured" by civil rights groups in the late 1960s, with Neal E. Devins, "The Civil Rights Hydra," *Michigan Law Review* 89 (1991): 1723–65, arguing that the original statute and early administration were consistent with a public-regarding account of administrative responsibility.

30. Richard A. Liroff, *Reforming Air Pollution Regulation: The Toil and Trouble of EPA's Bubble* (Washington, DC: Conservation Foundation, 1986); Richard A Liroff, *Air Pollution Offsets: Trading, Selling, and Banking* (Washington, DC: Conservation Foundation, 1980); Richard A. Liroff and G. Gordon Davis, *Protecting Open Space: Land Use Control in the Adirondack Park* (Cambridge, MA: Ballinger, 1981).

31. On the science of wetlands, reflected in the text, see Judy L. Meyer et al., *Where Rivers Are Born: The Scientific Imperative for Defending Small Streams and Wetlands* (Washington, DC: American Rivers and Sierra Club, February 2007). On the dramatic paradigm shift in ecological thinking between 1970–73 and the present, see Fred P. Bosselman and A. Dan Tarlock, "The Influence of Ecological Science on American Law: An Introduction," *Chicago-Kent Law Review* 69 (1994): 847–73, starting with the theory of the ecosystem as a mechanical system tending toward

harmony and order, which was the basis for the environmental laws of 1970–73, and tracing its replacement with a chaos theory driven, nonequilibrium approach.

32. On the sequential features of statutory interpretation and its dynamic features, see William N. Eskridge Jr., "Overriding Supreme Court Statutory Interpretation Decisions," *Yale Law Journal* 101 (1991): 331–455.

33. Clean Water Act Amendments of 1977, Public Law No. 95-217, 91 Stat. 1566 (1977); *Congressional Record* 123 (August 4, 1977): 26690 (Senate rejection of Bentsen amendment, 51–45); House Conference Report No. 95–830 (1977) (accepting the Senate's version of Corps jurisdiction over wetlands). See generally Kalen, "Commerce to Conservation," 897–905.

34. Endangered Species Act Amendments of 1982, Public Law No. 97-304, 96 Stat. 1411 (1982), codified at 16 U.S.C. § 1539(a) (permit system for "takings" incidental to lawful activities); Senate Report No. 97-418 (1982), 10; House Conference Report No. 97-835 (1982), 30–32. Compare *Sweet Home*, 515 U.S., 700–01 (majority opinion, relying on the 1982 ESA Amendments and the legislative history), with ibid., 729–30 (Scalia, J., dissenting and objecting to the Court's reliance on the legislative history of the 1982 amendments).

35. *Solid Waste Agency v. Army Corps of Engineers*, 531 U.S. 159 (U.S. Supreme Court, 2001); *Rapanos v. United States*, 547 U.S. 715, 759–87 (U.S. Supreme Court, 2006) (Kennedy, J., concurring in the judgment). Compare ibid., 715–58 (plurality opinion of Scalia, J.), reflecting a narrower view of the Corps' jurisdiction, with ibid., 787–810 (Stevens, J., dissenting), accepting the Corps' understanding of its statutory jurisdiction.

36. *Rapanos*, 547 U.S., 757–58 (Roberts, C.J., concurring); ibid., 811–12 (Breyer, J., dissenting), both calling for the agencies to engage in rulemaking; Benjamin H. Grumbles (assistant administrator for water, EPA) and John Paul Woodley Jr. (assistant secretary of the army (civil works)), Memorandum, "Clean Water Act Jurisdiction Following the U.S. Supreme Court Decision in *Rapanos v. United States & Carabell v. United States*" (June 6, 2007) (joint EPA/Corps guidance memorandum, not itself binding law but providing binding legal guidance).

37. Clean Air Act Amendments of 1970, Public Law No. 91-604, 84 Stat. 1676 (1970); Reorganization Plan No. 3, *Federal Register* 35 (1970): 15623 (creation of the EPA); Clean Air Act Amendments of 1977, Public Law No. 95-95, § 172(b)(6), 91 Stat. 685 (1977), codified at 42 U.S.C. § 7502(c)(5). For useful histories of federal air quality regulation, see Bruce A. Ackerman and William T. Hassler, *Clean Coal, Dirty Air: Or How the Clean Air Act Became a Multi-Billion Dollar Bail-Out for High Sulfur Producers and What Should Be Done About It* (New Haven: Yale University Press, 1981); Arnold W. Reitze Jr., "The Legislative History of U.S. Air Pollution Control," *Houston Law Review* 36 (1999): 679–741.

38. *Chevron, U.S.A., Inc. v. Natural Resources Defense Council*, 467 U.S. 837 (U.S. Supreme Court, 1984). On the Bator brief and its background, see Thomas W. Merrill, "The Story of *Chevron*: The Making of an Accidental Landmark," in Peter Strauss, editor, *Administrative Law Stories* (New York: Foundation Press, 2006), 398–429, especially 412–14. See also *Alabama Power v. Costle*, 636 F.2d 323, 397–401 (U.S. Court of Appeals for the D.C. Circuit, 1979) (Wilkey, J.) (arguing for the need for courts to

allow the EPA regulatory flexibility so that costs are not disproportionate to benefits).

39. *Chevron,* 467 U.S., 863–64; Justice Blackmun's Conference Notes for *Chevron,*
March 2, 1984, in The Papers of Harry A. Blackmun (Library of Congress, Madison
Building, Manuscript Collections), Box 397, Folder 7 (Justice Stevens's explanation
for his deferential vote); John Paul Stevens, "In Memoriam: Byron R. White," *Harvard Law Review* 116 (2002): 1–2 (Justice Stevens's account of the *Chevron* assign-
ment).

40. Compare Kenneth Starr, "Judicial Review in the Post-*Chevron* Era," *Yale Journal on
Regulation* 3 (1986): 283–312, arguing that *Chevron* was revolutionary, with Stephen
Breyer, "Judicial Review of Questions of Law and Policy," *Administrative Law Review*
38 (1986): 363–98, arguing that *Chevron* is contrary to traditional principles of administrative law. See also Antonin Scalia, "Judicial Deference to Administrative Interpretations of Law," *Duke Law Journal* 1989: 511–21 (agreeing with Starr).

　　Except where otherwise noted, the empirical generalizations in this part's text are
taken from William N. Eskridge Jr. and Lauren E. Baer, "The Continuum of Deference: Supreme Court Treatment of Agency Statutory Interpretation from *Chevron* to
Hamdan," *Georgetown Law Journal* 96 (2008): 1083–1226. On the deference regimes
applied by the Court in environmental cases between 1984 and 2006, see ibid., 1139
(table 14).

41. For an argument that *Chevron* deference requires lawmaking delegation, see Thomas
W. Merrill and Kristin E. Hickman, "*Chevron's* Domain," *Georgetown Law Journal*
89 (2001): 833–921. On the legitimacy-conferring nature of notice-and-comment rule
making, see Henry S. Richardson, *Democratic Autonomy: Public Reasoning About
the Ends of Policy* (New York: Oxford University Press, 2002). On the empowerment
of scientists within EPA, see E. Donald Elliott, "*Chevron* Matters: How the *Chevron*
Doctrine Redefined the Roles of Congress, Courts, and Agencies in Environmental
Law," *Villanova Environmental Law Journal* 16 (2005): 1–18, especially 11–12.

42. *Chevron,* 467 U.S., 863–64 (justifications for deference); *Motor Vehicle Manufactur-
ers Association v. State Farm Mutual Automobile Insurance Co.,* 463 U.S. 29 (U.S.
Supreme Court, 1983). See generally Gillian Metzger, "The Story of *Vermont Yan-
kee:* A Cautionary Tale of Judicial Review and Nuclear Waste," in Strauss, editor,
Administrative Law Stories, 124–67. For a narrow interpretation of *State Farm,* see
FCC v. Fox Television Stations, Inc., 129 S.Ct. 1800 (U.S. Supreme Court, 2009).

43. *Massachusetts v. EPA,* 549 U.S. 497, 527–32 (2007), interpreting 42 U.S.C. § 7521(a)
(1) (as amended in 1977 to reflect the precautionary principle) to require the EPA to
regulate greenhouse gas emissions if they can reasonably be anticipated to endanger
public health; ibid., 532–34, finding the EPA's refusal to give reasons for not considering greenhouse gases to endanger public health to be arbitrary and capricious. For
discussions of the Bush-Cheney administration's efforts to marginalize science in
environmental regulation, see Chris Mooney, *Republican War on Science* (New
York: Basic Books, 2005); Barton Gellman, *Angler: The Cheney Vice Presidency* (New
York: Penguin, 2008).

44. *Chevron,* 467 U.S., 865–66. For academic support for the presidential-accountability
justification for *Chevron* deference, see Mathew D. Adler, "Judicial Restraint in the

Administrative State: Beyond the Countermajoritarian Difficulty," *University of Pennsylvania Law Review* 145 (1997): 759–892, especially 875–76; David Barron and Elena Kagan, "*Chevron's* Nondelegation Doctrine," *Supreme Court Review* 2001: 201–54, especially 234–37; Lawrence Lessig and Cass R. Sunstein, "The President and the Administration," *Columbia Law Review* 94 (1994): 1–119, especially 105–06; Starr, "Judicial Review in the Post-*Chevron* Era," 312.

Academic critics of the presidential accountability justification for *Chevron* include Lisa Schultz Bressman, "Beyond Accountability: Arbitrariness and Legitimacy in the Administrative State," *New York University Law Review* 78 (2003): 461–556; Cynthia R. Farina, "Undoing the New Deal Through the New Presidentialism," *Harvard Journal of Law and Public Policy* 22 (1998): 227–38; Thomas O. McGarity, "Presidential Control of Regulatory Agency Decisionmaking," *American University Law Review* 36 (1987): 443–90; Peter L. Strauss, "Presidential Rulemaking," *Chicago-Kent Law Review* 72 (1997): 965–86. The Court's post-*Chevron* jurisprudence is consistent with the critics' reading. See *United States v. Mead Corp.*, 533 U.S. 218 (U.S. Supreme Court, 2001); *National Cable & Telecommunications Association v. Brand X Internet Services*, 545 U.S. 967 (U.S. Supreme Court, 2005).

For suggestions that *Chevron* deference is justified by agency responsiveness to current congressional, perhaps even more than presidential, preferences, see William N. Eskridge Jr. and John Ferejohn, "The Article I, Section 7 Game," *Georgetown Law Journal* 80 (1992): 523–64; Einer Elhauge, "Preference-Estimating Statutory Default Rules," *Columbia Law Review* 102 (2002): 2027–2161, especially 2126–28.

45. Our view that presidential accountability does not justify *Chevron* deference is not altered by arguments made by executive power enthusiasts that the president is more accountable to We the People because he is elected by a national vote and is alone accountable to national popular majorities. The president, chosen by an electoral college that frequently graduates preference outliers, does not necessarily reflect majoritarian preferences better than Congress does. See Cynthia R. Farina, "Faith, Hope, and Rationality or Public Choice and the Perils of Occam's Razor," *Florida State University Law Review* 28 (2000): 109–36, especially 128–29; Jide Nzelibe, "The Fable of the Nationalist President and the Parochial Congress," *UCLA Law Review* 53 (2006): 1217–74, especially 1231–46.

46. For critiques of White House pressure overriding scientific judgments, see Bressman, "Beyond Accountability," 506–11; Mooney, *Republican War on Science*. On the president's first-mover advantage, which we apply to agency guidances and rule making, see Terry M. Moe and William G. Howell, "The Presidential Power of Unilateral Action," *Journal of Law, Economics, and Organization* 15 (1999): 132–79; William G. Howell, *Power Without Persuasion: The Politics of Direct Presidential Action* (Princeton: Princeton University Press, 2003).

47. Martin van der Werf, "Endangered Species Act 'Gotta Be Fixed,' Foe Says," *Arizona Republic*, July 1, 1995, B1 (Cushman quotations in text). The Cushman anecdote and much of our analysis in text are drawn from Mark Sagoff, "Muddle or Muddle Through? Takings Jurisprudence Meets the Endangered Species Act," *William & Mary Law Review* 38 (1997): 825–993, an excellent treatment of the ESA on the ground.

48. Sagoff, "Takings Jurisprudence Meets the Endangered Species Act," 854–56 (Secretary Babbitt's conciliatory remarks and the regulatory response); FWS, "Endangered and Threatened Wildlife and Plants; Proposed Rule Exempting Certain Small Landowners and Low-Impact Activities from Endangered Species Act Requirements for Threatened Species," *Federal Register* 60 (July 20, 1995): 37419–23 (proposed regulations exempting small farmers etc. from the § 9 rules).

49. Compare *Sweet Home*, 515 U.S., 726–29 (Scalia, J., dissenting, based upon sponsor's explanations of the 1973 legislation), with ibid., 700–01 (majority opinion, supporting the agency's dynamic interpretation on the ground that the 1982 amendments accepted that construction and created a permit program to accommodate it).

50. *Rapanos*, 547 U.S., 732–38 (plurality opinion of Scalia, J.) (quotation in text); ibid. (Kennedy, J., concurring in the judgment); ibid., 800–05 (Stevens, J., dissenting).

51. On the conceded applicability of *Chevron* to the Corps' rules, see *Rapanos*, 547 U.S., 739 (plurality opinion of Scalia, J.); ibid., 758 (Roberts, C.J., concurring); ibid. (Kennedy, J., concurring in the judgment); ibid., 788 (Stevens, J., dissenting). For recent statements of the Court's superdeference to agency interpretations of their own regulations, see, e.g., *Gonzales v. Oregon*, 546 U.S. 243, 277–81 (U.S. Supreme Court, 2006) (Scalia, J., dissenting); *Auer v. Robbins*, 519 U.S. 452, 461–63 (U.S. Supreme Court, 1997) (Scalia, J.).

52. *Rapanos*, 547 U.S., 721 (plurality opinion of Scalia, J.) ("enlightened despot"); *Sweet Home*, 515 U.S., 714 (Scalia, J., dissenting) (protecting the "simplest farmer" from having his land "conscripted for national zoological use").

53. Eskridge and Baer, "Continuum of Deference," 1153–56. The pathfinding survey among law professors is Richard L. Revesz, "Environmental Regulation, Ideology, and the D.C. Circuit," *Virginia Law Review* 83 (1997): 1717–72, finding strong evidence of ideological voting by D.C. judges adjudicating challenges to EPA rules and other actions. See also Orrin S. Kerr, "Shedding Light on *Chevron*: An Empirical Study of the *Chevron* Doctrine in the U.S. Courts of Appeals," *Yale Journal of Regulation* 15 (1998): 1, 37–39 (1998), finding significant evidence of ideological voting in *Chevron* cases among the courts of appeals; Thomas J. Miles and Cass R. Sunstein, "Do Judges Make Regulatory Policy? An Empirical Investigation of *Chevron*," *University of Chicago Law Review* 73 (2006): 823–81, finding significant evidence of ideological voting by Supreme Court justices in *Chevron* cases decided between 1994 and 2005.

54. *Rapanos*, 547 U.S., 731 and note 3 (plurality opinion of Scalia, J.); ibid., 777 (Kennedy, J., concurring in the judgment) (quotation in text).

55. Dan M. Kahan, "Lenity and Federal Common Law Crimes," *Supreme Court Review* 1994: 345–428; William N. Eskridge Jr., "Overriding Supreme Court Statutory Interpretation Decisions," *Yale Law Journal* 101 (1991): 331–417, especially 344–48, 375–77 (the rule of lenity sets a good default rule, because criminal code constructions favoring criminal defendants are most likely to trigger congressional deliberation and override, while those disfavoring defendants have virtually no likelihood even to trigger congressional deliberations).

56. On the absolute duty to obey, see Owen M. Fiss, *The Civil Rights Injunction* (Bloomington: Indiana University Press, 1978), criticizing the rule of *Walker v. City of Birmingham*, 388 U.S. 307 (U.S. Supreme Court, 1967).

57. *Whitman v. American Trucking*, 531 U.S. 457, 468 (U.S. Supreme Court, 2001) (Congress does not "hide elephants in mouseholes"); *Chisom v. Roemer*, 501 U.S. 380, 396 (U.S. Supreme Court, 1991) (Congress would make a point, i.e., the dog would bark, if it were making a big change in the status quo), both discussed in Christopher Lynch, "School Desegregation and the 'Critter Canons': A Case Study" (Yale Law School Supervised Analytic Writing, 2008).

58. *Solid Waste*, 531 U.S., 173–74 (majority opinion of Rehnquist, C.J.). The notion that the avoidance canon trumps deference is hardly novel. For earlier examples, perhaps even stronger medicine than *Solid Waste*, see, e.g., *Department of Commerce v. U.S. House of Representatives*, 525 U.S. 316 (U.S. Supreme Court, 1999); *NLRB v. Catholic Bishop of Chicago*, 440 U.S. 490 (U.S. Supreme Court, 1979); *United States v. Witkovich*, 353 U.S. 194 (U.S. Supreme Court, 1957).

59. There is a great deal of empirical support for understanding justices' votes as merely expressing their political preferences. E.g., Lee Epstein and Jack Knight, *The Choices Justices Make* (Washington, DC: CQ Press, 1998); Jeffrey A. Segal, "Separation-of-Powers Games in the Positive Theory of Congress and Courts," *American Political Science Review* 91 (1997): 28–44.

60. For a spirited debate, with much agreement, over differences in Constitutional and statutory methodology, compare William N. Eskridge Jr., "Should the Supreme Court Read *The Federalist* But Not Statutory Legislative History?" *George Washington University Law Review* 66 (1998): 1301–23, with John Manning, "Textualism and the Role of *The Federalist* in Constitutional Adjudication," *George Washington University Law Review* 66 (1998): 1337–65; Stephen F. Williams, "Restoring Context, Distorting Text: Legislative History and the Problem of Age," *George Washington University Law Review* 66 (1998): 1366–69.

61. Jerry L. Mashaw, "Agency Statutory Interpretation," *Issues in Legal Scholarship, Issue 3: Dynamic Statutory Interpretation* (2002): Article 9, available at www.bepress.com/ils/iss3/art9 (viewed August 2008). See also Mashaw, "Norms, Practices, and the Paradox of Deference: A Preliminary Inquiry into Agency Statutory Interpretation," *Administrative Law Review* 57 (2005): 501–42.

62. For a similar departure from Professor Mashaw's view of administrative interpretation, see Trevor W. Morrison, "Constitutional Avoidance in the Executive Branch," *Columbia Law Review* 106 (2006): 1189–1259.

63. For a concise statement of the purposive approach, see Henry M. Hart Jr. and Albert M. Sacks, *The Legal Process: Basic Problems in the Making and Application of Law*, William N. Eskridge Jr. and Philip P. Frickey, editors (Westbury, NY: Foundation Press, 1994 [1958 tentative edition]), 1411–12.

64. Brief of the United States, *Rapanos* (Docket Nos. 04-1034 and 04-1384), 1–8; Brief of the Association of State and Interstate Water Pollution Administrators as *Amicus Curiae* in Support of Respondents, *Rapanos* (Docket Nos. 04-1034 and 04-1384), 7 (quotation in text). See also Brief of Former EPA Administrators as *Amici Curiae* in Support of Respondents, *Rapanos* (Docket Nos. 04-1034 and 04-1384) (arguing that most of the coverage of the CWA would be lost if the Court overruled the Corps' assertion of jurisdiction); Brief of [Thirty-three Listed] States et al. as *Amici Curiae* in Support of Respondents, *Rapanos* (Docket Nos. 04-1034 and 04-1384) (arguing

that states have relied on the Corps' longstanding assertion of broad wetlands juris-diction).

65. Compare *Rapanos*, 547 U.S., 732–33 and note 4 (plurality opinion of Scalia, J., selec-tively invoking *Webster's Second*), with Brief of the Honorable John D. Dingell et al., as *Amici Curiae* in Support of the Respondent, *Rapanos* (Docket Nos. 04-1034 and 04-1384), representing six Democrats and three Republicans who were key senators and representatives in the CWA of 1977 and arguing that Congress in 1977 ratified the Corps' broad understanding of "waters of the United States" and affirmatively *rejected* narrower understandings such as the one the *Rapanos* plurality ultimately adopted.

66. *Rapanos*, 547 U.S., 733–38 (plurality opinion of Scalia, J.) (discussion and quotation in text).

67. To take a classic exchange, *Green v. Bock Laundry Machine Co.*, 490 U.S. 504 (U.S. Supreme Court, 1989), we disagree with the archaeological approach to legislative intent pursued at great length in Justice Stevens's majority opinion, ibid., 505–27, and the rejection of all such materials in Justice Scalia's concurring opinion, ibid., 527–30. The best approach is the one in Justice Blackmun's dissenting opinion, ibid., 530–35, for it sought to understand Congress's purposes and values and reasoned from those to correct the scrivener's error that all nine justices recognized was the problem.

68. *Congressional Record* 119 (1973): 30162 (Representative Sullivan, ESA House floor manager) (quotation in text); ibid., 25,669 (similar comments by Senator Tunney, Senate floor manager); *Sweet Home*, 515 U.S., 726–29 (Scalia, J., dissenting), relying on these materials as strong evidence of statutory meaning.

69. Brief for Petitioners, *Sweet Home* (Docket No. 94-859), 31–40, an excellent treat-ment of the ESA's ongoing legislative history. See also Endangered Species Act Amendments of 1978, Public Law No. 95-632, 92 Stat. 3751 (1978); Endangered Spe-cies Act Amendments of 1982, Public Law No. 97-304, 96 Stat. 1411 (1982); House Conference Report No. 97-835 (1982), 30–32, explaining that the 1982 permit pro-gram was established as a safety valve for the department's harm-to-habitat regula-tion.

70. For an account of the Court's rebuffs from the political process when it ignored sub-sequent legislative signals, see William N. Eskridge Jr., "Reneging on History? The Court/Congress/President Civil Rights Game," *California Law Review* 79 (1991): 613–84.

71. For explication and critique of the Court's superstrong presumption of correctness for statutory precedents, see William N. Eskridge Jr., "Overruling Statutory Prece-dents," *Georgetown Law Journal* 76 (1988): 1361–1439.

72. *National Cable & Telecommunications Association v. Brand X Internet Services*, 545 U.S. 967, 982 (U.S. Supreme Court, 2005) (quotations in text); *Rapanos*, 547 U.S., 757–59 (Roberts, C.J., concurring); ibid., 776–78 (Kennedy, J., concurring in the judg-ment); ibid., 811–12 (Breyer, J., dissenting). See also *United States v. Mead Corp.*, 533 U.S. 218, 247 (U.S. Supreme Court, 2001) (Scalia, J., dissenting), citing *Chevron* defer-ence as a protection against "ossification" of statutory schemes because of *stare decisis*.

73. For recent examples of the Court's willingness to revisit Sherman Act precedents at the behest of the Department of Justice, see *Leegin Creative Leather Products v. PSKS, Inc.*, 551 U.S. 877 (U.S. Supreme Court, 2007); *State Oil Co. v. Khan*, 522 U.S. 3 (U.S. Supreme Court, 1997). In chapter 3, we offered a modest critique of *Leegin*, on the ground that the Court overruled a precedent that Congress had relied on and that plausibly contributed to, rather than undermined, the consumer-protection purpose the Court now attributes to the Sherman Act.

74. James Gray Pope, "Republican Moments: The Role of Direct Popular Power in the American Constitutional Order," *University of Pennsylvania Law Review* 139 (1990): 287–368, describing the 1970s groundswell of support for environmental protection as "republican moments." On Earth Day and the evolution of the environmental movement as complicated normative social movement, see Gottlieb, *Forcing the Spring.*

75. Pacific Legal Foundation Attorney Reed Hopper, "Op Ed on the Rapanos Settlement," *Detroit News*, available at www.rapanos.typepad.com (viewed March 26, 2009) (quotation in text).

76. For a thoughtful critique of the biodiversity norm and its uncertain future, see Sagoff, "Takings Jurisprudence Meets the Endangered Species Act," 902–12, 968–89. See also "Symposium: The Endangered Species Act: Thirty Years of Politics, Money, and Science," *Tulane Environmental Law Journal* 16 (2003): 257–444; Andrew P. Morris and Richard L. Stroup, "Quartering Species: The 'Living Constitution,' the Third Amendment, and the Endangered Species Act," *Environmental Law* 30 (2000): 769–810, especially 785–96 (useful policy critique of the ESA, in contrast to the authors' zany Constitutional argument).

CHAPTER 7. THE MONETARY CONSTITUTION
AND ADMINISTRATIVE EXPERIMENTATION

1. Thomas Hobbes, *Leviathan* (1651), chap. 13 (quotation in text). Hobbes famously opposed the political excesses of common lawyers and judges, specifically Edward Coke, who had been chief justice of the Court of Common Pleas and, later on, the King's Bench. But his deeper hostility was to the pretentions of the common lawyers, who sought to restrict the king's sovereign authority, and not to the values that the common law aimed at preserving. Hobbes thought those values better preserved in a system in which sovereignty was clear and undivided and, in England, controlled by the king through statutes rather than by the arcane and sophistic workings the "artificial reason" of the common lawyers.

2. Legal scholarship on the early monetary constitution is a scarce commodity, but most of it is superb, especially Claire Priest, "Currency Policies and Legal Development in Colonial New England," *Yale Law Journal* 110 (2001): 1303–1404.

3. The facts in the text are taken from the caption and opinion for the Court in *Hepburn v. Griswold*, 75 U.S. 603, 603–06 (U.S. Supreme Court, 1870), "The First Legal Tender Case," discussed in the second part of this chapter.

4. On Hamilton's sophisticated philosophy for supporting the First Bank, see David McGowan, "Ethos in Law and History: Alexander Hamilton, *The Federalist*, and the Supreme Court," *Minnesota Law Review* 85 (2001): 794–804.

5. On Jefferson's objections to the bank, see Paul Leicester Ford, editor, *The Writings of Thomas Jefferson* (New York: G. P. Putnam's Sons, 1892–99), 5: 284–89. On the serious Constitutional objections to the bank, see Paul Finkelman, "The Constitution and the Intentions of the Framers: The Limits of Historical Analysis," *University of Pittsburgh Law Review* 50 (1989): 349, 359–60. As Professor Finkelman points out, Madison's Constitutional opposition to the bank in 1791 was persuasive to very few members of Congress, half of whom had been directly involved in the drafting or ratification of the Constitution. Ibid., 360–64.

6. Act of Feb. 25, 1791, To Incorporate the Subscribers to the Bank of the United States, chap. 10, 1 Stat. 191 (1791); McGowan, "Ethos in Law and History," 804–19 (detailed account of the Constitutional debate between Hamilton and Jefferson).

7. Act of February 25, 1791, §§ 4, 11 (United States' participation in the Bank of the United States' equity and its board of directors). On the creation and early operation of the bank, see Richard Timberlake, *Monetary Policy in the United States* (Chicago: University of Chicago Press, 1978).

8. On the politics of the First Bank's demise in 1811, see Jeffery A. Jenkins and Marc Weidenmier, "Ideology, Economic Interests, and Congressional Roll-Call Voting: Partisan Instability and Bank of the United States Legislation, 1811–1816," *Public Choice* 100 (1999): 225–43.

9. Timberlake, *Monetary Policy in the United States*, chap. 2; Jenkins and Weidenmier, "Partisan Instability and Bank of the United States Legislation, 1811–1816" (discussing the realignment of political forces favoring and opposing the Second Bank).

10. James Madison, "Veto Message to the Senate of the First Bank Bill" (January 30, 1815), reprinted in Gaillard Hunt, editor, *The Writings of James Madison* (New York: G. P. Putnam & Sons, 1900–1910), 7:327–30 (quotation in text); Act of April 10, 1816, To Incorporate the Subscribers to the Bank of the United States, 3 Stat. 266 (1816); Jenkins and Weidenmier, "Partisan Instability and Bank of the United States Legislation, 1811–1816" (discussing the votes for and against the Second Bank).

11. *McCulloch v. Maryland*, 17 U.S. (4 Wheat.) 316 (U.S. Supreme Court, 1819). On the proliferation and importance of state-chartered banks, see Richard Sylla, John B. Legler, and John J. Wallis, "Banks and State Public Finance in the New Republic: The United States, 1790–1860," *Journal of Economic History* 47 (1987): 391–403.

12. *McCulloch*, 17 U.S. (4 Wheat.), 407 (analysis of Article I's grants of authority, first quotation in text); ibid., 421 (analysis of Necessary and Proper Clause; second quotation). After broadly construing Article I, § 8, along the purposive and liberal lines originally suggested by Alexander Hamilton, the chief justice then invalidated Maryland's effort to tax the bank as unconstitutional. Ibid., 425–37. Presumably, the latter holding represented a judgment that state taxation was inconsistent with the efficient operation of a federally chartered bank—but that was a judgment which was not made on the face of the statute and which Marshall teased out of the nature of things.

13. *Osborn v. Bank of the United States*, 22 U.S. (9 Wheat.) 738, 817–18 (U.S. Supreme Court, 1824) (arguing that the law permitting the bank to sue and be sued in the circuit courts of the United States was an implicit vesting of federal jurisdiction for any case brought by the Second Bank); ibid., 818–28 (broad interpretation of Article III); ibid., 871–72 (Johnson, J., dissenting) (quotation in text).

14. See Bray Hammond, *Banks and Politics in America from the Revolution to the Civil War* (Princeton: Princeton University Press, 1957), the classic account of the Second Bank and its role in the history of public finance. The policies of the Second Bank made clear the tensions between the (fiduciary) duties of the bank to its stockholders and its public mission. It received a substantial public subsidy every year in exchange for serving as a lender and depository for the federal government. As a private institution its interests sometimes ran counter to the public interest in preventing panics or maintaining a stable currency. Moreover, as Nicholas Biddle and other central bankers learned early on, performing a public duty, such as restricting credit to discourage speculation, is no guarantee of political popularity.

15. Jerry L. Mashaw, "Administration and 'The Democracy': Administrative Law from Jackson to Lincoln, 1829–1861," *Yale Law Journal* 117 (2008): 1568, 1587–98.

16. John Wood, *A History of Central Banking in Great Britain and the United States* (Cambridge: Cambridge University Press, 2005), 133 (quoting both Biddle and Benton); Robert A. Remini, *Andrew Jackson and the Bank War: A Study in the Growth of Presidential Power* (New York: Norton, 1967).

17. Veto Message of President Andrew Jackson of "A Bill to Modify and Continue the Act entitled 'An Act to Incorporate the Subscribers to the Bank of the United States'" (July 10, 1832), reprinted in James D. Richardson, editor, *A Compilation of the Messages and Papers of the Presidents, 1789–1897* (Washington, DC, 1900), 2:1139 (quotation in text). On the constitutional theory of the veto message, see Mashaw, "Administration and 'The Democracy,'" 1591–98.

18. The conventional account in the text, drawn from Hammond, *Banks and Politics in America*, is recognized and disputed in Peter Temin, *The Jacksonian Economy* (New York: Norton, 1969), whose account is disputed in Peter L. Rousseau, "Jacksonian Monetary Policy, Specie Flows, and the Panic of 1837," *Journal of Economic History* 62 (2002): 457ff.

19. Act of July 4, 1840, 5 Stat. 385 (1840) (creating the subtreasury system); Act of August 13, 1841, 5 Stat. 439 (1841) (repealing the 1840 act).

20. House Document No. 20, Twenty-seventh Congress, Second Session (December 21, 1841) (President Tyler's Exchequer bill); see generally Norma Lois Peterson, *The Presidencies of William Henry Harrison and John Tyler* (Lawrence: University Press of Kansas, 1989), 89–90; Leonard White, *The Jacksonians: A Study in Administrative History, 1829–1861* (New York: Macmillan, 1967) (1954), 43–44.

21. The creation of a private central bank had already been anticipated in Boston, where Suffolk Bank performed as an agent for the Boston banks in handling the notes of the many country banks. Effectively it created a uniform regional currency, imposed "reserve" requirements on country banks, and redeemed country notes when necessary. This system was soon copied by New York banks. After a few years the country banks themselves banded together to form an association that ended

the domination of the Suffolk Bank. Wood, *History of Central Banking*, 120–22. On the Polk presidency in general, see Paul H. Bergeron, *The Presidency of James K. Polk* (Lawrence: University Press of Kansas, 1987).

22. Bray Hammond, *Sovereignty and an Empty Purse: Banks and Politics in the Civil War* (Princeton: Princeton University Press, 1970), 22–23 (quotation in text).

23. National Banking Act of February 25, 1863, 12 Stat. 665 (1863), superseded by Act of June 3, 1864, 13 Stat. 99 (1864); Act of March 3, 1865, § 6, 13 Stat. 484 (tax on state notes); *Veazie Bank v. Fenno*, 75 U.S. (7 Wall.) 533, 548–49 (U.S. Supreme Court, 1869) (upholding these statutes based upon Congress's broad authority to create and regulate currency).

24. Act of February 25, 1862, § 1, 12 Stat. 345 (1862) (quotation in text); see Kenneth Dam, "The Legal Tender Cases," *Supreme Court Review* 1981: 367, 370–74 (excellent account of Civil War financing, from which our summary draws).

25. *Hepburn v. Griswold* (The First Legal Tender Case), 75 U.S. (6 Wall.) 603 (U.S. Supreme Court, 1870) (Chase, C.J., for a plurality of Justices); ibid., 626 (announcing Justice Grier's agreement with the plurality on the Constitutional issue). On the original meaning of the Coinage Clauses, the best source, and a very illuminating treatment of Reconstruction finance, is Dam, "Legal Tender Cases," 367–412. See also James Bradley Thayer, "Legal Tender," *Harvard Law Review* 1 (1887–88): 73–88.

26. First Legal Tender Case, 75 U.S., 626 (announcing that Justice Grier would have interpreted the statute narrowly but, upon reading the chief justice's opinion, agreed with the plurality on the Constitutional issue). On Chase's motivations for invalidating the legal tender law that he had lobbied for, and the public uproar after the decision was issued, see John Niven, *Salmon P. Chase: A Biography* (New York: Oxford University Press, 1995).

27. *Knox v. Lee* (The Second Legal Tender Case), 79 U.S. 457 (U.S. Supreme Court, 1871); see ibid., 529–44 (Justice Strong's repeated invocation of *McCulloch* and other Marshall opinions, for the propositions listed and quoted in text); ibid., 544–47 (rejecting original meaning arguments); ibid., 555–70 (Bradley, J., concurring) (even broader reading of the U.S. Bank case and the Necessary and Proper Clause).

28. Gretchen Ritter, *Goldbugs and Greenbacks: The Antimonopoly Tradition and the Politics of Finance in America, 1865–1896* (Cambridge: Cambridge University Press, 1997), 95 (quotation in text); ibid., 96–104 (detailed explanation of greenbackers' theory of public finance and currency).

29. On the vacillating GOP policies of the 1870s, see Ritter, *Goldbugs and Greenbacks*, 34–45.

30. *Juilliard v. Greenman* (The Third Legal Tender Case), 110 U.S. 421 (U.S. Supreme Court, 1884); ibid., 450 (quotation in text); Dam, "Legal Tender Cases," 390–408 (excellent legal and political analysis of the Third Legal Tender Case).

31. See Roger T. Johnson, *Historical Beginnings . . . The Federal Reserve* (Boston: Federal Reserve Bank of Boston, revised edition, 1999), 13–15. See also Gary Gorton and Donald J. Mullineaux, "The Joint Production of Confidence: Endogenous Regulation and Nineteenth-Century Commercial Bank Clearinghouses," *Journal of Money, Credit, and Banking* 19 (1987): 457–68.

32. James Livingston, *Origins of the Federal Reserve System: Money, Class, and Corporate Capitalism, 1890–1913* (Ithaca, NY: Cornell University Press, 1986). On the financial system and crises between 1873 and 1893, see generally John A. James, *Money and Capital Markets in Postbellum America* (Princeton: Princeton University Press, 1978); Richard E. Sylla, *The American Capital Market, 1846–1914: A Study of the Effects of Public Policy on Economic Development* (New York: Arno Press, 1975).

33. See generally Livingston, *Origins of the Federal Reserve System*, 159–71; Robert Craig West, *Banking Reform and the Federal Reserve, 1863–1923* (Ithaca, NY: Cornell University Press, 1974); Michael A. Whitehouse, "Paul Warburg's Crusade to Establish a Central Bank in the United States" (May 1989), available at www.minneapolisfed.org/pubs/region/89–05/reg895d.cfm (visited March 2008).

34. Livingston, *Origins of the Federal Reserve System*, 172–74. For a contemporary collection of assessments, see E. R. A. Seligman, editor, *The Currency Problem* (New York: Columbia University Press, 1908).

35. For an argument that the supporters of a European-style central bank had a limited view of public finance that hampered the design contained in the various reform proposals, see Allan H. Meltzer, *A History of the Federal Reserve: 1913–1951* (Chicago: University of Chicago Press, 2003), 52–64. Specifically, Meltzer argues that the reformers concentrated on the problems noted in our text but did not understand how a central-bank-run monetary policy affects production, inflation, and the entire economy. For a strong statement of the notion that Congress cannot limit the president's authority to discharge purely "executive" officials, see *Myers v. United States*, 272 U.S. 52 (U.S. Supreme Court, 1926) (Taft, C.J.).

36. See Livingston, *Origins of the Federal Reserve System*, 174–87, for the educational and political campaign of the new corporate capitalists and the headway they made in Congress; ibid., 188–212, for Senator Aldrich's 1911 central bank bill, patterned on Paul Warburg's 1906 proposal for a United Reserve Bank.

37. Ibid., 215–34.

38. Federal Reserve Act of 1913, Public Law No. 63-43, codified at 12 U.S.C. § 221 et al.; Johnson, *Historical Beginnings*, 16–34 (dramatic legislative history of Federal Reserve Act, which was enacted notwithstanding opposition from virtually all Republicans in Congress and many rural Democrats).

39. Meltzer, *History of the Federal Reserve*, 65–135 (detailed account of the Federal Reserve System's confused and blundering start).

40. See ibid., 67–82 (Federal Reserve Act's structure created a weak and confused agency; detailed account of Governor Benjamin Strong); ibid., 103–09 (arguing that the Fed's rate increase in 1920 drove the country into recession).

41. See ibid., 139–270 (detailed account of the tug of war between Strong and the board during the 1920s and, more important, the development of open market operations).

42. Irving Fisher, *The Stock Market Crash and After* (New York: Macmillan, 1930); Milton Friedman and Anna Schwartz, *A Monetary History of the United States, 1867–1960* (Princeton: Princeton University Press, 1963); Ben S. Bernanke, "The Macroeconomics of the Great Depression: A Comparative Approach," *Journal of Money, Credit, and Borrowing* 27 (1995): 1–28; James D. Hamilton, "Monetary

Factors in the Great Depression," *Journal of Monetary Economics 34* (1987): 145–69. For a useful account of subsequent scholarship and the current status of the Friedman and Schwartz thesis, see Remarks of Governor Ben S. Bernanke, at the Conference to Honor Milton Friedman, November 8, 2002, available at www.federalreserve. gov/BOARDDOCS/SPEECHES/2002/20021108/default.htm (visited March 2008).

43. Emergency Banking Relief Act of 1933, 48 Stat. 1 (1933); Joint Resolution of June 5, 1933, 48 Stat. 112 (1933). See also Gold Reserve Act of 1934, 48 Stat. 337 (1934), confirming Roosevelt administration financial initiatives after the Joint Resolution. See generally Barry Eichengreen, *Golden Fetters: The Gold Standard and the Great Depression, 1919–1939* (New York: Oxford University Press, 1992).

44. *United States v. Bankers Trust Co.*, 294 U.S. 240, 322 (U.S. Supreme Court, 1935) (McReynolds, J., dissenting) (first quotation in text); ibid., 326 (second quotation); ibid., 329 (third quotation).

45. Ibid., 307–08 (Hughes, C.J., delivering the opinion of the Court) (contracts are subject to the public interest); ibid., 311–16 (Congress was acting appropriately under its Coinage Clause power to regulate monetary policy).

46. Banking Act of 1935, Public Law No. 74-305, title I, 49 Stat. 684 (1935) (making the FDIC a permanent institution of government); ibid., title II (reaffirming and improving the Federal Reserve System). See generally Frederick A. Bradford, "The Banking Act of 1935," *American Economic Review* 25 (1935): 661–72.

47. See Sidney Hyman, *Marriner S. Eccles: Private Entrepreneur and Public Servant* (Stanford, CA: Stanford Business School, 1976); Meltzer, *History of the Federal Reserve*, 490–534 (Fed's contribution to the recession of 1937–38); ibid., 579–724 (dominance of Treasury over the Fed, 1941–51).

48. For blow-by-blow details leading up to the accord of March 4, 1951, see Meltzer, *History of the Federal Reserve*, 699–713.

49. See ibid., 737–45 (summing up the lessons for the Federal Reserve System from its history, 1914–51).

50. On the members and staff of the Federal Reserve Board, see John Turner Woolley, *Monetary Politics: The Federal Reserve and the Politics of Monetary Policy* (Cambridge: Cambridge University Press, 1984), 48–68, 88–107.

51. Act of February 20, 1946, chap. 33, 60 Stat. 23, codified at 15 U.S.C. § 1021 (Employment Act of 1946); Stephen Kemp Bailey, *Congress Makes a Law: The Story Behind the Employment Act of 1946* (New York: Columbia University Press, 1950); G. J. Santoni, "The Employment Act of 1946: Some History Notes" (Federal Reserve Bank of St. Louis, November 1986).

52. See Woolley, *Monetary Politics*, 154–80 (detailed account of the Fed's policy in the first term of the Nixon administration and its contribution to Nixon's reelection). Nixon administration scandals may have dominated monetary mismanagement in explaining the 1974 and 1976 elections.

53. Full Employment and Balanced Growth Act of 1978, Public Law No. 95-523, 92 Stat. 1887 (1978), codified at 15 U.S.C. §§ 3101–3152 (Humphrey-Hawkins Full Employment Act of 1978). On the effect of Humphrey-Hawkins and related legislation on the Federal Reserve's mandate, see John P. Judd and Glenn D. Rudebusch, "The Goals of U.S. Monetary Policy" (Federal Reserve Board of San Francisco, January 29, 1999).

54. Joseph B. Treaster, *Paul Volcker: The Making of a Financial Legend* (New York: Wiley, 2004); Alan Greenspan, *The Age of Turbulence: Adventures in a New World* (New York: Penguin, 2007), critically reviewed by Benjamin M. Friedman, "Chairman Greenspan's Legacy," *New York Review of Books*, March 20, 2008, 25–28.

55. See Neil Irwin, "Bernanke Urges Broader Powers For Central Bank; Critics Worry About Fed Losing Focus," *Washington Post*, August 23, 2008, D1, D3.

56. For many examples of the executive department's domination of the Fed between 1914 and 1951, see Meltzer, *History of the Federal Reserve*. For examples of post-1951 presidential influence and theoretical explanation for it, see Woolley, *Monetary Politics*, 108–30, 154–80. For an example of a much more spectacular regulatory failure, see Kevin McCoy, "He Blew a Whistle for Nine Years," *USA Today*, February 13, 2009, 1B–2B (the Securities and Exchange Commission ignored nine years of detailed warnings that the Bernie Madoff investment fund was a Ponzi scheme).

CHAPTER 8. THE ANTIHOMOSEXUAL CONSTITUTION AND ITS DIS-ENTRENCHMENT

1. The best biographical sources for José Sarria are Nan Alamilla Boyd, *Wide-Open Town: A History of Queer San Francisco to 1965* (Berkeley: University of California Press, 2003), 20–24, 56–62, 144–46; Vern L. Bullough, *Before Stonewall: Activists for Gay and Lesbian Rights in Historical Context* (New York: Haworth Press, 2002), 376–79; Michael R. Gorman, *The Empress Is a Man: Stories from the Life of José Sarria* (New York: Haworth Press, 1998).

2. On the striking parallels between America's antihomosexual constitution and Nazi Germany's, see William N. Eskridge Jr., *Gaylaw: Challenging the Apartheid of the Closet* (Cambridge, MA: Harvard University Press, 1999), 80–82.

3. 1850 California Statutes, chap. 99 (California's crime against nature law); *People v. Boyle*, 116 Cal. 658 (California Supreme Court, 1897) (crime against nature does not include oral sex). On the narrow application and interpretation of sodomy laws in the nineteenth century, see Jonathan Ned Katz, *Love Stories: Sex Between Men Before Homosexuality* (Chicago: University of Chicago Press, 2002); William N. Eskridge Jr., "*Hardwick* and Historiography," *University of Illinois Law Review* 1999: 643–49, 666–71.

4. On the collective panic of middle-class society confronted with visible communities of sexual and gender "variants," see Lisa Duggan, *Sapphic Slashers: Sex, Violence, and American Modernity* (Durham, NC: Duke University Press, 2002); Siobhan B. Somerville, *Queering the Color Line: Race and the Invention of Homosexuality in American Culture* (Durham, NC: Duke University Press, 2000); Jennifer Terry, *American Obsession: Science, Medicine, and Homosexuality in Modern Society* (Chicago: University of Chicago Press, 1999).

5. Eskridge, *Gaylaw*, 27–29, 338–41 (municipal cross-dressing laws in California and other states); Lillian Faderman and Stuart Timmons, *Gay L.A.: A History of Sexual Outlaws, Power Politics, and Lipstick Lesbians* (New York: Basic Books, 2006), 30–37 (Long Beach raid and legislative response to acquittals); Louis Sullivan, *From Female to Male: The Life of Jack B. Garland* (Boston: Alyson Publications, 1990) (evolving

enforcement of cross-dressing ordinances). The statutes mentioned in the text are 1915 California Statutes, chap. 586; 1921 California Statutes, chap. 848; 1903 California Statutes, chap. 87; 1923 California Statutes, chap. 69.

6. On sodomy law enforcement against consensual activities, see Eskridge, *Gaylaw*, 374 (app. C1) and 375 (app. C2); Faderman and Timmons, *Gay L.A.*, 71–104 (pervasive police harassment after World War II). On the sterilization law, see 1909 California Statutes, chap. 720, expanded by 1937 California Statutes, chap. 369, § 6624; California State Department of Mental Hygiene, *Sterilization Operations in California State Hospitals for the Mentally Ill, 1909–1960* (1962).

7. For antihomosexual regimes at the federal level before and right after World War II, see Eskridge, *Gaylaw*, 34–37. For antihomosexual regimes at the state level, see generally George Painter, *The Sensibilities of Our Fathers: The History of Sodomy Laws in the United States*, available at www.sodomylaws.org/sensibilities (state-by-state survey). Municipal-level surveys can be found in *Report of the Vice Commission of Maryland* (1915); The History Project, *Improper Bostonians: Lesbian and Gay History from the Puritans to Playland* (Boston: Beacon Press, 1998); The Vice Commission of Chicago, *The Social Evil in Chicago: A Study of Existing Conditions* (Chicago: Gunthorp-Warren Printing, 1911); George Chauncey Jr., *Gay New York: Gender, Urban Culture, and the Making of the Gay Male World, 1890–1940* (New York: Basic Books, 1994); Vice Commission of Philadelphia, *A Report of Existing Conditions, with Recommendations* (1913); Gary L. Atkins, *Gay Seattle: Stories of Exile and Belonging* (Seattle: University of Washington Press, 2003).

8. Bullough, *Before Stonewall*, 376 (Sarria's military career). On the cultural origins of the antihomosexual terror, see Robert Corber, *Homosexuality in Cold War America: Resistance and the Crisis of Masculinity* (Durham, NC: Duke University Press, 1997); George Chauncey Jr., "The Postwar Sex Crime Panic," in William Graebner, editor, *True Stories from the American Past* (New York: HarperCollins, 1993), 160–78.

9. 1939 California Statutes, chap. 447, § 5500 (original sexual psychopath law), expanded in 1945 California Statutes, chap. 138; 1951 California Statutes, chap. 1759; and 1955 California Statutes, chap. 757; John LaStala, "Atascadero: Dachau for Queers?" *Advocate*, April 26, 1972, 11, 13.

10. 1947 California Statutes, chap. 1124 (sex registration); 1949 California Statutes, First Extra Session, chap. 15 (Jan. 1950) (new penalties for sodomy); ibid., chap. 14 (new crime for loitering around a public toilet); ibid., chap. 34 (requiring registration of toilet loiterers and "lewd vagrants"); 1952 California Statutes, First Extra Session, chap. 23 (April 1952) (eliminating maximum sentence for sodomy). On Sarria's own account of his arrest, see Boyd, *Wide-Open Town*, 21–23. On the high level of police activity, see Project, "The Consenting Adult Homosexual and the Law: An Empirical Study of Enforcement and Administration in Los Angeles County," *UCLA Law Review* 13 (1966): 799 (arrest statistics); see ibid., 673–85 (excellent summary of California's antihomosexual criminal laws, 1966).

11. 1952 California Statutes, chaps. 389–90 (revocation of teaching certificates for homosexual crimes); E. Carrington Boggan et al., *The Rights of Gay People: The Basic*

ACLU *Guide to a Gay Person's Rights* (New York: Discus Books, 1975), 211–35 (various professional license disqualifications for homosexual crimes).

12. 1935 California Statutes, p. 1135 (no liquor licenses for "disorderly" establishments); 1955 California Statutes, chap. 1217 ("resort for perverts" law), invalidated in *Vallerga v. Department of ABC*, 53 Cal.2d 313 (California Supreme Court, 1959); Boyd, *Wide-Open Town*, 121–47 (draconian enforcement of licensing laws against gay bars, with the Black Cat as regulators' special target).

13. For detailed accounts of antihomosexual campaigns, see Allan Bérubé, *Coming Out Under Fire: The History of Gay Men and Women in World War II* (New York: Free Press, 1990); David K. Johnson, *The Lavender Scare: The Cold War Persecution of Gays and Lesbians in the Federal Government* (Chicago: University of Chicago Press, 2004) (federal civil service witch hunts); James T. Sears, *The Lonely Hunters: An Oral History of Lesbian and Gay Southern Life, 1948–1968* (Boulder, CO: Westview Press, 1997), 48–108 (Florida's Johns Committee).

14. For more details about the antihomosexual *Kulturkampf*, see Eskridge, *Gaylaw*, 17–97, as well as a state-by-state survey, ibid., apps. A1—A3 (state-by-state array of antihomosexual laws and ordinances).

15. Alfred C. Kinsey, Wardell B. Pomeroy, and Clyde E. Martin, *Sexual Behavior in the Human Male* (Philadelphia: W. B. Saunders, 1948); Alfred C. Kinsey, Wardell B. Pomeroy, Clyde E. Martin, and Paul Gebhard, *Sexual Behavior in the Human Female* (Philadelphia: W. B. Saunders, 1953), 8–21. On Kinsey as a moral crusader deploying science to assault traditional morality, see Paul Robinson, *The Modernization of Sex: Havelock Ellis, Alfred Kinsey, and William Masters and Virginia Johnson* (Ithaca, NY: Cornell University Press, 1989), as well as James H. Jones, *Alfred C. Kinsey: A Public/Private Life* (New York: W. W. Norton, 1997), 465–66, 518–33.

16. On the early homophile groups, see John D'Emilio, *Sexual Politics, Sexual Communities: The Making of a Homosexual Minority in the United States, 1940–1970* (Chicago: University of Chicago Press, 1983); Boyd, *Wide-Open Town*, 200–236 (San Francisco); Faderman and Timmons, *Gay L.A.*, 141–58 (Los Angeles). For their specific advocacy of sodomy repeal, see, e.g., "Daughters of Bilitis—Purpose," *Ladder*, October 1956, 1, 4; "A Report from the Legal Director, Mattachine Society," *San Francisco Mattachine Newsletter*, December 1955.

17. Gorman, *Empress Is a Man*, 162 (quoting Sarria).

18. Eric Marcus, *Making History: The Struggle for Gay and Lesbian Equal Rights, 1945–1990, An Oral History* (New York: HarperCollins, 1992), 135–36; Dudley Clendinen and Adam Nagourney, *Out for Good: The Struggle to Build a Gay Rights Movement in America* (New York: Simon & Schuster, 1999), 148–63; William N. Eskridge Jr., "Challenging the Apartheid of the Closet: Establishing Conditions for Lesbian and Gay Intimacy, Nomos, and Citizenship, 1961–1981," *Hofstra Law Review* 25 (1997): 840–42.

19. William N. Eskridge Jr., *Dishonorable Passions: Sodomy Law in America, 1861–2003* (New York: Viking, 2008), chap. 5; Joint Legislative Committee for Revision of the Penal Code, Penal Code Revision Project, Tentative Draft No. 1—Division 11: Crimes against Sexual Morality, Public Decency, and the Family (1967).

20. *Boutilier v. Immigration & Nationalization Service*, 387 U.S. 118 (U.S. Supreme Court, 1967). Chief Justice Warren's comment is taken from Conference Notes for *Boutilier* (1966 Term, Docket No. 440), in Douglas Papers, Library of Congress (Madison), Container 1391.

21. On the ability of gay rights groups to bring pressure against abusive police practices at the local level, see Boyd, *Wide-Open Town*, 209–12 (San Francisco); Faderman and Timmons, *Gay L.A.*; Johnson, *The Lavender Scare* (Washington, DC); Marc Stein, *City of Sisterly and Brotherly Loves: Lesbian and Gay Philadelphia, 1945–1972* (Chicago: University of Chicago Press, 2000); John D'Emilio, "Gay Politics, Gay Community: San Francisco's Experience," *Socialist Review* 55 (January/February 1981): 77–104; Steven A. Rosen, "Police Harassment of Homosexual Women and Men in New York City 1960–1980," *Columbia Human Rights Law Review* 12 (1980–81): 188ff.

22. Illinois decriminalized consensual sodomy when it adopted the MPC in 1961, but with virtually no public debate. Eskridge, *Dishonorable Passions*, chap. 4. New York adopted the MPC in 1965, but the legislature recriminalized consensual sodomy the same day. Ibid., chap. 5. Connecticut (1969), Colorado (1971), Oregon (1971), Hawaii (1972), Delaware (1972), Ohio (1972), North Dakota (1973), New Mexico (1975), Maine (1975), New Hampshire (1975), and Washington (1975) decriminalized consensual sodomy, with focused debate within their legislatures but little input from the general public. Ibid., chap. 6. Only California's sodomy reform in 1975 occurred after both a focused legislative debate and popular feedback.

23. Eskridge, *Dishonorable Passions*, chaps. 6–7 (detailed account of the sodomy reform efforts in New York, Texas, Idaho, Pennsylvania, and Michigan).

24. 1975 California Statutes, chap. 71, § 7; Interview by William N. Eskridge Jr. with former assemblyman Willie Brown, San Francisco (Embarcadero), January 10, 2005. See generally Eskridge, *Dishonorable Passions*, chap. 7, for a complete account of the Brown-Moscone Act.

25. California Proposition 6, § 3(b)(2) (1978) (Briggs Initiative), analyzed in Nan D. Hunter, "Identity, Speech, and Equality," *Virginia Law Review* 79 (1993): 1702–06; Executive Order No. B-54-79, April 4, 1979; 1977 California Statutes, chap. 339, §§ 1–2 (reaffirmation of different-sex marriage).

26. *Bowers v. Hardwick*, 478 U.S. 186, 194 (U.S. Supreme Court, 1986) (first quotation in text); ibid., 196–97 (Burger, C.J., concurring) (second quotation in text).

27. Eskridge, *Dishonorable Passions*, 256–62, arguing that the Georgia consensual sodomy law could have been invalidated under *Papachristou v. City of Jacksonville*, 405 U.S. 156 (U.S. Supreme Court, 1972).

28. Patrick Egan, Nathaniel Persily, and Kevin Wallsten, "Gay Rights," in Persily et al., editors, *Public Opinion and Constitutional Controversy* (New York: Oxford University Press, 2008), figure 5 (media coverage of AIDS and homosexual conduct runs parallel to public opinion favoring criminalization of such conduct).

29. Professor Robert Bork was an adamant opponent of the faculty's decision to add sexual orientation to its list of discriminations the Yale Law School required employers to disavow in order to take advantage of the law school's placement services. See Derek B. Dorn, "Sexual Orientation and the Legal Academy: The Experience at

Yale" (Yale Law School Supervised Analytic Writing, June 2002), 142–77. Judge Bork's opinion in *Dronenberg v. Zech*, 731 F.2d 1388 (U.S. Court of Appeals for the District of Columbia Circuit, 1984), anticipated the analytical structure and some of the rhetoric of the Supreme Court's majority opinion in *Bowers.*

30. E.g., Gina Kolata, "Lesbian Partners Find the Means to Be Parents," *New York Times,* January 30, 1989, A13, as corrected by Nan D. Hunter, "Lesbian Parents Prove to Be in No Way Inferior," *New York Times,* February 13, 1989, A20.

31. An excellent collection of public opinion polls regarding homosexuality and state policy is AEI Studies in Public Opinion, "Attitudes about Homosexuality and Gay Marriage" (compiled by Karlyn Bowman and updated as of October 27, 2006), available at www.aei.org/publications/pubID.14882,filter.all/pub_detail.asp (viewed January 2008).

32. *Commonwealth v. Wasson,* 842 S.W.2d 487, 494–96 (Kentucky Supreme Court, 1992); ibid., 497 (criticizing *Bowers* and refusing to follow its lead); Interview by William N. Eskridge Jr. with Ernesto Scorsone, Lexington, Kentucky, December 8, 2006.

33. Eskridge, *Dishonorable Passions,* chap. 9 (sodomy reform in Kentucky, Tennessee, Georgia, Montana, Rhode Island, and Arkansas).

34. The states with enforceable sodomy laws in 2003 were Alabama, Florida, Idaho, Kansas, Louisiana, Michigan, Mississippi, North Carolina, Oklahoma, South Carolina, Texas, Utah, and Virginia. See Eskridge, *Dishonorable Passions,* chap. 9. Employment discrimination bars are listed and discussed in Human Rights Campaign Foundation, *The State of the Workplace for Lesbian, Gay, Bisexual and Transgender Americans 2002* (2003); Nan D. Hunter, "Sexuality and Civil Rights: Re-Imagining Anti-Discrimination Laws," *New York Law School Journal of Human Rights* 17 (2000): 565–87.

35. The *amicus* briefs can be found and accessed at the end of the Westlaw display of the Court's opinions in *Lawrence v. Texas,* 539 U.S. 558 (U.S. Supreme Court, 2003) (Docket No. 02-102).

36. On the Danish law and its ripple effects in the United States, see William N. Eskridge Jr. and Darren Spedale, *Gay Marriage: For Better or For Worse? What We've Learned from the Evidence* (New York: Oxford University Press, 2006).

37. *Dean v. District of Columbia,* 653 A.2d 307 (District of Columbia Court of Appeals, 1995); *Baehr v. Lewin,* 852 P.2d 44 (Hawaii Supreme Court, 1993), both discussed in William N. Eskridge Jr., *The Case for Same-Sex Marriage* (New York: Free Press, 1996), 1–6, 100–104, 153–72. One of us (Eskridge) was counsel for the gay plaintiffs in *Dean.*

38. For the public reaction in Hawaii and the rest of the country, see David Orgon Coolidge, "The Hawaii Marriage Amendment: Its Origins, Meaning and Fate," *Hawaii Law Review* 22 (2000): 19–118; Andrew Koppelman, "Interstate Recognition of Same-Sex Marriages and Civil Unions: A Handbook for Judges," *University of Pennsylvania Law Review* 153 (2005): 2143–94 (state statutes and constitutional amendments barring same-sex marriage recognition). On the Defense of Marriage Act, Public Law No. 104-199, 110 Stat. 2419 (1996), see Andrew Koppelman, *The Gay Rights Question in Contemporary American Law* (Chicago: University of Chicago Press, 2002).

39. *Lawrence*, 539 U.S., 590, 599 (Scalia, J., dissenting) (end of morals legislation); ibid., 602–04 (adoption of "homosexual agenda," especially gay marriage).

40. For decisions rejecting state constitutional arguments for same-sex marriage, see *Hernandez v. Robles*, 855 N.E.2d 1 (New York Court of Appeals, 2006); *Lewis v. Harris*, 188 N.J. 415 (New Jersey Supreme Court, 2006); *Andersen v. King County*, 138 P.3d 963 (Washington Supreme Court, 2006); *Conaway v. Deane*, 932 A.2d 571 (Maryland Court of Appeals, 2007).

41. See William N. Eskridge Jr., *Equality Practice: Civil Unions and the Future of Gay Rights* (New York: Routledge, 2002).

42. Kees Waadijk, "Small Change: How the Road to Same-Sex Marriage Got Paved in The Netherlands," in Robert Wintemute and Maes Andenaes, editors, *Legal Recognition of Same-Sex Partnerships* (London: Hart, 2001), 437–64; William N. Eskridge Jr., "Comparative Law and the Same-Sex Marriage Debate: A Step-by-Step Approach to State Recognition," *McGeorge Law Review* 31 (2000): 641–72.

43. Eskridge, *Gaylaw*, 356 (App. B2), listing antidiscrimination ordinances; Governor Jerry Brown (California), Executive Order No. B-54-79 (April 4, 1979), prohibiting sexual orientation discrimination in state employment; *Gay Law Students Association v. Pacific Telephone & Telegraph Co.*, 24 Cal.3d 458 (California Supreme Court, 1979), interpreting the California Labor Code to bar job discrimination on the basis of sexual orientation, reaffirmed and elaborated in 1992 California Statutes, chap. 915, § 2.

44. E.g., *Rolon v. Kulwitzky*, 153 Cal. App. 3d 289 (California Court of Appeal, 1984), applying California Civil Code § 51 to bar antigay discrimination by public accommodations, explicitly codified in 2005 California Statutes, chap. 420, § 3. For another pro-gay statutory interpretation, see *Pryor v. Municipal Court*, 25 Cal.3d 238 (California Supreme Court, 1979), interpreting the California lewd vagrancy law to apply only to solicitation to engage in public sexual activities.

45. On the spread of the domestic partnership idea, see Raymond O'Brien, "Domestic Partnership: Recognition and Responsibility," *San Diego Law Review* 32 (1995): 163–220. On the proliferation of judge-approved second-parent adoptions in California from the early 1980s onward, see Jennifer Pizer, "What about the Children?" *Advocate*, November 9, 2001, 1; this practice was ratified in *Sharon S. v. Superior Court*, 31 Cal.4th 417, 438–40 (California Supreme Court, 2003), over objections that state recognition of lesbian and gay families was inconsistent with marriage and traditional family values. Ibid., 463–65 (Brown, J., concurring and dissenting).

46. 1999 California Statutes, chap. 588 (California Domestic Partnership Law), expanded to include almost all the legal rights and duties of marriage in 2003 California Statutes, chap. 421; proposed California Marriage License Nondiscrimination Act of 2005, Assembly Bill No. 849, 2005–06 Regular Session of the California Legislature, vetoed by Governor Arnold Schwarzenegger (as was a similar bill in 2007). See also California Family Code § 9000(b), (g), recognizing joint parental rights for registered domestic partners.

47. *In re Marriage Cases*, 183 P.3d 384 (California Supreme Court, 2008) (George, C.J.); ibid., 450–54 (sexual orientation is a "suspect" classification triggering strict scrutiny); ibid., 419–34 (lesbian and gay couples were denied a "fundamental" right to marry,

also triggering strict scrutiny). On the California Marriage Cases and their sequelae, see William N. Eskridge, "The California Supreme Court, 2007 Term—Foreword: The Marriage Cases, Reversing the Burden of Inertia in a Pluralist Constitutional Democracy," *California Law Review* 97 (2009).

48. *Goodridge v. Department of Public Health*, 798 N.E.2d 941 (Massachusetts Supreme Judicial Court, 2003); *Kerrigan v. Commissioner of Public Health*, 957 A.2d 407 (Connecticut Supreme Court, 2008); *Varnum v. Brien*, 763 N.W.2d 862 (Iowa Supreme Court, 2009). A News Release by the majority leader of the Iowa Senate and the speaker of the Iowa House of Representatives, April 3, 2009, praised the *Varnum* decision. Because amendment of the Iowa Constitution requires majority votes in two successive sessions of the legislature and then from the voters, it does *not* appear likely that its Constitution will be soon amended to override the *Varnum* opinion.

49. For legal scholars arguing for same-sex marriage from Constitutional precedent and principle, see, e.g., Eskridge, *The Case for Same-Sex Marriage*; Koppelman, *The Gay Rights Question in Contemporary American Law*; David A. J. Richards, *The Case for Gay Rights: From* Bowers *to* Lawrence *and Beyond* (Lawrence: University Press of Kansas, 2005), as well as the more philosophical treatment in Carlos Ball, *The Morality of Gay Rights: An Exploration in Political Philosophy* (New York: Routledge, 2003). Brigham Young University professor Lynn Wardle is the leading analyst rejecting these arguments. E.g., Lynn Wardle, "A Critical Analysis of Constitutional Claims for Same-Sex Marriage," *Brigham Young L. Rev.* 1996: 1–96.

50. For the small "c" constitutional erosion of support for different-race marriage bans between *Brown* (1954) and *Loving* (1967), see Randall Kennedy, *Interracial Intimacies: Sex, Marriage, Identity, and Adoption* (New York: Pantheon, 2003), 244–80.

51. The challenge to the validity of Proposition 8 was rejected in *Strauss v. Horton*, 207 P.3d 48 (California Supreme Court, 2009), discussed in Eskridge, "Marriage Cases."

52. Alexander M. Bickel, *The Least Dangerous Branch: The Supreme Court at the Bar of Politics* (New Haven: Yale University Press, 1962).

53. Compare *Hague v. Allstate Insurance Co.*, 486 U.S. 717 (U.S. Supreme Court, 1988) (permissive full faith and credit review of home state preferring its statutory policies to those of sibling state), with *Baker v. General Motors*, 522 U.S. 222 (U.S. Supreme Court, 1998); *Fauntleroy v. Lum*, 210 U.S. 230 (U.S. Supreme Court, 1908) (strict enforcement of full faith and credit for state court judgments rendered in an adversarial proceeding).

54. Parental Kidnapping Prevention Act of 1980 (PKPA), codified at 28 U.S.C. § 1738A; Defense of Marriage Act of 1996 (DOMA), codified at 28 U.S.C. § 1738C.

55. For recent lesbian custody cases where courts declined to read DOMA as overriding the PKPA, see *Miller-Jenkins v. Miller-Jenkins*, 912 A.2d 951 (Vermont Supreme Court, 2006); *Miller-Jenkins v. Miller-Jenkins*, 637 S.E.2d 330 (Virginia Court of Appeals, 2006) (review denied by Virginia Supreme Court).

56. On process rights that an accused sodomy or oral copulation felon would have enjoyed in California in 1965, see Eskridge, *Gaylaw*, 101–04; *Bielicki v. Superior Court*, 57 Cal.2d 602 (California Supreme Court, 1962) (recognizing a privacy right against police spying while one was occupying an enclosed toilet stall).

57. For details of the First Amendment payoff for LGBT minorities and their associations, see Eskridge, *Gaylaw*, 92–96 (1950s), 111–25 (1960s–70s); Richard A. Posner, "Ask, Tell," *New Republic*, October 11, 1999, 52–58 (reviewing *Gaylaw* and emphasizing this theme as the most promising example of judicial review from a general straight audience as well as a gay rights perspective).

58. *Stoumen v. Reilly*, 37 Cal.2d 713 (California Supreme Court, 1951), expanded in *Vallerga v. Department of ABC*, 53 Cal.2d 313 (California Supreme Court, 1959) (striking down the legislature's statutory response to *Stoumen*); *Pryor v. Municipal Court*, 25 Cal.3d 238 (California Supreme Court, 1979).

59. *Sharon S. v. Superior Court*, 31 Cal.4th 417 (California Supreme Court, 2003); *Elisa B. v. Superior Court*, 37 Cal.4th 108 (California Supreme Court, 2005); *Gay Law Students Association v. Pacific Telephone & Telegraph Co.*, 24 Cal.3d 458 (California Supreme Court, 1979).

60. California Constitution, article XVIII, § 3 (Constitutional amendments can be added by majority vote supporting an initiative submitted by a citizen petition); Eskridge, "The Marriage Cases," discussing the campaign to override the California Supreme Court's gay marriage decision, with particular reference to the materials on the Web site created by the supporters of Proposition 8, www.ProtectMarriage.org (last viewed March 15, 2009).

61. See Eskridge, "The Marriage Cases," for a legal analysis of the Yes-on-Eight argument that the *Marriage Cases* would have required public schools to teach children (without parental consent) that gay marriage is the same as straight marriage.

CHAPTER 9. THE NATIONAL SECURITY CONSTITUTION

1. The account of Abdul Razzaq Hekmati's life and the dueling accounts of his political activities are taken from press reports based on recently released Pentagon transcripts and interviews with sources in Afghanistan. See Carlotta Gall and Andy Worthington, "Time Runs Out for an Afghan Held by the United States," *New York Times*, February 5, 2008, A1, A10.

2. *Hamdi v. Rumsfeld*, 542 U.S. 507 (U.S. Supreme Court, 2004) (requiring some kind of due process for prisoners detained by the government in the war on terror); *Rasul v. Bush*, 542 U.S. 466 (U.S. Supreme Court, 2004) (Guantánamo prisoners such as Hekmati may bring habeas corpus action challenging their detention as unlawful); Gall and Worthington, "Afghan Held by U.S.," A10 (fate of Hekmati after *Hamdi* and *Rasul*).

3. For important statements of the hydraulic effect globalization has had and should have on Large "C" Constitutional understandings, see Oona A. Hathaway, "Treaties' End: The Past, Present, and Future of International Lawmaking in the United States," *Yale Law Journal* 117 (2008): 1236–1362; Peter J. Spiro, "Globalization and the (Foreign Affairs) Constitution," *Ohio State Law Journal* 63 (2002): 649–730.

4. For overviews of Vice President Cheney's philosophy of retaliation, intelligence gathering, and justice for accused terrorists, and its implementation through the various administrative experiments described in the text, see Barton Gellman, *Angler: The Cheney Vice Presidency* (New York: Penguin, 2008); Jane Mayer, *The Dark Side: The*

Inside Story of How the War on Terror Turned into a War on American Ideals (New York: Doubleday, 2008). For a normative account that is supportive of Cheney, see John Yoo, *The Powers of War and Peace: The Constitution and Foreign Affairs after 9/11* (Chicago: University of Chicago Press, 2005).

5. *Korematsu v. United States*, 323 U.S. 214 (U.S. Supreme Court, 1944) (opinion of the Court by Black, J.); ibid., 224–25 (Frankfurter, J., concurring) (first quotation in text). There is some ambiguity as to whether Justice Black's opinion was making a Constitutional argument. He said that the right to the polity's self preservation trumps anything in the Constitution; this suggests that the precept driving his opinion was preconstitutional; it precedes the Constitution and is a foundation for it.

6. Ibid., 244 (Jackson, J., dissenting) (first quotation in text); ibid., 244–45 (second quotation).

7. *Ex parte Mitsuye Endo*, 323 U.S. 283 (U.S. Supreme Court, 1944) (companion case to *Korematsu*), illuminatingly discussed in Patrick O. Guddridge, "Remember *Endo?*" *Harvard Law Review* 116 (2003): 1933–70.

8. The discussion in the text is taken from John Ferejohn and Pasquale Pasquino, "The Law of the Exception: A Typology of 'Emergency Powers,'" *International Journal of Constitutional Law* 2 (2004): 210–39. On Article 48 of the Weimar Constitution, see Clinton L. Rossiter, *Constitutional Dictatorship: Crisis Government in the Modern Democracies* (Princeton: Princeton University Press, 1948). On the Schmittian critique, see Carl Schmitt, *Political Theology: Four Chapters on the Concept of Sovereignty*, translated by George Schwab (Cambridge, MA: MIT Press, 1985) (1922); John P. McCormick, "The Dilemmas of Dictatorship: Carl Schmitt and Constitutional Emergency Powers," in David Dyzenhaus, editor, *Law as Politics: Carl Schmitt's Critique of Liberalism* (Durham, NC: Duke University Press, 1998), 217–24.

9. On Lincoln's response to the Civil War and Congress's ratification, see Daniel A. Farber, *Lincoln's Constitution* (Chicago: University of Chicago Press, 2003); David A. Barron and Martin S. Lederman, "The Commander in Chief at the Lowest Ebb—A Constitutional History," *Harvard Law Review* 121 (2008): 941–1112, especially 993–1025. For an argument in favor of such a Lincolnian (Statutory) Strategy in response to 9/11, see Oren Gross, "Chaos and Rules: Should Responses to Violent Crises Always Be Constitutional?" *Yale Law Journal* 112 (2003): 1011–34.

10. For a detailed explication of the theory of presidential power and duty held by Vice President Cheney and his adviser David Addington (as well as their allies), see Gellman, *Angler*, 131–93; John Yoo, *War by Other Means: An Insider's Account of the War on Terror* (New York: Atlantic Monthly Press, 2006). For a more pragmatic but still relatively Schmittian perspective, see Richard A. Posner, *Not a Suicide Pact: The Constitution in a Time of National Emergency* (New York: Oxford University Press, 2006).

11. Cheney and Addington's broad interpretation of the Commander-in-Chief Clause, U.S. Const. Art. II, § 2, is at odds not only with the views of Justice Jackson in *Youngstown Sheet & Cube Co. v. Sawyer*, 343 U.S. 579 (U.S. Supreme Court, 1952) (concurring opinion) but also with original Constitutional meaning and subsequent historical practice. See David J. Barron and Martin S. Lederman, "The Commander in Chief at the Lowest Ebb—Framing the Problem, Doctrine, and Original Understanding," *Harvard Law Review* 121 (2008): 689–800.

12. *Endo,* 323 U.S., 300 (quotation in text); ibid., 300–304 (rejecting the government's arguments that Congress had authorized or ratified the executive's continuing detention of concededly loyal citizens such as Mitsuye Endo).

13. Authorization for Use of Military Force Act of 2001, Public Law No. 107-40, 115 Stat. 224 (2001); USA Patriot Act of 2001, Public Law No. 107-56, 115 Stat. 272 (2001), which was revised and reauthorized in Public Law No. 109-177, 120 Stat. 192 (2006). On Schmittian gray holes, see David Dyzenhaus, *The Constitution of Law: Legality in a Time of Emergency* (Oxford: Oxford University Press, 2006).

14. Compare Guddridge, "Remember *Endo?*" (excellent analysis of the political and legal factors contributing to Justice Douglas's *Endo* opinion), with David A. Martin, "Judicial Review and the Military Commissions Act: On Striking the Right Balance," *American Journal of International Law* 101 (2007): 347–48, praising the productive "interbranch colloquy" that took place after 9/11.

15. Heidi Kitrosser, "'Macro-Transparency' as Structural Directive: A Look at the NSA Surveillance Controversy," *Minnesota Law Review* 91 (2007): 1163–1208; *Boumediene v. Bush,* 128 S.Ct. 2229 (U.S. Supreme Court, 2008), interpreting U.S. Constitution, Article I, § 9 (Habeas Corpus Suspension Clause) to trump congressional abrogation of habeas for suspected terrorists detained in Guantánamo Bay, Cuba.

16. Philip Bobbitt, *Terror and Consent: The Wars for the Twenty-First Century* (New York: Alfred A. Knopf, 2008); Stephen Holmes, *Matador's Cape: America's Reckless Response to Terror* (Cambridge: Cambridge University Press, 2007), 299–302; Geoffrey R. Stone, *War and Liberty: An American Dilemma, 1790 to the Present* (New York: W. W. Norton, 2007), as well as Stone, *Perilous Times: Free Speech in Wartime From the Sedition Act of 1798 to the War on Terrorism* (New York: W. W. Norton, 2004).

17. See William E. Scheuerman, "Emergency Powers and the Rule of Law After 9/11," *Journal of Political Philosophy* 14 (2006): 61–84, for an excellent and nuanced evaluation of our nation's non-Schmittian experience after 9/11.

18. Akhil Reed Amar, *The Constitution and Criminal Procedure: First Principles* (New Haven: Yale University Press, 1997).

19. For an excellent debate on the Bush-Cheney administration's assertion of executive power to handle "enemy combatants" under the new terms of the "war on terror," compare *al-Marri v. Pucciarelli,* 534 F.3d 213, 284–93 (U.S. Court of Appeals for the Fourth Circuit, en banc, 2008) (Williams, C.J., concurring in part and dissenting in part), supporting the president's authority on both statutory and Constitutional grounds, and ibid., 293–341 (Wilkinson, J., concurring in part and dissenting in part), a more theoretical defense, with ibid., 217–53 (Motz, J., concurring in part and dissenting in part), critical of the president's assertion of authority.

20. Moreover, the meaning of the Bill of Rights changed when the Reconstruction Amendments were added to the Constitution. Following the Bill of Rights' philosophy of creating process rights judicially enforceable against the federal government, the Fourteenth Amendment's Due Process or Privileges and Immunities Clause created process rights judicially enforceable against state governments. See Akhil Reed Amar, *The Bill of Rights: Creation and Reconstruction* (New Haven: Yale University Press, 1998); William Brennan, "The Bill of Rights and the States," *NYU Law Re-*

view 36 (1961): 761–78; Jerrold Israel, "Selective Incorporation Revisited," *Georgetown Law Journal* 71 (1982): 253–338.

21. For a statutory distinction, see Military Commissions Act of 2006, Pub. L. No. 109-366, § 948a(2), 120 Stat. 2600, 2601 (defining "enemy combatant"); ibid., § 948a(1) (defining "unlawful enemy combatant"). For discussion of broader understandings, see Richard H. Fallon Jr. and Daniel J. Meltzer, "Habeas Corpus Jurisdiction, Substantive Rights, and the War on Terror," *Harvard Law Review* 120 (2007): 2029–2112.

22. *Ex parte Quirin*, 317 U.S. 1, 39–45 (U.S. Supreme Court, 1942), rejecting the defendants' Fifth and Sixth Amendment claims, because they were "unlawful enemy combatants." For a lucid judicial defense of the president's position, see *al-Marri*, 534 F.3d, 293–341 (Wilkinson, J., concurring in part and dissenting in part).

23. *Brady v. Betts*, 316 U.S. 455, 465–67 (U.S. Supreme Court, 1942), surveying uniform state founding era override of common law rule barring representation at the indictment stage of felony cases; ibid., 467–72, surveying diverse state counsel appointment practice in 1942; *Johnson v. Zerbst*, 304 U.S. 458 (U.S. Supreme Court, 1938), requiring appointment of counsel for indigent defendants in federal criminal cases.

24. *Betts*, 316 U.S., 476–80 (Black, J., dissenting), including a forty-eight-state survey of state statutory and judicial practice in 1942; *Gideon v. Wainwright*, 372 U.S. 335 (U.S. Supreme Court, 1963) and Brief for Petitioner, 30–31, *Gideon* (1962 Term, Docket No. 155). On the evolution of the Court's right to counsel jurisprudence, see William N. Eskridge Jr., "Some Effects of Identity-Based Social Movements on Constitutional Law in the Twentieth Century," *Michigan Law Review* 100 (2002): 2210–11.

25. *Furman v. Georgia*, 408 U.S. 238 (U.S. Supreme Court, 1972) (per curiam); *Gregg v. Georgia*, 428 U.S. 153 (U.S. Supreme Court, 1976); *Coker v. Georgia*, 433 U.S. 584 (U.S. Supreme Court, 1977); Stuart Banner, *The Death Penalty: An American History* (Cambridge, MA: Harvard University Press, 2002), chaps. 9–11. For subsequent death penalty cases where the Court has explicitly relied on state statutory convergences, see *Kennedy v. Louisiana*, 128 S.Ct. 2641 (U.S. Supreme Court, 2008) (no death penalty for rape of a minor); *Roper v. Simmons*, 543 U.S. 551 (U.S. Supreme Court, 2005) (no death penalty for juvenile defendants); *Atkins v. Virginia*, 536 U.S. 304 (U.S. Supreme Court, 2002) (no death penalty for mentally disabled defendants).

26. *Baze v. Rees*, 128 S.Ct. 1520 (U.S. Supreme Court, 2008) (lethal injection as the method for imposing the death penalty, okay because of state statutory convergence); *Quirin*, 317 U.S., 41–42, invoking act of April 10, 1806, 2 Stat. 371 (statute quoted in text), derived from Resolution of the Continental Congress, August 21, 1776.

27. Executive Order on Detention, Treatment, and Trial of Certain Non-Citizens in the War on Terrorism, *Federal Register* 66 (November 13, 2001): 57833–36; ibid., 57833 (quotation in text); Department of Defense Military Order No. 1, available at www.defenselink.mil/news/Mar2002/d20020321ord.pdf (viewed February 2008); Mayer, *Dark Side*, 80–89 (the process by which Cheney and Addington pushed the military commissions idea and circumvented opposition).

For background and commentary on military commissions, see Louis Fisher, *Military Tribunals and Presidential Power: American Revolution to the War on Terrorism* (Lawrence: University Press of Kansas, 2005). For critical analyses of the procedures afforded, see Oona A. Hathaway, "*Hamdan v. Rumsfeld:* Domestic Enforcement of International Law," in John E. Noyes et al., editors, *International Law Stories* (New York: Foundation Press, 2007), 229–60; Jordan Paust, "Antiterrorism Military Commissions: Courting Illegality," *Michigan Journal of International Law* 23 (2001): 1–27; Neal K. Katyal and Laurence H. Tribe, "Waging War, Deciding Guilt: Trying the Military Tribunals," *Yale Law Journal* 111 (2002): 1259–1310.

28. Compare Adrian Vermeule, "Our Schmittian Administrative Law," *Harvard Law Review* 122 (2008): 1096–1149, arguing that even when Supreme Court decisions seem to set limits on the executive, those limits have no real bite in practice.

29. *Hamdi v. Rumsfeld*, 542 U.S. 507 (U.S. Supreme Court, 2004); *Rasul v. Bush*, 542 U.S. 466 (U.S. Supreme Court, 2004). For excellent commentary, see Jenny S. Martinez, "Process and Substance in the 'War on Terror,'" *Columbia Law Review* 108 (2008): 1013–92. For the post-*Hamdi* tribunals, see Memorandum of the Secretary of the Navy, Implementation of Combatant Status Review Tribunal Procedures for Enemy Combatants Detained at Guantanamo Bay Naval Base (July 29, 2004), adopting the procedures of Army Regulation 190-8, *Enemy Prisoners of War, Retained Personnel, Civilian Internees and Other Detainees* (November 11, 1997).

30. *Hamdan v. Rumsfeld*, 548 U.S. 557, 593–613 (U.S. Supreme Court, 2006) (plurality opinion, on this point, by Stevens, J.).

31. UCMJ Article 36(a)–(b) (quotations in text); *Hamdan*, 548 U.S., 615–25 (Stevens, J., for the Court), limiting *Yamashita v. United States*, 327 U.S. 1 (U.S. Supreme Court, 1949), which had allowed the trial of a Japanese general even though the process was a far cry from court-martial procedures.

32. National Security Act of 1947, Public Law No. 235, 61 Stat. 496 (1947), codified as amended at 50 U.S.C. § 401a(4). For an excellent and accessible overview, see Denis McDonough, Mara Rudman, and Peter Rundlet, *No Mere Oversight: Congressional Oversight of Intelligence is Broken* (Washington, DC: Center for American Progress, 2007).

33. Final Report of the Senate Select Committee to Study Governmental Operations with Respect to Intelligence Activities, book II (1976) ("Church Committee Report"), 104 (first quotation in text); ibid., 70 (second quotation). On the NSA and its abusive activities, see Senate Select Committee to Study Governmental Operations With Resort to Intelligence Activities, Ninety-fourth Congress, Second Session, *Hearings on National Security Agency and Fourth Amendment Rights* (1976).

34. *Katz v. United States*, 389 U.S. 347 (U.S. Supreme Court, 1967); *United States v. United States District Court*, 407 U.S. 297 (U.S. Supreme Court, 1972) (reserving the issue whether surveillance of foreign-sponsored surveillance activities fall within the Fourth Amendment); Kitrosser, "'Macro-Transparency' as Structural Directive."

35. Foreign Intelligence Surveillance Act of 1978, Public Law No. 95-511 (1978), codified at 50 USC §§ 1801 et seq.; ibid., § 1809 (criminalizing foreign surveillance not authorized by FISA); cf. 18 USC § 2511(2)(f) (FISA and specified provisions of the federal criminal code are the *"exclusive* means by which electronic surveillance . . . may be conducted"); USA Patriot Act of 2001, Public Law No. 107-56, §§ 206–08, 218, 115 Stat. 272, 282–83, 291 (2001) (amending FISA); Theodore W. Ruger, "Chief Justice

Rehnquist's Appointments to the FISA Court: An Empirical Perspective," *Northwestern University Law Review* 101 (2007): 239–58. On FISA's legislative history, see James Risen, *State of War: The Secret History of the CIA and the Bush Administration* (New York: Free Press, 2006), 44–59.

36. On the origins of the NSA domestic surveillance program in the wake of 9/11, see Gellman, *Angler*, 139–58; Mayer, *Dark Side*, 66–71.

37. The story of Goldsmith's reservations about the NSA's domestic wiretapping program and the internal battle between the Justice Department and the vice president's office is dramatically recounted in Gellman, *Angler*, 277–326; Mayer, *Dark Side*, 261–94.

38. Memoranda supporting and opposing the president's statutory and Constitutional justifications for the post-2001 NSA program are reproduced in David Cole and Martin S. Lederman, "The National Security Agency's Domestic Spying Program: Framing the Debate," *Indiana Law Journal* 81 (2006): 1355–1424.

39. Protect America Act of 2007, Public Law No. 110-55, 121 Stat. 552 (August 5, 2007); FISA Amendments Act of 2008, Public Law No. 110-261, 122 Stat. 2436 (July 10, 2008).

40. For thoughtful suggestions for updating FISA and taking greater advantage of our technological sophistication, but with post hoc privacy protections, see Bobbitt, *Terror and Consent*; Orin S. Kerr, "Updating the Foreign Intelligence Surveillance Act," *University of Chicago Law Review* 75 (2008): 225–43; Richard A. Posner, "Privacy, Surveillance, and the Law," *University of Chicago Law Review* 75 (2008): 245–60.

41. Gellman, *Angler*, 171–77.

42. Ibid., 177–80; Mayer, *Dark Side*, 171–81; United Nations Convention Against Torture and Other Cruel, Inhuman, or Degrading Punishment (1984); 18 U.S.C. §§ 2340–40A (codification of Convention, making torture a federal crime). See generally Ahcene Boulesbaa, *The U.N. Convention on Torture and the Prospects for Enforcement* (The Hague: M. Nijhoff, 1999).

43. Memorandum from Jay S. Bybee, Assistant Attorney General, to Attorney General Alberto R. Gonzales, Counsel to the President, "Standards of Conduct for Interrogation under 18 U.S.C. §§ 2340–2340A" (August 1, 2002) (quotations in text). The memorandum is reproduced as an appendix (document 1) to Karen J. Greenberg, editor, *The Torture Debate in America* (New York: Cambridge University Press, 2006). The subsequent memorandum to the Defense Department is Memorandum from Jay S. Bybee, Assistant Attorney General, to William J. Haynes, II, General Counsel of the Department of Defense, "Military Interrogation of Alien Unlawful Combatants Held Outside the United States" (March 14, 2003).

44. Scott Shane, "Waterboarding Used 266 Times on 2 Suspects," *New York Times*, April 20, 2009, A1, A10 (CIA waterboarded Abu Zubaida eighty-three times in August 2002 and Khlaid Shaihk Mohammed 183 times in March 2003).

45. Mayer, *Dark Side*, 200–202 (Guantánamo authorized to use harsh interrogation tactics); ibid., 202–12 (detailed description of psychological and physical abuse of Qahtani, with dubious payoff, according to Mayer).

46. The juxtaposition of the solicitor general's argument, "trust the executive," and the Abu Ghraib revelations on the same day comes from Hathaway, *"Hamdan v. Rumsfeld,"* 239.

47. Human Rights Watch, *United States: Abu Ghraib Only the "Tip of the Iceberg"* (April 2005), and *By the Numbers: Findings of the Detainee Abuse and Accountability Project* (April 2006), and *United States: "No Blood No Foul": Soldiers' Accounts of Detainee Abuse and Torture* (July 2006). For recent evidence and evaluation, based upon examinations of former detainees by trained medical personnel, see Physicians for Human Rights, *Broken Laws, Broken Lives: Medical Evidence of Torture by U.S. Personnel and Its Impact* (June 2008), available at http://brokenlives.info (viewed September 2008).

48. Jack Goldsmith, *The Terror Presidency: Law and Judgment Inside the Bush Administration* (New York: W. W. Norton 2007), 141–62 (account of Goldsmith's withdrawal of the Bybee-Yoo torture memorandum); Memorandum from Daniel Levin to James B. Comey, "Legal Standards Applicable Under 18 U.S.C. §§ 2340–2340A," December 30, 2004 (superseding the Bybee-Yoo memorandum), reproduced as an appendix (document 3) to Greenberg, editor, *Torture Debate in America*; Mayer, *Dark Side*, 295–306 (Levin subjects himself to waterboarding, finds the experience terrifying even for brief periods, and issues a revised memorandum on interrogation techniques).

49. Detainee Treatment Act of 2005, Public Law No. 109-148, title X, 119 Stat. 2739; ibid., § 1002(a) (confining interrogation techniques to those approved in the Army Field Manual); ibid., § 1003(a) (prohibiting cruel, inhuman, degrading treatment); Mayer, *Dark Side*, 319–23 (McCain Amendment and Addington's and Bradbury's attempted evasions); Dana Priest, "CIA Holds Terror Suspects in Secret Prisons," *Washington Post*, November 2, 2005, A1.

50. *Youngstown Sheet & Tube Co. v. Sawyer (The Steel Seizure Case)*, 343 U.S. 579 (U.S. Supreme Court, 1952); ibid., 637 (Jackson, J., concurring) (the three-zone analysis in text).

51. *Hamdan*, 548 U.S., 593 note 23 (opinion for the Court, following the Jackson *Steel Seizure* framework and noting that the solicitor general had acceded to that framework); ibid., 679–80 (Thomas, J., joined by Scalia, J., dissenting, but following the Jackson *Steel Seizure* framework). The most thorough analysis to date demonstrates that broad claims about the president's commander-in-chief power cannot be made from standard rule of law sources (the Constitutional text, original debates, early practice, Supreme Court precedent). See Barron and Lederman, "Commander in Chief . . . Original Understanding." Presidents tend to view their commander-in-chief authority very broadly, but until recent years they had almost always acknowledged that their authority was subject to congressional regulations. See Barron and Lederman, "The Commander in Chief . . . Constitutional History," 946–50.

52. Gordon Silverstein, *Imbalance of Powers: Constitutional Interpretation and the Making of American Foreign Policy* (New York: Oxford University Press, 1997), maintains that American courts have generally not stood up to the executive in foreign affairs cases. The Steel Seizure Case is highly exceptional in his view. Our superstatutory perspective requires amendment of his strong thesis, for judges are more likely to re-

sist the president through cautious statutory interpretations, as in *Hamdan*, than through liberal Constitutional rulings, as in the Steel Seizure Case.

53. On the president's first-mover advantage, see Terry M. Moe and William G. Howell, "The Presidential Power of Unilateral Action," *Journal of Law, Economics, and Organization* 15 (1999): 132–79; William G. Howell, *Power and Persuasion: The Politics of Direct Presidential Action* (Princeton: Princeton University Press, 2003), as well as Silverstein, *Imbalance of Powers*. On the recent legislative deliberations regarding wiretapping of international communications, see Protect America Act of 2007, Public Law No. 110-55, 121 Stat. 552 (August 5, 2007); FISA Amendments Act of 2008, Public Law No. 110-261, 122 Stat. 2436 (July 10, 2008).

54. Detainee Treatment Act of 2005, Public Law No. 109-148, § 1004, codified at 42 U.S.C. § 2000dd-1 (good faith defense for officials who torture alien detainees such as Hekmati).

55. Detainee Treatment Act of 2005, § 1005 (stripping alien detainees of their habeas corpus rights and allowing them limited access to the D.C. Circuit).

56. Military Commissions Act of 2006, Public Law No. 109-366, § 3, 120 Stat. 2600 (2006), adding new 10 U.S.C. §§ 948a to 950v; see 10 U.S.C. § 948q (notice); ibid., §§ 948k, 949c, and 949j (right to counsel); ibid., § 949m (conviction by two-thirds vote of the tribunal); ibid., § 948r (no self-incrimination and limited admissibility of statements secured under "debatably coercive" techniques); ibid., § 949a (discretion of presiding judge to admit hearsay and evidence secured without a warrant); ibid., § 950g (limited review of tribunal verdicts).

57. Gall and Worthington, "Afghan Held by U.S.," A10 (Hekmati's evidence demonstrating his innocence).

58. *Congressional Record* 101 (1955): 9972–73 (Geneva Conventions ratified 77–0). The other conventions ratified that day were Convention for the Amelioration of the Condition of the Wounded and Sick in Armed Forces in the Field (Geneva Convention No. I), August 12, 1949, 6 UST 3114, TIAS No. 3,362, 75 UNTS 31; Convention for the Amelioration of the Condition of the Wounded, Sick, and Shipwrecked Members of Armed Forces at Sea (Geneva Convention No. II), August 12, 1949, 6 UST 3217, TIAS No. 3,363, 75 UNTS 85; Geneva Convention Relative to the Treatment of Prisoners of War (Geneva Convention No. III), August 12, 1949, 6 UST 3316, TIAS No. 3,364, 75 UNTS 135; Convention Relative to the Protection of Civilian Persons in Time of War (Geneva Convention No. IV), August 12, 1949, 6 UST 3516, TIAS No. 3,365, 75 UNTS 287.

59. Third Geneva Convention Relative to the Treatment of Prisoners of War, 6 U.S.T. 3316 (1949); ibid., article 2 (coverage, quotation in text); ibid., article 5 (POW protections of Geneva III pertain until there has been determination otherwise by "competent tribunal"); ibid., article 3 (protections for persons detained and tried in connection with conflicts not of an international character).

60. For the administration's internal battle over the applicability of the Geneva Conventions to captured Afghans, see Gellman, *Angler*, 168–71; Mayer, *Dark Side*, 121–24, both of which discuss and quote from the January 25 memorandum.

61. *Hamdan*, 548 U.S., 625–35 (opinion for the Court, holding that Common Article 3 of the Geneva Conventions was applicable to Hamdan's case and was not satisfied); 641–43 (Kennedy, J., concurring in the Court's ruling and most of the plurality's

reasoning as regards Common Article 3); Gellman, *Angler*, 346–58 (account of internal executive department debate, 2005–06); Department of Defense, Directive 2310.01E, "Department of Defense Detainee Program" (September 5, 2006), available at www.washingtonpost.com/wp-srv/politics/documents/cheney/dod_directive _2310_01E.pdf (viewed April 16, 2009).

62. U.S. Constitution, Article I, § 7 (process for enacting statutes: bicameral approval and presentment to the president); ibid., Article II, § 2 (process for ratifying treaties: president negotiates, Senate ratifies by two-thirds vote); ibid., Article VI (both statutes and treaties are "supreme Law of the Land"). See also *Missouri v. Holland*, 252 U.S. 416 (U.S. Supreme Court, 1920), suggesting (quite controversially) that the president acting with the Senate under the Treaty Clause is not limited by the federalism constraints that confine Congress legislating under Article I, § 7.

63. Hathaway, "Treaties' End," 1252–71 (thorough empirical survey of American treaty and executive-congressional agreement practice); ibid., 1276–86 (original expectations for the Treaty Clause); ibid., 1286–92 (treaty practice in first one hundred years); Laurence Tribe, "Taking Text and Structure Seriously: Reflections on Free-Form Method in Constitutional Interpretation," *Harvard Law Review* 108 (1995): 1221–1303; ibid., 1249–78 (analysis of the Treaty Clause in the context of the whole Constitution, as well as some analysis of history and practice).

64. *Field v. Clark*, 143 U.S. 649 (U.S. Supreme Court, 1892); Peter Spiro, "Treaties, Executive Agreements, and Constitutional Method," *Texas Law Review* 79 (2001): 961–1035 (excellent analysis of *Field* as a rebuttal to Tribe's Constitutional case against congressional-executive agreements). See also Bruce Ackerman and David Golove, "Is NAFTA Constitutional?" *Harvard Law Review* 108 (1995): 799–929, arguing that the congressional-executive agreement supplanted treaties during the New Deal and afterward; Hathaway, "Treaties' End," 1292–1302 (arguing that the turning point toward congressional-executive agreements was *Field*-era tariff policy; the New Deal confirmed and expanded the *Field* revolution).

65. The leading briefs on the applicability of the Third Geneva Convention to Hamdan's appeal are Brief for Petitioner Salim Ahmed Hamdan, *Hamdan v. Rumsfeld*, 548 U.S. 557 (U.S. Supreme Court, 2006) (Docket No. 05-184); Brief for Respondents, *Hamdan* (Docket No. 05-184); Brief for the Association of the Bar of the City of New York and the Human Rights Institute of the International Bar Association as *Amici Curiae* in Support of Petitioner, *Hamdan* (Docket No. 05-184). For our own education, the most helpful submission was *Amicus Curiae* Brief of Retired Generals and Admirals and Milt Beardon in Support of Petitioner (Geneva Conventions—Judicial Deference), *Hamdan* (Docket No. 05-184).

66. The International Covenant on Civil and Political Rights (ICCPR), G.A. Res. 2200 A(XXI), December 16, 1966, 21 U.N. GAOR Supp. (No. 16), 999 U.N.T.S. 171, U.N. Doc. A/6316 (1966); Theodor Meron, "The Geneva Conventions as Customary Law," *American Journal of International Law* 81 (1987): 348–70; Jean-Marie Henckaerts and Louise Doswald-Beck, editors, *Customary International Humanitarian Law* (New York: Cambridge University Press, 2005).

67. *Restatement, Third, of the Foreign Relations Law of the United States* § 114 ("Where fairly possible, a United States statute is to be construed so as not to conflict with in-

ternational law or with an international agreement of the United States."); *Hamdan,* 548 U.S., 598–02 (UCMJ incorporates by reference the common law of war and Geneva Conventions into U.S. law).

68. Senate Committee on Foreign Relations, Eighty-fourth Congress, First Session, *Hearings on Geneva Conventions for the Protection of War Victims* (1955), 3–4 (testimony of Secretary of State Dulles) (first quotation in text); *Congressional Record* 101 (1955): 9960 (Senator Mansfield, D-MT) (supporting Geneva Conventions) (second quotation).

69. Department of the Army, Field Manual No. 27-10, "The Law of Land Warfare," chap. 3, § 1 ¶ 71 (Washington, DC, 1956) (adopting Geneva III's Article 5 verbatim) (first quotation in text); Army Regulation 190-8, "Enemy Prisoners of War, Retained Personnel, Civilian Internees and Other Detainees," § 1–5(a)(2) (1997) (second quotation in text); ibid., §§ 1–6, 3–7 ("competent tribunals" shall determine POW status); NWP 1–14M: The Commander's Handbook on the Law of Naval Operations § 11–7 (1995) (third quotation in text).

70. Department of State Bulletin, January 4, 1971, 10 (Nixon administration assurance that America would follow the Geneva Conventions for all combatants in Vietnam); Senator John McCain, Speech to the American Red Cross Promise of Humanity Conference, May 9, 1999, available at http://mccain.senate.gov/index/cfm?fuseaction=Newscenter.ViewPressRelease&Content_id=820 (viewed February 2008) (quotation in text); Milt Bearden, "When the CIA Played by the Rules," *New York Times,* November 4, 2005, A27.

71. On the strong opposition of JAG officials, from all service branches, to the Bush-Cheney administration's pullback from our nation's traditional adherence to the Geneva Conventions as the law of the land, see Memorandum from Alberto J. Mora, General Counsel, U.S. Dep't of the Navy, to Vice Admiral Albert Church, Inspector General, U.S. Dep't of the Navy, Statement for the Record: Office of General Counsel Involvement in Interrogation Issues (July 7, 2004), available at http://www.aclu.org/safefree/torture/29228res20040707.html; Letter from Retired Members of the U.S. Armed Forces and Former Officials of the Department of Defense, to Senator John Warner, Chairman, and Carl Levin, Ranking Member, Senate Armed Services Committee (September 12, 2006). See generally M. Cherif Bassioini, "Symposium: Torture and the War on Terror: The Institutionalization of Torture under the Bush Administration," *Case Western Reserve Journal of International Law* 37 (2006): 389–425; Jane Mayer, "The Memo: How an Internal Effort to Ban the Abuse and Torture of Detainees Was Thwarted," *New Yorker,* February 27, 2006.

72. ACLU reports poll saying that majority of Americans reject torture, September 2007, available at http://www.aclu.org/safefree/general/32084res20071004.html (last viewed April 7, 2008) (81 percent of respondents wanted the United States to make it clear that it opposes torture and follows the Geneva Conventions; 57 percent wanted to close Guantánamo and schedule trials in U.S. courts for the terrorist suspects held there); CNN Opinion Poll, November 6, 2007, available at http://www.cnn.com/2007/POLITICS/11/06/waterboard.poll/ (last viewed April 7, 2008) (69 percent of Americans polled considered waterboarding a form of torture, and 58 percent believed the United States should never be allowed to use the procedure to get information;

however, 40 percent said it would be okay for the government to use the technique to stop a terrorist attack); Steven Kull, "Americans on International Courts and Their Jurisdiction Over the U.S.," *World Public Opinion*, May 11, 2006 ("Two in three Americans say the United States should change the way it treats detainees in Guantánamo Bay, as prescribed by the UN Commission on Human Rights"); CBS News, "Poll: Doubts On Military Tribunals," New York, December 11, 2001 (82 percent of Americans polled believed that the executive should not have sole discretion in matters of national security, and that changes in policy should be made in Congress; also, 60 percent believed that terrorist suspects should be tried in criminal courts instead of military tribunals). But see Pew Research Center Poll, "Less Opposition to Gay Marriage, Adoption and Military Service," March 22, 2006, available at http://people-press.org/reports/display.php3?ReportID=273 (last viewed April 9, 2008) (showing that Americans are "divided evenly over whether they favor (44%) or oppose (43%) the government's policy of holding suspected terrorists at Guantánamo Bay without formal charges or trial").

73. Compare *Hamdan*, 548 U.S., 633–34 (plurality opinion, on the precise requirements of Common Article 3, by Stevens, J.), with ibid., 653–55 (Kennedy, J., concurring in the judgment and reserving decision on the precise requirements of Common Article 3, beyond the judgment that it reinforces the Court's UCMJ analysis), with ibid., 725–34 (Alito, J., dissenting from the plurality's and Justice Kennedy's analysis of Common Article 3).

74. Military Commissions Act of 2006, adding new 10 U.S.C. §§ 948a to 950v; see 10 U.S.C. § 948q (notice); ibid., §§ 948k, 949c, and 949j (right to counsel); ibid., § 949m (conviction by two-thirds vote of the tribunal); ibid., § 948r (no self-incrimination and limited admissibility of statements secured under "debatably coercive" techniques); ibid., § 949a (discretion of presiding judge to admit hearsay and evidence secured without a warrant); ibid., § 950g (limited review of tribunal verdicts).

75. Mayer, *Dark Side*, 326–35 (dismal assessment of the practical consequences of the Cheney-Addington aggressive response to 9/11).

76. Executive Order No. 13440, "Interpretation of the Geneva Convention's Common Article 3 as Applied to a Program of Detention and Interrogation Operated by the Central Intelligence Agency" (July 20, 2007), revoked by Executive Order No. 13493 (January 22, 2009); William Glaberson, "6 at Guantánamo Said to Face Trial in 9/11 Case," *New York Times*, February 9, 2008, A1, A8.

77. Department of the Army, Field Manual 2-22.3 (34–52), "Intelligence Interrogations" (September 6, 2006), available at www.fas.org/irp/doddir/army/fm2-22-3.pdf (viewed February 2008).

78. *Boumediene v. Bush*, 128 S.Ct. 2229 (U.S. Supreme Court, 2008). The same majority as in *Hamdan* (Justices Stevens, Kennedy, Souter, Ginsburg, Breyer) ruled that the MCA's revocation of the detainees' habeas rights was unconstitutional.

79. Gall and Worthington, "Afghan Held by U.S.," A10 (quotation in text).

CONCLUSION

1. For examples of engineering metaphors by authors discussing Constitutional design, see, e.g., Walter F. Murphy, "Designing a Constitution: Of Architects and Builders,"

Texas Law Review 87 (2009), 1303–37, as well as Donald S. Lutz, *The Principles of Constitutional Design* (Cambridge: Cambridge University Press, 2006); Sujit Choudhry, editor, *Constitutional Design for Divided Societies: Integration or Accommodation?* (Oxford: Oxford University Press, 2008).

2. John Ferejohn and Barry Weingast, "A Positive Theory of Statutory Interpretation," *International Review of Law and Economics* 12 (1992): 263–79 (quip in text); Jed Rubenfeld, *Freedom and Time: A Theory of Constitutional Self-Government* (New Haven: Yale University Press, 2001).

3. Our account of Sally Durán Armendáriz's life is taken from interview with Augustina (Sally) Durán Armendáriz by William N. Eskridge Jr. and Kevin Schwartz, Gilroy, California, August 13–14, 2007.

4. On the disinclination of the Supreme Court to stray too far from public opinion, see Nathan Persily, Jack Citrin, and Patrick Egan, *Public Opinion and Constitutional Controversy* (New York: Oxford University Press, 2008); William Mishler and Reginald S. Sheehan, "The Supreme Court as a Countermajoritarian Institution? The Impact of Public Opinion on Supreme Court Opinions," *American Political Science Review* 87 (1993): 87ff. For a theorization of the consequences of this phenomenon for public law, see William N. Eskridge Jr. and Philip P. Frickey, "The Supreme Court, 1993 Term—Foreword: Law as Equilibrium," *Harvard Law Review* 110 (1994): 4–84.

5. Larry D. Kramer, *The People Themselves* (Cambridge, MA: Harvard University Press, 2005), and Kramer, "The Supreme Court, 2000 Term—Foreword: We the Court," *Harvard Law Review* 115 (2001): 4–108. For other accounts sharply critical of the Court's Constitutional activism, see Gerald Rosenberg, *The Hollow Hope: Can Courts Bring About Social Change?* (Chicago: University of Chicago Press, second edition, 2008) (no); Jeremy Waldron, *Democracy and Disagreement* (Oxford: Oxford University Press, 1999).

6. Mark V. Tushnet, *Taking the Constitution Away from the Court* (Princeton: Princeton University Press, 1999).

7. We draw inspiration for *deliberation-respecting* judicial review from Alexander M. Bickel, *The Least Dangerous Branch: The Supreme Court at the Bar of Politics* (New Haven: Yale University Press, 1962); John Hart Ely, *Democracy and Distrust: A Theory of Judicial Review* (Cambridge, MA: Harvard University Press, 1980); Henry M. Hart Jr. and Albert M. Sacks, *The Legal Process: Basic Problems in the Making and Application of Law*, William N. Eskridge Jr. and Philip P. Frickey, editors (Westbury, NY: Foundation Press, 1994 [1958 tentative edition]). For an earlier expression of such a theory, see William N. Eskridge Jr. and Philip P. Frickey, "Quasi-Constitutional Law: Clear Statement Rules as Constitutional Lawmaking," *Vanderbilt Law Review* 45 (1992): 593–646, especially 630–32.

8. Deliberation-respecting judicial review has its closest allies in Martha Minow, *Making All the Difference: Inclusion, Exclusion, and American Law* (Ithaca, NY: Cornell University Press, 1990); Bruce Ackerman, "The Living Constitution," *Harvard Law Review* 120 (2007): 1737–1812 (published version of the 2006 Oliver Wendell Holmes Lectures); Michael C. Dorf and Barry Friedman, "Shared Constitutional Interpretation," *Supreme Court Review* 2000: 61–107; Oona A. Hathaway, "Treaties' End: The

Past, Present, and Future of International Lawmaking in the United States," *Yale Law Journal* 117 (2008), 1236–1362; Victoria Nourse, "The Vertical Separation of Powers," *Duke Law Journal* 49 (1999): 749–802; Robert C. Post and Reva B. Siegel, "Legislative Constitutionalism and Section 5 Power: Policentric Interpretation of the Family and Medical Leave Act," *Yale Law Journal* 112 (2003): 1943–2059.

9. Akhil Reed Amar, *America's Constitution: A Biography* (New York: Random House, 2005).

10. For a small sample of classic works that take Constitutional text and structure seriously, see, e.g., Akhil Reed Amar, *The Constitution and Criminal Procedure: First Principles* (New Haven: Yale University Press, 1997), and *The Bill of Rights: Creation and Reconstruction* (New Haven: Yale University Press, 1998); Steven G. Calabresi and Chistopher S. Yoo, *The Unitary Executive: Presidential Power from Washington to Bush* (New Haven: Yale University Press, 2008); Vicki Jackson, "Holistic Interpretation: *Fitzpatrick v. Bitzer* and Our Bifurcated Constitution," *Stanford Law Review* 53 (2001): 1259–1310; Paul Heald and Suzanna Sherry, "Implied Limits on the Legislative Power: The Intellectual Property Clause as an Absolute Constraint on Congress," *University of Illinois Law Review* 2000: 1119–97; John F. Manning, "The Eleventh Amendment and the Reading of Precise Constitutional Texts," *Yale Law Journal* 113 (2004): 1663–1750; Nourse, "Vertical Separation of Powers"; William Michael Treanor, "Taking Text Too Seriously: Modern Textualism, Original Meaning, and the Case of Amar's *Bill of Rights*," *Michigan Law Review* 106 (2007): 487–543; Carlos Manuel Vázquez, "Sovereign Immunity, Due Process, and the *Alden* Trilogy," *Yale Law Journal* 109 (2000): 1927–81; John Choon Yoo, *The Powers of War and Peace: The Constitution and Foreign Affairs after 9/11* (Chicago: University of Chicago Press, 2005); Ernest A. Young, "*Alden v. Maine* and the Jurisprudence of Structure," *William & Mary Law Review* 41 (2000): 1601, 1630–64. See also recent work by more senior scholars, such as Laurence Tribe, "Taking Text and Structure Seriously: Reflections on Free-Form Method in Constitutional Interpretation," *Harvard Law Review* 108 (1995): 1221–1303.

11. For some leading statements of original meaning theories of Constitutional interpretation, see Robert H. Bork, *The Tempting of America: The Political Seduction of the Law* (New York: Free Press, 1989); Antonin Scalia, *A Matter of Interpretation* (Princeton: Princeton University Press, 1997); Steven G. Calabresi, "The Tradition of the Written Constitution: A Comment on Professor Lessig's Theory of Translation," *Fordham Law Review* 65 (1997): 1435–56; Vasan Kesavan and Michael Stokes Paulsen, "The Interpretive Force of the Constitution's Secret Drafting History," *Georgetown Law Journal* 91 (2003): 1113–1214; Michael McConnell, "Originalism and the Desegregation Decisions," *Virginia Law Review* 81 (1995): 947–1140.

For a statement of the dilemma faced by original meaning theory, see Nathan Persily, "Introduction," in Persily et al., editors, *Public Opinion and Constitutional Controversies*; Barry Friedman and Scott B. Smith, "The Sedimentary Constitution," *University of Pennsylvania Law Review* 147 (1998): 1–90 (arguing that original meaning theories must consider the entire sweep of America's Constitutional history).

12. *District of Columbia v. Heller*, 128 S.Ct. 2783 (U.S. Supreme Court, 2008).

13. Ibid., 2788–2802 (Scalia, J., for the Court), detailed examination of evidence pertaining to the original meaning of Second Amendment's text; ibid., 2797–99, tradition-based evidence confirming and deepening linguistic evidence of original meaning; Brief of *Amici Curiae* Academics for the Second Amendment in Support of the Respondents [Ratification and Original Public Meaning], 14–17, *Heller* (Docket No. 07-290); Joyce Lee Malcolm, *To Keep and Bear Arms: The Origins of an American Right* (Cambridge, MA: Harvard University Press, 1994).

   For evidence from professional linguists and historians that cuts against Justice Scalia's reading of the words of the Second Amendment, see Brief for Professors of Linguistics and English Dennis E. Barron, Richard W. Bailey, and Jeffrey Kaplan in Support of Petitioners, 18–28, *Heller* (Docket No. 07-290); Brief of *Amici Curiae* Jack N. Rakove, Saul Cornell [and 12 Other Eminent Legal Historians of the Founding Era] in Support of Petitioners, *Heller* (Docket No. 07-290); Saul Cornell, "The Original Meaning of Original Understanding: A Neo-Blackstone Critique," *Maryland Law Review* 67 (2007), 150–65, a survey of 115 late eighteenth-century texts using term "bear arms"; David Yassky, "The Second Amendment: Structure, History, and Constitutional Change," *Michigan Law Review* 99 (2000): 588, 618, same result for Library Congress database, 1774–1821. Justice Scalia replied that "keep and bear arms" has a broader meaning than "bear arms." *Heller*, 128 S.Ct., 2793–94. But see ibid., 2827–31 (Stevens, J., dissenting), responding to Scalia's reply. For a critique of Justice Scalia's opinion by a historian, see Saul Cornell, "Originalism on Trial: The Use and Abuse of History in *District of Columbia v. Heller*," *Ohio State Law Journal* 69 (2008): 625–40.

14. Justice Douglas's opinion in *Griswold v. Connecticut*, 381 U.S. 479 (U.S. Supreme Court, 1965), created a marital privacy right within the "penumbras" of the First, Third, Fourth, and Fifth Amendments. Although following a different methodology, Justice Scalia's opinion in *Heller* reaches a very similar result. Specifically, he reads the Second Amendment to protect an individual's right to keep handguns in the home for self-defense purposes—a reading that links the Second Amendment with the Third Amendment, barring the quartering of troops in people's homes; the Fourth Amendment, protecting against unreasonable searches and seizures within the home (especially); the Fifth Amendment, which bars the government from "taking" one's home except for a public purpose and with just compensation; and perhaps even the First Amendment, whose rights of individual self-expression and association might have a connection to defense of oneself and one's family within the home.

15. Sir William Blackstone, *Commentaries on the Laws of England* (Oxford: Clarendon Press, 1765), 1:175–76 (quotation in text).

16. Brief for *Amici Curiae* 55 Members of the U.S. Senate, the President of the U.S. Senate, and 250 Members of the U.S. House of Representatives, *Heller* (Docket No. 07-290), authored by Stephen Halbrook, adapted from his article "Congress Interprets the Second Amendment," *Tennessee Law Review* 62 (1995): 597–641; see also William N. Eskridge Jr., "Guns and Sodomy: Tradition as Democratic Deliberation and Constitutional Interpretation," *Harvard Journal of Law and Public Policy* 32 (2008), 193–218.

17. For the 1892 statute, see Act of July 13, 1892, chap. 159, 27 Stat. 116 (1892), as amended by Act of March 3, 1901, chap. 854, § 855, 31 Stat. 1189, 1328 (1901) (first two quotations

in text); *Congressional Record* 23 (1892): S5788 (Senator Mills, objecting to the proposed bill) (third quotation); ibid., S5789 (Senator Wolcott, defending the bill). The 1932 statute is Public Law No. 275, 47 Stat. 650 (1932); Senate Report No. 575, Seventy-second Congress, First Session (1932), 3 (fourth quotation); accord, House Report No. 767, Seventy-second Congress, First Session (1932), 2 (similar language).

18. Act of October 16, 1941, chap. 445, 55 Stat. 742 (1941); Halbrook, "Congress Interprets the Second Amendment," 618–31 (collecting quotations from various legislators to give the flavor of the 1941 debates, including the quotation in text, from Representative Hall of New York).

19. Act of October 21, 1968, Public Law No. 90-618, § 101, 82 Stat. 1213 (1968) (first quotation in text); Act of May 19, 1986, Public Law No. 99-308, 100 Stat. 449 (1986); ibid., § 1(b)(1)(A) (second quotation); ibid., §107, 100 Stat. 460 (preempting state laws barring interstate travel with lawful firearms).

20. Gun Free Zones Act of 1990, part XII of Public Law No. 101-647, 104 Stat. 4789 (1990), codified at 18 U.S.C. § 922(q); *United States v. Lopez*, 514 U.S. 549 (U.S. Supreme Court, 1995), lucidly defended in Steven G. Calabresi, "'A Government of Limited and Enumerated Powers': In Defense of *United States v. Lopez*," *Michigan Law Review* 94 (1996): 752–831. For an analysis emphasizing the deliberation-inducing features of judicial review, see *Lopez*, 514 U.S., 578 (Kennedy, J., concurring); Brief of the National Conference of State Legislatures, National Governors' Association, National League of Cities [et al.], as *Amici Curiae* in Support of Respondent, *Lopez* (Docket No. 93-1260). For skepticism about the Court's enforcement of federalism limitations generally, see *Lopez*, 514 U.S., 603–15 (Souter, J., dissenting), and under then-existing doctrine, ibid., 615–44 (Breyer, J., dissenting).

21. Violence against Women Act of 1994, § 40302, 108 Stat. 1941–42, codified at 42 U.S.C. § 13981, invalidated in *United States v. Morrison*, 529 U.S. 598 (U.S. Supreme Court, 2000). For an accounting of the multifarious costs of gender-motivated violence in the voluminous congressional record, see ibid., 628–40 (Souter, J., dissenting). On the malleability of the Court's new economic/noneconomic distinction and the likelihood that it would prove no more workable than past lines previous Courts had drawn, see ibid., 640–55.

22. Philip P. Frickey and Steven S. Smith, "Judicial Review, the Congressional Process, and the Federalism Cases: An Interdisciplinary Critique," *Yale Law Journal* 111 (2002): 1707–56, especially 1744–45. See also William W. Buzbee and Robert A. Schapiro, "Legislative Record Review," *Stanford Law Review* 54 (2001): 87–161; Ruth Colker and James J. Brudney, "Dissing Congress," *Michigan Law Review* 100 (2001): 80–144; Robert C. Post and Reva B. Siegel, "Equal Protection by Law: Federal Antidiscrimination Legislation after *Morrison* and *Kimel*," *Yale Law Journal* 110 (2000): 441–526.

23. For a short introduction, with leading cases, for the Court's jurisprudence for these open-textured provisions, see Daniel A. Farber, William N. Eskridge Jr., and Philip P. Frickey, *Cases and Materials on Constitutional Law: Themes for the Constitution's Third Century* (St. Paul, MN: Thomson/West, third edition, 2003), 59–423 (Equal Protection Clause), 425–592 (fundamental rights protected by the Due Process Clause), 922–53 (Eleventh Amendment), 967–1000 (Federalism, Intergovernmental Immunities), 1000–1037 (Dormant Commerce Clause).

24. Henry Paul Monaghan, "Stare Decisis and Constitutional Adjudication," *Columbia Law Review* 88 (1988): 723–73; Ernest Young, "Rediscovering Conservatism: Burkean Political Theory and Constitutional Interpretation," *North Carolina Law Review* 72 (1994): 619–723, especially 689–93 (quotation in text). See also David A. Strauss, "Common Law Constitutional Adjudication," *Chicago Law Review* 63 (1996): 877–935 (similar); Cass R. Sunstein, *One Case at a Time: Judicial Minimalism on the Supreme Court* (Cambridge, MA: Harvard University Press, 1999) (similar).

25. Justice Harlan Fiske Stone, "The Common Law in the United States," *Harvard Law Review* 50 (1936): 12–13 (quotation in text); accord, James Landis, "Statutes as the Sources of Law," in *Harvard Legal Essays* (Cambridge, MA: Harvard University Press, 1934), 213 (urging revival of civil law concept "equity of a statute," under which statutory principles would be the basis for resolving related issues). Here is how Roscoe Pound characterized the proper judicial regard for "legislative innovation": "They might receive it fully into the body of the law as affording not only a rule to be applied but a principle from which to reason, and hold it, as a later and more direct expression of the general will, of superior authority to judge-made rules on the same general subject; and so reason from it by analogy in preference to them." Roscoe Pound, "Common Law and Legislation," *Harvard Law Review* 21 (1908): 385–86.

26. For an excellent account of the Second Amendment through the prism of Reconstruction, see Akhil Reed Amar, Comment, "*Heller,* HLR, and Holistic Legal Reasoning," *Harvard Law Review* 122 (2008): 145–90, especially 173–77.

27. *Griswold v. Connecticut,* 381 U.S. 479 (U.S. Supreme Court, 1965) (announcement of a Constitutional privacy right in a decision striking down only law in the nation barring contraception use by married couples); *Eisenstadt v. Baird,* 405 U.S. 438, 453 (U.S. Supreme Court, 1972) (broadening the *Griswold* marital privacy right, to assure "the *individual,* married or single," freedom from "unwarranted governmental intrusion into matters so fundamentally affecting a person as the decision whether to bear or beget a child"); *Roe v. Wade,* 410 U.S. 113 (U.S. Supreme Court, 1973), reaffirmed and narrowed by *Planned Parenthood v. Casey,* 505 U.S. 833 (U.S. Supreme Court, 1992). On the political as well as legal history of the contraception-abortion cases, see David J. Garrow, *Liberty and Sexuality: The Right to Privacy and the Making of Roe v. Wade* (New York: Macmillan, 1994). See also *Gonzales v. Carhart,* 127 S.Ct. 1610 (U.S. Supreme Court, 2007), upholding the federal Partial-Birth Abortion Act, a law that echoed a state statutory convergence.

28. *Bowers v. Hardwick,* 478 U.S. 186 (U.S. Supreme Court, 1986) (upholding consensual "homosexual sodomy" laws against privacy attack); *Lawrence v. Texas,* 539 U.S. 558 (U.S. Supreme Court, 2003) (striking down consensual sodomy laws as inconsistent with the privacy right). For the social, political, and legal campaigns behind *Bowers* and *Lawrence,* see William N. Eskridge Jr., *Dishonorable Passions: Sodomy Law in America, 1861–2003* (New York: Viking, 2008).

29. *Brown v. Board of Education,* 347 U.S. 483 (U.S. Supreme Court, 1954). On the institutional dynamics see Mark Tushnet, *The NAACP's Legal Strategy against Segregated Education, 1925–1950* (Chapel Hill: University of North Carolina Press, 1987); Dennis J. Hutchinson, "Unanimity and Desegregation: Decisionmaking in the Supreme

Court, 1948–1958," *Georgetown Law Journal* 68 (1979): 1–44. On state desegregation before *Brown*, see "Educational Segregation in the U.S. Prior to Brown v. Board of Education," available at en.wikipedia.org/wiki/File:Educational_separation_in_the_US_prior_to_Brown_Map.svg (viewed December 2009).

30. *Naim v. Naim*, 87 S.E.2d 749 (Virginia Supreme Court, 1955) (reaffirming the constitutionality of its miscegenation law after *Brown*), *appeal dismissed*, 350 U.S. 985 (U.S. Supreme Court, 1956); Alexander M. Bickel, *The Least Dangerous Branch: The Supreme Court at the Bar of Politics* (New Haven: Yale University Press, 1962), 174 (explaining the Court's *Naim* disposition); *Loving v. Virginia*, 388 U.S. 1 (U.S. Supreme Court, 1967) (striking down the Virginia law). On the twentieth-century history of miscegenation laws, including the repeal of most of them after *Naim* and before *Loving*, see Randall Kennedy, *Interracial Intimacies: Sex, Marriage, Identity, and Adoption* (New York: Pantheon, 2003), 244–80.

31. See William N. Eskridge Jr., "Some Effects of Identity-Based Social Movements on Constitutional Law in the Twentieth Century," *Michigan Law Review* 100 (2002): 2062–2407, especially 2124–44, for the argument in text, that the Supreme Court's sex discrimination jurisprudence reflects overwhelming popular support for the general principle in the ERA, but with caveats for issues like same-sex marriage, the exclusion of women from the draft, and state support for women in the workplace.

32. *Craig v. Boren*, 429 U.S. 190, 198 (U.S. Supreme Court, 1976) (quotation in text); *Baker v. Nelson*, 409 U.S. 810 (U.S. Supreme Court, 1972) (summary rejection of Constitutional sex discrimination challenge to same-sex marriage bar); *Califano v. Webster*, 430 U.S. 313 (U.S. Supreme Court, 1977) (one of several cases where the Court allowed remedial benefits just to women); *Rostker v. Goldberg*, 453 U.S. 57 (U.S. Supreme Court, 1981) (allowing Congress to exclude women from draft registration; dicta accepting the exclusion of women from combat). See Eskridge, "Social Movements," 2138–43 (tying these and other decisions to the main arguments made by Mrs. Schlafly against the ERA).

33. *Geduldig v. Aiello*, 417 U.S. 484 (U.S. Supreme Court, 1974); Equal Employment Opportunity Commission, "Guidelines on Discrimination Because of Sex," *Federal Register* 37 (April 5, 1972): 6835–37 (EEOC's initial effort to bar employer discrimination against workers because of pregnancy, codified at 29 C.F.R. § 1604.10).

34. *Nevada Department of Human Resources v. Hibbs*, 538 U.S. 721 (U.S. Supreme Court, 2002) (quotation in text). Compare Brief for the Petitioner, at 44–45, *Hibbs* (Docket No. 01-1368), arguing that the Family and Medical Leave Act of 1993 was not remedying Constitutional violations, citing *Geduldig* and *Gilbert*, and so was not a proper exercise of Congress's XIV Amendment, § 5, powers, with Brief for the United States, *Hibbs* (Docket No. 01-1368), assuming that failure *both* to provide pregnancy leaves for women *and* to provide parental leaves for mothers and not fathers raised equal protection concerns.

35. *Hibbs*, 538 U.S., 736 (first quotation in text); ibid., 737 (second quotation); ibid., 750–51 (Kennedy, J., dissenting), discussing *Geduldig*.

36. Ibid., 750–51 (Kennedy, J., dissenting); ibid., 741 (Stevens, J., concurring in the judgment); Transcript of Oral Argument, *Hibbs*, January 13, 2003, at 49, 2003 WL 145272 (Associate Solicitor General's concession, based upon *Geduldig*).

37. The Supreme Court ruled that states could not exclude Mexican Americans from juries in *Hernandez v. Texas*, 347 U.S. 475 (U.S. Supreme Court, 1954), but as late as 1971 federal district judges were dismissing Constitutional lawsuits alleging school discrimination on the basis of Mexican ethnicity. E.g., *Alvarado v. El Paso Independent School District*, 326 F.Supp. 674 (U.S. District Court for the Southern District of Texas, 1971), reversed and remanded, 445 F.2d 1011 (U.S. Court of Appeals for the Fifth Circuit, 1971).

38. Compare John Hart Ely, *Democracy and Distrust: A Theory of Judicial Review* (Cambridge, MA: Harvard University Press, 1980), 136–40, 160–61 (defending *Brown* because it protects "discrete and insular minorities" politically marginalized because of "prejudice"), with Michael J. Klarman, "The Puzzling Resistance to Political Process Theory," *Virginia Law Review* 77 (1991): 747, 788–819 (defending *Brown* because people of color were systematically denied political participation under apartheid).

39. Compare *Parents Involved in Community Schools v. Seattle School District Number 1*, 551 U.S. 701 (U.S. Supreme Court, 2008) (Chief Justice Roberts's plurality opinion rejecting race-based plans for voluntary desegregation), with ibid., 782–98 (Kennedy, J., concurring in part and in the judgment) (supporting the diversity goal and allowing race-based considerations sometimes), with ibid., 803–76 (Breyer, J., dissenting) (supporting the discretion of local school boards to seek actual integration and to use race-based criteria to do it).

40. Ely, *Democracy and Distrust*. The theory in the next paragraph of text is a narrower version of Ely's famous "representation-reinforcing" theory of judicial review. Our theory focuses on the democratic access provisions of the Constitution (the first prong of Ely's theory) and does not incorporate the protection of the "discrete and insular minorities" prong of Ely's theory.

41. For an abbreviated catalogue of textually based "fundamental" Constitutional rights, see *Buckley v. Valeo*, 424 U.S. 1 (U.S. Supreme Court, 1976) (per curiam) (political contributions); *Brandenburg v. Ohio*, 395 U.S. 444 (U.S. Supreme Court, 1969) (expressive conduct, including cross burning); *Duncan v. Louisiana*, 391 U.S. 145 (U.S. Supreme Court, 1968) (jury trial in criminal cases); *Harper v. Virginia Board of Elections*, 383 U.S. 663 (U.S. Supreme Court, 1966) (voting); *Pointer v. Texas*, 380 U.S. 400 (U.S. Supreme Court, 1965) (right to confront opposing witnesses); *Malloy v. Hogan*, 378 U.S. 1 (U.S. Supreme Court, 1964) (no self-incrimination); *Reynolds v. Sims*, 377 U.S. 533 (U.S. Supreme Court, 1964) (one person, one vote); *New York Times v. Sullivan*, 376 U.S. 254 (U.S. Supreme Court, 1964) (nonreckless but untruthful criticisms of public figures); *Gideon v. Wainwright*, 372 U.S. 335 (U.S. Supreme Court, 1963) (right to counsel in felony prosecutions); *NAACP v. Alabama*, 357 U.S. 449 (U.S. Supreme Court, 1958) (freedom of association).

42. Among the leading cases are *Guinn v. United States*, 238 U.S. 347 (U.S. Supreme Court, 1915) (invalidating discriminatory literacy test for voting); *Moore v. Dempsey*, 261 U.S. 86 (U.S. Supreme Court, 1923) (expansive understanding of federal habeas review for "mob dominated" proceeding); *Powell v. Alabama*, 287 U.S. 45 (U.S. Supreme Court, 1932) (right to counsel in capital proceedings); *Brown v. Mississippi*, 297 U.S. 278 (U.S. Supreme Court, 1936) (invalidating convictions based on coerced

confessions); *Smith v. Allwright*, 321 U.S. 649 (U.S. Supreme Court, 1943) (invalidating whites-only primary); *Shelley v. Kraemer*, 334 U.S. 1 (U.S. Supreme Court, 1948) (invalidating racially restrictive property covenant). For discussions of these and other cases, and a skeptical evaluation of their contribution to southern justice, see Michael J. Klarman, *From Jim Crow to Civil Rights: The Supreme Court and the Struggle for Racial Equality* (Oxford: Oxford University Press, 2004), chaps. 2–4.

43. On the importance of the Warren Court's criminal procedure and First Amendment protections for gay rights, see William N. Eskridge Jr., *Gaylaw: Challenging the Apartheid of the Closet* (Cambridge, MA: Harvard University Press, 1999); Richard A. Posner, "Ask, Tell," *New Republic*, October 11, 1999, 52–58.

44. *Hernandez v. Texas*, 347 U.S. 475 (U.S. Supreme Court, 1954) (ruling that the state cannot bar Mexican Americans from jury service); *San Antonio Independent School District v. Rodriguez*, 411 U.S. 1 (U.S. Supreme Court, 1974) (rejecting Constitutional challenge to Texas's education-funding system even though it perpetuated extreme inequalities in educational experience for Anglo- versus Latino- and African American schoolchildren); Voting Rights Act Amendments of 1975, Public Law No. 94-73, title III, 89 Stat. 402 (1975), codified as amended at 42 U.S.C. § 1973aa-1a (protecting language-minority voters against discrimination and assuring most such voters access to voting materials in their language).

45. Senate Report No. 94-295, 25–30 (1975), reprinted in 1975 *U.S. Code Congressional and Administrative News*, 791–97 (summarizing the evidence before Congress in 1975). See also *Katzenbach v. Morgan*, 384 U.S. 641 (U.S. Supreme Court, 1966) (upholding against Constitutional attack 1965 act's assurance of language-assistance for Puerto Rican–educated voters who did not speak English); *Oregon v. Mitchell*, 400 U.S. 112 (U.S. Supreme Court, 1970) (upholding against Constitutional attack 1970 act's preemption of all state literacy tests).

46. *Hernandez v. New York*, 500 U.S. 352 (U.S. Supreme Court, 1991) (reaffirming earlier rule against ethnicity-based exclusions from juries but allowing strikes of all "Hispanic" jurors because they were bilingual); Brief for the Mexican American Legal Defense and Education Fund, the Commonwealth of Puerto Rico, Department of Puerto Rican Community Affairs in the United States, as *Amici Curiae* in Support of Petitioner, *Hernandez* (Docket No. 89-7645), especially the appendices.

47. Alec Stone Sweet and Jed Mathews, "Proportionality Balancing and World Constitutionalism" (draft January 2008). See also Alec Stone Sweet, *The Judicial Construction of Europe* (Oxford: Oxford University Press, 2004), and *Governing with Judges: Constitutional Politics in Europe* (Oxford: Oxford University Press, 2000); Ran Hirschl, *Towards Juristocracy: The Origins and Consequences of the New Constitutionalism* (Cambridge, MA: Harvard University Press, 2004).

48. Hiroshi Motomura, "Immigration Law after a Century of Plenary Power: Phantom Constitutional Norms and Statutory Interpretation," *Yale Law Journal* 100 (1990): 545–613.

49. *Wong Yang Sung v. McGrath*, 339 U.S. 33 (U.S. Supreme Court, 1950); see Motomura, "Phantom Constitutional Norms," 564–600 (surveying dozens of federal appellate decisions applying the phantom norms approach). For some post-Motomura immigration decisions following this approach, see, e.g., *Zadvydas v. Davis*, 533 U.S.

678, 696–99 (U.S. Supreme Court, 2001); *INS v. St. Cyr*, 533 U.S. 289 (U.S. Supreme Court 2001).

50. For examples of the avoidance canon in action, see, e.g., *Gonzales v. Oregon*, 546 U.S. 243, 268–69 (U.S. Supreme Court, 2006); *NLRB v. Catholic Bishop of Chicago*, 440 U.S. 490 (U.S. Supreme Court, 1979). For commentary, see Eskridge and Frickey, "Quasi-Constitutional Law"; John Copeland Nagle, "*Delaware and Hudson* Revisited," *Notre Dame Law Review* 72 (1997): 1495–1518; Adrian Vermeule, "Saving Constructions," *Georgetown Law Journal* 85 (1997): 1945–77.

For a big collection of the Supreme Court's canons, see William N. Eskridge Jr., Philip P. Frickey, and Elizabeth Garrett, *Cases and Materials on Legislation: Statutes and the Creation of Public Policy* (St. Paul, MN: West, fourth edition, 2007), appendix B, 29–34 (listing dozens of Constitution-based canons).

51. For a deliberation-inducing explanation of the avoidance canon, see Philip P. Frickey, "Getting from Joe to Gene (McCarthy): The Avoidance Canon, Legal Process Theory, and Narrowing Statutory Interpretation in the Early Warren Court," *California Law Review* 93 (2005): 397–464.

52. 34 Stat. 808, 809 (1906), codified in D.C. Code § 1303.43 (quotation in text).

53. See Henry M. Hart Jr. and Albert M. Sacks, *The Legal Process: Basic Problems in the Making and Application of Law*, William N. Eskridge Jr. and Philip P. Frickey, editors (Westbury, NY: Foundation Press, 1994 [1958 tentative edition]), 1374, for a leading statement of the purposive approach to statutory interpretation.

54. Thurman W. Arnold, *The Bottlenecks of Business* (New York: Reynal & Hitchcock, 1940). For explications of the Dormant Commerce Clause along the lines we develop in the text, see Donald Regan, "The Supreme Court and State Protectionism: Making Sense of the Dormant Commerce Clause," *Michigan Law Review* 84 (1986): 1091–1286; Mark V. Tushnet, "Rethinking the Dormant Commerce Clause," *Wisconsin Law Review* 1979: 125ff. For a scathing critique, see Lisa E. Heinzerling, "The Commercial Constitution," *Supreme Court Review* 1995: 217–76.

55. *United Haulers Association, Inc. v. Oneida-Herkimer Solid Waste Management Authority*, 550 U.S. 330 (U.S. Supreme Court, 2007).

56. *Ex parte Endo*, 323 U.S. 283, 300 (U.S. Supreme Court, 1944) (quotation in text); *Hamdan v. Rumsfeld*, 548 U.S. 557 (U.S. Supreme Court, 2006). Further inspiration for an accountability meta-canon are Justice Robert Jackson's dissenting opinion in *Korematsu v. United States*, 323 U.S. 214, 244–45 (U.S. Supreme Court, 1944), and his concurring opinion in *Youngstown Sheet & Cube Co. v. Sawyer*, 343 U.S. 579 (U.S. Supreme Court, 1952). Both opinions are analyzed at length in chapter 9.

57. *Hamdi v. Rumsfeld*, 542 U.S. 507 (U.S. Supreme Court, 2004) (requiring some kind of due process for prisoners detained by the government in the war on terror); *Boumediene v. Bush*, 128 S.Ct. 2229 (U.S. Supreme Court, 2008).

58. The *Carolene* meta-canon is articulated and defended in William N. Eskridge Jr., *Dynamic Statutory Interpretation* (Cambridge, MA: Harvard University Press, 1994), 151–54, as well as "Public Values in Statutory Interpretation," *University of Pennsylvania Law Review* 137 (1989): 1007–1104, especially 1032–34.

59. *Richardson v. Ramirez*, 418 U.S. 24 (U.S. Supreme Court, 1974); National Voter Registration Act of 1993, Public Law No. 103-31, 107 Stat. 77, codified at 42 U.S.C. §

1973gg-6(a)(3)(B); Help America Vote Act of 2002, Public Law No. 107-252, 116 Stat. 1666, codified at 42 U.S.C. § 15483(a)(2)(A)(ii)(1). National legislation has been proposed to limit state ability to disenfranchise felons. E.g., Count Every Vote Act of 2005, Senate Bill No. 450, 109th Congress (2005).

On the effect of felon-disenfranchisement laws, see Christopher Uggen and Jeff Manza, "Democratic Contraction? Political Consequences of Felon Disenfranchisement in the United States," *American Sociological Review* 67 (2002): 777–82; *Hayden v. Pataki*, 449 F.3d 305, 355–57 (U.S. Court of Appeals for the Second Circuit, en banc, 2006) (Barrington Parker, J., dissenting); David Crary, "Ratio of Americans Behind Bars Tops 1 in 100," *USA Today*, February 29, 2008, 3A (reporting survey of incarcerated persons by Pew Survey).

60. 42 U.S.C. § 1973(a) (original § 2 of the 1965 act, first quotation in text); ibid., § 1973(b) (new § 2(b), added by the 1982 amendments, second quotation). For an excellent debate among the judges of the eminent Second Circuit as to whether § 2 should be read literally, see *Hayden v. Pataki*, 449 F.3d 305 (U.S. Court of Appeals for the Second Circuit, en banc, 2006).

INDEX

567